JAZZ AND AMERICAN CULTURE

Almost immediately after jazz became popular nationally in the United States in the early twentieth century, American writers responded to what this exciting art form signified for listeners. This book takes an expansive view of the relationship between this uniquely American music and other aspects of American life, including books, films, language, and politics. Observing how jazz has become a cultural institution, widely celebrated as "America's classical music," the book also never loses sight of its beginnings in Black expressive culture and its enduring ability to critique problems of democracy or speak back to violence and inequality, from Jim Crow to George Floyd. Taking the reader through time and across expressive forms, this volume traces jazz as an aesthetic influence, a political force, and a representational focus in American literature and culture. It shows how jazz has long been a rich source of aesthetic stimulation, influencing writers as stylistically wide-ranging as Langston Hughes, Eudora Welty, and James Baldwin, or artists as diverse as Aaron Douglas, Jackson Pollock, and Gordon Parks.

MICHAEL BORSHUK is Associate Professor of African American Literature and Director of the Humanities Center at Texas Tech University. He is the author of *Swinging the Vernacular: Jazz and African American Modernist Literature* (2006), which won the Texas Tech University President's Book Award for Outstanding Faculty Publication. He has written widely on African American literature, American modernism, and music. For ten years he wrote on jazz for *Coda* magazine.

CAMBRIDGE THEMES IN AMERICAN
LITERATURE AND CULTURE

Twenty-first-century America puzzles many citizens and observers. A frequently cited phrase to describe current partisan divisions is Lincoln's "A house divided against itself cannot stand," a warning of the perils to the Union from divisions generated by slavery. America seems divided in almost every way, on almost every attitude. Civic dialogue on issues often seems extremely difficult. America is an experiment always in process, a remarkable union of 300 million diverse people covering all races and faiths. As a forum in which ideologies and interpretations abound, Literary Studies has a role to play in explanation and analysis. The series **Cambridge Themes in American Literature and Culture** addresses the key cultural themes that have brought America to its current moment. It offers a summation of critical knowledge on key cultural themes as well as an intervention in the present moment. This series provides a distinctive, authoritative treatment of the key literary and cultural strains in American life while also pointing in new critical directions.

Titles in the Series

Apocalypse and American Literature and Culture
Edited by John Hay, *University of Nevada*

War and American Literature
Edited by Jennifer Haytock, *SUNY–Brockport*

Climate and American Literature
Edited by Michael Boyden, *Uppsala University*

Gender in American Literature and Culture
Edited by Jean Lutes, *Villanova University, and* Jennifer Travis, *St. John's University*

The City in American Literature
Edited by Kevin R. McNamara, *University of Houston – Clear Lake*

Race in American Literature and Culture
Edited by John Ernest, *University of Delaware*

JAZZ AND AMERICAN CULTURE

EDITED BY

MICHAEL BORSHUK

Texas Tech University

Shaftesbury Road, Cambridge CB2 8EA, United Kingdom

One Liberty Plaza, 20th Floor, New York, NY 10006, USA

477 Williamstown Road, Port Melbourne, VIC 3207, Australia

314–321, 3rd Floor, Plot 3, Splendor Forum, Jasola District Centre, New Delhi – 110025, India

103 Penang Road, #05–06/07, Visioncrest Commercial, Singapore 238467

Cambridge University Press is part of Cambridge University Press & Assessment, a department of the University of Cambridge.

We share the University's mission to contribute to society through the pursuit of education, learning and research at the highest international levels of excellence.

www.cambridge.org
Information on this title: www.cambridge.org/9781009420198
DOI: 10.1017/9781009420167

© Cambridge University Press & Assessment 2024

This publication is in copyright. Subject to statutory exception and to the provisions of relevant collective licensing agreements, no reproduction of any part may take place without the written permission of Cambridge University Press & Assessment.

First published 2024

Printed in the United Kingdom by TJ Books Limited, Padstow, Cornwall

A catalogue record for this publication is available from the British Library

Library of Congress Cataloging-in-Publication Data
NAMES: Borshuk, Michael, editor.
TITLE: Jazz and American culture / edited by Michael Borshuk.
DESCRIPTION: [1.] | New York : Cambridge University Press, 2023. | Series: Cambridge themes in American literature and culture | Includes bibliographical references and index.
IDENTIFIERS: LCCN 2023022801 | ISBN 9781009420198 (hardback) | ISBN 9781009420167 (ebook other)
SUBJECTS: LCSH: Jazz – History and criticism. | Influence (Literary, artistic, etc.) – History – 20th century. | Jazz – Social aspects – United States. | Jazz – Political aspects – United States. | Music and literature – History.
CLASSIFICATION: LCC ML3508 .J37 2023 | DDC 781.650973–dc23/eng/20230606
LC record available at https://lccn.loc.gov/2023022801

ISBN 978-1-009-42019-8 Hardback

Cambridge University Press & Assessment has no responsibility for the persistence or accuracy of URLs for external or third-party internet websites referred to in this publication and does not guarantee that any content on such websites is, or will remain, accurate or appropriate.

Contents

List of Contributors   *page* viii
Acknowledgments   xv

    Introduction: A Brief History of Jazz in American Culture:
    Five Moments from Jim Crow to George Floyd   1
    Michael Borshuk

PART I   ELEMENTS OF SOUND AND STYLE

1   Improvisation   21
    Ajay Heble

2   Scat and Vocalese   35
    Chris Tonelli

3   Jazz as Intertextual Expression   49
    Charles Hersch

4   How to Watch Jazz: The Importance of Performance   64
    Michael Borshuk

PART II   AESTHETIC MOVEMENTS

5   Jazz Age Harlem   81
    Fiona I. B. Ngô

6   "Hard Times Don't Worry Me": The Blues in Black Music
    and Literature in the 1930s   96
    Steven C. Tracy

7   A Fool for Beauty: Modernism and the Racial Semiotics
    of Crooning   110
    Michael Coyle

8	Free Jazz, Critical Performativity, and 1968 *Michael Hrebeniak*	127

PART III   CULTURAL CONTEXTS

9	Jazz Slang, Jazz Speak *Amor Kohli*	145
10	Jazz Cool *Joel Dinerstein*	159
11	The Institutionalization of Jazz *Dale Chapman*	173
12	Jazz Abroad *Jürgen E. Grandt*	187

PART IV   LITERARY GENRES

13	Orchestrating Chaos: Othering and the Politics of Contingency in Jazz Fiction *Herman Beavers*	203
14	"Wail, Wop": Jazz Poetry on the Page and in Performance *Jessica E. Teague*	219
15	Jazz Criticism and Liner Notes *Timothy Gray*	234
16	Jazz Autobiography *Daniel Stein*	248
17	Jazz and the American Songbook *Katherine Williams*	262

PART V   IMAGES AND SCREENS

18	"The Sound I Saw": Jazz and Visual Culture *Amy Abugo Ongiri*	277
19	Love, Theft, and Transcendence: Jazz and Narrative Cinema *Krin Gabbard*	291
20	Reinstating Televisual Histories of Jazz *Nicolas Pillai*	305

21	Documentary Jazz/Jazz Documentary *Will Finch*	319
22	Two Dark Rooms: Jazz and Photography *Benjamin Cawthra*	338

Bibliography 352
Index 393

Contributors

HERMAN BEAVERS is the Julie Beren Platt and Marc E. Platt President's Distinguished Professor of English and Africana Studies at the University of Pennsylvania, where he has taught since 1989. He teaches courses in twentieth- and twenty-first-century African American literature and creative writing. Professor Beavers's most recent poems have appeared in *The Langston Hughes Colloquy, MELUS, Versadelphia, Cleaver Magazine, The American Arts Quarterly,* and *Supplement, Volume 2*. His poems are anthologized in the volumes *Obsession: Sestinas for the Twenty-First Century* (University Press of New England, 2014), *Remembering Gwendolyn Brooks* (Moonstone Press, 2017), *Who Will Speak for America?* (Temple University Press, 2018), and *Show Us Your Papers* (Mainstreet Rag Press, 2020). His chapbook, *Obsidian Blues*, was published in 2017 by Agape Editions as part of its Morning House Chapbook Series. His latest books are *Geography and the Political Imaginary in the Novels of Toni Morrison* (Palgrave Macmillan, 2018) and *The Vernell Poems* (Moonstone Press, 2019).

MICHAEL BORSHUK is Associate Professor of African American Literature and Director of the Humanities Center at Texas Tech University. He is the author of *Swinging the Vernacular: Jazz and African American Modernist Literature* (Routledge, 2006) and many essays and book chapters on African American literature, American modernism, and music. His most recent project is a guest edited special issue, *Steely Dan at 50*, for *Rock Music Studies*. From 1999 to 2009, he wrote on jazz regularly for *Coda* magazine.

BENJAMIN CAWTHRA is Professor of History at California State University, Fullerton. He is the author of *Blue Notes in Black and White: Photography and Jazz* (University of Chicago Press, 2011) and *Herb Snitzer: Photographs from the Last Years of Metronome* (Sheldon Art

Galleries, 2008) and articles on Miles Davis, Wynton Marsalis, Duke Ellington, and photographer/curator Lee Tanner. He has curated exhibitions on Davis and on the photography of Snitzer, Kathy Sloane, and William Gottlieb and was an on-camera consultant for Stanley Nelson's film *Miles Davis: Birth of the Cool* (2019).

DALE CHAPMAN is Associate Professor of Music at Bates College. His research primarily centers on the political economy of contemporary music. His book, *The Jazz Bubble: Neoclassical Jazz in Neoliberal Culture*, was published with the University of California Press in 2018. His work has appeared in the *Journal of Popular Music Studies*, the *Journal of the Society for American Music*, *Popular Music*, the *Oxford Handbook of Sound and Image in Digital Media* (2013), the *Oxford Handbook of Music and Advertising* (2020), and the Bloomsbury collections *Cybermedia: Science, Sound,* and *Vision* (2021) and *Transmedia Directors: Artistry, Industry, and New Audiovisual Aesthetics* (2019).

MICHAEL COYLE is Professor of English at Colgate University, Founding President of the Modernist Studies Association, and a past president of the International T. S. Eliot Society. He has published widely on modernist poetry and modernist cultural history – within which his attention to jazz history developed as a special focus. He has lectured on jazz history and African American music at events sponsored by the Smithsonian and the Rock & Roll Hall of Fame, as well as at numerous professional conferences. Faculty Adviser to and Jazz DJ for WRCU radio station, he served as a regular jazz record reviewer for *Cadence* magazine for fifteen years. The development and reception of jazz tradition remains a long-term interest.

JOEL DINERSTEIN is the author of five books, three of them on cool – *Jazz: A Quick Immersion* (Tibidabo, 2020), *The Origins of Cool in Postwar America* (University of Chicago Press, 2017), *American Cool* (Prestel, 2014), *Swinging the Machine: Modernity, Technology, and African-American Culture* (University of Massachusetts Press, 2003) – and a brand study, *Coach: A Story of New York Cool* (Rizzoli, 2016). His TED Talk on cool, "Why Cool Matters," is on YouTube. He was the curator of *American Cool* (2014), an acclaimed exhibit of 100 icons at the National Portrait Gallery. He has served as a consultant for jazz and popular music for HBO's *Boardwalk Empire*, the National Endowment for the Humanities, and the New Orleans Jazz Museum. He is a professor in the English Department of Tulane University in New Orleans.

x   *List of Contributors*

WILL FINCH'S research focuses on relationships between music and screen media. His doctoral thesis presented the first analysis of music and sound in the BBC's off-beat arts documentary strand *Arena* (1975–present) – on the means by which *Arena* constructs ideas about music, and on the uses the series itself makes of music. He is currently working on an eco-critical history and analysis of sound and music at the BBC's Natural History Unit and the ways they have shaped popular experiences and understandings of "nature."

KRIN GABBARD teaches the occasional course in the Jazz Studies program at Columbia University. In 2014 he retired from Stony Brook University where he had, since 1981, taught classical literature, film studies, and literary theory. His books include *Psychiatry and the Cinema* (American Psychiatric Press, 1999), *Jammin' at the Margins: Jazz and the American Cinema* (University of Chicago Press, 1996), *Black Magic: White Hollywood and African American Culture* (Rutgers University Press, 2004), *Hotter Than That: The Trumpet, Jazz, and American Culture* (Faber & Faber, 2009), and most recently, *Better Git It in Your Soul: An Interpretive Biography of Charles Mingus* (University of California Press, 2016). He is also the editor of *Jazz among the Discourses* (Duke University Press, 1995). Now that he is retired, he spends most of his time practicing the trumpet and working crossword puzzles.

JÜRGEN E. GRANDT is an independent scholar residing in Switzerland. The author of numerous articles in African American and American studies, he has also penned *Kinds of Blue: The Jazz Aesthetic in African American Narrative* (Ohio State University Press, 2004) and *Shaping Words to Fit the Soul: The Southern Ritual Grounds of Afro-Modernism* (Ohio State University Press, 2009). His most recent monograph is *Gettin' Around: Jazz, Script, Transnationalism* (University of Georgia Press, 2018).

TIMOTHY GRAY is Professor of English at College of Staten Island, City University of New York. His books include *Gary Snyder and the Pacific Rim: Creating Countercultural Community* (University of Iowa Press, 2006), *Urban Pastoral: Natural Currents in the New York School* (University of Iowa Press, 2010), *Moonchild: Poems* (FootHills, 2013), and *It's Just the Normal Noises: Marcus, Guralnick, No Depression, and the Mystery of Americana Music* (University of Iowa Press, 2017). He is currently writing a book on Soft Rock (due from University of Iowa Press in 2025).

List of Contributors

AJAY HEBLE is the Founding Director of the International Institute for Critical Studies in Improvisation and Professor of English in the School of English and Theatre Studies at the University of Guelph. His research has covered a full range of topics in the arts and humanities and has resulted in sixteen books published or in press, numerous articles or chapters, and over 100 graduate students and postdoctoral fellows trained and mentored. He was the Founding Artistic Director of the award-winning Guelph Jazz Festival and Colloquium (he served in that capacity for twenty-three years, retiring in 2016) and is a founding coeditor of the peer-reviewed journal *Critical Studies in Improvisation/ Études critiques en improvisation*. Heble is also an accomplished pianist with a long background as a performer. His first CD, a live set of improvised music called *Different Windows*, with percussionist Jesse Stewart, was released on the IntrepidEar label in 2001. His recent recordings include *Hold True (Accroche-Toi)*, *The Time of the Sign*, and *Le gouffre/ The Chasm*, all with his improvising quartet The Vertical Squirrels (and released on the Ambiances Magnétiques label).

CHARLES HERSCH is Emeritus Professor of Political Science at Cleveland State University. He is the author of *Democratic Artworks: Politics and the Arts from Trilling to Dylan* (State University of New York Press, 1998), *Subversive Sounds: Race and the Birth of Jazz in New Orleans* (University of Chicago Press, 2007), and *Jews and Jazz: Improvising Ethnicity* (Routledge, 2017).

MICHAEL HREBENIAK is a lecturer in film poetics at University College London and Convenor of the New School of the Anthropocene, a higher-educational experiment dedicated to confronting biopolitical emergency through the arts. He previously taught at Cambridge University and the Royal Academy of Music, and has worked as a documentary film producer and jazz journalist. His first book, *Action Writing: Jack Kerouac's Wild Form* (Southern Illinois University Press), was published in 2006, and he has continued to write on the Beats, as well as contributing chapters to edited collections on cinema, visual culture, jazz, and ecopoetics. He is currently writing a book for the British Film Institute on the BBC Arena strand and his first feature-length film, *Stirbitch: An Imaginary*, was premiered at the Heong Gallery in Cambridge in 2019.

AMOR KOHLI is Associate Professor and Chair of the Department of African and Black Diaspora Studies at DePaul University. Kohli's publications include essays on Black writers published in scholarly journals such as *Callaloo, MELUS*, and *Journal of Commonwealth Literature*. His work has also appeared in edited collections, including *Beat Drama: Playwrights and Performances of the "Howl" Generation* (Bloomsbury, 2016) and *The Black Imagination, Science Fiction, and the Speculative* (Routledge, 2011). His most recent publication is as editor of *A Beat Beyond: Selected Prose of Major Jackson* (University of Michigan Press, 2022).

FIONA I. B. NGÔ is Associate Professor in American Studies at the University of Virginia, specializing in transnational US cultural and intellectual history, with particular attention to music, aesthetic cultures, refugees, and other aftereffects of war. *Imperial Blues* (Duke University Press, 2014) focuses on the role of imperialism in shaping the gendered, racial, and sexual logics of Jazz Age New York. With Elizabeth Stinson, Ngô coedited a special issue of *Women & Performance* called "Punk Anteriors," also contributing an article titled "Punk in the Shadow of War," which takes on Los Angeles's early punk scene through the lenses of space, violence, political economy, imperialism, and racial formation in the critical years following the official end of war in Vietnam. Ngô has coedited a special issue of *positions* on "Southeast Asian Diaspora" with Mimi Thi Nguyen and Mariam Lam, and published an article called "Sense and Subjectivity" concerning the figure of the Cambodian refugee in *Camera Obscura*.

AMY ABUGO ONGIRI is Professor and Director of Ethnic Studies at the University of Portland. Their work focuses on visual culture at the intersection of race, gender, and identity and their book *Spectacular Blackness: The Cultural Politics of the Black Power Movement and the Search for a Black Aesthetic* (University of Virginia Press, 2009) explores the cultural politics of the Black Power movement, particularly the Black Arts movement's search to define a "Black Aesthetic." Their academic work has been published in *College Literature, Journal of African American History, Camera Obscura, Postmodern Culture, Black Filmmaker, The Los Angeles Review of Books*, and *Nka: The Journal of Contemporary African Art*. In addition to academic publications, they have also published creative nonfiction in *Black Girl Dangerous, Mutha Magazine, Glitterwolf, Black Lesbian Love Lab*, and the *Rad Families* anthology.

NICOLAS PILLAI is Assistant Professor of Creative and Critical Practice at University College Dublin. He currently serves as the university's Academic Lead on Creative Futures Academy, a €10-million project funded by Ireland's Human Capital Initiative. He is managing editor of *Jazz Research Journal* and a BBC Four documentary based on his research won Best Music Programme at the 2020 Broadcast Awards. Publications in progress include the edited collection *Rethinking Miles Davis* (Oxford University Press, forthcoming) and a short play, *Albert Ayler's Ghost* (published in *Jazz Research Journal*, 2022).

DANIEL STEIN is Professor of North American Literary and Cultural Studies at the University of Siegen, Germany. He is the author of *Music Is My Life: Louis Armstrong, Autobiography, and American Jazz* (University of Michigan Press, 2012) and *Authorizing Superhero Comics: On the Evolution of a Popular Serial Genre* (Ohio State University Press, 2021), and coeditor of the special issue *Musical Autobiographies* of *Popular Music & Society* (2015). He is a member of the Collaborative Research Center 1472 *Transformations of the Popular*, funded by the German Research Foundation, and is one of the editors of *Anglia: Journal of English Philology*.

JESSICA E. TEAGUE is an associate professor of English at the University of Nevada, Las Vegas, and author of *Sound Recording Technology and American Literature, from the Phonograph to the Remix* (Cambridge University Press, 2021). The intersections between literature, sound, and technology are the focus of her research. Her teaching, like her scholarship, is interdisciplinary and engages with modernism, sound studies, jazz and popular music, theatre and performance, new media, and African American studies. Her work has been published or is forthcoming from venues such as *American Quarterly*, *Sound Studies*, *SoundingOut!*, and *MELUS*. Dr. Teague has also been the recipient of fellowships from the American Council of Learned Societies and the Harrison Institute at the University of Virginia. She is currently working on a new book about the history of jazz in Las Vegas.

CHRIS TONELLI is Assistant Professor of Music at the University of Groningen and the author of *Voices Found: Free Jazz and Singing* (Routledge, 2020). He has also published essays on the sociopolitical effects of human vocal sound in the journals *Music & Politics* and *Yearbook for Traditional Music*. He is a community music practitioner, soundsinger, and improvising choir leader who has founded several "Vocal Exploration" Choirs/Gatherings, as well as a research associate with the International Institute for Critical Studies in Improvisation. He also works in the field of popular music studies, researching mimesis/pastiche, transnational dynamics, and musical masculinities.

STEVEN C. TRACY is a distinguished university professor at the University of Massachusetts Amherst. He has been writing about African American vernacular music for over fifty years. Author, editor, coeditor, and introducer of thirty books, he also has a reputation as a significant harmonica player and singer.

KATHERINE WILLIAMS primarily works on jazz, popular music, music and gender, and music and geography. Her work has been published in *Jazz Perspectives* and *Jazz Research Journal*, which she also edited from 2018 to 2021. Her published books include the *Cambridge Companion to the Singer-Songwriter* (Cambridge University Press, 2016), *Singer-Songwriter Handbook* (Bloomsbury, 2017), and the monograph *Rufus Wainwright* (Equinox, 2016). Between 2014 and 2020, she was Lecturer in Music and Head of Performance at the University of Plymouth, UK.

Acknowledgments

Sometime after I'd assembled this volume's roster of contributors and shared that list with everyone involved, one of them wrote back enthusiastically, "This is quite a big band you put together!" This is the perfect way to assess the collective excellence of the writers whose work follows here. Each of them, as unique as the soloists in a great ensemble, brings a vital perspective to the history of jazz and American culture. I am exceedingly grateful for their participation and their insight into the wide-ranging, century-plus context we explore together.

I am thankful to Ray Ryan, our commissioning editor at Cambridge University Press, for helping to shape the book's concept, and for his patience and support during its development. I also owe much to Edgar Mendez for his help in moving the project toward publication.

I am very grateful to my colleagues and friends in the Department of English and the Humanities Center at Texas Tech University, for their intellectual company and unfailing encouragement. Finally, my work on this project, like everything I do, is dedicated with love and gratitude to my family for all the ways they support me. For my mother, Leslee, my sister, Jenny, and in memory of my father, Tom; and especially for Jess and Tommy, always.

Introduction
A Brief History of Jazz in American Culture: Five Moments from Jim Crow to George Floyd

Michael Borshuk

I begin with the following five events to introduce the variety of contexts that *Jazz and American Culture* explores. Scholarly studies on jazz often narrate the form's development as a series of innovators acting in singular moments of performance, on stage or on record. This tendency is one way to contain an otherwise unruly set of musical developments and curtail a range of competing cultural discourses into tidier understandings. It might seem like I've succumbed to that academic temptation here – collating a cluster of myths and presenting them with certainty as the authoritative historical record. Instead, I ask you to see these five moments not as signposts on a straight and certain path through the history of jazz and American culture, but rather as a handful of nodes from which a much messier story might extend.

August 10, 1920: Mamie Smith Records "Crazy Blues"

This wasn't even Mamie Smith's first recording session.

That came earlier, on Valentine's Day, when the vaudeville singer cut two tracks for Okeh Records and promptly produced a notable first: the earliest documented recording by a Black woman.[1] Backed by Okeh's house band, the Rega Dance Orchestra, Smith created a record that some heard as "indistinguishable from white pop music fare of the period."[2] (Incidentally, Okeh had actually wanted the Jewish-American entertainer Sophie Tucker, but conceded to Smith because Tucker was unavailable.)

Smith's pedestrian debut certainly didn't even evince the manic energy of the first jazz recordings, released a few years earlier by the all-white Original Dixieland Jazz Band (ODJB). Over 1917 and 1918, the ODJB emerged as unlikely pioneers, after the Creole cornetist Freddie Keppard turned down RCA Victor's invitation to record and they took the offer instead. Their ragged, risible jazz on 78s like "Livery Stable Blues" (with its simulated animal sounds) has long been eclipsed in listeners' memories by other early jazz records. But while the ODJB didn't offer innovation in these early efforts, they at least brought some *oomph*. Nevertheless, Smith had challenged the recording industry's Jim Crow economics, and the record's modest sales opened the door for a momentous second act.

In August, Smith returned to the studio with pianist Perry Bradford, who had composed her featured song, "Harlem Blues," for the stage show, *Maid of Harlem*.[3] Bradford liked to tinker with the blues form while hanging out at the Colored Vaudeville Benevolent Association on Lenox Avenue. As Samuel Charters and Leonard Kunstadt suggest, Bradford's love of the blues – a vernacular form rooted in Southern expression – didn't sit especially well with his Harlem contemporaries. "To them the blues stood for everything they had tried to leave behind them."[4] For the new session, Bradford renamed "Harlem Blues" to "Crazy Blues" – allegedly to make the composition appear new. He'd been selling Okeh on the value of the blues for some time. Most importantly, he wanted to release recordings of African American vernacular music performed by Black musicians, not made palatable to white buyers by white performers. Bradford later recalled having argued that Smith "sings jazz songs with more soulful feeling than other girls, for it's only natural with us."[5]

This time Mamie performed with Black musicians, the Jazz Hounds, after Bradford declared the Rega Orchestra idiomatically unsuitable.[6] The difference between the two sessions was palpable. "Crazy Blues" crackles by comparison.[7] Rhythmically less rigid, it possesses more of the gut-bucket sass we associate now with early jazz aesthetics. Its lyrics are bold, as well. In the most shocking verse – which Bradford excised for sheet music publication – Smith bellows, "I'm gonna do like a Chinaman ... get myself some hop / Get myself a gun ... and shoot myself a cop."[8] Smith the blueswoman was imagining (though articulated through the denigrating language of unchecked Orientalism) getting stoned and reciprocating the violence police rained down on Black citizens. For this reason, Adam Gussow has called "Crazy Blues," "an insurrectionary social text," part of "an evolving social discourse of black revolutionary violence in the broadest sense – which is to say, black violence as a way of resisting white violence and a repressive social order."[9]

All of this – the sonic, the social – resonated with record buyers, especially African Americans. In a month the record sold 75,000 copies; some estimate its eventual total sales to have reached one million.[10]

The record's success also cleared a space for the emergence of many African American innovators in blues and jazz. As Daphne Brooks summarizes, the wild returns on Smith and Bradford's collaboration "provided Black artists with access – though still heavily mediated by white executives – to recording their own music," while also changing the aesthetic terms of American popular music by admitting "musical innovations [which] were the manifestation of a brutal, centuries-long, blood-soaked struggle to be regarded as human in the West."[11] After "Crazy Blues" became a smash, Okeh hired the Black pianist and composer Clarence Williams to direct a new "race records" division. The ensuing releases – Okeh's 8000 series of 78 rpm sides – included early recordings by King Oliver's Jazz Band, featuring Louis Armstrong, and later, Armstrong's own much-fêted Hot Five records.

Other companies followed suit. "Crazy Blues" launched the race records industry – promoting Black music to Black listeners, and with this development came a comprehensive documentation of the Black innovators who now define our understanding of early jazz. As Amiri Baraka commented in his 1963 study of Black music, *Blues People*, "Crazy Blues" spoke back to a conspicuous absence wherein "jazz had rushed into the mainstream without so much as one black face."[12] Without Smith's commercial triumph, which redefined a market, there is no easy passage toward what has become the early jazz canon, those records that followed from Armstrong, Duke Ellington, or Bessie Smith.

Beyond unsettling segregation's racially restricted access to economic reward, "Crazy Blues" also participated in the era's changing discourses about African American art and Black self-definition. In 1925, Alain Locke gave name to these game-changing cultural turns in his essay, "The New Negro."[13] There, he summarized postwar changes in African American life through artistic developments and an ideological shift among African Americans toward greater political assertiveness.[14] In Locke's narration, the New Negro had moved north and moved urban amid the century's seismic migrations – just as the blues idiom as an aesthetic counterpart had traveled from its Southern vernacular birthplace to the Northern recording studio or the New York stage. Locke himself did not assert this connection, though in retrospect, the import of the nearly simultaneous emergence of the New Negro and the blues idiom seems fairly obvious. Rather, Langston Hughes was among a culturally insurgent minority when he called out in 1926: "Let the blare of Negro jazz bands and the bellowing voice of Bessie Smith singing Blues penetrate the closed ears of the colored near-intellectuals until they listen and perhaps understand."[15] Locke took a decade to extol the cultural value of these brassy innovations. In his later study, *The Negro and His Music* (1936), he admits of jazz, "It is now part

Negro, part American, part modern; a whole period of modern civilization may ultimately be best known and understood as 'The Jazz Age.'"[16]

Later scholars have offered corrections to the Harlem intelligentsia's slow awakening. Notably, Angela Y. Davis appraises the work of Bessie Smith, Ma Rainey, and Billie Holiday – three Black women whose careers built on Mamie Smith's early success – as "divulg[ing] unacknowledged traditions of feminist consciousness in working-class black communities."[17] Explaining the missing attention to Black women blues singers in political-aesthetic writings of the Harlem Renaissance, Davis writes, "because women like Bessie Smith and Ida Cox presented and embodied sexualities associated with working-class black life – which, fatally, was seen by some Renaissance strategists as antithetical to the aims of their cultural movement – their music was designated as 'low' culture, in contrast, for example, to endeavors such as sculpture, painting, literature, and classical music."[18] The popularity of these vernacular performances exposed the limits of middle-class intellectuals' articulation of new Black identities.

Davis reminds us how this challenge went beyond class and gender. The exploratory vernacular space that jazz and blues opened also allowed for a reconsideration of sexual identity. Recordings by Black women celebrated queer intimacy and depicted departures from heterosexual norms without apology. In "Prove It on Me Blues,"[19] for example, Ma Rainey sings slyly, "Went out last night with a crowd of my friends / They must've been women, 'cause I don't like men."[20] Lucille Bogan explores the butch character of the "bulldagger" in her 1935 recording, "B.D. Woman's Blues."[21] Offstage, Ma Rainey, Bessie Smith, and Ethel Waters maintained relationships with women. The immensely popular Gladys Bentley cut blues records for Okeh and drew big crowds for her live shows in Harlem. Bentley performed in drag and delighted audiences with her bawdy improvisations, at times flouting moral restrictions by adding verses about "sodomy" to familiar Broadway tunes.[22]

In short, American listeners were certainly alive to the novelty and invigorating difference of Black music after the war, even if it took some people time to hear properly just how important jazz and blues were to the century's ongoing revolutions.

March 1939: Billie Holiday Premieres "Strange Fruit" in Performance at Café Society

The song began as a poem composed by schoolteacher Abel Meeropol. Billie Holiday wasn't even the first to perform it.

Meeropol taught for years at DeWitt Clinton High School in the Bronx, a school whose past students include jazz musicians George Duvivier, Herbie Nichols, and Fats Waller. Meeropol was also a political activist and a prolific writer (of literature, of music) under the pen name Lewis Allan. In the latter role, he earned famous admirers like Ira Gershwin and Thomas Mann, and wrote other works that remain in the collective consciousness. (His later composition "The House I Live In," co-written with Earl Robinson, was recorded by Frank Sinatra and Paul Robeson, among others.) In 1937, Meeropol published the anti-lynching poem "Bitter Fruit" in a union magazine called *The New York Teacher*. Afterwards, he set the text to music himself. The song became a favorite among the New York left, performed in intimate settings by anti-Fascists and union members. When Robert Gordon – an entertainment director from Café Society, where Holiday was headlining – heard it, he brought it to Lady Day.[23]

At Café Society, Holiday performed in a setting intended to challenge racism's hold on the New York entertainment landscape. Black performers had been visible in the city's cabarets for decades, but patronage often conformed to Jim Crow's restrictions. Duke Ellington and Cab Calloway had headlined Harlem's Cotton Club, but that venue's racial policing ensured that the clientele listening were exclusively white. For Café Society, owner Barney Josephson wanted inclusive patronage, encouraging jazz appreciation in a progressive setting. (The club's famous slogan was "the Right Place for the Wrong People.") As Josephson recalled later, "I often wondered how Billie Holiday, for instance, who always kept one eye on the door when she sang, must feel when singing in a place where her own people were not permitted in. But if they were welcomed and seated at ringside tables, wouldn't that make a difference in Billie's performance and others also?"[24]

Holiday's inaugural performance of "Strange Fruit" has been dramatized once onscreen, by Diana Ross in 1972's *Lady Sings the Blues*,[25] where the premiere is cast as an expression of Holiday's personal anguish. Fictionalizing the sequence of events, *Lady Sings the Blues* has Holiday touring the South with a white band. When she takes an impromptu break from the tour bus to relieve herself in the wild, she stumbles across a traumatized Black family cutting a lynched family member down from a tree. Stunned, Billie returns to the bus and urges the driver to leave. As "Strange Fruit" opens in underscore, we're presented with a long look at her grieving face looking out the bus window, before the scene cuts to a mournful Holiday in performance. Overall, Ross's Holiday is frail and the scene presents "Strange Fruit" as a plaintive wail rather than a protest song. In the more recent *The United States vs. Billie Holiday*, singer Andra Day evokes a bolder Billie when "Strange Fruit" finally appears (in a concert hall setting, not Café Society) during the film's second half.[26] Day's gaze meets the camera fiercely and she offers the first verse acapella. Here, we have a hint of the song's historical audacity. But even this version diminishes the song's legacy through a preceding montage: showing a drug-addled Holiday trying to overcome her debilitating addiction. Ultimately, in both films, "Strange Fruit" dramatizes the singer's internal wrestling with adversity, rather than emphasizing how she transformed Meeropol's text into an adversarial stance.

As both Hilton Als and Farah Jasmine Griffin have pointed out, there is a disturbing critical discourse that dismisses Holiday's agency by doubting her awareness of her own political importance. Some writers, they note, insult Holiday as an undisciplined simpleton – a drug addict who, in Griffin's words, "was semiliterate, read only comic books, and was barely capable of understanding the meaning of the song 'Strange Fruit.'"[27] Misrepresenting Holiday as a tortured savant, these takes fail to understand her genius in performance. Again, to quote Griffin: "In performance her charisma made each member of her audience feel as though she were singing directly to them, expressing exactly what they were feeling. Even during the final years of her life, when her voice was practically gone, Holiday was still capable of rendering a lyric with profound meaning and drama."[28]

Reading Holiday as theatrical does not imply a thespian in the conventional sense, meaning an actor with a clearly delineated offstage life, who inhabits a different character under the lights. Holiday's great talent was to produce art that was embodied, understood always through the effect of her onstage presence or the mediated double of its recorded simulation. Her musical approach recalls what Fred Moten labels "the freedom drive that animates black performances."[29] In song, her performance of Blackness, of womanhood, of Black womanhood, and her self-aware presentation of those subject positions in relationship to the limiting or violent ways social forces positioned her, exemplifies, again in Moten's words, "the improvisation through the opposition of spirit and matter that is instantiated when the object, the commodity, sounds."[30] Others may have tried to make Billie Holiday an object – of exploitation, of destruction – but her embodied performance counters that violence.

Among the myths Holiday proposes in her autobiography is her claim to have co-authored "Strange Fruit." In her telling, Holiday was presented with the poem and was actively involved in "turn[ing] it into music."[31]

Introduction 7

While this tale of origins is a tall one, it is worth remembering Als's suggestion that Holiday is the song's *auteur* even if she wasn't its author.[32] In other words, the example of Holiday reminds us how jazz as comprehensive performance complicates the stable way we think of authorship and artistic creation. Holiday also didn't write the many great tunes she performed from the American Songbook. But are "All of Me" or "I Cover the Waterfront" any less her creation for not having written the words or music?

Summer, 1955: RCA Victor Releases the Eponymous *Count Basie*, a Long-Playing Compilation of Previously Unreleased Count Basie Material, with Cover Art by Andy Warhol

It's certainly not Basie's most canonical release.

Reviewing RCA Victor's *Basie* for *Billboard* magazine on July 2, 1955, an unsigned critic admitted it might be a "must for Basie fans," but that the band was "by no means at its peak" when the recordings were made, 1947 to 1950.[33] While the music wasn't as essential as the early 78s with Lester Young or the hit mid-century long-playing records (LPs) such as *April in Paris* or *The Atomic Mr. Basie* still to come, there was something notable that buyers wouldn't have realized at the time. The line drawing of Basie on the album's cover was by a professional illustrator named Andy Warhol.

Warhol had already done illustrations for nonjazz records after his 1949 arrival in New York. His first LP commission was *A Program of Mexican Music* by Carlos Chavez, a Columbia release sponsored by the Museum of Modern Art. The Basie commission is in keeping with Warhol's Bauhaus-derived merger of art and design. Its stylized portrait of the Count with a cigarette in his mouth and his hat at a rakish angle anticipates a series of important developments: in Warhol's career, in jazz marketing, and in the broader place the music was coming to occupy in American life.

The Basie drawing looks ahead to Warhol's increasing emphasis on American icons. In later depictions of American celebrity – Elvis, Marilyn, Jackie O – he deployed commercial techniques to forge an aesthetic that stylized the famous in bright colors. Intriguingly, it was for a jazz record commission – saxophonist Paul Desmond's 1963 LP *Take Ten* – that Warhol initially used his signature silkscreen technique, to render Desmond's portrait.[34] Warhol saw a reciprocal relationship between professional assignments and the Pop style that made him internationally famous. As Pop became ubiquitous, its influence, unsurprisingly, spread back to commercial contexts. Look at Philip Chiang's Warholesque hand-colored silkscreen portrait of Ahmad Jamal for the jazz LP *Ahmad Jamal '73*, or Warhol's own silkscreen album covers for American divas Liza Minnelli, Diana Ross, or Aretha Franklin.[35]

More generally, the 1955 *Basie* image reminds us how the LP cover was becoming its own artistic medium. The advent of cover artwork on LPs – a far cry from the brown paper wrapping on earlier 78s – was important for collapsing the distance between jazz as popular music and high modernism's abstruse energy. In aestheticizing the product by incorporating the bold styles of twentieth-century art, cover artists placed the hi-fi system and the museum in conversation.

Of course, modern artists had been inspired by jazz in the past: Stuart Davis imagined the music by incorporating both Matisse's bold colors and Cubism's play with form in works like *Swing Landscape* (1938); Piet Mondrian visualized the intricate rhythms of New York piano players in *Broadway Boogie Woogie* (1942–43). By the 1950s, the relationship between jazz and visual modernism was more mutual. Jazz album covers might feature recognizable works by the zeitgeist's boldest innovators, as with the appearance of Jackson Pollock's *White Light* on the cover of Ornette Coleman's *Free Jazz* in 1960. In other examples, LP covers featured facsimiles of abstract expressionist work. Think, here, of the iconic S. Neil Fujita graphics that graced the covers of Dave Brubeck's *Time Out* and Charles Mingus's *Mingus Ah Um*, both from 1959.

In reading the sleeve art for Sonny Rollins's 1960 album *Way Out West*, Michael Jarrett proposes a "theory of album covers," suggesting that they "represent – encode in visual form – the myths associated with music […] and] contribute to the construction of those myths. They are part of the process that imbues music with meaning, gives it voice."[36] But the visual encoding at work on jazz album covers was not a simple importing of aesthetic significance from the art world by opportunistic designers. Rather, in the century's middle decades, practitioners across these expressive contexts were breaking down traditional hierarchies collectively. Dizzy Gillespie could shake his butt leading an orchestra through a ludic performance of "Salt Peanuts" in the 1946 film, *Jivin' in Be-Bop*, but he and Charlie Parker also brought bop to exclusive concert spaces like Carnegie Hall in 1947 or Toronto's Massey Hall in 1953. In the early sixties, Warhol and Roy Lichtenstein admitted the soup can and the comic book to the collective visual vocabulary of modern art. These examples reveal how porous the boundaries between art and the popular had become.

But jazz music's place in the loftier neighborhoods of American culture was sometimes still tenuous in the century's middle decades. Some were clear on the music's importance. In 1961's *The Beer Can by the Highway*, for instance, John A. Kouwenhoven read jazz (in all its musically varied "subspecies," as he was careful to note) as akin to the New York skyline, "a tension of cross-purposes" whose outcome was consistently "a dazzling precise creative unity."[37] Yet elsewhere, jazz had also not completely shaken its earlier rebellious associations. In 1957's "The White Negro," Norman Mailer adapted the historical racism of earlier white reactions to jazz, depicting the music as undisciplined, playfully threatening, and overtly sexual. In jazz, Mailer saw only a riotous (and in his mind, welcome) break from civilization, which Black creators had kindly bestowed on hip white listeners.[38] On television, Henry Mancini's jazz-themed score for *Peter Gunn* reminded viewers of the music's link to the seedier parts of the urban landscape through which the show's title detective repeatedly ventured.

The music was vital in these years to the kind of critical inquiry from outside which animates modern art across expressive forms. In its newer styles – bebop, the emerging free jazz – it still lived somewhat on the margins, but this was useful, inspiring bohemian poets and avant-garde painters. As William B. Scott and Peter M. Rutkoff write, "In Greenwich Village, at the Café Bohemia and the Village Vanguard, and, later, at the Five Spot on Cooper Square, beat poets, abstract artists, and hip college students in black turtlenecks, assembled, listened, and debated their distress all night."[39] These populations operated in constant exchange.

Jazz was still the object of competing cultural interpretations at mid-century, but more people were understanding the music as one of the great American contributions to modernist art.

April 7, 1997: Wynton Marsalis Wins the Pulitzer Prize for Music for His Long-Form Composition *Blood on the Fields*

The award's aesthetic prejudices were embedded right there in its mission statement: "For distinguished musical composition by an American in any of the larger forms including chamber, orchestral, choral, opera, song, dance, or other forms of musical theatre, which has had its first performance in the United States during the year."

Awarded annually since 1943, the Pulitzer Prize for Music carried with it a set of implied criteria that leaned toward European and classical, including a conservative conceptualization of "composition." Wasn't Charlie Parker spontaneously "composing" labyrinthine inventions in performance on the bandstand nightly in the forties and fifties? As the Pulitzer language made clear, significance was a byproduct of "larger forms" – symphonic, operatic – and less determined by cultural provocation or paradigm-shifting radicalism. Bebop, free jazz: these were significant, but they weren't award-worthy compositional contexts.

In 1965, the Pulitzer music jury proposed a special lifetime citation to commend Duke Ellington for his substantial body of work as a composer. This departure from the norm was rejected outright by the Pulitzer's advisory committee – a slight to Ellington, and to jazz broadly, that led two jury members (Robert Eyer and Winthrop Sargeant) to resign in protest.[40] The always debonair Ellington took the offense in stride, quipping famously, "Fate is being kind to me. Fate doesn't want me to be too famous too young."[41] But speaking more expansively with jazz writer Nat Hentoff, Ellington was clear on the reasons for his undervaluing: "Most Americans still take it for granted that European music – classical music, if you will – is the only really respectable kind."[42] Duke sidestepped the more volatile question of racism, but others have not in revisiting the controversy. In a recent *New York Times* piece about jazz critic Ted Gioia's campaign to have the 1965 prize awarded to Ellington posthumously, John McWhorter comments, "it strikes me as unlikely that racism wasn't part of why the Pulitzer board disregarded the jury's decision in Ellington's case."[43]

If in the mid-sixties the idea of a jazz artist being worthy of such a high honor was still contentious, what a difference a few decades made. On April 7, 1997, the Pulitzer for music was awarded to trumpeter and composer Wynton Marsalis for his sprawling jazz oratorio, *Blood on the Fields*, a Lincoln Center commission that revisited the experience of enslaved Black people. Marsalis's pioneering status as the first jazz honoree was not completely surprising, given his career trajectory. In 1983, for example, he had attained a music industry first by winning Grammy awards in both classical and jazz categories in the same year. (A year later, he repeated the feat.) For jazz, Marsalis championed a neoclassical approach that incorporated historical styles from early New Orleans to 1960s post-bop. But Marsalis's catholic attitude excluded later developments: jazz-rock fusion, free avant-garde playing, hip-hop. In the press, he was outspoken about his exacting criteria. The jazz tradition was expressively Black, rooted in blues tonalities and swing rhythms. The Marsalis orthodoxy was acoustic. He insisted that jazz resist the diluting lure of amplification or less serious aesthetic borrowings from the popular genres. "They call Miles' stuff jazz," Marsalis riffed in a 1982 *Down Beat* interview, referring to Miles Davis's recent synthesizer-driven pop and funk. "That stuff is not jazz, man. Just because somebody played jazz at one time, that doesn't mean they're still playing it."[44] In a 1984 Grammy acceptance speech, Marsalis dedicated his award to Armstrong, Parker, and Thelonious Monk, whom he claimed "gave an art form to the American people that cannot be limited by enforced trends or bad taste."[45] Allegedly, when Davis first met Marsalis in the 1980s, he sneered to the younger trumpeter, "So here's the police…"[46]

The 1990s saw the emergence of an institutional arm to support Marsalis's neoclassical ambitions. In 1991, with Marsalis as artistic director, Jazz at Lincoln Center (JALC) became an official department of the venerable arts establishment, building on four years of earlier concert programming. Five years later, JALC was inducted as "the first new constituent of Lincoln Center since the School of American Ballet joined in 1987."[47] In both the abstract and the material, jazz had become an American institution. Marsalis's efforts – which he conceptualized in conversation with his mentors, African American writers Albert Murray and Stanley Crouch – looked to confer classical legitimacy to jazz, the effects of which included a new generation of like-minded acoustic musicians or cultural documents such as Ken Burns's epic 2001 documentary *Jazz*.

But not all were enamored with these developments. A wide array of jazz artists increasingly positioned themselves outside the aesthetic and economic orbit of projects like Lincoln Center. This assembly, whom the scholar Herman Gray calls "the jazz left," resisted the invitation to calcify the music in nostalgic repertories.[48] Others criticized Jazz at Lincoln Center's avowed emphasis on Black aesthetic qualities and African American artists. In 1995, the critic Terry Teachout characterized JALC as an extension of what he called Murray and Crouch's "Crow Jim" cultural criticism, whose view of jazz history amounted to "reverse racism."[49]

In 1997, the Pulitzer jury did not shy from acknowledging the importance of race and African American historical experience to the artistic triumph of *Blood on the Fields*. As Howard Reich recalled later, he and his fellow jurors, in their report to the Pulitzer board, called special attention to the "power with which [the oratorio] expresses the pain and promise of the black experience in America."[50] Significantly, Reich also remembered how Marsalis's incorporation of jazz aesthetics – on their own terms – led to substantial changes in evaluation standards. Marsalis's score had, in Reich's words, "featured pages and pages of white space," where the composer intended individual players in his orchestra to improvise. By 1998, the Pulitzer board's guidelines for submission included "a score of the non-improvisational elements of the work" – a minor shift that challenged the prize's historical fixation on through-composition. These developments allowed for musical elements central to African American expressive traditions. By 2004, the Pulitzer board publicly announced more changes – in a statement subtitled "It's Time to Alter and Affirm" – including a complete relaxing of the requirement to submit a score at all, which the board acknowledged "will provide sufficient latitude for improvisational work."[51]

This led the way to the honoring of more jazz representatives, with Ornette Coleman in 2006, and Henry Threadgill in 2016, as well as the award's first hip-hop honoree, Kendrick Lamar in 2018.

September 7, 2020: James Carter Performs "Lift Every Voice and Sing" in a Socially Distanced Performance at the Detroit Jazz Festival

The summer had been painful and tumultuous.

The coronavirus pandemic disrupted everyday life amid its global growth since early March. The virus's mortal effects had thrown into stark relief persistent inequalities subtended by race, ethnicity, and class across the world. By Labor Day, of the nearly 200,000 documented American deaths by COVID-19, people of color – especially Black and Indigenous – had been most disproportionately harmed.[52] The pandemic was vicious to the jazz world, claiming, by mid-summer, pianist Ellis Marsalis, trumpeter Wallace Roney, guitarist Bucky Pizzarelli, bassist Henry Grimes, and saxophonists Lee Konitz and Manu Dibango.[53] Those musicians spared by the virus were affected dramatically by a world cast into unexpected lockdown: gigs canceled, clubs shuttered.

In late May, Minneapolis police constable Derek Chauvin murdered George Floyd, a Black motorist whose death was captured on cellphone video and circulated throughout the world. Floyd's murder added to a growing list of African American citizens killed by police (or would-be police, like Florida vigilante George Zimmerman) over the previous decade. Trayvon Martin, Michael Brown, Freddie Gray, Philando Castile, Breonna Taylor, Ahmaud Arbery. Floyd's death, seen over and over on screens while much of the country sat at home in lockdown, was a tipping point. Americans across identities took to the streets in protest throughout the summer, often clashing violently with police in riot gear.

Amid this volatile context, organizers of the Detroit Jazz Festival looked to salvage the largest free jazz festival in the United States, hosted every Labor Day weekend since 1980. With an eye to safety, the DJF planned a socially distanced event. They would assiduously test and mask all participating artists and staff, host performances without in-person audiences, and livestream the proceedings online for a global viewership.[54]

On Labor Day, toward the festival's conclusion, homegrown saxophonist James Carter took the stage with his organ trio. Carter had been wowing DJF audiences for three decades, showing off his otherworldly chops in various ensembles. But this homecoming was different; his trio hadn't played together in months. Earlier in the summer, Carter, along with his cousin and fellow Detroit jazz legend, violinist Regina Carter, spoke with Herb Boyd in *Down Beat* about the year's turmoil. Both artists directly referenced the ongoing pandemic and the Black Lives Matter-driven response to Floyd's murder. As the saxophonist summarized, grimly, "The pandemic, poverty and the police have brutally assailed the Black community."[55]

Carter's September set came, coincidentally, on Sonny Rollins's ninetieth birthday, and days after Charlie Parker's centennial on August 29th. Carter paid homage to both, opening with Parker's bebop standard "Confirmation," returning to the Parker songbook later with "Parker's Mood," and remembering Rollins and John Coltrane together through their 1957 collaboration "Tenor Madness." In these, Carter revealed how jazz continues to narrate its own history through echo and sonic reproduction. Jazz improvisation, which incorporates elements from shared vocabularies developed over time, allows individual soloists to embody their forebears, summoning past performances – as Carter did in these examples – in the current moment. Toward the close of the set, Carter invoked this transhistorical impulse again, performing a spirited version of the hymn "Lift Every Voice and Sing," the "Black national anthem," composed by James Weldon Johnson with his brother J. Rosamond Johnson just after the turn of the last century. The rendition was searing, an articulation of the year's pain in both elegiac and encouraging turns.

In her 2018 history of "Lift Every Voice," Imani Perry thinks through the song's ever-changing meaning, especially across time. Perry writes:

> Even as it was embraced by widely divergent political actors, some aspects of its meaning were and are resilient. It tells the singer to see herself or himself as emerging magnificently through struggle. It nurtures an identity rooted in community. It is a song that moves regionally and internationally, yet holds fast to a sense of particular belonging.[56]

Carter's September 2020 performance achieved these various resonances. He used the allusive power of multiple well-traveled song-texts to acknowledge the specificity of Black experience and to invite others' witnessing and commitment for change. The sound of his horn from Detroit carried listeners back through time, but also traversed geographies, moving through digital media to remind us of jazz music's ongoing power to affirm, critique, and surprise.

Jazz is wonderful in its contradictions: esoteric and antic, palliative and inflammatory, conservative and radical in its aesthetic standards and practices. Jazz has also always offered a record of the most volatile parts of American life and has regularly responded to the injustices and acts of violence that animate those upheavals. For over a century, its power has been simultaneously aesthetic and political. This, despite any ongoing critical, commercial, or institutional attempts to make it appear "serious" or less "dangerous," or to contain its persistent willfulness.

Many commentators have posited that jazz is an ideal model for democracy – an idea that several contributors in the following pages scrutinize. This view of jazz often proceeds from understanding the art form as a negotiation among diverse musical voices improvising together, in the service of performing an organic, satisfying whole. But what's lost in this sometimes overly romantic narrative is how often jazz has been a vital critique of American democracy as historical practice. Jazz observes no fidelity to the text nor fixation on stability. A musician who plays a song "straight," without personal flair, without an eye to opening the tune up to a series of sonic questions, is largely seen as going against the music's unspoken expectations. All of this is to say, emphatically, there's no constitution that jazz improvisers return to over and over again with rigid, originalist zeal.

Though I close with reminders about the always unfinished project that jazz – by its own aesthetic imperatives – constitutes, I also celebrate, paradoxically, the authoritative way the following chapters lead us through that uncertainty. This volume is history open to debate, a guidebook with competing directions. Expansive in its many conversations, *Jazz and American Culture* is every bit as provocative as the context it examines.

Notes

1 Eileen Southern, *The Music of Black Americans: A History*, 3rd ed. (New York: Norton, 1997), 369. The first Black recording star was George W. Johnson, a formerly enslaved singer and whistler whose documented career begins with a series of wax cylinders around 1890. For more on Johnson, and other early Black recording artists, see Tim Brooks, *Lost Sounds: Blacks and the Birth of the Recording Industry, 1890–1919* (Urbana and Chicago: University of Illinois Press, 2004).
2 Chris Albertson, *Bessie Smith*, revised and expanded ed. (New Haven: Yale University Press, 2003), 24.

Introduction 15

3 Samuel B. Charters and Leonard Kunstadt, *Jazz: A History of the New York Scene* (Garden City, NY: Doubleday, 1962), 83.
4 Ibid., 82.
5 Perry Bradford, *Born with the Blues: Perry Bradford's Own Story* (New York: Oak Publications, 1965), 118.
6 Charters and Kunstadt, *Jazz*, 85.
7 Mamie Smith, "Crazy Blues" (Okeh 4169, 1920).
8 Adam Gussow, "'Shoot Myself a Cop': Mamie Smith's 'Crazy Blues' as Social Text," *Callaloo* 25.1 (2002), 10–11. Gussow cites the detail about removing the lyric from the sheet music from Bradford, *Born with the Blues*, 154. I cite the song's lyrics from Gussow's transcription on pages 38–39 of his article.
9 Gussow, "Shoot Myself a Cop," 10.
10 Ted Gioia, *The History of Jazz*, 2nd ed. (New York: Oxford University Press, 2011), 16. These numbers are cited in most historical narrations of "Crazy Blues" and its success. Gussow speculates that the million figure may be slightly suspect, and might include other kinds of sales, like sheet music or other artists' versions. See Gussow, "Shoot Myself a Cop," 40 n2.
11 Daphne A. Brooks, *Liner Notes for the Revolution: The Intellectual Life of Black Feminist Sound* (Cambridge, MA: Harvard University Press, 2021), 334. For more of Brooks's commentary on "Crazy Blues," see "1920, August 10: Mamie Smith Becomes the First Black Woman to Make a Phonograph Record," in Greil Marcus and Werner Sollers, eds., *A New Literary History of America* (Cambridge, MA: Harvard University Press, 2009), 545–50.
12 Amiri Baraka (LeRoi Jones), *Blues People: The Negro Experience in White America and the Music that Developed from It* (New York: Morrow, 1963), 100.
13 In its initial published form for the periodical *The Survey Graphic*, Locke titled this essay "Enter the New Negro," before shortening the title for its eventual book publication in his edited collection of the same name.
14 Alain Locke, "The New Negro," in Alain Locke, ed., *The New Negro*, 1925 (New York: Touchstone, 1997), 3–16.
15 Langston Hughes, "The Negro Artist and the Racial Mountain," 1926, in Angelyn Mitchell, ed., *Within the Circle: An Anthology of African American Literary Criticism from the Harlem Renaissance to the Present* (Durham, NC: Duke University Press, 1994), 59.
16 Alain Locke, *The Negro and His Music* (Washington, DC: The Associates in Negro Folk Education, 1936), 90.
17 Angela Y. Davis, *Blues Legacies and Black Feminism* (New York: Pantheon, 1998), xi.
18 Ibid., xiii.
19 Ma Rainey, "Prove It on Me Blues" (Paramount 12668, 1928).
20 Davis, *Blues Legacies*, 39.
21 Lucille Bogan [Bessie Jackson], "B.D. Woman's Blues," Rec. March 7, 1935, *Complete Recorded Works in Chronological Order, Vol. 3* (Document Records BDCD-6038, 1993); Eric Garber, "Gladys Bentley: The Bulldagger Who Sang the Blues," *OutLook: National Lesbian and Gay Quarterly* 1 (1988), 58.

22 Garber, "Gladys Bentley," 55. For more on Bentley, especially as a representative artist of "queer modernism," see Patricia Yaeger, "Editor's Note: Bulldagger Sings the Blues," *PMLA*, 124.3 (2009), 721–26.
23 David Margolick, *Strange Fruit: Billie Holiday, Café Society, and an Early Cry for Civil Rights* (Philadelphia: Running Press, 2000), 33–37.
24 Barney Josephson, with Terry Trilling-Josephson, *Café Society: The Wrong Place for the Right People* (Urbana: University of Illinois Press, 2009), 110.
25 Sidney J. Furie, dir., *Lady Sings the Blues* (Paramount, 1972).
26 Lee Daniels, dir., *The United States vs. Billie Holiday* (Lee Daniels Entertainment, 2021).
27 Farah Jasmine Griffin, *If You Can't Be Free, Be a Mystery: In Search of Billie Holiday* (New York: The Free Press, 2001), 15; see also, Hilton Als, "Foreword," in David Margolick, *Strange Fruit: Billie Holiday, Café Society, and an Early Cry for Civil Rights* (Philadelphia: Running Press, 2000), 9–11.
28 Griffin, *If You Can't Be Free*, 17.
29 Fred Moten, *In the Break: The Aesthetics of the Black Radical Tradition* (Minneapolis: University of Minnesota Press, 2003), 12.
30 Ibid., 13.
31 Billie Holiday, with William Dufty, *Lady Sings the Blues*, 1956 (New York: Broadway Books, 2006), 94.
32 Als, "Foreword," 12–13.
33 "Reviews and Ratings of New Popular Albums," *Billboard*, July 2, 1955, 28.
34 Blake Gopnik, *Warhol* (New York: Ecco, 2020), 268. See also Guy Minnebach, "The Bossa Nova Cover No One Knew Was a Warhol: Paul Desmond's Take Ten," *Andy Earhole*, October 13, 2019, https://warholcoverart.com/2019/10/13/the-bossa-nova-cover-no-one-knew-was-a-warhol-paul-desmonds-take-ten/.
35 See Joaquim Paulo and Julius Wiedenmann, eds., *Jazz Covers*, Vol. I & II (Cologne: Taschen, 2012), and Paul Maréchal, ed., *Andy Warhol: The Complete Commissioned Record Covers*, 2nd ed. (Munich: Prestel, 2015).
36 Michael Jarrett, "The Tenor's Vehicle: Reading *Way Out West*," in Krin Gabbard, ed., *Representing Jazz* (Durham, NC: Duke University Press, 1995), 272.
37 John A. Kouwenhoven, *The Beer Can by the Highway: Essays on What's "American" About America* (Garden City, NY: Doubleday, 1961), 52.
38 Norman Mailer, *The White Negro* (San Francisco: City Lights Books, 1957).
39 William B. Scott and Peter M. Rutkoff, *New York Modern: The Arts and the City* (Baltimore: Johns Hopkins University Press, 1999), 288.
40 Theodore Strongin, "2 Pulitzer Jurors Resign in Protest," *New York Times*, May 13, 1965, https://timesmachine.nytimes.com/timesmachine/1965/05/13/97200854.pdf.
41 Howard Klein, "Ellington Denied Pulitzer Citation," *New York Times*, May 5, 1965, www.nytimes.com/1965/05/05/archives/ellington-denied-pulitzer-citation-advisory-board-turns-down-bid-by.html.
42 Quoted in Nat Hentoff, "This Cat Needs No Pulitzer Prize," 1965, in Mark Tucker, ed., *The Duke Ellington Reader* (New York: Oxford University Press, 1993), 363.

43 John McWhorter, "Duke Ellington Deserves the 1965 Pulitzer Prize," *New York Times*, July 20, 2022, www.nytimes.com/2022/07/20/opinion/duke-ellington.html.
44 A. James Liska, "Wynton and Branford Marsalis: A Common Understanding," *Down Beat*, December 1982, available at https://wyntonmarsalis.org/news/entry/a-common-understanding-wynton-and-branford-marsalis-interview-downbeat-december-1982.
45 Richard Harrington, "Wynton Marsalis, Young Lion of Jazz," *Washington Post*, December 15, 1984, www.washingtonpost.com/archive/lifestyle/1984/12/15/wynton-marsalis-young-lion-of-jazz/85901b90-3f36-4bd7-b300-0a9ca6e67240/.
46 Joachim-Ernst Berendt and Günther Huesmann, *The Jazz Book: From Ragtime to the Twenty-first Century*, 7th ed. (Chicago: Lawrence Hill Books, 2009), 169.
47 "History of Jazz at Lincoln Center," http://jazz.org/history.
48 See Herman S. Gray, *Cultural Moves: African Americans and the Politics of Representation* (Berkeley: University of California Press, 2005), especially chapter 3.
49 Terry Teachout, "The Color of Jazz," September 1995, www.commentary.org/articles/terry-teachout/the-color-of-jazz/.
50 Howard Reich, "The Story Behind the First Pulitzer for Jazz," *Nieman Reports*, https://niemanreports.org/articles/the-story-behind-the-first-pulitzer-for-jazz/.
51 "The Pulitzer Prize for Music: It's Time to Alter and Affirm," June 1, 2004, www.pulitzer.org/files/musicchanges.pdf.
52 See www.cdc.gov/nchs/covid19/mortality-overview.htm, and www.kff.org/other/state-indicator/death-rate-by-raceethnicity/?currentTimeframe=0&sortModel=%7B%22colId%22:%22Location%22,%22sort%22:%22asc%22%7D.
53 Kyra Phillips and Deenu Zara, "Human toll of COVID-19 Touches Every Corner of the Jazz World," *ABC News*, June 12, 2020, https://abcnews.go.com/Entertainment/human-toll-covid-19-touches-corner-jazz-world/story?id=71178081.
54 Frank Alkyer, "Inside the Detroit Jazz Festival's Bubble," *Down Beat*, September 8, 2020, https://downbeat.com/news/detail/inside-the-detroit-jazz-festivals-bubble.
55 Herb Boyd, "Setbacks Are Not Defeats for James Carter, Regina Carter," *Down Beat*, July 21, 2020, https://downbeat.com/news/detail/setbacks-defeats-carters.
56 Imani Perry, *May Forever We Stand: A History of the Black National Anthem* (Chapel Hill: University of North Carolina Press, 2018), xiv.

PART I

Elements of Sound and Style

CHAPTER 1

Improvisation

Ajay Heble

In his address at the founding rally of the Organization of Afro-American Unity in June 1964, Malcolm X drew an explicit analogy between the Black musician's ability to engage in musical improvisation and the development of new social and political forms that would help "create a new society and make some heaven right here on this earth" for African American people.[1] "I've seen it happen," he declared. "I've seen black musicians when they'd be jamming.... [T]hat black musician, he [*sic*] picks up his horn and starts blowing some sounds that he never thought of before. He improvises, he creates."[2] For Malcolm, this act of improvising was "the only area on the American scene where the black man has been free to create."[3]

Improvisation, Malcolm was pointing out, is a musical practice, yes, but it is also, importantly, a vital social practice. Indeed, Minister Malcolm counseled that there was much to be learned from the innovative working models of improvisation developed by Black musicians, much to be understood about how improvisation might offer resources for hope, social transformation, and Black mobility: "[I]f given intellectual independence," Black people – and Malcolm was forthright on this point – could do the same thing as Black musicians; they "can come up with a new philosophy that nobody has heard of yet. [They] can invent a society, a social system, an economic system, that is different from anything that exists or has ever existed anywhere on this earth. [They] will improvise.... And this is what you and I want."[4]

In September of that same year, Martin Luther King Jr. penned some remarks for the opening of the Berliner Jazztage, a new jazz festival in Berlin (later to be known as JazzFest Berlin). "Jazz speaks for life," Dr. King remarked in his address. He continued:

> When life itself offers no order and meaning, the musician creates an order and meaning from the sounds of the earth which flow through his instrument.

It is no wonder that so much of the search for identity among American Negroes was championed by Jazz musicians. Long before the modern essayists and scholars wrote of racial identity as a problem for a multiracial world, musicians were returning to their roots to affirm that which was stirring within their souls. Much of the power of our Freedom Movement in the United States has come from this music. It has strengthened us with its sweet rhythms when courage began to fail. It has calmed us with its rich harmonies when spirits were down. And now, Jazz is exported to the world. For in the particular struggle of the Negro in America there is something akin to the universal struggle of modern man. Everybody has the Blues. Everybody longs for meaning. Everybody needs to love and be loved. Everybody needs to clap hands and be happy. Everybody longs for faith.

In music, especially this broad category called Jazz, there is a stepping stone towards all of these.[5]

Heaven right here on this earth for Black people.
A new society the likes of which we haven't yet seen.
The creation and development of order and meaning in a multiracial world.
Jazz as a stepping stone towards love.

These, of course, are extraordinary claims, but it is perhaps no coincidence that two of the most iconic figures and activists in the US Civil Rights Movement would, in that same year, turn to this kind of language about Black music to describe their vision of a future society. Recall that 1964 was a landmark year for Civil Rights in America, the year that saw the Civil Rights Act of 1964 legislate an end to segregation in public places and a ban on employment discrimination on the basis of race, color, religion, sex, or national origin. It was the year that Dr. King would be named "Man of the Year" in *Time*, the year that he would go on to win the Nobel Peace Prize. But, we should remember, 1964 was also the year during which Nina Simone would release her searing "Mississippi Goddam," an indictment of racially motivated acts of violence, including the murder of Civil Rights activist Medgar Evers in Mississippi and the white supremacist terrorist bombing of the 16th Street Baptist Church in Birmingham, Alabama, that killed four Black girls.[6] Soon to become an anthem for the Civil Rights Movement, the song declared, "They keep on sayin' 'go slow' / But that's just the trouble," insisting that the imperative from moderate factions of the Civil Rights Movement to "do things gradually" would, in fact, only "bring more tragedy."[7] During these turbulent times, Dr. King and Minister Malcolm surely knew that, despite the new legislation, there was much work to be done. Both recognized that their hopes, their visions, their dreams for a future society would not be achieved on the basis of legislation alone. They understood that the realities associated with struggles for civil rights and social justice would not be easily accommodated by the bureaucracy that administers them, or by the complications of domestic and international policies, politics, or priorities. Both saw and heard in the practices of Black musicians something far from the reaches of conventional forms of institutionalized power, yet something equally powerful, something profoundly urgent and expansive.

These claims about jazz music's social force have been echoed in the words and insights of a number of thinkers. In his book *Dangerous Crossroads*, George Lipsitz, for instance, tells us that jazz, at least in some of its most provocative historical instances, has been about "relentless innovation" rather than "static tradition." "The principal practices that define [the genre]," Lipsitz suggests, have "offered cultural, moral, and intellectual guidance to people all over the world."[8] John Gennari has similarly written that one of jazz's defining features has been "its role as a progenitor of new forms, an inventor of new languages, a creator of new ways to express meaning. The blue notes, microtones, polyrhythms, and extended harmonies of jazz constitute a musical vocabulary and grammar that cannot be accurately represented by the standard notational systems of Western music."[9] More recently, jazz critic Nate Chinen writes in his book *Playing Changes: Jazz for the New Century*, "Jazz has always been a frontier of inquiry, with experimentation in multiple registers. That's as true now as it has ever been."[10] Throughout jazz history, improvisation has been a vital part of this vocabulary and grammar, a core component of the music's commitment to "relentless innovation." From the polyphonic group extemporizations of early styles, through the featured solos within Swing Era arrangements, to bebop's harmonic steeplechase or the open form experiments that followed, jazz musicians have privileged departures from through-composed scores and fixed or predetermined musical texts.

This chapter will consider the ideological and aesthetic stakes of these departures, exploring how the music's emphasis on improvisation constitutes both an ongoing impetus for artistic innovation and perhaps its most relevant challenge to the American status quo. In reframing standards for musical virtuosity, for instance, jazz has often cleared a cultural space for validating otherwise marginalized Black innovators, from Louis Armstrong to Charlie Parker to Ornette Coleman. On a more philosophical level, improvisation, as the speech from Malcolm X referenced earlier would suggest, also allows for a critique of existing discourses, subjecting the rigidity of those discourses to reformulation through an articulation of other possible futures.

"What We Play Is Life": Playing the Changes

Improvisation in jazz involves musical practices that accent and embody real-time invention, creative decision-making, risk-taking, and collaboration. If it can be said to have a standard form, the form is perhaps best captured in Chinen's book title: *Playing Changes*. The phrase refers to the creation and development of on-the-spot melodic statements over a set of fixed chord progressions. A composed melodic line, called the "head," typically begins and ends the piece, with musicians in between those beginning and end points taking turns crafting solos over the chord changes. In early New Orleans style jazz, collective improvisation involved the polyphonic interaction of "front line" melodic instruments engaging in a kind of call-and-response conversation.[11] Gunther Schuller has characterized the improvisation that took place during these days of early jazz as generally taking the form of embellishments of the melody.[12] Later forms of the music, while still relying on fixed chord progressions, would come to emphasize greater variation and more extemporization of new melodies,[13] leading to what Amiri Baraka, referring to the role that Louis Armstrong played in "moving jazz into another era," would call "the ascendency of the soloist."[14]

When asked to describe the style of music his band played, Armstrong would famously declare, "What we play is life," perhaps suggesting to his listeners that even when he was improvising within the familiar diatonic confines of the music and soloing over conventional chord changes, there was, as I have pointed out elsewhere, much in his oeuvre that was already breaking free from that familiar structure: "the slides, the capacity (legendary in his performances) to spin endless breaks, the high tessituras, the rhythm."[15] These examples perhaps remind us of what Armstrong's biographer, the American musicologist Thomas Brothers, calls the "socially conditioned details of sonic practice."[16] He puts it this way:

> Armstrong grew up surrounded by freak music, pitch bending, heterophony, and collective improvisation. Most important was the format I refer to as "fixed and variable," a musical model that is still ubiquitous in sub-Saharan Africa, from which enslaved people brought it to the New World. The model works like this: one instrument (or group of instruments) plays a repeated rhythmic figure. This "fixed" level orients the listener or dancer, while the "variable" instrument or group brings the music to life by departing from the figure in interesting ways.[17]

"Aspects of the fixed and variable model," Brothers argues, "are key to hearing [Armstrong's] music, as well as to understanding how it was socially conceived."[18] Just as Armstrong found "interesting ways" to depart from the fixed elements in the music he played, so too, as Brothers documents, did the trumpeter find compelling (and often under-appreciated) strategies to engage in a skillful negotiation of the musical and social legacies of slavery in America.

"We Invented Our Own Way": The Sonic Symbolism of Bebop

If Armstrong's newness was signaled both via his stylistic innovations as a soloist and through the ways he departed from the fixed elements in the music he played, then the fabled music associated with Charlie "Bird" Parker, Dizzy Gillespie, Thelonious Monk, and others that came to be known as bebop would prove to be a (if not *the*) pivotal moment in the development of jazz in American culture. Now axiomatic in its role as the dominant institutionalized model of pedagogical inquiry in jazz studies across North America, bebop, during its heyday, was seen as taking the music into some largely uncharted (and, for some, bewildering) territory. Improvising trombonist and educator George E. Lewis explains:

> Bop improvisers, like earlier generations of jazz improvisers, used "heads," or precomposed melodic material as starting points for a piece. Bop heads, however, as Gridley points out, "resembled little or nothing that the average listener had heard before" (165). In a further abstraction, bebop improvisers felt no obligation to use the melodic material of the "head" as material for improvisational transformation. Instead, the underlying harmonic sequence, usually subjected to extensive reworking by the improvisers, became the basis for improvisation. Often this harmonic material was appropriated from the popular show tunes of the day, linking this music with earlier jazz styles. The musicians often "signified on" the tunes, replacing the melodic line with another, then naming the new piece in an ironic signifying riff on Tin Pan Alley as well as upon the dominant culture that produced it.[19]

I have written elsewhere about bebop's stylistic innovations, about Bird's flight into chromaticism, how he "played notes in his improvisations which nobody had dared to acknowledge except perhaps as passing harmonies. The flattened fifth, for instance, the devil itself in music, became a stylistic device that characterized much of what Parker, Gillespie, and other boppers were doing."[20] What is interesting here is that bebop's challenge to the status quo was "not limited to musical concerns."[21] Lewis points to how the "sonic symbolism" associated with improvisation for African American musicians is "often constructed with a view toward social instrumentality.... New improvisative and compositional styles are often identified with ideals of race advancement and, more important, as resistive ripostes to perceived opposition to black social expression and economic advancement by the dominant white American culture."[22]

Improvisation during the bebop era, in short, became part of a pronounced strategy for African American musicians to sound off against oppressive structures of fixity through what poet, novelist, and cultural theorist Nathaniel Mackey has called "black linguistic and musical practices that accent variance, variability."[23] Mackey's words are taken from an essay in which he riffs on Baraka's well-known argument in "Swing – From Verb to Noun" on white appropriation of Black music. Mackey explains: "'from verb to noun' means, on the aesthetic level, a less dynamic, less improvisatory, less blues-inflected music, and, on the political level, a containment of black mobility, a containment of the economic and social advances that might accrue to black artistic innovation."[24] By contrast, says Mackey, "the movement from noun to verb ... linguistically accentuates action among a people whose ability to act is curtailed by racist constraint."[25]

Describing the after-hours jam sessions that took place during the 1940s at Minton's, the legendary New York City club known for the significant role it played in the development of bebop, Gillespie remembered:

> What we were doing at Minton's was playing, seriously, creating a new dialogue among ourselves, blending our ideas into a new style of music. You only have so many notes, and what makes a style is how you get from one note to the other.... We invented our own way of getting from one place to the next.... Musically, we were changing the way that we spoke, to reflect that way that we felt. New phrasing came in with the new accent. Our music had a new accent.[26]

"We invented our own way," Gillespie says. "We were changing the way we spoke, to reflect the way that we felt."[27] These words that accentuate action and mobility also seem strikingly similar to the claims from Malcolm X about the Black musician blowing sounds never before heard, about creating new ways of expressing meanings through improvising. In his "Improvised Music after 1950" essay, Lewis quotes from composer-improviser Anthony Braxton, who makes a related point to underscore the argument about how jazz's radical departure from conventional sources of musical meaning during this period had extramusical resonances: "[B]ebop," Braxton asserts, "had to do with understanding the realness of black people's actual position in America."[28]

"The Most Radical Ideas": To Hear the Sounds of Change

I have long been drawn to the argument that struggles for social change often take as one of their most salient manifestations an allegiance to performance practices that cannot readily be scripted, predicted, or compelled into orthodoxy, that cannot be accommodated within habitualized frameworks of assumption.[29] Improvisation has been a core part of this argument for aggrieved peoples. And in the context of jazz and its role in American culture, improvisation as both a musical innovation and a vital social practice has had a long and illustrious history, especially for African American musicians as they have sought to sound off against systems of fixity and oppression. If we agree with historian Robin Kelley's assessment that "[t]he most radical ideas often grow out of a concrete intellectual engagement with the problems of aggrieved populations confronting systems of oppression,"[30] then there is, I suggest, much to be learned from the innovative working models of improvisation developed by creative practitioners in jazz.

One of the most well-known examples that comes to mind in the context of the arguments I am rehearsing can be found in the work of saxophonist John Coltrane, and how, in particular, he would, over the course of several years, improvise upon the popular show tune "My Favorite Things." Many critics have written about Coltrane's renditions of the tune, how he signified upon it in creative ways to express a Black sensibility. I believe the point is worth reemphasizing here. Indeed, I would suggest that Trane's continued reworkings of the tune encapsulate, in miniature, the trajectory of his lifework, offering a kind of microcosm for the sense of movement, the momentum, that served to characterize his career and its wider social implications. If his early iterations of the tune will now sound familiar to most listeners who have come to know the song as it was popularized by Julie Andrews in *The Sound of Music*, by the time he came to record the nearly hour-long rendition on *Live in Japan* in 1966, the improvisations would become so extreme, so far out, that the song would be barely recognizable. Pushing the outer limits of the music and only touching down on the familiar melody for tantalizingly brief moments, Coltrane's *Live in Japan* rendition of "My Favorite Things" uses improvisation to subject our settled habits of response and judgment to a process of ongoing inquiry.[31]

In her essay "Doubleness and Jazz Improvisation," ethnomusicologist Ingrid Monson writes about how African American jazz artists have used irony to transform popular Euro-American songs into vehicles for jazz improvisation, with, again, perhaps the most oft-cited and well-known example being Coltrane's version of "My Favorite Things." Monson's concern is "to show the way in which improvising musicians articulate worldviews, identities, and aesthetics through manipulation of musical resources that signal matters of cultural significance."[32] Improvisational music, she says, "is a form of social action." "Musicians articulate cultural commentary with sound itself."[33] In this context, Monson draws on Henry Louis Gates Jr.'s concept of "Signifyin(g)," a term that, at the most general level, says Monson, Gates uses "to mean any transformation that employs an African-American mode of figurative expression."[34] She argues, "Coltrane's version of 'My Favorite Things' turns a musical theater tune upside down by playing with it, transforming it, and turning it into a vehicle for expressing an African-American-based sensibility."[35] Moreover, Monson is forthright in pointing out that "Coltrane would have been well aware of the emphasis on 'white' things in the lyric – girls in white dresses, snowflakes on eyelashes, silver white winters, cream-colored ponies. In 1960 – a year of tremendous escalation in the Civil Rights Movement and a time of growing politicization in the jazz community – Coltrane quite possibly looked upon the lyrics with an ironic eye."[36] Philosopher Eric Lewis, in his own analysis of Coltrane's reworkings of "My Favorite Things," puts it this way: "Sure, the superficial meaning of 'My Favorite Things' is still present, or perhaps accessible," he writes. "One can still hear, so to speak, the ode to 'warm woolen mittens,' but can anyone really take the sonic onslaught of the version performed in Tokyo to really be *about* the pleasures enjoyed by coming-of-age Austrian aristocrats during World War II?" Lewis concludes: "Not only does Coltrane clearly alter the apparent meaning of 'My Favorite Things' via his complex act of formal revision – via his signifyin(g) – but, so many argue and I agree, he *intended* these meaning revisions, for they are in keeping with his own accounts of his practices, and the practices of many like-minded musicians at the time."[37]

Coltrane, in short, was using improvisation as part of his ongoing search for new ways to announce the sounds of change. With his increasingly radical departures from conventional sources of musical meaning in jazz, his taking of giant steps into the outer limits of improvisational sound, he offers us an exemplary instance of how the social force of improvised music resides, at least in part, in its capacity to trouble the assumptions (and the expectations of fixity) that have been inculcated through dominant systems of knowledge production. In contrast to the institutionalized silencing of Black voices in canonical representations of history, the process that Malcolm X famously referred to as "whitening,"[38] Coltrane deliberately introduces scorching solos, dissonances, and free form improvisations into hegemonic, historically laden sonorities. In place of stability and predictability, he experiments with improvisation in an effort to create a space for the articulation and the revaluing of dissonant histories, histories that are out of tune with dominant and whitewashed epistemic orders.

"Time to Try the Impossible": Utopias *in Sound*

Far from coming out of nowhere, far from having no necessary connection to anything that has come before, improvisation, as the examples I have touched on here suggest, is connected in complex ways to vital questions about representations of history and the production of knowledge in American culture. In his book about the influential musicians' collective, the Association for the Advancement of Creative Musicians (AACM), George E. Lewis stresses this point when he tells us that "the insistence by blacks that music has to be 'saying something' [is] part of a long history of resistance to the silencing of the black voice. Indeed," he argues, "as might be expected from a people whose genetic, historical, and cultural legacies were interrupted through sustained, systematized violence, every effort was made by the musicians to recover rather than to disrupt historical consciousness."[39] Lewis is writing here specifically about African American experimental musical practices, and, in such a context, as I have written elsewhere, his reminder that "black musicians felt that music could effectuate the recovery of history itself,"[40] serves as a vital corrective to some widely held and oft-institutionalized assumptions about improvised forms of music-making.[41] And if many Black artists turned to improvisation in an effort to "effectuate the recovery of history," then it is worth noting too that many of these same artists saw and heard improvisation as an expression of other possible futures. Indeed, one of the best-known groups associated with the AACM, the Art Ensemble of Chicago, has used the slogan "Great Black Music: Ancient to the Future" to name and describe their music.

The critic and activist bell hooks suggests that "African American performance has been a site for the imagination of future possibilities."[42] Elsewhere, I have considered this comment as a prompt to write about the lifework of composer-improviser and bandleader Sun Ra, including his claims to hail from another planet:

> [Ra's] out-ness, his fondness for blasting off into what other African American improvising artists might have called "destinations out," needs to be seen and heard as a kind of (social and sonic) expression of black mobility.

Ra's performances, often featuring a quasi-theatrical improvised romp through the history of African American music, from the early forms of swing (remember that Ra played with Fletcher Henderson) to bebop, free jazz, and – well, yes – far, far beyond into the outer-space noisiness of who-knows-where, were themselves statements about a mobility of practice, expressions both of unspoken, erased, or whitewashed black histories and of unwritten, unscripted futures. The "somewhere there" of improvisation was, for Ra, part of black music's resistance to capture and fixity, its noisiness and clamorousness part of a refusal to give in to the kind of culture of acquiescence or non-participation that resigns itself to the way things are because (or so we are too often told), no other future is possible.[43]

Ra once famously declared, "The possible has been tried and failed. Now it's time to try the impossible."[44] What does it meant to give the impossible a chance? What might such an effort look (and sound) like? If improvisation, for Ra, was a vehicle to enact the impossible futures that many could only envision, a social location through which he could embody his belief that another future, perhaps even an impossible one, was, indeed, worthy of his commitment, a similar belief that improvisation can sound alternative futures is evident in the work of other notable jazz improvisers. I am drawn – to cite just one recent example – to the work of another AACM member, Nicole Mitchell. During a keynote talk for the Improvisation, Community, and Social Practice project, Mitchell spoke about the role that improvised and experimental music has played in creating a kind of utopia *in sound* for African Americans during a time when they could not have it in reality.[45] In an interview with Ellen Waterman, Mitchell speaks explicitly about musical improvisation as a social practice that allows her to dream of "other worlds."[46] Riffing on a phrase in a poem written about her by Kalamu ya Salaam, Mitchell suggests that the line "I dreamed of other worlds" suggests an ability "to take blankness or nothingness and create a combination of what's familiar and what's unknown, or what's never existed before, with creativity." She explains: "That's why I love to improvise. Because improvisation is a practice that allows you not to be focused on the smallness of who you are and your reality, but to actually experience the greatness of possibility and surprise and spontaneity."

"Where Do We Go from Here?": Improvisation's Giant Steps

Let's take a moment to rewind back to 1964 and turn up the volume on the speeches from Malcolm X and Martin Luther King Jr., with which I began. For jazz, it was, in many ways, a banner period: Thelonious Monk would grace the cover of *Time* magazine in February of that same year.

And just a few years earlier, as Tammy Kernodle writes, jazz improvisation was taking some giant steps into largely uncharted territory:

> In December 1960 alto saxophonist Ornette Coleman recorded the controversial album *Free Jazz: A Collective Improvisation* within the vibrant political milieu of John F. Kennedy's presidency and the radical wave of activism sparked by student sit-ins throughout the South. Conceived in a sonic blueprint of collective improvisation between two quartets that had no preset key, tonal system, or melodies, *Free Jazz* embodied a full articulation of Coleman's vision of jazz experimentation. Listeners were inundated with forty minutes of continuous improvisation – something that had never been captured on vinyl. It was radical, transgressive, and foreshadowed the social and cultural unrest of the 1960s.[47]

Radical, transgressive sounds never before captured on vinyl. The greatness of possibility and surprise and spontaneity. Time to try the impossible. Again, phrases about the music that echo some of the views expressed by both Malcolm X and Martin Luther King Jr. Indeed, as discussed elsewhere in this volume, many similar ideas about the vital new forms of expression enacted in musical improvisation throughout jazz history have proved attractive to writers and artists (Beat poets, abstract expressionist painters), who have looked to the music as a way to invigorate their own genres.[48] In the sounds of change embodied, enacted, and activated in improvisational practices throughout the history of jazz, I continue to hear a vital social force. I hear improvisation in jazz not mainly as an element of style and sound, but rather as a "social and cultural location."[49] Now, lest I seem overly optimistic and utopian in my assessment of improvised music's social and political efficacy, we need only to be reminded of the troubled times during which I am writing these words. Earlier this year, in May 2020, the brutal murder of George Floyd by Minneapolis police sparked outrage and mass protests across the planet. In the months since then, millions of protesters under the banner of the Black Lives Matter movement have continued to stand up against police killings and the systemic and structural anti-Black racism that causes them to occur. It seems clear that the question posed in the title of Dr. King's 1967 book, *Where Do We Go from Here?*, remains fundamentally unanswered. It is clear that there is much work still to be done. Clear that we are a far cry from the "equality" that Nina Simone so urgently called for in "Mississippi Goddam." Clear, too, that musical improvisation cannot offer a magical cure-all for the social problems we face now or in the future. Still, I must admit that I continue to be inspired by the role that improvisation has played throughout the history of jazz, inspired by the vital challenge the music has posed to the American status quo, to dominant and whitewashed orders of knowledge production, to racist constraint. I am not going to apologize for that. Indeed, the sonic activism of contemporary jazz improvisers such as William Parker, Matana Roberts, and Kamasi Washington, to name only a few, may be even more outspoken, more expansive, than the activism of their predecessors. Improvisation, in short, continues to be a vital form of Black social expression in jazz today. It continues to inhabit the American cultural landscape in ways that offer resources for hope, for Black mobility, and for the promise of a new society "that is different from anything that exists or has ever existed anywhere on this earth." And this, as Malcolm X put it to his listeners during his prescient address in June 1964, "is what you and I want."

Notes

1. Malcolm X, "The Founding Rally of the OAAU," 1964, in *By Any Means Necessary* (New York: Pathfinder, 1992), 64.
2. Ibid., 63.
3. Ibid., 64.
4. Ibid.
5. Martin Luther King, Jr., "On the Importance of Jazz: Opening Address to the 1964 Berlin Jazz Festival," WCLK, www.wclk.com/dr-martin-luther-king-jr-importance-jazz.
6. LaShonda Barnett, ed., *I Got Thunder: Black Women Songwriters on Their Craft* (Cambridge, MA: Da Capo Press, 2007).
7. Nina Simone, "Mississippi Goddam," *Nina Simone in Concert* (Phillips 600–135, 1964).
8. George Lipsitz, *Dangerous Crossroads: Popular Music, Postmodernism and the Poetics of Place* (London: Verso, 1997), 178.
9. John Gennari, "Jazz Criticism: Its Development and Ideologies," *Black American Literature Forum* 25.3 (1991), 449.
10. Nate Chinen, *Playing Changes: Jazz for the New Century* (New York: Vintage, 2019), xi.
11. For more detail on the New Orleans front line, see e/Prime Media & Randy Fertel, "Musical Threads in Early Jazz," *A Closer Walk*, https://acloserwalknola.com/historical-context/musical-threads-early-jazz/.
12. Gunther Schuller, *Early Jazz: Its Roots and Musical Development* (Oxford: Oxford University Press, 1968), 73–74.
13. P. N. Johnson-Laird, "How Jazz Musicians Improvise," *Music Perception* 19.3 (2002), 415–42.
14. Amiri Baraka. [LeRoi Jones], *Blues People: The Negro Experience in White America and the Music That Developed from It* (New York: Morrow, 1963), 155.
15. Ajay Heble, *Landing on the Wrong Note: Jazz, Dissonance, and Critical Practice* (New York: Routledge, 2000), 34.

16 Thomas Brothers, *Louis Armstrong: Master of Modernism* (New York: Norton, 2014), 7.
17 Ibid., 6–7.
18 Ibid., 7.
19 George E. Lewis, "Improvised Music after 1950: Afrological and Eurological Perspectives," *Black Music Research Journal*, 16.1 (1996), 94.
20 Heble, *Landing on the Wrong Note*, 37.
21 Lewis, "Improvised Music," 95.
22 Ibid., 94.
23 Nathaniel Mackey, "Other: From Noun to Verb," *Representations* 39 (1992), 52. See also, Jesse Stewart, "No Boundary Line to Art: 'Bebop' as Afro-Modernist Discourse," *American Music* 29.3 (2011), 332–52.
24 Mackey, "Other," 52.
25 Ibid., 53.
26 Dizzy Gillespie with Al Fraser, *To Be or Not to Bop* (New York: Da Capo, 1979), 140–41.
27 Ibid., 141.
28 Quoted in Lewis, "Improvised Music," 95.
29 Heble, *Landing on the Wrong Note*, 83.
30 Robin D. G. Kelley, *Freedom Dreams: The Black Radical Imagination* (Boston: Beacon, 2002), 9.
31 John Coltrane, "My Favorite Things," 1966, *Live in Japan* (Impulse GRD-4-102, 1991).
32 Ingrid Monson, "Doubleness and Jazz Improvisation: Irony, Parody, and Ethnomusicology," *Critical Inquiry* 20.2 (1994), 292.
33 Ibid., 313.
34 Ibid., 290.
35 Ibid., 298.
36 Ibid.
37 Eric Lewis, *Intents and Purposes: Philosophy and the Aesthetics of Improvisation* (Ann Arbor: University of Michigan Press, 2019), 255; original emphasis.
38 Malcolm X, with Alex Haley, *The Autobiography of Malcolm X* (New York: Grove Press, 1965), 175.
39 George E. Lewis, *A Power Stronger Than Itself: The AACM and American Experimental Music*, (Chicago: University of Chicago Press, 2008), 41.
40 Ibid., 42.
41 Among the assumptions I have in mind, think of how improvisation is often seen as involving adherence to neither convention nor protocol, as tolerating no system of constraint, as requiring no prior thought, coming out of nowhere, simply being made up on the spot. See Daniel Fischlin, Ajay Heble, and George Lipsitz, *The Fierce Urgency of Now* (Durham, NC: Duke University Press, 2013), 33.
42 bell hooks, "Performance Practice as a Site of Opposition," in Catherine Ugwu, ed., *Let's Get It On: The Politics of Black Performance* (Seattle: Bay Press, 1995), 220.

43 Ajay Heble, "Introduction," in Ajay Heble, ed., *Classroom Action: Human Rights, Critical Activism, and Community-Based Education* (Toronto: University of Toronto Press, 2017), 4.
44 Quoted in John Szwed, *Space Is the Place: The Lives and Times of Sun Ra* (New York: Pantheon, 1997), 192.
45 Nicole Mitchell, "Improvisation, Community, and Social Practice," Keynote Address, Lex Non Scripta, Ars Non Scripta: Law, Justice, and Improvisation Conference, McGill University, Montreal, Quebec, 2009.
46 Ellen Waterman, "'I Dreamed of Other Worlds': An Interview with Nicole Mitchell," *Critical Studies in Improvisation / Études critiques en improvisation* 4.1 (2008), www.criticalimprov.com/index.php/csieci/article/view/510.
47 Tammy L. Kernodle, "Beyond the Chord, the Club, and the Critics: A Historical and Musicological Perspective of the Jazz Avant-Garde," in Danielle A. Jackson and Simone Austin, eds., *Creative Black Music at the Walker: Selections from the Archives* (Minneapolis: Walker Art Center, 2020), https://walkerart.org/collections/publications/jazz/creative-black-music-introduction/. For more on the relationship between Coleman's *Free Jazz* and the social and cultural upheavals of the 1960s, see Michael Hrebeniak's chapter in this volume (Chapter 8).
48 For more on this, see Daniel Belgrad, *The Culture of Spontaneity: Improvisation and the Arts in Postwar America* (Chicago: University of Chicago Press, 1998).
49 Lewis, "Improvised Music," 93.

CHAPTER 2

Scat and Vocalese

Chris Tonelli

Recently, I saw a social media post by a professional jazz musician. He shared a video of a young professional old-time musician performing a solo fiddle and buck dance piece with several sung verses. He complimented her rhythm, then added his "expert" opinion – she should nix the vocals. His opinion met resistance: others disagreed, and one argued that (1) old-time music is inclusive and everyone present is usually invited to sing, and (2) her vocal qualities were aesthetically normative in the genre, a genre that, perhaps, he did not understand. His response to the first argument was she should not sing because she "is simply not a good vocalist" and "that is the real, and musical, fact of the matter."[1] His response to the second was perhaps even more of a refusal – he clicked the laughing emoji.

I begin this way to remind us of self-righteous universalism in music and the ways it has impinged upon singing practices. It sets a trap for those of us who want to hear or practice forms of singing Othered as unmusical. Music is a reification. What qualifies as music in various cultural spaces differs and, thus, that abused and abusive word "musical" can never draw universal divides. Certain musicians gain capital from positioning themselves as authorities with the right to speak universally about what is and isn't musical, but it's a trap; when they say something is musical we need to translate their universalism into what it really is – a mere statement of preference cloaked as fact.

Lindon Barrett reminds us of the violent history of aesthetic universalism in his book *Blackness and Value*. He includes a passage from John Miller Chernoff's *African Rhythm and African Sensibility* worth re-presenting here:

> People from Western cultures historically have had a difficult time understanding anything African. Those who dislike African music respond to it in several ways. Some say that they are bored, that the music is so monotonously repetitive that it just dulls the sense. Others, alternatively, say that the music is so complicated rhythmically that they get confused and cannot make any sense of it. These people are likely to add that because they cannot

figure out any pattern, they feel threatened that either the monotony or the confusion might take them over, and they do their best to ignore the unpleasantness. Less tolerant people have felt their sanity or their morals challenged, and in the past some of them even took the truly remarkable step of forbidding Africans to make music.[2]

In the second chapter of *Blackness and Value*, Barrett invokes this history of musical policing as he constructs a theory of how African diasporic singing voices have unsettled exclusivist notions of vocal and human value. In his framework, he opposes the (African American) "singing" voice to what he calls the "signing voice," a voice that self-privileges and dehumanizes its Other(s) by hearing its own connectedness to literacy as evidence of a human status that, it implies, not all humans possess and not all human vocal utterance affirms. Conversely, the "singing" voice humanizes bodies Othered as less-than-human when vocalization affords a sense of value that does not align with exclusivist hegemonic notions of value.

Though the anecdote I began with is not equivalent to the histories Barrett evokes, they are related. The signing voice exists in a mutual relationship of reinforcement with self-privileging universalizations of "the musical." Barrett's work asserts the connection between the signing voice, arguments asserting the nonmusicalness of forms of music, and culturally specific beliefs about property, and invokes scat singing to explain these connections:

> scatting abandons meaningful speech altogether and turns freely and ludically to the charged instrumentality of voice – an Other, novel realm of meaning. In the context of this tradition, the ludic corporeality of the singing voice suggests that the dominant act of monopolizing voice amounts not so much to monopolizing meaningfulness itself as the transcendent symbol of the most fully human but, instead, the monopolizing of a particular kind of bodily production – the capacity of the body and of a culture to engage in a particular kind of work that is, in turn, a particular kind of self-representation. It amounts to an attempt to monopolize no more than the power of speech and literacy as tied to a *civic* vision in which "property might be seen as the foundation and determinant of social and political personality."[3]

In other words, our sense that our musics are musical and Others' aren't, or our sense we possess a signing voice Others don't have access to, is fueled by a desire to own something our Others don't, and we need this feeling, in part, because we live in a culture that normalizes private property. Scat emerges, in the view of this passage, from a playful place where this anxious need for ownership does not manifest and where value can emerge without the need for exclusion.

For Barrett, understanding music, singing, and scat means understanding how their sounds contribute to processes of empowerment and disempowerment, how meanings come to be articulated with these sounds, and how senses of self and Otherness are reshaped via these articulations. He points us to one of the most important processes scat, and music in general, can contribute to – resistance to processes of dehumanization. However, what styles of vocalization have been and have done exceeds a focus on this function. My opening anecdote reminds us that while jazz has been, and is still occasionally, the singing Other to a dominant signing voice, jazz is also now an institutionalized force asserting itself as a signing genre, Othering other musics, even other forms of jazz, as unmusical. In this chapter, I will follow Barrett by thinking about what scat has achieved and afforded. However, I will focus on how scat and vocalese have functioned as *both* singing and signing voice, how they have empowered *and* Othered listeners and singers.

What scat, or any music, has been and done is largely unknowable. I seek to draw us not into a sense that we *possess* an understanding of scat and vocalese; rather, I seek to draw us into a space where we can foster a broad, unfinished sense of how these vocal sounds may have mattered and may matter in the future. I offer reflections too fragmented to be taken as "the" history of these two vocal practices. I hope these fragments unsettle existing histories of the practices and offer other ways to think about what scat and vocalese have been and done.

Is Pre-Scat Scat Scat Too?: Scat in the Bright Shadow of Blackface Minstrelsy

The term scat has an unclear origin, but it was popularized in conjunction with the recording often positioned as the beginning of scat: Louis Armstrong's 1926 Hot Five recording of "Heebie Jeebies." This origin myth states Armstrong dropped his lyrics as he was recording and compensated with an asemantic vocal improvisation, giving birth to scat. The subsequent sheet music for "Heebie Jeebies" labelled the corresponding section a "'Skat' Chorus" and the term began to be used frequently in the ensuing years.[4]

What might be most interesting about this origin story is how it has offered some license to overlook pre-1926 vocal predecessors. And as much as that might impoverish our historical understanding, it has significantly helped distance post-"Heebie Jeebies" scat from associations afforded by earlier popular song, which was largely dominated by the norms of blackface minstrelsy. In the paragraphs that follow, I'll discuss aspects of this prehistory; if this might taint your sense of what scat means, there is a precedent and logic to skipping this section.

Armstrong acknowledged he scatted long before "Heebie Jeebies."[5] Also, many pre-1926 recordings document asemantic melodic sequences of vocables in jazz-related musics. Michael G. Garber discusses how another "nonsense syllable singing practice" called eephing "[f]rom the 1890s onward … cropped up in almost every entertainment venue of the time."[6] Garber observes pre-"Heebie Jeebies" scat-like singing on recordings by singers like Gene Greene, Cliff "Ukulele Ike" Edwards, Don Redman, Bert Williams, Al Jolson, Ethel Waters, Noble Sissle, and Arthur Collins and Byron Harlan. Others have expanded this list: Brent Hayes Edwards also points to recordings by Bo Diddly and Carlton Coon and Joe Sanders, and Brian Rust mentions recordings by Johnny Marvin, Gene Austin, Lee Morse, and one of Fred Hall's Sugar Babies, as well as Armstrong's 1924 recording of "Everybody Loves My Baby" with Fletcher Henderson.[7] The line between these vocal performances and scat (if one is imposed at all) will be drawn in different places by different listeners. Garber parses these practices into "yodeling on nonsense syllables; humming; melismatic singing on a single open vowel (ah, oh, uh); traditional European nonsense syllables ("fa la," "tra la loo," etc.); mock foreign languages; laughter – not just chuckles or giggles but "ha-ha-ha" sung in rhythm and, often, on pitch; imitations of animal sounds; and, particularly germane to the later rhetoric surrounding scat singing, imitations of musical instruments."[8] While listeners might be inclined to hear much of this as scat or protoscat, others – especially those invested in policing a narrow sense of what counts as scat – will hear it as distinct from scat.

Garber documents how eephing involved vocables related to the phrase "Eepha-Soffa-Dill." These were common in ragtime music and he traces how vaudevillian Gene Greene's recordings (1911–17) of "King of the Bungaloos" incorporate eephing in ways that "closely parallel conventional practices of post-'Heebie-Jeebies' scat singing."[9] He points out "King of the Bungaloos" was part of a trend of songs about African royalty and argues these were part of "a vogue in show business, particularly among African American performers and songwriters who presumably were trying to avoid the violent and poverty-stricken images of earlier blackface dialect songs."[10] In "King of the Bungaloos," the protagonist finds out he is the successor to the throne of his ancestral home on the Nile and he fantasizes about this in cartoonish terms, including having an array of African animals as servants. Given the commonality of blackface minstrel norms at the time, it is likely Greene's asemantic utterances were heard, by some listeners, in primitivist fashion, as the nonsensical utterances of a racialized "inferior," despite Garber's suggestion that such songs resisted more violently denigrating blackface imagery. The song Garber presents as the first to contain an eeph phrase, the 1903 song "Ephasafa Dill," is similar in this regard: "the locution is presented as the constant utterance of an African American child (described with the now-offensive terms 'pickaninny' and 'coon')."[11] While pre-"Heebie Jeebies" asemantic vocal practices were diverse and afforded a contradictory array of meanings and subjectivating energies, proximity to blackface minstrel tropes coupled with the problematic notion that asemantic utterance is tied to "the primitive" meant that part of the work these vocals did was to provide a space in which racist imaginaries could be felt and undergirded.

The "Heebie Jeebies" myth helped distance post-1926 scat singers from readings of scat as an extension of minstrelsy. However, Armstrong's work itself engages with a minstrel-influenced performance persona that at times embodied demeaning stereotypes for the benefit of a racist white gaze.[12] For the listener attuned to this reading, Armstrong's scatting, or scat in general, may be heard as a tool in the service of those stereotypes. By contrast, counter-readings of these personae also exist, like Gary Giddins's argument that as Armstrong embodied these stereotypes he employed an "absurdist humor" that helped "demolish" them.[13] Thus, the same scat could be heard as a vehicle for embodying stereotypes to mark them as tropes to be critiqued and abandoned.[14] In the shadow of minstrelsy, scat has been heard as trafficking in primitivist stereotypes while providing a resistance to them from within. And, of course, in other ears, that shadow is not audible and those sounds ring out amid some other brightness.

Multivocality, Mythopoetics, and Marketing Ploy (with a Floy Floy)

Barrett draws on Portia Maultsby's affirmation that African diasporic voices traditionally "bring intensity to their performance by alternating lyrical, percussive, and raspy timbres; juxtaposing vocal and instrumental textures; changing pitch and dynamic levels; alternating straight with vibrato tones and weaving moans, shouts, grunts, hollers, and screams into the melody."[15] Barrett's singing voices don't have to reject a Eurological ideal of vocal purity to function as "singing voices," but he implies that the voices Maultsby describes have historically been rejected by and have countered the power of the signing voice. These distinct sounds, the social functions they serve, and the ideologies attached to them have shaped what scat and vocalese have been and done.[16]

Let's consider another singer at the center of many scat histories, Ella Fitzgerald. Often what listeners value about her scat is "perfect intonation."[17] Rather than focusing on how her scat manifests the African diasporic vocal aesthetics invoked above, these listeners focus on a more institutionally powerful Eurological vocal aesthetics of intonational and timbral purity. Fitzgerald's scat seems to have helped to manifest a signing voice; it has helped give rise to a vocal jazz culture that argues: "There is a difference between scat singing and scat singing that has musical integrity and sounds good."[18] This quotation opens a 2015 journal article by Michele Weir intended to help guide young singers into scatting. Unlike in Barrett's work, what makes a vocal performance significant in Weir's article is not the voice's ability to chip away at hegemonic power, but its ability to manifest sounds "experts" hear as musical. The first singer Weir mentions is "the great Ella Fitzgerald," and this is unsurprising given Fitzgerald's fame and association with "perfect intonation."[19] The only other singers the article mentions (as singers at least – Dizzy Gillespie comes up but with no mention of his singing) are "Darmon Meader from the New York Voices and Jon Hendricks from Lambert, Hendricks, & Ross."[20] They are praised for their "great control" and ability to fluently "navigate the harmony."[21]

The invocation of Hendricks, one of the major figures in the history of vocalese, is also unsurprising. Vocalese is the inverse of scat; a semantics emerges there out of asemantic instrumental jazz solos. From the early 1950s, vocalists such as Eddie Jefferson and King Pleasure began lyricizing instrumental solos and performing and recording their lyricizations. Vocalese criticism often marvels at the virtuosity, intonation, and harmonic sophistication of these performances, but also sometimes focuses on dimensions like the verbal dexterity involved in the composition of the lyrics and the value of local communities formed around this practice.

Though Weir's article does not Other specific music, its notion of "musical integrity" is connected to both the ideologies with which I opened the chapter and Barrett's signing voice (especially when Weir employs literary metaphors in her universalizing explanation of what makes scat sound good).[22] Institutionalized scat/vocalese voices only become signing voices when they help manifest a sense of the valuelessness of Other voices and we need to understand this signing authority is not, of course, the only affordance these more Eurological scat voices help manifest. We also need to understand that while the values of this corner of the vocal jazz world often dominate discourse about this music, the music of singers like Fitzgerald can be appreciated for other qualities it possesses and social functions it has served. For just one example of Fitzgerald's use of timbral complexity related to the Afrological aesthetics Maultsby describes, listen to the singer's multiphonic scatting midway through her March 20, 1966 performance of "How High the Moon."[23]

While her 1945 Decca recording of "Flying Home" is celebrated as the breakthrough that took Fitzgerald's scatting on commercial recording from an "ornamental novelty" – that is, used sparingly in sections that were usually less than ten bars – to an "artform" in itself (taking the foreground throughout a full track), her earlier scat recordings also served social functions that are part of scat history. One of these is the undermining of the racial imaginary manifested by the categorical divisions of the music industry. Her version, with the Ink Spots, of "Cow-Cow-Boogie," begins with Fitzgerald singing the opening verse and then moving into ten bars of scat. Unusual among her recordings, the scat is not foregrounded; rather, it functions as the background to Orville "Hoppy" Jones's spoken verse. This subordinate musical function is part of what scat has been and done; also significant is the fact that the song's lyrics are about (and some actually manifest) the fusion of cowboy yodeling and scat. The song describes a singer raised in Harlem who relocated to Santa Fe, a "swing half-breed," who sings, in "a knocked out Western accent with a Harlem touch."[24] While listeners might hear this song as an absurd hybrid, a combination of the music industry's categories of "race" and "hillbilly" that in its absurdity reinforces the (problematic) divide between the two, others may be reminded of or introduced to the long and widely ignored history of Western Swing music, blues yodeling, or other music that challenges the binaristic racial imagination of American music industry categories.

Such recordings often, in part because of their commercial success ("Cow Cow Boogie" was a hit in 1944), stand at odds with the values of jazz modernisms that have largely determined what qualifies for inclusion in jazz canons.[25] Ronald Radano has argued that jazz histories have been "[d]ominated by hagiographic portraits, patronizing celebrations of performative mastery, and bloodless formal analyses of a canonical repertory."[26] He associates this with a jazz modernism that portrays "jazz not as a complicated and contested cultural moment, but as a fixed, essential form ("real jazz") that endured a barrage of influences as it moved inexorably toward self-realization."[27] Jazz modernists devalue and obscure jazz that doesn't fit into a fixed, universalized progress narrative of the "self-realization" of the artform and modernism is, for Radano, in one sense of the term, "a social category" defined by its perpetuation of "elitist categories of art."[28] While many of the critical attitudes of jazz modernisms address valid concerns, they also often contribute to the creation of elitist, misogynist and/or ableist manifestations of the signing voice and to marginalization of jazz that may have mattered in ways that don't align with the concerns of these modernisms.[29] The relative lack of vocal jazz in jazz canons and jazz institutions is one such marginalization.[30]

Other social functions that scat performs are the unsettling of reductive categorical norms of embodiment and of hegemonic notions of how we should employ and gain pleasure from vocalization. In a July 1947 *Down Beat* review of the "Lady Be Good/Flying Home" single, the author marvels at the way Fitzgerald tosses in "sly digs at Dizzy, Babs, Slam, Hamp, Leo Watson and others by singing variations on their better-known ideas."[31] Stuart Nicholson points out that this is both a "practice that she would follow for the rest of her life" and one she shared with Leo Watson, a vocalist Nicholson argues "showed Ella that scat need not remain in hock to Armstrong. It could be developed and personalized."[32] The ways scat singers have employed vocal material that audiences experience as incoherent in relation to their sense of how the racialized, gendered, classed, abled body of the performer should sound is critically important. James D. Hart, writing about scat in 1932, commented: "Wordless mimicry of well-known sounds arouses the blood of listeners to say this is 'hot stuff.'"[33] When singers employ sounds listeners hear as belonging to other genders or to nonhuman objects or instruments, it potentially elicits the powerful emotional effect to which Hart alludes, brought on, perhaps, by the ways these moments prompt listeners to denaturalize their notions about what kinds of voices belong to what kinds of bodies. As well, it may inspire listeners to understand that societal vocal norms compel us to abandon the pleasurable vocal fluidity and exploration in which children often engage, alienating ourselves, in the name of normativity, from a broad array of our bodily potentials and the pleasures they might afford. Scat singers (legitimized, outsiders, and new practitioners from Cab Calloway to Babs Gonzales, Dizzy Gillespie, Joe Carroll, Sarah Vaughn, Jackie and Roy, Richard Boone, Al Jarreau, Shooby Taylor, Ledisi, and many others) have unsettled and subjectivated listeners with their sounds. These responses and their socio-political implications are the lifeblood of music's significance.

Like Barrett, Clyde Taylor also theorized scat's challenge to "Western bias toward logocentrism" (his parallel concept to Barrett's "singing voice" is his notion of the "mythophone").[34] Taylor draws parallels between scat and asemantic sound poetry, pointing to the potential for subjectivating, anti-hegemonic energies to emerge from asemantic utterance, particularly when emerging from peoples historically robbed of ancestral language cultures. Understanding these animating energies and the way they get into thought, feeling, and action is key to understanding much of what scat and vocalese have been and done. Scat in bebop culture often materialized asemantic utterances with the morphology of words. Word-like manifestations, like those of Slim Gaillard, may have been even more palpable refusals of the signing voice than other scat-related vocalizations because they closely resemble while seemingly refusing the word. However, it is important to note that bop talk also led to practices of pushing these asemantic utterances towards the semantic. Singers like Gaillard and Babs Gonzales turned their scat utterances into slang languages and sold dictionaries that decoded the semantics they attached to their seemingly asemantic utterances; we can cultivate a more diverse sense of the affordances of scat and vocalese by ending this largely celebratory section acknowledging that bop language was also a vehicle through which more crass or exploitative commercializations of bebop took place.[35]

Silent Articulations: Poetry's Shaping of Scat

Scat's construction of meaning does not occur only via encounters with sound. References to music in other media also have an effect. To bring this fragmented reflection towards its end, I'll consider how scat's meanings have been shaped by poetry.

Whenever the phonetics of scat are incorporated into poetry, the results modulate the meanings scat affords and bring the reader (or listener in the case of performance poetry) into new embodied interactions with scat. Langston Hughes's poetic incorporation of scat framed scat as an activist expression. The nine poems in his poetic suite *Montage of a Dream Deferred* (1951) that incorporate scat each produce this effect distinctly. The opening poem, "Dream Boogie," ends with a scat interjection – "*Hey, pop! / Re-bop! / Mop! / Y-e-a-h!*" – that is thrust into ambiguity by an earlier question asking "*You think / It's a happy beat?*"[36] The suggestion that these seemingly joyful utterances could be called into question as such sets the stage for suggestions in the later poems of what scat might express. "Children's Rhymes" ends with: "Oop-pop-a-da! / Skee! Daddle-de-do! / Be-bop! / Salt peanuts! / De-dop!"[37] This scat concludes a poem about Black children lacking the opportunities and protections white children receive. The sudden shifts from topical semantic poetry into asemantic scat assert a relation between the topical content and the scat. Thus, the scat comes to contain in some way the grievance that dominates the poem. Before *Montage* concludes, the same process occurs in relation to masculine economic anxiety (in "Question [2]" and "What? So Soon!"), drug addiction ("Flatted Fifths"), unjust incarceration ("Jam Session"), forced military service ("Tag"), and antisemitism ("Likewise").

A similar but distinct process unfolds in the poetry of Haki Madhubuti. Whereas scat in *Montage* seems juxtapositional and ambiguous, in Madhubuti's work it manifests asemantic representation of near-specific narrative action. His poem "For Black People" (1968) depicts the passage from oppression, to resistance, to utopia. In the resistance phase scat conveys the dynamism of actions occurring, thanks to its placement between serial narrative descriptions of action.[38] The result: certain scat sounds become imbued with the possibility of expressing the actions and feelings of resistance.

Amiri Baraka's poetry makes extensive use of asemantic phonetics, some of which refer specifically to scat. Often, Baraka reinforces connections between scat, Blackness, and Africanness. In his 1995 collection *Wise, Why's, Y's*, in a poem entitled "You Wants To Know Why?" Baraka frames both bebop and scat as "African / American Bloods / Speaking still / pure African."[39] This brief statement about scat precedes a longer exploration, "Speech #38 (or Y We say it this way)," where Africanness is invoked, but also humanness and Blackness.[40] Gillespie's, Calloway's, and Gaillard's scat are referenced. Gaillard appears in lines 7–8 via references to his bop language ("oroonie" and "McVouty"). He is evoked again in line 81 via a reference to his 1938 song "Flat Foot Floogie (with a Floy Floy)" followed with the lines "Human light / in your / African / Eyes."[41] Here scat is heard as a manifestation of humanness; "light" marks scat as a radiant force.

"Speech #38" ends by negating the difference between scat singer, bebop musician and "Black poet"; the musicians invoked become "Black poet" in these final lines.[42] The poem begins with textualizations of Gillespie's scat phrases and references to his scat-like song titles.[43] These channel scat phonetics into the reader's body. To read the first lines – "OoBlahDee / Ooolyacoo / Bloomdido / OoBopShabam" – silently or out loud (as one might be tempted to given the potential tactile pleasures involved) is to attend closely to the morphology of these assemblages and feelings/meanings they might generate.[44] The experience might be even more likely than a "musical" performance to create an intimacy between listener and scat utterance, as their body is the only body present to contain and become articulated with the utterance.

So Many More Scats to Be Scholarshipped

Scat has been Othered and institutionalized; it has functioned as the singing and the signing voice. What scat and vocalese have been and done is a complex untellable story and we benefit from reminding ourselves that when we feel we know that story is when our knowledge is at its most untrustworthy.

What the voice can do today and in the future is more important for us than what it has done, but we prepare ourselves to help the voice have a greater positive impact tomorrow when we understand more about what voices have been and done. Scat and vocalese do not cover all the categories of jazz vocalization; vocal jazz also includes Leon Thomas's soularfone, the ethereal wordless vocals of singers like Sheila Jordan and Ingrid Sertso, Clark Terry's mumbles, and the soundsinging I discuss in my book *Voices Found: Free Jazz and Singing*. Contemporary singers such as Fay Victor blur the lines between these categories, but this could also be said of many early scat singers. Certain contemporary scat singers sing in ways more strongly coded as belonging to the past, and recordings from previous eras accrue these associations and are subject to our constantly renegotiating senses of what bygone eras were and mean.[45]

So, we should never be fully sure of our sense of what a music is or has done or buy into belief our musical opinions are musical facts. There is always more to learn about what any given music has been, and in jazz studies there is no doubt that the voice has been understudied and undertheorized. To know more about what voices have mattered and why, we need to do more research and cast away the universalisms that close us off from what other listeners have felt, thought, and heard.

Notes

1 To protect the participants, I refrain from citation here.
2 John Miller Chernoff, *African Rhythm and African Sensibility: Aesthetics and Social Action in African Musical Idioms* (Chicago: University of Chicago Press, 1979), 27–28. Quoted in Lindon Barrett, *Blackness and Value* (Cambridge: Cambridge University Press, 1998), 61.
3 Barrett, *Blackness and Value*, 80. The quotation closing this quote is from J. G. A. Pocock, *Virtue, Commerce, and History: Essays on Political Thought and History, Chiefly in the Eighteenth Century* (Cambridge: Cambridge University Press, 1985), 122.
4 Michael G. Garber, "Eepha-Soffa-Dill and Eephing: Found in Ragtime, Jazz, and Country Music, from Broadway to a Texas Plantation," *American Music* 35.3 (2017), 373.

5 Chris Tonelli, *Voices Found: Free Jazz and Singing* (New York: Routledge, 2020), 77–78.
6 Garber, "Eepha-Soffa-Dill," 343.
7 Brent Hayes Edwards, "Louis Armstrong and the Syntax of Scat," *Critical Inquiry* 28.3 (2002), 619. Bo Diddly should not be confused with Bo Diddley. Rust's "list" is described in Stuart Nicholson, *Ella Fitzgerald: The Complete Biography* (New York: Routledge, 2014), 89–90. Nicholson cites a personal letter from Rust as the source. Rust's discography *Jazz and Ragtime Records (1897–1942)* (Highlands Ranch: Mainspring Press, 2002) provides further context.
8 Garber, "Eepha-Soffa-Dill," 345.
9 Ibid., 356.
10 Ibid., 357.
11 Ibid., 350. Garber explains Eepha-Soffa-Dill was associated with infant sound (358).
12 See Jeremy F. Lane, *Jazz and Machine-Age Imperialism* (Ann Arbor: University of Michigan Press, 2013), 83, or Krin Gabbard, *Jammin' at the Margins: Jazz and the American Cinema* (Chicago: University of Chicago Press, 1996), 120.
13 Gary Giddins, *Satchmo: The Genius of Louis Armstrong* (Cambridge, MA: Da Capo Press, 1988), 8.
14 See Tonelli, *Voices Found*, 79–81.
15 Portia K. Maultsby, "Africanisms in African-American Music," in Joseph E. Holloway, ed., *Africanisms in American Culture* (Bloomington: Indiana University Press, 1990), 191–92. Quoted in Barrett, *Blackness and Value*, 79–80.
16 See George E. Lewis, "Improvised Music after 1950: Afrological and Eurological Perspectives," *Black Music Research Journal* 16.1 (1996): 91–122.
17 Nicholson quotes a review – No author, "Ella Fitzgerald: Lady Be Good/Flying Home," *Down Beat* 14.14 (July 2, 1947), 15 – praising her "perfect" intonation (91) as well as Mel Torme singling Fitzgerald out as the one singer who doesn't have to "work doubly hard to emit those random notes in scat singing with perfect intonation" (Torme, quoted in Nicholson, *Ella Fitzgerald*, 89).
18 Michele Weir, "The Scat Singing Dialect: An Introduction to Vocal Improvisation," *The Choral Journal* 55.11 (2015), 29.
19 Ibid.
20 Ibid., 30.
21 Ibid.
22 See, for example, "Songs generally begin with an initial melodic statement … and conclude with a motive that has the sense of *end of paragraph*" (Weir, "The Scat Singing Dialect," 34–35).
23 See www.youtube.com/watch?v=1GUmxnYheKo.
24 Ink Spots and Ella Fitzgerald, "Cow Cow Boogie" (Decca Records 18587A, 1944). Composed by Don Raye, Gene De Paul, and Benny Carter. The problematic term "half-breed" likely appears via the Western theme and the frequent appearance of that term in discourse, related to settler colonialist relationships with American Indian and First Nations people, that has filtered

into the Western genre. While the history of the term is complex, it is worth noting that it was often pejorative and aided in the reification of racist racial imaginaries. It likely did so in the reception history of this song too, though it also aligns awkwardly, given the term's history, with celebration of third spaces that denaturalize binaries that reify those same racist racial imaginaries.
25 Nicholson, *Ella Fitzgerald*, 79–80, notes "Cow Cow Boogie's" success was under the direction of Jack Kaap and that, shortly after, Milt Gabler took over determination of the songs Fitzgerald would record for Decca and championed the new direction of "Flying Home."
26 Ronald M. Radano, "Review: Jazz, Modernism, and the Black Creative Tradition," *Reviews in American History*, 21.4 (December, 1993a), 672.
27 Ibid. For more on jazz and modernism, especially related to the history and reception of crooning, see Michael Coyle's chapter in this volume (Chapter 7).
28 Ronald M. Radano, *New Musical Figurations: Anthony Braxton's Cultural Critique* (Chicago: University of Chicago Press, 1993b), 3.
29 For more on jazz modernism and Fitzgerald's early career, see Christopher J. Wells, "'A Dreadful Bit of Silliness': Feminine Frivolity and Ella Fitzgerald's Early Critical Reception," *Women and Music: A Journal of Gender and Culture* 21 (2017), 43–65.
30 Weir's article addresses this institutional imbalance ("The Scat Singing Dialect," 29). For another discussion of modernism devaluing vocal jazz see my discussion of Maggie Nicols in *Voices Found*, 33–34.
31 "Record Reviews," *Down Beat*, 14.14 (July 2, 1947), 15. The quote refers to Dizzy Gillespie, Babs Gonzales, Slam Stewart, and Lionel Hampton.
32 Nicholson, *Ella Fitzgerald*, 90.
33 James D. Hart, "Jazz Jargon," *American Speech* 7.4 (1932), 247. Quoted in William Bauer, "Louis Armstrong's 'Skid Dat De Dat': Timbral Organization in an Early Scat Solo," *Jazz Perspectives*, 1.2 (2007), 135. Bauer's work offers a valuable analysis methodology specific to the study of scat.
34 Clyde Taylor, "'Salt Peanuts': Sound and Sense in African/American Oral/Musical Creativity," *Callaloo* 16 (1982), 2–3.
35 Babs Gonzales' first autobiography discusses this. He recounts Capitol Records reproducing and distributing his "Bop Dictionary" without his consent. See Babs Gonzales, *I, Paid My Dues* (East Orange: Expubidence Publishing Corp, 1967), 60. These dictionaries of personalized slang are outgrowths of earlier compiling and/or commercializing of jazz slang like Carl Cons's November 1935 *Down Beat* column "The Slanguage of Swing: Terms the 'Cats' Use" or *Cab Calloway's Hepster Dictionary*, published in 1938. For more on jazz and language, see Amor Kohli's chapter in this volume (Chapter 9).
36 Langston Hughes, *Montage of a Dream Deferred*, 1951, in Arnold Rampersad and David Roessel, eds., *The Collected Poems of Langston Hughes* (New York: Vintage, 1994), 388.
37 Ibid., 390.
38 Haki R. Madhubuti, "For Black People," 1968, in *GroundWork: New and Selected Poems* (Chicago: Third World Press, 1997), 97–103.
39 Amiri Baraka, *Wise, Why's, Y's* (Chicago: Third World Press, 1995), 98.

40 Ibid., 123–27.
41 Ibid., 126. "Human" here is used in contrast to "Ape" as the reference to "Floogie" is made via the lines "The Ape said, / "Floogie, / Lucy, Baby!" The seeming reference to Gaillard as "The Ape" may refer to Gaillard's appearance in the 1968 film *Planet of the Apes* as well as to the practice of dehumanizing Black subjects in white supremacist culture using images of nonhuman primates.
42 Ibid., 127.
43 "OoBlahDee" references Gillespie's 1949 recording "In the Land of Oo-Blah-Dee." "Ooolyacoo" resembles the title of Gillespie's 1947 scat recording "OOL-YA-KOO." "Bloomdido" references a Charlie Parker composition he recorded in 1950 with the Dizzy Gillespie Quartet.
44 Baraka, *Wise, Why's, Y's*, 123.
45 See www.youtube.com/watch?v=W6prPMxTHAA where Ledisi scats in styles she refers to as "Old School" and "New School."

CHAPTER 3

Jazz as Intertextual Expression

Charles Hersch

What might "intertextuality," an often disputed term usually applied to literary texts, teach us about jazz?[1] Existing analyses of intertextuality in music encompass multiple genres, from symphonies and rock "covers" to hip-hop sampling, but there have been surprisingly few treatments of jazz. Here I argue that major variants of intertextuality often miss what is most important to jazz – the way jazz has served as a vehicle for both the transmission of tradition and a dialogue within it and with other genres – and suggest that Bakhtin's dialogism illuminates those neglected intertextual features. I then explore the manifold ways jazz is intertextual and more broadly what this suggests to us about the music's relationship to individuality, tradition, and the larger social context.

In its broadest sense, intertextuality indicates that any text inevitably refers to other texts. Coined by Julia Kristeva, the term in its earliest incarnations was associated with post-structuralist approaches to literature like Roland Barthes's "death of the author," a mode of reading that foregrounds varied textual relationships and effects above a meaning intended by the work's creator.[2] According to Barthes, "it is language which speaks, not the author," the latter a mere "scriptor," through whom language anonymously flows.[3] A second version of intertextuality derives from Harold Bloom's notion of "the anxiety of influence," which argues that "strong poets," fearful of being mere imitators, transform the texts of their predecessors to assert their own originality.[4] Commentators on classical music have often utilized Bloom to show how composers competitively rework materials from previous musical giants to "push their precursors aside and clear creative space for themselves" and "remake the past."[5]

Yet post-structuralist and Bloomian notions of intertextuality are of limited applicability to jazz. While the erasure of the subject/author helped liberate literary criticism from a rigid metaphysics of the self, its unaltered application to a music born out of a struggle against dehumanization is problematic. Unlike the post-structuralist version of intertextuality,

Bloom grants agency to artists, but his framework rests on assumptions not fully applicable to a music steeped in African American culture: namely, competitive individualism and a belief that traditions threaten individuality. Competitiveness exists in jazz, in practices like "cutting contests," but equally important in African American culture is an ethic of empathy and mutuality, in which (in Martin Luther King Jr.'s words, drawing on Martin Buber), "'I' cannot reach fulfillment without 'thou.' The self cannot be self without other selves."[6] Within this framework, adherence to tradition and the expression of individuality are not mutually exclusive. There are artists and critics who call into question or even seek to dismantle the jazz tradition, at times in opposition to Wynton Marsalis and Jazz at Lincoln Center.[7] But as George Lewis points out, Black musicians are less likely to want to extinguish the past from music, since much of their familial and cultural history was erased by slavery and racism.[8] Many jazz musicians do not fear "imitation" in Bloom's terms but instead draw sustenance from a tradition that at its best accommodates individuality and group solidarity.[9]

In this vein, there exists an African American model of intertextuality that sees individual utterances as bounded by, yet not reducible to, a larger tradition and sees in jazz a paradigm for a healthy relationship between individual and tradition, text and intertexts. For Ralph Ellison, when jazz musicians improvise, they define themselves simultaneously as individuals and as part of "a chain of tradition," so that "the jazzman must lose his identity even as he finds it," innovating within a larger "frame."[10] Henry Louis Gates, Jr. also emphasizes the artist's active engagement with tradition through "signifyin(g)," "repetition with a signal difference," in which African American artists take practices from the dominant culture and transform them for their own purposes.[11] Going beyond Ellison's evolutionary model, Gates stresses the way innovative artists rewrite the tradition and the fact that the tradition is always multiple and unstable. For Gates, like Ellison, jazz is a paradigm for this process of intertextuality, asserting that "there are so many examples of Signifyin(g) in jazz that one could write a formal history of its development on this basis alone," citing artists from Jelly Roll Morton to John Coltrane who use techniques like theme and variation or call and response.[12]

Gates explicitly draws on Bakhtin, and I wish to more fully utilize the Russian theorist to expand on Gates's dialogic, African American version of intertextuality. In my view, Bakhtin's notion of dialogue provides a framework for understanding how jazz improvisation is intertextual, which illuminates aspects missed by post-structuralist and Bloomian approaches. Like post-structuralists, Bakhtin emphasizes the way language shapes us from the inside, because we "live in a world of others' words,"[13] and each of those words is "permeated with the interpretations of others."[14] But Bakhtin, unlike post-structuralists, emphasizes the way speakers can make the words of others (partially) their own through what he calls "re-accenting," in which we put our own stamp on them.[15]

Jazz scholars like David Brackett, Alan Stanbridge, Gary Tomlinson, and Tony Whyton have analyzed the intertextuality of jazz using dialogism and/or signifyin(g), focusing on the way a performance of a tune engages with previous versions, its meaning changing by coming into contact with other texts and contexts.[16] Drawing on their work as well as my own reading of Bakhtin, I show how jazz musicians intertextually "re-accent" or "signify" in their use of quotations, licks, style, and repertory.

Admittedly, the centrality of improvisation to jazz complicates the applicability of intertextuality. When a musician improvises over the same tune hundreds (or more) times over the course of a lifetime, is each performance a separate "text" or a variation on one text? Ingrid Monson argues that jazz improvisation "has nothing in common with a text," because it is composed through ongoing interaction, preferring the term "intermusicality" – "aurally perceptible relationships that are heard in the context of particular musical traditions" – to intertextuality.[17] Yet her analysis of intermusicality shares the central idea of intertextuality: something within one text – whether a melody, a quotation, or timbre – refers to or evokes something from another one.[18] In contrast to her statement, though consistent with her practice, here I see repeatable features of jazz performances as "texts" and the relationships among them as "intertextuality."

Quoting

Musical quotation – the insertion of one musical text into another – occurs in every genre, but is ubiquitous in jazz. Charlie Parker quoted from a vast array of sources, from popular songs of his time ("Over There," "Buttons and Bows," "Why Was I Born") to folk or traditional melodies ("I Dream of Jeannie with the Light Brown Hair," "Three Blind Mice," "Oh Come, All Ye Faithful") to classics or light classics from Stravinsky, Grieg, Bizet, Wagner, Rossini, Johann Strauss, and others. He also quoted jazz melodies – sometimes his own compositions, and sometimes the work of older players like Armstrong ("West End Blues").[19] Such musical quoting is intertextuality in its purest form.

Jazz musicians quote for a variety of reasons. Occasionally improvisers use quotes to convey a literal message. When an attractive woman came into the club, Parker quoted "A Pretty Girl Is a Melody;" when another musician felt the rhythm section was wobbling, he would quote "I Got Rhythm" or "I Didn't Know What Time it Was."[20] In a round of "trading fours," with Johnny Griffin, Dexter Gordon quotes "Anything You Can Do I Can Do Better," to communicate a playful boast.[21] More often, musicians quote for humorous or ironic intent, like "quoting a trite popular tune within a sophisticated solo … or shifting a solo's mood unexpectedly."[22]

In one of the few sustained treatments of the subject, Krin Gabbard argues that bebop jazz musicians used quotes to position themselves in relation to either European classical music or other jazz artists, depending on what was quoted.[23] For Gabbard, quotation from the light classics, as in Parker's often-deployed "Country Gardens" lick, represents an ironic, avant-garde gesture that serves, like a modernist collage, to "break the illusion of organic art," and "signifies on the fatuous, bourgeois art music by emphasizing the passion and complexity of the new Afro-American art music."[24] (Gabbard does acknowledge that the effect on the audience depends on their previous knowledge: Some would miss the reference, others would take it and enjoy it at face value, and "a select group of initiates will catch the irony of a black jazz artist dipping into the sedate repertoire of a completely different milieu."[25]) Evoking Bloom's "anxiety of influence," however, he argues that quoting an improvised phrase or composition by another jazz musician has an entirely different valence, showing "the ambivalent relationship that each generation of jazz musicians bears to the preceding ones."[26] These quotations, rather than ironically critiquing, both reaffirm the tradition and modify it in Ellison-like fashion.

Jazz musicians certainly quote to poke fun at mainstream culture or to stand out from their forebears. Yet there are other possible motivations, including a love of the quoted melody, which may simply pop into the mind of the improvisor in a particular context. More importantly, quoting can be a means not just to criticize through parody or irony but to connect to the larger tradition. John Murphy in "Jazz Improvisation: The Joy of Influence" specifically rejects Bloom as inapplicable to jazz and sees jazz quotation instead as tradition-affirming.[27] For Murphy, quotation, rather than seeking to obliterate or surpass predecessors, instead "emphasizes the connection."[28]

Murphy overstates the case a bit, ignoring the tradition-puncturing strand in jazz. For example, *Blue*, a 2014 album by the band Mostly Other People Do the Killing, questions the value of the tradition altogether, by "quoting" the whole canonical album *Kind of Blue* – that is, reproducing it in its entirety, note for note, drumbeat for drumbeat. Band member Moppa Elliott has described the album as in part a response to the dangers inherent in the canonization of jazz and the way jazz history can "kind of creep up and consume you if you let it."[29] Yet *Blue*, says Elliot, simultaneously plays homage to the tradition and raises questions about the role of improvisation in jazz; the subtle, irreproducible aspects of a musicians' technique; and the importance of context in a musical performance's meaning. The sheer multiplicity of implications of this particular "quote" shows that no singular explanation will suffice.

Alongside this iconoclasm, testimony by musicians shows that many quote to engage with the jazz tradition. Saxophonist Joe Henderson, according to Murphy, has described the practice as "having a conversation with *somebody*" (original emphasis) and traced its origins to the process of transcribing canonical solos to learn to improvise.[30] Similarly, multi-instrumentalist Arthur Rhames describes quoting as paying homage. "Being able to quote from songs and solos is always part of a mature artist because he's aware of the contribution of others and its impact, how it is."[31] Some even feel that inserting a quote from a great player establishes one's credibility, validating one's lineage.[32] Quotations also allow the audience to connect to the tradition, giving them something familiar to hold on to.[33] Quoting can also be a means to expand the jazz tradition or build bridges to other genres, as when Parker quotes Stravinsky.

Equally important, musicians transform ("re-accent") quotations and make them their own, altering them melodically, rhythmically, or harmonically. Murphy shows how improvisers like Henderson use quotes as the basis of their own improvisation. Sometimes this is done in a spirit of humor or irony. Bill Evans would quote "Take Me Out to the Ball Game," shifting the melody to make it sound humorous,[34] while Parker displaced the "Habanera" phrase (from Bizet's *Carmen*), ending on the "wrong" note for comic effect.[35] And when ending a solo with the "Country Gardens" lick he would pompously extend the trill, heightening the irony.[36] But more often the purpose of the alteration is to contribute to a conversation by means of a hybrid construction, taking part of the original and adding something of one's own. When Henderson quotes and expands upon previous statements by musicians, whether recorded ones or those on the bandstand, he does so "not to refute them or to mock them, but to repeat them in altered versions in order to continue the dialogue."[37] In "re-accenting" these quotes, musicians thus reaffirm Bakhtin's central idea that in creative uses of language we both connect with larger discourse (and culture) and make that discourse in part our own. This transformation of the ideas of others to make them one's own is the key to the jazz vocabulary ("licks") as well.

Licks

Licks – common phrases used in jazz improvisation – are by nature intertextual, as they are passed from one improviser to another, and often have their origins in canonical solos by jazz greats. (Of course, some licks are simply musical patterns that a player might improvise spontaneously or learn from an exercise book, but what matters is the existence of a cultural discourse that shows up in many variations rather than conscious knowledge of its origin.)[38] Every player uses licks, for they are a way of learning the tradition and the genre, and can also provide filler material when inspiration runs dry.[39] Though some players embrace licks wholeheartedly and others try to avoid them, they are inevitable, for playing jazz phrases is what makes one a jazz musician, as Dizzy Gillespie acknowledged by stating trumpeter Fats Navarro "could have never completely broken away from my influence, no more than I could've broken away from the influence of Roy Eldridge, or Roy from the influence of Louis Armstrong."[40] An aspiring bebop saxophonist in the 1950s could not have avoided playing Charlie Parker's lines any more than one can completely bypass common verbal expressions like "hello" in everyday conversation.

Merely stringing together licks from one's favorite player can make one a "clone," usually seen as unimaginative copycats. But even innovators started by absorbing the others' vocabulary, as when in an early recording Parker quotes a long excerpt from a Lester Young solo.[41] And merely using others' licks does not make one a clone, because there are multiple innovators at any given time, allowing one to choose and blend one's influences to forge an individual style. According to Arthur Rhames, most players, though not great innovators, nevertheless possess "the ability to take different musical perspectives" embodied in other musicians' licks and "integrate them into their own."[42]

But the task of truly integrating the jazz vocabulary into one's own improvisations to create a musical personality is not an easy one. Josh Schneider compared it to language learning; at first you learn "words," that eventually "naturally" combine into larger statements when improvising.[43] Sometimes people at first practice putting a phrase in the same spot in the tune every time ("force feeding"), until it "becomes ingrained in you because you practice it so much. It becomes a natural habit when you improvise."[44] This process calls to mind Aristotle's argument that developing good habits creates a more virtuous self – though at first such habits feel artificial, if they are part of one's aspired-to character, they eventually become part of one's identity.[45] On the other hand, habit can be a hindrance as well; players complain that sometimes when they want to develop their own musical ideas more fully, they find it difficult to avoid using ingrained licks.[46] Thus, using licks has the capacity to engender a stronger self-identity but also to prevent its growth.

Players avoid the mere repetition of licks and the concomitant rigid musical personality by transforming a phrase to make it their own, just as one might do with a quote but more extensively, so it becomes a springboard for creativity.[47] Emily Remler claimed you could take one Wes Montgomery lick and "base ten million of your own licks, or a whole solo, on that one thing." Walter Bishop, Jr. described working to make Bud Powell lines his own "in the same idiom, playing with the same kind of feeling and intensity,"[48] while Gillespie suggested one could make individualized variations on a Eldridge line, saying "Ah, then, you could also go here instead of going there."[49] According to Rhames, it is like adopting the speaking style of another person to express your own ideas. Rhames took Coltrane licks "to get the feeling of the line, the phrasing, which allowed me to understand how Trane was talking when he played. What I wanted was the form, the basket that he was using, but the contents I wanted to fill myself."[50]

Jazz musicians' creative utilization of another's phrases in the service of self-expression taps into a larger tradition of such transformations in African American oral performance. According to Bruce Rosenberg, "Spiritual" black preachers in the South and Southwest use "patterned sequences of formulas" in their oral sermons, "stitching together ... several traditional themes" from the Bible and elsewhere, creating through unique "expression, gesture, and dramatic intonation" a whole that is both spontaneous and formulaic, personal and tradition-affirming.[51] According to Barry Brummett, this intertextuality is a feature of "Afrocentric culture," which "expects that texts will borrow from other texts freely," as when King's speeches drew upon "the Bible, proverbs, maxims, and his other speeches."[52] A particular repertory of formulas together makes a genre, to whose intertextuality I now turn.

Style and Genre

Genre, according to Charles L. Briggs and Richard Bauman "is quintessentially intertextual," illustrating how our speech, and thus our selves, are constructed from pre-existing vocabularies and models.[53] As Bauman puts it, a genre is "a constellation of systemically related, co-occurrent formal features and structures that serves as a conventionalized orienting framework for the production and reception of discourse."[54] As part of a genre, a text is in its production and reception "mediated through its intertextual relationship with prior texts".[55]

Repeatable elements of a musical genre include harmony, rhythms, melodic features, tempo, and repertory. In this sense jazz itself is a genre as are styles like bebop and swing. Even the sounds that define particular genres can be intertexts, like a bluesy guitar riff or a Coltrane-like saxophone squeal. An instrument's sound, Bennett Hogg argues, evokes "culturally learned listener expectations" and associations through "sonic intertextuality."[56]

Genres also limit musicians' use of intertextuality, because too many (musical) utterances from "outside" the genre threaten the listenability or even intelligibility of a performance. As Bakhtin emphasizes, genres structure all communication, even at its freest, and its rules are not created by the individual but instead given to him or her.[57]

On the other hand, the judicious use of generic intertextuality, incorporating material from other genres, simultaneously asserts individuality and affirms tradition. Andrew Kluth argues that saxophonist Joe Farrell's performance on "Moon Germs" is creative not – as in the Western notion of the "original" genius – due to pure novelty but rather by "synthesiz[ing] ... extant surrounding elements into a unique voice tempered with labor and imagination."[58] For Kluth, in "Moon Germs" Farrell "appropriated" and "synthesized" elements from various jazz styles and from rock, creating an "intertextual palimpsest."[59] Farrell gives listeners enough familiar generic features (blues harmony, a clear written melody, and melodic minor modes) to feel comfortable and oriented, which allows him to introduce more unfamiliar and demanding ones (diminished patterns and quartal harmony).[60] "Moon Germs" is thus "shot through with intertextual significance relating to the jazz world, but ... also works to incorporate new and/or appropriated texts to potentially increase its capacity for the construction of meaning."[61] According to Kluth, works of jazz like these use vocabulary from a variety of genres to affirm existing "social reality while simultaneously transcending it from within."[62]

Generic intertextuality also occurs when jazz musicians improvise on tunes from other genres. According to René Rusch, Brad Mehldau's version of Radiohead's "Paranoid Android" both draws on and transforms the Radiohead intertext. The transfer to solo piano changes the feeling of the tune, and Mehldau uses jazz techniques, including improvisations on the song's motives, to both express the original song and to put his own stamp on it. Rusch shows how Mehldau "recontextualizes" and "transforms" Radiohead's musical statements, creating a dialogue between the old and new material, "encouraging us to rehear and rediscover the original through its cover."[63]

Genres' intertextuality, according to Briggs and Bauman, has political implications. "Genres have strong historical associations" and "bear social, ideological, and political-economic connections" – for example, connections with certain social groups[64] – and "different genres implicate different subject positions and formations."[65] The maintenance or breaching of generic boundaries thus has social meaning. Genres can be used to uphold the established order, reinforcing the authority of existing texts, their ways of thinking and feeling, and the social forces behind them.[66] Conversely, the breaking of generic boundaries or the creation of new genres can give voice to new subjectivities and empower social groups, creating new sets of texts and intertextual relations.

Briggs and Bauman's analysis of genres and their social meanings has two implications for jazz and intertextuality. First, the debates over what "jazz" is necessarily implicate larger societal issues, as when Paul Whiteman's attempt to "make a lady out of jazz" sought to rescue it from associations with lower classes, African Americans, and unregulated sexuality. One thinks also of attempts to separate "real" jazz from "commercialism," something that was seen in the "trad versus swing" debate of the 1930s and the canon wars of the 1980s. In the latter case, Wynton Marsalis and associates, drawing on an unlikely mixture of Black nationalism and Reaganesque conservatism, sought to protect "pure" jazz from too much generic intertextuality. For Marsalis, pop music is simply a "low level realization of sex," representing the lowest common denominator. Thus jazz-rock fusion in his view encourages democracy's tendency to see every desire and opinion as worthy of equal respect, whereas jazz embodies and encourages that which is objectively highest and most admirable in human beings.[67] In contrast, as we shall see, many of today's jazz musicians, in a sense harking back to the fusion of the 1960s and 1970s so despised by Marsalis, embrace genre mixing. Second, blurring genre boundaries can represent an act of signifying, confronting a "foreign" or "other" speech, that has political meaning. When early jazz musicians in New Orleans signified on European forms like waltzes and marches to create jazz, they were inserting themselves into American culture and transforming it.[68] The breakdown of genres and the rise of new ones begins with intertextuality, and new genres allow new social groups and concepts of the self, to speak. Today's looser, more intertextual genres represent a more cosmopolitan and diverse world.

Standards and Repertory

Another intertextual feature of jazz is its use of "standards" – a body of tunes over which generations of jazz musicians have improvised. Not all jazz styles utilize standards, but much of canonical jazz is based on them. Monson shows how particular canonical performances invest tunes with associations that they carry with them, which are then evoked in the minds of knowledgeable listeners when they hear a later improvisation on that tune; a listener hearing "Body and Soul" inevitably compares it with previous versions, like Coleman Hawkins's classic rendition or Coltrane's revisioning of it decades later.[69] Performances of standards are adaptations, like remakes of canonical films, and thus are, according to Linda Hutcheon, "inherently 'palimpsestuous' works, haunted at all times by their adapted texts."[70]

As with quoting, the "adaptation" – the performance of a standard – can exhibit a variety of attitudes toward the "original" (canonical) version(s), from homage to parody. As Hutcheon puts it, the question is "what one *does with* the other text."[71] A rote version of a standard is less individual and expressive than a more adventurous reworking, like pianist Art Lande's "Angel Eyes" (1977), guitarist Derek Bailey's "Stella by Starlight" (2002), and guitarist Mary Halvorson's "Solitude" (2015), which take some features of a standard – usually its melody and harmonic framework – and radically rework others, combining the familiar with the unsettling.[72] In each of these three performances, the musician applies his or her own idiosyncratic stylistic devices, including tone clusters (Lande), dissonant voicings and percussive plucking (Bailey), and wide reverb (Halvorson) to the tune, making it simultaneously recognizable as a jazz standard and the artist's own expression. The vast majority of performances are neither rote reproductions nor avant-garde deconstructions, but something in between; however, to quote Hutcheon again, "Whatever the motive, from the adapter's perspective, adaptation is an act of appropriating and salvaging, and this is always a double process of interpreting and then creating something new."[73]

Jason Moran's recent work illustrates how jazz musicians' use of intertextuality both affirms and makes more permeable stylistic, and by implication, social/political/ethnic boundaries. His 2015 performance *In My Mind: Monk at Town Hall, 1959* showcases music from the earlier pianist's famous concert but also utilizes video of historical photographs and recorded conversations from those sessions.[74] Moran's performance of "Little Rootie Tootie" opens with a black and white video simulating a television screen (complete with "snow") while the audience listens to a recording of a rehearsal for the original concert, where Monk explains that he wants the whole band to play his solo from the original recording of the tune (thus creating an intertextual performance itself). Then Moran begins, accompanied by a recording from the same session of Monk tapping his feet to the tune. Solos featured in the performance pay homage to Monk (Moran's features a long silence and percussive block chords) but incorporate a more modern harmonic vocabulary as well, bridging the time periods.

In other performances, Moran utilizes a different form of intertextuality – combining (sub-)genres to both affirm tradition and undermine it. In his 2015 "Fats Waller Dance Party" performance in Paris, Moran begins by playing "Honeysuckle Rose" similar to the original recording, but the tune then morphs into funk, with chunky electric bass, the rhythmic emphasis moving from 1 and 3 to 2 and 4, with 16th note based drumming.[75] At a certain point the feeling of the original gets lost until Moran brings back the melody insistently on piano, in which case the funk and the original style come together, rhythms speaking to each other across the generations. By the end we hear Waller differently, as a precursor of James Brown. Another "Fats Waller Dance Party" performance incorporates Latin devices and Cecil Taylor-esque avant-garde tone clusters into Waller as well.[76]

In performances like these Moran uses stylistic, generic, and repertory-based intertextuality to make the case for jazz as a far-reaching but ultimately unified continuum from its beginnings to the present. In doing so he emphasizes continuity and change, text and intertext, utterance and re-accentuation. Having studied with Andrew Hill and Jaki Byard, Moran himself is a self-described "fourth-generation Earl Hines." "You *hear* your tribe in the music that you like.... They call you."[77] But the point is not to reproduce the past but to make it one's own; even when playing Waller, Moran emphasizes, "I'm doing new production on old pieces. I'm actually changing the music, too."[78] What matters is "the context you're going to put the music in." Your influences "only give you enough to get to the door. They don't tell you what to say once you get inside the door."[79] Contemporary musicians like Moran, then, weave various "sonic languages" into a widely expanded intertextuality, representing voices from a range of races, classes, and genders.[80] Like Bakhtin's Dostoevsky, these musicians give voice to the past and present, as well as to the "*latent, unuttered future Word*," all in dialogue with one another.[81]

In the end, neither the Bloomian struggle for influence nor the poststructuralist triumph of the play of language do justice to the complexities of intertextuality in jazz. Intertextuality is instead a window into the rich and ever-changing relations among a musician, previous musical texts and traditions, and the social context, including the backgrounds and expectations of listeners. Jazz musicians constantly incorporate the musical utterances of others into their own performances, affirming Bakhtin's notion that "our speech ... is filled with others' words," and "each utterance is filled with echoes and reverberations of other utterances to which it is related."[82] In doing so, they connect with a larger tradition, but through recontextualization and re-accenting use those utterances for self-expression and sometimes to push against cultural boundaries. Thus intertextual jazz performances – and there are no other kinds – simultaneously express the musicians and engage with the larger whole(s) of which they are a part.

Notes

1 The author would like to thank Ken Prouty and Tony Whyton for their helpful suggestions in the writing of this essay.
2 See Julia Kristeva, "Word, Dialogue and Novel," 1966, in Toril Moi, ed., *The Kristeva Reader* (New York: Columbia University Press, 1986), 34–61.
3 Roland Barthes, "The Death of the Author," 1968, in *Image-Music-Text*, trans. Stephen Heath (London, Fontana, 1977), 143–45.
4 Harold Bloom, *The Anxiety of Influence: A Theory of Poetry*, 2nd ed. (New York: Oxford University Press, 1997), 5.
5 Joseph N. Straus, "The 'Anxiety of Influence' in Twentieth-Century Music," *The Journal of Musicology* 9:4 (1991), 447. For another example of Bloom's "anxiety of influence" in classical music scholarship, see Kevin Korsyn, "Toward a New Poetics of Musical Influence," *Music Analysis* 10.1–2 (1991), 3–72.
6 Martin Luther King, Jr. *Where Do We Go from Here: Chaos or Community?* (Boston: Beacon Press, 1967), 180.
7 See Stuart Nicholson, *Is Jazz Dead? (Or Has It Moved to a New Address)* (New York: Routledge, 2005). For more on the institutionalization of jazz, see Dale Chapman's chapter in this volume (Chapter 11).
8 George E. Lewis, "Improvised Music after 1950: Afrological and Eurological Perspectives," *Black Music Research Journal* 16:1 (1996), 109.
9 Charles Hersch, *Democratic Artworks: Politics and the Arts from Trilling to Dylan* (Albany: State University of New York Press, 1998), 106–20.
10 Ralph Ellison, "The Charlie Christian Story," 1958, in *Shadow and Act* (New York: Random House, 1964), 234, 189.
11 Henry Louis Gates, Jr., *The Signifying Monkey: A Theory of African-American Literary Criticism* (New York: Oxford University Press, 1988), xxiv.
12 Ibid., 104–5.
13 M.M. Bakhtin, *Speech Genres & Other Late Essays*, Vern W. McGee, trans., Caryl Emerson and Michael Holquist, eds. (Austin: University of Texas Press, 1986), 145.
14 M.M. Bakhtin, *Problems of Dostoevsky's Politics*, Caryl Emerson, Ed. and Trans. (Minneapolis: University of Minnesota Press, 1984), 202.

15 M.M. Bakhtin, *The Dialogic Imagination*, Caryl Emerson and Michael Holquist, trans. (Austin: University of Texas Press, 1981), 293. See also, Bakhtin, *Speech Genres*, 89.
16 David Brackett, *Interpreting Popular Music* (Berkeley: University of California Press, 2000), 34–74; Alan Stanbridge, "A Question of Standards: 'My Funny Valentine' and Musical Intertextuality," *Popular Music History* 1.1 (2004), 83–108; Gary Tomlinson, "Cultural Dialogics and Jazz: A White Historian Signifies," in Katherine Bergeron and Philip V. Bohlman, eds., *Disciplining Music: Musicology and Its Canons* (Chicago: University of Chicago Press, 1992), 64–94; Tony Whyton, *Beyond a Love Supreme* (Oxford: Oxford University Press, 2013). For citations to other musical scholars who have used Bakhtin, see Charles Hersch, "Unfinalizable: Dialog and Self-Expression in Jazz," in Nicholas Gebhardt, Nichole Rustin-Paschal, and Tony Whyton, eds., *The Routledge Companion to Jazz Studies* (New York: Routledge, 2018), 374n.3.
17 Ingrid Monson, *Saying Something: Jazz Improvisation and Interaction*, Chicago: University of Chicago Press, 1996, 80, 128.
18 Ibid., 97–98, 115–17.
19 Thomas Owens, "Charlie Parker: Techniques of Improvisation, Vol. 1," Unpublished dissertation (University of California, Los Angeles, 1974), 29–30.
20 Paul Berliner, *Thinking in Jazz: The Infinite Art of Improvisation* (Chicago: University of Chicago Press, 1994), 469, 254.
21 Dexter Gordon, "Blues Up and Down," *Great Encounters* (CBS-Columbia LP: JC 39578, 1979). The quotation appears at 10:40 in the track.
22 Berliner, *Thinking in Jazz*, 258.
23 Krin Gabbard, "The Quoter and His Culture," in Reginald T. Buckner and Steven Weiland, eds., *Jazz in Mind: Essays on the History and Meanings of Jazz* (Detroit: Wayne State University Press, 1991), 92–111.
24 Ibid., 93, 100, 103–4.
25 Ibid., 94.
26 Ibid., 105.
27 John P. Murphy, "Jazz Improvisation: The Joy of Influence," *The Black Perspective in Music* 18:1–2 (1990), 7–19.
28 Ibid., 10.
29 Quoted in Brad Cohan, "Mostly Other People Do the Killing Interview: 'If We Wanted to Make People Mad, That's Easy,'" *Time Out*, November 14, 2014, www.timeout.com/newyork/music/mostly-other-people-do-the-killing-interview-if-we-wanted-to-make-people-mad-thats-easy. See also "Kind of, Kind of Blue: A Conversation with Mostly Other People Do the Killing," *PopMatters*, September 14, 2014, www.popmatters.com/185662-kind-of-kind-of-blue-a-conversation-with-mostly-other-people-do-the--2495616921.html, where Moppa Elliott talks about the way canonization "kind of kills" classical music.
30 Murphy, "Jazz Improvisation," 15.
31 Quoted in Berliner, *Thinking in Jazz*, 104.
32 Berliner, *Thinking in Jazz*, 249.

33 Murphy, "Jazz Improvisation," 9.
34 Berliner, *Thinking in Jazz*, 258.
35 Owens, "Charlie Parker," 29.
36 Ibid.
37 Murphy, "Jazz Improvisation," 13.
38 Ken Prouty, personal communication.
39 Berliner, *Thinking in Jazz*, 249, 270.
40 Dizzy Gillespie with Al Fraser, *To Be or Not to Bop* (New York: Da Capo, 1979), 487.
41 Charlie Parker, tenor sax, "Shoe Shine Boy" [aka "Yardin' with Yard"/"Shoe Shine Swing"], Rec. February 15, 1943, *The Complete "Birth of the Bebop"* (Stash Records CD ST-CD-535, 1991). Parker's solo is available as an excerpt at www.youtube.com/watch?v=8391neI3uV4.
42 Quoted in Berliner, *Thinking in Jazz*, 138.
43 Quoted in Berliner, *Thinking in Jazz*, 184.
44 Harold Ousely, quoted in Berliner, *Thinking in Jazz*, 173.
45 Aristotle, *The Nicomachean Ethics*, in Hugh Tredennick and Jonathan Barnes, eds. (New York: Penguin, 1976), 31–32.
46 Berliner, *Thinking in Jazz*, 206.
47 For such techniques, see Hal Crook, *How to Improvise* (Rottenburg, Germany: Advance Music, 1991).
48 Quoted in Berliner, *Thinking in Jazz*, 142.
49 Gillespie, *To Be or Not to Bop*, 489.
50 Quoted in Berliner, *Thinking in Jazz*, 143.
51 Bruce A. Rosenberg, "Oral Sermons and Oral Narrative," in Dan Ben-Amos et al., eds., *Folklore: Performance and Communication* (Berlin: DeGruyter, 1975), 77–78.
52 Quoted in Brian L. Ott and Cameron Walter, "Intertextuality: Interpretive Practice and Textual Strategy," *Critical Studies in Media Communication* 17.4 (2000), 443 n3.
53 Charles L. Briggs and Richard Bauman, "Genre, Intertextuality, and Social Power," *Journal of Linguistic Anthropology* 2.2 (1992), 147.
54 Richard Bauman, *A World of Others' Words* (New York: Wiley, 2004), 3.
55 Ibid., 4.
56 Bennett Hogg, "Enactive Consciousness, Intertextuality, and Musical Free Improvisation," in David Clarke and Eric Clarke, eds., *Music and Consciousness: Philosophical, Psychological, and Cultural Perspectives* (New York: Oxford University Press, 2011), 88.
57 Bakhtin, *Speech Genres*, 78, 80–81.
58 Andrew J. Kluth, "Intertextuality and the Construction of Meaning in Jazz Worlds: A Case Study of Joe Farrell's 'Moon Germs,'" *Journal of Jazz Studies* 12.1 (2019), 56.
59 Ibid., 58–60.
60 Ibid., 63–66.
61 Ibid., 67.
62 Ibid., 68.

63 René Rusch, "Crossing Over with Brad Mehldau's Cover of Radiohead's 'Paranoid Android': The Role of Jazz Improvisation in the Transformation of an Intertext," *Music Theory Online* 19.4 (2013), https://mtosmt.org/issues/mto.13.19.4/mto.13.19.4.rusch.html.
64 Briggs and Bauman, "Genre," 147.
65 Bauman, *A World of Others' Words*, 6.
66 Briggs and Bauman, "Genre," 148.
67 See Charles Hersch, "Reconstructing the Jazz Tradition," *Jazz Research Journal* 2.1 (2008), 13–14.
68 Charles Hersch, *Subversive Sounds: Race and the Birth of Jazz in New Orleans* (Chicago: University of Chicago Press, 2007), 124–64.
69 Monson, *Saying Something*, 98. Also see examples in Brackett (2000) ("I'll Be Seeing You"), Stanbridge (2004) ("My Funny Valentine"), and Robert Walser, "'Out of Notes': Signification, Interpretation, and the Problem of Miles Davis," in Krin Gabbard, ed., *Jazz Among the Discourses* (Durham, NC: Duke University Press, 1995), 165–88 ("My Funny Valentine").
70 Linda Hutcheon, *A Theory of Adaptation* (New York: Routledge. 2006), 6.
71 Ibid., 20, original emphasis.
72 Art Lande, "Angel Eyes," *The Eccentricities of Earl Dant* (1750 Arch Records S-1769, 1977); Derek Bailey, "Stella by Starlight," *Ballads* (Tzadik TZ 7607, 2002); Mary Halvorson, "Solitude," *Meltframe* (Firehouse 12 Records FH12-04-08-021, 2015).
73 Hutcheon, *A Theory of Adaptation*, 20.
74 Jason Moran, piano, *In My Mind: Monk at Town Hall, 1959*, Rec. March 28, 2015 for *Jazz Night in America* (NPR), www.youtube.com/watch?v=JqhH-OUXyrY&t=683s.
75 Jason Moran, piano, "Fats Waller Dance Party: Live at Paris Jazz Festival," Rec. July 5, 2015, www.youtube.com/watch?v=z6-db4p9tL8.
76 Jason Moran, piano, "Fats Waller Dance Party – Middelheim 2015," Rec. August 2015, www.youtube.com/watch?v=TZjZ7mFir28. Another of Moran's experiments in generic intertextuality, "Muldrow Meets Mingus," featured singer/rapper/producer Georgia Anne Muldrow with a group doing Mingus tunes, often reconfigured with funky backbeats. See Bill Beuttler, *Make It New: Reshaping Jazz in the Twenty-first Century* (Amherst, MA: Lever Press, 2019), 24.
77 Quoted in Beuttler, *Make It New*, 43.
78 Ibid., 28.
79 Ibid., 45.
80 Ibid., 42.
81 Bakhtin, *Problems of Dostoevsky's Politics, 90*.
82 Bakhtin, *Speech Genres*, 89, 91.

CHAPTER 4

How to Watch Jazz
The Importance of Performance
Michael Borshuk

While academic reactions to jazz were long dominated by a methodology drawn from musicology, attentive to composition and transcribed solos as forms for interpretation, scholarship over the past few decades – amid the interdisciplinary shift of "the New Jazz Studies" – has articulated in ever more assertive terms that "meaning" in jazz depends not only on *what* is played, but *how*.[1] Examples of this turn include Dana Reason's assertion that "meaning [in jazz improvisation can be] located in the ways in which improvisers situate their bodies, change their facial expressions, and use their voices to accompany notes, gestures, silences or phrases;"[2] or Vijay Iyer's imperative for the music's critics to "explode" the idea of the "narrative" as the dominant way to understand meaning in jazz.[3] As Iyer proposes in counterpoint, the meaning of jazz performance extends to the music's "traces of embodiment."[4] Paul Berliner has written on the aesthetic functionality of gesture and movement in jazz soloing – how musicians externalize improvisational flow in acts of bodily display. "Although sound serves as the principal medium binding improvisers to audience," Berliner writes, "the audience typically responds to the inseparable mixture of the music created by improvisers and their theatrical image or stage presence."[5] Berliner suggests that apprentice improvisers are as attentive to gesture and physical movement in formulating their personal style as they are to timbre and phrasing. "Learners ... study the subtle dance moves with which artists support improvisations, the gestures imbuing their creations with rhythmic swing and sometimes dramatizing features of performance."[6]

Indeed, as these examples suggest, a more comprehensive approach to understanding the jazz aesthetic should foreground the range of contexts and performative elements that inform the music's creation. Jazz is not only music. While its improvisatory nature has always allowed artistic experimentation and political expression through innovation on music-as-text,[7] jazz performance, broadly understood, turns also on a more comprehensive sense of play that includes theatrical elements, self-presentation, and visual codes. In this chapter, I suggest that jazz musicians have always been aware of themselves not just as conduits for sound, but as physical performers who often enact their artistry onstage, in film, in photographs, for watchful audiences. As jazz great Sonny Rollins once remarked, "To me it is very important to put on a show: I believe what we do is theatre."[8]

While I situate this revised focus within the emergence of the New Jazz Studies in the 1990s, an attention to musical expression's embodied elements appears in broader scholarly discussions as well. David Clowney and Robert Rawlins, for example, argue that aesthetic philosophy would be better served by an expanded understanding of music by admitting other codes into the discussion. They "see music as a form of human communication, embodied and social."[9] To do so, they encourage philosophers to make room for the spectacular elements of music-making which earlier scholars might have dismissed as merely extramusical "showing off." Among the artists they consider are jazz musicians Rahsaan Roland Kirk and Ella Fitzgerald. But even with this declared attention to the "social," Clowney and Rawlins do not scrutinize the specific historical contexts and political vicissitudes I would posit are central to the birth and development of jazz practice.

Fundamentally, that is, we should interpret the social and political stakes of embodied transactions by understanding jazz performance within the context of Black diasporic expression – as, in part, a rejoinder to the historical antagonisms and inequalities brought on by white supremacy. Jazz is a musical performance tradition whose major innovations have been inaugurated historically by African American creators and, as such, is inseparable from broader African American cultural traditions. In this, jazz is especially important because Black musicians' awareness of their own performing bodies as "canvases of representations" (to use a phrase from Stuart Hall) has helped generate the performative ripostes these artists have made to the complex of white voyeurism, surveillance, and violence that produced the lived experience of "race" in America.[10] As the performance studies scholar Harry J. Elam, Jr. summarizes:

> From the arrival of the first African slaves on American soil, the discourse on race, the definitions and meanings of blackness, have been intricately linked to issues of theater and performance. Definitions of race, like the processes of theater, fundamentally depend on the relationship between the seen and unseen, between the visibly marked and unmarked, between the "real" and the illusionary.[11]

To return to the history of jazz performance with a concentrated attention to its visual aspects and intersections with theatrical performance, then, is to understand the long intervention the music's practitioners have made within the spectacular ways race and identity have been constructed and contested in American life. And in restoring the visual and the embodied to our understanding of jazz, we adhere to Paul Gilroy's important call that we move past the "idea and ideology of the text and of textuality as a mode of communicative practice which provides a model for all other forms of cognitive exchange and social interaction."[12]

So what does a performance-driven search for meaning in jazz look like? Broadly, it would consider the aesthetic and political importance of jazz musicians' visual self-presentation (especially through fashion) and their onstage performance styles (including gesture, posture, and the suggestion of dramatic persona); and the appearance of jazz musicians in photography, television, and film. To juxtapose these various elements in a comprehensive interpretation expands our understanding of jazz, and enables us to consider more profoundly how African American jazz innovators have challenged conventions in the arts, the marketplace, and the political sphere – especially through an improvisational sense that bridges music with self-aware physicality.

But we must also not lose sight of the complexity of exchange across subject positions. Just as non-Black musicians have participated in a broad jazz tradition by adapting sonic elements originating in Afro-diasporic practices, artists of other identities have picked up the visual and gestural elements I mark as "Black" here. "Cool," for example, as a mode of theatrical understatement has a long history across the Black diaspora – recognizable, famously, in the self-consciously restrained performance styles of African American musicians like Lester Young and Miles Davis. As Robert Farris Thompson suggested decades ago, what began as an embodied philosophical approach to manage social crisis on the African continent evolved into a vernacular expressive style among Black Americans. "Mystical coolness in Africa," Thompson writes, "has changed in urban Afro-American assertions of independent power. But the functions, to heal and gather strength, partially remain."[13] Fittingly, younger African Americans negotiating the threats to personal safety that came with participation in Civil Rights Era protests "looked to Miles Davis as a model for how to think and behave under pressure."[14] However, white musicians like Chet Baker and Stan Getz also incorporated a cool aesthetic of stylized self-possession into their performance demeanors, reminding us that the adoption of gestures or modes of physical comportment does not always read the same across context and identities.[15]

It would also be culturally shortsighted to conceive of "theatricality" in jazz as governed by Western drama's traditional bifurcation between performer and audience. As Bertram D. Ashe cautions, jazz as a component of longstanding African American vernacular practice depends on interaction between those performing and those who respond. Improvisers feed off the encouraging energy of nightclub and festival patrons, or signify against antagonistic vibes from disinterested listeners. The antiphonal energies at work between all involved remind us that, in Ashe's words, "in a sense, there *is* no audience as such."[16] Even in the stagiest moments of jazz performance, there is no fourth wall separating the improvisers at work and the crowds they seek to please. At the same time, to name jazz as theatre bucks against other aspects of the music's dominant discourses. As John Gennari writes: "[I]f jazz authenticity hinges on believing that the music is defined by its truthfulness, its sincerity and integrity, jazz then is fundamentally at odds with the idea of *performance*, especially insofar as the idea of performance attaches itself to traditions of the theatrical, in particular blackface minstrelsy and its long legacy."[17]

With these qualifications in sight, we might turn to other examples to explore jazz performance as an embodied extension of Black expressive practices. Consider, for example, Thelonious Monk's longstanding tendency to dance in performance, often rising from the piano during a set to bounce or pirouette while other bandmates soloed.[18] Monk's dancing is an excellent example of what Jacqui Malone identifies as a central property defining African American movement to music – the process, to use Malone's phrase, of making rhythm *visible*.[19] As Malone argues, following earlier critics like John Miller Chernoff, the explicit relationship between music and physical movement is one of the most recognizable Africanisms in the historical development of an African American expressive style.[20] Summarizing the relationship of physical movement to musical performance across a range of African traditions, and noting this contrast with European practices, Malone summarizes:

> Most European conceptions of art would separate music from dance and both music and dance from the social situations that produced them. Most traditional African conceptions, on the other hand, couple music with one or more other art forms, including dance. And most Africans experience music as part of a multidimensional social event that may take place in [a variety of public spaces].[21]

Malone's cultural history of African American vernacular dance – a category I am suggesting we use to include less easily contextualized performances like Monk's movements – emphasizes the African foundation at the heart of Black American vernacular performance, especially in the understanding that, from an African diasporic perspective, physical movement and music are necessarily inextricable. To connect jazz performance strategies to their prehistorical origins through this long purview is to ascribe meaning to these performative moments in more complicated ways. That is, Monk's movement extends elements foundational to a vernacular tradition in African American music, rather than just exist independently as the incidental actions of one artist on one stage. This is not to propose, of course, that Monk was always *consciously* trying to evoke West African practice in his onstage actions. It is only to recognize, in Malone's words, that the discourse around African retentions in African American culture "has evolved beyond a search for specific elements to the recognition of shared cultural processes of creativity, based on the notion that 'art moves within people' and that cultural continuity is never completely broken."[22] Or as Thompson suggests, the recognition of continuity sometimes depends on instinct. In Thompson's words, "there is no evidence machine.... But the machinery plugs into intuition and the spirit."[23]

In addition, to contextualize jazz as performance – as opposed to looking only at the musical form divorced from context – renders the social importance of these various onstage tendencies more clearly. Reading Monk's frequently misunderstood physical movements as an extension of a long vernacular practice redeems his performance style from the specter of denigration and calls attention to how often insulting readings of his onstage persona (as primitive, as unhinged) have turned on white supremacist ideas about the untutored Black artist.

Beyond historicizing individual performance processes, a longer chronological view also allows us to challenge broad misconceptions about jazz clouded by archaic hierarchies. As Bruce Johnson suggests, one of the reasons that jazz was historically denigrated by early white American and European critics is because of its opposition to a post-Enlightenment mind/body binary. Johnson writes: "[N]otwithstanding the crucial importance of the sound recording in the dissemination of jazz, the body is the primary site of the music."[24] Thus, to restore an awareness of the body challenges the hegemony of what George E. Lewis calls "Eurological critical perspectives" with regard to African American music. As Lewis summarizes, Eurological perspectives – which he poses in opposition to Afrological points of view – too often present "a series of ongoing critiques of their construction of 'jazz,'" in what inevitably seems like a collective "attempt to create ... an 'epistemological other.'"[25] To redress this, we must always be conscious of the aesthetic importance of embodied and visual elements: Monk's dancing and sartorial flair, Louis Armstrong's facial expressions and signature white handkerchief, Billie Holiday's white gardenia and cool delivery, Sun Ra's Afrofuturist costuming and theatrics, or Wynton Marsalis's restoration of the second-line funeral procession in concert hall performances.

Marsalis is particularly useful for developing this argument about the organic relationship between theatricality and jazz musical performance. Consider two different performances, recorded on video twelve years apart. The first features Marsalis in a quartet setting, appearing at Spain's Festival de Vitoria-Gasteiz in 1987. Accompanied by his then working ensemble of Marcus Roberts on piano, Robert Hurst on bass, and Jeff "Tain" Watts on drums, the trumpeter performs a formidable rendition of John Coltrane's "Giant Steps."[26] Worth noting is that as he works through this post-bop standard, Marsalis's comportment rehearses the physical calm that Miles Davis brought to the stage in the 1950s and 60s. His carriage is stable, erect. There is little motion beyond a slight dip of the head here and there for rhythmic emphasis, and the quick movement of his fingers on the horn. When he closes his solo and yields to Roberts on piano, Marsalis turns and walks soberly to the side of the stage, away from the camera. Later, when Roberts finishes, the trumpeter returns just as plainly. He restates Coltrane's famous chord-jumping melody and brings the performance to an understated close. In the second performance, from 2009's Jazz in Marciac festival, Marsalis's demeanor has changed completely. Here, the trumpeter offers another standard, the 1921 Tin Pan Alley hit, "The Sheik of Araby," performed this time with an octet in the breezy, polyphonic style of early jazz.[27] After a brassy trumpet fanfare to introduce a conventional solo round, Marsalis spends the closing choruses of the tune sliding in and out of dialogue with the rest of his front line. Appropriate to the New Orleans feel, Marsalis replaces the thin, nimble tone of his "Giant Steps" performance with a much more gutbucket sound, employing the slides, grunts, and growls of his earliest jazz antecedents. Physically, he completes this variation through gesture and posture. Here, the trumpeter and his fellow improvisers are seated in a loose semi-circle, their legs spread and their bodies somewhat slack. Marsalis himself is considerably more animated than in the earlier performance. He tilts, he furrows his bow, he taps his foot, and he shakes his head in antic response to some of his own musical lines. The theatrical effect of these moves in combination is undeniable: "The Sheik of Araby" comes off as looser, bluesier. It is a playful reconstruction of the presumed laidbackness we would expect in an after-hours jam session. And yet, the setting reminds us that this effect is effortful in its simulation. Like the earlier performance, Marsalis and company appear here before a European audience in a festival setting. The field of differences between the two moments of onstage activity are meaningful for calling attention to Marsalis's construction of onstage character as anything but "natural." In the 1987 appearance, as he evokes jazz modernism of the 1960s, his impassivity is a matter of actorly discipline; in the Marciac performance, any suggestion of casualness or spontaneity results directly from the trumpeter's conscious self-presentation and performance choices.

The difference between Marsalis's two performances here emphasizes the illusory nature of what many assume about jazz in performance: namely, that what musicians do at the gestural level is little more than, as Peter Elsdon calls it, "the externalization of the personal interior"[28] – which I would add is often mistaken as a straightforward revelation of the "authentic self" or the "soul." Instead, I am suggesting that improvisers are always actively constructing musical identities by assembling elements from an already-in-existence corporeal grammar that precedes them.[29] In the example of the two Marsalis performances, this grammar may shift according to the style of the music being played. Bebop and post-bop command impassive poses; earlier styles proceed from a very different gestural language, marked more by affected ebullience and animation.

The performance studies scholar Philip Auslander gives us a language for explaining these theatrical modes in the concept he calls "musical personae." As Auslander argues, critical understandings of musical performance must continue to move beyond musicology's traditional disciplinary dichotomy, in which the musical work is worshipped and the performance itself is disdained. He writes:

> When we hear a musician play, the source of the sound is a version of that person constructed for the specific purpose of playing music under particular circumstances. Musical performance may be defined, using [David] Graver's terms as *a person's representation of self within a discursive domain of music*. I posit that in musical performance, this representation of self is the direct object of the verb *to perform*.[30]

Suggesting a way to think of musical work and musical performance more continuously, Auslander proposes a third term that binds the two: *musical persona*. "What musicians perform first and foremost," Auslander writes, "is not music, but their own identities as musicians, their musical personae."[31]

As the application of Auslander's idea exemplifies, our understanding of jazz benefits significantly from incorporating performance studies methodologies. Another useful borrowing is Richard Schechner's concept of

How to Watch Jazz: The Importance of Performance 71

"restored behavior," which Schechner uses to define the very parameters of performance activity itself. On one level, Schechner's "restored behavior" enables us to see how jazz musicians' artistic activities, bracketed as they are by the stage, might necessarily suggest an ongoing self-awareness about audience, artifice, and gesture. Secondly, the idea helps establish how the embodied practices of jazz relate back to the context of social ritual – in this case, how the physical aspects of jazz musical performance originated and developed out of expressive traditions at the heart of African Americans' negotiation with the inequalities of American racism. First developed at length in 1985's *Between Theater and Anthropology*, Schechner's "restored behavior" articulates a tangible set of criteria for defining "performance" as a phenomenon, and also reads those specific acts within a number of material contexts: the social, the anthropological, the political.[32]

Schechner imagines performance as a broad human activity that can never be divorced from its conscious and unconscious antecedents. Performing constitutes the "restoration of behavior" because in so many different contexts – from a theatrical performance to a religious ritual to a simple wave hello – we are acting within the context of models, traditions, and routines that precede us. As Schechner writes in a later articulation of the idea:

> Restored behavior is "out there," separate from "me." To put it in personal terms, restored behavior is "me behaving as if I were someone else," or "as I am told to do," or "as I have learned." Even if I feel myself wholly to be myself, acting independently, only a little investigating reveals that the units of behavior that comprise "me" were not invented by "me."[33]

This awareness here of both the temporal context and the importance of antecedent to individual moments of performance is useful, in that it opens up a series of critical frames through which so many acts might be interpreted.

In particular, Schechner's exploration of what we might call the "not-me"-ness of performance, an exaggerated self-consciousness that comes out of the awareness of being perceived, is especially germane to a consideration of jazz as social theater. The long performance tradition that led to jazz began with expressive acts by Black subjects, whose actions affirmed life and voiced resistance against white supremacy's violence. Both the policing mechanisms and ideological scaffolding of race itself turn on the specular and the voyeuristic. As W. E. B. Du Bois famously suggested in 1903's *The Souls of Black Folk*, the legacy of this concentrated surveillance was the peculiar phenomenon of African American double-consciousness: the exaggerated self-awareness that Black people had been forced to adopt.[34] As Toi Derricotte adds, within that voyeuristic context, gesture became a fundamental means for the Black subject to challenge the menace of the white person's gaze. As Derricotte eloquently suggests, "Language and body have to contort themselves in order to embody the painful meanings of double consciousness. Often black people can only say in tone, in nuance, in the set of the mouth, or in the shifting of the eyes what language alone cannot say. Perhaps because of the ambivalence we feel about language, we must put the body itself to use."[35]

Black jazz musicians built on longstanding vernacular traditions that addressed this voyeuristic context. But they also formulated a theatrical and then mediated tradition that deformed historical notions of Blackness and redressed misrepresentation through an embodied tradition aware of its own artifice. Daphne Brooks's work in performance studies helps us develop this conversation. Brooks proposes the term "'Afro-alienation acts,' [in which] the condition of alterity converts into cultural expressiveness and a specific strategy of cultural performance."[36] Here, Brooks references both Bertolt Brecht's ideas of the self-consciously alienating performance of avant-garde theatre, and the collective historical alienation of Black diasporic subjects, which she acknowledges by quoting from Du Bois. "In Afro-alienation," she writes, "the 'strange' situation of 'looking at one's self through the eyes of others' evolves into" a more Brechtian phenomenon, "the enlivened position of 'looking at being looked at ness.'"[37] Brooks's "Afro-alienation" theorizes a tradition that extends through the varied theatrical elements evident in jazz performance. This is important since jazz was initially a theatrical phenomenon, staged nationally on a touring circuit for over a decade before it became a recorded musical tradition.[38]

In time, jazz musicians became some of the earliest African American celebrities of the media age. These Black artists were validated on terms that challenged white European aesthetic criteria and the denigrating lens of malicious racism. Celebrity also gave these performers the illusion of being accessible "real" people to a broad public, even as the acts that generated that celebrity in the first place turned often on theatrical conventions. Thus, generations of Americans feel they knew figures like Armstrong or Holiday or Duke Ellington because of these performers' visibility, while the self-consciously constructed aspects of these artists' demeanors escaped audiences at large. One need only weigh the affable onstage Armstrong character – courting audiences through deference and humor – against the more political and profane private man preserved in hours and hours of home-recorded tapes in the Armstrong archives to see how one contextual frame alone is too limited to understand the "full" Armstrong performance.[39]

Moreover, while onstage jazz performance may appear easily understood in aesthetic-functional terms – the bandleader cued the rest of the group back in after her solo with a nod of the head; the drummer twirled his sticks to advertise his impeccable rhythm – we arrive at a more compelling narrative of the jazz aesthetic's historical relationship to American reality if we broaden our frame. Take, again, the example of Miles Davis. On the one hand, Davis's restoration of behavior onstage was a phenomenon tied to his expressive style. As I mentioned above, his impassive body language and reserved gestures helped construct the performance of understatement central to the theatricalization of "cool." And yet, other aspects of the Davis stage demeanor, like his refusal to announce song titles to audiences or his mid-century tendency to perform with his back to the crowd, might be more broadly conceived. To think about them in political terms, that is, against the precedent of white expectations for Black men in America before Davis's fame at the onset of the Civil Rights Movement is to see these "units of behavior" (to use Schechner's language) as inherently related to a series of more sober offstage concerns. These moments of performance were tethered to Davis's everyday militancy on behalf of Black equality, not to be divorced from, say, his campaigns to see African American musicians paid better or his unflinching challenges to the violence of white supremacy.

To close, I want to make the case that sometimes the most dramatic effects produced in jazz performance arrive primarily out of the peculiar context in which the performance occurs. To do so, I offer a brief look at a specific performance: saxophonist Ornette Coleman's 1979 television appearance with his group Prime Time on NBC's *Saturday Night Live* (*SNL*).[40] At the time of the episode, Coleman was long famous in jazz for his innovations in open form improvisation. Here, the saxophonist showcased what had become a new direction in his music – namely, an expansion of his "harmolodic" theory with a younger, electric ensemble. In simplistic terms, Coleman's harmolodics looked to free music from its various traditional centers, arguing instead that harmony, melody, and rhythm might all co-exist in open-ended arrangement, without a prescribed melodic line, a fixed sequence of chord changes, or a common pulse to bind the musicians' various contributions.[41] In practice, then, Coleman's ensemble juxtaposed improvised lines and rhythmic textures continually. The effect of this – as displayed in the group's television performance of Coleman's "Times Square" – was not just to extend his earlier boundary-pushing experiments with free jazz but to rattle generic expectations to the core. Coleman's Prime Time was "plugged in," with electric bass and two electric guitars. Their musical vocabulary in "Times Square" drew all at once from postwar jazz, contemporary funk, and 1970s punk and its descendants. But while this particular amalgamation might suggest an affinity with other "edgy" popular music guests from the period – including New Wave acts like Devo or Talking Heads, both of whom also appeared on *SNL* that season – the engagement carried the intellectual weight of Coleman's long reputation for artistic experimentation and his expressed modernist influences. With this background in mind, Coleman's performance marks itself as sympathetic to the energy of its popular music moment but something more conspicuously lofty as well.[42]

Coleman's impassive comportment during the five-minute *SNL* appearance reaffirms jazz as "serious" and modern. Standing at the center of his fellow musicians in X-formation, Coleman plays with head bowed and eyes closed, avoiding any direct engagement with the camera for the song's duration. While this aloof posturing is familiar to postwar jazz – perceived as one of the defining stances musicians like Charlie Parker and Davis contributed to the music's changing reception – it is much less common in the staging of contemporary popular music. As such, Coleman's heightened calm works in direct tension with the energy audiences might have expected from Prime Time's jangling up-tempo funk. (For a contrasting pop music example, consider how convulsive and playfully aware of the camera Talking Heads lead singer David Byrne is in performance on an *SNL* episode that aired two months earlier.)

At the same time, Coleman's performance also resists the antiquated jazz feel of pianist Eubie Blake and singer-dancer Gregory Hines, who appeared together on *SNL* a few weeks prior.[43] That performance coincided with the Broadway run of the show *Eubie!*, a repertory showcase for many of Blake's most famous songs. Indeed, host Gary Busey alludes to the museum quality of that production by framing Hines and Blake as "classical artists" in his introduction. The display that follows – Hines's overly reverent demeanor and buoyant tap performance, Blake's jaunty unaccompanied stride piano solo – foregrounds the historical. Here, jazz and its various expressive corollaries are safely confined to an innocuous rendering of collective memory.

Coleman's presentation, on the other hand, keeps alive historical performance strategies without fully framing them as of-the-past. His studied detachment from the camera, for instance, theatricalizes modernist gravity and Black aesthetic urgency, expressive energies that first emerged in the same post-World War I period Hines and Blake memorialize in anodyne terms. At the same time, Prime Time's vibe is aesthetically current, as marked by bassist Jamaaladeen Tacuma's popping, danceable groove and his bobbing up and down in the background. In all, by eschewing purely vintage appeal, Coleman and company mark jazz music's vitality and relevance to 1979's mediated, punky present. This is even clear sartorially: while Hines appeared in a necktie and buttoned-up waistcoat, Coleman is much more *au courant* in a collarless shirt and bright purple suit with fashionably flared trousers.

Furthermore, opening up the critical frame on Coleman's *SNL* performance one more level, to observe its relationship to other parts of the episode, introduces other provocative resonances. In a bizarre juxtaposition, Coleman was the musical guest alongside Milton Berle as guest host. Berle's appearance was heavily steeped in nostalgia, a quality marked early on by the 1950s-themed *Texaco Star Theater* cold open or announcer Don Pardo's introducing Berle as "Mr. Television himself." While these aspects of the show are somewhat unsurprising, given *SNL*'s perennial self-reflexive engagement with television's generic conventions past and present, Berle's reliance on the corny and culturally insensitive clichés of his era generated much friction between the two historical points. Among the hackneyed sexist and racist jokes of Berle's monologue, for example, are groaners like "I'm so unlucky that if they sawed a woman in half I'd get the part that eats," or (directed at one of the band's African American musicians) "It's the Black guy! You're lucky, pal, you can walk home at three in the morning." (As a racist joker, moreover, Berle is wide-ranging. Later he quips, "A flash just come over the air. 404 Puerto Ricans in a crash. The bed broke.") Repeatedly, the comedian's mincing laughter after each punchline bespeaks how oblivious he is to his jokes' dated nature – especially in the ideological assumptions on which they turn. Berle's archaic aesthetic reaches a musical fever pitch late in the show, when he performs a schmaltzy rendition of Kurt Weill's "September Song," drawing out the lyrics in a shivering vibrato, and closing to a standing ovation that he had prearranged with some members of the audience.[44]

Now, reinsert Coleman's complicated musical performance into this cringe-worthy throwback to the show business standards of yesteryear. The unforeseen consequence of the curious scheduling is the varied way that Prime Time's appearance provides a critical counterpoint to so many aspects of the surrounding episode, both aesthetic and political. Coleman's impassivity contrasts the amped-up artifice Berle brings back from 1950s television; the forward-looking aesthetic of Prime Time's harmolodic experimentation opposes Berle's remarkably unhip torch song; the saxophonist's Black modernist seriousness offers a riposte both to Berle's casual assumption of white supremacist sympathies and his endless obsequious appeals to the audience.

All of these unforeseen antagonisms call attention to the critical benefits of interpreting jazz performance through the ever-expanding lenses of either the New Jazz Studies or performance studies. Indeed, the Coleman *SNL* performance is also evidence of traditional jazz studies' shortcomings in another way. Coleman and Prime Time recorded a full album's worth of material in New York just a week and a half after the *SNL* appearance, but various business complications kept that music unreleased until 1982, after Coleman switched record labels. Thus, for a few years, the greatest public access to Prime Time's harmolodic innovations came from their five minutes on national television here, rather than the document to which scholars would historically be likely to turn: an audio recording. Finally, as my concentration on the incongruity of Berle and Coleman emphasizes, a comprehensive attention to the impact of happenstance moments of concurrence enables us to arrive at other political effects in jazz performance, some of which, as I suggested, do not depend entirely on an artist's explicit intentions.

Notes

1 For introductions to the "New Jazz Studies," see Mark Tucker, "Musicology and the New Jazz Studies," *Journal of the American Musicological Society*, 51.1 (1998), 131–48, and Sherrie Tucker, "Deconstructing the Jazz Tradition: The 'Subjectless Subject' of New Jazz Studies," in David Ake, Charles Hiroshi Garrett, and Daniel Goldmark, eds., *Jazz/Not Jazz: The Music and Its Boundaries* (Berkeley: University of California Press, 2012), 264–84.
2 Dana Reason, "Navigable Structures and Transforming Mirrors': Improvisation and Interactivity," in Daniel Fischlin and Ajay Heble, eds., *The Other Side of Nowhere: Jazz, Improvisation, and Communities in Dialogue* (Middletown, CT: Wesleyan University Press, 2004), 73.
3 Vijay Iyer, "Exploding the Narrative in Jazz Improvisation," in Robert G. O'Meally, Brent Hayes Edwards, and Farah Jasmine Griffin, eds., *Uptown Conversation: The New Jazz Studies* (New York: Columbia University Press, 2004), 395.
4 Ibid.
5 Paul Berliner, *Thinking in Jazz: The Infinite Art of Improvisation* (Chicago: University of Chicago Press, 1994), 459.
6 Ibid., 460.
7 For more on these intertextual resonances, see Charles Hersch's chapter in this volume (Chapter 3).
8 Quoted in Keith Shadwick, "Brave New World," *Jazzwise*, March 2007, 37.

9 David Clowney and Robert Rawlins, "Pushing the Limits: Risk and Accomplishment in Musical Performance," *Contemporary Aesthetics*, 12.1 (2014), https://digitalcommons.risd.edu/liberalarts_contempaesthetics/vol12/iss1/15/.
10 Stuart Hall, "What Is This 'Black' in Black Popular Culture?," in Gina Dent, ed., *Black Popular Culture* (Seattle: Bay Press, 1992), 27.
11 Harry J. Elam, Jr., "The Device of Race: An Introduction," in Harry J. Elam, Jr. and David Krasner, eds., *African American Performance and Theater History: A Critical Reader* (Oxford: Oxford University Press, 2001), 4.
12 Paul Gilroy, *The Black Atlantic: Modernity and Double Consciousness* (London: Verso, 1993), 77.
13 Robert Farris Thompson, *African Art in Motion: Icon and Act* (Berkeley: University of California Press, 1974), 45.
14 Farah Jasmine Griffin and Salim Washington, *Clawing at the Limits of Cool: Miles Davis, John Coltrane, and the Greatest Jazz Collaboration Ever* (New York: St. Martin's Press, 2008), 4.
15 For more on cool as an African American expressive style rooted in Afro-diasporic traditions, see Joel Dinerstein's chapter in this volume (Chapter 10).
16 Bertram D. Ashe, "On the Jazz Musician's Love/Hate Relationship with the Audience," in Gena Dagel Caponi, ed., *Signifyin(g), Sanctifyin', and Slam Dunking: A Reader in African American Expressive Cultures* (Amherst: University of Massachusetts Press, 1999), 278 (original emphasis).
17 John Gennari, "'Wacky Post-Fluxus Revolutionary Mixed Media Shenanigans': Rethinking Jazz and Jazz Studies Through Jason Moran's Multimedia Performance," in Nicholas Gebhardt, Nichole Rustin-Pascal, and Tony Whyton, eds., *The Routledge Companion to Jazz Studies* (New York: Routledge, 2019), 122.
18 To witness examples of this, see Harald Heide Steen, Jr., dir., *Monk in Oslo* (Norwegian Broadcasting Corporation, 1966), available at www.youtube.com/watch?v=RINHNEMtm_k&t=46s; or Thelonious Monk, "Evidence," Rec. 1963, www.youtube.com/watch?v=qweSlfP6BtI.
19 Jacqui Malone, *Steppin' on the Blues: The Visible Rhythms of African American Dance* (Urbana: University of Illinois Press, 1996).
20 See, for example, John Miller Chernoff, *African Rhythm and African Sensibility* (Chicago: University of Chicago Press, 1979), 33–37.
21 Malone, *Steppin' on the Blues*, 10.
22 Ibid., 24.
23 Robert Farris Thompson, *Aesthetic of the Cool: Afro-Atlantic Art and Music* (Pittsburgh: Periscope, 2011), 68.
24 Bruce Johnson, "Hear Me Talkin' to Ya: Problems of Jazz Discourse," *Popular Music*, 12.1 (1993), 3.
25 George E. Lewis, "Improvised Music after 1950: Afrological and Eurological Perspectives," *Black Music Research Journal*, 16.1 (1996), 103.
26 Wynton Marsalis Quartet, "Giant Steps," Rec. July 17, 1987, www.youtube.com/watch?v=2XrdiOY_Uxk.

27 Wynton Marsalis, "Jazz in Marciac 2009," Rec. August 6, 2009, www.youtube.com/watch?v=ZBJ-MmTA-eU&t=392s.
28 Peter Elsdon, "Listening in the Gaze: The Body in Keith Jarrett's Solo Piano Improvisations," in Anthony Gritten and Elaine King, eds., *Music and Gesture* (Aldershot: Ashgate, 2006), 194.
29 Elsewhere I have written about how we might give name to some of these grammatical elements through the example of what I call "the tilt." See Michael Borshuk, "'The Sound of Jazz as Essential Image:' Television, Performance, and the Modern Jazz Canon," *Jazz Research Journal*, 12.1 (2018), 12–35.
30 Philip Auslander, "Musical Personae," *TDR*, 50.1 (2006), 102. Original emphasis.
31 Ibid.
32 See Richard Schechner, *Between Theater and Anthropology* (Philadelphia: University of Pennsylvania Press, 1985), especially chapter 2.
33 Richard Schechner, *Performance Studies: An Introduction*, 2nd ed. (New York: Routledge, 2012), 34.
34 W. E. B. Du Bois, *The Souls of Black Folk*, 1903 (Oxford: Oxford University Press, 2007), 8–9.
35 Toi Derricotte, *The Black Notebooks: An Interior Journey* (New York: Norton, 1997), 162.
36 Daphne A. Brooks, *Bodies in Dissent: Spectacular Performances of Race and Freedom, 1850–1910* (Durham, NC: Duke University Press, 2006), 4.
37 Ibid., 5
38 Alyn Shipton, *A New History of Jazz*, rev. ed. (New York: Continuum, 2007), 50.
39 See Ben Alexander, "'For Posterity': The Personal Audio Recordings of Louis Armstrong." *The American Archivist*, 71.1 (2008), 50–86.
40 *Saturday Night Live*, April 14, 1979, with guests Milton Berle and Ornette Coleman, NBC Television.
41 To read Coleman's own theorization of "harmolodics," especially in relationship to Prime Time, see Ornette Coleman, "Prime Time for Harmolodics," *Down Beat*, July 1983, 54–55.
42 For more on jazz on television, see Nicolas Pillai's chapter in this volume (Chapter 20).
43 *Saturday Night Live*, March 10, 1979, with guests Gary Busey, Eubie Blake, and Gregory Hines, NBC Television.
44 Tom Shales and James Andrew Miller, *Live from New York: The Complete, Uncensored History of Saturday Night Live as Told by Its Stars, Writers, and Guests* (New York: Little, Brown, 2008), 138.

PART II

Aesthetic Movements

CHAPTER 5

Jazz Age Harlem

Fiona I. B. Ngô

When Louis Armstrong relocated to New York from Chicago in 1929, he recorded Fats Waller's "(What Did I Do to Be So) Black and Blue?," a song that has grown to be seen as one of the quintessential songs of Black America, enunciating racial violence that occurs in everyday and extraordinary ways.[1] From the extended trumpet opening that follows through choruses and a verse to Armstrong's vocals, the song evokes a universalized Black experience of abject poverty, as seen in Andy Razaf's lyrics:

> Cold, empty bed, springs hard as lead,
> Feel like old Ned, wish I was dead
> All my life through, I've been so black and blue.

Armstrong simultaneously forwards a sense of hopefulness through lyrical humor ("Even the mouse ran from my house") and the expressive energy of his trumpet. The song evokes the everyday discomfort of living in poverty *and* the everyday joys of living. The performance matches the effects of structural racism and inequality with a means for survival and a space for creatively countering narratives of racism.

The universalization of "Black and Blue" expressed in Armstrong's version of the tune does so through the concealment of the experience of Black women. Razaf's original lyrics include whole verses skipped by Armstrong, verses that highlight the plight of Black women, particularly as regards skin tone, poverty, and sexuality. Joel Vance notes that:

> [Black and Blue] was written by Waller and Razaf for a Harlem nightclub floor show. The producer of the revue told Waller and Razaf that the show needed an interpolated number, a scene of a black girl in bed moaning over the trials of being a black, and that the tune and lyrics should be 'funny.' Waller and Razaf didn't see anything humorous in the assignment. Tom [Waller] composed a *via dolorosa* melody, while Razaf wrote lyrics that made a statement for the whole race and its place in society: 'What did I do/To be so black and blue?'[2]

Here Vance understands the original lyrics as reflecting a wider racial experience with no need to conceal women from the narrative.

Ethel Waters, in the same year she began performing with Benny Goodman, 1930, recorded a version of "Black and Blue?" that acts to call out race men for their preference for light-skinned women. Significantly, Waters changes Razaf's original line: "Browns and yellers all have fellers" to "All the race fellers crave high yellers."[3] Here Waters takes a line that is already about the politics of sexuality and skin privilege within the Black community, and points specifically to the race men, who are ostensibly interested in racial uplift, but for whom Black masculinity has a very particular meaning, which works to exclude many from the narrative of power. As Hortense Spillers writes in a reading of race men interested in light-skinned women in Gwendolyn Brooks's *Maud Martha*, "African-American men's community has yet, it seems, to come to terms with its profoundest impulses concerning African-American women and their 'Africanity.'"[4] Waters applies a similar critique, asserting how Black women's skin color can prevent them from financial security and love, even within the Black community. Across its various iterations, "Black and Blue?" demonstrates the undoing of racialized gender and sexuality, where Armstrong travels between a progressive Black masculinity and an invisible femininity, and Waters questions the universality of Blackness.

What both versions show is that to understand the universality of Blackness is to understand the instability of gender categories in the way that they are known and in the way that they come into being. Here I propose that the intersections of racialized, classed, and sexualized gender are "fugitive." For this reading I draw upon two ideas of the fugitive to understand the politics of cultural production during the Harlem Renaissance. The first mode comes from Stefano Harney and Fred Moten, who describe "fugitive enlightenment" as both the "life stolen by the enlightenment" and the "life stolen back" from the enlightenment.[5] The way they describe the activeness of fugitivity comes not from trying to repair, "not finishing oneself, not passing, not completing."[6] For them, the fugitive is an active engagement with enlightenment constructions, where life and creativity emerge from repressive circumstances and ideologies. The second mode of my understanding of fugitivity comes from scholar C. Riley Snorton in *Black on Both Sides*, where he draws on Harney and Moten and Spillers. Snorton understands fugitivity in relationship to the "ungendering of blackness" – that is, that flesh is fungible and thus becomes "a mode for fugitive action."[7] For Snorton, the relationship of fungibility to fugitivity helps us "focus on modes of escape, of wander, of flight that exist within violent conditions of exchange."[8] Considering these performances of "Black and Blue?" as fugitive action, we see both performances as simultaneously fleeing the strictures and violence of everyday life and moving towards new futures outside the systems of racial oppression, through the use of, and reimagining of, the meanings of racialized gender.[9]

I hope to understand musical resistance beyond a reclamation of heteropatriarchal masculinity; rather, because epistemologies of Blackness mark out gender as mutable, we need another avenue for understanding how resistance happens. In complicating what and how resistance might happen, how life might be sustained, we must not ignore the circumstances of Black life as we celebrate Black performance, or even Black genius. In recognizing that creative work, along with fugitive ontological modes of Blackness, emerges from iterations of everyday violence compels us to better understand the relationship of aesthetics and politics as embedded within the necropolitical. Black creative arts in the Jazz Age and beyond are a practice in promoting Black life.

To do this work, I have divided this chapter into three sections. The first further explores the notion of fugitive gender, offering that the purposeful instability caused through the relationship between gender and Blackness created the conditions of possibility in everyday life for Black folks. The second section excavates the meanings of Duke Ellington's cosmopolitan dandyism as seen in the 1929 film *Black and Tan*. Ellington, known for his sartorial flair, sexual attractiveness, and innovative musical compositions and arrangements, bore the markings of fugitive gender as he navigated Harlem: its apartments, stages, and death beds. The final section considers the fugitive sociality of rent parties, informal musical venues born of necessity and delight, which served the community of Harlem by providing shelter, food, entertainment, and sexual pleasure.

Fugitive Gender

As a mode of survival, Harlem's residents crossed gender's threshold every day as seen in dress, work, dating, and moving about the city. As singers narrated a sexually and gender diverse Harlem, they demonstrated how this was a common part of life though one that was viewed as suspicious by city aldermen, the police, and vice investigators. This section continues the work of Nicole Rustin and Sherrie Tucker, who write of the "mutability and surprise" that come from "gender and jazz" as categories, demonstrating how gender play provided opportunity in the context of difficult material circumstances.[10]

Bessie Smith, whom musicologist Gunther Schuller dubbed "the first great urban-blues singer, and therefore the first important jazz singer,"[11] told stories of everyday life that incorporated the transgression of gender boundaries. Philadelphia-based Smith regularly traveled into New York, becoming a fixture of the Renaissance as she performed on stage and recorded with many of Harlem's musical luminaries. A song written and recorded by Smith in 1927, "Foolish Man Blues," has been hailed as an example of a queer blues that connects fugitivity with "cross-gendered modes of escape."[12] In the opening verse Smith sings that men are "Acting like a bunch of women, they just gabbing, gabbing, gabbing away," and at the end of the second she continues, "There's two things got me puzzled/ There's two things I can't understand/ That's a mannish-acting woman and a skipping, twisting woman-acting man."[13] These lines assert gender as fungible in acknowledging that cross-gendered forms are employed in everyday situations. Scholars often focus on the latter of these two verses, resisting readings of other parts of the song which may seem more heterosexual.[14] Understanding the song's gender play, however, also queers its ending, which otherwise may seem a problem for a queer reading. The song ends with a man who has been indiscreet in saying he has kissed a girl. If we know already that gender categories are mutable, then the song's ending fails to preclude queer relationality. Smith forwards queerness as an everyday occurrence in Black life: the quotidian moments of talking to friends, difficult romantic relationships, and the breaking of trust.

Performances the Board of Aldermen read as "wild" and attempted to ban in 1926, featured Black performers embracing queer sexualities and gender mutability.[15] Gladys Bentley also performed various gendered, sexed, and sexualized viewpoints in the course of her stage act. Arriving in New York when she was just sixteen years old, Bentley quickly began holding court at popular night spots while other pianists were on break. Her talents were soon recognized, as she booked standing gigs on bustling 133rd Street. Billed variously as Gladys Bentley or Bobbie Minton, she charmed audiences with outrageous lyrics and charismatic sing-a-longs. She became famous for singing overtly sexualized lyrics of her own invention to the tunes of popular songs. She was equally as famous for her sparkling attire. As Bentley herself later described, "I wore immaculate white full dress shirts with stiff collars, small bow ties and skirts, oxfords, short Eton jackets and hair cut straight back."[16] At the Clam House she could be seen in a dazzling white tuxedo, a top hat, and a cane as she drew in the smart set night after night. Bentley's style of dress, as well as her flexibly gendered naming practices, were commercially viable *and* a threat to the city's social order. Additionally, Bentley's fugitive performance happened both on stage and in everyday life where she strode along the sidewalks of Manhattan in suits.[17] Like Ethel Waters and Bessie Smith, Bentley took men and women as lovers. She even married a white woman in a public ceremony.[18] The performative traces created during her stage show saw a life beyond the walls of nightclubs.

Her performances themselves were mesmerizing, drawing in sizable, enthusiastic audiences. Indeed, her livelihood was predicated on her clothing (on and off stage) and her songs of sexual transgression. When she began at the Mad House her salary was a respectable $35 a week plus tips. Soon her salary jumped to $125 a week when she moved to the Clam House, attracting patrons such as Heywood Broun and Carl Van Vechten as well as luminaries such as the Prince of Wales and industrialist J. P. Morgan in for her shows.[19] Audiences were not only engaged by her startling appearance, but were also pleasantly shocked by her bawdy lyrics, Wilbur Young commented that:

> Some of those lyrics would be so rank that the house lady would look on in despair while Gladys, not content with merely singing them herself ... would encourage the paying guests to join in on the chorus, which they did willingly. At this stage, it was just a matter of time before the house got raided.[20]

Bentley belted out challenging lyrics to the audiences and encouraged their participation. Bentley effectively led audiences in the reordering of their bodies and, thus, their identities, through both the perlocutionary forces that marked any performance and the illocutionary forces that emanated from the voices of audience members themselves. The audience, then, could follow Bentley in taking on various subject positions that both enforced and went against conceptions of their own identities.

Because Bentley boldly embodied her ungendering, any tune Bentley sang had the potential to be a fugitive performance. This could be fairly evident when she combined "Sweet Georgia Brown" and "My Alice Blue Gown" into a new tune about anal sex, but part of the entertainment derived from this tactic came from providing a familiar context with well-known popular tunes and subverting the comfort they afforded with highly sexualized lyrics.[21] Bentley, then, infused and discovered sexuality, and even queer sexualities, in the fabric of the everyday. Songs that combined Tin Pan Alley-style tunes like "My Alice Blue Gown," which spoke to forms of white femininity, with the raw Black sexuality associated with the blues, described a space for racial mixing organized around sexuality.

Bentley, in providing a mix of racial codes in the music she performed, destabilized categories of race in performance, providing for audiences starved for the realization of the instability that marked modernity.

These types of performances were anathema to city fathers and also to some Black intellectuals, who preferred forms of Black masculinity that adhered to a heteropatriarchal order. That is to say, that performances like Armstrong's, Waters's, Smith's, and Bentley's were not universal strategies for exploring the boundaries of Blackness as an ontological and epistemological position. One such leader was W. E. B. Du Bois, whom Hazel Carby contends "clearly believed that women (and, I will argue, certain men whom he regarded as having compromised their masculinity) could become the mediators through which the nation-state oppressed black men."[22] This version of respectable racial uplift contrasted significantly with the singers and writers who embraced gendered fugitivity to negotiate public space, providing alternatives to a social order that relied upon particular types of gendered and racialized power.

Fugitive Labor

"Black and Tan" night clubs featured Black entertainers performing for mostly white audiences. This Jim Crow-style arrangement structured labor even in the most glorious of venues. From the Cotton Club stage in the middle of Harlem, Duke Ellington and his orchestra evoked places and people from the South to the South Pacific. Tensions bubbled between Ellington's elegant arrangements and the club's primitivist themes; between the space of the urban north juxtaposed against arrangements and tunes meant to evoke the deep south. Ellington trafficked in a cosmopolitan dandyism, drawing musical inspiration from jazz styles out of New Orleans, St. Louis, and Chicago; classical music structures and melodic forms from composers such as Chopin and Debussy; spirituals and hymns; and from Tin Pan Alley hits.[23] His musical voraciousness helped create entire worlds from the Cotton Club stage as he accompanied skits set in jungles, dance numbers evoking the orient, or small dramas set in Harlem apartments. His cosmopolitanism, described through his personal and compositional style, feminized him. While discourses around Black masculinity often cast Black men as hypersexual and hypermasculine, we must also remember that in the 1920s, one conversation around Blackness drew from sociologists Robert Park and Ernest Burgess naming Black people the "lady among the races." According to Roderick Ferguson, Park and Burgess saw "African Americans' racial temperament" as particularly feminized because of their artistry and propensity for expression.[24] As a leader of the Harlem music scene, Ellington embodied this sort of "racial temperament," pushing the instability of gendered racial categories in tandem with his cosmopolitan acumen.

When Ellington co-starred in the 1929 Dudley Murphy film *Black and Tan* with his then real-life girlfriend, Fredi Washington, he had already been performing at the Cotton Club for almost two years.[25] The Ellington and Bubber Miley composition "Black and Tan Fantasy" provides the basis for the film's story of two struggling artists in Harlem. As the film opens onto a Harlem apartment scene, the viewer finds Ellington at the piano playing chords that echo Frédéric Chopin's "Piano Sonata no. 2 in B-flat Minor, Op. 35 (Marche Funèbre)," as trumpeter Arthur Whetsol stands next to Ellington, learning to play his part with Harmon mute in hand. The sequence forecasts death with the quote from Chopin's "Funeral March" during the opening credits and through that first scene. As the film points out, mortality guides artists' lives in a Jim Crow labor system, where health must be sacrificed in order to pay rent and to create.

Not all those impoverished are created equal. The film casts Ellington, Washington, and Whetsol as cosmopolitan characters through their juxtaposition with Black manual laborers. While Ellington and Whetsol rehearse, the camera cuts to two repo men checking an address and entering the building. This comic duo – shabbily dressed, illiterate, bribed by alcohol – contrast with Ellington and Whetsol. Whetsol is impeccably dressed in a suit and matching hat. While Duke's outfit here mirrors one of the workers, with a shirt and vest, Ellington also sports an undone tie and his feather-adorned fedora is visible atop the piano. Ellington here exists in a space between the men who perform manual labor and the dandified artist. Though both work to make ends meet – and Ellington is clearly *not* making ends meet – there is a palpable difference between them, as Ellington plays the intellectual, the artist, the composer, the rational, against the repo men as silly, comedic, manual laborers. The contrast provides an approach for understanding Ellington as artistic and feminized, as someone whose gender expression is mutable in his elegance.

These distinctions are amplified as news arrives: just as the repo men move in to take the piano, Fredi Washington enters, a vision of the New Woman, announcing she's lined up a club show in which she will dance and Ellington's band will play. In a display of female financial independence, she first offers the repo men five dollars each to leave the piano, which they refuse, but end up accepting, instead, a bottle of gin as a bribe. While the mutability of gender is posed here as exciting, innovative, and attractive, it happens amid new legal definitions of personhood. As Imani Perry writes, describing the effects of laws proposed at the end of the nineteenth century:

> In the public imaginary the "new woman" was twinned with the images of "dandies": decadent and deviant men, feminine men, who were likewise a threat for their visible transgression of gender ideals.... The new woman and new man were features of urban landscapes. They breached ideals of femininity and masculinity. And both knowledge and law were produced that could account for them and sort them within the gender hierarchy.[26]

Jim Crow laws created nonwhite people not simply as marginalized, but without the legal status of personhood; Blackness created a landscape of fluid gender categorization and associated characteristics that could propel people into peril.

As the film moves to the famous Cotton Club, the viewer understands the club's daring spectacles within a context of racial segregation and death. The nightclub sequence reveals how Ellington's cosmopolitanism played out on stage, as he sits, tuxedo-clad at the piano surrounded by abstracted palm trees. The scene mirrors Ellington's actual work at the club. The Cotton Club hired Ellington in 1927, after King Oliver turned down the gig. As part of this extended engagement, Ellington composed songs for various skits, dance numbers, and singers.[27] According to jazz historian Martin Williams:

> Some of the sketches and production numbers in the Cotton Club shows were lurid affairs, with "jungle" nonsense, or sheiks kidnapping fair maidens, etc., and the music occasionally had to be bizarre and always immediate in its effect. Ellington approached his tasks with his own kind of urbane but optimistic irony, and he could use preposterous titles like *Jungle Nights in Harlem* for the benefit of the "slumming" white crowds at the club at the same time that he was expanding the sonorities, the color, the orchestrational resources of his ensemble and creating a memorable and durable music.[28]

Song titles from Ellington's repertoire in this era show this diversity of race, location, and exoticism, including "Arabian Lover," "Yellow Dog Blues," "Tishomingo Blues," "Jungle Jamboree," "Maori" (A Samoan Dance), and "Wang Wang Blues."[29] His agility with genres and ability to pull on the history of Western music, regional styles of jazz, and musical tropes that recalled various parts of the globe, brought his cosmopolitan style to bear sonically. Here imperial logic inhabits the cosmopolitan film setting, where exotic representations of race and nation provide consumable versions of primitivism and orientalism.[30] While the spirit of these songs engages imperial logic, the Black performers are identified with exoticized people rather than the people who inhabit the colonial center, a position claimed by the white audience. These performances, then, open a space for racialized resistance, even as they reiterate imperial fantasies.

Over the course of the nightclub performance, tension mounts between Black cultural production and economies of Black death. From the stage, the band rips through "The Duke Steps Out" and "Black Beauty" before Washington emerges on stage to shimmy to "The Cotton Club Stomp" while suffering from a weak heart. Near the tune's end, she collapses on stage – spinning, spiraling, and clutching her breast. Club workers remove her as the club manager marches on stage to demand that the band continue playing the next number: "Get the show on!" The band launches into a few seconds of "Flaming Youth" before Ellington realizes that something is seriously wrong with Washington and storms off the stage. Here, the stakes of working are life and death. Washington, who wants Ellington and herself to be able to support themselves and their careers, puts her life on the line to work. The club manager demands labor beyond death.

The last scene of the short film takes place around Washington's death bed, where a wonderfully orchestrated version of "Black and Tan Fantasy" is played. The scene fulfills the film's opening promise of death as Harlem's Hall Johnson Choir join Ellington's band, cast in extremes of shadow and light. The role of the Hall Johnson Choir sets the film version of "Black and Tan Fantasy" apart from the numerous other recorded versions because it changes the arrangement so drastically, incorporating the choir's singing of the traditional Black spiritual, "Same Train," a dirge about waiting at the station to take the same train as those ancestors who have died before you. As "Same Train" closes, Fredi turns toward the piano and asks, "Duke, will you play 'Black and Tan Fantasy'"? This time, the song begins with piano, trumpet, and the choir, which now sings a variation of "The Holy City," the song upon which Bubber Miley partially based the melody for "Black and Tan Fantasy." Whetsol's trumpet again recalls the Chopín as he sets the melodic theme for the number. So, the listener is left with a mix of an eighteenth-century piano sonata, a nineteenth-century spiritual, and the contemporary jazz style of a growling trumpet.

The mix of influences in this version of "Black and Tan Fantasy," speaks to Ellington's cosmopolitanism, and it also speaks to how Black artists navigated race and racialized genealogies of cultural creation. While there is utility in naming forms as originating through histories of Blackness, another politics emerges when Black artists display a range of creative influence that stretches across the globe and across centuries. That is, many imagine jazz as a "Black music" or as quintessentially African American in compositional form, improvisation, roots, and performances. If this were true, it would still be important to understand the racialization of music as something that is not static or unchanging. If we understand race and racial definition as mutable, and the movement of people and art across borders as opportunities to shift form and definition, then we also must consider the wide range of influence and the broad, international conversation that an artist like Ellington engaged. My argument here is meant to be distinguished from ones such as French jazz historian André Hodeir, who acknowledges that jazz emanates from multiple musical sources, but who also ultimately argues that "[t]he universality of jazz may be due in part to these occidental elements, since Western culture has followed the example of Western civilization in spreading its influence over the entire world."[31] Ellington's mix of influences speaks more to racial systems and histories at work in the creation of African American life and experience. He demonstrates his knowledge of European musical forms, but here they specifically play the necropolitical part of the threat of death for Black people. Fredi expires with the tune, reminding us of Christina Sharpe's words that Black people live "in spaces where we were never meant to survive, or have been punished for surviving and for daring to claim or make spaces of something like freedom."[32]

Fugitive Sociality

The opening to *Black and Tan* tells a wider story about the precarious conditions that managed life and death in Harlem. Rents were high, apartment buildings were over-crowded, and premature death was rampant. Even within these conditions, Harlemites created spaces of pleasure, musical composition, dancing, and eating. Harlem rent parties were born of financial necessity. As an article in *Negro World* had it, "The environment in which these negroes live is a steel vise, restricting their natural freedom. In the house-rent parties, with the aid of liquor and music, they make a mad effort to recapture the abandon of the past, but dawn comes and with it the responsibilities of a modern economic system that cannot be shirked."[33] That economic and legal system limited what buildings and neighborhoods Black folks could inhabit as new migrants from the South moved into Harlem. Once in Harlem, they paid above-market rents, and were forced to share apartments, making Harlem one of the most densely populated places on earth with over 330 people per acre.[34] Additionally, as historian Gilbert Osofsky notes, "High rents and poor salaries necessarily led to congested and unsanitary conditions."[35] From 1923–27, Harlem's mortality rate was 42 percent higher than elsewhere in New York, more than one in ten infants died, and the tuberculosis rate was 2.5 times that of the city overall.[36] Out of these circumstances, Harlemites responded with strategies for survival: parties held within, despite of, and in opposition to their deteriorating living conditions. These jazz-infused parties served as sites of fugitive creativity and sociality, expressions of life emerging from the circumstances of death.

Held to help pay rent, feed others, employ musicians, and provide pleasure, rent parties skirted the line between the licit and the illicit, and thus were spaces of "fugitive sociality," as performance studies scholar Shane Vogel has named them.[37] Called by various names – buffet flats, chitterling struts, parlor socials – rent parties provided private entertainments outside legal or moral guidelines, often challenging sexual norms to a different degree than public stage shows. Black performances in these spaces also participated in the ontological undoing of Blackness by exploring multiple means of sexual expression. Fugitive sociality and fugitive gender both rely on notions of social order: for Vogel, this occurs within spaces that straddle legality and illegality, where sexual horizons open, and for Snorton, the fugitive is derived from histories of uneven power expressed in the ungendering of Blackness. In my reading, I would like to consider these techniques to understand these spaces of music within the landscape of Black life. At these semi-private sites of Black performance, the fungibility of gender drove and expressed fugitive sociality and sexuality exceeded the space of the stage, encircled, and recruited the audience as participants, entertainers, and sexual partners.

Wallace Thurman evoked the sexualized, racialized, and classed atmosphere of a typical rent party in *Negro Life in New York's Harlem*, a sociological survey:

> Saturday night comes. There may be only piano music, there may be a piano and drum, or a three or four-piece ensemble. Red lights, dim and suggestive, are in order. The parlor and the dining room are cleared for the dance and one bedroom is utilized for hats and coats. In the kitchen will be found boiled pigs feet, ham hock and cabbage, hopping John (a combination of peas and rice), and other proletarian dishes.[38]

The music and lighting recontextualized the apartment space, while the food marked the party as particularly racialized and classed, drawing on Southern history as a nod to Black migration patterns following World War I. For Thurman, living rooms were sexualized through "barbarous and slow" music accompanied by "dancers [who] will use their bodies and the bodies of their partners without regard to the conventions.

There will be little restraint."[39] If restraint guided public space, then rent parties moved beyond the social possibilities of stage performances. How dancers moved, according to Thurman, implies a challenge to the public social order. In this way, the partygoers subverted notions of acceptable sexuality through both display and the hypersexuality mapped onto Black bodies.

The music that guided those bodies also stretched musical norms and, in turn, the social and political imagination of Blackness. Bessie Smith's "Soft Pedal Blues" (1925), for example, situates these parties within the underground economy of performance in Harlem.[40] Despite the economic pressures of institutionalized racism, revelers, musicians, and other performers created their own spaces for artistic expression outside of white-owned clubs. The song speaks to a wider culture of sexuality during the Harlem Renaissance that embraced the fluidity of gender categorization and expanded sexual identification and practice. Smith begins, "There's a lady in our neighborhood who runs a buffet flat," calling in double entendre to the party's smorgasbord of sexual delights. Ruby Walker Smith, Bessie Smith's niece described one such party: "Buffet flats," she observed, "is nothing but faggots and bulldaggers, and an open house. Everything goes in that house!"[41]

The "soft pedal" of Smith's song refers to the dampening pedal on the piano, which is meant to make the piano quieter; however, as these parties were often dances, piano playing was audible to partygoers and neighbors alike. In these spaces of fugitive sociality, Harlem's famous stride piano players – Waller, Willie "The Lion" Smith, Earl Hines, Ellington, James P. Johnson – honed their craft in ways that exceeded business hours and the technical and content restrictions of commercial recordings. Entertainment hosted in apartments did not have to be commercially viable or follow the strictures of law and police surveillance in the same way public performances did. While the spaces were still surveilled, it was usually from noise complaints rather than continual police inspection. This meant that pianists could play songs that included much more improvisation because they were not confined by the temporal limits of recording technology. They could also explore sexual themes and lyrics that needed to be cleaned up elsewhere. Waller, for example could perform "(I Wish I Could Shimmy Like) My Sister Kate," to a room full of dancers. The song itself often had improvised lyrics that were both hypersexual and queer in nature. A queer rendering, for example, appears in Ma Rainey's 1926 recording of "Sissy Blues," where the shimmy shake of Sister Kate becomes the sissy Miss Kate of the title. Rainey sings,

"My man's got a sissy, his name is Miss Kate / He shook that thing like jelly on a plate."[42] The musical ungendering of these Kates, as reflected in the sexualized atmosphere of rent parties, is based in forms of fugitive gender that spring to life in the context of sexual pleasure. The pressing of gender that occurs through music and space pushes up against housing laws and profiteering, laws that guide decency in public and in cultural production, and food insecurity and health conditions that threatened the foundations of life and livelihood. Jazz Age music materialized through these precarious conditions of institutionalized poverty, reaching beyond the city and into the future of jazz.

Notes

1. Louis Armstrong "(What Did I Do to Be So) Black and Blue?" Rec. July 19, 1929 (Okeh 8714, 1929). Fred Moten also ties this to its reference in Ellison's *Invisible Man* in his text *Black and Blur* (Durham, NC: Duke University Press, 2017).
2. Joel Vance, *Fats Waller: His Life and Times* (London: Robson Books, 1979), 59.
3. Ethel Waters, "(What Did I Do to Be So) Black and Blue?" Rec. April 1, 1930 (Columbia 2184-D, 1930).
4. Hortense Spillers, *Black, White, and in Color: Essays on American Literature and Culture* (Chicago: University of Chicago Press, 2003), 139–41.
5. Stephano Harney and Fred Moten, *The Undercommons: Fugitive Study and Black Study* (Wivenhoe, UK: Minor Compositions, 2013), 28.
6. Ibid.
7. C. Riley Snorton, *Black on Both Sides: A Racial History of Trans Identity* (Minneapolis: University of Minnesota Press, 2017), 11–12.
8. Ibid., 57.
9. A number of Black feminists have theorized mutable versions of gender. These terms include: "Vestibular" from Hortense J. Spillers, *Black, White, and in Color: Essays on American Literature and Culture* (Chicago: University of Chicago, 2003) and Imani Perry, *Vexy Thing: On Gender and Liberation* (Durham, NC: Duke University Press, 2018), 37; "Aberrational" from Roderick A. Ferguson, *Aberrations in Black: Toward a Queer of Color Critique* (Minneapolis: University of Minnesota Press, 2013); and "Plasticity" from Zakiyah Iman Jackson, *Becoming Human: Matter and Meaning in an Antiblack World* (New York: New York University Press, 2020), 10.
10. Nicole T. Rustin and Sherrie Tucker, "Introduction," in Nichole T. Rustin and Sherrie Tucker, eds., *Big Ears: Listening for Gender in Jazz Studies* (Durham, NC: Duke University Press, 2008), 8.
11. Gunther Schuller, *Early Jazz: Its Roots and Musical Development* (New York: Oxford University Press, 1968), 226.
12. Snorton, *Black on Both Sides*, 56.

13　Bessie Smith, "Foolish Man Blues," Rec. October 27, 1927, *Bessie Smith: The Complete Recordings*, vol. 3 (Columbia Records C2K47474, 1992).
14　See the work of Eric Garber, "A Spectacle in Color: The Lesbian and Gay Subculture of Jazz Age Harlem," in Martin Bauml Duberman, Martha Vicinus, and George Chauncey, Jr., eds., *Hidden from History: Reclaiming the Gay and Lesbian Past* (New York: New American Library, 1989), 320.
15　Fiona I. B. Ngô, *Imperial Blues: Geographies of Race and Sex in Jazz Age New York* (Durham, NC: Duke University Press, 2014), 44.
16　Gladys Bentley, "I Am a Woman Again," *Ebony*, August 1952, 94.
17　Bentley attests to having felt more comfortable in boys' clothes since she was young and still living at home with her parents in Philadelphia. See Bentley, "I Am a Woman Again," 96.
18　Eric Garber reports the wedding ceremony in "Gladys Bentley: The Bulldagger Who Sang the Blues," *OutLook: National Lesbian and Gay Quarterly* 1 (1988), 58–59.
19　Bentley, "I Am a Woman Again," 92, 94. Garber reports that her salary increased only to $100, but his source for this is not footnoted. See "Gladys Bentley," 55.
20　Garber, "Gladys Bentley," 55.
21　Ibid.
22　Hazel Carby, *Race Men* (Cambridge, MA: Harvard University Press, 1998), 33.
23　Both Ellington and Louis Armstrong would later achieve a grand sense of cosmopolitanism during the Cold War era as they toured the world. See Penny M. Von Eschen, *Satchmo Blows Up the World: Jazz Ambassadors Play the Cold War* (Durham, NC: Duke University Press, 2004).
24　Ferguson, *Aberrations in Black*, 56–58.
25　Dudley Murphy, dir., *Black and Tan*, RKO, 1929.
26　Perry, *Vexy Thing*, 68–69.
27　Martin T. Williams, *The Jazz Tradition* (New York: Oxford University Press, 1983), 105–6.
28　Ibid., 106–7.
29　Duke Ellington, "Jungle Nights in Harlem," Rec. June 4, 1930, and "Arabian Lover," Rec. May 3, 1929, *Duke at the Cotton Club* (RCA 6127, 2000). "Jungle Jamboree," Rec. July 29, 1929, "Maori (A Samoan Dance)," Rec. February 21, 1930, and "Wang Wang Blues," Rec. October 27, 1930, *Early Ellington: The Complete Brunswick and Vocalion Recordings of Duke Ellington, 1926–1931* (Decca GRD-3-640, 1994). Ellington was not alone in this endeavor to create exotic music for stage shows. Fletcher Henderson, for example, wrote and performed, "He Wasn't Born in Araby, But He's a Sheikin' Fool," Rec. April 1924, *Fletcher Henderson and the Blues Singers: Complete Recorded Works in Chronological Order, Vol. 2, 1923–1924* (Document Records DOCD-5343, 1995). For more on Fletcher Henderson's role in developing the music of the Harlem Renaissance, see Schuller, *Early Jazz*, 252–79.
30　For more on imperial logic and orientalisms see Ngô, *Imperial Blues*, 6.
31　André Hodeir, *Jazz: Its Evolution and Essence* (New York: Grove Press, 1956), 46–47.

32 Christina Sharpe, *In the Wake: On Blackness and Being* (Durham, NC: Duke University Press, 2016), 130.
33 "Harlem House Parties Inspire New Play," *Negro World* (February 9, 1929), 7.
34 Gilbert Osofsky, *Harlem: The Making of a Ghetto; Negro New York, 1890–1930* (New York: Harper & Row, 1971), 140.
35 Ibid., 136.
36 Ibid., 141.
37 Shane Vogel, *The Scene of the Harlem Cabaret: Race, Sexuality, Performance* (Chicago: University of Chicago Press, 2009), 18–19, 112, 121.
38 Wallace Thurman, *Negro Life in New York's Harlem: A Lively Picture of a Popular and Interesting Section* (Girard, KS: Haldeman-Julius Publications, 1928), 42.
39 Ibid.
40 Bessie Smith, "Soft Pedal Blues," Rec. May 14, 1925 (Columbia 14075-D, 1925).
41 Ruby Walker Smith interview with Chris Albertson, "Life on the Road, I," *Bessie Smith: The Final Chapter, The Complete Recordings, Vol. 5.* (Columbia/Legacy, C2K 57546, 1996).
42 Ma Rainey, "Sissy Blues," 1926, *Ma Rainey: Complete Recorded Works in Chronological Order, Volume 3, c. December 1925–c. June 1926* (Document Records DOCCD-5583, 1997).

CHAPTER 6

"Hard Times Don't Worry Me"
The Blues in Black Music and Literature in the 1930s
Steven C. Tracy

> People is ravin bout hard times, tell me what it's all about.
> People is holl'in bout hard times, tell me what it's all about.
> Hard times don't worry me, I was broke when they first started out.
> Lonnie Johnson, "Hard Times Ain't Gone No Where" (1937)[1]

The 1920s (or rather 1916–30, amid the so-called "First Great Migration") delivered 1.6 million African Americans from southern soil to northern pavement. It was fueled by unrelenting Jim Crow oppression in the South; World War I and *Chicago Defender* fever promoting good jobs and better conditions in the North; and rampant industrialization that made the Northern city seem like a panacea, however illusory. Films like Oscar Micheaux's *The Girl from Chicago* (1932) and *Birthright* (1939) explored rural–urban cultural tensions.[2] Indeed, while Ida Cox was singing the "Chicago Bound Blues (Great Migration Blues)" in 1923, many singers had changed their tunes by the 1930s.[3] Optimism, both authentic and manufactured, came packaged within bulging "Black Belts" as multiple families crammed into single apartments, with bitterly cold heat and barely running water, high rents, and limited opportunity. A subtler, more sinister racism found a fair number of hot music singers longing for "Good Old Bygone Days," as Charles and Effie Tyus sang in 1924.[4] There were many who imagined reciprocal mobility and a return "home": "Goin' Back to Texas" (Memphis Minnie & Kansas Joe, 1929), "I'm Going Back to Tennessee" (Leroy Carr, 1929), "Going Back to Memphis" (Memphis Jug Band, 1930), "Going Back Home" (Leroy Carr 1935), "Goin' to Richmond" (Jimmie Strothers 1936), "Goin' Back to Alabama" (Eddie Kelly 1937), "Going Back to Florida" (Amos Easton 1937), and "Going Back to Arkansas" (Big Bill Broonzy 1938, and Washboard Sam 1940).[5] Rosa Henderson's "Down South Blues" (1923) and Sonny Boy Williamson's "Down South"

(1938), the latter with the immortal lines "Well, now I'm goin back down South, where the weather fits my clothes," present veiled nostalgia, while Henderson's "Back Woods Blues" describes the stark indignity of making the second-class citizen trip back South.[6] By 1929, "the panic was on," "times was getting tight," and belly button was being introduced to backbone by the "Miss Meal Cramp" described by Alec Johnson.[7] Thus, with the evidence of hardship more obvious, the 1930s were known less for migration, the "Second Great Migration" of five million African Americans occurring largely between 1940 and 1970.[8] In the 1930s, many people were instead migrating in the bread lines and soup lines, from one barrel-fire to another, from dollars to doughnuts. To destitution.

The blues and its sister jazz had been perfect for expressing the radically new sensibility emerging out of the war to end all wars (1914–18). Something new was needed, that could plumb the depths of the horrors of Old World violence while improvising a new era of African American artistry emerging from the minstrel shadows to the hot music forefront. Everyone seemed to discover the blues – white audiences, country music fans, classical music experts, and writers such as Carl Sandburg, T. S. Eliot, Langston Hughes, and Howard W. Odum. The music inspired a new literature, one that was neatly structured, yet loose and free, and one in which Langston Hughes, through poems such as "The Weary Blues," had become a master, even as it was T. S. Eliot who garnered popular praise as a jazz poet.[9]

The blues was also the perfect music for what was called the Depression era – though, as Lonnie Johnson pointed out, the era's sudden deprivations were not so unprecedented for African Americans. They had known such socioeconomic conditions long before white Americans began to inhabit unsanitary Hoovervilles, cover themselves with "Hoover blankets" (i.e., the daily newspaper) and slip "Hoover leather" pieces of cardboard in their bottomless shoes. These early-decade neologisms name-checked an unpopular president, and were lent literary currency in the decade-ending *The Grapes of Wrath* (1939) by John Steinbeck. But hunger, joblessness, and poverty did not come in a vacuum. The phrase "hard times" itself was ubiquitous in the blues, a euphemism, perhaps, for the racism and sexism behind the perennial hard times endured by masses of African Americans. For a number of reasons, the blues gave voice to many conflicting or incongruous emotions in a way that virtually no other genre could, unless that agent was itself mingled with the blues, such as the sometimes-harrowing Appalachian country sound of Dock Boggs, or Bill Monroe and Ralph Stanley's high lonesome wails. Loneliness, starvation, panic, heartache, frustration, despair, absurdity – they were all hallmarks of the blues even before Mamie Smith's vocal hit "Crazy Blues" (1920) helped create a much larger stage than vaudeville and tent shows had provided for earlier blues superstars like the brilliant pianist and blackface comedian Butler May, who died in 1917.[10] And yet the music also provided opportunities: to comment, be it tragically, seriously, ironically, or humorously; to reach out; to exhort; to express anger; to celebrate creativity in the face of limitation, perseverance in the face of adversity. To *laugh* together, with people who have experienced, or are experiencing, or who *will* experience what you feel, and need some downhome genius to help them express it.

In the 1930s, Harlem was still clearly a prime hotspot for the intense early jazz style known as hot music – as well as the other aesthetic forms it influenced. Cab Calloway and his Missourians replaced Duke Ellington at the Cotton Club, with a hot "hi-de-ho" and "hee-dee-hee" scorching the musical landscape. Only now, more and more, hot was under the collar, with anger at the failure of American society to manage its economic duties properly, address its racial issues honestly, and advance a feminist/womanist agenda equitably. These failures amounted to the continuing failure of American democracy. Hughes expressed it thusly in *Esquire* in 1936: "Let America be America Again ... ("America never was America to me.")."[11] Hughes, a representative Black American of his generation, articulated his criticism through the combination of a powerful oral tradition, increasing educational opportunities, and expanding expressive platforms. On August 20, 1930, Hughes brought forth in *Amsterdam News* his first new expression of hot music in the new decade through the poem "Rent-Party Shout: For a Lady Dancer," a raucous ride through a woman's emerging self-assertion.[12] At the same time, Hughes and Zora Neale Hurston were tackling the play *Mule Bone* together, though *togetherness* is a relative term given the legendary tensions that arose during the collaboration. Hughes also published his first novel, *Not Without Laughter* that same year, portraying a young boy, Sandy, whom America is failing economically, socially, and spiritually, while the women who raise him negotiate a difficult path through a classist, racist, and sexist world. It was the beginning of the 1930s, and Hughes still had the blues – to feel, to express, to model, and to champion.

With a few notable exceptions, Hughes's plays of the 1930s do not employ hot music substantively. Leslie Sanders notes that c. 1963 Hughes and his editor Webster Smalley retroactively changed musical references from the 1930s to the 1920s in 1935's *Little Ham*. They replaced a dance called "truckin,"[13] the Ubangi Club, and a connection to entertainer

Gladys Bentley, who appeared at the Ubangi Club in 1934–35,[14] to 1920s references,[15] and employed a character called "the hot stuff man," whose "stuff" would have been hot in the musical sense.[16] W. C. Handy's "St. Louis Blues" gets a look-in in Hughes's play, too.[17] Hughes employed references to Handy's famous composition throughout his career, in *Not Without Laughter*, "Maker of the Blues" (1942), and *First Book of Jazz* (1955). A program note reported that it was not a play of serious import, but "just to laugh and in laughing to be happy,"[18] extending a sensibility common to *Not Without Laughter* and *Mule Bone*, though the novel takes a much more serious turn than this local color play.

Much more interesting and notable for its use of blues is Hughes's "*Don't You Want to Be Free?*" Premiering in a Harlem loft on April 12, 1938 and first published in *One Act Play Magazine* in October 1938, it was a striking example of aesthetic and community success in its blending of leftist politics, racial history, folklore, personal poetry, and music. The individual elements of the play were fluid and immediately adaptable to the performance context, seeking to involve audience and current events to provoke personal and timely responses. The experimental combination of various performance genres provided a unified ambience and vision, aided by Hughes's production notes, which counseled to use "a rapid moving-picture technique of one scene flowing directly into another,"[19] and further blends the play's panoramic historical vision. Providing both African American folk songs such as "Go Down, Moses,"[20] "Nobody Knows the Trouble I've Seen,"[21] "John Brown's Body,"[22] "I Couldn't Hear Nobody Pray,"[23] "In That Great Gettin' Up Mornin',"[24] and "Trouble, Trouble, I Has 'Em All My Days,"[25] alongside his own poems, such as "Song for a Dark Girl,"[26] and "Cross,"[27] and especially blues and gospel poems like "Bound No'th Blues" and "The Weary Blues,"[28] Hughes gives the play a clear sense of the individual's relationship to the community, the poem to the folk roots. This is an element that African American aesthetics have always embraced, traceable back to West African roots, and to Hughes's earliest poems, such as "The Negro Speaks of Rivers." The title of the poem refers to the singular "Negro," but the poem's capitalization of the word and discussion throughout emphasizes that this is a collective spirit. As such, the individual is connected to the group in an essential, and grammatical, way. Influenced by plays such as Elmer Rice's *The Adding Machine* (1923) and Clifford Odets' *Waiting for Lefty* (1935), Hughes created an "impressionistic"[29] and immersive theater experience that was public and private, exterior and interior, generalized and personal.

Hughes deals with the blues and spirituals deliberately in an unburnished state. As his stage directions insist, the spirituals are to have a "natural, simple, mellifluous and rhythmic quality to be heard in the singing of any humble NEGRO church."[30] Hughes, of course, is not referring to the Pentecostal or COGIC institution, which would be more emotional and demonstrative, such as that captured by Hurston on a field trip to Florida. Hughes is also very specific about the blues sequence:

> The blues sequence should be accompanied by an expert, old-time, stomp-down blues-piano player who should continue the same rhythm throughout the entire sequence, playing softly but steadily through the spoken portions. The action of the blues sequence should be in time to the music, the characters walking and moving in tempo.[31]

Clearly, Hughes has different effects in mind to distinguish the two different genres. The spirituals are just that – spiritual in an internal, "humble" way, and presented pleasingly. The blues, on the other hand, are to be played by a "stomp-down" pianist, suggesting a rough and tumble style for "dancing or carousing" with an unvarying and "steady rhythm."[32] Hughes argues for the blues as a genre that deals realistically with everyday issues in the Black community and that provides an unwavering rhythm to which the masses can march, in step toward their freedom.

Staged and published just before John Hammond staged the first *From Spirituals to Swing* concert in December 1938 to celebrate African American musical history from a politically progressive perspective, Hughes's play captures the musical zeitgeist. By connecting the "working class,"[33] the "radical,"[34] the "union ... agitator,"[35] and attempts to "organize"[36] with the increasing interracial appreciation of African American music like the blues, Hughes unites contemporary aesthetic, social, and political concerns, such as the worldwide perception of Black big band music as representatively American. In ironic counterpoint, Hughes juxtaposes the statement "I want to be free"[37] with the lynch rope that is the only "character" that continually occupies and dominates the stage.[38]

Across genres, Hughes demonstrated his thorough knowledge of the blues song form. The classic AAB pattern consists of a sung thought or line, roughly repeated, and followed by a third line that end rhymes with the first two. Though there are ample variations, this is the primary form used in commercially recorded blues, as well as in Hughes's blues poems, such as "Hard Luck," "Hey!," and "Hey! Hey!" For example, as Peg Leg Howell sang in "Rock and Gravel Blues" (1928):

> Honey, let's go to the river and sit down.
> Honey let's go to the river and sit down.
> If the blues overtake us, jump overboard and drown.[39]

Nonetheless, while Hughes emphasized form he also sought to capture oral performance elements, generating both oral performances and poems that crossed expressive borders. Thus, one must approach his work at the intersection of the oral and the written form to capture its full complexity.

For example, Hughes's blues poems are consistent with the blues tradition in terms of recognizing the frequent medial caesura by breaking the "line" in two, allowing the "repeat" line to be improvised with small differences that alter the drama of the line, and providing common eight- and twelve-bar AAB patterns:

> I works all day
> Wid a pick an' a shovel
> Comes home at night,--
> It ain't nothin but a hovel.[40]

> I'm goin' down to the railroad
> And lay my head on the track
> Goin' down to the railroad,
> Lay my head on the track,
> If I see the train a-comin',
> I'm gonna jerk it back.[41]

Hughes also employs a vaudeville-style blues with a slightly expanded structure and a theatrical female speaker:

> I ain't got no heart no mo'
> Next time a man comes near me
> Gonna shut and lock my door,
> Cause they treats me mean—
> The ones I love.
> They always treats me mean.[42]

He uses the less common ABB stanza pattern in two circumstances, both of which reference slavery times, a technical anachronism since the blues did not formally exist then, though Hughes seems to be making a connection between slavery and the blues.[43] As he suggests, the spirit of the blues existed before it became "codified," so to speak, in its recognized forms.

Hughes further partakes of another element common to the blues tradition, this time with his own blues poems – he mixes the lyrics of two of his poems together in one. Of course, variant versions of songs that do this are common in folklore, and specifically in the blues, so Hughes's strategy here is entirely consistent with the fluidity of blues tradition. Hughes provides us with a sense of the adaptability of the blues, with its improvisational quality, an aesthetic that might lend itself to sociopolitical strategies as well. Hughes starts a lyric with a stanza from "Bound No'th Blues," interpolates the poem "Hey!," and then uses another stanza from "Bound No'th Blues"[44] to complete the lyric. "Hey!" presents the fulcrum on which the contributions from "Bound No'th Blues" precariously balance. That is, the migration North, as related to the period of the first Great Migration, 1916–30, presented participants with wearying burdens, even amid optimism about better conditions in the North. In between two stanzas that discuss these concerns comes "Hey!" to present a sense of the momentous change that is coming, here represented by night's encroaching darkness. Still, the lyric suggests that darkness will not necessarily bring something bad – as is traditional with the symbolism of darkness as ignorance and danger. It brings the *unknown*, and it brings an ambiguous – part fearful, part hopeful – feeling.

It is no accident that the sequence ends with the symbol of the hopping toad. Traditionally, toads have symbolized transformation and renewal, restlessness, and fertility. Hughes provides us here with a pseudo-folkloric depiction of the small animal, frantic in its hopping, but nonetheless persevering over a long journey. The migration itself represented the transformation, renewal, restlessness, and fertility of the suffering, hopeful masses, small in their individual hopes and dreams, but mighty in their collective changing of themselves and their country. And, of course, the migration of the blues from South to North brought significant continuity and stability, even while significant urban alterations, as the modernists would say, made it new and made it whole. The sequence sung by the "Boy" beginning with the picture frame lyric, and ending with the refusal to commit the suicide he considered represents a similar composite: several different poems by Hughes that connect to the tradition, diverge from it individually, and become whole again in the way that they are so easily juxtaposed with continuity. In this sense, the blues tells an individual and collective story, infinitely variable and yet crucially connected. Blues lyrics, after all, are not always narrative – in fact they are frequently lyrical and sometimes progress in a nodal rather than logically coherent fashion – like Life.

When Sterling Brown came to Howard in 1929, he continued a tradition started by his father forty years before, a venerable succeeding a venerable, bringing new roots and branches to African American culture and the ways it would be performed and studied. Young Master Sterling was a rogue and a raconteur filled with toasts and dozens along with an impressive array of literatures. The elder Brown, a professor of theology, possessed great moral courage and toughness. Sterling A. was schooled in the ways of white folks and the ways of Black folks, rich and poor, and the wary negotiation between these overlapping and sometimes antagonistic traditions.

Brown's study of literature and folklore offered him wisdom, style, and intelligence, and he had his eyes open for all of these wherever he went. When he named a poem "Ma Rainey," which he did in 1930, he didn't intend a simple characterization of Ma Rainey, or a caricature or anecdote, he meant *This is Ma Rainey*, in all her three-dimensional glory, *in the flesh!* And Ma Rainey was important enough to have been commemorated within the genre, in the song "Ma Rainey" by Memphis Minnie. The annunciation of and arrival of Ma Rainey was an event of the first magnitude for poor sharecroppers and laborers hungry not only for victuals but for the arrival of a recording star of the "race," someone who could demonstrate Black genius through the distinctive, dynamic music born out of the talent of the "common" person. The tent and stage shows that traveled throughout Black communities brought much-needed relief from back-breaking labor, especially when that relief came in the form of "Ma" Rainey, dubbed "the Mother of the Blues," "the Assassinator of the Blues" – she who could evoke and soothe and destroy the existential blues with aplomb unavailable to other performers. She was the big maternal, a figure of comfort and care, though also a gaudy fashion plate and ruler of the socio-sexual domain in all its diversity.

Ma, born Gertrude Pridgett, in 1886, had begun appearing with Pa Rainey in 1906,[45] one of a number of blues singers emerging at a similar time – so she was not alone as a matriarchal head in the blues family tree. But what Ma had in particular was a deep South, low-down, singing style that was full of swamps, turpentine mills, and toting and lifting and rolling that told the whole story from the inside, but trumpeted that tale back outside in a demonstration of strength, endurance, invention, and beauty. Memphis Minnie's song typifies a response to Rainey's presence:

> I was thinking about Ma Rainey, wonder where could Ma Rainey be
> I was thinking about Ma Rainey, wonder where could Ma Rainey be
> I been looking for her, even been in old Tennessee
>
> She was born in Georgia, traveled all over this world
> She was born in Georgia, traveled all over this world
> And she's the best blues singer, peoples, I ever heard
>
> When she made "Bo Weavil Blues," I was living way down the line
> When she made "Bo Weavil Blues," I was living way down the line
> Every time I hear that record, I just couldn't keep from crying

> Hmmmm, hmmmmm
> Hmmmm, hmmmmm
> Hmmmm, hmmmmmmmm
>
> People it sure look lonesome since Ma Rainey been gone
> People it sure look lonesome since Ma Rainey been gone
> But she left little Minnie to carry the good works on[46]

Rainey, of course, did not travel the entire world, but she traveled the world Memphis Minnie knew and could imagine. "Bo Weavil Blues" was a hit for Rainey, expressing the troubles of poor sharecroppers. Minnie's reference to being down the line may well evoke red light districts and prostitution, milieus that Minnie may have known intimately.[47] Apparently, Minnie means to say that Rainey's performance took her back to other places and times and troubles, away from a tougher urban life to the rural setting where Rainey reigned. Importantly, Rainey's artistry activated Minnie, like the audience in Brown's poem, to become a blues singer, too. In the song, Rainey even provokes Minnie into a stanza-long wordless humming of the blues, an oral, but nonsemantic, tribute to Rainey's legacy.

In the famous poetic tribute, Brown is careful to capture with the opening adverb the complete Ma Rainey experience as it unfolds in the communities Ma blows into like a tornado. Although one's arrival is not necessarily a life-changing event, Brown blows reveille by announcing that arrival from the outset. This sets in motion a chain of events that reverberates in the communities for miles around. When Ma comes to town, she doesn't merely arrive, she "goes to town," "[does] her stuff" (line 8) in a way no one else can.[48] Touring troupes would sometimes throw parades or play baseball games to make each show a grander event. Rainey's status as "Mother of the Blues" prefigures this grandness. The mother was there when the blues was born. Her title suggests an intimate familiarity with African American life, loss, struggle, and survival. And yet she is also referenced in the familiar, "Ma." She is as close as a cakewalk into town, but at the same time exalted, burgeoning from a historical distance, past barracoons, past slave pens, middle passage, invasive examinations, and becoming captive to tribal neighbors and rapacious Europeans. As Zora Neale Hurston acknowledged, "You got to go there to know there"[49] – and you could hear it in every nuance and inflection of Ma's sound and phraseology. We don't even need the name of the town, or the numbers of the people choogling in line. Ma was there. It was homecoming.

Significantly, Ma comes to town, making a journey that the townsfolks need, too. This is an idea to remember toward the poem's end, when the two entities physically approach each other with reverence born of familiarity, and familiarity born of excitement. The short, breathless lines with which Brown begins the poem portray anticipation across a diverse, though clearly Black, audience. Significantly, the words are spoken in dialect, but not the hackneyed dialect of inferior practitioners, not "a jingle in a broken tongue."[50] Brown's dialect is not comic or fractured, but communicative, allowing the meaning to emerge by denying linguistic rigidity. The single sentence opening section is exuberant and words like "flivverin'" and "picknickin'" capture all of the vernacular buzz surrounding Ma's visit. This one person, this Ma, will cast her net and pull in not just the bigwigs and muckety mucks, but hillsides and wharves full of anonymous, voiceless people, uniting the famous and the unknown in a celebration of self. One way or another, they will get to see Ma, be it via mule, train, car, or foot power. And this is not just in particular places, but "anyplace" (line 3), "anywheres" (line 18), a magical phenomenon across the disaster-haunted land.

The second section of the poem features longer lines, which slows the tempo. The eight lines last from twelve to sixteen syllables, a marked contrast with the earlier eighteen lines of five syllables or less. Significantly, the words do revisit the mild dialect of the earlier section. It is as if Brown is answering the criticism that dialect poetry constitutes a limited genre by using language whose energy is tonally more expressive. Thus, the folks are "a-laughin' an' a-cacklin'" (line 21), while others hold in "aches and miseries" (line 24), until the show informally begins with smiles and piano runs that announce the festivities.

Interestingly, the folks who arrive from lumber camps and cornrows command the power of "roaring water" (line 22) and "wind" that rules their workplaces. The poem pairs the force of nature symmetrically with the force of humanity come to hear their own. It is a symbiotic relationship that Brown describes among people, environment, and the great heroine who blends them all together. The first shot of Ma presents a smiling blues singer – one who drives away the blues with buoyant artistry, rather than weeping or moaning. Her smiles are decorated by gold teeth, a popular method of decoration deemed gauche by the upper classes but a sign of wealth among the poor. For Ma, the gold-toothed grin was a part of her persona as a blues diva and queen. Brown, of course, had met Ma, so his familiarity with Ma's smiles is authentic, as is his knowledge of Long Boy, who actually played piano with Ma for a time. Just as there is nothing out of line with Ma's "gold toofed" smiles, neither is anything awry with Long Boy's black and yellow keys. One assumes here the piano provided for the gig is an old one, exhibiting wear and tradition. The white keys would be yellow from pounding, rubbing, tickling, trilling, and tinkling, though the black remains intact. Symbolically, the spectrum from black to yellow covers the range of "mulatto" colors, denoting the varied Black experiences touched by the blues.

The poem's third section returns to the prosody of the first part – returning to shorter lines as the audience begins to have a conversation with Ma in the first-person plural. Here the audience offers Ma's own lyrics for Ma to sing now, telling her what they want. Important is "Little and Low," a traditional blues lyric descriptor completed by "built up from the ground." Ma, in fact, recorded a song with Blind Blake entitled "Little Low Mamma Blues" in 1926 that evokes the person described in the poem – she was, in fact, short, little, and low, with gold-toothed smiles.[51] While Ma is singing a song to keep the expectant audience strong, she also inaugurates a creative ritual through the performance: the audience admonishes "Sing us 'bout de hard luck" and "Sing us 'bout de lonesome road." They do not say sing *to* us or sing *about* us, but *sing us*, as if they are being sung into existence. The blues lyric performed is a vivifying act, marshalling the power of the audience, nature, the tradition, and Ma, thus setting the stage for the poem's magnificent fourth part. Brown masterfully uses African American Vernacular English (AAVE) to express the communal and intimate meanings that Standard English cannot.

In part four, the speaker addresses a character in the text, an audience member. Importantly, Brown's quotation marks determine who is actually talking. The audience member says, "She jes' catch hold of us, somekindaway. She sang Backwater Blues one day" (lines 41–42). It is the same gentle vernacular spoken by the poem's narrator, uniting the two speakers through language. Interestingly, Brown has Ma sing a song she did not record. Indeed, the song was associated with Bessie Smith, a "rival" of Ma's, though this does not preclude Ma from having sung the song. Nine other Black recordings of the song exist from Bessie's time, along with four more by white country performers.[52] What it does emphasize is Brown's recognition of this particular song's importance. "Backwater Blues" is assumed to be about the 1927 Mississippi flood, though it was recorded "two months before the levees broke in the southern states."[53] Part of the point here seems to be that, even though it is "Bessie's" song, Ma can sing it because she embodies blues tradition, and the flood was a mass disaster. Ma has the emotional background and the technique to adapt and perform it in a way that moves the audience "somekindaway." The audience member also recognizes that she unites the group, in "catch[ing] hold of *us*" (emphasis added). But something interesting transpires in the following lines: first, the quotation marks do not close; second, italics indicate that Ma is singing the song as the audience member reports it; third, the audience member returns to speak some lines that are not italicized. Brown unites the voice of the audience member with that of Ma, demonstrating to whom the song belongs, experientially and spiritually: the community, and the landscape of the lowlands – remember Ma is little and low – and the vast distance between the hills and the lowland swamps. The isolation, the homelessness, and the terror characterizes African American existence as the singer attempts to transcend the tragedy of the flood. The following three lines are not a part of Ma's performance, lacking the italics of the song lyrics. Still, the three lines partake of the performances and spirit of the blues by following a rough 12-bar AAB stanza pattern that makes the response of the audience part of the call and response and then makes Ma's response to the audience a part of the performance, too. Importantly, instead of the crowd following the star outside, Ma follows the crowd. This is significant in that it indicates how song-crowd-performer antiphony completes the blues experience, indicating how important each part is to the unifying process. By changing the word "somekindaway" to "dataway," Brown indicates that the process has been spiritually and definitively fulfilled.

By the 1930s, the important work in blues poetry by Langston Hughes and others through the 1920s found new expression in the continuing experimentation of writers like Hughes and Brown, Richard Wright, and Frank Marshall Davis. As the musical genre changed, so did the written work on which it was based. Hughes and Brown both continued to work the genre in written form for the rest of their lives, as did other artists such as Sonia Sanchez, Sherley Anne Williams, and Amiri Baraka, all intent upon joining tradition to innovation, mainstream to multi-streams, aural to visual. It is important to have as broad and deep an understanding of the developments in the types of blues in order to keep pace with the changing nature of blues music and poetry.

Notes

1 Lonnie Johnson, "Hard Times Ain't Gone No Where" (Decca 7388, 1937).
2 Oscar Micheaux, dir., *The Girl from Chicago* (Micheaux Film, 1932); Oscar Micheaux, dir, *Birthright* (Micheaux Film, 1939).
3 Ida Cox, "Chicago Bound Blues (Great Migration Blues)," 1923, *Complete Recorded Works, Vol. 1.* (Document DOCD 5322, 1995).
4 Charles and Effie Tyus, "Good Old Bygone Days," 1924, *Vocal Duets: Complete Recorded Works in Chronological Order (1924–1931)* (Document 5526, 1997).
5 Memphis Minnie and Kansas Joe, "Goin' Back to Texas," 1929, *Complete Recorded Works 1929–1934 Vol. 1* (Document DOCD 5028, 1991); Leroy Carr, "I'm Going Back to Tennessee," 1929, *Leroy Carr Vol. 2* (Document DOCD 5135, 1992); Memphis Jug Band, "Going Back to Memphis," 1930, *Memphis Jug*

Band Vol. 3 (Document DOCD 5023, 1991); Leroy Carr, "Going Back Home," 1935, *Leroy Carr Vol. 6* (Document DOCD 5139, 1992); Jimmie Strothers, "Goin' to Richmond," 1936, *Red River Blues* (Travelin' Man TM CD 08, 1991); Eddie Kelly, "Goin' Back to Alabama," 1937, *Carolina Blues 1937–1947* (Document DOCD 5168, 1993); Amos Easton [Bumble Bee Slim], "Going Back to Florida," 1937, *Bumble Bee Slim Vol. 8* (Document DOCD 5268, 1994); Big Bill Broonzy, "Going Back to Arkansas," 1938, *Big Bill Broonzy: Complete Recorded Works in Chronological Order, Vol. 8* (Document DOCD 5130, 1993); Washboard Sam, "Going Back to Arkansas," 1940, *Complete Recorded Works in Chronological Order, Vol. 4* (Document DOCD 5174, 1993).

6 Rosa Henderson, "Down South Blues," 1923, *Rosa Henderson: Complete Recorded Works in Chronological Order, Vol. 1* (Document DOCD 5401, 1995); Sonny Boy Williamson, "Down South," 1938, *Sonny Boy Williamson: Complete Recorded Works in Chronological Order, Vol. 1* (Document DOCD 5055, 1991); Rosa Henderson, "Back Woods Blues," 1924, *Rosa Henderson: Complete Recorded Works in Chronological Order, Vol. 2* (Document DOC 5402, 1995).

7 Alec Johnson, "Miss Meal Cramp Blues," 1928, *Mississippi String Bands and Associates, 1928–1931* (Document BDCD 6013, 1991).

8 William H. Frey, "The New Great Migration: Black Americans Return to the South, 1965–2000," *The Brookings Institution*, May 2004, 1–3.

9 For more on the history of jazz poetry, see Jessica E. Teague's chapter in this volume (Chapter 14).

10 Lynn Abbott and Doug Seroff, *The Original Blues* (Jackson, MS: University Press of Mississippi, 2017), 309; Mamie Smith, "Crazy Blues," Okeh 4169, 1920.

11 Langston Hughes, "Let America Be America Again," 1936, in Arnold Rampersad and David Roessel, eds., *The Collected Poems of Langston Hughes* (New York: Vintage, 1994), 189.

12 Langston Hughes, "Rent-Party Shout: For a Lady Dancer," 1930, in Rampersad and Roessel, *The Collected Poems of Langston Hughes*, 130.

13 Langston Hughes, *Little Ham*, 1935, in Leslie Catherine Sanders and Nancy Johnston, eds, *The Collected Works of Langston Hughes: Volume 5, The Plays to 1942: Mulatto to The Sun Do Move* (Columbia, MO: University of Missouri Press, 2002), 259–65.

14 Sheldon Harris, *Blues Who's Who: A Biographical Dictionary of Blues Singers*, 1979 (New York: Da Capo, 1981), 43.

15 Leslie Catherine Sanders, "Introduction: *Little Ham*," in Sanders and Johnston, *The Collected Works of Langston Hughes*, 196.

16 Hughes, *Little Ham*, 221–23.

17 Ibid., 264–65.

18 Sanders, "Introduction: *Little Ham*," 196.

19 Langston Hughes, "Don't You Want to Be Free?," 1938, in Sanders and Johnston, *The Collected Works of Langston Hughes*, 573.

20 Ibid., 545.

21 Ibid., 546.

22 Ibid., 547.

23 Ibid., 549.
24 Ibid., 551.
25 Ibid., 554.
26 Ibid., 549–50.
27 Ibid., 552.
28 Ibid., 552–53.
29 Ibid., 570.
30 Ibid., 572.
31 Ibid.
32 Stephen Calt, *Barrelhouse Words: A Blues Dialect Dictionary* (Urbana: University of Illinois Press, 2009), 233.
33 Hughes, "Don't You Want to Be Free?," 551.
34 Ibid., 565.
35 Ibid., 566.
36 Ibid., 567.
37 Ibid., 544.
38 Ibid., 540, 570.
39 Peg Leg Howell, "Rock and Gravel Blues" (Columbia 14320-D, 1928).
40 Hughes, "Don't You Want to Be Free?," 554.
41 Ibid., 555.
42 Ibid.
43 Ibid., 543, 544.
44 Ibid., 552–53.
45 Abbott and Seroff, *The Original Blues*, 162.
46 Memphis Minnie, "Ma Rainey," 1940, *Complete Recorded Works 1935–1941 in Chronological Order, Vol. 5* (Document BDCD 6012, 1991).
47 Paul Garon and Beth Garon, *Woman with Guitar: Memphis Minnie's Blues* (New York: Da Capo, 1992), 127.
48 Sterling Brown, "Ma Rainey," 1932, in Michael S. Harper, ed., *The Collected Poems of Sterling A. Brown* (Evanston, IL: TriQuarterly Books, 1980), 62–63.
49 Zora Neale Hurston, *Their Eyes Were Watching God*, 1937 (New York: Harper, 1990), 183.
50 Paul Laurence Dunbar, "The Poet," 1903, in Joanne M. Braxton, ed., *The Collected Poetry of Paul Laurence Dunbar* (Charlottesville: University of Virginia Press, 1993), 191.
51 Ma Rainey, "Little Low Mama Blues," 1926, *Complete Recorded Works in Chronological Order, Vol. 4* (Document DOCD 5584, 1997).
52 Bessie Smith, "Backwater Blues," Rec. February 17, 1927 (Columbia 14195-D, 1927). For more detail on "Backwater Blues" and its many versions, see David Evans, "High Water Everywhere: Blues and Gospel Commentary on the 1927 Mississippi River Flood," in Robert Springer, ed., *Nobody Knows Where the Blues Come From: Lyrics and History* (Jackson, MS: University Press of Mississippi, 2006), 24–25.
53 Ibid., 25.

CHAPTER 7

A Fool for Beauty
Modernism and the Racial Semiotics of Crooning

Michael Coyle

In 1963, John Coltrane was in the middle of what we celebrate today as his classic quartet period. With McCoy Tyner on piano, Jimmy Garrison on bass, and Elvin Jones on drums, Coltrane was pushing restlessly into a jazz future that threatened to turn the previous half century of recordings into mere souvenirs – quaint and not necessarily worth keeping. In 1961, he joined this quartet with a new kind of big band in the *Africa/Brass* sessions; in 1962, he recorded the modal album, *Coltrane*, as well as *Live at the Village Vanguard*; and 1963 began with two more universally acclaimed recordings, including the legendary record with Duke Ellington – a record where jazz tradition and jazz modernism proved still capable of speaking a common language (the other album was *Impressions*, which despite its enduring popularity represented not a single session but something the label put together comprising two live tracks and two studio tracks). But what came next surprised Trane's band as much as it did fans and critics: Coltrane made his first and only album with a vocalist.

In fact, even the vocalist, crooner Johnny Hartman, was by his own account "a little reluctant."[1] Hartman hadn't made a studio recording for nearly four years. That record, *And I Thought about You* (1959), had been his first since December 1956 and "even though it contained some of Hartman's best work" it "went essentially unheard," in part because the attention of popular audiences was on the new youth musics of the era and in part because the independent Roost label was in financial trouble so that the album "was in print only for a minute and a half."[2] Hartman then compounded his troubles: "instead of contributing to the promotion of *And I Thought About You*, Hartman left the country," flying to England in January 1959. But his subsequent explanation is both poignant and telling: "I decided to go overseas because there just wasn't any work for a black ballad singer."[3] Note that Hartman calls himself a "balladeer" rather than a "crooner," because the latter term would have seemed impossibly quaint to postwar American audiences, white or Black.

But then again, as Gregg Akkerman observes, Hartman also avoided referring to himself as a "jazz singer" when admitting "that rock music had overtaken whatever genre he was a part of: 'When rock came to the fore, jazz musicians, singers, and supper club singers took a back seat. I went to Europe to stay employed.'"[4] Indeed, as Howard Goldstein observes in the *Online Grove Dictionary of Music*, "by the end of the 1960s, crooning was practically extinct as a distinct performance style."[5] So then the inescapable question is why a leading champion of modernity would have tapped a crooner rather than a defiantly modern and political singer like, say, Abbey Lincoln or Oscar Brown, Jr., someone consciously developing an uncompromisingly Black style?

To date, Allison McCracken's *Real Men Don't Sing: Crooning in American Culture* remains the authoritative study of crooning as a cultural phenomenon and I am indebted to her work in several respects.[6] McCracken notes that "*crooning* reached North American shores through blackface minstrelsy; minstrels first popularized the term in the nineteenth century as a descriptor for the living, protective murmurs of the black slave woman singing to her infant charge."[7] The music industry was, however, eager to separate this style from its Black origins: "Publishers and songwriters worked to broaden their nets by de-emphasizing specific racial, ethnic, and political song content and stressed instead the universal and generic romantic courtship that could appeal across social categories. One strategy of the new industry was to redefine existing terms to broaden their meaning with the public; while *mammy* never lost its specific association with African Americans, *crooning* did."[8] This effacement effectually made possible the subsequent transgressiveness of this now apparently innocuous form, even as it prepared the basis for the subsequent backlash against it:

> Crooners were mostly young men who softly sang love songs into microphones, most popularly over the radio; they gave crooning its modern and still current meaning, "to sing popular, sentimental songs in a low, smooth voice, especially into a closely-held microphone." Their melodies were catchy and familiar, and their lyrics were generally innocuous and inoffensive. Their songs contained no explicit social agenda and were far less ribald than typical vaudeville fare. The top stars were either Irish or Italian American, and although predominantly Catholic, they were all "white" in the increasingly ethnically assimilated and racially segregated urban entertainment landscape of the time.[9]

McCracken's emphasis is on "the erotics of male passivity and submissiveness" that characterized the work of the earliest crooners.[10]

This emphasis marks one of McCracken's most important contributions to our understanding of American crooning. In fact, even though McCracken identifies the first crooner as the "Original Radio Girl," Vaughn De Leath (born Leonore Vonderlieth in 1894), it seems to me important to note that, in the modern era at least, female singers have always been expected to express vulnerability.[11] Men were not, and that the earliest crooners did so was part of the transgressive thrill occasioned by their performances. This sense of the transgressive informs McCracken's particular interest in the cultural work that crooning did before the heteronormative backlash at the end of the Jazz Age. Her note that the "top stars" of crooning's heyday "were all 'white'," however, suggests further questions.

McCracken demonstrates that crooning's African American origin was not so much obscure to white audiences as it was deliberately obscured by the industry. Crooning was in this way read as "white" – by Black audiences as well as white – in the same kind of essentializing move that led early audiences to hear jazz as "Black" whatever the ethnicity of the performers. Two factors might explain the curious time lag between the commercial success of crooning and the earliest recordings of it by Black singers. The first of these is cultural. Male singing in African American culture seems always to have included the use of falsetto – it is there right from the beginning in the recorded work of Charley Patton (1891–1934). Like crooning, falsetto performance can convey vulnerability, but as Dana Cypress remarks, at the same time it also represents a display of very masculine control.[12] Falsetto singing thus represents different things to Black audiences than does crooning, as well as having an organic relation to African American culture and not being reliant on electronic technology. The second factor is less cultural than a simple matter of economics – the dependence of crooning on access to pricey technology, as well as industry prejudices about the taste of Black audiences. No less important would have been the threat to public morality, especially to the virtue of white women, that crooning was perceived to represent, perceptions that would have made crooning more dangerous for Black singers. Even twenty years later, a 1950 photo of Billy Eckstine being mobbed by a throng of young white women nearly ended his career.[13] But Eckstine's example also exemplifies how, when Black crooners emerged, they quickly pushed a form that was often regarded by the industry as mere novelty into something that made more serious claims on popular attention. Black male vocalists pushed the style to new levels of significance which black audiences have continued to value.

We might say that the African American preservation of crooning as a style represents another queering of the trope. At the same time that crooning was being separated from its Jazz Age transgressiveness, it was acquiring for African American audiences what Pierre Bourdieu has called "cultural capital."[14] For Black audiences, crooning came to represent not so much transgression but assimilation: an achievement of modernity, the moving beyond not just the forms of African American folk music but also the popularized forms of those musics in what was already being remembered as "the Jazz Age." For African American communities, the white appropriation of Black styles (ragtime, blues, gospel, boogie-woogie, jazz, rock 'n' roll) came inexorably bundled up with white attempts to define the meaning of Blackness. The Black adoption of crooning represented a resistance to such racialist and racist impositions of identity as well as new opportunities for self-definition. Like the 32-bar pop song format, crooning was distinctly modern, insistently urban, and predominantly white. That the cultural threats crooning once seemed to pose to American culture were not inflected by questions of race helped shape its enduring attraction for urban, Black audiences.

The first Black crooners established themselves after the collapse of the Jazz Age and after the Black-led emergence of swing. By the mid-thirties most Black swing bands featured a crooner. In 1934, for instance, Charles Holland (1909–87) was recording with the Fletcher Henderson Orchestra. A lyric tenor whose classical ambitions were blocked by his race, he nevertheless landed roles in Virgil Thomson and Gertrude Stein's opera *Four Saints in Three Acts* (1934) and the Warner Bros. feature film *The Green Pastures* (1936) before eventually settling in France.[15] Holland's classical ambitions frame his performances as a crooner: he wanted to make art; he wanted respect for his art. Like his somewhat tragic employer, Fletcher Henderson, whose best work has long been collected under the title *A Study in Frustration*, he wanted recognition more than mere popularity. He wanted to make serious music.[16]

But arguably the band that played the most important role in moving crooning across the color line was Duke Ellington's. After his manager and sometime vocalist, Irving Mills, pushed him through the "jungle band" phase that established his international reputation, Duke never again worked with a blues singer or a shouter of any kind. What Ellington wanted from his vocalists was class and sophistication – and he got it. However, apart from Ivie Anderson, with her remarkable enunciation and poised elegance, he didn't tend to employ vocalists for very long. His first records to feature a crooner came early, in 1930, possibly at Mills's suggestion, and with white crooners.

That Ellington's first recordings with crooners crossed the color line also reminds us that crooning was initially a style understood as white. Ellington made his first crooning sides with a vocalist who sometimes stepped in for Irving Mills on "jungle band" numbers – Dick Robertson. Robertson was more accustomed to rhythm numbers, but he adapted, and between April and October of 1930 he cut eight sides with Duke, including a fine recording of Eubie Blake and Noble Sissle's "Memories of You." The next month, Duke cut two sides with Smith Ballew (1902–84), the novelty "Nine Little Miles from Ten Tennessee" and then the kind of tender ballad with which Ballew so excelled – "I'm So in Love with You." Ballew's voice sounds ethereal even today in its gender fluidity, which makes his having become one of the first onscreen singing cowboys especially interesting as a sign of the times. Ballew did his most affective work with others, but Duke seems not to have been especially impressed and in his next recording session replaced him with another white crooner named Sid Garry (1901–73). Garry recorded three songs with Duke, including (in January 1931) a new version of "I'm So in Love with You," a song Duke had recorded with Ballew just six weeks earlier. In this fevered period, made all the more feverish by record companies rendered desperate by the stock market crash and looking to find something – anything – that would sell, other white crooners made similarly brief stops with Duke.[17] In February of 1932, Bing Crosby himself joined Duke and cut two takes of W. C. Handy's "St. Louis Blues." Perhaps inevitably, the rising white singer got top billing over the established Black band leader, but it remains surprising that Crosby and Duke collaborated on a song that was even then receding into tradition, associated with a bygone era, rather than recording a love ballad or even a current song. That neither Crosby nor Duke was especially interested in the blues suggests the decision was made by the producer. Critic Brian Zimmerman has noted how "the dark, shadowy harmonies of Ellington's horn arrangements [render] Crosby's coppery baritone in a new light," but be that as it may the experiment was not repeated and, in July of that year, Duke hired his first Black crooner.[18]

According to *The Baltimore Afro-American*, "Ray Mitchell was discovered by Ellington in Cincinnati where he was a staff singer at radio station WLW."[19] Otherwise, we don't know much about Mitchell. Audiences in the thirties didn't either – the *Pittsburgh Courier* identifies him as "Wesley Mitchell."[20] What we do know is that he toured with Ellington, getting a special notice for a performance at the Howard Theater; that his time with the band ended in December of 1932; and that before he left or was fired he made one recording with the Ellington orchestra, an obscure ballad identified on the record label simply as "Stars."[21] The recording opens with Barney Bigard softly playing the melody in the lower octaves of his clarinet before the brass section comes in growling, reminding us how recently the orchestra had been billed as "the jungle band"; that "jungle" sound similarly reaffirms the connection of crooning to the Jazz Age. Mitchell croons confidently but sensitively, a baritone voice sweet in its upper register. Formally there is nothing new in this performance, but culturally, in the racial ambiguity of Mitchell's delivery and its distance from (as Ethel Waters would sing in 1935) the "hotcha, *je ne sais quoi*–cha" that so often marked Black singing in the twenties, it is very new indeed.[22] Mitchell's tenure with Ellington was short but historically significant. The record's sound owes much to earlier work but was nevertheless a sign of things to come. Perhaps it suited Ellington that his crooner was unknown and so comparatively faceless: given the panic that crooning excited in the mid- to-late twenties, it is easy enough to imagine how a Black crooner would have been received.

But by 1933 crooning had already been assimilated into mainstream culture – in large part because it had been heteronormalized – and in the years that followed, the crooners with whom Duke worked were without exception Black. Louis Bacon (1904–67) was next, joining Ellington in September 1933. Bacon, too, was a baritone but his singing owed as much to Louis Armstrong as it did to Crosby – unsurprising perhaps given that he also played trumpet. His voice can be heard on "Rude Interlude" (1933), "Dear Old Southland" (1933), and, finally, "I'll Come Back for More" (1939).[23] He didn't come back for more, however, because later that year Duke hired Herb Jeffries (1913–2014), who became the first male vocalist and the first crooner to establish himself in the band for the long term. Like Ballew, Jeffries was a singing cowboy, but for Black audiences he was *the* singing cowboy, famed as "the bronze buckaroo." He was a polished crooner in the post-Crosby fashion – his baritone could handle the occasional rhythm number but unlike Ivie Anderson he didn't really swing. When his cinematic career called him away Duke replaced him with Al Hibbler (1915–2001), another baritone, but able to take on the more visceral music that African American audiences craved even before the Swing Era postwar collapse. What remained consistent through the revolving door of Ellington's male vocalists is that Duke expected modern sophistication. In this regard, his tastes helped shape the enduring popularity of crooning for Black audiences, not just in jazz but in the various forms of R&B that have flourished ever since. Duke never hired Johnny Hartman, but Hartman established his career by mastering this cultural-stylistic language.

Because it wasn't, of course, only an Ellington thing, and by 1963, it wasn't even a swing thing. Earl Coleman (1925–95), for instance, made his name singing with Charlie Parker, perhaps the chief architect of bebop, which is to say jazz modernism. We might remember, too, vocalist Lee Richardson (1926–99), whom Hartman was hired to replace when Richardson left Dizzy Gillespie's band; and, of course, there is the beloved figure of Nat "King" Cole (1919–65), who began his career as a pianist focused on rhythm numbers, but found massive stardom when producers took him from behind the piano and put him at the microphone in front of the band.

By the 1940s, African American crooners were commercially and artistically rivaling their white counterparts, singers like Ray Eberle, or the still-popular Crosby, or, of course, the young Frank Sinatra. I want to pause over Sinatra because the break in his career suggests a marker for the postwar divergence of Black and white crooners. Sinatra made his first recordings between 1940 and 1942 as a vocalist for Tommy Dorsey – not coincidentally one of the few white band leaders to have emerged in the twenties, survived the collapse of the Jazz Age, and found new success in the Swing Era. Sinatra remained an old-fashioned baritone crooner even after leaving the Dorsey band and going solo in 1943. For nearly a decade thereafter his style remained unchanged. But popular tastes shifted quickly after the Second World War and by 1952 Sinatra seemed washed up. His reinvention of himself as a swinging hipster in 1952–53 thus represented more than a surprising personal success – it was a sign of the times. His self-reinvention was necessary because *white* audiences had tired of crooning.

But African American music was developing in different directions and Billy Eckstine (1914–93), who like Hartman had debuted with the Earl Hines Orchestra, offers the paradigmatic example. Eckstine was a suave baritone sex symbol and embodied a new Black masculinity. Founding and fronting the first bebop big band, Eckstine was hugely important in marking crooning as still *modern*, separating it from Jazz Age roots and – no less than Sinatra after him – associating it with postwar American optimism. In many performances, like his 1947 release of "Everything I Have Is Yours," Eckstine could make crooning swagger. Sonny Burke's orchestra behind him is big but, amplified by the microphone, his voice – even crooning – carries over it. The orchestra isn't there to sweeten the tune but to chromaticize it, to give it edge, so that we feel the risk entailed in Eckstine's offering *everything*. This offering is sign of the vulnerability that twenty years remained a hallmark of male crooning. Nevertheless, in its every aspect this recording represented Black pride when doing so was – even more than it remains today – a political act.[24]

Eckstine's success helps illuminate why crooning held such appeal for African American audiences. For nearly three decades, crooning remained a sign of modernity and a sign of art overtly distinguishing itself *as* art. Initially an instrumental music, when after a few years bop finally connected with vocalists, the style it chose was that of the crooners: including many of the names I just recited and leading at last to Hartman. Crooning appealed to Black audiences precisely because of its distance from African American folk tradition. It seemed more open to future promise than to historical tribulation.

Hartman was among the younger singers who stepped through the door Eckstine opened. If he lacked Eckstine's charisma and swing, he was capable of unmatchable sensitivity and nuance. A singing contest victory at the Apollo in 1946 had won Hartman a week's engagement with the Earl Hines Orchestra. That week turned into a year, during which time he also recorded a couple of sides with Marl Young's String Ensemble – the first recordings of his career.[25] In November 1947, he cut five more sides under Hines's direction. It is striking how much Hartman even then already sounded fully formed and mature. "Midnight in New Orleans" is blues in form but tonally distant from the jump blues that dominated Black radio immediately after the war.[26] Big Joe Turner, perhaps the greatest shouter of them all, recorded "Hollywood Bed" that year; Wynonie Harris recorded "Good Rockin' Tonight" – the song that less than ten years later would put him out of work when it was covered by Elvis Presley; and Jimmy Liggins and His Drops of Joy delivered "Hep Cat Boogie."

We can see then that even at the start of his career Hartman beat against prevailing currents. Working with Hines, though, he was in good company. The Hines Orchestra could swing like nobody's business, but in 1947 Hines was remaking himself as a modernist – as Dizzy Gillespie recognized when contending that "the modern piano came from Earl Hines."[27] Like Ellington, Hines had little interest in vocalists, so Hartman's short stay is typical. He recorded four songs with Hines in 1947 and two more in 1953 – and that was it. These six songs were enough, however, to establish Hartman as a serious jazz vocalist. A good thing, too, since Hines broke up his band early in 1948 – the "Earl Hines Orchestra" with which Hartman recorded a final two songs in 1953 was really just a sextet. In this regard, the Hines orchestra met the same fate as most American dance bands in 1947, breaking up or going on hiatus as Americans voted with their feet and sought out new dances and new musics. Hartman was then working in the midst of a profound transformation driven both by forces outside of jazz and also by forces from within, as figures from Bird, Diz, and Monk through Ornette, Mingus, and Coltrane struggled to establish jazz as a serious art music.

I am hardly the first to ask why a leading champion of modernity would want to record with a crooner. The question was posed at the time to Coltrane himself, who couldn't quite put his motivation into words: "I just felt something about him; I don't know what it was. I like his sound, I thought there was something there I had to hear, so I looked him up and did that album."[28] The liner notes to the 1995 CD reissue of *John Coltrane and Johnny Hartman* were written by Alfred Bennett (A. B.) Spellman, a poet and music critic associated with the Black Arts Movement. Spellman offers that Coltrane was interested in the challenge of how to translate the "energy-formed vernacular" of his recent music "to the more articulate but more restrictive form of the song." Besides, Spellman continued,

> Trane had been recording little else lately. His latest two releases were *Ballads* (Impulse A-32) and *Duke Ellington & John Coltrane* (Impulse A-30), which were about 2/3 ballads. … His ballad style is increasingly becoming as subtle as his uptempo blues playing is dynamic, as witness "Autumn Serenade." The vernacular translates quite well; is, in fact, the same language.[29]

Spellman's observation that Coltrane had recently been playing lots of ballads is useful, but more interesting still is his conviction that Trane and Hartman were speaking "the same [vernacular] language." It would be a mistake to see Coltrane's ballads in some kind of binary opposition to the urgent questing of something like *A Love Supreme*. The majesty of Coltrane's vision was not limited to any one form. More in keeping with his art is his tendency to obsess over a form until he had exhausted it of further possibility. *A Love Supreme* (1965) came two years after the album with Hartman. It is a four-part, through-composed suite. The suite is a more open form than a ballad, although each of the four parts observes its own organic integrity, but *A Love Supreme* was the last formal music that Coltrane made. After that comes *Ascension* (1966) and, ultimately, *Interstellar Space* (recorded in 1967, but not released until 1974), the album titles themselves suggesting Trane's trajectory. We can imagine, then, that Coltrane felt challenged by the formal limits of the ballad. But still, Coltrane could have recorded ballads with any number of singers. But why a crooner? Why Johnny Hartman?

It is sometimes suggested that Coltrane would have remembered Hartman from the Dizzy Gillespie Orchestra, where a young Coltrane worked from 1949–51, but in fact their time there didn't overlap: Hartman had left the Gillespie band by April of 1949 and Coltrane wasn't hired until that November. The answer to our question isn't then biographical any more than it's casual. The answer must be aesthetic in nature and being aesthetic inevitably must be semiotic. The answer involves a certain vision of beauty and the implications that follow from African American artists aspiring to principles of beauty that are so rarified, so demanding, so difficult. In the case of this recording, the difficulty emerges as a modern artist tries to hold onto a once but no longer commercial form and produce art.

This effort might seem untimely to say the least. As the Civil Rights Movement was gathering strength in 1962 and 1963, so too was the racist violence often marshalled by state forces to oppose it. In March 1960, students from Augusta's historically Black Paine College initiated the direct-action phase of the city's Civil Rights Movement when they organized sit-ins at area department stores. And in the very month that Coltrane and Hartman were recording, Martin Luther King and the Southern Christian Leadership Conference were planning "Project C" ("C" for Confrontation) and launching the Birmingham Campaign. That campaign landed King behind bars, where he wrote his stirring "Letter from Birmingham Jail." He delivered his "I Have a Dream" address on the 29th of that August, less than three weeks before white supremacists bombed the 16th Street Baptist Church on September 15, 1963, murdering four children and wounding more than twenty others. In the context of this passionate, globally significant struggle, the recording of an album of quiet ballads might seem escapist indulgence, if not outright counter-revolutionary, but recall Angela Davis's analysis of Billie Holiday's 1939 recording of "Strange Fruit":

> Billie Holiday was not herself directly involved in the political developments of the thirties that served as the backdrop for her own cultural contribution. She was among the host of artists who moved into the stream of political radicalization by following paths carved out by their art, rather than by explicit political commitments.[30]

We might think of the Coltrane-Hartman collaboration in similar terms. For both, staying true to their art, refusing to cater to anyone else's expectations about what Black music should sound like, was their most profound political statement.

One of the most celebrated white writers of "protest music" or, as he preferred, "topical songs," was Phil Ochs, and ironically it was this singer who had devoted his career to social commentary who wrote,

> I must be home again soon.
> To face the unspoken unguarded thoughts of habitual hearts
> a vanguard of electricians a village full of tarts
> who say you must protest you must protest
> it is your diamond duty
> ah but in such an ugly time the true protest is beauty[31]

Ochs's oft-quoted line, "in such ugly times the only true protest is beauty," isn't an aesthete's complaint against bourgeois banality so much as a reaffirmation of the old avant-garde dream of what Viktor Shklovsky called "defamiliarization." Art, Shklovsky contended more than a century ago, has the power to open us to the possibility of change by disrupting the mechanisms of habit, to enable us to see or experience the familiar world as though for the first time.[32] Shklovsky's theory may be historically specific, and we can grant that art functions in different ways in different places at different times, but in the postindustrial world, which is also not coincidentally the period of white, global hegemony, it is broadly resonant. What use is political song, Phil Ochs asks, if it only reinforces the habitual feelings of its audience? And what good is a vanguard of technicians or electricians who focus solely on the transference of power through circuits that are already in place? The challenge to the modern artist is to restore our fullest capacity for human feeling. The challenge to the vanguard is to rewire our semiotic circuits, to redirect the currents of our collective feeling.

Neither Coltrane nor Hartman needed semiotics to know that in 1963 it was still an act of defiance for a Black artist to insist on their identity as an artist. *John Coltrane and Johnny Hartman* was such a work, despite the fact that it has always been almost universally lauded. It is a quiet record made in an increasingly noisy world. It affirms a new era by revisiting standards made in an earlier era that would not have welcomed them (in this context Billy Strayhorn's world-weary "Lush Life" represents a special intervention). The album comprises six tracks, all of them ballads, but a seventh track was recorded, dropped from the album, and the tapes of it mysteriously lost.[33] That track was Mongo Santamaria's "Afro Blue." Composed less than four years earlier, in 1959, with lyrics subsequently added by Oscar Brown, Jr., the song celebrates Black beauty:

> Dream of a land my soul is from
> I hear a hand stroke on the drum
> Shades of delight
> Cocoa hue
> Rich as the night
> Afro blue

The song is not overtly political and it is a call to action only in the sense that it is a celebration of love and of a shared identity. Hartman had never recorded such a song before, but its melancholy spirituality was perfectly in keeping with where Coltrane was traveling. Akkerman relates the story of the tape's rediscovery in 2005 and the legal struggles that to this day have prevented its issue. But Barry Kernfeld, former editor of the *New Grove Dictionary of Jazz*, has heard them and published his response. Although this album "is by far the most gorgeous session of jazz I have ever heard in my life," Kernfeld concluded, Hartman's "'Afro Blue' was 'not a great recording.' Despite the existence of lyrics to this originally instrumental song, Hartman's vocals are heard 'repeatedly intoning the title – but no lyric – over the group performance'." "Given the propensity for traditional lyricism on the other six songs," Akkerman's synopsis of Kernfeld concludes, "this experimental and minimalistic 'Afro Blue' was left off the album."[34] We can't know why Hartman didn't sing the full lyric and only time will tell whether his repeated intoning of the title was meant to function like Coltrane's spontaneous chanting in *A Love Supreme* or whether the experiment simply didn't work. But the fact the song was recorded at all, and that it was apparently the most experimental performance of a brilliant recording session is revealing. So, too, is Hartman's later comment to pianist Tony Monte that "the executives at ABC-Paramount (the original owners of Impulse) considered the album, at the time, to be no more than a 'throw-away.'"[35] The label execs, too, were apparently nonplussed by Coltrane's interest in a crooner.

John Coltrane and Johnny Hartman has long since entered the realm of myth. It was Hartman himself who in 1982 later recounted that five of the six tracks on the album were completed in one take; Akkerman gently suggests that Hartman "was recalling the session nineteen years later with a romanticized view worthy of the album's then-known stature."[36] In fact, as Akkerman explains, "the evidence proves that there were alternate takes of *every* track ... [and] three full-length takes of "You Are Too Beautiful."[37]

The longest track on the album, "You Are Too Beautiful" is by no means an obvious choice for a jazz performance, yet it seems to me the most exquisitely realized track on the album. Written in 1932 for the 1933 film, *Hallelujah I'm a Bum*, by lyricist Lorenz Hart and composer Richard Rodgers, it was first performed by Al Jolson. In this film, Jolson played a bum, but Jolson had made his name as the highest-grossing blackface minstrel in history, over-emoting and shouting through it all. Hartman's persona, here as always, is the furthest thing from down and out, and his voice exchanges the joke in Jolson's performance ("I am too drunk with beauty") for vulnerability and sensitivity. There is no irony in Hartman's performance – except perhaps in his reimagining the song for a new age and moving it beyond its problematic history. Where Jolson's character, outside ordinary society because derelict and poor, is a joker, Hartman's persona reveals deep sincerity inside an aesthete's removal. In Hartman's performance, beauty is the ultimate value. He wishes not to possess his beloved but merely to appreciate her perfection:

> You are too beautiful, my dear, to be true
> And I am a fool for beauty
> Fooled by a feeling that because I have found you
> I could have bound you too
>
> You are too beautiful for one man alone
> For one lucky fool to be with
> When there are other men
> With eyes of their own to see with
>
> Love does not stand sharing
> Not if one cares
> Have you been comparing
> My every kiss with theirs
>
> If, on the other hand, I'm faithful to you
> It's not through a sense of duty
> You are too beautiful
> And I am a fool for beauty

In Hartman's performance, the lover demonstrates his worthiness less by his accepting that others see what he sees than by his understanding that beauty cannot be possessed – only appreciated. The recording begins with four bars from the quartet. Coltrane playing obbligato lines based on the chords and the melody of the song; Tyner feeds the chords to which Garrison supplies the roots; Jones lays out until the instrumental break after the second chorus. There's nothing radical about any of this, gorgeous as it is, but even still the band never really plays "the head," the jazz musician's term for the first part of a melody, or at least of its principal ideas. In fact, it's Coltrane's restraint here that is the most remarkable aspect of his accompaniment. And though by 1963 Trane had been playing modally for several years, on this record "the harmony is crystal clear without any of the obfuscations you typically get from 'modal' playing, where it's often difficult to tell what the chord is 'supposed to be' at any moment."[38] Akkerman suggests that this playing represents a kind of strategic restraint:

> In 1961, jazz writer John Tynan scathingly referred to John Coltrane's recent recordings as "anti-jazz," "horrifying," and "gobbledegook." Taking umbrage at this criticism and others similar in tone, Impulse Records producer and chief executive Bob Thiele steered Coltrane toward making

a series of albums featuring ballads and standard tunes. As described in his autobiography, *What a Wonderful World*, Thiele said, "We decided to straighten these guys out once and for all by showing them that John was as great and complete a jazz artist as we already knew, and it was one of the few times he accepted a producer's concept."[39]

Akkerman's contextualizing of this record as a response to the old guard is helpful. Thiele's hunch was a good one. It took time for audiences to recognize the genius of, say, *A Love Supreme*, but as we noted above, about the only people who didn't immediately see the greatness of *John Coltrane and Johnny Hartman* were the label execs at ABC-Paramount. Nevertheless, the feel of this performance differs dramatically from the many pop versions of the song. As Hartman sings, individual words seem to melt into pure sound. There is, in fact, something very "meta" about his delivery, so that this song which is *about* beauty comes to embody it in every phrase. Crooning emphasizes the aesthetic experience of voice itself, foregrounding the sound of the voice over the melody line, being there just as a means of delivering the lyric – the sound of the voice for its own sake.

Crooning, then, represented something very different from the kind of vocal record that Coltrane's management had urged him to make. It was almost antithetical to the directions of contemporaneous popular vocals. But then Black crooning had always represented a kind of counter tradition, laying a claim to unpossessable beauty. By the early twenty-first century, crooning has established itself among the most enduring of African American vocal styles, and it continues to attract singers of extraordinary talent. Hartman struggled in the last part of his career almost as hard as he did the first, turning to songwriters of the rock era in hopes of managing something like relevance in a world where jazz was no longer a popular music. Those records have their own virtues, but they never rose to the achievement of his record with Trane. But Hartman's emphasis on artistry can still be heard in the work of any number of distinguished African American crooners after him, inside jazz and out: Johnny Mathis, Arthur Prysock, Lou Rawls, Teddy Pendergrass, Barry White, Luther Vandross, Freddie Cole, Andy Bey, Allan Harris, Nicholas Bearde, even Gregory Porter will sometimes croon. What crooning signifies has changed a great deal since its disruptive emergence a century ago. Indeed, in yet another sign that origin isn't destiny, crooning's troubled emergence is of little interest to the African American artists who continue to develop it and perform it as a style of ever-changing modernity.

Notes

1. Gregg Akkerman, *The Last Balladeer: The Johnny Hartman Story* (Toronto: Scarecrow Press, 2012), 116.
2. Ibid., 104–5.
3. Ibid., 106.
4. Ibid., 107.
5. Howard Goldstein, "Crooning," *Grove Music Online*, www-oxfordmusiconline-com.exlibris.colgate.edu/grovemusic/view/10.1093/gmo/9781561592630.001.0001/omo-9781561592630-e-0000006867?rskey=bJFMeF&result=1.
6. Allison McCracken, *Real Men Don't Sing: Crooning in American Culture* (Durham, NC: Duke University Press, 2015).
7. Ibid., 16.
8. Ibid., 18.
9. Ibid., 2.
10. Ibid., 33.
11. De Leath's first performance was of the minstrel tune, "Swanee River," over New York's 2XG in January 1920. Subsequently she broadcast regularly over WJZ. See McCracken, *Real Men Don't Sing*, 80–85.
12. Professor Dana Cypress, Department of English, Colgate University, in a private communication with the author, April 30, 2023. Every era of African American music provides rich examples: Bill Kenny in the 1930s, Alex Sharp in the 1940s, Clyde McPhatter in the 1950s, Smokey Robinson in 1960s, Eugene Record or Philip Bailey in the 1970s, Prince in the 1980s, to name only a few outstanding examples.
13. See Michael Eli Dokosi's account of this scandal: https://face2faceafrica.com/article/how-a-photo-of-singer-billy-eckstine-offended-the-white-community.
14. Bourdieu's fullest discussion of "cultural capital" can be found in his *Distinction: A Social Critique of the Judgment of Taste* (New York: Routledge, 1986). For a perceptive and imaginative deployment of Bourdieu's work on the critique of music, see Carl Wilson's contribution to the 33 1/3 series, *Celine Dion's Let's Talk about Love: A Journey to the End of Taste* (New York: Continuum, 2007). Wilson is particularly interested in the processes by which we attach meaning to music.
15. Marc Connelly and William Keighley, dir., *The Green Pastures* (Warner Bros., 1936).
16. *A Study in Frustration: The Fletcher Henderson Story* is a 4-LP compilation of studio recordings by the Fletcher Henderson Orchestra from 1923 to 1938 (Columbia CXK 85470, 1961).
17. On the near collapse of the record industry and the rise of radio in the 1930s, see https://medium.com/@Vinylmint/history-of-the-record-industry-1920-1950s-6d491d7cb606
18. Brian Zimmerman, "Song of the Day," *Jazziz*, February 12, 2020: www.jazziz.com/song-of-the-day-bing-crosby-with-the-duke-ellington-orchestra-st-louis-blues/

19 Steven Lasker, Liner notes, *The Complete 1932–1940 Brunswick, Columbia and Master Recordings of Duke Ellington and His Famous Orchestra* (Mosaic Records MD11-248, 2010). For these details about the mysterious Ray Mitchell, I am indebted to David Palmquist, editor of *Ellington on the Web*: http://tdwaw.ellingtonweb.ca/TDWAW.html#Yr1932.
20 "Jolly," "Harlem Show and Duke at Howard," *The Pittsburgh Courier*, December 10, 1932, 11.
21 Duke Ellington and His Famous Orchestra, "Stars" (Brunswick A-9331, 1932). The title as given on the record is simply, "Stars," and the writing credit as "Parker." The legal title for the song is "The Moon, the Stars, and You" (Travis R. Parker, 1933) and the authors are Travis Parker and Lou Gold. A note from *The Duke Ellington Society of Sweden* usefully reminds us that there was once serious tension between jazzers and crooners. Bo Haufman quotes Eddie Lambert's contemporaneous review of Ray Mitchell's recording with Duke: "An inane popular song called 'Stars,' recorded for Brunswick with guest vocalist Ray Mitchell, is among the more forgettable segments of this year's output. 'Stars' does at least have the distinction of marking the end of the policy of using guest vocalists – usually of an abysmal quality – for the band's popular recordings, and Mitchell rounds off the series in an entirely appropriate fashion." Besides Lambert's obvious prejudice against crooners, I am struck by his perception of "a policy of using guest vocalists": the singers in this period of Duke's work were not simply "guests" – they were programmatically white. See https://ellington.se/wp-content/uploads/2021/01/Bulle-19-4.pdf
22 Ethel Waters, "The Hottentot Potentate" (Liberty Music Shop L-188, 1935); words and music by Howard Dietz and Arthur Schwartz.
23 Duke Ellington and His Orchestra, "Rude Interlude," Rec. September 26, 1933 (Victor 24431, 1933); Duke Ellington and His Orchestra, "Dear Old Southland," Rec. December 4, 1933 (Victor 24501, 1934); Rex Stewart and His Orchestra, "I'll Come Back for More," Rec. March 20, 1939 (Vocalion 5448, 1940). The latter record credits Ellington as composer but does not credit him on piano.
24 Billy Eckstine, "Everything I Have Is Yours" (MGM Records 10259, 1948).
25 Marl Young's String Ensemble, "The Songs You Sing/Always To-Gether" (Sunbeam S-108, 1947).
26 Earl ("Fatha") Hines and Orchestra, *Midnight in New Orleans* (MGM Records 10329, 1949).
27 Dizzy Gillespie, with Al Fraser, *To Be or Not to Bop* (New York: Da Capo, 1979), 486.
28 Quoted in Frank Kofsky, *Black Nationalism and the Revolution in Jazz* (New York: Pathfinder Press, 1970), 237.
29 Alfred Bennett Spellman, Liner Notes, *John Coltrane and Johnny Hartman*, 1963 (Impulse GRD 157, 1995). Available online at http://albumlinernotes.com/Coltrane_And_Hartman.html
30 Angela Y. Davis, *Blues Legacies and Black Feminism* (New York: Pantheon, 1998), 192.

31 Phil Ochs, Liner Notes, *Pleasures of the Harbor* (A&M 133, 1967).
32 Viktor Shklovsky, "Art as Technique" (1917), available in English translation at https://paradise.caltech.edu/ist4/lectures/Viktor_Sklovski_Art_as_Technique.pdf
33 Akkerman, *The Last Balladeer*, 124–25.
34 Ibid., 124.
35 Ibid., 125.
36 Ibid., 123.
37 Ibid.
38 Ben Rosen, private message, August 5, 2022. Rosen also notes that on this track Coltrane gives the solo to Tyner, keeping his own presence minimal. In writing this essay I owe special thanks to others as well. It was Deirdre Manion Coyle who successfully tracked down the few notices about the mysterious Ray Mitchell. And to Kara Rusch, aka Slim of Cadence Records, I owe thanks for her careful readings of successive drafts and for her many challenges to untested theories. Finally, as readers have doubtless noticed, I am deeply indebted to Tom Lord's *A Jazz Discography*, www.lordisco.com/.
39 Akkerman, *The Last Balladeer*, 115.

CHAPTER 8

Free Jazz, Critical Performativity, and 1968
Michael Hrebeniak

> Many of us would say that [the occupation of Columbia] was a turning point in our own politicization, if not radicalization. I got drafted, deserted, was on the run for 30 days, and they put me in the stockade for 30 days. As soon as I got out I was on the run again for three years, one month, and five days, and wanted by the F.B.I. I went to San Francisco and started a very radical avant-garde African jazz group called Juju.[1]
>
> James 'Plunky' Branch, *Columbia University student and saxophonist*

On April 23, 1968, hundreds of Columbia University students, mostly allied to the Students for a Democratic Society and Students' Afro-American Society, took direct action against their university's collusion with racist and militaristic policies by barricading themselves inside five campus buildings. Two demands were issued: Columbia must end construction of a symbolically segregated gymnasium in the nearby Black neighbourhood of Morningside Park ("Gym Crow Must Go!") and disaffiliate with the Institute for Defense Analyses, which conducted weapons research for deployment in Vietnam.

The occupation featured a typically heterogeneous ensemble of the disaffected: polemical and earnest, leaderless but gathered around a common purpose. A collection of testimonies, *A Time to Stir: Columbia '68*, published as a fifty-year commemoration of the rebellion, gives an insight into the protagonists' exhilaration as the boundaries of permitted behavior are rendered porous. The suddenly available practices of freedom – joyous, sensual, ludic – demand concomitant responsibility, as we witness the negotiations of power among alert participants who must improvise decisions at speed. The negation of a psychic economy of alienation and sacrifice seems achievable, albeit temporarily.

Not since the 1964–65 Berkeley Free Speech Movement had a major university campus been shut down by its students. The 1968 uprisings had started in February when a civil rights demonstration at South Carolina State University turned deadly with the massacre of three Black students by state troopers. Whereas in March students at Howard University in Washington, DC staged a four-day sit-in, Harlem had blown on the night of Martin Luther King, Jr.'s assassination on April 4th. Columbia had evicted more than 7,000 Harlem residents from university-controlled properties, 85 percent of whom were African American or Puerto Rican. Three years earlier, Malcolm X had been slaughtered in the Audubon Ballroom forty blocks to the north, a site that would host further confrontation with Columbia officials a quarter of a century later in response to the university's bull-headed plans to flatten the site for a biotech research center.

For Black Americans, the 1960s had long been established as the decade of insurgence. The cry of "Burn, baby, burn!" reverberated across US cities and was echoed in the title of Archie Shepp's 1965 LP, *Fire Music*, as fury at racial injustice catalyzed nationwide protests and a militant shift within Black consciousness movements. In 1961, white supremacists had retaliated to the demand for civil rights by burning Black churches across the South. When a congregation in Birmingham was bombed two years later, leaving four girls dead, John Coltrane, the vanguard improviser of his generation, responded to the atrocity with the somber "Alabama," its hymnal shape derived from the cadences of a speech by King.[2] In publicly demonstrating solidarity with the struggle, Coltrane moved within a continuum extending back to the arrival of the first slaves on American soil, in which "sorrow songs," as named by W. E. B. Du Bois,[3] carried coded messages of resistance. By the time of the Columbia occupation, the need for tactical secrecy was long obsolete. Hamilton Hall, renamed "Malcolm X Hall" by its occupiers, remained "Black only" during the disciplined week-long hold-out under the leadership of SAS, which assumed representation of Harlem's working-class community and the moral center of the uprising. A press conference held on the hall's steps by H. Rap Brown and Stokely Carmichael, the respective current and former leaders of the Student Nonviolent Coordinating Committee (SNCC), declared that this act stood for the entire spectrum of Black self-determination struggles.

The occupation would meet a bloody end at the hands of New York's Tactical Patrol Force, whose teargassing and clubbing of protestors, bystanders, and faculty members alike was indiscriminate and gleeful. This revealed to the students an empirical difference between the theory and militarized practice of constitutional law, as well as the prerogatives of the *New York Times*, which printed a front-page story the next day calling the 700 arrested students barbarians, alongside staged photographs of vandalism in the President's office. But the bust served only to galvanize Columbia's students for a fresh insurrection, with an incendiary effect on colleges across the States. Taking Columbia as a prototype for nonviolent civil disobedience, this was a formidable and transformative popular revolt that would swarm across the world and, in some cases, spur general strikes to serve as a potent rejoinder to the business civilization and its supporting military dictatorships.

In *The Action Image of Society: On Cultural Politicization*, the Swiss sociologist Alfred Willener appraised the Spring 1968 revolutions across the United States and Europe through a dialectic across the binaries of "action" and "theory." Using the empirical apparatus of questionnaires, polls, and colloquia, he interviewed scores of student activists and professorial spectators during what he called the "socially hallucinatory period."[4] His thesis, shared with Henri Lefebvre, was that these "intersectional" insurgencies transcended the vocabulary and conceptual framework of political science to comprise "a crisis in Marxist thought and perhaps even a break with Marxism."[5]

The observations and aspirations voiced by his participants led to a series of unquantifiable, nonpositivist conclusions. What Willener observed as the "demands and denunciations" of May vaulted economics and expressed "the desire for joy," the emancipation from "boredom" perceived as oppression, and a preoccupation with features of "ruins, crumbling and fragmentation" characteristic of Dada and Surrealism.[6] Willener cited ubiquitous messages of street graffiti – "art & culture is dead;" "Let us create our daily lives" – and noted an aperture to possible socialities afforded by experimentation across avant-gardes that, with the exception of Jean-Luc Godard's films, were expressly American in origin.[7]

His purview was the New York performance scene defined by composer John Cage and choreographer Merce Cunningham; the Happenings of Jackson MacLow built upon *Performance Piece No. 1* staged at Black Mountain College in 1952; the embodied feminist praxis of Carolee Schneeman and Laurie Anderson; the canvases of Robert Rauschenberg and Jasper Johns; Judith Malina and Julian Beck's Living Theater; and, most significantly of all, the atonal forms of ensemble improvisation pioneered by a new generation of African American jazz musicians across the burgeoning New York loft scene, all of which dramatized social and psychic experience and illuminated the liberatory prerogatives of the immediate present. Willener spoke of a shared emphasis on "process" that united free jazz musicians, poets, artists, and political dissenters, each expressing "a revolutionary desire for social emancipation ... the emancipation of the non-formal ... the desire to avoid being confined within a particular school, within existing rhythmic patterns."[8] "Either we are at the antipodes of politics," he claimed, "or it is a new way of seeing politics."[9]

Homologous traits included alternative perceptions of space and time in social practices; new constitutions of subjectivity in relation to power; the bridging of internal and external ecologies; the downgrading of dialectical procedures in considerations of agency; and a release from the obligations of linear narrative and mimesis, where the realization of meaning, through either emotional absorption or psychological identification, was actively deprived. Willener's "Action-Image" was instead rooted in the engagement with chance operations, discontinuities, rhizomes, nonhierarchical collaborative groupings and the practices of everyday life. In each instance, the performance of text, sound, body, or paint might work free of any representational function as an object of knowledge, to be experienced instead in its materiality, alterity, and exteriority.

This milieu had its roots in a series of aesthetic developments that sought to emulate jazz practices across the American arts in the postwar decades. The commitment to improvisation within a symbolic economy of desire lay at the core of Beat Generation writing: of Jack Kerouac's "spontaneous prose" and of Allen Ginsberg's insistence (paraphrasing Blake) on "first thought best thought."[10] Kerouac's work was styled around the emulation of bop's leading practitioners and steeped in the music's esoteric and ritualistic character. In his 1950 essay, "Projective Verse," Charles Olson reiterated Kerouac's concern with a transferable gestalt of extemporization by speaking of "COMPOSITION BY FIELD" determined by content alone, "as opposed to inherited line, stanza, over all form: the closed form of poem."[11] In 1947, Olson had been appointed Rector of Black Mountain College, an institution founded by John Andrew Rice in 1933 to foster interdisciplinary collaborative community, and oriented towards a Bauhaus ethos exemplified by Annie and Josef Albers. With Olson's election it took on a new direction, coalescing an extraordinary group of American artists and teachers, including Cage and Cunningham, writers M. C. Richards, Robert Creeley, and Robert Duncan, painters Willem de Kooning, Franz Kline, and Jacob Lawrence, drama theorist, Eric Bentley, and the theoretician of comprehensive anticipatory design science, Richard Buckminster Fuller.

The arts of Black Mountain circled around no exhaustive definition, but all shared a sense of the Aristotelean reach of *poetics* across forms alongside Olson's idea of the "projective" – from the Latin, *proicere*, "throw forth" – with its emphasis on action, indeterminacy, and mobility. Such qualities were less typically associated with literary composition than with the ensemble activity of bebop, the results of which crystallize through the impromptu binding of apparently unrelated shards at bewildering speed. But in Olson's ambit the poet was immersed in a process of becoming and regarded as a maker, recovering the etymological origins of *poein*. The poem was its own subject or being rather than a vehicle for a higher message. Energies emerged and were shaped within the work to accomplish its design. Across life and art, "ONE PERCEPTION MUST IMMEDIATELY AND DIRECTLY LEAD TO A FURTHER PERCEPTION," demanded Olson:

> It means exactly what it says, is a matter of, at all points (even, I should say, of our management of daily reality as of the daily work) get on with it, keep moving, keep in, speed, the nerves, their speed, the perceptions, theirs, the acts, the split second acts, the whole business, keep it moving as fast as you can, citizen. And if you also set up as a poet, USE USE USE the process at all points, in any given poem always, always one perception must must must MOVE, INSTANTER, ON ANOTHER![12]

As Creeley affirmed, a poem's "structure [is] possessed of its own organisation [which] in turn derives from the circumstances of its making."[13] The upshot was an act of transformation of self, of sociality, of history. Such a stance converged with the work of contemporary New York painters blazing a similar trail. In 1948, Jackson Pollock placed his canvas on the floor and abandoned the traditional means of applying paint in a celebration of art as performance. His previous practice of incarnating forms within sign systems was now displaced by marks or gestures, corresponding to no external prior reference, either symbolic or representational. Pollock spoke of being "in the painting," which had "a life of its own."[14] The result would be the most striking innovations in pictorial space since Picasso and Braque. As Harold Rosenberg, who coined the term "Action Painting," explained:

> At a certain moment the canvas began to appear to one American painter after another as an arena in which to act – rather than as a space in which to reproduce, re-design, analyze, or "express" an object, actual or imagined. What was to go on the canvas was not a picture but an event. The painter no longer approached his easel with an image in his mind; he went up to it with material in his hand to do something to that other piece of material in front of him. The image would be the result of this encounter.[15]

The commonalities with jazz, a music realized instantaneously that owes its expressive power to contingency, are clear. In his essay, "Hunting Is

Not Those Heads on the Wall," Amiri Baraka contended that the burnished rehearsal of a previous improviser's technique carried no inventive potency, regardless of the prototype's revolutionary impact. "A saxophonist who continues to 'play like' Charlie Parker," he stressed, "cannot understand that Parker wasn't certain that what happened had to sound like that."[16] This is the imperative that excited artists across forms: a thrilling tension between the freedom of blowing and the imperatives of order; an application of procedures that cannot forecast guaranteed results. The notion of perpetual rehearsal, signified in the name of Charles Mingus's group, the Jazz Workshop, sheds that anguished search for perfectibility in completion with a definitive interpretation rendered neither possible nor desirable. This way of thinking about the creative act – which is avowedly more than just reheated romanticism – would have a constellational effect. Whereas Creeley told Olson that he was "more influenced by Charley [sic] Parker, in my acts, than by any other man, living or dead … Bird makes Ez look like a school-boy, in point of rhythms,"[17] jazz, in turn, articulates the Action/Projective impulse within a collaborative setting. By 1968 its lessons would be discharged on an overtly political plane in a culmination of that decade's unparalleled social and psychic shifts.

And yet, while continuities across these diverse formations can be mapped, and the shared aesthetic-political ruptures characterizing the work of artists like Creeley and Pollock or Baraka and Mingus traced, the profoundly different circumstances of their creative production cannot be overlooked. Jazz might offer a connective tissue between multiple vanguard contexts through its privileging of indeterminacy and capacity for irreverence, but the music cannot be disaggregated from the contemporary material inequalities conferred by race, which also extend to the more stealthy valorizations of canonicity. George E. Lewis argues, for example, that seemingly obvious points of correspondence across racial lines between postwar musical innovators like Parker or John Cage were frequently muted by the perpetuation of Eurocentric codes by white artists and critics alike. Lewis observes that:

> texts documenting the musical products of the American version of the move to incorporate real-time music-making into composition often present this activity as part of "American music since 1945," a construct almost invariably theorized as emanating almost exclusively from a generally venerated stream of European cultural, social, and intellectual history – "the Western tradition."[18]

In such appraisals, a denial of the impact of African American forms on the work of European and Euro-American composers is commonly asserted.[19] Cage himself could be dismissive of improvisation in general, and jazz in particular, eroding the potential to assert fertile connections between Black and white avant-garde energies by casting jazz as Western classical music's "epistemological other."[20] On the other side of this racial divide, Eric Porter notes how Charles Mingus "recognized that categories such as 'jazz' and 'classical' were constructs informed by racialized ideas about virtuosity and genius that, in turn, contributed to inequality in the music business."[21] Any consideration of the history of race in the United States would necessarily indicate that not all vanguard propositions were understood in their moment on equal terms.

In 1959 the Texan saxophonist Ornette Coleman opened to an eruption of controversy at the Five Spot in New York's East Village with a white plastic alto and a new principle: "the pattern for the tune will be forgotten, and the tune itself will be the pattern, and won't have to be forced into conventional patterns."[22] Relinquishing standard song-forms and piano harmonies, Coleman proceeded to dismantle boundaries for individual and collective extemporization, courting surprise and re-evaluating "a musical syntax which although derived from Charlie Parker was a copy of no one."[23] Gunther Schuller, an early supporter, identified the "complete freedom" of his conception, while noting the evolution of his materials from bop:

> His musical inspiration operates in a world uncluttered by conventional bar lines, conventional chord changes, and conventional ways of blowing or fingering a saxophone. Such practical 'limitations' did not even have to be overcome in his music; they somehow never existed for him. Despite this – or more accurately, *because* of this – his playing has a deep inner logic. Not an obvious surface logic, it is based on subtleties of reaction, subtleties of timing and color that are, I think, quite new to jazz.[24]

Reflecting the practice of his working quartets featuring trumpeter Don Cherry, bassist Charlie Haden, and either Ed Blackwell or Billy Higgins on drums, the 1959 studio dates *Tomorrow Is the Question* and *The Shape of Jazz to Come* advocate atonal self-regulation without the limitation of a strict pulse. Coleman's disposal of regimented chorus and chordal mass, sources of prescriptive reference that direct soloists into running acrobatically through a harmonic maze, serve only to enhance communication. "Music is for our feelings," asserted the saxophonist. "I think jazz should try to express more kinds of feeling than it has up to now."[25] Moving beyond the contemporary modal innovations of Gil Evans, Miles Davis, and John Coltrane, Coleman assigns an absolute plasticity to jazz that disregards questions of idiomatic category. "My melodic approach is based on phrasing," he maintained:

and my phrasing is an extension of how I hear the intervals and pitch of the tune I play. There is no end to pitch. You can play flat in tune and sharp in tune. It's a question of vibration. My phrasing is spontaneous, not a style. A style happens when your phrasing hardens. Jazz is the only music in which the same note can be played night after night but differently each time. It's the hidden things, the subconscious that lies in your body and lets you know: you feel this, you play this.[26]

Dispensing with the abstracting of melody, harmony, and rhythm into exclusive elements, Coleman implicitly applied Buckminster Fuller's concept of "Synergy" in design, "which means the behavior of whole systems unpredicted by the behavior of any of its parts taken separately, requir[ing] the reversal of our present system of compartmentalization of knowledge and of going from the particular toward the ever more special."[27] As Julian Cowley observed, such a correlation was more than coincidence. The altoist expressed profound admiration for Fuller, attending lectures through the 1960s and 1970s, and dedicating several compositions to him. Coleman's idiosyncratic "Harmolodic" system, which "eliminate[s] styles and past categories" and "allows a person to use a multiplicity of elements to express more than one direction at one time,"[28] suggests a musical translation of Fuller's vision of the global ordering of utilities – a realization of techno-anarchistic society that maximizes individual freedom by discarding patterns of private ownership adjusted to specialization.[29] In his essay, "The Music of the New Life," Fuller argued that "in the world of music and in the world of art, human beings have attained much spontaneous and realistic coordination,"[30] his point being that the benign, liberatory potential of technology may be realized only after the collective adoption of new modes of understanding and behavior, to which musicians are most closely attuned.[31] Casting the uniformity of parts into disarray through open-ended heterophony, Coleman's explosive approach put Fuller's theories to an aesthetic test.

Whereas his 1959 LPs revealed fewer signs of traditional organization, Coleman assumed unprecedented risk the following year with his double-quartet recording, *Free Jazz*. Answering Cage's call for jazz musicians to quit the reiteration of singular measures and apply the lessons of Charles Ives's Fourth Symphony, where "everything is happening at the same time,"[32] the improvisers of *Free Jazz* connect to an equilibrium of different lines without obligation to take their place within or in opposition to ascendant group meters. Coleman likened this orchestration process to that of Jackson Pollock's painting: in a tidy symmetry the painter gave the title *Free Form* to one of his 1946 works, while Coleman and Atlantic

Free Jazz, Critical Performativity, and 1968   135

Records reproduced his *White Light* (1952) on the LP's gatefold sleeve. With permutations shifting and sliding in response to ever-new situations, the variety of ensemble exchanges stands as an analogue of the "all-over" design of Pollock's canvases, as noncadential disjunctions counteract the linear unfolding of sound and subsume the Western emphases on peaks and troughs, centers and margins. Moods alternate erratically between austere experiment and facetious parody. Riffs and quotes drawn from gospel, blues, swing, and contemporary composition are re-mediated on a collage footing, converging at a volatile juncture of carnivalesque declassification. The juxtapositional impulse would be given an increasingly thematic emphasis in the new jazz, recalling the Dada treatment of trace elements and exacerbated in the collision of swing, showmanship, atonality, astrology, Egyptian mythological tract, and electronics deployed by Sun Ra's Arkestra.

Indeed, broader jazz-parallels can be drawn to the 1916 example set by Arp, Ball, Janco, and Tzara at the Cabaret Voltaire of countering World War I propaganda by dismantling received codes, engaging in free play with existing signs and creating new ones without anterior meaning: a means of revealing the ideological basis of prevailing reasoning and resisting the bourgeois spectacle of collective homicide.[33] In *The Freedom Principle*, John Litweiler remarks upon the "Dada atmosphere" of a 1967 gig by the Roscoe Mitchell Quartet,[34] whose members maintained links with Ra's organization through the Association for the Advancement of Creative Musicians. A further offshoot, the Art Ensemble of Chicago, echoed the Arkestra in performances that resembled a sermon, drama, and stand-up comedy routine all at once. With its tribal makeup and idiosyncratic couture, the Ensemble generated a rolling slide-show of aural and visual images – forests seething with life, village fiestas, traffic jams, arguments, stampedes – built upon references from every jazz era. Having worked in St. Louis carnival ensembles as well as blues and bop bands, trumpeter Lester Bowie was a central contributor to both the AEC and Mitchell's Quartet. His exuberant amalgams of the incongruous recalled the freedom claimed for the novel in Ishmael Reed's *Yellow Back Radio Broke-Down*, a book whose hero is called "crazy dada nigger" by a social realist commentator.[35]

In the same vein, Amiri Baraka, author of "Black Dada Nihilismus" – a poem built upon the distanced ventriloquism of overdetermined voicings of racial and sexual violence ascribed to Black males – branded the rhythm and blues "barwalkin'" saxophonist, Big Jay McNeely "the first Dada coon of the age" in his short story "The Screamers." Lying on his back and producing an animalistic wail through his horn, he is compared to Marcel Duchamp's "L.H.O.O.Q." – "the Mona Lisa with the moustache."[36] And in *Down and In*, Sukenick referred to a party thrown by poet-trumpeter Ted Joans and attended by Charlie Parker, "dedicated to Surrealism, Dada, and the Mau."[37] Designated "the only Afro-American surrealist" by Andre Breton, Joans advocates in his 1970 volume *Afrodisia* a weave of Black Nationalism, jazz, and outmoded carnality.[38] A related ambience informed the description of a street fight in Chester Himes's novel *A Rage in Harlem* where slash-wounds yield not blood, but "old clothes" and "dried printer's ink from the layers of old newspapers."[39] "I thought I was writing realism," Himes declared. "It never occurred to me that I was writing absurdity. Realism and absurdity are so similar in the lives of American blacks that one cannot tell the difference."[40] Indeed, the political implications of what Baraka named "Afro-Surrealism" are crucial here. Developing the term out of his reading of Henry Dumas's writing, Baraka argues that Afro-Surrealism's "broken quality" – that is, its departure from conventional modes of representation – is "a function of change and transition."[41] Or as Robin D. G. Kelley adds in *Freedom Dreams*, "Contrary to popular belief, surrealism is not an aesthetic doctrine but an international revolutionary movement concerned with the emancipation of thought."[42]

The satirical clout of the absurd and gratuitous and the distortion of semantic reference here implicitly function as critiques of the available models of Black representation in mass America. In the instance of jazz prior to the mid-1960s, such attacks were often necessarily oblique, the explicit references to slavery, the Sharpeville Massacre, and Greensboro lunch counter protests in Max Roach's *We Insist! Freedom Now Suite* (1960);[43] Charles Mingus's excoriating response to the summoning of the National Guard by the Governor of Arkansas to prevent the racial integration of Little Rock High School in "Fables of Faubus";[44] and Archie Shepp's elegy for Malcolm X, "*Malcolm, Malcolm, Semper Malcolm*"[45] standing as fairly exceptional within the era. But if ideology is taken as the total sum of semiotic activity within a culture, the nihilistic gesture might equally qualify as a tactical resistance of the condition of alterity assigned to African Americans. This extends from innumerable ballad readings by Charlie Parker that feature a bathetic ripping of Grainger's *English Country Garden* as a four-bar coda, to Shepp's sarcastic anti-rendering of "The Girl from Ipanema" (*Fire Music*, 1965). Such performances have little to do with traditional rhetorical patterns, but serve to enforce duplicity and disjunction in the face of white audience demands for gratification. The recourse to Dada that Willener recognized within the 1968 uprisings herein takes on a dialectical role in relation to normative social codes. From a cultural space of absence, Black subjectivities might potentialize through forms of critical performativity that render elusive any conception of authenticity through mimesis.

Coleman was alive to the political implications of retreat from patterns of "re-cognition," and as Willener notes, the saxophonist's "improvisation takes place entirely in melodic action" with "no obligation to keep or depart from a prior reference." The jazz performer's self-pluralization, achieved through quoting from a glossary of styles recalling the musical personalities of predecessors, leads to the "redefining of known elements, elements that have just been played and experienced, while inventing new elements in the course of the activity itself."[46] In *Free Jazz* the altoist encourages his fellow musicians to abandon given orders of representation and, instead, "relate to the emotion, the pitch, the rhythm, the melody of a theme without relating to chords or bar divisions."[47] The constraints of standard roles – soloist, accompanist, timekeeper – yield to a model of fluid interchange that Willener termed "the dialectical synthesis created by a group or individual."[48] In line with Bruno Latour's analysis of the scientific laboratory as a site of distributed labour and knowledge production, such a performance involves equally complex and intricate overlapping agencies, while also maintaining particular hierarchies of responsibility and authorship.[49] *Free Jazz*, however, arguably dramatizes a more sophisticated series of dialectical micro-shifts within the alignments of autonomy, which might stand as a metaphorical critique of power relations in a society that customarily subjugates active community to the demands of routinization, specialization, and spectatorism. The band's collective improvisation initiates ways of music-making that recover the possibilities of collaborative, nonalienated labor in the face of an industrial technocracy marked by speed, efficiency, and surveillance. Permutations shift in response to ever-new situations, resisting the architecture of fixed system to suggest a non-teleological set of effects or eternal middle, with sonic propositions begun without knowledge of their ending. As Baraka suggested, with reference to the noncadential contributions of trumpeter Don Cherry, "the completion of one statement simply reintroduces the possibility of more."[50]

The listener, too, is inducted into a state of emergence as the breach between the performer and audience dissolves within a depersonalizing field. The experience is marked by a proliferation of excess: discontinuous and querulous; disordered and perilous. This is reflected in the titles of many 1960s LPs – Eric Dolphy's *Out to Lunch* and *Out There*, Jackie McLean's *Destination Out*, Freddie Hubbard's *Breaking Point* – which convey a Dionysian vertigo, bridging aesthetic, psychological, and political terrains. Superficially, this recalls the ceremonial ecstasy of West African spirit possession but this is not a return to ritual, which is a conservative technology for the reproduction of social orders positioned as inevitable, universal, and unchanging. Such recordings render us constantly aware of the mechanics of performance through their frustrations of expectancy, leaving a form of communication described by Jacques Attali as "use and exchange-time as lived and no longer stockpiled."[51] This is a music "drawn towards an unknown praxis," to cite Roland Barthes,[52] one situated outside the given criteria for the production and reception of sound that can be defined as "operationality, spectacle, accumulation or value."[53] *Free Jazz* vigorously extricates itself from these codes of sacrifice, representation, and repletion to emerge as activity in itself. Reflecting the militant mood of Black America, Coleman's band repudiates the consumption ethic of the mainstream jazz scene to symbolize the improviser's refusal of constraint, imposed by what Attali defines as:

> a concern for maintaining tonalism, the primacy of melody, a distrust of new languages, codes or instruments, a refusal of the abnormal – those characteristics common to all totalitarian regimes.[54]

The de facto censorship of jazz throughout the twentieth century indeed testifies to the affront suffered by the authoritarian sense of order when confronted by the example of a flexible collaboration of individuals reworking materials drawn from diverse cultures and ignoring distinctions between popular and learned, European and Black.[55] Goebbels had generated performance instructions in Nazi Germany restricting syncopated rhythms to a maximum of eight bars and forbidding the pitching of saxophones in higher registers and trumpets with mutes, lest they reduce their "noble" sound to a "Jewish-Freemasonic yowl."[56] Lord Reith, the first chairman of the BBC, was delighted by this and lamented in his diary that Britain "should be behind in dealing with this filthy product of modernity."[57] Soviet propaganda of the early 1950s used similar tactics to demonize American culture, identifying the playing of saxophones with murder and treason, and an allegiance to jazz over the next three decades continued to qualify as a resistance gesture. In September 1986, five Czechoslovakian free improvisers were indicted in Prague on trumped-up charges of engaging in "unauthorised business enterprises," and subsequently imprisoned.[58] As Theodor Adorno, whose grasp of jazz was less than enlightened, argued:

> In music, too, one should ask why men, as soon as they are free, get the feeling that *things must be put into good order*.... They imagine that order must

be imposed on freedom from the outside, that it must be restrained rather than allowed to organise itself, without obeying any heteronome criterion, which would mutilate the demands to develop itself freely.[59]

The prodigious levels of invention underscoring the jazz continuum testify to the fact that improvisation is not merely ad hoc performance in lieu of preconceived design, but a way of potentializing countermodels, both aesthetic and social, at a point where forms remain provisional.[60] It embodies Deleuze's location of form at a "plane of immanence ... within a given multiplicity: where unifications, subjectifications, rationalizations, centralizations have no special status; and where we witness the extension and unfolding of its lines, the production of something new."[61] The music's projective impetus necessarily remains foreign to the category of completion, being neither digestible, transcendent, nor productive in terms of its use value. The result, in Willener's words, "exteriorize[s] a whole potential of energy, since expression in sound is no longer inhibited by any taboos."[62] The 1968 insurgency moves within this performance episteme: a cultural imagination of synthesis anchored in the "emancipation of the non-formal," and an "immediate exteriorisation of life ... from structure to action."[63]

The historical determinism of the Third International thus gives way to the consideration of improvisation as a means of testing and scrambling social practices and regulations inscribed as normative, and complicating the relations between intention and expression. In Michael McClure's view, the collective experience of the protests shattered the resistance of local bureaucratic power and assigned "a challenge that allows new openings for glandular, organic, hormonic, intellective energies," a surge against "biological ignominy," and the beginning not only of "the long march through the institutions" – in Rudi Dutschke's phrase – but of "a new relation with nature."[64]

Under such circumstances, the "role of the organization" is diminished – or perhaps elevated – to "that of the interpreter of spontaneity," writes Willener by way of a conclusion,[65] reflecting the aegis of the *Congress on the Dialectics of Liberation* ("to demystify human violence in all its forms, and the social systems from which it emanates, and to explore new forms of action")[66] held in Camden's Roundhouse in 1967, and preempting the shock encounter of the New York avant-garde and French philosophy at the *Schizo-Culture* colloquium at Columbia in 1975. Thinking expressly through jazz, performativity becomes the subject of study *and* its means. This is not to rejuvenate the economy of the spectacle, but to realign what Pierre Bourdieu called the "durably installed generative principle of regulated improvisations" that define the "habitus" – his term for the matrix of practices and representations that socially "appear as realised myth."[67] "We were all living together, and we called it a commune," recalled Hilton Obenzinger of the Columbia occupation. "The spirit was of cooperation; everyone had to make decisions together; everyone had to speak; everyone had to act as a group."[68]

The imperative is to forge new paradigms "ethico-aesthetic in inspiration," to quote Felix Guattari, wherein "the reconquest of a degree of creative autonomy in one particular domain encourages conquests in other domains – the catalyst for a gradual reforging and renewal of humanity's confidence in itself starting at the most miniscule level."[69] The euphoric example of free jazz – as metaphor, as enactment – is salutary. In their own practice of collective improvisation, the participants in the 1968 uprisings across the United States and Europe "rediscovered procedures that had been practised at earlier times and in other places";[70] putting them on the edge of becoming otherwise; threatening the stability of body-mind's habitual patterns and coding; and producing vital new modes of sociability and encounter without the impediments of hierarchy or classification.

Notes

1 Quoted in Paul Cronin, ed., *A Time to Stir: Columbia '68* (New York: Columbia University Press, 2018), 32.
2 John Coltrane, "Alabama," *Live at Birdland* (Impulse A-50, 1964).
3 W. E. B. Du Bois, *The Souls of Black Folk*, 1903 (Oxford: Oxford University Press, 2007), 167–69.
4 Alfred Willener, *The Action-Image of Society*, trans. A. M. Sheridan-Smith (London: Tavistock, 1970), 32.
5 Ibid., 77.
6 Ibid., 196.
7 Ibid., 216.
8 Ibid.
9 Ibid., 83.
10 Michael Hrebeniak, *Action Writing: Jack Kerouac's Wild Form* (Carbondale: Southern Illinois University Press, 2006), 181–83.
11 Charles Olson, "Projective Verse," *Selected Writings* (New York: New Directions, 1966), 16.
12 Ibid., 17.
13 Robert Creeley, "Introduction," Charles Olson, *Selected Writings* (New York: New Directions, 1966), 7.
14 Jackson Pollock, "My Painting," *Possibilities*, No. 1, Winter 1947–48, 79.
15 Harold Rosenberg, *The Tradition of the New* (New York: Horizon, 1960), 25.
16 Amiri Baraka, "Hunting Is Not Those Heads on the Wall," 1964, in Donald Allen and Warren Tallman, eds., *Poetics of the New American Poetry* (New York: Grove, 1973), 380.

17 Charles Olson and Robert Creeley, *The Complete Correspondence, Volume IV*, ed. George Butterick (Santa Barbara: Black Sparrow, 1980), 157.
18 George E. Lewis, "Improvised Music after 1950: Afrological and Eurological Perspectives," *Black Music Research Journal* 16.1 (1996), 92.
19 Ibid.
20 Ibid., 103.
21 Eric Porter, *What Is This Thing Called Jazz?: African American Musicians as Artists, Critics, and Activists* (Berkeley: University of California Press, 2002), 107.
22 Ornette Coleman, Liner notes, *The Shape of Jazz to Come* (Atlantic SD-1317, 1959).
23 A.B. Spellman, *Four Lives in the Bebop Business*, 1966 (New York: Limelight, 1985), 79.
24 Gunther Schuller, Liner notes, Ornette Coleman, *The Shape of Jazz to Come* (Atlantic SD-1317, 1959).
25 Coleman, Liner notes, *Shape*.
26 Quoted in Wilfred Mellers, *Music in a New Found Land: Themes and Developments in the History of American Music*, 1965 (London: Faber, 1987), 346.
27 Richard Buckminster Fuller, *Earth Inc.* (New York: Doubleday/Anchor, 1973), 176.
28 Ornette Coleman, "Harmolodic = Highest Instinct: Something to Think About," in Paul Buhle, et al., eds., *Free Spirits: Annals of the Insurgent Imagination* (San Francisco: City Lights, 1982), 120, 119.
29 Julian Cowley, "The Art of the Improvisers: Jazz and Fiction in Post-Bebop America," *New Comparison*, 6 (1988), 195.
30 Richard Buckminster Fuller, *Utopia or Oblivion: The Prospects for Humanity* (New York: Bantam, 1969), 95.
31 Cowley, "The Art of the Improvisers," 196–97.
32 Michael Zwerin, "A Lethal Measurement," 1966, in Richard Kostelanetz, ed., *John Cage: An Anthology* (New York: Da Capo, 1991), 163.
33 Cowley, "The Art of the Improvisers," 198.
34 John Litweiler, *The Freedom Principle: Jazz after 1958* (New York: Morrow, 1984), 177.
35 Ishmael Reed, *Yellow Back Radio Broke Down* (New York: Doubleday, 1969), 35.
36 Amiri Baraka, "The Screamers," 1967, in William J. Harris, ed., *The LeRoi Jones/Amiri Baraka Reader* (New York: Thunder's Mouth, 1999), 175.
37 Ronald Sukenick, *Down and In: Life in the Underground* (New York: Beech Tree, 1987), 50.
38 Ted Joans, *Afrodisia* (New York: Hill & Wang, 1970).
39 Chester Himes, *A Rage in Harlem, 1957* (London: Penguin, 2011), 60–61.
40 Qtd. in James Campbell, *Paris Interzone* (London: Secker and Warburg, 1994), 122.
41 Amiri Baraka, "Henry Dumas: Afro-Surreal Expressionist," *Black American Literature Forum* 22.2 (1982), 165.
42 Robin D.G. Kelley, *Freedom Dreams: The Black Radical Imagination* (Boston: Beacon Press, 2002), 5.

43 Max Roach, *We Insist! Max Roach's Freedom Now Suite* (Candid CJM 8002, 1961).
44 Charles Mingus, *Charles Mingus Presents Charles Mingus*, (Candid CJM 8005, 1961).
45 Archie Shepp, *Fire Music* (Impulse AS-86, 1965).
46 Willener, *Action-Image of Society*, 230.
47 Coleman, Liner notes, *Shape*.
48 Willener, *Action-Image of Society*, 238.
49 Bruno Latour and Steve Woolgar, *Laboratory Life: The Construction of Scientific Facts* (Princeton, NJ: Princeton University Press, 1986).
50 Amiri Baraka, *Black Music* (New York: Morrow, 1968), 170.
51 Jacques Attali, *Noise: The Political Economy of Music*, trans. Brian Massumi (Minneapolis: University of Minnesota, 1985), 135.
52 Roland Barthes, *Image-Music-Text*, trans. Stephen Heath (London: Fontana, 1977), 105.
53 Attali, *Noise*, 135.
54 Ibid., 8.
55 Cowley, "The Art of the Improvisers," 197–98.
56 Josef Škvorecký, "Foreword," *The Bass Saxophone*, trans. Kaca Polackova-Henley (London: Picador, 1980), 10.
57 Marista Leishman, *My Father – Reith of the BBC* (Edinburgh: Saint Andrew Press, 2006), 148.
58 Hrebeniak, *Action Writing*, 270.
59 Theodor Adorno, *Night Music: Essays on Music 1928–1962*, trans. Wieland Hoban (Calcutta: Seagull, 2017), 331, original emphasis.
60 Michael Hrebeniak, "Jazz and the Beat Generation," in Steven Belletto, ed., *The Cambridge Companion to the Beat Generation* (Cambridge: Cambridge University Press, 2017), 251–52.
61 Gilles Deleuze, *Negotiations*, trans. Martin Joughin (New York: Columbia University Press, 1995), 145–46.
62 Willener, *Action-Image of Society*, 242.
63 Ibid., 231, 234, 235.
64 Michael McClure, "Wolf Net," *Io*, No. 20 (1974), 166–72.
65 Willener, *Action-Image of Society*, 175.
66 Poster for the International Congress on the Dialectics of Liberation, London, 1967.
67 Pierre Bourdieu, *Outline of a Theory of Practice*, trans. Richard Nice (Cambridge: Cambridge University Press, 1977) 78.
68 Quoted in Cronin, *A Time to Stir*, 124.
69 Felix Guattari, *The Three Ecologies*, trans. Ian Pindar and Paul Sutton, 1989 (London: Continuum, 2007), 69.
70 Willener, *Action-Image of Society*, 230.

PART III
Cultural Contexts

CHAPTER 9

Jazz Slang, Jazz Speak

Amor Kohli

In an 1884 essay, Walt Whitman turned his attention to American slang. Within it, this celebrator of the American vernacular cautions that language "is not an abstract construction of the learned, or of dictionary-makers, but it is something arising out of the work, needs, ties, joys, affections, tastes of long generations of humanity and has its bases broad and low, close to the ground."[1]

Although Whitman's take predates jazz's emergence, his sensitivity to language is attuned – as was his poetry – to the rhythms and patterns of American vernacular life. The slang – also variously known as "jive," "hip speech," and "jazz talk," – from the communities, people, and "broad and low, close to the ground" spaces in which jazz bloomed has substantially permeated American speech. Foremost among its sources is Black vernacular, the influence of which on American speech more broadly cannot be overstated. Words and phrases such as "hip," "cool," (as all-purpose word), "dig," "gig," "split" (to leave), "later" (as salutation), are still widely understood expressions originating in jazz scenes.[2]

While there is a clear analogical relationship between jazz making and verbal conversation, there is also a long, mutual relationship between jazz and the making and remaking of language.[3] A music history characterized by continual stylistic change and innovation is echoed in a corresponding "slanguage." The peculiar way that jazz musicians spoke became a touchstone for the expression and understanding of jazz scenes and subcultures. Among fans, the musicians one followed, the way one dressed, the dances one knew, and the slang one spoke figured into a cultural calculus outlining a comprehensive way of being.

Dizzy Gillespie pithily notes that "bebop language came about because some guy said something and it stuck. Another guy started using it, then another one, and before you knew it, we had a whole language."[4] While Gillespie presents a fairly mundane but accurate understanding of how slang can develop, the wide reach of jazz slang occurred due to a broader

145

and more complex array of factors and arenas. Jazz slang permeates American culture and reflects the experience of Black musicians who created new worlds within language itself. Jazz slang has provided a venue for protesting white supremacy, exploring artistic playfulness, and expressing the energy of improvisation.

Commonly, however, approaches to jazz slang consider it as a rebellious response to the historical oppression of Black people. The role of rebellion in the development of a jazz vernacular has been central to critical discussions since the 1940s. This understanding situates jazz slang as symbolizing – if not actually embodying – a tradition of Black protest, whether protective, assertive, or defiant.

The history of Black expression in the United States is built around the need to develop ways of articulating ideas that cloak their true meanings and avoid the opprobrium of white Americans. This protective, coded language allows for simultaneous expression and concealment of Black desires for freedom or rebellion as a means to freedom. Escape has long been a key expression of protest. This is perhaps most obviously embodied in the Great Migration, during which millions of Black Americans expressed their discontent by leaving the American South for the North, for possibility that had previously been only a whispered aspiration. Examples of this covert speech can be found in the Negro Spirituals, through which Black people could, through analogical coding, collectively express their deeply rooted desires for freedom and deliverance from bondage. Within this schema, for instance, Black Americans were coded as the Biblical Israelites and the Ohio River, which marked passage to the nonslave states, as the River Canaan. Black people not only expressed desire for freedom but also a coded desire for retribution; punishment of enslavers (often "Pharoah" in the spirituals) occupied a notable space in these songs. Slaveholders, desiring pliancy, would harshly punish straightforward Black collective utterances of freedom and retribution but would not necessarily grasp the analogies in spirituals. In fact, such codes were also not innately clear to all Black hearers, and it was necessary to develop an underground system of collective communication in order to initiate listeners into, and subsequently pass down via the group, this coded language of liberation and redress.

There are clearly significant differences between the roles and development of jazz slang and the spirituals, especially regarding the social and political situation of Black Americans by the 1920s, but the parallels are important. The threat of social, economic, and political repression certainly did not disappear as the United States entered the Jazz Age, but slang allowed Black jazz musicians to continue to talk about whites, nightclub officials, and authority figures openly, if not straightforwardly. Slang not only shielded jazz musicians from repression but also helped to protect their creative innovations. The drummer Baby Dobbs explains jazz musicians' wariness of white musicians who would pick up new sounds and techniques from which they, well-meaning or not, could, more easily profit than could Black musicians, given music industry racism: "We used to call white musicians 'alligators'.... That was the way we'd describe them when they'd come around and we were playing something that we didn't want them to catch on to. We'd say 'watch out, there's an alligator!'"[5]

During the mid-1940s, when writers like Earl Conrad suggested that jazz slang serves a protective function because it is created "in self-defense,"[6] the evolution of bebop shifted the language (and music) to a more consciously oppositional stance, reflecting Black Americans' willingness and ability to more forthrightly express political feelings and desires. The political mood in Black areas of the urban North had grown increasingly assertive. Depression-era activism and campaigns such as "Don't Buy Where You Can't Work" and the Double-V Campaign, along with antiracist campaigns in the *Chicago Defender* and other Black press, all contributed to this political mood.

As bebop developed, it was quickly perceived as a protest music, one that Amiri Baraka would, in his epochal book *Blues People*, describe as music that, through its "willfully harsh, *anti-assimilationist* sound,"[7] arguably captures the ideological stance of its creators. Bebop's militant idiom is assertive but more increasingly becomes read as a defiant refusal of the expectations of mainstream American society, a refusal inspiring a generation of young whites, including many writers and artists. As Robert S. Gold argues in his influential *A Jazz Lexicon*, the "totality of his experience in America stamped the Negro with a psychology demanding not only a unique and rebellious music but a unique and rebellious way of speaking."[8] For Gold and other like-minded commentators, Black transformations of standard American English reflected attempts to at once claim English for Black uses and decouple the language from ideas and associations that have historically come at Black people's expense. Thus, this language encompasses a protest against historical oppression and a refusal to work within the accepted bounds of lexical understanding. In this, words are recast with irregular meanings and usage, including semantic inversions, in order to register a protest or complaint against mainstream American society.

Black Americans' transformational practice of English generated vibrant attempts to pull linguistic and musical innovations closer together. It has long been understood that, as the musician and scholar Archie Shepp notes, "Black music has transmitted the seeds of Black experience far more effectively than mere words acquired second hand."[9] Yet, new words and ways of speaking still emerged as musicians applied similar expressive techniques and attitudes to their linguistic play. Gillespie expresses as much, connecting historical linguistic practices to the creative expansiveness in the new music of the 1940s: "As black people, we just naturally spoke this way.... As we played with musical notes, bending them into new and different meanings that constantly changed, we played with words. Say sumpin' hip, Daddio."[10]

Jazz slang's playful innovation has not garnered the same attention as its use as protest, coded or direct. This may reflect an unwillingness to understand creativity as politically effective. Particularly given the sociopolitical stakes of Black American existence, "mere" playful creativity that exists for its own sake and pleasure might be understood as an ill-affordable luxury. Jazz slang indicates the irrepressible desire to create without specific purpose or direction. This creative impulse, even outside of the bounds of accepted lexical, structural, or logical associations, has long been central to Black creative endeavors, including language and music. In his preface to his important handbook of jive, Dan Burley acknowledges the limitations of his writerly, cataloguing project, especially given Black expression's relentlessly innovative drive: "That is why the effort has been put forth to present Jive, both written and spoken, as employed by its actual proponents, even though this form is continually undergoing a process of change, a kind of evaluation in which new words and phrases are tried and old ones are discarded as obsolete."[11] Black music and language inhabit similar performative impulses and what Burley outlines here closely echoes many musicians' descriptions of jazz-making, including Gillespie's comment above. Creativity as "play" – a category that includes tactics such as experimentation, iconoclasm, revision, mockery, floridity, inversion – is a vital, rejuvenating force. Rather than understanding jazz slang as evidence of rejecting civilization or evincing civilization's degradation, we might see slang, actually, as evidence of the creative wellsprings from which civilization develops. Jazz musicians' assertion of lexical freedom may not have been initiated for such lofty goals – they may not, after all, have set out to create a new language – but even creating without motive or direction illustrates a primordial social well as aesthetic force.

The term "jazz" itself, while its etymological history is disputed, is often argued to have originated as slang. The word may have derived from a term used to call for heightened energy or liveliness. Others argue that "jazz" originated from a slang term for ejaculate, which hews to the long-standing association of this music with the seedier parts of life, associations hounding jazz well into its maturation in the twentieth century. Associations of jazz with deviance, immorality, and savagery have dampened over time and have usually, in the United States, been funneled into related moral panics over newer Black musical styles.

While jazz has a long history of primitivist aspersions on the music, reflecting racist ideologies, similar general condemnations have been directed towards slang, considered by some to be a debasement of linguistic purity and propriety. The audaciousness of jazz slang, particularly, has been distorted to promulgate a racist narrative positing Black people as incapable of the mental acuity necessary to "properly" speak English. The sounds and structures of Black music and language have been castigated as the inability (as opposed to unwillingness) of Black people to play or speak "properly," thus providing dubious evidence of Black inferiority.

Some have balked at the use of "slang" to describe these words, reasoning that this label hinders the elevation and evaluation of Black speech as legitimate language. Unfortunately, these efforts often do not adequately account for the power, reach, and nuanced creativity historically central to the development and dissemination of slang. The elevating impulse is understandable and arguably necessary due to the longstanding dismissal of Black expression. By and large, however, longing for respectability is not a hallmark of slang usage. Clarence Major outlines the dilemma in *Juba to Jive*, a dictionary of Black vernacular speech: "Slang has never had a consistently good reputation…. But it also happens to be the most alive aspect of our language. My goal then – at least in part – was to help bring to the language we call slang a better name, a better reputation; and also to suggest, by the example of this dictionary, how intrinsic it is to the quest of human culture to express and to renew itself."[12] Slang is nonstandard by design, and jazz slang speakers – whether musicians or fans – often reveled in that outlandishness as they unknowingly created the American vernacular of the twentieth century.

The linguist Julie Coleman identifies a few major conditions supporting the creation and dissemination of new slang words and phrases. The first, in response to a military emphasis on group conformity and submergence of the individual, is a "heightened desire for self-expression."[13] As Coleman points out, the use of slang words can allow "conscripted servicemen to grumble about food, equipment, and those in authority over them. They also offered the opportunity to use humour to enliven the dull routine of daily life."[14] A second condition is that, in most instances, the speakers of slang usually exist on "the lower rungs of a hierarchy ... [but] slang offers the possibility for minor rebellion that won't usually meet with serious consequences."[15] A third necessary factor is that slang creators must have a sense of a group identity. Those feelings of connection are often codified through an in-group language. That slang often contains words, phrases, and ways of speaking that help to address the fourth condition Coleman lays out: the "oppressed group must have a sense that their situation is unfair or unreasonable, usually because they've experienced greater freedom or hope to in the future."[16] Coleman's criteria clearly reflect the African American social reality. In addition, the conditions dovetail with two significant historical functions of Black speech: protection and protest. That slang's major function is to allow the powerless to comment on the powerful and the oppressive dynamic they reinforce has long been a hallmark of Black speech, and this impulse carries over into jazz speak.

The question of whether Black speech and jazz slang are synonymous or not is a contested one. Even if not identical, the two have often been used interchangeably. However, while African American vernacular is a language, jazz speak is clearly categorizable as slang. Jazz speak includes, for example, the presence of certain kinds of technical, underground, or even illicit talk. The argot of other subcultures, most notably drug subcultures, enter into jazz speak distinct from African American vernacular English. Also, as occasional reference to "Harlemese" indicates, what is today considered jazz speak is an argot that developed in Black urban areas of the United States and grew exponentially during the Great Migration.

Jazz slang – much like the music and people from which it originates – has been feared, derided, mocked, imitated, studied, and finally, absorbed into the fabric of American culture. But how did this slang – meant for a relatively small, insular set – become mainstream?

Its beginnings in jazz circles can be traced to before the 1930s, but the movement of swing music and culture into the American mainstream marked a sharp upsurge of jazz speak in the everyday language of young Americans. Afterwards, jazz speak increasingly developed in American popular culture, continuing into the "jive" speak of the 1940s, the linguistic innovations of Beat Generation writers and "hipsters" in the 1950s, the consciously countercultural movements of the 1960s, and on into the long, contemporaneous hip-hop moment, which has generated its own styles of talk indebted to jazz speak's earlier innovations.

Black vernacular speech more generally, particularly from urban areas of the United States during the Great Migration, has so powerfully affected American speech that it can be difficult to separate one from the other, even if the mainstream often lags behind. Given the nature of slang, by the time the mainstream is hip to the language, its innovators have moved on to new phrases and approaches. Opacity is often desired by slang users who deploy exclusive language to ensure open communication amongst themselves, especially when those they wish to exclude are within earshot. Slang is not merely informal, but "conspicuously divergent."[17] Baraka describes speech as "the way one describes the natural proposition of being alive."[18] Slang, by extension, describes the desired proposition of being consciously and ostentatiously apart.

The appeal of slang's obfuscation was challenged by jazz's increasing visibility. Fans clearly reveled in the humor and inventiveness of jazz speak. Youth, invested in embracing styles and sounds distinguishing them from their parents, were often drawn to the dual gift of exclusivity and adult consternation. While exclusivity has a marketable allure, the idea of access to the exclusive is powerfully exploitable. Jazz, by the 1930s, wielded a notable commercial power and access to jazz speak played a significant role. Even when this commercial power waned later in the twentieth century, young fans drawn to rock'n'roll continued to apply language first created in jazz circles.

Rick McRae notes that by the late 1930s, at the height of swing's popularity, as swing musicians established a broad visibility through highly publicized tours, appearances in motion pictures, and the growth of national radio networks, jazz talk moved past being "seen as an incomprehensible argot spoken only within a small clique on the fringes of society" and instead became "the norm among swing fans throughout the country."[19] The 1930s are also when the scholar Clyde Taylor places "the first developed stage of hipness," as this period marks a convergence of the development of a "hip"-suffused mass media popular culture with the emergence of "the first large generation of Black youths born in urban centers [who] picked up hip speech as part of their normal language acquisition."[20] During this time, hip (often spelled "hep" until the 1940s) speech had become an intrinsic part of the American vernacular.

This period saw an efflorescence of glossaries and articles dedicated to understanding jazz talk. Rendering this language – and by extension, access to an intelligible insiderness – to a broader public was first undertaken by magazine writers and linguistics scholars. Many early investigations into jazz slang appeared in the form of glossaries and word-lists, both in mainstream media outlets such as *Down Beat* and in scholarly journals like *American Speech*. These texts were often both informational and instructional, outlining potential etymologies for jazz speak and explanations for the novice. This lexicographical emphasis obscures the fact that jive originated and mostly existed in spoken form. Gold discusses this broader problem in his dictionary, noting that the "great difficulty in tracing jazz words to their sources stems not only from the dynamic and prolific coinage of the argot, but also from the fact that jazz terms rarely appear in those written records upon which the makers of dictionaries are necessarily so dependent."[21] However, writers of these word-lists often employed unclear or suspect methodologies – stating some version of "I spoke to some jazz musicians I had access to," or its opposite: "such-and-such musician told me he'd never heard of these words." Moreover, given slang's reinforcement of insider/outsider relationships and Black Americans' often self-protective uses of covert language, it is reasonable to question how candid Black musicians in the 1930s would have been when approached by white academics and magazine writers seeking access to their private language. Also, the initiation of a much wider audience into the slang would simultaneously signal to some the need for new slang.

Given the spaces in which jazz developed and the ready willingness of critics and cultural commentators to support visions of jazz as inseparable from a criminal underworld or the decline of Western civilization, these compendia of jazz words and phrases highlight how jazz talk combines "black English with the jargons of gambling, prostitution, larceny, music and dance."[22] By the 1950s, scholars were paying similar attention to a variety of slang terms originating in subcultural groups often the sources of moral panics – homosexuals, college students, criminals, and illicit drug users. The vogue for these sorts of publications – and their impact – can be surmised by the fact that H. L. Mencken, in a 1948 supplement to *The American Language* (1919) included information on "jive" terminology. Pitching this slang as "an amalgam of Negro slang from Harlem and the argots of drug addicts and the pettier sort of criminals, with occasional additions from the Broadway gossip columns and the high-school campus," he adds, in a familiarly problematic vein, that the language got its "start among jazz musicians, many of them Negroes and perhaps more of them addicts."[23] Whether Mencken's including jazz slang is grudging or not, clearly the attention paid to this slang since the 1930s indicates its necessary place in any discussion of "American language." After dismissing as "romantic exaggeration"[24] the developing thesis that jazz slang developed from a tradition of Black linguistic, self-protective coding, Mencken concludes by wrongly forecasting "there is every indication that jive is not long for this life."[25]

Slang was important to the marketing and growth of jazz. As slang relies on exclusivity, the potential for inclusion through unlocking the codes of a Black jazz subculture – to become, in other words, *hip* to the scene – attracted many jazz fans. This was especially true of young white Americans drawn to often stereotypical and shallow ideas of sonic and symbolic freedom which jazz suggested. Understanding the lingo was not only desirable and powerful but vendable, as it coincided with the identification of youth as a social category and market force in the postwar era. Beginning with the inclusion of a glossary in the first published autobiography by a Black jazz musician, Louis Armstrong's 1936 *Swing That Music*, musicians directly played a role in distributing and demystifying jazz speak for a broader reading public.[26]

After Armstrong, musicians often refer to saxophonists Lester Young and Ben Webster as some of the most inventive wielders of jazz slanguage. Cab Calloway, however, first and best capitalized on the allure of jazz slang when he published, in 1938, the first edition of a dictionary of jazz speak, *Cab Calloway's Cat-alogue: A Hepster's Dictionary* (later editions would be titled *Cab Calloway's Hepster's Dictionary: Language of Jive*). Co-written with Calloway publicist Ned Williams, this dictionary would become, by its sixth edition in 1944, the "official" jive reference publication for the New York Public Library, a distinction that Calloway and later commentators would proudly trumpet, putting aside the question of how easily the NYPL's imprimatur sat with hipness. At any rate, Calloway's dictionary was designed to capitalize on his ebullient personality and international fame.[27] The *Dictionary* was included with Calloway sheet music, sold as standalone booklets, and reprinted in the show business weekly *Variety* in June, 1938. The 1944 edition was appended to Calloway's 1976 autobiography.

Although the slang developing in Harlem jazz scenes was central to his 1931 hit, "Minnie the Moocher," Calloway and his management team judiciously omitted drug references (vital to decoding "Minnie") from the *Hepster's Dictionary* and later editions. As Alyn Shipton argues, "there were some aspects of jive talk that needed to remain private, in order not to discourage innocent fans and record buyers."[28] Jazz speak was essential for Calloway's performative identity and, as his team appreciated, for his bottom line. Calloway's playful dictionary provides definitions for under 250 words and phrases, with little other discussion. In 1939, refiguring himself as "Professor Calloway," he would publish a companion handbook, *Professor Calloway's Swingformation Bureau*. Calloway's texts eschew any talk of protest, instead presenting the jazz musician as "a happy-go-lucky artist who gave his entire life to his music."[29] The stated goal of these publications was celebrating the jazz musician as a "new hero of public life" who "appealed to millions of Americans who wanted to know more about the way he lived and spoke, and what interested him."³⁰ That the explicit function was to decode jazz speak for a much broader audience supports Calloway's interest in celebrating it as a vernacular open to "millions of Americans." It is, as he writes, "a fact that the American language has absorbed many of the quaint expressions that have had their origin in the Harlem section of New York City."³¹

One of the more impactful publications was *Really the Blues*, the 1946 memoir by jazz musician "Mezz" Mezzrow. Among the musicians' books using jazz slang – and containing glossaries – Mezzrow's had arguably the largest role in widely disseminating jazz slang. It had a powerful effect on the young readers and writers who would make up the Beat Generation. (In a somewhat ironic twist, Mezzrow would have nothing good to say about bebop, a touchstone of the Beats.) Mezzrow, a Jewish jazz musician from Chicago, began his musical career there in the 1920s, a fertile time and place for the effusion of jazz slang. Mezz relocated to New York in the late 1920s as the Swing Era and its attendant speechways were having a considerable impact on American culture and society.

Much is made – not unproblematically – celebrating Mezzrow's embrace and claiming of Black culture and Black personhood.³² He was famed in the jazz scene, deeply steeped in its lingo and subculture. As a mark of distinction, the slang term "mezz" referred to cannabis of the highest quality, which Mezzrow was known to procure for many musicians. (Calloway's *Dictionary* once again stops short by defining "mezz" as "anything supreme, genuine."³³) His investment in the slanguage of jazz musicians is apparent in his memoir. The book's lively tone relies heavily on slang and includes a section written entirely in jive, translated in an appendix, with an extensive glossary to guide the under-initiated.

Really the Blues was a substantial success and, as Scott Saul maintains, its "influence in the postwar period – on the Beats, the jazz audience, and American culture more generally – should not be underestimated."³⁴ A television program based on the book aired on NBC in 1953, assuring its exposure to potentially millions of viewers. In 1952, the book sold over 20,000 copies and continued selling impressively even beyond the late 1950s.³⁵ As with Calloway's dictionary, the publishers relied on jazz slang as a marketing technique banking on insider allure. What was attractive and lucrative was the access to the linguistic codes of jazz musicians' speech and, in the vein of Mezzrow himself, a self-styled "voluntary Negro," access, through a facility with purportedly authentic Black speech, to Blackness itself.

The press – mainstream, trade, and Black – was notable in bringing jazz slang to a national readership. Music and entertainment publications such as *Variety* (which also created a show-biz slang it peppered throughout its pages) and *Down Beat* regularly used jazz slang in its pages, while mainstream periodicals such as *Time* and *Life* published articles – often panicked or mocking – about jazz musician and jazz fan subcultures, focusing particularly on their outlandish fashion and customs. If the music and accompanying styles engendered derision and fear in the white, mainstream press, the Black press, often due to the pressures of respectability politics, avoided embracing these styles and customs, sometimes matching their white counterparts in mockery. However, widely read columnists for Black newspapers would, beginning in the 1940s, increasingly write in jazz slang, introducing Black people across the nation – particularly those outside of New York – to the new and ever-evolving urban argot. Even Adam Clayton Powell's short-lived leftist newspaper, *People's Voice*, included a column, "Home Boy Says," written in jive and accompanied by a translation. Larger Black newspapers, based in big cities, but with a national reach, had a significant impact on this spread. Langston Hughes's weekly "Simple" columns, from the Chicago *Defender*, in which everyman Jesse B. Semple spoke in everyday Harlemese, was consumed by many readers outside of Chicago or Harlem. Similarly, the Pittsburgh *Courier's* "Billy Rowe's Notebook" also had a national reach. Rowe's exceedingly popular column made liberal use of jazz slang, so much so that the Foreword to Cab Calloway's *Dictionary* explicitly acknowledges only Rowe's column as a key source for "some of the new expressions."[36] Finally, Dan Burley, while editing the New York *Amsterdam News* also wrote a popular column on Harlem nightlife, "Back Door Stuff," which incorporated urban jazz slang. While "Back Door Stuff" helped the spread of jazz slang across the nation, Burley's greatest achievement in this area was the 1944 publication of *Dan Burley's Original Handbook of Harlem Jive*. This book, purportedly written at Hughes's urging, collected pieces in and about this slanguage. Burley's book contains jive definitions and parody translations of literary works into jive, including a soliloquy from William Shakespeare's *Hamlet* ("To Dig, or not to Dig, Jack, that's the Question"[37]), Joyce Kilmer's "Trees" ("I think I shall never dig / A spiel as righteous as a twig"[38]), and Clement Clarke Moore's "A Visit from St. Nicholas" – a/k/a "The Night Before Christmas" ("Twas the dim before Nicktide, and all through the Crib"[39]). Additionally, the handbook's attention to the aesthetic and political aspects of jazz slang led one critic to characterize Burley's *Handbook* and its sequel, *Diggeth Thou?* as "works of civil rights advocacy," and "exposés of the Black urban situation."[40] Burley's influential historical perspective greatly distinguished his work from most other jazz slang publications.

Another substantive vehicle for the popularization of jazz slang was radio; as an oral/aural medium, it stands opposed to the written dictionaries and word-lists. Radio amplified the jazz idiom across the country, which helps jazz/hip speech become synonymous with Black speech, especially for many Americans who could then more easily consume Black culture without first-hand interaction with Black people. The "disk jockey" as a personality arose in the late 1940s, and both white and Black DJs heavily based their personae on jazz musicians' patter. White DJs practiced what William Barlow calls "racial ventriloquy on the nation's airwaves."[41] Not only did they use the slang, but they also patterned their vocal inflections and intonations on Black speech. This allowed radio stations to hew to a segregationist ideal by hiring white men who "sounded Black." However, there were white DJs, notably "Symphony Sid" Torin, who were deeply knowledgeable, respectful boosters of the music. Ultimately, Black DJs such as Dr. Hepcat (Lavada Hurst) in Austin, Texas and Chicago's Al Benson and Daddy O'Daylie (Holmes Daylie) were hired for their facility with the vernacular of their Black audiences, their "mastery of the latest street slang, or 'jive talk,' and their ability to speak in rhymes."[42] These radio stations often had a very wide broadcasting area, and they spread jazz talk, which was eagerly adopted by young listeners across the nation. As jazz's once-secret slanguage was heard across the country, it left some bewildered and angry; others, particularly in the younger generation, eagerly adopted it as a form of rebellion against the racist, classist, and stuffy mainstream American status quo.

As it has always been, jazz slang remained, if not a language of protest, then a language of distinction. This would link jazz slang to youth marketing, particularly through the categories of the "rebel," the Beat, and that market force that has felt inexorable since its inception, the teenager. While the longstanding desire of jazz fans to be hip and not square often depended on the ability to master the language developed by jazz musicians, we do begin to see a shift, as youth are drawn more to rhythm and blues and, then, rock'n'roll, to the language becoming less overtly identified with the musicians and increasingly as the expression of their fans. To be sure, musicians still often created the slang, but the slang becomes a more general youth slang. The inventive audaciousness of jazz slang, however, continued to impact American society and its language well after jazz ceased to become a significant market force. The tradition of Black linguistic dynamism aligned with Black musical innovation persists and is most readily evident in the language developed within the context of hip-hop music and culture.

Notes

1. Walt Whitman, "Slang in America," *The North American Review*, 141 (1885), 431.
2. For more on "cool," in particular, see Joel Dinerstein's chapter in this volume (Chapter 10).
3. For a discussion of this analogy, see Charles Hersch's chapter in this volume (Chapter 3).
4. Dizzy Gillespie, with Al Fraser, *To Be or Not to Bop* (New York: Da Capo, 1979), 280–81.
5. William "Baby" Dodds, as told to Larry Gara, *The Baby Dodds Story*, 1959 (Alma, MI: Rebeats Publications, 2002), 51.
6. Earl Conrad, "Foreword," in Dan Burley, *Dan Burley's Jive*, Thomas Aiello, ed. (DeKalb, IL: Northern Illinois University Press, 2009), 8.
7. Amiri Baraka (LeRoi Jones), *Blues People: Negro Music in White America* (New York: Morrow, 1963), 181, original emphasis.
8. Robert S. Gold, *A Jazz Lexicon* (New York: Knopf, 1964), xiv.
9. Archie Shepp, "Foreword," in Ben Sidran, *Black Talk* (New York: Da Capo, 1981), xvii.
10. Gillespie, *To Be or Not to Bop*, 281.
11. Dan Burley, *Dan Burley's Jive*. Thomas Aiello, ed., 1944, 1959 (DeKalb, IL: Northern Illinois University Press, 2009), 11.
12. Clarence Major, *Juba to Jive: A Dictionary of African American Slang* (New York: Penguin, 1994), xxvii.
13. Julie Coleman, *The Life of Slang* (New York: Oxford University Press, 2012), 50.
14. Ibid., 51.
15. Ibid.
16. Ibid., 52.
17. Richard M. Hogg, *The Cambridge History of the English Language* (New York: Cambridge University Press, 1992), 221.
18. Amiri Baraka (LeRoi Jones), *Home: Social Essays*, 1966 (New York: Ecco Press, 1998), 168.
19. Rick McRae, "'What Is Hip?' and Other Inquiries in Jazz Slang Lexicography," *Notes*, 57.3 (2001), 581.
20. Clyde Taylor, "The Language of Hip: From Africa to What's Happening Now," *First World* (January/February 1977), 29.
21. Gold, *A Jazz Lexicon*, xvii.
22. Neil Leonard, "The Jazzman's Verbal Usage," *Black American Literature Forum*, 20.1–2 (1986), 151.
23. H. L. Mencken, *The American Language: An Inquiry into the Development of English in the United States, Supplement Two*, 1948 (New York: Knopf, 1962), 704.
24. Ibid., 705.
25. Ibid., 712.
26. For more on the importance of jazz autobiography as a genre, see Daniel Stein's chapter in this volume (Chapter 16).

27 Nate Sloan, "Constructing Cab Calloway: Publicity, Race, and Performance in 1930s Harlem Jazz," *The Journal of Musicology*, 36.3 (2019), 373.
28 Alyn Shipton, *Hi-De-Ho: The Life of Cab Calloway* (New York: Oxford University Press, 2010), 107.
29 Cab Calloway and Bryant Rollins, *Of Minnie the Moocher and Me* (New York: Thomas Y. Crowell Company, 1976), 264.
30 Ibid.
31 Ibid.
32 See Gayle Wald's critique, "Mezz Mezzrow and the Voluntary Negro Blues" in her *Crossing the Line: Racial Passing in Twentieth Century U.S. Literature and Culture* (Durham, NC: Duke University Press, 2000), 53–81.
33 Calloway and Rollins, *Of Minnie*, 258.
34 Scott Saul, *Freedom Is, Freedom Ain't: Jazz and the Making of the Sixties* (Cambridge, MA: Harvard University Press, 2009), 41.
35 Ibid.
36 Calloway and Rollins, *Of Minnie*, 252.
37 Burley, *Dan Burley's Jive*, 33.
38 Ibid., 74.
39 Ibid., 28.
40 Ibid., xxii.
41 William Barlow, *Voice Over: The Making of Black Radio* (Philadelphia: Temple University Press, 1999), 9.
42 Ibid., 104.

CHAPTER 10

Jazz Cool

Joel Dinerstein

Jazz musicians disseminated the modern usage of *cool* in post-World War II urban America and it caught on so quickly – in the streets and subcultures, among Beats and bohemians – as to be ubiquitous by the 1960s. Like most in-group slang, the meanings of the spoken word "cool" were initially contextual and situational. To understand it, a person needed to hear it spoken, and it helped to know the speaker. Cool's ambiguity was part of its power and mystery – as a word, a concept, and an aesthetic. Robert Farris Thompson, the art historian of the Black Atlantic, long ago traced cool to its roots in Central and West Africa, showing how *cool* was a major aesthetic modality by which African culture(s) became transmuted into African American expressive culture, from sports to language to dance.[1] Here I will trace *cool*'s route into American society through its primary linguistic and stylistic creators, Black jazz musicians.

Iconic tenor saxophonist Lester Young first invoked the colloquial phrase "I'm cool" to mean he felt safe and relaxed in his own style. The phrase projected an emotional mode both psychological and situational: he meant "I'm *keeping it together* – in mind and spirit – against oppressive social forces." The modern usage of cool first surfaced within African American Vernacular English (AAVE) in the 1930s as a term for calming someone down from emotional stress: as Big Bill Broonzy sang to a woman in "Let Me Dig It" (1938), "Let me *cool* you, baby / before the ice man come."[2] Young was an original and idiosyncratic creator of slang and repurposed the word to mean a calm center, a near-Buddhist cerebral space, a balanced mind. Thompson traced cool to the Yoruba concept of *itutu* or spiritual balance, and already we can see a resonant correspondence in Young's usage.[3]

By interviewing all the living figures of the postwar scene in Greenwich Village, Lewis MacAdams created an oral history of cool's emergence in his 1999 book *The Birth of The Cool: Bebop, The Beats, and the American Avant-Garde*. MacAdams recalled how as an alienated teenager in his hometown, Dallas, he first heard the word "cool" – in its modern context – on a rhythm and blues radio show in 1952. It was initially abstract and inchoate: "What did I mean, then, when I thought that the Beats were cool? I had no idea. I just liked *the feeling* when I said the word." He later unraveled its evocative allure: "'*Cool' meant not only approval, but kinship.* It was a ticket out of the life I felt closing in all around me; it meant the path to a cooler world."[4] This *cooler world* was an ideal bohemia, a community of kindred spirits interested in innovation, self-liberation, and tolerance.

Given cool's emergence amid Jim Crow's strict segregation and systemic racism, *keeping it together* was no small matter. Ralph Ellison claimed *cool* characterized Black survival and cultural resistance – the combination of "resistance to provocation" and "coolness under pressure" were together "indispensable values in the struggle [for freedom]."[5] The daily stress of second-class citizenship and caste exclusion led to African American men invoking the need to *be cool* until things changed – or until overt political protest arose. The jazz cool of *surviving-with-dignity* has been supplanted in public memory by its abstract positive qualities, however, as when bassist Esperanza Spalding introduced her 2016 performance at the Obama White House by saying, "Jazz is urban cool."[6]

In 1940s New York, the epicenter of the jazz world, African American cool was most recognizable as an embodied projection of *stylish stoicism*. Style here signifies in two ways. First, there is the impassive, nearly blank public demeanor that symbolized a refusal to "Uncle Tom" in front of white people (that is, to smile or defer). Second, there is the necessary creation of an individual artistic voice to be considered a true jazz musician. In a nation that treated African Americans as a collective racial type with fixed negative traits, asserting one's individuality in music was a proclamation of selfhood, equality, and cultural citizenship. As for stoicism, this blank face represented philosophical detachment as a response to constant state-sanctioned oppression. To take a few examples: the New York Police Department (NYPD) regularly suspended jazz musicians' cabaret cards for any infraction, removing their ability to play clubs; FBI agent Harry Anslinger maintained a personal vendetta against Billie Holiday for her nonviolent drug use; Miles Davis was arrested for helping a white woman into her car under a marquee with his name on it; Black male jazz musicians were often arrested just for being in a car with a white woman.[7]

Emblematic jazz compositions with cool in the title appear throughout the twenty-year period between 1940 and 1960, but not before. For cool as an act of strategic silence and stoicism, there was Erskine Hawkins's "Keep Cool, Fool" (1941)[8] and Count Basie's "Stay Cool" (1946).[9] For cool as an ideal state of relaxation, there was Fats Navarro's "Everything's

Cool" (1946)[10] and Charlie Parker's "Cool Blues" (1947).[11] For cool as a projection of style in public, there was Sonny Clark's "Cool Struttin'" (1958)[12] and Ray Brown's "Cool Walk" (1958).[13] After the white American appropriation of *cool* diluted its in-group meanings, young Black men replaced cool with "chill" in the early 1980s. The contemporary phrase "just chillin'" has for precedent Lester Young's "Just Coolin'" in 1945.[14] The lexical similarities are obvious.

In addition, "hot music" and "hot jazz" were common genre designations for uptempo jazz between 1917 and 1945, with "hot" meaning emotional or exciting. The main soloist in a big band was known as its "hot man," designated to drive audiences (and the band) to thrilling heights at live performances. French scholar Hugues Panassié's *Hot Jazz: The Guide to Swing Music* (1936)[15] was one of the first full-length studies of jazz, followed by Frederic Ramsey, Jr. and Charles Edward Smith's *Jazzmen: The Story of Hot Jazz Told by the Men Who Created It* (1939),[16] and "The Case for Hot Jazz" (1941), a classical musician's argument for its formal innovative qualities.[17] *Esquire* magazine then released an annual set of records featuring its jazz poll winners under *Esquire's All American Hot Jazz* (1944–47). *Le Jazz Hot* was the genre's name in France and, in Germany, just "hot jazz."[18]

The opposite of hot, *cool* represented the reclaiming of jazz by African Americans, and within this new formulation, the "cool man" replaced the "hot man." In his essential jazz memoir, *Really the Blues*, Mezz Mezzrow notes the hostility jazz musicians felt towards the experience of fans standing under soloists and yelling, "Get hot! Get hot!" This reinforced the framing of jazz musicians as entertainers rather than artists, and for Black musicians, the racist perception whites carried of them as "happy darkies," serving their emotional needs for escape and excitement.[19]

The reign of "hot music" came to a decided end by 1950. In 1949, jazz's main journal *Down Beat* offered $1,000 to come up with an alternative to jazz or hot music, "a new word to describe the music from dixieland through bop." The panel of judges chose "crewcut music" as the best term; "Americana" was the runner-up. These absurd choices were seemingly chosen to reboot jazz with a clean-cut white image, associating it with big band swing's wartime importance to soldiers and civilians alike. Both "crewcut" and "Americana" would have served to erase jazz's African American origins and artistry, as voted by white jazz fans.[20]

In the 1950s, the crossover of cool as word and concept was noticed, and *noted*, by every Beat writer on the scene. Jack Kerouac spent his nights at jazz clubs and wrote a letter to Neal Cassady of his new "theory of cool" in 1950. "A *raw mind* and a *cool mind* are two different minds," he wrote, where "the raw mind is associated with the physical life ... [and] the cool mind is the *intellectual* emphasis."[21] In the first Beat novel, John Clellon Holmes's *Go* (1952), the narrator identifies cool as the emblematic term of the new postwar mood – it meant "pleasant, somewhat meditative, and without tension," and young people were acting "cool, unemotional, withdrawn."[22] In 1953's *Junky*, William Burroughs registered this "all-purpose word" in "the new hipster vocabulary," observing its special use to indicate a safe environment ("any situation not hot with the law"), where "the heat" means the police.[23] *Cool* was such a new slang term that it did not appear in Mezzrow's glossary in *Really the Blues* (1946), Cab Calloway's popular *Hepster's Dictionary*, or Zora Neale Hurston's "Story in Harlem Slang" (1942).

Yet within a single twenty-year period, cool became "*the* protean word" of the jargon of jazz musicians, according to Robert S. Gold's definitive dictionary, *A Jazz Lexicon* (1964). Gold needed two pages to cover all the connotations of cool; in addition, there was a page each for "uncool" and "cool it." Gold quoted *Down Beat* and *Esquire*, academic articles by sociologists and jazz critics, jazz novels such as Kerouac's *On the Road* and Ross Russell's *The Sound* (1961).[24] Russell described "the new jargon" as something of a "secret language passed among them [jazz fans] like a kind of black-market currency." He also noted that *cool* was something "close to the heart of [jazz musicians'] philosophy." A drummer in *The Sound* passes along this advice to a young musician: "You just have to know where you stand and play it cool. Play it cool, that's the main thing, man, play it cool, *play it cool.*"[25]

Jazz was the dominant urban subculture of the post-World War II era and musicians' slang was cool's first rebel code. There is some precedent for the modern usage of jazz musicians in English, Thompson noted in 1972, then presented the difference in a convincing chart, "The Concept 'Cool' in Select West and Central African Languages." In each of thirty-five languages, "cool" means "spiritual balance" or "to be silent" (or "still"), with "be cool" meaning "being calm" or "to be composed."[26] In addition, West and Central African musical practices conceptualize hot and cool rhythms within its drumming traditions: *cool rhythms* are relaxed, steady, and supportive; *hot rhythms* are propulsive, aggressive, and heated. In short, this African concept of cool has linguistic, musical, and physiological aspects, later adapted by African Americans in similar ways.[27]

Jazz slang such as "cool" was an underground *lingua franca* in the 1950s, yet *linguistic* racism refuses to recognize the impact of jazz slang on American society. Etymologies of cool still more often trace it through the *Oxford English Dictionary* (*OED*) rather than African American vernacular culture.[28] This is despite the fact that Thompson's work on African diasporic aesthetics is widely recognized, and even UK sociologist Jim McGuigan's *Cool Capitalism* (2009) takes West African concepts such as *itutu* as cool's grounding concept.[29]

Among jazz musicians, cool referred to four specific things: a relaxed (chill) style of performance and self-presentation; a Black American translation of West African concepts such as *itutu*, a Yoruba term meaning spiritual balance; an existential mode of *being-in-the-world;* an *aesthetic* in music involving an innovative set of sonic preferences (see next section). For more than a generation, *cool* was a symbolic matrix – complex, elusive, and multi-layered – until corporate advertising and marketing flattened cool's subcultural energy. Yet the vestiges of *jazz cool* remain in the vernacular when anyone says, "Cool!" or "I'm cool with it."

The Cultural Politics of Cool

From Simone de Beauvoir to leftist UK historian Eric Hobsbawm to Czech novelist Josef Škvorecký, European writers helped establish the association of jazz with freedom – freedom of individual voice, freedom of expression (Duke Ellington's phrase), creative freedom within the form (improvisation), freedom *from* top-down artistic control. For example, New Orleans jazz was the sound of freedom in postwar Paris after the end of the Nazi occupation, with Beauvoir reporting that Louis Armstrong's performance in 1946 made "the youth mad with enthusiasm."[30] Škvorecký's novels and essays chronicle the fervor of Czech youth for jazz in defiance of its ban under Nazi- and Soviet-backed regimes, even documenting German musical prohibitions against "Negroid excesses in tempo (so-called hot jazz) or in solo performances."[31] Films such as *Swing Kids* and the documentary *Swing Under the Swastika* show jazz's appeal to German youth.[32] In his study of jazz in the Soviet Union, S. Frederick Starr called jazz and Bolshevism "the two revolutions of 1917," only one of which concerned freedom.[33] Hobsbawm's essays on jazz artists appeared alongside his critiques of capitalism and technology; he considered the art form vital to understanding the twentieth century.[34]

"Jazz turned the Cold War into a *cool* war," in German historian Reinhold Wagnleitner's evocative phrase. Both the Soviet Union and Nazi Germany banned jazz since neither ideology had a "sonic weapon" to counter its ensemble individuality and dialogic ritual.[35] In formal musical terms, jazz is the antithesis of collective ideologies due to the artistic freedom built into the musical form. No totalitarian government of the twentieth century developed such innovative artistic forms, only American popular culture as created by African Americans. This political validation of jazz as democracy was first theorized in the late 1940s, then developed intellectually by cultural critics Ralph Ellison and Albert Murray.[36]

Beauvoir visited jazz clubs in New York and New Orleans in 1947. Her experience led to her claim that jazz was a new *type* of art form – improvisatory, self-excavating, direct, in-the-moment. "Compared with art, poetry, and printed music, jazz has the privileged emotional impact of a communication that is immediate and fleeting, like the very moments it transfigures."[37] She found white Southern audiences racist in their treatment of musicians as entertainers, but the musicians kept their cool. "It's here in these modest clubs [in New Orleans], among these unknown musicians, ... that jazz achieves its true dignity: there's no entertainment, no exhibitionism, no commercialism – for certain men, it's a way of life and a reason for being."[38]

In 1955, Norman Mailer observed that *British* cool was a class ideal while *American* cool was focused in and through the individual. An Englishman "had to be cool because to be cool is for the English the *social* imperative." Yet he understood American cool as something achieved by an individual *in-the-moment*: "Americans are more primal; for us to be *cool in action* is the basic thing." Mailer's idol, Ernest Hemingway, had established a definition of courage, "grace under pressure," that often stood in as well for cool.[39] What Mailer failed to notice was that jazz musicians had transformed cool into a Black word, an in-group term infused with West African values and musical practices. As early as 1962, Black novelist William Marvin Kelley alerted *New York Times* readers to the importance of jazz slang in an op-ed, "If You're Woke, You Dig it."[40]

Jazz cool represented the recuperation of individuality in the arts from the century's collective ideologies of Communism, fascism, and state capitalism. Such embodied *cool* was performed nightly by the era's iconic figure, the improvising jazz musician. *Cool* named a new matrix of cultural resistance, an underground that subverted the era's American triumphalism, blind patriotism, and military-industrial complex. Yet the inversion of "jazz cool" is also key to understanding the term, the genre known as "cool jazz."

The Cool Aesthetic

The primary meaning of cool among jazz musicians, as Gold wrote in *A Jazz Lexicon*, was an aesthetic one: it meant "restrained and relaxed" socially, but in terms of jazz, "artistic expression within a frame of restraint."[41] Gold extended this idea by framing the word cool as "[the] *linguistic* parallel of the new post-World War II *musical* temper (more relaxed, cerebral, sophisticated)."[42] The secret of a *cool aesthetic* is the contrast of embodied relaxation in the artist that creates excitement in the listener.

Cool jazz was a musical turn away from bebop's virtuosity and high-speed conversations, its extended solos and angular runs, even its core African American musical practices such as blues and percussive emphasis. Cool jazz can be seen as a small-combo continuity of big bands: it expanded the latter's emphasis on melody, lyrical sensibility, and arrangements, but added more space for soloing. Some of these ideas came from white big bands such as Claude Thornhill's Orchestra, ensembles that muted the rhythmic brassiness of Count Basie, Duke Ellington, or even Benny Goodman.

In effect, the cool aesthetic represented an *aestheticizing of detachment*. The cool aesthetic favors melody and emphasizes flow, restraint, and expression over power, vibrato, and virtuosity. There is an element of withdrawal and resignation here often associated with the common heroin use of postwar jazz musicians across racial lines. If bebop's abrasive sound and angular rhythms "reflected a protest against the position of the Negro [and] against the position of the Negro entertainer," according to jazz producer Orrin Keepnews, then *cool jazz* reflected an inward turn marked by guild as much as race.[43] The partnership of Miles Davis and Gil Evans marks an origin point in the *Birth of the Cool* recordings, with future cool jazz avatar Gerry Mulligan as the third composer.[44] Yet the cool *aesthetic* followed from the expressive individual sound and solos of Lester Young.

Young and Billie Holiday together established the minimalist power of understatement synonymous with *playing it cool*: Young created its modern sound, while Holiday's vocal phrasing and swinging built upon his innovations. As a technique, the *cool* aesthetic favors fewer notes timed for affect *and* effect. By accenting only certain words or notes through rhythmic nuance and a sophisticated manipulation of musical space, the duo created a low-key late-night emotional sphere. Young's sound revolutionized the tenor saxophone with its cool tone, long, flowing lines, and behind-the-beat rhythmic approach; Holiday discarded her early bluesy approach for the Youngian model.

Miles Davis picked up their example in the late 1940s such that the cool aesthetic came to represent an individual musician's state of equipoise within jazz improvisation. Davis's muted trumpet floated apart and aloof, a melodic mist attracting the rhythm section to itself. To French existential writer Boris Vian, Davis's romantic trumpet was "a monk's sound," the sonic register of "somebody who is part of the century but who can look at it with serenity." To be *jazz* cool, a musician floated buoyantly above the groove yet remained rhythmically grounded. "[It] takes a healthy sense of balance," Vian wrote of Davis's solos, to create "such complex constructions" and yet "land on your feet."[45]

When baritone saxophonist Gerry Mulligan moved to Los Angeles, he pursued the cool aesthetic in a combo format: lighter tone, muted horns, more structure, shorter solos. During a residence at a club called The Haig, he teamed with trumpeter Chet Baker, whose sparse romantic solos, much influenced by Davis, provided a perfect foil. Mulligan spent six months in jail for heroin possession, and in his absence, Baker became a singer and a *bona fide* pop star. In hits such as "Let's Get Lost," we again hear jazz as urbane pop music.

The Mulligan-Baker quartet was the big bang of cool jazz and their sound evokes a *very* laid-back post-World War II Los Angeles: relaxed tempos, cool sonorities, floating melodies, light swing, fluid solos, soft Latin rhythms. LA musicians experimented with a synthesis of bebop and swing because they were more invested (than bebop musicians) in "the depth and profundity of big band music," trumpeter Art Farmer recalled.[46] There were small big bands on albums such as *Art Pepper + Eleven*, or *Gerry Mulligan and His Tentette*.

Cool jazz was sometimes called "West Coast jazz," and was long considered a white musical style by critics, a misconception that ignored its interracial bands and shared musical influences. Musically, LA musicians shared five lodestars: for solos, Young's melodic imagination and Charlie Parker's harmonic complexity; for tonal colors, Duke Ellington and arranger Gil Evans; for swinging equilibrium, the Count Basie rhythm section. Art Pepper, for instance, created a tenor saxophone sound and style that synthesized Young and Parker.

In the 1950s, Frank Sinatra retooled the cool jazz aesthetic into a global style. Sinatra adapted from Holiday her artistic genius in narrating songs as if they were short stories. In addition, Sinatra and Lester Young were musical friends and recognized their common cool cause. "I knew Lester well," Sinatra recalled. "We were close friends, and we had a mutual admiration society ... I took from what he did, and he took from what I did." Young admired how Sinatra told a story and, of equal importance, how he swung. "If I could put together exactly the kind of band I wanted ... Frank Sinatra would be the singer," Young said in 1956.[47] If Sinatra was America's mainstream male culture hero in the 1950s, selling Vegas cool across media formats, Young was the cool avatar of the jazz underground.[48]

The major white saxophonists of cool jazz all claim Young as their major influence: Stan Getz, Paul Desmond, Art Pepper, Lee Konitz. Getz often went up to visit Young at the Alvin Hotel to ask how he produced his signature effects, both aesthetically and sonically.[49] Miles Davis learned from Young how to "flood the tone" of his trumpet, then in a key innovation, he amplified his romantic, detached sound by putting the bell of his horn up against the microphone.[50] In his autobiography, Davis also claimed Sinatra's voice and phrasing was a major influence.[51]

In the late 1950s, jazz dovetailed with bossa nova, a genre that might be called *Brazilian* cool jazz. Built on Antônio Carlos Jobim's compositions, Sinatra's vocal style, Brazilian rhythms, and jazz improvisation, Stan Getz recorded two breakthrough classics: *Getz/Gilberto* with Brazilian guitarist João Gilberto and *Jazz Samba* with American guitarist Charlie Byrd. Both Sinatra and Ella Fitzgerald recorded albums of Jobim compositions, while East Coast saxophonists such as Cannonball Adderley, Ike Quebec, and Eddie Harris all made bossa nova albums in a five-year period of transnational exchange. This global cool aesthetic remains integral to any archaeology of cool.

Cool and Rebellion

For Lewis MacAdams, the example set by a trio of martyrs in 1954–55 – Charlie Parker, James Dean, and Jackson Pollock – triggered what he called "the age of cool." Just as young Beat poets such as Ted Joans and Bob Kaufman scrawled "Bird lives" on New York's subway walls, so too did Dean and Pollock project what MacAdams calls "the myth of tragic cool … that cool was a caged thing waiting to be freed."[52] In effect, a cool rebel leaves behind an artistic vapor trail, a legacy that becomes for others a flag of future rebellion. As Albert Camus distilled this process, "I rebel, therefore we exist."[53]

Jazz cool can be thought of as an American version of existentialism, except the musicians were the exemplars, not the writers: Ross Russell once called jazz musicians "America's organic existentialists."[54] In their nightly public assertion of the *self-in-resistance*, individual jazz musicians performed the kind of existential freedom called for by French philosophers. Camus wrote the first historical study of rebellion in Western culture, *The Rebel: A Study of Man in Revolt* (1951), and American authors intuited the connection between jazz, rebellion, and existentialism. From James Baldwin and Ralph Ellison to Beat novelists, there was an outpouring of poems, essays, and stories featuring jazz protagonists between 1950 and 1965 (e.g., Baldwin's "Sonny's Blues," John Clellon Holmes's *The Horn*, the essays in Ellison's *Living with Music*).[55] During a period of Western existential crisis, that is to say, following the revelations of

Auschwitz, Hiroshima, and the Soviet labor camps, writers were drawn to the nightly self-creation (and improvisation) of jazz musicians.

The Black jazz musician was the emblematic figure of existential cool, whether through an individual resistance to an oppressive white supremacist nation, or paradoxically, as artistic creators of a new Afro-Western musical culture. In this sense, as a symbol of rebellion, the jazz musician was global culture's first nonwhite rebel. Having been dehumanized at every level, Black men made a value of cool through rituals of self-affirmation that Albert Murray called "survival technology."[56] These rituals of survival – including in-group music, style, humor, and slang as coded language – provided the stylistic elements for the aestheticization of detachment necessary for a new existential attitude of *being-in-the-world*.[57]

When white jazz fans appropriated cool as a term, it still carried qualities of authenticity, innovation, and rebellious community. Soon, however, cool morphed into a rogue American sensibility. Zen and Beat poet Gary Snyder defined cool among San Francisco bohemians as "our ongoing in-house sense of [being] detached, ironic, fellaheen hip, with an outlaw/anarchist edge."[58] Novelist Ken Kesey often called the Merry Pranksters' cross-country road trip "the search for a kool place."[59]

As developed by jazz musicians, *cool* became the modern American synonym for rebellion: those following the status quo are *uncool*, almost by definition. In contemporary global terms, *cool* remains a myth for iconic rebels providing an innovative cultural charge. Yet the word *cool* was so stripped of its original in-group meanings – then became so commodified and diluted – that young Black men transmuted *cool* into *chill*.

Cool began as an African American word, concept, and streetwise philosophy in post-World War II jazz culture. *Jazz cool* was a form of rebellious self-expression predicated on emotional self-control (i.e., stoicism) channeled into artistic endeavor. The legacy of the concept is that cool remains the supreme compliment of American culture. Even now, to emphasize the pronoun in "*he's* cool" or "*she's* cool" carries a social charge of style, stoicism, and authenticity, of a person who has developed and walks an edge all one's own.

Notes

1. Robert Farris Thompson, *Aesthetic of the Cool: Afro-Atlantic Art and Music* (Pittsburgh: Periscope, 2011), 28–30.
2. Big Bill and the Memphis Five, "Let Me Dig It" (Vocalian 04591, 1938). An early documentation of cool as an African American word of aesthetic approval

can be found in Zora Neale Hurston's short story, "The Gilded Six-Bits," 1933, in *The Complete Stories* (New York: Harper Perennial, 2008), 89–90.
3 The Great Migration was a period of rich vernacular ferment among African Americans especially among musicians. See *Cab Calloway's Catologue: A Hepster's Dictionary* (New York: Cab Calloway, Inc., 1938); Dan Burley's *Original Handbook of Harlem Jive* (New York: Dan Burley, 1944); and the glossaries at the end of Zora Neale Hurston's "Story in Harlem Slang," *American Mercury*, July 1942, 84–96; and Mezz Mezzrow's *Really the Blues* (with Bernard Wolfe, 1946, New York: Citadel, 2001). See also Joel Dinerstein, "Lester Young and the Birth of Cool," in Gena Dagel Caponi, ed., *Signifyin(g), Sanctifyin' and Slam Dunking* (Amherst: University of Massachusetts Press, 1999), 239–76. For more on jazz and language, see Amor Kohli's chapter in this volume (Chapter 9).
4 Lewis MacAdams, *Birth of the Cool: Beat, Bebop, and the American Avant-Garde* (New York: Free Press, 2001), 13–14, original emphasis.
5 Ralph Ellison, "The World and the Jug," 1963–64, in *The Collected Essays of Ralph Ellison*, ed. John F. Callahan (New York: Modern Library, 2003), 161.
6 Esperanza Spalding, "On the Sunny Side of the Street," January 2016, www.youtube.com/watch?v=TQtXo4tiZxs.
7 Gerald Horne, *Jazz and Justice: Racism and the Political Economy of the Music* (New York: Monthly Review Press, 2019), 50, 119, 142, 231–32.
8 Erskine Hawkins, "Keep Cool, Fool," Bluebird B-11049, 1941.
9 Count Basie, "Stay Cool," Columbia DC 368, 1946.
10 Fats Navarro and His Bop Boys, "Everything's Cool," Rec. September 6, 1946, Savoy 941, 1949.
11 Charlie Parker Quintet feat. Errol Garner, "Cool Blues," Dial 1015, 1947.
12 Sonny Clark, *Cool Struttin'*, Blue Note LP 1588, 1958.
13 Ray Brown, *This Is Ray Brown*, Verve LP V-8290, 1958.
14 Lester Young, *The Greatest*, Intro Records LP 603, 1951.
15 Hugues Panassié, *Hot Jazz: The Guide to Swing Music* (New York: M. Witmark & Sons, 1936).
16 Frederic Ramsey, Jr. and Charles Edward Smith, *Jazzmen: The Story of Hot Jazz Told in the Lives of the Men Who Created It* (New York: Harcourt Brace, 1939).
17 Louis Harap, "The Case for Hot Jazz," *Musical Quarterly* 27.1 (1941), 47–61.
18 See also Charles Edward Smith, "Collecting Hot," *Esquire*, February 1934, 96, 148, and "Collecting Hot: 1944," *Esquire*, February 1944, 27, 98–100; William H. Kenney, "Le Hot: The Assimilation of American Jazz in France, 1917–1940," *American Studies* 25.1 (Spring 1984), 1–25; Michael J. Budds, ed., *Jazz and the Germans: The Influence of 'Hot' American Idioms on Twentieth Century German Music* (Hillsdale, NY: Pendagron, 2002).
19 Mezzrow, *Really the Blues*, 141–42.
20 For the magazine's own summary of this crisis in jazz, see "A History as Rich as Jazz Itself," https://downbeat.com/site/about/P6. It is also worth reading the original articles on this contest. See also Ted Gioia, "When They Had a

Contest to Rename Jazz," *The Honest Broker*, June 7, 2022, https://tedgioia.substack.com/p/when-they-had-a-contest-to-rename.
21 Ann Charters, ed., *Jack Kerouac: Selected Letters, 1940–1956* (New York: Penguin 1996), 231–32, original emphasis.
22 John Clellon Holmes, *Go*, 1952 (New York: Thunder's Mouth Press, 1997), 209.
23 William S. Burroughs [William Lee], *Junkie: Confessions of an Unredeemed Drug Addict [Junky]* (New York: Ace, 1953), 120.
24 Robert S. Gold, *A Jazz Lexicon* (New York: Knopf, 1964), 65–67.
25 Ross Russell, *The Sound* (London: Cassell, 1961), 11, 74.
26 Thompson, *Aesthetic of the Cool*, 17.
27 John Miller Chernoff, *African Rhythm and African Sensibility* (Chicago: University of Chicago Press, 1979), 30–115; John Collins, *West African Pop Roots* (Philadelphia: Temple University Press, 1992), 1–15; see Thompson, *Aesthetic of the Cool*, passim.
28 See the *OED* entry on "cool," for example, to see etymologies traced to medieval and Renaissance English with little reference to African or African American philosophical traditions: www.oed.com/viewdictionaryentry/Entry/40978.
29 Jim McGuigan, *Cool Capitalism* (London: Pluto Press, 2009), 2–3.
30 Simone de Beauvoir, *A Transatlantic Love Affair: Letters to Nelson Algren* (New York: New Press, 1998), 185.
31 Josef Škvorecký, "Foreword," in *The Bass Saxophone*, trans. Kaca Polackova-Henley (London: Picador, 1980), 10; Josef Škvorecký, *Talkin' Moscow Blues: Essays about Literature, Politics, Movies, and Jazz* (New York: The Ecco Press, 1988), 86–87.
32 Thomas Carter, dir., *Swing Kids*, Hollywood Pictures, 1993; John Jeremy, dir., *Swing Under the Swastika*, Yorkshire Television, 1988.
33 S. Frederick Starr, *Red and Hot: The Fate of Jazz in the Soviet Union* (New York: Limelight, 1994). Beauvoir documents the role of New Orleans jazz in revitalizing (postwar) Paris in her novel, *The Mandarins* (Paris: Gallimard, 1954).
34 See Eric Hobsbawm [Francis Newton], *The Jazz Scene* (London: MacGibbon & Kee, 1959).
35 Reinhold Wagnleitner, "Jazz – The Classical Music of Globalization, Or: When the Cold War Morphed into the Cool War," in Astrid M. Fellner, Susanne Hamscha et al., eds., *Is It 'Cause It's Cool?: Affective Encounters with American Culture* (Vienna: Lit Verlag, 2013), 51–53.
36 See Sidney Finkelstein, *Jazz: A People's Music* (New York: The Citadel Press, 1948); John A. Kouwenhoven, *Made in America: The Arts in Modern Civilization* (New York: Anchor, 1962); Ralph Ellison, *Shadow and Act* (New York: Random House, 1964), Albert Murray, *Stomping the Blues* (New York: Da Capo, 1976). This idea reached national exposure through Wynton Marsalis's public discourse arguing about jazz as democracy, especially in the 2001 Ken Burns documentary *Jazz*. Bassist Kabir Sehgal toured with Maralis

Jazz Cool

and wrote a full-length extension of the mutual influence of jazz and democracy in *Jazzocracy: Jazz, Democracy, and the Creation of a New American Mythology* (Mishawaka, IN: Better World Books, 2008).

37 Simone de Beauvoir, *America Day by Day*, 1954, trans. Carol Cosman (Berkeley: University of California Press, 1999), 226.
38 Ibid., 225–26.
39 Norman Mailer, Box 1014, Folder 1, Norman Mailer Papers, Harry Ransom Center (HRC), University of Texas-Austin.
40 William Marvin Kelley, "If You're Woke You Dig It," *New York Times*, May 20, 1962, Section SM, 45.
41 Gold, *A Jazz Lexicon*, 66.
42 Ibid., 65–66.
43 Orrin Keepnews, *The View from Within* (New York: Oxford University Press, 1988), 39.
44 Miles Davis, Birth of the Cool (Capitol LP T-762, 1957).
45 Vian's review was entitled "The Ears of a Faun," an allusion to Debussy's "Afternoon of a Faun," and an attempt to create equivalence between jazz and classical music. See Boris Vian, *Round about Close to Midnight: The Jazz Writings of Boris Vian*, Mike Zwerin, ed., (London: Quartet, 1988), 76–77.
46 Quoted in Clora Byant and Buddy Collette et al., eds., *Central Avenue Sounds: Jazz in Los Angeles* (Berkeley: University of California Press, 1998), 264.
47 Young and Sinatra, quoted in Will Friedwald, *Sinatra! The Song Is You* (New York: Da Capo, 1997), 405; Young quoted in Nat Hentoff, "Pres," 1956, in Lewis Porter, ed., *A Lester Young Reader* (Washington DC: Smithsonian Press, 1991), 163.
48 *The New Yorker* called Young "the pres of cool" in their report of the 1954 Newport Jazz Festival, using the nickname Billie Holiday gave him, short for being "the president of all the saxophonists." Lillian Ross, "You Dig It, Sir?," 1954, in Robert Gottlieb, ed., *Reading Jazz* (New York: Vintage, 1999), 700. Just a year before, jazz vocalist Annie Ross sang in "Jackie" (1953), *"I sure dug Pres / I thought that / he was real cool."* Annie Ross, "Jackie," Rec. September 14, 1953 (Prestige 879, 1954). Jack Kerouac revered Young as "the cultural master of his [musical] generation," the key to its "mysteries as well as masteries," the cultural leader of its "styles [and] sorrows." Jack Kerouac, *Visions of Cody*, 1972 (New York: Penguin, 1993), 393.
49 Frank Büchmann-Møller, *You Just Fight for Your Life: The Story of Lester Young* (Westport, CT: Greenwood, 1990), 210.
50 Miles Davis, with Quincy Troupe, *Miles: The Autobiography* (New York: Simon and Schuster, 1990), 99.
51 Ibid., 70.
52 MacAdams, *Birth of the Cool*, 60.
53 Albert Camus, *The Rebel: An Essay on Man in Revolt*, 1951 (New York: Vintage 1991), 104.
54 Ross Russell, "Lester and Alienation," Ross Russell Papers, Box 5, Folder 5, Harry Ransom Center, University of Texas-Austin.

55 James Baldwin, "Sonny's Blues," *Partisan Review*, 24.3 (1957), 327–58; John Clellon Holmes, *The Horn* (New York: Random House, 1958); Ralph Ellison, *Living with Music: Ralph Ellison's Jazz Writings* (New York: Modern Library, 2002).
56 Murray, *Stomping the Blues*, 42.
57 I developed Murray's phrase "survival technology" into a critical term for a broader continuum of African American culture in Joel Dinerstein, *Swinging the Machine: Modernity, Technology, and African-American Culture between the World Wars* (Amherst: University of Massachusetts Press, 2003), 22–23 and *passim*.
58 Quoted in MacAdams, *Birth of the Cool*, 180.
59 The documentary of the Merry Pranksters' cross-country bus trip is named for this quest, *Magic Trip: Ken Kesey's Search For A Kool Place*, dir. Allison Ellwood and Alex Gibney (Magnolia Pictures, 2011).

CHAPTER 11

The Institutionalization of Jazz

Dale Chapman

On Dr. Martin Luther King Jr. Day in 2013, the performing arts district in downtown San Francisco was the site of a milestone in the twenty-first-century development of jazz as a cultural institution. On that day, the local jazz community saw the opening of the SFJAZZ Center, a shimmering, modern complex that reportedly constitutes the first free-standing edifice in the United States dedicated entirely to jazz performance and education. SFJAZZ, under the direction of Randall Kline, was founded in 1983 as the concert series Jazz in the City, but it has grown to become a major arts organization, understood in jazz circles as a West Coast response to Jazz at Lincoln Center in New York.[1]

The opening concert for the Center, whose construction was made possible by $64 million in donations, featured such artists as Joshua Redman, Bill Frisell, Miguel Zenón, Regina Carter, and Jason Moran.[2] The SFJAZZ Center could be understood as the architectural distillation of the contradictory ideological dynamics of public arts institutions in the early twenty-first century. The building's full-length windows, clean lines, and ample illumination, which allow Center activities to be seen by passersby on the street, seem tailored to fulfill the populist vision articulated by SFJAZZ Operations Executive Officer Felice Swapp, who notes that, "[i]t's all about making sure that artists and audiences can see each other and participate in one big zone of energy."[3] This populist bent also manifests itself in the Center's decentralized organizational structure and forward-looking programming, which work to position the Center as a less fusty philanthropic alternative to its Eastern seaboard competitors. Its programming is developed by a series of temporary resident artistic directors, with several of the artists featured in the opening concert serving as resident directors in the Center's inaugural season.[4] One representative concert from that season took place in May of 2013, when pianist Jason Moran featured his Bandwagon ensemble accompanying eight of the Bay Area's top skateboarders, performing freestyle tricks on a large half-pipe set up onstage. The event was an elegant manifestation of the venue's creative posture – under Kline, the goal of the Center has been to look aggressively *outwards*, to the vitality of the Bay Area community and its national and international contexts.[5]

For all its putative openness, though, the Center's sleek architecture, which houses a café, rehearsal space, digital lab, and intimate 80-seat space alongside its 700-seat auditorium, also concretizes the Bay Area's massive concentrations of wealth – the capital campaign behind the Center's construction relied heavily upon donations from Silicon Valley entrepreneurs, ten of whom gave upwards of one million dollars. As such, it has managed to tap into an emergent donor class that has only recently begun to contribute to this kind of cultural philanthropy.[6] The magnanimity of the region's tech multimillionaires may in some cases have been driven by a sense of ideological identification with jazz as a cultural product. Kline recalls that Srinija Srinivasan, a former board member of SFJAZZ and early Yahoo! employee, would cite jazz performance as a powerful analogy for Silicon Valley entrepreneurial culture: "In the Valley people work together in small teams and feed off each other's ideas. It requires highly sophisticated training, and you have to improvise."[7] Here, the SFJAZZ Center is rendered in the tech sector's flattering self-image: the philanthropic surplus of the region's dynamic capital flows is recast in material form, as a transmutation of Silicon Valley's claims to hip, transparent accessibility.

Jazz Institutions

I focus at length on the SFJAZZ Center in order to illustrate something of the complex dynamics of jazz music's institutionalization. To speak of institutions is usually to invoke an idea of brick-and-mortar establishments, and the organizations that inhabit and sustain them; the SFJAZZ Center is nothing if not a powerful instance of the ways that finance capital and nonprofit philanthropy converge in a concrete iteration of jazz music's self-perpetuation, inscribed in the built environment of San Francisco. However, as Silicon Valley's romanticization of jazz would suggest, an institution is as much an idea as it is a thing: the institutionalization of a musical genre is, above all else, the formalization of a narrative about the genre, and of the value system that the narrative embodies.

The growth of jazz institutions in the United States over the past century tracks closely with the changing ideas that we have about the music's import. Between the 1920s and 1960s, for instance, the phenomenon that

Paul Lopes refers to as the "rise of a jazz art world" follows the contours of jazz music's reception as it migrates from an underground, transgressive context shaped by racist moral panic to one invoking a modernist conception of jazz as serious art, in which the priorities of an emerging class of professional musicians comes to predominate.[8] The shifts in context that Lopes describes here help us to understand the music's new visibility in classical recital halls and mid-century college curricula, as well as the support it would come to receive by way of philanthropy or state subsidy. A second narrative tension shaping the music's institutionalization pertains to the temporal orientation of jazz history: Do we conceive of jazz as a music of futurity, either associated with perpetual revolutionary self-fashioning (in the modernist mode), or with the postmodern dismantling of genre barriers or cultural hierarchies? Or do we understand jazz as a tradition to be preserved, with our contemporary efforts dedicated to the curation of the music's past lineage, imagined as a stable and finite musical canon?[9]

The present discussion on this subject can in no way be comprehensive. But in what remains of the chapter, I would like to touch upon two moments in the institutionalization of jazz in the United States since the Second World War, to discern what their supporting narratives can tell us about shifting conceptions of jazz institutionalism, and its reflection of broader ideas about the music's role in American and global musical culture. These narratives must always be held in tension with the political economy of jazz music's institutionalization: the viability of any institution depends entirely upon whether its guiding ideas can be easily translated into philanthropic patronage, state support, private investment, or buy-in from an engaged public. In this sense, the history of jazz institutions is closely bound up in the funding mechanisms that, in concert with their conceptual frameworks, establish the organizations' conditions of possibility.

While one could argue that an account of jazz institutions should include the spread of for-profit jazz venues and the record companies' engagement with the music, my two examples derive from the nonprofit sector of higher education.[10] In contrast to the stories that buttress the financial interests of club owners and artists and repertoire (A&R) executives, the stories that public sector and nonprofit institutions tell about the music serve the interests of a different range of stakeholders, from the college administration looking to diversify its music department course offerings beyond the Western classical canon, to the government-run museum, looking to derive from the music's legacy a microcosm of American exceptionalism or a signifier of its pluralism. None of which is to say that these outcomes of institutionalization are wholly disconnected from the music's relation to the market. In the contemporary context of neoliberalism, where even nonprofit institutions operate with an eye to market logics, the circulation of jazz discourses in the meetings of museum boards or college curriculum committees can be leveraged by market actors in ways that are powerful, if often indirect.[11] Finally, in jazz culture, these questions of political economy are never wholly extricable from questions of race. Even where the formalization of jazz music's recognition and commemoration takes the form of a deliberate celebration of Black cultural legacies, institutionalization operates as a response to the structural violence of white supremacy – its perpetuation of a context in which some musics, some legacies, some lives are made to matter more than others.

Marshall Stearns and the Institute of Jazz Studies

In many ways, the history of the nonprofit jazz institution begins in earnest with the decade following the end of the Second World War. This period saw a confluence of factors that would, at least in theory, make the postwar environment particularly congenial for the music's institutionalization: for one thing, the emergence of the bebop subgenre intensified existing narratives about jazz being a "serious" art music. The angular, fiendishly virtuosic stylistic innovations of bebop, performed largely (though by no means exclusively) for audiences of seated, raptly listening club audiences (in contrast to the dance-centered audiences and venues of the Swing Era), began to remake the jazz world in modernism's image, distancing the music from its association with swing's dancehalls and juke joints.[12] This period of emergent modernism in jazz, and its concomitant redefinition as an "art world" buttressed by claims to artistic seriousness, coincided with a broader set of developments in the public sphere that facilitated the drive towards institutionalization at the country's research universities, in particular creating new spaces for those musics that could be promoted as candidates for institutionalization. In the postwar period, the passage of the G.I. Bill, which subsidized college tuition for millions of soldiers returning home from the Second World War, created a new impetus for the assertive public funding of the nation's universities.[13] In the same moment, the fields of historical musicology, ethnomusicology, and music theory each followed a postwar trajectory in which discourses from the natural and social sciences were employed to shore up each discipline's claims to legitimacy: ethnomusicology's investment in a behaviorist model of anthropology (see Alan Merriam on ethnomusicology as "sciencing about music"),[14] together with the rigid formalism and positivism that characterized postwar work in music theory and musicology, respectively, gesture towards a Cold War environment in which social scientific discourses of empiricism or scholarly objectivity could enhance an institution's prestige, and (consequently) its prospects for public funding.[15]

The postwar institutionalization of jazz in the United States stands in a complex and contradictory relation to these developments. One might assume, given music academia's mid-century embrace of new music, that a set of discourses that located postwar bebop in relation to the angular aesthetics and rigid formalism of mid-century modernism would also render it an attractive candidate for institutionalization.[16] And yet despite these affinities, formal recognition of the music in higher education was slow to emerge.[17] We see much of these tensions embodied in the foundation and early development of the Institute of Jazz Studies (IJS), presently housed on the Newark campus of Rutgers University. The IJS project was the brainchild of Marshall Stearns, a widely published jazz critic with a PhD in medieval literature from Yale, who was teaching courses on jazz history at Hunter College in the early 1950s. As Mario Dunkel points out in his work on the subject, Stearns encountered resistance in his initial push to locate funding for a proposed "Institute of Modern American Music"; having pursued an unsuccessful campaign to secure funding for the Institute in 1948 (with queries directed to the Ford Foundation, the Carnegie Corporation, and the Rockefeller Foundation, among others), Stearns was left to his own fiscal devices to get the nascent institution off the ground. In a letter that Stearns sent to the National Association for the Advancement of Colored People (NAACP) in 1950 to appeal to them for support in his campaign, he indicated that "[f]inancing the Institute poses a *problem* that I am in the throes of attacking";[18] this "problem," a problem of establishment suspicion of a music legacy centered upon Black creative production, posed a sufficient impediment to the foundation of the IJS that it remained housed (together with its already impressive recording collection) in Stearns's own "spacious apartment" in Greenwich Village for the first fifteen years of its existence, made available by appointment twice a week, until it was relocated to its present permanent home in Newark in 1966, shortly after Stearns's death.[19]

The context that Stearns faced in the early 1950s was one in which no narrative of legitimacy was yet sufficiently established to render the music safe for significant state, nonprofit, and philanthropic support. The rejection of Stearns's proposal by numerous philanthropic foundations took place in spite of Stearns's use of language that soft-pedaled its jazz focus (the first mention of jazz in this cryptic proposal for an "Institute of Modern American Music" was on p. 5), and his use of patriotic rhetoric specifically calibrated to navigate the McCarthyist ideological waters of the early Cold War.[20] What is almost certainly at work here is both a context of racialized moral panic surrounding the reception of bebop (the nascent genre's modernism was initially overshadowed by its stereotyping as a transgressive drug subculture), as well as the more subtle operation of what Phillip Ewell has recently called the "white racial frame" of musical studies, which would likely have informed the abiding assumptions of mid-century philanthropy – the Eurocentrism of prevailing establishment conceptions about musical aesthetics was sufficient here to disqualify the recognition of "Modern American Music" of any kind, let alone one in which jazz would figure prominently.[21]

In this respect, the narrativizing of jazz that we encounter in Stearns's scholarly writings from the 1950s and 1960s (including, among other texts, his crucial 1956 book *The Story of Jazz*), which provide a template for jazz historiography that has echoed down to the present, is noteworthy for its balancing of a celebration of the music's African diasporic legacy on the one hand, and its pointed imbrication in a legitimating discourse of Eurocentric "complexity" on the other.[22] Stearns's approach in such writings seems to be to situate jazz music's rhythmic components as a function of the music's ostensibly direct alignment with West African musical aesthetics, to which he assigns a degree of *rhythmic* complexity understood as the counterpart to European classical music's *harmonic and formal* complexity. At the same time, Stearns's discourse about jazz music's *harmonic* complexity (which he located in bebop) is for its part imbricated in an evolutionary model that positions this complexity as tracking with, though not quite yet equaling, that of Western art music:

> In terms of harmony, jazz has developed along the same lines as classical music, but more recently and rapidly. It still lags behind. Today Bop roughly parallels the period in classical music which followed Wagner and Debussy, and ninths and augmented fourths (jazz musicians call them flatted fifths) appear over and over again in the solos as well as the accompaniments.[23]

Stearns's preoccupation with setting both jazz music's rhythmic and harmonic components in relation to the Western classical tradition (with each of these neatly assigned to "African" and "European" musical precedents, respectively) functions as a clear legitimating discourse, marshalling the cultural capital of formalist analysis in a manner similar to Gunther Schuller's roughly contemporaneous interpretation of Sonny Rollins's *Saxophone Colossus* track "Blue 7" through the lens of "thematic improvisation."²⁴

Stearns's effort to harness comparisons to Western classical music as a legitimating discourse for jazz clearly serves as an important move in its own right, but it also makes clear the degree to which such narratives become an important vector for securing material support at critical moments in the founding of new institutions. As Dunkel points out, such Stearns initiatives as his book, *The Story of Jazz*, his lectures on jazz at Hunter College and NYU, and his well-regarded Jazz Roundtable sessions of the early 1950s (in which practicing jazz artists, critics, and scholars were brought together with established classical musicians in a spirit of collaborative discussion) taken together, modeled the kind of work that his proposed Institute of Jazz might do, "secur[ing] a place for jazz as a U.S. national achievement, thereby contributing to the music's legitimacy apart from the whims of the music market."²⁵

As I noted above, the nonprofit institutionalization of jazz often becomes precisely about the conviction that a music whose worth is self-evident should be protected from commercial trends.²⁶ Such an assumption is implicit, for instance, in the project of Jazz at Lincoln Center (JALC), which despite its heavy reliance upon corporate benefactors has promised to offer jazz the same protection from the market that has long been afforded to the "common practice" Western concert repertory programmed by its established classical parent.²⁷ Across the gamut of postwar jazz institutionalization, these initiatives have raised the question of which genres are seen to have earned this material buffer against the vicissitudes of the market, and why. In the case of jazz, both Cold War-era jazz advocates in the 1950s and JALC's celebrants since the 1990s have advanced a populist rhetoric that sometimes contradicts their more elitist appeals regarding the music's aesthetic complexity or sophistication. Even as Stearns, Martin Williams, and Schuller employed music theory formalism to certify the music's claims to classical legitimacy, the State Department Jazz Ambassador tours of the period (in which Stearns played a key role) deployed jazz as an effective weapon of diplomacy precisely by celebrating its embodiment of freedom, its practice of a democratic impulse that was seen to challenge both Soviet authoritarianism and the rigid aesthetic hierarchies of Soviet officialdom (which assigned legitimacy only to classical music).²⁸ Likewise, JALC artistic director Wynton Marsalis, building upon the sensibilities of such thinkers as Stanley Crouch, Ralph Ellison, and Albert Murray, has powerfully wedded jazz history to ideologies of American exceptionalism by positioning the music as a metaphor for democracy itself.[29] Jazz, by such a reckoning, is at once hailed as the most universal of American aesthetic forms, *and* deemed to be a rare, vulnerable treasure, deserving protection from a commercial sphere that stubbornly refuses to translate such universalism into market share.

Terri Lyne Carrington and the Institute of Jazz and Gender Justice

At the other end of this remarkable period of institutionalization, the jazz community has witnessed the establishment of an Institute of Jazz and Gender Justice (IJGJ) at the Berklee College of Music, founded by renowned jazz drummer Terri Lyne Carrington in 2018.[30] In a period of productive intellectual ferment surrounding issues of race, gender, sexuality, and their intersections, the IJGJ proceeds from the foundational question: "What would jazz sound like in a culture without patriarchy?"[31] This vision, which situates aesthetics and politics in intimate relation to one another, further promises that the Institute will

> focus on equity in the jazz field and the role that jazz plays in the larger struggle for gender justice. The institute will celebrate the contributions women have made in the development of the art form as well as frame more equitable conditions for all pursuing careers in jazz in an effort to work toward a necessary and lasting cultural shift in the field.[32]

If it is true, as I suggested at the outset of this chapter, that the institutionalization of jazz is about the formalization of specific narratives about the music's history and value systems, what are we to make of the formation of an institu[tion] of jazz and gender justice? In a sense, the establishment of projects like the IJGJ are aimed at dismantling the negative effects of institutionalization itself – the very history of jazz music's institutions, as with their more longstanding counterparts in the classical world, is bound up in the legacies of sexism, racism, and structural violence that have been so endemic to institutionalization writ large. With respect to gender, for instance, such institutional projects as Martin Williams's *Smithsonian Collection of Classic Jazz*, or even the more recent recording anthology released to supplement the Ken Burns *Jazz* series, have tended to reinforce a conception of the jazz canon in which women factor in primarily as vocalists, largely bracketed off from the comparative prestige of instrumental jazz creativity.[33]

More recently, the scrutiny that journalists and activists have devoted to the issue of sexual violence in contemporary film studios, media multinationals, tech sector corporations, universities, or opera houses under the banner of the #MeToo movement has been applied to various corners of the jazz world, and to the culture of toxic masculinity that has circulated in its vicinity.[34] Targets of scrutiny have included conservatories or university jazz studies departments, including the school where the IJGJ resides: a 2017 report in the *Boston Globe* cited a toxic culture of permissiveness among Berklee's instructors surrounding issues of sexual harassment and abuse, with "[a]dministrators at the renowned music school [having] tolerated lecherous behavior ... often silenc[ing] the accusers through financial settlements with gag orders attached."[35] The egregious culture of silence at jazz conservatories cannot, of course, be laid at the feet of jazz alone; it is a common feature of classical conservatories, where the longstanding model of instruction by private lessons predominates, that students are often doubly vulnerable before the power imbalance of the private lesson (where instructors are vested with enormous pedagogical authority, itself grounded in patriarchal assumptions) and the opportunities that isolation provides for abuse. Beyond the question of sexual harassment and abuse, there are a variety of more subtle manifestations of misogyny at jazz conservatories and schools of music. Just to cite one instance among many, a blog post by vibraphonist Sasha Berliner demonstrates how men's homosocial networks have worked to systemically exclude women from participation in the most valuable pedagogical and professional opportunities.[36]

The project of the IJGJ is at one level *counterinstitutional*, in that its design is calibrated to address the ill effects of the music's half-century of institutionalization. But the IJGJ also leverages formal, institutional power to counter the myriad ways that informal networks and informally disseminated attitudes have stood in the way of women's full participation in the jazz world; after all, the informal male networks that Berliner locates in jazz conservatories replicate even more perniciously exclusionary networks in the jazz community at large. And so the initiatives of the IJGJ mobilize along two fronts, undoing both the discursive patterns of jazz patriarchy and the formal mechanisms that have amplified and installed those patterns in American jazz officialdom. Pushing back on the exclusively male canon of conventional jazz education, program founder Terri Lyne Carrington leads a student ensemble dedicated to programming the work of women composers; the ensemble coursework proceeds, too, from a pedagogical approach in which the exclusivity of conventional jazz instruction is dismantled. For Carrington, "[l]earning collaborative skills in an environment that's more equitable and mixed is a key for transforming the culture" of jazz.[37] Carrington also continues to oversee a five-week intensive summer session for young women musicians, in which a program of mentorship, advocacy, and empowerment serves as a springboard for launching the professional careers of performers historically excluded from the music industry. As a further addition to Berklee's music curriculum, Aja Burrell Wood, the program's managing director, teaches a liberal arts class entitled "Music and Society: Jazz Gender and Justice," which approaches jazz history through a feminist lens. Another project on the IJGJ's agenda is to produce a book of jazz standards by women composers, and to enhance the college's archival materials on women jazz artists.[38] All such efforts look to reverse the all-male homosocial networks that jazz conservatories cultivate, to challenge the exclusivity of the all-male canon of artists that they perpetuate, and to proactively cultivate a jazz community in which all subject positions are respected and welcomed.[39]

Conclusion

Ironically, what perhaps binds together the three cases of jazz institutionalization I outline in the present chapter – the instances of the SFJAZZ Center, the Institute of Jazz Studies, and the Institute of Jazz and Gender Justice – is that each of them, for different reasons, stands in a complicated relation to the very idea of institutionalization. For Marshall Stearns and the IJS, the first decade of the Institute's activities took place in spite of the unwillingness of the country's major philanthropic foundations to extend the same recognition and support for jazz that they gave to classical music organizations as a matter of course; this refusal, proceeding from the logic of the white racial frame, withheld financial capital, and thus the imprimatur of institutional permanence, from a genre that continued to be seen through the pathologizing lens of mid-century racism. However, for the organizations at the other end of our timeline, SFJAZZ and the IJGJ, the imprimatur of institutional permanence is something that needs to be as much resisted as cultivated, precisely because of the complicated baggage that accompanies institutionalization. In the self-conscious hipness of the SFJAZZ project, we see a West Coast organization struggling to disentangle jazz programming from the classicizing impulse of conventional concert-hall formalism, and thus from the respectability politics that the contemporary nonprofit jazz establishment has wielded to secure its own interests.[40] In the affirmative feminist ethos of the IJGJ, on the other hand, we see a concerted effort to extricate jazz practices from the patriarchal assumptions that continue to shape interpersonal relations on the bandstand, representations of the music's historical canon, and the very conditions of possibility for women and nonbinary artists. As we proceed into the twenty-first century, the story of jazz music's institutionalization will continue to be bound up in these dynamics of consolidation and contestation.

Notes

1. Andrew Gilbert, "In the Bay Area, A New Jazz Mecca," *Jazz Times* (January/February 2013), 11. Among the small number of available scholarly discussions thus far on SFJAZZ, see Dhirendra Mikhail Panikker, "'Sound Come-Unity': Post-9/11 Brown and the Politics of Intercultural Improvisation," PhD dissertation, University of California at Riverside, 2019, and Arathi Govind, "'An Undeniable Presence': Racial Justice Work among South Asian American Musicians," PhD dissertation, University of California at Berkeley, 2019, 99–103, both of which focus on the artist residencies of Vijay Iyer.
2. Nate Chinen, "SF Jazz Center Opens in California," *New York Times*, January 24, 2013, http://artsbeat.blogs.nytimes.com/2013/01/24/sfjazz-center-opens-as-temple-of-jazz-in-california/.
3. Gilbert, "In the Bay Area," 12.
4. Paul de Barros, "SF Jazz Center a West Coast oasis for the genre," *Seattle Times*, February 3, 2013, www.seattletimes.com/entertainment/sf-jazz-center-a-west-coast-oasis-for-the-genre/.
5. Richard Scheinin, "Jason Moran's New Trick: Skateboarding at SFJazz," *San Jose Mercury News*, May 2, 2013, www.mercurynews.com/ci_23132144/jason-morans-new-trick-skateboarding-at-sfjazz.
6. The anchor donation of $20 million, officially anonymous, is generally acknowledged to have been a gift from Robert Mailer Anderson, who is the son-in-law of Robert Miner, the co-founder of Oracle (Gilbert, "In the Bay Area," 12). On the Bay Area tech establishment and their relationship with philanthropy, see Keith Matheny, "Techies Can Appear Slow to Embrace Philanthropy," *USA Today*, June 18, 2012, Money, p. 5b; and Larry Popelka, "Google and Other Tech Companies Need Lessons in Local Philanthropy," *Bloomberg Businessweek*, April 22, 2014, www.businessweek.com/articles/2014-04-22/google-and-other-tech-companies-need-lessons-in-local-philanthropy.
7. Gilbert, "In the Bay Area," 12.
8. Paul Lopes, *The Rise of a Jazz Art World* (Cambridge: Cambridge University Press, 2002), 46–95.
9. Scott DeVeaux, "Constructing the Jazz Tradition: Jazz Historiography," *Black American Literature Forum* 25.3 (1991), 525–60.
10. For a dissertation that examines the work of a variety of nonprofit jazz/improvised music institutions, see Kimberly Hannon Teal, "Living Traditions: Embodying Heritage in Contemporary Jazz Performance," PhD dissertation, Eastman School of Music, University of Rochester, 2012.
11. Eitan Y. Wilf, *School for Cool: The Academic Jazz Program and the Paradox of Institutionalized Creativity* (Chicago: University of Chicago Press, 2014).

12 Scott DeVeaux, *The Birth of Bebop: A Social and Musical History* (Berkeley: University of California Press, 1997), 202–207. For a discussion that complicates the idea of bebop as a decisive historiographic break with dance culture, see Christopher J. Wells, "'*You* Can't Dance to It': Jazz Music and Its Choreographies of Listening," *Daedalus* 148.2 (2019), 36–51.
13 John Thelin, "Higher Education and the Public Trough: A Historical Perspective," Edward P. St. John and Michael D. Parsons, eds., *Public Funding of Higher Education: Changing Contexts and New Rationales* (Baltimore: Johns Hopkins University Press, 2004), 31–34.
14 Alan Merriam, *The Anthropology of Music* (Evanston, IL: Northwestern University Press, 1964), 25.
15 Theodore M. Porter, "Foreword: Positioning Social Science in Cold War America," in Mark Solovey and Hamilton Cravens, eds., *Cold War Social Science: Knowledge Production, Liberal Democracy, and Human Nature* (New York: Palgrave Macmillan, 2012), ix–x; Joseph Kerman, *Contemplating Music: Challenges to Musicology* (Cambridge, MA: Harvard University Press, 1986), 42–45, 74–75.
16 See Michael Hrebeniak's chapter in this volume (Chapter 8) for a discussion of jazz within the context of the American postwar avant-garde.
17 Wilf, *School for Cool*, 69.
18 Mario Dunkel, "Marshall Winslow Stearns and the Politics of Jazz Historiography," *American Music*, 30.4 (2012), 468.
19 Edward Berger, David Cayer, Henry Martin, and Dan Morgenstern, eds., "A Photo Gallery: The Institute of Jazz Studies Celebrates Its First Fifty Years," in *Annual Review of Jazz Studies 12:2002* (Lanham, MD: Scarecrow Press, 2002), 117.
20 Dunkel, "Marshall Winslow Stearns," 490.
21 Philip A. Ewell, "Music Theory and the White Racial Frame," *Music Theory Online*, 26.2 (2020), https://mtosmt.org/issues/mto.20.26.2/mto.20.26.2.ewell.html.
22 For a discussion of Stearns's analysis of West African cultural retentions in contemporary jazz, see Ken Prouty, *Knowing Jazz: Community, Pedagogy, and Canon in the Information Age* (Jackson, MS: University Press of Mississippi, 2012).
23 Marshall Stearns, "Rebop, Bebop, and Bop," *Harper's*, April 1, 1950, 93.
24 On the relationship between Stearns's *Story of Jazz* and Schuller's later work, see Prouty, *Knowing Jazz*, 94. For Schuller's analysis of "Blue 7," see Gunther Schuller, "Sonny Rollins and the Challenge of Thematic Improvisation," *Jazz Review* 1.1 (1958), 6–11, 21. For an account of the high modernist ideologies informing the formalism of Schuller's "Blue 7" analysis, see Benjamin Givan, "Gunther Schuller and the Challenge of Sonny Rollins: Stylistic Context, Intentionality, and Jazz Analysis," *Journal of the American Musicological Society*, 67.1 (2014), 169–70.
25 Dunkel, "Marshall Winslow Stearns," 486.
26 In jazz education, though, this has long operated alongside a conflicting discourse of pragmatic market orientation (Wilf, *School for Cool*, 171).

27 George E. Lewis, *A Power Stronger Than Itself: The AACM and American Experimental Music* (Chicago: University of Chicago Press, 2008), 444.
28 Penny Von Eschen, *Satchmo Blows Up the World: Jazz Ambassadors Play the Cold War* (Cambridge, MA: Harvard University Press, 2006), 95.
29 Eric Porter, *What Is This Thing Called Jazz?: African American Musicians as Artists, Critics, and Activists* (Berkeley: University of California Press, 2002), 326–27; Mark Laver, "Freedom of Choice: Jazz, Neoliberalism, and the Lincoln Center," *Popular Music and Society* 37.5 (2014), 538–56.
30 Amelia Mason, "Berklee's Institute of Jazz and Gender Justice Aims to Combat Sexism in Jazz," *WBUR.org*, April 9, 2019, www.wbur.org/artery/2019/04/09/berklees-institute-of-jazz-and-gender-justice-sexism-jazz.
31 Berklee College of Music, n.d., "Berklee Institute of Jazz and Gender Justice," www.berklee.edu/jazz-gender-justice.
32 Ibid.
33 Lara Pellegrinelli, "Separated at 'Birth': Singing and the History of Jazz," in Nichole Rustin and Sherrie Tucker, eds., *Big Ears: Listening for Gender in Jazz Studies* (Durham, NC: Duke University Press, 2008), 32–34.
34 For an account of the #MeToo movement, and an overview of the legal conditions which surround sexual harassment and sexual violence in the United States, see Deborah L. Rhode, "#MeToo: Why Now? What Next?," *Duke Law Journal* 69.2 (2019), 377–428. On the longstanding sexism of the jazz world, and its marginalization of women, see for instance the collected interviews with women jazz artists in Wayne Enstice and Janis Stockhouse, eds., *Jazzwomen: Conversations with Twenty-One Musicians* (Bloomington: Indiana University Press, 2004).
35 Kay Lazar, "Berklee Let Teachers Quietly Leave after Alleged Sex Abuse, and Pushed Students for Silence," *Boston Globe*, November 8, 2017, www.bostonglobe.com/metro/2017/11/08/berklee-college-lets-teachers-quietly-leave-after-alleged-sexual-abuse-students-least-one-found-another-teaching-job/yfCkCCmdJzxkiEgrQK4cWM/story.html. Women recount similar experiences at other institutions; see for example Kalia Vandever, "Token Girl," Medium.com, March 16, 2018, https://medium.com/@kaliamariev/token-girl-564457c86f13
36 Sasha Berliner, "An Open Letter to Ethan Iverson (and the Rest of Jazz Patriarchy)," SashaBerlinerMusic.com, September 21, 2017, www.sashaberlinermusic.com/sociopoliticalcommentary-1/2017/9/21/an-open-letter-to-ethan-iverson-and-the-rest-of-jazz-patriarchy. For a more general scholarly overview of issues facing women in contemporary jazz, see, for example, Yoko Suzuki, "Two Strikes and the Double Negative: The Intersections of Gender and Race in the Cases of Female Jazz Saxophonists," *Black Music Research Journal*, 33.2 (2013), 207–226.
37 Gail Mitchell, "Drummer Terri Lyne Carrington Talks Berklee Institute of Jazz, Gender Equity: It 'Is Everybody's Work,'" *Billboard.com*, May 7, 2019, www.billboard.com/articles/business/8510413/terri-lyne-carrington-talks-berklee-institute-jazz-gender-justice.

38 Ibid.
39 Jazz scholar Tracy McMullen is presently studying the working methods of IJGJ as part of an ACLS Frederick Burkhardt Residential Fellowship, with a particular interest in the institution's grounding in Black feminist thought. See Tom Porter, "Music Professor McMullen Heading to Berklee on Prestigious Fellowship," Bowdoin.edu, April 6, 2020, www.bowdoin.edu/news/2020/04/music-professor-mcmullen-heading-to-berklee-on-prestigious-fellowship.html. See also Tracy McMullen, "Jazz Education after 2017: The Berklee Institute of Jazz and Gender Justice and the Pedagogical Lineage," *Jazz & Culture*, 4.2 (2021), 27–55.
40 Porter, *What Is This Thing Called Jazz?*, 320; Lewis, *A Power Stronger Than Itself*, 442–43.

CHAPTER 12

Jazz Abroad

Jürgen E. Grandt

In the summer of 1932, Langston Hughes hurried to the Brooklyn pier of "the North German Lloyd, loaded down with bags, baggage, books, a typewriter, a victrola, and a big box of Louis Armstrong, Bessie Smith, and Ethel Waters records."[1] He had signed a four-month contract as a script writer and dialogue coach for a movie dramatizing southern race relations, *Black and White*, to be shot in Moscow. As he sailed across the Atlantic aboard the *Bremen*, he couldn't have known yet that the ill-fated project was to propel him on a journey around the planet. Throughout his wanderings, the "Harlem Victrola" wasn't just the poet's steadfast road buddy, but the "race records" it was spinning afforded him an instant connection to the *human* race everywhere he went, from Berlin to Moscow, across the vast expanse of the Soviet Union, and on to Japan.[2] Even in Ashgabat, the "dust-laden" provincial capital of Turkmenistan, did Hughes's Harlem Victrola sound the bond of a common humanity transcending race and culture, class and nationality: "Perhaps it was because of music that my room became a kind of social center. Everywhere, around the world, folks are attracted by American jazz. A good old Dixieland stomp can break down almost any language barriers, and there is something about Louis Armstrong's horn that creates spontaneous friendships."[3] During this sojourn, the local apparatchiks pressured Hughes to join the Communist Party, but he declined, citing "the fact that jazz was officially taboo in Russia, being played only at the declassé Metropol Hotel, and very badly there." Against the ideological objections of his hosts, Hughes simply insisted, "'It's *my* music,' I said, 'and I wouldn't give up jazz for a world revolution.' The Russians looked at me as if I were a decadent bourgeois writer and let it go at that. But they liked my jazz records as much as I did, and never left the room when I played them."[4]

Hughes's Harlem Victrola in Ashgabat sounds the (ostensible) paradox of jazz abroad. On one hand, jazz has often been perceived as indubitably, authentically "Black," a racially encoded expression. Hughes certainly heard "his" music also in this way, as the sounds of Black folk, using it to stake out his cultural membership and individual self-determination. On the other hand, jazz's inherent multivalences oscillate on transnational frequencies that have resonated and continue to resonate with all kinds of folk all over the world. The story of jazz abroad, then, is also the story of Blackness on the move, a journey perpetually navigating a course between authenticity and hybridity, individuation and polyvocality, originality and imitation. This jazz dialectic amplifies Blackness as a floating signifier and allows for the performance of fluid, transnational identities that defy homogenizing taxonomies of race, class, culture, or nationhood.[5] The "social center" Hughes hosted in Ashgabat with his Harlem Victrola as its node is emblematic of this jazz dialectic: jazz – and jazz abroad especially – is (paradoxically) both a distinctly Black American art form and at the same time a world music long before we had a term for it. After all, Jelly Roll Morton, who boasted to have invented jazz, pointed to the "Spanish tinge" as its distinguishing trait.[6]

But Morton didn't take jazz abroad, nor was Hughes the first to do so. In fact, ever since the advent of technological sound reproduction, musicians from the African diaspora had been touring the Old World regularly – and they recorded, too: Black artists had cut almost 2,000 different discs and cylinders in European studios when the era of acoustic recording came to an end in the mid-1920s.[7] But on December 27, 1917, a troop transport arrived in the port of Brest on the rugged coast of Brittany, carrying soldiers from the 369th Infantry Regiment, which would gain fame and glory as the Harlem Hellfighters. Among them was a lieutenant from Alabama who, ironically, bore the name of the continent on which he was to fight. James Reese Europe fronted a regimental band that played music like no other – a merry mix of ragtime, marches, and blues, the Hellfighters' proto-jazz delighted everyone wherever they performed.[8] Heralding Hughes's claim to ownership, Europe declared categorically upon his return from the battlefields, "We won France by playing music which was ours and not a pale imitation of others...."[9]

The 369th spurred not only an insatiable appetite for syncopation all over the continent, but its performance and reception both also manifested the jazz dialectic at play already, in that the Hellfighters reminded Europeans that they were still alive after all. Europe himself, as well as his audiences, heard (and saw) in his music a purportedly authentic Blackness. At the same time, Europeans quickly recognized that these sounds of otherness afforded them, too, a novel avenue of self-expression after the devastation wrought by the Great War had seemingly maimed not only the soldiers in the trenches of Verdun and the Somme, but also Western culture as a whole. Consequently, dances such as the shimmy, the foxtrot, or the black bottom spread across the continent, and jazz fever soon raged even in the chaotic Weimar Republic. Novelist Klaus Mann observed, with a mixture of fascination and repugnance characteristic of the age, that "Jazz was the great balm and narcotic of a disconcerted, frustrated nation. The fever was indomitably expansive – a mass frenzy akin to certain contagious excesses in the Dark Ages."[10] The virus didn't spare academia either – in fact, the world's first jazz course was offered at the Hoch Conservatory in Frankfurt am Main, which began accepting students in January of 1928 and was directed by Hungarian cellist Mátyás Seiber. Seiber's primary instrument already indicates that not all viruses causing jazz fever in the 1920s were actually jazz in a strict sense; in Frankfurt, Seiber and his faculty simply grafted a muddled understanding of the music onto the classical conservatory tradition.[11] Ernst Krenek, the creator of the "jazz opera" *Johnny spielt auf*, which took the nation by storm, would later admit, "Real jazz was unknown in Europe. We gave the name jazz to anything that came out of America."[12]

And what came out of America was Black music galore, "real" jazz included. Revues like *Chocolate Kiddies* (containing songs penned by Duke Ellington) and, of course, the *Revue Nègre* starring the mesmerizing Josephine Baker, blanketed Europe with jazzy entertainment. In the orchestra backing "La Baker" was an experienced reed player from New Orleans, Sidney Bechet. Bechet had actually come to Europe once before – he was the featured soloist in Will Marion Cook's Syncopated Orchestra, whose 1919 performance in London's venerable Royal Philharmonic Hall created a sensation and prompted Swiss conductor Ernst-Alexandre Ansermet to pen what is still considered the first serious discussion of jazz by a classically trained musician.[13] In the pages of the *Revue Romande*, Ansermet predicted that "the whole world will swing along tomorrow" to the sounds he had heard emanate from the bell of Bechet's instrument.[14] His article also reacts, already, to the jazz dialectic: he heard the Syncopated Orchestra as distinctly "other," yet at the same time, his enthusiasm was ignited also by the fact that Bechet, great lover of opera that he was, liked to weave quotes from famous arias into his solos.[15] Bechet would settle in France permanently in 1950, recording and touring prolifically until his death nine years later. Playing mostly with goggle-eyed young Frenchmen, the first jazz ambassador explained his choice of domicile thus: "I felt when I settled in France that it was nearer to Africa," so even in Europe, "there's so much Negro music *waiting*."[16]

The music hadn't waited long at all to become institutionalized there.[17] In the fall of 1931, five French college students formed the Jazz Club Universitaire, the world's first jazz association. Quickly renamed Hot Club de France by its founding president, Hugues Panassié, the association spawned a radio show, a record label, several magazines, as well as copycat hot clubs in virtually every country in Western Europe, and in jazz's homeland, the USA. Amazingly enough, the Hot Club's activities continued under Nazi occupation – the wily Panassié managed to broadcast jazz music by simply giving American songs French titles. His successor, Charles Delaunay, used the association as a front to funnel information to British intelligence. Codenamed "Benny" by his handler, his ring of informants in the resistance was "Cart" in a nod to alto saxophonist Benny Carter. The Gestapo finally caught up with Delauney in 1943; though he was set free again, several other Hot Club members were summarily sent to the gas chamber.[18]

So the City of Light was darkening during the war. Hughes had visited it just before the Wehrmacht set the continent ablaze. In December of 1938 he arrived from besieged Madrid, where he had left his entire record collection at the Alianza Hotel with his friends, who were using his Harlem Victrola to drown out the rumble of Falangist bombardments. Now, Hughes couldn't help but notice the jazz dialectic still in full swing: "All over Paris that winter there was Negro music ... and French jazz bands all over town were trying their best to beat it out like the Negroes."[19] On a whim, though, the poet decided to take in a production of Saint-Saëns's *Samson et Dalila* at the Paris Opera on New Year's Eve. Making his way back to his hotel – "an Ethiopian hotel" no less – that snowy night, Hughes understood that a cataclysm was looming: "Would the world really end? 'Not my world,' I said to myself. 'My world will not end.'"[20] He was right: it didn't.

To be sure, the Axis muted the jazz dialectic, bringing the music's parade around the planet to a slow crawl. Nonetheless, amidst the carnage and genocide, jazz abroad survived, and survived in the unlikeliest of places. In Tokyo, for instance, Hattori Ryōichi had been dubbed "Japan's Cole Porter" by the patrons of the uniquely Japanese institution of the *jazz kissa*, coffee shops devoted exclusively to the consumption of hot java and recorded jazz. Now, with all of them shuttered, he simply grafted swing arrangements onto traditional folk songs, which in turn led to the profoundly ironic situation that the only place in the empire where jazz could be played legally were the radio studios of state-owned NHK. At the same time, Hattori was a member of one of the many para-governmental associations conceived to rid Japanese culture of everything Anglo-American; how active he was in this role remains unclear – he may have joined as a matter of professional survival, as many others did – but later he liked to relay how he smuggled "Tiger Rag" into the vastly popular NHK propaganda broadcast "Light Music Hour" by pulling a Panassié and branding it an old Malayan folk ditty about big cat hunting.[21] In the north German port city of Hamburg, intrepid young jazz fans, keenly monitored by Nazi authorities, were known as "Swingheinis," while in the Sudetenland, Czech trumpeter Eric Vogel and his Ghetto Swingers delighted the SS henchmen operating the Theresienstadt concentration camp and were featured in a propaganda movie shot on location. Vogel survived the Shoah, but many of the Swingers didn't.[22] Meanwhile, back in occupied France, Belgian-born Jean "Django" Reinhardt, a Romany guitarist with a stupendous technique despite having lost the use of two fingers in a wagon fire, fronted the Quintette Hot Club de France, pioneering the first jazz style to originate outside of the United States, "jazz manouche." Despite the constant threat of deportation and extermination hovering over him – after all, Reinhardt was a "gypsy" *and* a practitioner of "entartete Kunst" – jazz manouche flourished: the music's rabid fanbase even had its own moniker, the "Zazous," and the guitarist's composition "Nuages" became the unofficial anthem of wartime France, selling well over 100,000 copies in the first year of its release alone.[23] Reinhardt's success during the occupation was possible also because he enjoyed the protection of a jazz-loving first lieutenant in the Luftwaffe.[24] The jazz dialectic had not stopped swinging after all.

In the wake of Germany's surrender something like the golden age of jazz globalization emerged, also thanks to US troops being stationed all over the world. Policymakers in Washington, however, feared that they were losing the cultural Cold War as the escalating civil rights conflict in the South presented them with an embarrassing image problem in their propaganda efforts against the Red Menace. The State Department therefore launched the "Jazz Ambassadors" program, deploying Dizzy Gillespie on an eminently successful swing through the Middle East in 1956. Other state-sponsored tours soon followed, but the acute paradox of America trotting out its Black jazz stars to paint a picture of harmonious democracy while racial violence raged at home was not lost on the ambassadors. At one point, the trumpeter rebuffed an official briefing and scoffed, "I've got three hundred years of briefing. I know what they've done to us, and I'm not gonna make any excuses."[25] Clearly, the jazz dialectic is not coopted easily, nor does it need to carry a diplomatic passport. His second ambassadorial outing took Gillespie – who had already put Afro-Cuban jazz on the map – to Brazil. One night, he sat in with the house band in Rio de Janeiro's Gloria Hotel and played his boppish trumpet over the combo's traditional samba. Three young locals happened to be in the audience that night, Astrud and João Gilberto and Antônio Carlos Jobim. Astrud was still a teenager, the others in their twenties, but this fleeting encounter between bop and samba inspired them to use Black American jazz to put a new twist on Brazilian pop music, and millions of listeners all over the world would soon learn to blame their romantic entanglements on the bossa nova.[26] The bossa nova wave started on the shore of the Copacabana, but in 1963 Jobim and the Gilbertos rode it all the way to the A&R Recording Studios in New York City, where they were paired with tenor saxophonist Stan Getz. Released the following year, *Getz/Gilberto* became an international juggernaut. Women in Minneapolis as much as in Milan wanted to *be* the girl from Ipanema, and men from Tokyo to Toledo wanted to *meet* her. The attraction endures – in the summer of 2019, the album peaked at number ten in the French iTunes album charts.[27]

As the jazz dialectic was drawing many crisscrossing routes on the world map, its most cogent cartography was proffered by Martin Luther King, Jr. The same year *Getz/Gilberto* hit record stores, the preacher from Atlanta noted in his 333-word opening address to the (west) Berliner Jazztage that:

> now, Jazz is exported to the world. For in the particular struggle of the Negro in America there is something akin to the universal struggle of modern man. Everybody has the blues. Everybody longs for meaning. Everybody needs to love and be loved. Everybody needs to clap hands and be happy. Everybody longs for Faith. In music, especially that broad category called Jazz, there is a stepping stone toward all of these.[28]

How precisely the jazz dialectic came to encompass the entire planet around mid-century is exemplified by two seemingly very different albums but a year apart. Pianist Randy Weston's *Uhuru Afrika*, recorded in November of 1960, is a homage to the fledgling independence movement on the continent and one of the first sustained fusions of American jazz with African musics, with liner notes courtesy of none other than Langston Hughes.[29] On the album sleeve, the poet clearly accentuates the Afrocentric bent of the music when he declaims at the outset that jazz was "back home" after "American recordings have penetrated to the furthest jungle jukebox."[30] Nonetheless, the music's homecoming exemplifies the jazz dialectic, perpetually oscillating between the authentic and the polyglot. The voices of Martha Flowers and Brock Peters who intone Hughes's own lyrics to "African Lady" are positively operatic, and the album closes with a nod to the blues, the father of American jazz, yet even here the jazz dialectic won't be channeled readily: "Kucheza Blues" tumbles out of the speakers in a 3/4 time signature – or, as a fast waltz time, shortening the distance between Lagos and Vienna considerably.[31]

Trumpeter Benny Bailey delivers a blistering solo on "Kucheza Blues," but after the Weston session he, alongside baritone saxophonist Sahib Shihab, hightailed it to Cologne, West Germany, to record the debut album of the Kenny Clarke-Francy Boland Big Band, *Jazz Is Universal*.[32] Released in 1962 but recorded the year before, there is actually very little "universal" about the music – the opener picks up where *Uhuru Afrika* left off, with the blues, though "Box 703, Washington, D.C." is in the more conventional 4/4 time signature and penned by the Belgian co-leader. The album sounds as thoroughly "American" as the geographic coordinates of the opening track's title. The liner notes were authored by Willis Conover, whose map charts a different set of trajectories of the jazz dialectic than Hughes's: "The presence in the Clarke-Boland band of thirteen personalities from seven nations, playing in Germany for an Italian producer – and, now, released for Americans by a Turkish impresario – is all the evidence anyone needs" that jazz had indeed gone global with this unit, "the world's most representative stamp collection."[33] Conover's explications were explicitly aimed at proving that geography didn't much matter; Hughes, in turn, was commissioned to nudge the jazz dialectic in a particular geographic direction, to demonstrate that jazz was indeed (also) African. In both cases, though, the repositioning is as much discursive as musical, as the liner notes tether the inherent transnational mobility of jazz music to specific cultural reference points: Hughes's "jungle juke box" – his Harlem Victrola come "home" – in the case of *Uhuru Afrika*, the international stamp collection Conover sees assembled in the Cologne recording studio for *Jazz Is Universal*. This pair of albums, then, traces how the jazz dialectic oscillates between the authentic and the cosmopolitan: Benny Bailey's trumpet can travel to Africa and become even more "authentically Black" somehow. Here, Blackness matters, according to Hughes. But Bailey's trumpet can also travel to Europe, play in the same section next to Turkman Muvaffak "Maffy" Falay, and produce jazz where Blackness, as Conover insinuates, does not matter in the least. In both big bands, Bailey remains Bailey, retaining his musical individuality.

The trumpeter would contribute to many more stamp collections as he relocated first to Sweden, then to Holland, and was just one in a veritable flood of Black jazz expatriates. Bechet, of course, had been revered in France; bebop pioneer Bud Powell lived and recorded there for four years, and fellow bopper Oscar Pettiford moved to Denmark. Tenor saxophonists in particular seemed to favor Europe: Lucky Thompson, Don Byas, Johnny Griffin, Ben Webster, Hank Mobley, and Dexter Gordon sought to escape Jim Crow, changing musical tastes, addiction, or all of these together. For his part, Stan Getz was dodging the Internal Revenue Service (IRS) in Scandinavia. But of all the tenorists migrating to the Old World, Long Tall Dexter enjoyed the most successful career. Settling eventually in Valby, a district of Copenhagen, he founded a family and recorded steadily for the Dutch SteepleChase label. "I could breathe," he said simply of his fourteen years as an expat.[34] Remarkably, almost none of the many African American jazzers sojourning in Europe changed their style. Gordon never veered from the hard bop he had perfected prior to his move and apprenticed many eager acolytes who made the pilgrimage to the transnationally named Jazzhus Montmartre in the Danish capital. One of them was pianist Tete Montoliu, for whom navigating the jazz dialectic was a piece of cheese cake: "basically we Catalonians are all black," he flatly declared – a statement not without its irony, for Montoliu was born blind.[35]

While Gordon held court at the Jazzhus with Montoliu comping behind him, occasionally sharing the stage with Benny Bailey, much ink was being spilled over the supposed "emancipation" of European jazz from its American parent, signaled most decisively so by German "Kaputtspieler" Peter Brötzmann's earthshaking sophomore album, *Machine Gun*.[36] Its cacophonic free improvisations, which in 1968 sounded to most ears like the ultimate severance from the music's roots, a fundamental repositioning or perhaps outright suspension of the jazz dialectic, weren't really that. The riff section at the end of "Responsible," for example, sounds much more like New Orleans than Wuppertal and serves as a reminder that the octet's radical free jazz is also a tribute to the dialectic that has characterized jazz from its very beginnings in the Crescent City: for Brötzmann as much as for Bechet, the search for individual self-expression can succeed only in an ongoing creative interplay within a supportive and responsive, if not to say "responsible," collective.[37] A year after Brötzmann's aural assault, as if in counterpoint, Manfred Eicher founded the record label ECM (Edition of Contemporary Music) in Munich and perfected a "Nordic" soundscape of cool, spacious, and meditative clarity, summed up in the label's slogan, "The most beautiful sound next to silence."[38] But the very same jazz dialectic that underscored *Machine Gun* is readily audible on the vast majority of ECM releases, too, starting with the very first one: in looking to be *Free at Last*, pianist Mal Waldron is accompanied in his musical journey from the studio in Ludwigsburg toward self-determination by Mississippi-born drummer Clarence Becton and the Swiss Isla Eckinger on bass.[39]

Of course, the jazz dialectic doesn't rove only between the New World and the Old. Six years before Brötzmann appeared to perforate American jazz with his brass Browning, a South African pianist finally managed to escape the apartheid regime and, thanks to a well-connected concert promoter, found himself in frigid, snowy Zurich of all places. Abdullah Ibrahim (then still going by Dollar Brand) and his trio were soon joined by others like Louis Moholo, Dudu Pukwana, Chris McGregor, or Johnny Dyani, and turned the city by the Limmat into the epicenter of South African township jazz. For the next two years, their home base was the Café Africana, a dingy dive in Zurich's red-light district that operated without a liquor license but sported gaudy decorations born of colonialist fantasies. When Duke Ellington dropped in one night, he was so impressed by what he heard that he immediately brokered a record deal for Ibrahim.[40] The group's sets in the Africana would often be preceded by another piano trio, fronted by a young, wide-eyed Irène Schweizer, one of the very few women looking to gain a foothold on the European jazz scene. For the autodidact Schweizer, who had started out jamming to old Dixieland records before she began copying Junior Mance solos, Ibrahim's township jazz was a revelation:

> The piano was very percussive, the sound seemed raw and archaic overall, it looked wild and unclean. The sound pattern was rather monotonous, it sounded foreign to European ears. But it was just this monotony, the courage for radical reduction that the South Africans had, that gave their music a trippy character. For me, those nights were like being in a spiritual witch's cauldron, their jazz exploded all the norms we knew from the Americans. It swept me up, and I literally soaked up and internalized this style of playing.[41]

Schweizer's description is once again resonant with the jazz dialectic. To her, Ibrahim's township jazz was initially "foreign," other – Black. But its sonic Blackness was anything but hermetic, and her internalization of it helped her formulate her own musical language, a different, uniquely personal jazz idiom, not an emulation of the hard bop stylings of Mance, nor a copy of Ibrahim's pianism, nor an adaptation of Cecil Taylor, whom she would discover shortly after the Africana shuttered. The jazz dialectic has a way of coming full circle, and so the third millennium has seen the First Lady of European jazz piano regularly touring South Africa (where *Uhuru Afrika* was banned for three decades) in a duo with her old confrère Moholo.[42]

Thus, the 1960s internationalized jazz for good. Today, the echoes of Langston Hughes's Harlem Victrola continue to reverberate as if to turn the entire planet into a jazzy "social center." Chilean Melissa Aldana, for example, is one of the very few contemporary tenor saxophonists who has crafted an original voice on the instrument; her ex-husband, Jure Pukl, hails from Slovenia and is an equally individual player and composer. Both were already much too accomplished artists in their own right to have participated in the inaugural Michael Brecker International Saxophone Competition, held in Eliat, Israel, in August of 2019 – the winner, altoist Alex Hahn, flew in from Los Angeles, runner-up Alex Weitz from Miami, and third-place finalist Artem Badenko was born and raised in Russia.[43] Virtuoso guitarist Lionel Loueke made the challenging leap from Benin to New York City, where he has released a string of albums for Blue Note, jazz's most iconic record label, itself founded by two refugees from Germany back in 1939. Trumpeter extraordinaire James Morrison keeps the flame of Australian trad jazz burning brightly, but also co-leads the fusion combo On the Edge together with Simon Stockhausen, son of Karlheinz, and occasionally shares the frontline with didgeridoo player William Barton. And when keyboarder Tigran Hamasyan is not pounding out punk bop in the Big Apple's Lower West Side clubs, the Armenian roams the remote mountain valleys around Mount Ararat in search of inspiration for his next release on Eicher's ECM. Such a vibrant jazz life has sprouted in Europe over the last half century that many believe the most innovative music is nowadays made there. By 2006, even *Down Beat* finally had to listen to what was happening in the Old World and with the Swedish e.s.t. put a European group on its cover for the first time in the storied history of the seventy-two-year-old magazine.[44]

Of course, many African American artists also continue to represent jazz abroad. Singer Dee Dee Bridgewater has been calling France home for many years now. Fusion pioneer Billy Cobham's imposing drum set is pitched in Switzerland these days when he's not on tour. But it's perhaps Washington, D.C. native Coco Rouzier who describes the abiding jazz dialectic best. The Bangkok-based chanteuse was already a seasoned veteran of the circuit in southeast Asia when she finally got the chance to record:

> An album, a collaboration, a multicultural international appointment with my long-awaited destiny. This was what this recording project meant to me. The opportunity to bare my soul. My chance encounter with Werner T. Fischer in Beijing was as natural as a downbeat on a Friday night in NYC. He was the white-haired foreigner with an easygoing style that played the blues in a jazzy way. ... After so many years of music business darkness, the light is finally on for this black American soul singer. I will always be forever grateful that I went to that blues club in Beijing.[45]

Five years after Swiss guitarist Fischer first heard the singer perform on the tiny stage of the legendary Café CD Blues, he flew Rouzier out to Zurich, billeted her in a cozy chalet where they rearranged a bushel of her songs and a couple of standards for jazz sextet, and recorded *The Light Is On* with his aptly named band, Travelogue, in a studio near Lake Lucerne, smack dab in the middle of the Alps. Rouzier's long journey only proves yet again what Langston Hughes already knew: when the jazz dialectic swings, *really* swings, "Trouble / Mellows to a golden note" – be that in Brooklyn or Berlin, Buenos Aires or Beijing.[46]

Notes

1. Langston Hughes, *I Wonder as I Wander*, 1934 (New York: Hill and Wang, 1993), 69.
2. Ibid., 150.
3. Ibid., 109, 114.
4. Ibid., 122, emphasis added.
5. Jürgen E. Grandt, *Gettin' Around: Jazz, Script, Transnationalism* (Athens: University of Georgia Press, 2018), 18–20.
6. Quoted in Alan Lomax, *Mister Jelly Roll: The Fortunes of Jelly Roll Morton, New Orleans Creole and "Inventor of Jazz"* (Oakland, CA: University of California Press, 1973), 62.
7. Rainer E. Lotz, "Early African-American Entertainers," in Francisco Martinelli, ed., *The History of European Jazz: The Music, Musicians, and Audience in Context* (Sheffield: Equinox, 2018), 642–43.
8. Reid Badger, *A Life in Ragtime: A Biography of James Reese Europe* (New York: Oxford University Press, 2007), 162–63.; E. Douglas Bomberger, *Making Music American: 1917 and the Transformation of Culture* (New York: Oxford University Press, 2018), 202–4.
9. Quoted in "A Negro Explains 'Jazz,'" *Literary Digest*, April 26, 1919, 28.
10. Klaus Mann, *The Turning Point: Thirty-Five Years in This Century*, 1942 (New York: Marcus Weiner, 1984), 86.
11. Wolfram Knauer, *"Play Yourself, Man!" Die Geschichte des Jazz in Deutschland* (Stuttgart: Reclam, 2019), 66–68.
12. Quoted in J. Bradford Robinson, "Jazz Reception in Weimar Germany: In Search of a Shimmy Figure," in Bryan Gilliam, ed., *Music and Performance During the Weimar Republic* (Cambridge: Cambridge University Press, 1994), 113.
13. Rashida K. Braggs, *Jazz Diasporas: Race, Music, and Migration in Post-World War II Paris* (Oakland, CA: University of California Press, 2016), 12–13.
14. Ernst-Alexandre Ansermet, "Bechet and Jazz Visit Europe, 1919," in Ralph de Toledano, ed., *Frontiers of Jazz*, 3rd ed., (Gretna, LA: Pelican, 1994), 118.
15. John Chilton, *Sidney Bechet: Wizard of Jazz*, 1987 (New York: Da Capo, 1996), 45–46.

16 Sidney Bechet, *Treat It Gentle*, 1960 (New York: Da Capo, 1978), 194, 207. Original emphasis.
17 For more on the institutionalization of jazz, see Dale Chapman's chapter in this volume (Chapter 11).
18 Michael Dregni, *Django: The Life and Music of a Gypsy Legend* (New York: Oxford University Press, 2004), 180–81; Mario Dunkel, "Constructing the American Hugues Panassié," in Julius Greve and Sascha Pöhlmann, eds., *America and the Musical Unconscious* (New York: Atropos, 2015), 93–96; Braggs, *Jazz Diasporas*, 67–70.
19 Hughes, *I Wonder*, 401.
20 Ibid., 402, 405.
21 E. Taylor Atkins, *Blue Nippon: Authenticating Jazz in Japan* (Durham, NC: Duke University Press, 2001), 133–57; Michael Pronko, "Quiet about It – Jazz in Japan," in Nicholas Gebhardt, Nichole Rustin-Paschal, and Tony Whyton, eds., *The Routledge Companion to Jazz Studies* (New York: Routledge, 2019), 272–74.
22 Mike Zwerin, *Swing under the Nazis: Jazz as a Metaphor for Freedom* (New York: Cooper Square, 2000), 24–29; Knauer, "Play Yourself, Man!," 111–27.
23 Dregni, *Django*, 166–69.
24 Zwerin, *Swing under the Nazis*, 43–52, 151–55.
25 Dizzy Gillespie and Al Fraser, *To Be or Not to Bop* (New York: Da Capo, 1979), 414.
26 Penny M. Von Eschen, *Satchmo Blows Up the World: Jazz Ambassadors Play the Cold War* (Cambridge, MA: Harvard University Press, 2004), 32–41; Eduardo Vicente, "Bossa Nova and Beyond: The Jazz as Symbol of Brazilian-Ness," in Nicholas Gebhardt, Nichole Rustin-Paschal, and Tony Whyton, eds., *The Routledge Companion to Jazz Studies* (New York: Routledge, 2019), 296–99.
27 iTunes Charts, (n.d.), www.itunescharts.net/fra/artists/music/stan-getz-joao-gilberto/albums/getzgilberto/; Marc Meyers, Liner notes: "Disquiet Nights of Reluctant Stars," Stan Getz and João Gilberto, *Getz/Gilberto*, 1964 (Verve 80020749-02 CD, 2014), 12–13.
28 Quoted in Bruce Jackson and David Demsey, "Source Uncovered for Martin Luther King Jr. Jazz Quote," *Down Beat*, January 2011, 62.
29 Robin D.G. Kelley, *Africa Speaks, America Answers: Modern Jazz in Revolutionary Times*. (Cambridge, MA: Harvard University Press, 2012), 53–64.
30 Langston Hughes, Liner notes, Randy Weston, *Uhuru Afrika*, 1961 (Roulette WPCR-29214 CD, 2017).
31 Randy Weston, *Uhuru Afrika*, 1961 (Roulette WPCR-29214 CD, 2017).
32 Kenny Clarke and Francy Boland, *Jazz Is Universal*, 1962 (Rhino WPCR-27191 CD, 2012).
33 Willis Conover, Liner notes, Kenny Clarke and Francy Boland, *Jazz is Universal*, 1962 (Rhino WPCR-27191 CD, 2012).
34 Maxine Gordon, *Sophisticated Giant: The Life and Legacy of Dexter Gordon* (Oakland, CA: University of California Press, 2018), 152.

35 Dexter Gordon, "Cheese Cake," Rec. June 11, 1964, *Cheese Cake* (SteepleChase SCCD 36008 CD, 1990); Joachim Ernst Berendt and Günther Huesmann, *The Jazz Book: From Ragtime to the Twenty-First Century*, 7th ed. (Chicago: Lawrence Hill, 2009), 390.
36 Peter Brötzmann, *Machine Gun*, 1968 (FMP CD 24 CD, 1990).
37 Knauer, *"Play Yourself, Man!,"* 260–3.
38 Immanuel Brockhaus, "Organizing Emotions in Time: Klangästhetik und Studiotechnologie im ECM Sound der frühen Jahre, 1970–1980," *European Journal of Musicology*, 16.1 (2017), 94–106.
39 Mal Waldron, *Free at Last*, 1970 (ECM 1001 831 332-2 CD, 1991).
40 Kelley, *Africa Speaks*, 149–55.
41 Quoted in Thomas Wyss, "Das archaische Herz der Finsternis." *Tages-Anzeiger*, November 25, 2009, 30.
42 Gitta Gsell, dir., *Irène Schweizer*, (RECK Filmproduktion/Intakt, 2006); Christian Broecking, *Dieses unbändige Gefühl der Freiheit: Irène Schweizer – Jazz, Avantgarde, Politik* (Berlin: Broecking Verlag, 2016), 51–53.
43 Michael Brecker International Saxophone Competition, https://breckercompetition.org/.
44 Stuart Nicholson, *Jazz and Culture in a Global Age* (Boston: Northeastern University Press, 2014), 152–53, 253; Måns Wallgren, "Sweden: 1970–2000," Francisco Martinelli, ed., *The History of European Jazz: The Music, Musicians, and Audience in Context* (Sheffield: Equinox, 2018), 217–23.
45 Coco Rouzier, Liner notes, Werner Fischer's Travelogue, *The Light Is On* (PBR Jazz PBR J300 CD, 2015).
46 Langston Hughes, "Trumpet Player," 1949. Arnold Rampersad and David Roessel, eds., *The Collected Poems of Langston Hughes* (New York: Vintage, 1994), 339.

PART IV
Literary Genres

CHAPTER 13

Orchestrating Chaos
Othering and the Politics of Contingency in Jazz Fiction

Herman Beavers

In his book *Subversive Sounds*, Charles Hersch cites an 1890 story in *The New Orleans Mascot*, expressing the newspaper's anxious criticism of "a nigger band" in the city's tenderloin district, decrying the dangers that would arise from "encouraging racial boundary crossings."[1] The story continues, "Here male and female, black and yellow, even white meet on terms of equality and abandon themselves to the extreme limit of obscenity and lasciviousness."[2] Jazz's opponents listened and "heard the racial and ethnic mixing in the music itself," its "European harmonies sullied by African rhythmic and tonal devices."[3]

It should come as no surprise, then, that in the years following World War I, a number of commentators bemoaned that the United States was entering a state of crisis. Just as the years following Reconstruction were the product of a racist imaginary that cast each and every Black man as a rapist-in-waiting, jazz's most insistent critics used words like "pathological," "infection," "virus," "epidemic," and "cancer," endeavoring to associate the music with physical malady.[4] Neil Leonard cites an article from the period stating that "The counters of music stores are loaded with this virulent poison which in the form of a malarious [sic] epidemic is finding its way into the homes and brains of our youth."[5] As such, jazz became the object of heavy public surveillance. Efforts to invalidate the music meant that the proponents of jazz were faced with analogies situated at the intersection of biologically inflected metaphors and racist intent. Characterizing jazz music as a "contagion" was also a way to articulate the dangers posed by racial difference such that jazz constituted a failure of the American cultural "immune system." Anne Shaw Faulkner's "Does Jazz Put the Sin in Syncopation?" from a 1921 edition of *Ladies Home Journal* asks, "Can music ever be an influence for evil?" And she concludes, "What instincts are then aroused by jazz? Certainly not deeds of valor or martial courage."[6]

These early responses to jazz indicate how the music formed a social nexus constituted by racial anxiety and cultural innovation. In his influential essay "Other: From Noun to Verb," Nathaniel Mackey proposes that "cultural diversity *is* cultural, that it is a consequence of actions and assumptions that are socially – rather than naturally, genetically – instituted and enforced."[7] Mackey distinguishes two forms of othering, "artistic othering" and "social othering." In his view, the former has to do with "innovation, invention, and change upon which cultural health and diversity depend and thrive." The latter, on the other hand, "has to do with power, exclusion, and privilege, the centralizing of the norm against which otherness is measured, meted out, marginalized."[8] Because jazz has so much to do with the individual's relationship to modernity itself, representations of jazz reflect very high stakes because they inevitably dramatize precarity. If, as Mackey insists, artistic othering occurs in the face of social othering's effort to nullify the musician's humanity, then humans playing the music are perpetually engaged in the act of managing contingency. The jazz musician's body is contingent upon performance as a way to manage the hegemonic exigencies imposed by inequality and alienation. But we might go further since this means that representations of jazz music, particularly in fiction, often suggest that jazz musicians find themselves in a state of exigency created by their need to survive economically, to find ways to master their instrument, and the necessities of improvisation and originality.

When the body is brought into this equation, what must be accounted for is the jazz musician's ability to manage contingency in the wake of past injury. In *The Wounded Storyteller*, sociologist Arthur W. Frank describes his desire to make use of people's stories about illness as one of wanting to "think with story."[9] It is not my contention that this process is always realized in jazz fiction. However, I insist that jazz musicians, and their ability to make their playing analogous to thinking with stories, means bodies playing the music need to be conversant with strategies for managing life at the point where contingency and exigency meet. Orchestration accompanies all those instances where the body is undone, rendered susceptible within the space of an identity that is contested on both racial and gendered fronts. The jazz musician's body is contingent upon performance as a way to manage the impositions created by misfortunes of all sorts.

We find such a postulation in James Baldwin's classic short story, "Sonny's Blues" (1957). I focus attention here on two aspects of the story: Sonny's drug addiction and his return to the jazz scene. In a letter to his brother (a middle-class teacher with no ties to the jazz life), Sonny writes, "I don't want you to think it had anything to do with me being a musician. It's more than that. Or maybe less than that."[10] Here, Baldwin suggests that drug addiction signalizes crisis. But that crisis is not contingent upon a binary of musician/nonmusician. Rather it is a crisis that must be read within a complex web of relations and Sonny's body serves as a way to register both affliction and the inchoate forces that can be mobilized, if not to overcome, then to nullify it, if only momentarily.

Baldwin's depiction of jazz involves first defamiliarizing the reader with what the music represents. This is signaled by his choice of narrator, the older brother of a jazz pianist named Sonny. The narrator has never understood Sonny's attraction to jazz, feeling that jazz musicians are nothing more than "good time people."[11] Upon Sonny's return to New York from a detoxification facility upstate, the narrator "watch[es] Sonny for signs" of relapse and wonders if he will be "safe."[12] As the narrator directs a brotherly gaze at Sonny, he remembers a story his mother relates about his uncle's death. His father has never spoken of his dead brother, run over by a car full of drunk white men, although he continues to grieve over the loss. The narrator's interpretation is that his father had failed to take care of the brother and thus has suffered because he wonders if "every white man he [sees is] the man that killed his brother."[13]

But this is a misinterpretation reflecting the narrator's inability to understand the difference between exigency and contingency. The narrator's interpretation of his mother's tale, which is both family history and parable, leads him to believe that it his fraternal duty to prevent Sonny's fall back into drugs, as if his sole duty is keeping trouble at bay. He believes that he has been tasked by his mother to keep Sonny safe from harm, but what she has deemed to be of greater importance is to *accept* him, irrespective of any trouble he finds.

He does not recognize this imperative because he casts himself in opposition to the exigency Sonny's addiction represents. It is only his daughter's death – from polio – that makes Sonny's trouble "real." As the narrator falls deeper and deeper into despair, he slowly realizes that his own recovery is contingent on his ability to listen. Baldwin begins "Sonny's Blues" with the narrator reading about Sonny's addiction and arrest in the newspaper. Chronologically, the story opens in the spring prior to his daughter's death later that fall. However, it is not, as the narrator believes, a matter of *thinking through* his injury, but *listening to* what that injury can tell him. But because his stewardship of Sonny involves telling him how to behave, the most fundamental aspect of acceptance eludes him, which is evidenced when Sonny declares, "I hear you, but you never hear anything I say."[14]

Baldwin's story is deeply concerned with the acquisition of sonic literacy. But such a state is often reached by unsavory means and thus exposes the racial fault lines running through American expressive culture and the body politic. This can often only be understood in the midst of the kinds of border crossing that tests – if not revealing the instability outright of – cultural norms around the management of racial difference. In some of the earliest jazz fictions this often took the form of confronting the exigencies produced by the presence of the racial Other. For example, Julian Street's "The Jazz Baby," first published in 1922, features a family of comfortable means in which the son, Chet, much to his parents' dismay, opens a musical case containing a saxophone, distinguished by the fact that it is "quadruple gold plate over triple silver plate," and then, "holding it as if to play, he be[gins] to shuffle, undulating his body in a negroid manner," before playing a tune titled "Home-Brew Blues."[15] For whites endeavoring to represent human experience in fiction, especially in the years just after World War I, few evinced concern with how Black people see the world, even as the Black body provoked levels of racial anxiety assuming a plurality of forms.

Street portrays jazz as a vehicle of social and racial masquerade that leads Chet's mother, Elsa, to appear at the vaudeville show of their local club under the stage name "The Painted Jazzabel." "[B]reezing" onstage wearing a "filmy evening gown," Elsa's face "suggest[s] a carved mask, very pretty and almost human in expression; eyebrows penciled to a narrow line, cheeks freshly tinted, lips like scarlet poppy petals, hair like a shock of yellow uncurled ostrich plumes."[16] Elsa adopts the posture of a burlesque performer and her costume is "accentuated by two large boxes dangling at the end of dog chains," as she sits at the piano and proceeds to play and sing – much to the dismay of her neighbors, friends, and son – a tune called "Booful Baboon Babe."[17] Street's depiction of jazz reflects the racial anxieties of whites and it intimates that the music's most salient feature (and therefore, the danger it poses) lies in its ability to devalue whiteness as it leads aficionados to embrace racial difference, looser morals, and freer social habits. It is no surprise, then, that after Elsa's performance, mother and son decide that jazz music is a form of self-debasement, reflecting mainstream attitudes about the music and dramatizing jazz's influence on the social behavior of whites. For reference, Faulkner proffers, "Never before have such outrageous dances been permitted in private as well as public ballrooms," implying that jazz has the power to rend the US social fabric.[18]

For all its preoccupation with giving readers a window into the world of jazz, jazz fiction often portrays modern life as a product of risk, invention, momentum, friction, profit, loss, and heartbreak. Because jazz is synonymous with contingency, the need to engage in acts of social and artistic invention, jazz fiction often portrays the music as it takes place in a local context. Indeed, the preponderance of jazz fiction situates musicians somewhere on a continuum that features weekend players at one end with virtuoso, professional players at the other, and a wide range of players and ensembles in between. Hence, "local" need not be a synonym for unprofessionalism or weak musicianship. As James Lincoln Collier points out:

> Ordinary local jazz players whether they work in jazz full-time or not, lead the same sort of daily life that most Americans do: a routine job, marriage and family life with the normal ups and downs; births, deaths, commuting train, vacation trips, the flu, office parties ... [Playing jazz] heals the battered ego, provides a sense of being on the inside of something, a feeling of doing something wholly worthwhile.[19]

Collier's observation is equally suggestive of how jazz musicians appearing in fiction are often solidly located in the world of work. Hence, when jazz musicians are depicted on stage, they are almost always engaged in the act of paid labor. While it may not lead to a handsome amount of money, the stories often dramatize what it means to be either a musician who plays jazz because they can or one who plays because they must. In highlighting jazz as a local iteration that reflects a particular set of issues surrounding playing, writers of jazz fiction complicate what, starting in the 1920s, is an increasingly volatile public sphere.

In C. W. Smith's "The Plantation Club" (1977), Curtis "Stoogie" Goodman lands in a nameless town in New Mexico, just long enough "to recoup the means to move on," after the band he has been touring with "collapse[s] in El Paso."[20] But the means elude him and he is stranded, with no hope of escape, his life reduced to stark contrasts: "Mornings he washed dishes at the Winslow Café," the narrator relates, "Three nights a week he played at The Plantation, a nightclub in our small black ghetto."[21] The narrator, a young white boy who aspires to become a jazz musician, describes the life he and his best friend, Terry, have lived as being the near polar opposite of Stoogie's lived experience, where they inhabit clean, well-lighted places free of squalor and want. When narrator and Terry park across the street from the club, he observes, "Now and then a black face poked its way into our vision, but we made no offers, asked no questions" and subsequently walking to the door of the club, he feels a small flash of anxiety: "The uncharted territory around the building hid conspirators whose razors flashed at the corners of my eyes."[22] Further, it should not be lost on the reader that the club is called "The Plantation," a detail which proposes that jazz and the Black musicians playing it are in a constant state of devalued labor.

Painfully aware of the radical differences between the lives of the Black musicians he seeks to emulate and the privilege that curls in and around his life, the narrator concludes, "My greatest sorrow to date was having lost my first love to another at age fifteen."[23] What lends this commentary its poignance is that the narrator's whiteness reduces jazz to being about the acquisition of technique, suggesting the ease with which racial difference can be ignored or dismissed – or worse, fetishized. Something to be compensated for but never confronted for its own sake.

Don Asher's "The Barrier," opens with its narrator's realization that "the blacks had something I was in dire need of," as if it is their duty to provide that desired object without compensation, or even the bestowal of respect.[24] The narrator has become aware of the "widening chasm separating the levels of rhythmic propulsion achieved by black and white musicians."[25] Jamming with Black musicians, the narrator calls off a tune, only to hear a Black musician say derisively, "That's one of your white-boy tunes."[26] A Black bass player makes the distinction between the narrator's choice of music and "tunes with relaxed, more fluid structures," like "Georgia on My Mind," which allows musicians to "climb inside it, feel its bones," while what he refers to as a "Caucasian tune is boxy, four-squared, forc[ing the musician] into corners."[27]

A similar sentiment is expressed in Evan Hunter's novel *Streets of Gold*, which features a white, blind piano player named Iggie, who's cut his teeth listening to Art Tatum's music, and who is allowed to sit in with three Black musicians in what he describes as a "toilet," a place where musicians on the descent find themselves.[28] Accompanied by his uncle, who announces, "It's full of niggers ... Let's get out of here," Iggie wants to meet his idol, Biff Anderson, a mid-level Black jazz pianist, more interested in the woman sitting next to him, than he is in schooling the young man.[29] After allowing him to sit at the piano and play a couple of Tatum tunes, Biff lets him stay at the piano while the Black musicians get set up. They launch into a Johnny Mercer tune, but unfamiliar with the slang the musicians use to direct him, and totally unaware that by this time, in 1944, the music of Tatum is considered well out of date, Iggie plays in the lower registers of the piano with his left hand, "pounding out [a] steady four/four rhythm" as he hears the bass player playing identical chords.[30] After the song ends, the bass player says, "Well, you ain't a F-sharp piano player, that's for sure ... But you know what you can do with that left hand of yours, don't you."[31]

Baffled, Iggie asks Biff why the bass player has dismissed him. Biff proceeds to explain the difference between the bebop music the Black musicians are trying to play and Iggie's Tatum-inspired style. Though he is proud of his left hand, he has no clue that he has insulted the band until Biff explains:

> You want to know why the boys shot you down, it's 'cause you put them in prison, man, you put them in that old-style bass prison, and they can't play that way no more.... Sam wants to walk the bass line himself, he don't want to be trapped by no rhythm the *piano* player's layin' down, he don't even want to be trapped by the *drummer* no more.[32]

Iggie has no understanding of what it means to play the "shell" of a chord, to allow the horn player to "blow pure and fast and hard," without being forced into a corner by ornate chords and pounding rhythms in his left hand. Biff describes how bebop maven Bud Powell plays a C-minor seventh chord: "all he plays are the C and the B flat. With his pinkie and thumb, you dig? He leaves out the insides, he just gives you the shell."[33] He directs Iggie to go to 52nd Street, where bebop has become the dominant style. When Iggie declares that he still wants to play like Tatum, Biff tells him, "[I]f you're startin' out *now*, for Christ's sake, don't start with something, already *dead*. Go to the Street, man. Fifty-Second Street, dig what the cats are doing."[34]

What each of these stories endeavor to communicate is that it is Black musicians who set the trends and dominate the bandstand. Each of the characters in Smith's, Asher's, and Hunter's stories find themselves disoriented, feeling as though they have landed in a foreign country speaking in a broken tongue. Stories such as these do more than describe what happens when a new musical paradigm supplants an old one, they likewise insinuate that whiteness, contrary to what it means in other endeavors, is neither a source of instant respect nor a marker of cultural authenticity. But these stories also make an equally important assertion regarding notions of racial essentialism, the belief that a musician's racial background imbues her with an innate understanding of jazz as what Guthrie Ramsey terms "race music."[35]

The protagonist in Asher's "The Barrier" eventually garners respect from his fellow musicians, but what he refers to as the barrier is, in effect, how he rationalizes his inability to play among "schooled, confident, nerveless musicians," suspecting "that the skills required for entry – so deeply ingrained in the Negro experience of despair, anger, and struggle – might lie forever beyond my reach."[36] But what he misses, and only slowly realizes, is that the skills the Black musicians put on display are not the product of natural gifts, nor are they fixated on the anger and despair the protagonist projects onto them. Rather, they have mastered their craft by woodshedding and by testing their skills in the cutting contests that happen after hours. The protagonist wants to play jazz at what happens to be a time of stylistic and instrumental innovation; in this instance, the shift from swing music as the dominant cultural signifier of jazz to bebop.

The stories by Smith, Hunter, and Asher, with their white protagonists finding themselves in the midst of Black musicians whose playing they admire and seek to emulate, acquire an additional level of clarity when understood within the context of social and artistic othering.[37] But as John McCluskey's 1990 story, "Lush Life," set in 1955, suggests, Black musicians embody discipline. Earl Ferguson, leading America's Greatest Band, with the help of composer and arranger Billy Cox, creates music that works "an easy magic. Few could weave sounds the way they could, few could get twelve voices, twelve rambunctious personalities, to shout or moan as one."[38] Driving in the "scout car," ahead of the bus carrying the band, Earl and Billy talk about women, their bandmates, and work out arrangements for the next night's gig. The rules of the band are simple: "[I]f you missed the bus and could not make practice the next day, you were fined fifty dollars. If you missed the date because you missed the bus or train, you were fired."[39] Here is a near-total reversal of the state of affairs that inhered in jazz's earliest incarnations.

Readers find a radical contrast to the professional routines of Ferguson's big band in James Reed's "The Shrimp Peel Gig" (1997), which features a professional musician who has "barely escaped the school band routine," where leading an elementary or high school band pays the bills. The story's narrator has "beat the small business odds," by getting a contract repairing horns for a school district. "I'm doing all right," he says as he prepares to play a gig, "The work is steady. I teach a few lessons. I play a few gigs."[40] Reed's story is distinguished by its near flawless description of the part-time musician's life. Here, Hank Leitner and the Starliners is a band composed almost completely by musicians with day jobs. One is a retired actuary "who took the buyout when it came."[41] Another, a trumpeter, teaches junior high school. Trombonist Murph, the narrator's best friend and frequent bandmate on gigs, "improvises counterpoint that looks gorgeous in transcription," and plays "'Caravan' like Bach had written the tune instead of Ellington."[42]

In stories like these, we find a love of playing wrapped in a pragmatic sensibility that refuses to allow musicians to dream of playing full-time. In J. F. Powers's "He Don't Plant Cotton" (1943), drummer Baby and piano player Dodo (who doubles as a bartender) play "Dodo's Blues," a number the piano player modestly calls "nothing," despite the fact that he can sit "gently worming music" from a battered upright piano.[43]

Just as Baldwin's Sonny is restored to a state of wholeness when he finds his "blues," so too is Dodo able to transcend his physical and social limitations to become synonymous with sound, to carve a space of freedom in the midst of degradation.

Baby and Dodo play with a Black female piano player named Libby for a group of increasingly surly white southerners from out of town. They insist that the band play "Ol' Man River" over and over, which the band resists. At one point, a white man touches Libby on the arm and says, "When I do that to you, that means 'Stop' ... Some of the boys want to hear that 'Ol' Man River some more."[44] The situation grows increasingly tense, with Libby insisting she and Baby will "play it for you later on."[45] But the white patron grabs her again, demanding, "You gotta play it right now. For a bunch of boys from down South. They all got a hankerin to hear that 'Ol' Man River' some more."[46] Another white man adds, "So you best play it," as he leans on the upright, "On account of I'm gonna take and give ear. We kinda like how that old song sounds up North. Whacha all need. The drummer will sing."[47] Libby responds by saying, "We ain't comin'," and gets up from the piano, putting her overcoat on over her red dress, while Baby disassembles his drum kit. As they continue to pack up, Libby looks at Baby and declares, "I won't change," to which Baby replies, "You don't have to."[48] The story's title, then, is ultimately a delineation of the line Black musicians are forced to toe: between a subservient reincarnation of "the darky" springing from the white Southern racist imaginary, or the defiant artist who refuses to sacrifice Black dignity for the sake of employment.

Powers's story is a direct descendant of Eudora Welty's classic story, "Powerhouse" (1941), which posits a rather ironic take on racial border crossings. Growing out of Welty's experience hearing jazz great Fats Waller in concert as a young woman in Mississippi, the story involves a musician nicknamed Powerhouse, whose band, The Tasmanians, plays for a white audience, as Blacks are forced to stand outside in the rain to hear.[49] Powerhouse, like many Black musicians in stories by white authors, is the very embodiment of excess, meaning that he exists in the liminal space between exigency and contingency.

As the narrator describes it, Powerhouse and His Tasmanians are playing at a "white dance" but "nobody dances," and so "Everybody just stands around the band and watches Powerhouse," which is suggestive for how whites apprehend Powerhouse and his musicians – as sources of spectacle, to be watched and consumed rather than understood as a source of rhythmic motion.[50] The narrator's racism is thinly veiled, couched as it is in stereotype and racial fascination. While this racial bias is evident, it is also clear that the band represents a kind of Black exceptionalism. "Powerhouse is not a show-off like the Harlem boys, not drunk, not crazy – he's in a trance; he's a person of joy."[51] Though he has a "look of hideous, powerful rapture on his face," is "monstrous," and "is in motion every moment" the narrator concludes "you need to see him" whether you've heard him on records or not. His sound is at once "obscene" and capable of "send[ing] everybody into oblivion."[52]

Powerhouse is distinguished, then, by the fact that he exists in a space constituted out of social transgression, joyousness, and racial mystery. Soon, the conversation turns back to Powerhouse's dead wife, Gypsy. But in an interesting turn, the band begins to imagine what led to her demise, and soon it becomes clear that all the talk about the wife's death is purely speculative, playful even. As this movement between on- and offstage life indicates, Powerhouse, dead wife or not, has an inner life of which the whites are neither aware nor care to understand. Welty's point is that jazz occurs at the interstitial site of race ritual and freedom. Though Blacks are not allowed inside to listen to the music, those who have followed Powerhouse and the band to the World Café have been privy to the band's performance of speculative ideation. Thus, their racial subordination is nullified, if only momentarily. That Welty allows the reader to be privy to this circumstance does not mean that she succeeds in altering the white reader's perspective when it comes to racial bigotry, but it does show an attempt to portray a space where the band's speculative approach to performance shields the most important parts of themselves away from the deleterious effects of racism and segregation.

Artistic othering is manifest in those moments when the individual finds herself empowered to overcome the inertia of everyday life. What makes this notion of a piece with my current discussion is the fact that against the backdrop of everyday life, Mike Featherstone posits what he terms "heroic life," arguing that it "cuts a swathe [sic] through [everyday life's] dense facticity."[53] Because jazz musicians most often appear in jazz fiction as heroic figures, I'm intrigued by the prospect that jazz fiction functions as a rumination on how human beings navigate the thicket of signification we have come to understand as everyday life. As Featherstone points out, we can perhaps best locate the jazz musician within the context of what sociologist Georg Simmel referred to as "the adventure." As Simmel would have it, "the adventure falls outside the usual continuity of everyday existence which is disregarded on principle." Further, the adventurer has "a different time sense which entails a strong sense of the present and disregard for the future."[54] And perhaps most poignantly, Featherstone points to Simmel's declaration that in the adventure "we abandon ourselves to the 'powers and accidents of the world, which can delight us, but in the same breath can also destroy us.'"[55] Featherstone describes everyday life as "a residual category into which can be jettisoned all irritating bits and pieces which do not fit into orderly thought."[56] Though it is equally possible to argue that everyday life is finally the canvas upon which representation is projected, Featherstone suggests that the "taken-for-grantedness" of the everyday is how we come to understand the jazz musician's rejection of uniformity and repetition in favor of improvisation and reinvention.

If jazz narratives have a recurring theme, it might revolve around the difficult, if not insurmountable, task of consciously trying to carry tradition forward by becoming an original contributor. Here, the story turns on the musician's effort to distinguish his (or her) individuality via the particulars of *their sound*, as if nothing matters to them but making the audience understand that the story they seek to relate is theirs and theirs alone. But what distinguishes this brand of playing is its ability to evoke the *familiar* while expressing the *new*. As Ralph Ellison observes, each "true jazz moment (as distinct from the uninspired commercial performance) springs from a contest in which each artist challenges all the rest; each solo flight, or improvisation, represents (like the successive canvasses of a painter) a definition of his identity: as individual, as member of the collectivity, and as a link in the chain of tradition."[57]

This is exemplified in "Sonny's Blues," where the plot's most insistent element addresses the inherent relationship between sound and human experience. The narrator's concern for Sonny reduces him to a place onto which the shame of drug addiction (and thus the futility of his life as a musician) is visually mapped. This prevents the narrator from accessing Sonny's story for any other purpose. His inability to ascertain Sonny's attempts to describe his experience demonstrates a failure of sonic literacy that can only be managed by altering his relationship to music. If our ability to negotiate the public domain is contingent on what resources we bring with us, then in that moment when Sonny begins to play, the narrator must realize that all he knows about music is "that not many people ever really hear it."[58] Even in those moments "when something opens within, and the music enters, what [is] corroborated, are personal, private vanishing evocations."[59]

It is at this point in the story where the narrator's resistance to jazz is supplanted by an important epiphany. But it is also, from a fiction writer's standpoint, a moment where the danger of intruding on the character's perspective becomes palpable. So, moving forward from the passage above, the narrator continues:

> But the man who creates the music is hearing something else, *is dealing with the roar rising from the void and imposing order on it as it hits the air.* What is evoked in him, then, is of another order, more terrible because it has no words, and triumphant, too, for that same reason. And his triumph, when he triumphs, is ours.[60]

Sonny's performative act provides the catalyst for the narrator to adopt a quality of observation and assessment that eluded him earlier in the story. As Sonny wrestles with his piano, trying to recover his public voice, he likewise seeks a way to move his body out of the visual confinement the narrator has imposed upon him in order to occupy a sonic space, where his voice assumes a custodial relation not only to his own body, but the bodies of the audience as well. When Sonny's voice is restored, an instance which the other members of the combo have anticipated, Creole, the bass player and Sonny's mentor, steps "forward to remind them that what they were playing was the blues."[61] And the narrator recognizes, all of a sudden that the music is

> not about *anything very new*. He and his boys up there were keeping it new, at the risk of ruin, destruction, madness, and death, in order to find ways to make us listen. For while the tale of how we suffer, and how we are delighted, and how we may triumph is never new, it always must be heard.[62]

Baldwin enacts an important shift between the narrator and Sonny, from a purely visual mode to one sustained by the sonic. What I wish to emphasize for our purposes here is the manner in which the jazz musician creates a symbiosis between himself and the audience, an instance where the performative generates a collective (if only transient) freedom. Baldwin further suggests the challenge for the jazz musician is not so much one of transcending the body as fixing its limitations within sonic discourse. The jazz musician's body constitutes the regenerative potential that can help the listener resist the dictates of shame and disillusionment.

It could be argued, then, that jazz fiction often highlights the manner in which musicians – and sometimes the audience – function at the intersection of exigency and contingency, where dire circumstances are held at bay by the musician's ability to take risks, commit herself to mastering her craft, and pushing past previously established limits, some of which occur in the artistic imagination and others that are located squarely in and around the musician's body. Considering the working conditions in which jazz musicians have been forced to work, it should come as no surprise that they experience high levels of stress that have historically been managed through acts of self-medication.

As I mentioned above, jazz fiction's focus on jazz musicians of all stripes offers readers a glimpse into the musician's tacit ability to wring meaning out of everyday encounters. But we should also be mindful of those instances when the jazz musician is constituted as a tragic figure, whose presence evokes a sense of pathos largely because she has difficulty managing everyday life. An example of this can be found in John A. Williams's 1961 novel, *Night Song*, which features a supporting character named Richie "Eagle" Stokes, whose life and career are reminiscent of Charlie Parker's artistic odyssey.[63] Stokes is a brilliant musician whose heroin addiction puts him into a severe state of decline. We see how the banalities and indignities associated with everyday life in a racist United States come into direct conflict with the contingencies associated with artistic inventiveness when Stokes has a confrontation with a police officer while standing outside a club. The moment recalls Miles Davis's fateful encounter with New York police officers outside Birdland in 1959 – which left Davis bloodied and in jail – as the confrontation unfolds in the same way: a police officer, not liking the sight of a Black man who exudes self-possession and confidence, decides to escalate the encounter till a fight ensues and he beats Stokes with his nightstick. This exigent circumstance forces readers to understand that for all his talent and renown, "Eagle" Stokes is viewed by the cop as an uppity Black man who must be put in his place. In this moment, Eagle's ability to manage contingency has little utility, rendering his status as a star jazz musician moot.

In her book *Risk*, sociologist Deborah Lupton describes the need on the part of certain individuals to engage in risky behaviors, noting that some "people ... cultivate risks as a means of undermining ontological security," in order to put on a "display of daring, resourcefulness, skill, and sustained endeavour, where people are only too aware of the risks involved."[64] Lupton describes this sort of behavior, borrowing from fellow sociologist David Lyng, as "edgework." She continues:

> Edgework incorporates the notion that risk-taking activities are about exploring the edges that exist along boundaries, a form of boundary negotiation. These boundaries may include those between sanity and insanity, consciousness and unconsciousness, life and death and an ordered sense of self and environment against a disordered sense of self and environment.

Edgework is also

> characterized by an emphasis on *skilled performance* of the dangerous activity, involving the ability *to maintain control over a situation that verges on complete chaos* that requires, above all, "mental toughness," the ability not to give in to fear.[65]

If everyday life is distinguished by exigency's potential for unmanageability, the heroic is distinguished by its resistance to inertia and its deployment of contingencies to avoid disaster. The heroic is marked by an impulse toward orchestrating chaos, not necessarily to transform it into order but rather to use it to frame the quest for the extraordinary. When writers of jazz fiction seek to employ this impulse in the service of narrating the liberatory struggle occasioned by modernity, a circumstance emerges reminiscent of Albert Murray's observation in *The Hero and the Blues*, when he insists, "The story teller works with language, but even so, he is a song and dance man ... whose fundamental objectives are also those of the bard, the minstrel, and the ballad maker, which incidentally are also those of the contemporary American blues singer."[66]

Jazz fiction is often distinguished, as we see with "Sonny's Blues," "Powerhouse," "Lush Life" and a host of other stories, by the quality of community that emerges when like-minded individuals, all of whom understand that "risk-takers [can] find a communal spirit" and who thus come to see themselves in an elite collective of the skilled and tough-minded.[67] It may be this aspect of jazz that makes it such an attractive subject for fiction writers because, at root, stories about musicians able to live life's terms but never accept them are suggestive of the ways that jazz is a cultural enterprise almost wholly devoted to democratic norms that reaches its zenith at the crossroads of possibility and chaos.

Notes

1 Charles B. Hersch, *Subversive Sounds: Race and the Birth of Jazz in New Orleans* (Chicago: University of Chicago Press, 2007), 5.
2 Ibid.
3 Ibid.
4 Russell L. Johnson, "'Disease Is Unrhythmical': Jazz, Health, and Disability in 1920s America," *Health and History*, 13.2 (2011), 14.
5 Neil Leonard, *Jazz: Myth and Religion* (Oxford: Oxford University Press, 1987), 10.
6 Anne Shaw Faulkner, "Does Jazz Put the Sin in Syncopation?" 1921, in Robert Walser, ed., *Keeping Time: Readings in Jazz History*, 2nd ed. (New York: Oxford University Press, 2014), 27, 29.
7 Nathaniel Mackey, "Other: From Noun to Verb," *Representations*, 39 (Summer 1992), 51.
8 Ibid.
9 Arthur W. Frank, *The Wounded Storyteller: Body, Illness, and Ethics* (Chicago: University of Chicago Press, 1997), 23.

10 James Baldwin, "Sonny's Blues," *Partisan Review* 24.3 (1957), 332.
11 Ibid., 341.
12 Ibid., 336.
13 Ibid., 339.
14 Ibid., 344.
15 Julian Street, "The Jazz Baby," 1922, in Sascha Feinstein and David Rife, eds., *The Jazz Fiction Anthology* (Bloomington: Indiana University Press, 2009), 422–23.
16 Ibid., 440–41.
17 Ibid., 441.
18 Faulkner, "Does Jazz Put the Sin in Syncopation?," 27.
19 James Lincoln Collier, *Jazz: The American Theme Song* (New York: Oxford University Press, 1995), 268–69.
20 C. W. Smith, "The Plantation Club," 1977, in Marcela Breton, ed., *Hot and Cool: Jazz Short Stories* (New York: Plume, 1990), 200.
21 Ibid.
22 Ibid., 202.
23 Ibid., 206.
24 Don Asher, "The Barrier," 1982, in Sascha Feinstein and David Rife, eds., *The Jazz Fiction Anthology* (Bloomington: Indiana University Press, 2009), 1.
25 Ibid.
26 Ibid.
27 Ibid., 2.
28 Evan Hunter, "From *Streets of Gold*," 1974, in Art Lange and Nathaniel Mackey, eds., *Moment's Notice: Jazz in Poetry and Prose* (Minneapolis, MN: Coffee House Press, 1993), 87.
29 Ibid., 86.
30 Ibid., 95–96.
31 Ibid., 96.
32 Ibid., 99, original emphasis.
33 Ibid., 99.
34 Hunter, "From *Streets of Gold*," 100, original emphasis.
35 Guthrie Ramsey, *Race Music: Black Music From Bebop to Hip-Hop* (Berkeley: University of California Press, 2003).
36 Asher, "The Barrier," 4.
37 But this also represents a near-total reversal of the state of affairs that inhered in jazz's earliest incarnations. From the early to the mid-twentieth century, Black musicians had to endure segregated musicians' unions, and clubs, as well as the negative assessment aimed at them by white musicians who were deemed to be more professional and better musicians.
38 John McCluskey, "Lush Life," 1990, in Sascha Feinstein and David Rife, eds., *The Jazz Fiction Anthology* (Bloomington, IN: Indiana University Press, 2009), 345.
39 Ibid., 341.

40 James Reed, "The Shrimp Peel Gig," 1997, in Sascha Feinstein and David Rife, eds., *The Jazz Fiction Anthology* (Bloomington: Indiana University Press, 2009), 373.
41 Ibid.
42 Ibid., 372.
43 J. F. Powers, "He Don't Plant Cotton," 1943, in Marcela Breton, ed., *Hot and Cool: Jazz Short Stories* (New York: Plume, 1990), 82, 81.
44 Ibid., 87.
45 Ibid., 88.
46 Ibid.
47 Ibid., 88–89.
48 Ibid., 90.
49 Eudora Welty, "Powerhouse," 1941, in Sascha Feinstein and David Rife, eds., *The Jazz Fiction Anthology* (Bloomington, IN: Indiana University Press, 2009), 457.
50 Ibid., 454.
51 Ibid., 452.
52 Ibid., 452–53.
53 Mike Featherstone, *Undoing Culture: Globalization, Postmodernism and Identity* (London: Sage, 1995), 55.
54 Ibid., 59.
55 Ibid.
56 Ibid., 55.
57 Ralph Ellison, "The Charlie Christian Story," 1958, in *Shadow and Act* (New York: Random House, 1964), 234.
58 Baldwin, "Sonny's Blues," 356.
59 Ibid.
60 Ibid., my emphasis.
61 Ibid., 357.
62 Ibid., my emphasis.
63 John A. Williams, *Night Song* (New York: Farrar, Straus and Cudahy, 1961). For a discussion of the 1967 film adaptation of this novel, *Sweet Love, Bitter*, see Krin Gabbard's chapter on jazz film in this volume (Chapter 19).
64 Deborah Lupton, *Risk*, 2nd ed. (London: Routledge, 2013), 206. Here Lupton quotes, in part, from Anthony Giddens, *Modernity and Self-Identity: Self and Society in the Late Modern Age* (Stanford: Stanford University Press, 1991), 132.
65 Lupton, *Risk*, 214, my italics.
66 Albert Murray, *The Hero and the Blues* (Columbia, MO: University of Missouri Press, 1973), 21.
67 Lupton, *Risk*, 208–9.

CHAPTER 14

"Wail, Wop"
Jazz Poetry on the Page and in Performance
Jessica E. Teague

Say the words "jazz poetry" and one might imagine a 1950s coffeehouse featuring a beret-wearing hipster, bongo drums, and finger snaps. But, beatniks aside, jazz music has powerfully inspired American poets for a hundred years. Far from being a Jazz Age relic, or some minor offshoot of modernism, jazz has been a central and ongoing concern for modern and contemporary poetry. Many of the biggest names in the tradition – Hughes, Williams, Kerouac, Ginsberg, Baraka – were explicitly indebted to jazz music, and many more leading poets today continue to write jazz poetry. That jazz poetry has produced so many anthologies is perhaps a testament to the form's saliency.[1] But what is it about jazz that has been so appealing to poets?

With so many different examples and expressions, the genre of jazz poetry is difficult to define. In his introduction to *Jazz Poetry*, Sascha Feinstein suggests that "a jazz poem is any poem that has been informed by jazz music. The influence can be in the subject of the poem or in the rhythms, but one should not necessarily exclude the other."[2] Feinstein offers a useful starting point, but defining jazz poetry simply as a relationship of influence imposes an unnecessary limit. I am interested in the reciprocal relationship that emerged between music and poetics, and in the possibility that the music itself, especially lyrics, might be a form of poetry.[3] As Robert G. O'Meally writes in *The Jazz Cadence of American Culture*, there is a "two-way road from jazz to the other arts and back."[4] Nowhere is this tension more apparent than in the performance of jazz poetry. The centrality of performance for much jazz poetry requires us to consider how poetry and jazz are in conversation. This means placing performances and recordings of poetry – what Meta DuEwa Jones refers to as *"rituals of recital"* – on even footing with print forms.[5] Analyzing poetry that inhabits the interstices of print, recording, and performance requires what I call *resonant reading* – a practice of extended technique for close listening and close reading that encourages us to think across the mediated divide.[6] After all, jazz poetry emerges almost simultaneously with jazz itself, appearing at the same time as the earliest jazz records. In this chapter, I will sketch a brief history of the development of jazz poetry over the course of the twentieth century and point toward a more expansive way of thinking about the relationship between jazz and poetics.

Hughes, Harlem, and Beyond: A Chronology of Jazz Poetry

Although it is hard to say with certainty who wrote the first jazz poem, Langston Hughes frequently billed himself as the "original jazz poet" (a title conferred by Arna Bontemps). Other writers, including Vachel Lindsay and Hart Crane, made reference to jazz in poems published before Hughes's, but few would dispute Hughes's title. In his 1926 manifesto "The Negro Artist and the Racial Mountain," Hughes advocated for African American poetry based in jazz and blues: "Let the blare of Negro jazz bands and the bellowing voice of Bessie Smith singing the Blues penetrate the closed ears of the colored near-intellectuals until they listen and perhaps understand."[7] His own poems, such as "The Cat and the Saxophone (2 a.m.)" from *The Weary Blues* (1926), exemplify the sense of conversation and interplay between music and poetry. In this particular poem, Hughes samples the lyrics of "Everybody Loves My Baby" (music by Spencer Williams, lyrics by Jack Palmer) and weaves them into a nightclub portrait:

> EVERYBODY
> Half-pint,—
> Gin?
> No, make it
> LOVES MY BABY
> corn.   You like
> liquor,
> don't you, honey?
> BUT MY BABY
> Sure.   Kiss me,
> DON'T LOVE NOBODY
> daddy.
> BUT ME.[8]

The poem is compact yet sophisticated; the collage of lyrics with the couple's nightclub banter evokes what it was like not only to hear the music but also to hear it in a culturally inscribed setting: the nightclub. To read it visually on the page, one might imagine hearing the music in the background like a soundtrack because Hughes offsets the lyrics in all-caps. But reading the poem aloud produces a more jarring effect as the lyrics and conversation splice into and interrupt one another. The jagged rhythms that result almost recall Harlem stride piano, which Fats Waller used to great effect on his own recording of the tune. Hughes's quotation of the lyrics, however, also elevates their own poetic qualities – in addition to the quippy vernacular tone, the song's bubbling alliteration lends the melody its percussive sense of syncopation. Hughes's poetry is deceptively simple, and yet it is often just as fragmented and allusive as the high modernist poetry of his contemporary T. S. Eliot.

Though Vachel Lindsay (who in an apocryphal origin story claimed to "discover" Hughes as a busboy in a Washington, D.C. hotel) was often noted as a "jazz" poet who made African American rhythms the subject of many poems, he himself resisted the term and disliked the music. While his poem "The Jazz of This Hotel" is often anthologized, it is worth noting that the poem itself "curses" jazz.[9] For white writers, jazz in the 1910s and 20s was associated with sex; the music stood in for moral decay. This was true for e. e. cummings, whose musing on jazz dancers from 1925 recounts "the weightless svelte drifting sexual feather / of your shall i say body?"[10] The intoxicating rhythms of jazz music was a source of both inspiration and anxiety. David Yaffe has referred to this as the "fetishization of jazz by poets."[11] However, we might also think about this anxiety as the difference between jazz and the so-called *Jazz Age*. Although Alain Locke wittily pointed out that "the Negro, strictly speaking, never had a jazz age," jazz among white listeners and poets was the embodiment of cultural crisis.[12]

On the other hand, poets of the Harlem Renaissance like Hughes, Claude McKay, Helene Johnson, Sterling Brown, Jean Toomer, Melvin Tolson, and others, saw the music for its complex expressive properties and its deep roots within African American culture, often noting the ironies of white audiences' exploitative attitudes toward Black musicians and dancers. McKay's sonnet "The Harlem Dancer" (1922) depicts exotic sounds and the movements of the dancer but also reveals tragedy with its devastating volta: "But looking at her falsely-smiling face, / I knew her self was not in that strange place."[13] Sterling Brown's "Cabaret" (1932) likewise depicts the ironies of a black and tan 1927 Chicago floor show glorifying the "Muddy Waters" of the old South as the Mississippi River flooded its banks and displaced thousands of actual African Americans.[14] By contrast, Helene Johnson's "Poem" shifts the gaze from a white male audience to a Black female point of view and transforms exploitation into adoration: "Gee, boy, I love the way you hold your head, / High sort of and a bit to one side, / Like a prince, a jazz prince."[15] Johnson's poem is a form of joyful identification, solidarity, and love whose innocent "Gee, boy" refrain defangs sexual desire. Like Hughes's more exuberant poems of that era, Johnson and other Harlem poets drew upon the scenes and sounds of jazz and blues as a way to celebrate Black culture and forge a new poetics. In this regard, many blues songs themselves can be considered part of the poetic canon, especially those penned by Ma Rainey, Bessie Smith, W. C. Handy, and Robert Johnson. The refrain of Handy's "Hesitating Blues" ("Can I get you now ... or must I hesitate"), for example, later became the leitmotif of Hughes's masterwork *Ask Your Mama: 12 Moods for Jazz* (1961).

With the arrival of bebop, the interplay between jazz and poetry continued to evolve and a new generation of postwar poets entered the scene. Perhaps no poem embodies bop rhythms so elegantly as Gwendolyn Brooks's 1959 poem "We Real Cool" with its compact, enjambed lines and ironic tone ("We real cool. We / Left School").[16] In Brooks's own performative readings of the poem, her clipped aspirations of "We" at the end of each line feel like the bop articulations of early Miles Davis.[17]

By the 1950s, the practice of reading poetry to jazz, which arguably began in Harlem with Hughes in the 1920s, was reinvigorating poetry circles from New York's bohemian cafes in Greenwich Village to the galleries and bookstores of San Francisco. Poets like Kenneth Patchen and Kenneth Rexroth made their reputations reading to jazz (even recording albums), and laid the foundation for the Beat poets. Rexroth, who was a critical figure in igniting the San Francisco Renaissance, frequently organized poetry readings and emceed Allen Ginsberg's infamous 1955 reading of *Howl* at the Six Gallery. For Beat writers like Ginsberg and others, jazz represented a rebellious spirit for a generation of (mostly white) hipsters "who poverty and tatters and hollow-eyed and high sat up smoking in the supernatural darkness of cold-water flats floating across the tops of cities contemplating jazz."[18] Ginsberg later claimed that the phrasing of *Howl* took inspiration from jazz saxophonist Lester Young.[19]

Jazz music was particularly central to the poetry of Jack Kerouac, who stated in the headnote for *Mexico City Blues*: "I want to be considered a jazz poet blowing a long blues in an afternoon jam session on Sunday."[20] Critical hot takes on Kerouac have complained (at times with good reason) that he didn't really understand the music; Rexroth panned *Mexico City Blues* calling it "naïve effrontery."[21] Strictly speaking, Kerouac's blues poems are *not* blues; instead, they aspire toward the raw unpolished jam session – a space reserved for more exploratory playing. (Kerouac was known to have frequented the open jam sessions that had become much more central to the development of jazz since at least the 1940s.) Taken in this light, these 242 choruses might be heard for their playful, homophonic rhythms. Kerouac riffs on everything from F. Scott Fitzgerald's *Tender is the Night* ("Tender is the marlin spike, / Tender is the sea") to Charlie Parker ("'Wail, Wop' – Charley[sic] burst / His lungs to reach the speed / Of what the speedsters wanted").[22] On the page, Kerouac's poems for Parker are exalting and rhythmic, but his recorded readings of these poems, accompanied by Steve Allen's noodling piano, render the lines nostalgic rather than evocative of bebop.[23]

The celebrity of Kerouac and Ginsberg tends to overshadow the centrality of African American poets to the Beat movement, which included Bob Kaufman (cofounder of *Beatitude*), Ted Joans, and LeRoi Jones/Amiri Baraka. Renegade street poets like Kaufman, in particular, are only now receiving renewed attention.[24] As a poet in the oral tradition, Kaufman rarely wrote down his early works. In poems like "Bagel Shop Jazz," depicting one of his many brutal arrests by San Francisco police, Kaufman resituates jazz in the postwar era as more than a backdrop for "Coffee-faced Ivy Leaguers" with "cool hipster smiles"; instead, the "beat" is the rhythm of resistance in the face of existential crisis.[25] As he declaims in "War Memoir," "Jazz – listen to it at your own risk."[26] For Black Beat writers, the music signified a spiritual and liberatory possibility.

The Black Arts Movement, which arguably began when poet LeRoi Jones broke with the Beats, decided to change his name to Amiri Baraka, and moved uptown to Harlem in 1965 following the murder of Malcolm X, was a kind of antidote to the apolitical Beats.[27] As the aesthetic manifestation of Black Nationalism and Black Power, the Black Arts Movement was also emblematic of a schism in the poetry community, between jazz as an aesthetic gesture and a political one. In his 1965 manifesto poem "Black Art" Baraka militantly calls for "poems that kill" and "Poems that wrestle cops into alleys / and take their weapons leaving them dead"; in his performative recording of the poem on the album *Sonny's Time Now* with Sunny Murray, Albert Ayler, and Don Cherry, his screams are matched by the free jazz squeals of horns and drums.[28] Baraka's "Ps" are so percussive that at times they clip the signal of the recording, and his vocal reproductions of sirens and gunshots perform the violence for which he calls. Recordings became a key vehicle for poetry; that Baraka is acutely aware of his medium is evident, and his avant-garde practices reimagined the possibilities for poetry readings, performances, and recordings.

This is especially apparent on *It's Nation Time*, his 1972 album on Motown's Black Forum label, which incorporates a range of musical accompaniment from African drumming, to free jazz, to R&B. The poetics of *It's Nation Time* are stereophonic and hail the opening of new Black sonic spaces.[29]

Of course, Baraka was not the only poet of this era to record. Albums such as *Boss Soul* (Folkways 1972) by Sarah Webster Fabio and Jayne Cortez's *Celebrations and Solitudes* (Strata-East 1974) blend spoken-word and music. (Maya Angelou had earlier recorded *Miss Calypso* in 1957.) Beyond Baraka, jazz was a catalyst and key expressive mode for poets as various as Sonia Sanchez, Nikki Giovanni, Haki R. Madhubuti (Don Lee), and others.

Of the various cross-directional projects of the era, we might look especially to the music and writings of Sun Ra. As both Brent Hayes Edwards and John Szwed have noted, Sun Ra's visionary approach to music was rooted in the literary and the poetic.[30] Though Sun Ra never published his poetry with a commercial press, he distributed it on broadsides and in pamphlets that accompanied his records; he recited it and chanted it and made poetry part of the "space of ritual performance," as Edwards puts it.[31] As a "space age poet," Sun Ra's poetry plays along the edges of language to open new and impossible realms – we hear this not only in the chants of his albums like *Space Is the Place* but also in poems like "The Outer Darkness":

> black is space
> the outer darkness
> the void direction to the heavens
> each spaceport is a heaven
> in that, it is a haven
> the music of the outer darkness is
> the music of the void
> the opening is the void
> but the opening is synonym to the
> beginning[32]

Aligning Blackness with outer space, Sun Ra marks himself as a progenitor of Afrofuturism. Other musicians also wrote poetry to accompany their musical works, including John Coltrane, Charles Mingus, Archie Shepp, and Cecil Taylor.

As jazz itself became less mainstream in the 1960s and 70s with the rise of rock, R&B, and later hip-hop, its place within and influence on poetry changed. One might argue that hip-hop absorbed certain elements of jazz poetry and transformed it into something else entirely. Certainly the recordings of spoken word poetry to music in the 1970s by artists such as the Last Poets and Gil Scott-Heron would presage hip-hop's emergence, and one can hear the resonance between jazz poets like Baraka and Cortez and early hip-hop artists like Afrika Bambaataa, Public Enemy, and the Native Tongues. Slam poetry, which emerged in the 1980s and 90s, arguably has roots in the vocal practices of jazz poets as well, and traces its birth to a Chicago jazz club.[33]

And yet, jazz poetry did not just disappear or become absorbed by other forms. Jazz as aesthetic practice, as folk practice, as political practice resonates still in contemporary circles, especially in African American poetry. Nathaniel Mackey, inspired by the long form innovations of musicians such as Coltrane, Rahsaan Roland Kirk, Ornette Coleman, and Don Cherry, has written open-ended serial poems that he has referred to as the "long song." These works, namely *Song of the Andomboulou* and *Mu*, explore the cosmology of the Dogon of West Africa. Aesthetically and spiritually, his serial poems are insistently recursive, and as Mackey explains in his Preface to *Splay Anthem* (2006), "Earlier moments can be said to die and live on as echo and rearticulation, riff and recontextualization, alteration and reconception."[34] Similar attitudes toward the music can be found in the poetry of Yusef Komunyakaa, Fred Moten, Harryette Mullen, and others.

This sense of echo or riff is especially present in Kevin Young's *Jelly Roll: A Blues* (2003), which inhabits the world of Jelly Roll Morton, even if the poems are not about him. Following a narrative arc of romance, infidelity, and lost love, Young (a member of the Dark Room Collective) pays homage to poets like Hughes and Toomer and evokes the slangy bounce of 1920s song lyrics. In "Errata," for example, he playfully misspells words within common pop song platitudes about love: "I live you so much / it perts! // Baby, jive me gust / one more bliss."[35] And yet these are very contemporary poems; the enjambment and internal rhymes of the second section feel closer to those of hip-hop. Young moves between these traditions seamlessly. The ongoing impact of the jazz poetry tradition on the emergence of hip-hop is often understated, and yet it is discernibly present – just look to a contemporary artist like Kendrick Lamar's collaboration with jazz saxophonist Kamasi Washington as an example. We also find echoes of the jazz and blues in the work of more traditional contemporary poets, such as Tyehimba Jess and Morgan Parker. Although jazz poetry is sometimes treated as a periphery or offshoot of modern poetry, it has been central to some of the most important poetic movements. In order to offer a sense of the prevailing themes and modes of jazz poetry, in the next section I offer two snapshots of transhistorical approaches to the poetry: the elegiac strain (and, in particular, poems about John Coltrane), and lyrics versus the lyric (looking especially to Billy Strayhorn's "Lush Life").

Modes: Odes and Elegies

Perhaps the most dominant mode of jazz poetry falls into the category of ode or elegy, with poems written *to* or *for* just about every famous musician from Bessie Smith to Charlie Parker and beyond.[36] Some recount particular performances or recordings, some function as hagiography, others lament a musician's untimely death. Frank O'Hara's well-known poem for Billie Holiday, "The Day Lady Died," mostly recounts a walk along a New York street to get a shoeshine and a hamburger, and in fact, it has little to do with Billie Holiday until he sees her picture in a newspaper announcing her death. The photo triggers a memory that transports him to a past moment listening to Holiday while "leaning on the john door in the 5 SPOT / while she whispered a song along the keyboard / to Mal Waldron and everyone and I stopped breathing."[37] The poem not only crystallizes a particular performance, but Holiday's effect on the listener.

Figures like Holiday have inspired dozens of poems, but there is likely no muse more potent that John Coltrane. Baraka, Sanchez, Cortez, Madhubuti, Cornelius Eady, Elizabeth Alexander, Mullen, and Mackey have all written poems that either elegiacally celebrate or spiritually extend the sound and feeling of Coltrane's music. Or as Sanchez put it, "my favorite things // is u/blowen // yo/favorite/things."[38] Writing about the persistence of Coltrane poems from the 1960s to the present, Meta DuEwa Jones (quoting Henry Lacey) notes that "homage to John Coltrane became an expected piece in the repertoire of succeeding black poets, in part because Coltrane 'epitomized the serious and committed Black artist' and in part because his iconic status within black communities virtually required it."[39] Following his premature death in 1967, Coltrane's musical legacy has lived on through poetry.

In his long poem, "AM/TRAK," Amiri Baraka works *with* and *against* the mode of elegy by simultaneously memorializing important moments in Coltrane's life, yet calling for him to "Be" and to "live!" Primarily written in the present tense, the poem calls to Coltrane ("Trane"), "Oh / blow," as though to evoke his presence on the page.[40] Through these exclamatory wails, Baraka self-consciously attempts to emulate the sound of protest that he hears in Coltrane's music. The desire to conjure the muse into existence demonstrates how Baraka works against the sense of *absence* left by Coltrane's death.

This aesthetic of absence and loss pervades jazz and blues, and is a key mode of its poetics. Interestingly, the feeling of premature loss even imbues Coltrane poems written prior to his death, such as Michael S. Harper's "Dear John, Dear Coltrane," originally written in 1966: "So sick / you couldn't play Naima, / so flat we ached / for song / you'd concealed / with your own blood."[41] But the figure of Coltrane and his music brings out competing valences of life, death, loss, and love, and in Baraka's "AM/ TRAK" there is also the sense that Coltrane is *not* gone. At the end of the poem, referring to Coltrane's 1965 album, Baraka notes that "And yet last night I played *Meditations* / & it told me what to do"[42]. This record ultimately answers Baraka's desire to bring Coltrane into existence and reinforces Baraka's own will to *live*. The poem offers a kind of corollary to Baraka's earlier liner notes for *Coltrane Live at Birdland*, which assert that all his music is "live" because of that "daringly human quality to John Coltrane's music that makes itself felt, wherever he records."[43]

Cortez's recording of "How Long Has Trane Been Gone," from *Celebrations and Solitudes* (a series of duets between bass and voice), also offers an elegy for Coltrane, but rather than dwell on his death, Cortez uses the occasion to issue a call for Black Art that celebrates Black history. She calls out the club owners and radio DJs who seem to no longer care about Black music: "How long how long has that Trane been gone."[44] Over the course of the track, John Coltrane becomes a father figure for the Black community:

> John palpitating love notes
> in a lost-found nation
> within a nation
> His music resounding discovery[45]

Rhythmically, through the modulation of her voice and the repetition of the short riff-life phrase *How long has this Trane been gone*, Cortez also borrows from Coltrane's signature sound and phrasing. In performance, her repetitive riffs are followed by long breathless improvisatory lines. Although it goes underacknowledged, Coltrane himself was a sometimes-poet, and the phrasing of "Psalm," the final track of his monumental album *A Love Supreme* (1965), follows the poem Coltrane wrote for the liner notes: "I will do all I can to be worthy of Thee O Lord. / It all has to do with it. / Thank you God. / Peace."[46]

Lyric versus Lyrics

One of the most perplexing aspects of so many of the anthologies of jazz poetry is how seldom they include song lyrics.[47] This omission is almost certainly related to the fact that the literary canon does not typically include song lyrics – just think of the feathers ruffled when Bob Dylan won the 2016 Nobel Prize in Literature. Yet although the lyrics of jazz standards churned out by Tin Pan Alley have often been derided for their shallow themes and repetitive jingles, many offer surprisingly rich examples of lyrical brilliance.[48] Among jazz lyrics that take up the political one might look to Billie Holiday's 1939 rendition of "Strange Fruit" based on the anti-lynching poem by Abel Meeropol. Cole Porter's marvelous ballad "Miss Otis Regrets" (1934) offers a sinister inversion of a lynching narrative. In the context of civil rights, Charles Mingus's "Fables of Faubus" and Nina Simone's "Mississippi Goddam" stand out for their vehement protest and lyrical economy.[49]

But perhaps these are thin ways to think of the value of lyrics. The tension between lyrics and lyric poetry might best be explored through the allusive interplay between these genres. For example, the lyrics of Billy Strayhorn's "Lush Life" (1933/1949) in relation to Elizabeth Alexander's "Billy Strayhorn writes 'Lush Life'" (2002) and Morgan Parker's "Lush Life" (2017).

As a long-form song that eschews traditional song forms, Strayhorn's tune has been hailed by Ted Gioia as a "perfect composition … one in which the melodic phrases, harmonies, and poetic sentiments are each unconventional yet sublime."[50] An anti-love song, "Lush Life" is narrated by a persona who has (or so it seems) given up the lush life:

> I used to visit all the very gay places,
> Those come-what-may places,
> Where one relaxes on the axis of the wheel of life
> To get the feel of life
> From jazz and cocktails[51]

The song is full of double-entendres. The "lush" from the title evokes both luxuriance and drunkenness. Even the appearance of the term "gay," though still used to mean lighthearted and carefree in the 1930s, likely held a coded meaning for Strayhorn, who was open about his homosexuality. The image of the wheel is especially vivid and serves as a model for the persona's journey. The axis at the center stays still while everything else whirls around it, experiencing the rush and speed of life without actually participating in it. But the moment one steps out onto the spinning wheel, as the singer does, they are at risk of being thrown off entirely.

These intricately woven metaphors elevate Strayhorn's lyrics, and enjambment and internal rhyme give them a slightly backbeat balance, similar to the underlying swing of syncopated music. This technique also gives the poem its lush sense of abundance, provoking the lyric to literally overflow the line: "Now life is awful again / A troughful of hearts could only be a bore."[52] Singers have struggled to interpret the song not just because of its notoriously difficult melody but because of the ambiguity of the lyrics. Nat King Cole's version feels downright melancholy. Ella Fitzgerald's take captures some of the droll humor. But when Strayhorn himself sings it, it sounds like a farce tinged by a deeply ironic smile; playing to a live audience in 1964, Strayhorn enunciates the hard G's of "wrong," provoking the crowd to chuckle.[53]

Many have wondered whether "Lush Life" was autobiographical; Strayhorn, who was Duke Ellington's staff arranger and composer, famous for penning songs like "Take the A Train," was not known for moderation and died at age 51 from esophageal cancer. In reality, Strayhorn wrote the piece when he was still in his late teens. In her poem, "Billy Strayhorn Writes 'Lush Life,'" Elizabeth Alexander plays upon the ambiguous connection between the song lyrics and the biographical details of Strayhorn's life. Like the song, Alexander's poem draws upon images of decadence and waste to illustrate the thin line between violence and laughter. An "Empty ice-cream carton / in a kitchen garbage can" at first appears to be the waste left over from an evening shared by Strayhorn and his mother, whom his father has beaten again, but the line is revised to "Up all night / eating ice-cream, you made your mother laugh."[54] The stanzas are interrupted by the song's haunting refrain-like line:

            ly
Life   *is lone*

Alexander's quotation imitates the phrasing of the ascending melodic line, and the space after "life" indicates its duration. Like the playing of a standard, Alexander's poem uses Strayhorn's song as the point from which to spin her own improvisations on the theme of Strayhorn's own *lush* life. This visual attempt to represent the song's melody parallels the way in which a jazz musician might hint at, or return to the melodic line for a brief moment in the middle of an improvised solo.

More recently Morgan Parker's take on "Lush Life" remixes the song for the twenty-first century. Parker samples Strayhorn's lyrics obliquely: "A trough of hearts meets me in the anxious sun / I could rot here."[55] Contemporary readers (and listeners) to Parker's poems might well miss the reference to the jazz standard. But the voice of the persona in Parker's "Lush Life" owes much to the persona of Strayhorn's original. "I take music self-stirred," Parker writes with droll humor.[56] The poem evokes a sense of future-nostalgia, longing for love and connection but inevitably undercut by various iterations of the lush life with its potential lovers who "wash up on a barstool."[57] As a poem set within a collection dominated by allusions to the pop singer Beyoncé, Parker's "Lush Life" is surrounded by meditations on Black womanhood in the twenty-first century. Beyoncé, for whom many of the poems are written, is both a metaphor for all Black women and a kind of stock figure of perfection, and in that sense she's not unlike the blues-woman figure and muse of so much earlier poetry. "Lush Life" is not Parker's only poem that references jazz. She gives her poems titles from jazz standards, like "Ain't Misbehaving" (by Fats Waller), or "So What" (by Miles Davis). The rhythms of her poetry are contemporary but also have the jagged syncopations of jazz.

As examples, this trio of poems is particularly emblematic of jazz poetry: the lyrics that might be treated as poems in their own right (Strayhorn), the elegiac memorializing of a musician (Alexander), and the more obliquely referential (Parker). That song lyrics are often sidelined in studies of jazz poetry may have something to do with the sidelining of women and queer figures more generally in the jazz tradition – songs are typically the purview of the "girl singer" (to invoke the dismissive appellation). But these particular examples of the intertwined nature of contemporary lyric poetry and the lyrics of jazz standards help to illustrate the extent to which songs must be considered within the tradition of modern poetry. Although literary histories of American poetry may periodize jazz poetry as a microgenre of the Harlem Renaissance or the Beat generation, jazz continues to be a vibrant poetic mode.

Notes

1 See, for example, Sascha Feinstein and Yusef Komunyakaa, eds., *The Jazz Poetry Anthology* (Bloomington: Indiana University Press, 1991) and its sequel *The Second Set: The Jazz Poetry Anthology, Volume 2* (Bloomington: Indiana University Press, 1996); Art Lange and Nathaniel Mackey, eds., *Moment's Notice: Jazz in Poetry & Prose* (Minneapolis: Coffee House Press, 1993); Kevin Young, ed., *Jazz Poems* (New York: Knopf, 2006); and Stephen Cramer, ed., *Turn It Up! Music in Poetry from Jazz to Hip-Hop* (West Brattleboro, VT: Green Writers Press, 2020).
2 Sascha Feinstein, *Jazz Poetry: From the 1920s to the Present* (Westport, CT: Greenwood Press, 1997), 2.
3 Other scholars have offered more expansive definitions of jazz poetry that extend to music and lyrics; see, for example, Barry Wallenstein, "Poetry and Jazz: A Twentieth-Century Wedding," *Black American Literature Forum*, 25.3 (1991), 595–620.

4 Robert G. O'Meally, ed., *The Jazz Cadence of American Culture* (New York: Columbia University Press, 1998), xiv.
5 Meta DuEwa Jones, *The Muse Is Music: Jazz Poetry from the Harlem Renaissance to Spoken Word* (Urbana: University of Illinois Press, 2011), 6.
6 For elaboration of *resonant reading* as a methodology, see Jessica E. Teague, *Sound Recording Technology and American Literature, from the Phonograph to the Remix* (Cambridge: Cambridge University Press, 2021), 15–20.
7 Langston Hughes, "The Negro Artist and the Racial Mountain," 1926, Angelyn Mitchell, ed., *Within the Circle: An Anthology of African American Literary Criticism from the Harlem Renaissance to the Present* (Durham, NC: Duke University Press, 1994), 59.
8 Langston Hughes, *The Weary Blues*, 1926 (New York: Knopf, 2017), 9.
9 For more on Lindsay's attitude toward jazz, see Feinstein, *Jazz Poetry*, 17–19.
10 e. e. cummings, "God Pity Me Whom(God Distinctly Has)," 1925, in Kevin Young, ed., *Jazz Poetry* (New York: Knopf, 2006), 31.
11 David Yaffe, *Fascinating Rhythm: Reading Jazz in American Writing* (Princeton: Princeton University Press, 2009), 103.
12 Alain Locke, *The Negro and His Music* (Washington, DC: The Associates in Negro Folk Education, 1936), 87.
13 Claude McKay, "The Harlem Dancer," in *Harlem Shadows: The Poems of Claude McKay* (New York: Harcourt Brace, 1922), 42.
14 Sterling Brown, "Cabaret," 1932, in Michael S. Harper, ed., *The Collected Poems of Sterling Brown* (Evanston, IL: TriQuarterly Books, 1980), 111–13.
15 Helene Johnson, "Poem," 1922, in Kevin Young, ed., *Jazz Poems* (New York: Knopf, 2006), 28.
16 Gwendolyn Brooks, "We Real Cool," 1959, in Kevin Young, ed., *Jazz Poems* (New York: Knopf, 2006), 45.
17 To listen to Brooks read "We Real Cool," visit https://poets.org/poem/we-real-cool.
18 Allen Ginsberg, *Howl and Other Poems*, 1956 (San Francisco: City Lights Publishers, 2002), 9.
19 Joel Dinerstein, *The Origins of Cool in Postwar America* (Chicago: University of Chicago Press, 2017), 19.
20 Jack Kerouac, *Mexico City Blues (242 Choruses)* (New York: Grove, 1959).
21 Kenneth Rexroth, "Discordant and Cool," *The New York Times*, November 29, 1959, https://archive.nytimes.com/www.nytimes.com/books/97/09/07/home/kerouac-mexico.html. See also, for example, Robert Creeley's Introduction to Kerouac's *Book of Blues* (New York: Penguin, 1995), ix, xi.
22 Kerouac, *Mexico City Blues*, 30, 243.
23 Jack Kerouac and Steve Allen, *Poetry for the Beat Generation* (Dot Records DLP 3154, 1959).
24 Kaufman's resurgence follows the publication of *The Collected Poems of Bob Kaufman* (San Francisco: City Lights Books, 2019), Billy Woodberry's documentary about Kaufman, *And When I Die, I Won't Stay Dead* (Rosa Filmes, 2015), and recent essays like Justin Desmangles' essays on Kaufman for SF Moma (https://openspace.sfmoma.org/2017/11/bob-kaufmans-african-dream/).

25 Bob Kaufman, *Collected Poems of Bob Kaufman*, Neeli Cherkovski, Raymond Foye, and Tate Swindell, eds. (San Francisco: City Lights Books, 2019), 11.
26 Ibid., 39.
27 For a less apocryphal, more elaborate narrative of the origins of the Black Arts Movement as emerging in the early 1960s out of Black poetry collectives like Umbra (in New York) and magazines like *The Cricket* see Brent Hayes Edwards, *Epistrophies: Jazz and the Literary Imagination* (Cambridge, MA: Harvard University Press, 2017), 127–33.
28 Amiri Baraka, "Black Art," 1965, in Paul Vangelisti, ed. *Transbluesency: The Selected Poems of Amiri Baraka/LeRoi Jones (1961–1995)* (New York: Marsilio Publishers, 1995), 142; Sonny Murray [Sunny Murray], *It's Sonny's Time* (Jihad Productions 663, 1965).
29 Imamu Amiri Baraka, *It's Nation Time – African Visionary Music* (Motown/Black Forum B 457L, 1972). I write at length about the stereophonic poetics of *It's Nation Time* in *Sound Recording Technology and American Literature*, 150–63.
30 Edwards, *Epistrophies*, 126.
31 Ibid., 135.
32 Sun Ra, *This Planet Is Doomed: The Science Fiction Poetry of Sun Ra* (New York: Kicks Books. 2011), 58.
33 For more about slam poetry, see Javon Johnson. *Killing Poetry: Blackness and the Making of Slam and Spoken Word Communities* (New Brunswick: Rutgers University Press, 2017).
34 Nathaniel Mackey, *Splay Anthem* (New York: New Directions, 2006), xiii.
35 Kevin Young, *Jelly Roll: A Blues* (New York: Knopf, 2005), 51.
36 In the Appendix to *The Jazz Poetry Anthology*, Sascha Feinstein and Yusef Komunyakaa include a list of musicians who appear in the poems (Bloomington: Indiana University Press, 1991, 279–284). See also Sascha Feinstein, *A Bibliographic Guide to Jazz Poetry* (Westport, CT: Greenwood Press, 1998).
37 Frank O'Hara, *Lunch Poems* (San Francisco: City Lights Books, 1964), 26.
38 Sonia Sanchez, "a/coltrane/poem," in Sascha Feinstein and Yusef Komunyakaa, ed., *The Jazz Poetry Anthology* (Bloomington: Indiana University Press, 1991), 183.
39 Jones, *The Muse Is Music*, 103. Jones has suggested that "Conjuring Coltrane serves as the vehicle for resurrecting black bodies from the deafening, deadening clutches of historical erasure" (86). With special attention to the formal and prosodic features of jazz poetry, Jones argues that "Poetic forms that are influenced by music, like the Coltrane poem, seek to transcend the boundaries of both speech and music to inhabit intangible realms of the spiritual, the emotional, and the soulful" (88).
40 Amiri Baraka, "AM/TRAK," 1979, in William J. Harris, ed., *The LeRoi Jones/Amiri Baraka Reader* (New York: Thunder's Mouth, 1991), 267–72. For a discussion of this poem within the context of Baraka's music criticism, see Timothy Gray's chapter in this volume (Chapter 15).
41 Michael S. Harper, *Dear John, Dear Coltrane* (Pittsburgh: University of Pittsburgh Press, 1970), 75.

42 Baraka, "AM/TRAK," 272.
43 Amiri Baraka, Liner notes, John Coltrane, *Live at Birdland* (Impulse A-50, 1964).
44 Jayne Cortez, *Celebrations and Solitudes* (Strata East SES-7421, 1974); Jayne Cortez, *Jazz Fan Looks Back* (New York: Hanging Loose Press, 2002), 14.
45 Cortez, *Jazz Fan Looks Back*, 15.
46 John Coltrane, *A Love Supreme*, 1965 (Impulse A-77).
47 Kevin Young's collection *Blues Poems* (New York: Knopf, 2003) is a notable exception and includes a number of blues lyrics.
48 For a discussion of Tin Pan Alley songwriting, see Katherine Williams's chapter on the American Songbook in this volume (Chapter 17).
49 For an excellent reading of Nina Simone's resistance to generic categorization, see Daphne Brooks, "Nina Simone's Triple Play," *Callaloo*, 34.1 (2011), 176–97.
50 Ted Gioia, *The Jazz Standards: A Guide to the Repertoire* (New York: Oxford University Press, 2012), 250.
51 Billy Strayhorn, "Lush Life," 1933/1949, in Kevin Young, ed., *Jazz Poems* (New York: Knopf, 2006), 68.
52 Young, *Jazz Poems*, 69.
53 Billy Strayhorn, *Billy Strayhorn* (Musica Jazz 2MJP 1055, 1987).
54 Elizabeth Alexander, "Billy Strayhorn Writes Lush Life," *Ploughshares* 28 (Spring 2002), 10.
55 Morgan Parker, *There Are More Beautiful Things Than Beyoncé* (Portland, OR: Tin House Books, 2017), 11.
56 Ibid.
57 Ibid.

CHAPTER 15

Jazz Criticism and Liner Notes

Timothy Gray

Jazz liner notes enjoyed their heyday in the decades following World War II. Part publication relations blitz, part advertisement, part advance directive for hipsters, part forum for writers hoping to match chops with the musicians they adored, liner notes accomplished several tasks at once. Liner notes existed before the LP era in boxed sets of 78 rpm discs, and afterwards, too, in the jewel cases of compact disc releases. But this art form began to lose steam in the 1970s, and more so after 2000, when digitalized delivery of music deprioritized the special qualities of albums, including cover art and sleeve notation.

This chapter offers a sampling of the liner note genre and showcases some of its practitioners, whose style and expertise varied widely. Some think that liner note writers routinely exceeded whatever musicians intended to communicate, and it is true that, in response, some musicians took to writing their own liner notes. At their best, liners provide illuminating details, allowing listeners to learn how sounds come together in the studio or on stage. Regardless of who wrote them, or in what manner, liner notes are a key component of jazz history.

"Let's Put Something on the Back"

The earliest liner notes appeared in boxed sets of 78 rpm discs made to look like keepsake photo albums, hence the popularization of the term. Two early "albums," from 1940, featured *New Orleans Jazz* and *Chicago Jazz*.[1] Notes for the New Orleans set underscored its historical import. "Today we can look back at more than a half century of jazz development," Charles Edward Smith writes. Tracking musical development up the Mississippi and Missouri Rivers to Chicago and Kansas City, Smith makes sure novices picking up the album will know to locate the cradle of jazz in New Orleans, where Louis Armstrong and Sidney Bechet "played together on advertising wagons ... a long, long time ago."[2] George Avakian announces a different agenda on *Chicago Jazz*, aiming to "set down on wax" a style "recognized as the greatest advance of white musicians in the essentially colored art of hot jazz."[3] As its producer, Avakian reveals the album's "arduous preparation" over several months.[4] As often occurred in the liner note genre, "the act of assembling or recording the album itself became a subject of interest, and the recording circumstances themselves sometimes became the subject of an album's annotations."[5] The liner writer likewise demands pride of place. The playful attitude in the Chicago scene is underscored by Avakian's mirthful descriptions ("the boys go into a corking finale" in one piece, while in another a trombonist "[comes] out of the fourth chorus like a surfboard into his own solo"), and by his jokey profiles of the musicians (cornetist Jimmy McPartland "looks like an All-American fullback – the kind co-eds go for," while clarinetist Pee Wee Russell is caricatured as a "long-faced St. Louis man with shoe button eyes.")[6]

The "long-playing" albums arrived in 1948, issued in a 10" format, featuring multiple tracks totaling fifteen minutes of music per side, outdoing the temporal limitations of 78 rpm discs before surrendering to 12" LPs a few years later. The first batch of 10" LPs issued by Columbia, where Avakian now worked, featured pedestrian notation by George Dale, the company publicist. But once the 12" LP emerged, and musicians had room for extended solos, there was a concomitant expansion of liner notes seeking similar sophistication and innovation. During a 1951 session, a producer waved Zoot Sims to keep going, to continue his solo. Sims was cooking, and the new format meant he was no longer constrained by three-minute tracks. Excited by what he heard, Prestige Records owner Bob Weinstock visualized the album (*Swingin' with Zoot Sims*), telling Ira Gitler, "Let's put something on the back. You're the writer and you know Zoot. Write something about the music and the musicians." From that point forward, Marc Meyers has asserted, jazz was regarded as "serious performance art," and "albums as unified concepts."[7] Gitler went on to become one of jazz's most prolific liner note writers in the 1950s and 1960s. He was matched by several others, including Leonard Feather, a musician and composer who doubled as a producer and a professional critic.

Feather lent his talents to many classic Blue Note releases in the bop era. He was not as incessantly witty as some liner writers, but he had his moments. Annotating the Art Blakey Quintet's *A Night at Birdland* (1954), Feather recalls Blakey's famous announcement that he was present when Dizzy Gillespie wrote "Night in Tunisia" "in Texas, on the bottom of a garbage can." To which Feather slyly adds, "The sanitation department can take a deep bow."[8] Occasionally, Feather tries too hard to be funny, as evidenced by the lingo and tasteless puns accompanying Paul Chambers's *Whims of Chambers* (1957). "I would call Chambers a gas," Feather writes, "except that it is depressing to think about gas chambers; so perhaps a bolder word may be permitted. Chambers, as his fellow-musicians have been saying ever since they heard his very first solo, is a bitch."[9] Usually, though, Feather assumes a debonair style, summoning literary references to John Milton on the Chambers album, for example. Feather situates each recording within the context of its production, or culture at large. On the sleeve of Cannonball Adderley's *Somethin' Else* (1958), for instance, Feather defends a solo by sideman Miles Davis against an "insensitive article in *Ebony* stating that 'Negroes are ashamed of the blues,'" rejoining that Davis evokes "the new, the deeper and broader blues of today." Further, he calls Davis's choice of title, *Somethin' Else*, a "phrase of praise," adopting it himself to champion the album.[10] Feather is also inclined to let musicians own their message. Annotating Bud Powell's classic set, *The Scene Changes* (1959), Feather devotes a good deal of space to the tune "Broderick," dedicated to the pianist's young son. "It is virtually a nursery rhyme," Feather writes, "valuable in the reflection of a seldom-considered aspect of Bud's personality, his life as a family man." The kicker, though, is when Feather describes Powell's reaction as he is shown the cover photo, which reveals his son peering across the keyboard: "Call the album *The Scene Changes*."[11] Similarly, Feather has Lee Morgan explain in notes for *The Sidewinder* (1964) that the album is not named after a snake, but after "the bad guy" on television shows.[12] In each liner note, Feather expands on that album's context.

Gunther Schuller was another multifaceted contributor to the jazz world. A French horn player and conductor, a composer of classical and jazz music, and president of the New England Conservatory, he moved easily among genres. In a 1957 lecture at Brandeis, he coined the term "Third Stream" to refer to a new kind of music that was part classical, part jazz, yet truly neither. In 1959, Schuller served as sound editor for Ornette Coleman's *The Shape of Jazz to Come*, but thereafter he focused on writing, composing liner notes and critical works like *Early Jazz* (1968) and *The Swing Era* (1991). In a review of Sonny Rollins's *Saxophone Colossus*, Schuller praises the musician's "thematic improvisation," providing listeners a new standard for jazz innovation, while also, according to Gary Giddins, "[assuring] the album's status as an untouchable classic."[13] Indeed, the eclectic Schuller adapted to the standard of whatever recording he described. In liner notes for *Ornette!* (1961), Schuller rescues Coleman from critics who deem him a "poor melodist." On the contrary,

Schuller declares that Coleman's music is "all melody"; it is simply free of "wallpaperlike cliches," and "beholden only to its own innermost logic and discipline."[14] In notes for *The Legendary Buster Smith* (1960), Schuller seeks justice for a different kind of saxophonist, recounting the time he traveled to Dallas with the Metropolitan Opera Orchestra and used his time off to track down the elusive alto player. Anticipating the "in-search-of" sagas that accompanied "comeback" recordings of Southern musicians in the Blues Revival, Schuller tells a shaggy-dog story of searching for Buster Smith in communities where few had telephones. After locating Smith and arranging a session with Atlantic, Schuller waits out the next phases of "Operation Buster," including a no-show on the first recording date. "Of course, I was dealing here with a peculiarly Southern characteristic!" Schuller explains. "Everything is very, very easygoing down there, and if we don't do something today, why there's always tomorrow or the day after."[15] While Schuller's notes for *Ornette!* operate on a theoretical plane to bolster the stature of free jazz, and his liners for Charles Mingus's *Tonight at Noon* (Atlantic 1964) serve similarly to elevate an unconventional composer to the ranks of Duke Ellington, his motivation on *The Legendary Buster Smith* is to provide an impression of how raw, yet how precious, are fugitive recordings of talented musicians facing hardscrabble circumstances.

Gitler rivals Feather as a prolific writer of liner notes. Gitler wrote reviews and criticism for a vast array of periodicals, including *Down Beat*, but his masterworks appeared on the back of jazz LPs. Gitler is famous for coining the phrase "sheets of sound," to describe John Coltrane's utterly free genius, in liner notes for *Soultrane* (Blue Note 1958). Coltrane subsequently told A. B. Spellman that his "sheets of sound" had been his attempt to imitate Thelonious Monk's unconventional piano runs while performing with Monk at the Five Spot.[16] Gitler was trying to translate Coltrane's virtuosic striving into words, and it was he who first asked Coltrane about that striving in an interview.[17] We know that Schuller coined the term "thematic improvisation" when reviewing *Saxophone Colossus*, but in his liner notes for that album, Gitler supplies his own power, likening Rollins to the Colossus of Rhodes, toppled by an earthquake in 224 BC, before suggesting that Rollins himself "has caused several movements on the seismograph of jazz in the past few years."[18] Gitler could also appreciate mellow moods, as he did on the Modern Jazz Quartet's *Django* (1956): "Just set at 33 1/3 and let them simmer on your turntable ... 'Very tasty.'"[19] He occasionally edged toward chauvinism, as evident in his annotations for Dexter Gordon's *Gettin' Around* (1965): "Gordon caresses Anthony

Newley's "Who Can I Turn To … as if he is holding a beautiful woman in his arms"[20]; or in his notes for Al Cohn and Zoot Sims' *Body and Soul* (1976): "[Jaki] Byard delineates 'The Girl from Ipanema' without quite revealing her original contours but tells us a lot about the inner woman."[21] All the while, Gitler played it smooth. He warmed to pop stylings heralding smooth jazz when reviewing Wes Montgomery's *Down Here on the Ground* (1968). "The way Wes is positioned in relation to his backing is an easy-listening delight," he moons. "The combination of the purely sweet and the naturally funky is constantly rewarding."[22]

In many ways, Nat Hentoff mirrored Gitler, writing for multiple publications (including the *Village Voice*) while composing a large body of liner notes. Hentoff did artists and repertoire (A&R) work, too, producing Max Roach's epic *We Insist! Freedom Now Suite* (1960) and writing its liners, which unpacked the album's political aesthetics, from Coleman Hawkins's atonal saxophone to Abbey Lincoln's haunting vocals. "There is still much to be won in America," Hentoff says about "Tears for Johannesburg," the final track. "But, as the soloists indicate after Abbey's wounding threnody, there will be no stopping the grasp for freedom anywhere."[23] Hentoff's special quality, Tom Piazza maintains, was his "large sensitivity and empathy for musicians; he was an intimate of some musicians who couldn't stand any critics at all, most notably Charles Mingus."[24] Accordingly, in notes for Mingus's eccentric masterpiece, *The Clown* (1957), Hentoff defends the irascible composer as an "open human being" whose "initial instinct is to strike from his hurt."[25] Hentoff adopts an existentialist tone common among jazz writers, and in this realm he reigned supreme. He loved authenticity, and he had an affinity with misunderstood outsiders, not just Mingus, but Ornette Coleman, too. In liners for *Tomorrow Is the Question* (1959), an admiring Hentoff explains how Coleman's eccentricity initially intimidated bandmate Don Cherry, who recoiled at seeing the saxophonist wearing an overcoat in 90-degree Los Angeles.[26] Hentoff also emphasized the impact of "taste" and authenticity as jazz LPs broke new ground across genres. Hentoff assures listeners that Donald Byrd's gospel-inspired LP, *A New Perspective* (1964), "is not a tongue-in-cheek, oh-how-soulful-I-am session. Nor is it an attempt to somehow mix old time religion, rhythm and blues and stomping jazz into a hopeful ride on the best-selling charts." It is instead a result of Byrd's "research into American negro history."[27]

Whitney Balliett, Ralph Gleason, Martin Williams, and Robert Palmer were other important mid-century jazz critics, and each wrote liner notes aligning with their worldviews. Balliett and Gleason wrote columns at the

New Yorker and the *San Francisco Chronicle*, respectively, and in their liners we glimpse the influence of their day jobs. Balliett avoided hip lingo, crafting a relatively dense or academic style when annotating LPs as diverse as *The Gerry Mulligan Quartet* (Pacific Jazz 1955), the Billy Taylor Trio's *Evergreens* (ABC Paramount 1956), and Joe Turner's *Boss of the Blues* (Atlantic 1956). Balliett prized nuance, as when he equates Mulligan's melodies with high-toned literature favored by *New Yorker* readers. "Writing a pure and ingratiating melody is like putting together a sentence that, by virtue of its perfectly chosen and arranged parts, has grace, rhythm, and meaning," he said of Mulligan.[28] Ralph Gleason had different literary proclivities, preferring the Beats and Bob Dylan, hosting the latter for a rambunctious 1965 press conference on KQED-TV (home to Gleason's *Jazz Casual* broadcasts). In his liner notes, Gleason exuded street cred. He appreciates the "good groove" that comes alive in the "witching hour" in notes for Nat King Cole's *After Midnight* (Capitol 1957),[29] and he replicates the laid-back aura of West Coast performance when annotating *Miles Davis in Person, Saturday Night at the Blackhawk, San Francisco, Volume 2* (Columbia 1966) and *John Handy Recorded Live at the Monterey Jazz Festival* (Columbia 1966). Martin Williams covered a different beat in his role as "dean of American jazz critics."[30] He cofounded *Jazz Times* with Nat Hentoff, directed jazz programs at the Smithsonian, and published the influential history *The Jazz Tradition* (1970). Along with Schuller, Williams won a Grammy for Best Album Notes in 1985 for *Big Band Jazz*, and he was an expert on swing. But his liner notes for Ornette Coleman's *The Shape of Jazz to Come* (1959) prove that he appreciated a "new thing" when he heard it. Robert Palmer, far younger than the others, was a polymath: a musician, a musicologist, a producer, and an unabashed fan of blues and world music. In the 1970s and 80s, he served as critic for the *New York Times* and *Rolling Stone*. Like Balliett, Palmer fixated on nuance, and he was especially good at describing unconventional tonalities. He praised McCoy Tyner for his "touch" on *Sahara* (1972) and underscored that message by quoting Tyner: "on a piano you can sound like water, like mountains, like so many things."[31] Palmer's eccentric and optimistic worldview infuses his notes for Julius Hemphill's *Dogon A.D.* (1978), an album that promises "unity of one world of black culture and of the word or sound or drumbeat which created this world and best expresses it."[32]

Amiri Baraka (LeRoi Jones) achieved fame in the 1960s as a poet, playwright, and Black Power activist. He was also a perceptive music critic, repeatedly emphasizing the culturally specific perspective necessary to make and appreciate Black music. Renowned for two iconic books of criticism – *Blues People* (1963) and *Black Music* (1968) – Baraka also penned one of the era's most passionate liner notes. His notes for Coltrane's *Live at Birdland* (1964) begin with a succinct appraisal: "One of the most baffling things about America is that despite its essentially vile profile, so much beauty continues to exist here."[33] Baraka hears in Coltrane a soundtrack for his own quest, recalling times he rushed through the ugliness of the New York City subway system only "to hear a man destroy all of it completely, like Sodom, with just the first few notes from his horn." Other members of the classic Quartet earn recognition, too, notably drummer Elvin Jones, who has Coltrane and pianist Tyner scrambling to keep pace, until they seem "driven, almost harassed." Most memorably, Baraka describes moments when he too feels harassed by the "mad ritual drama" Jones performs on the skins: "Beautiful has nothing to do with it, but it is (I got up and danced while writing these notes, screaming at Elvin to cool it)." The mood is more muted, but just as intense, once Baraka gets to "Alabama," the haunting tune Coltrane recorded shortly after the 16th Street Baptist Church bombing in Birmingham in 1963:

> [w]hat we're given is a slow delicate introspective sadness. Almost hopelessness, except for Elvin, rising in the background like something out of nature … a fattening thunder, storm clouds or jungle war clouds. The whole is a frightening emotional portrait of some place, in these musicians' feelings. If that "real" Alabama was the catalyst, more power to it, and may it be this beautiful, even in its destruction.

Listening to Coltrane is not just entertaining; it's transformative. "If you can hear, this music will make you think a lot of weird and wonderful things," Baraka exudes, concluding these notes. "You might even become one of them."

Stanley Crouch, a contributor to Baraka's late 1960s music journal, *The Cricket*, was a high-profile critic in ensuing decades, writing for the *Village Voice* and *Jazz Times* while composing a fair number of liners. Crouch deviated from Baraka insofar as he grew to favor African American traditionalism over "New Thing" experimentalism. Annotating Thelonious Monk's reissue compilation *At the Five Spot* (1977), Crouch downplays Monk's late-fifties innovations to promote a long-view conservatism. "What made [Monk] avant-garde," Crouch reasons, "was his determination to sustain the power of the tradition rather than reduce it to clichés, trends, novelties, or uninformed parodies."[34] Crouch proceeds to cite Albert Murray's *Stomping the Blues* as his lodestone, before labeling Monk "the Picasso of Jazz." Crouch's notes to Booker Ervin's *The Freedom and Space Sessions*

(1979) serve the same impetus. Crouch praises Ervin for having "studied the instrument and the tradition," and rejoices that, within his quartet's 1960s performances, "one can hear not only the sound of liberation but the sound of deliberation. These players are never content to reduce a musical situation to the level of primal scream therapy." Ervin's sideman Jaki Byard, meanwhile, is lauded not just for his improvisations, but for having "amalgamated the past" in traditionalist fashion.[35]

Crouch found his one true muse when Wynton Marsalis came to New York from New Orleans, by way of Art Blakey's Jazz Messengers. In liner notes for the trumpeter's debut, *Wynton Marsalis* (1982), Crouch calls the phenom "one of the most remarkable young musicians to appear in jazz since the early 1960s."[36] It is a nice compliment, but it notably erases two decades of innovative talent (in free jazz, New Thing, and jazz fusion). Unfazed, Crouch worships Marsalis "as an indication of the fresh development in a music plagued and battered by fusion for the last few years," and calls the trumpeter part of "a growing body of young, serious jazzmen ... committed to becoming first-class jazz artists." Ensuing years found Crouch "increasingly playing Boswell to Marsalis's Johnson."[37] Whether he was positioning Marsalis's *The Majesty of the Blues* (RCA 1989) within Albert Murray's canon (as he had done with Monk) or describing Marsalis's lullaby passages in *The Magic Hour* (Blue Note 2004) in bland humanist terminology, Crouch was a neo-traditionalist of the first order, and he didn't suffer fools gladly. "Stanley the Grouch," his detractors called him.

"The Scene Changes"

Outside the hands of the major critics, liner notes ranged from the ridiculous to the sublime. Pitfalls ensued when writers tried too hard to be hip. Willis Conover's notes to the Ahmad Jamal Trio's *Volume IV* (1958) take jive to a new level:

> You can skip this and start listening to the music. At that, you're one up on me, because as I write this the advance tapes haven't arrived yet ... you know, the tapes of the music on this LP that I'm supposed to listen to so I can write about it? It's all right, though. I was at the Spotlite when this session happened, so I can write Authoritative.[38]

Securing his own hip authority, Ralph Gleason ended his liner notes to Miles Davis's *Saturday at the Blackhawk* LP with the nod and wink of one "who hereby assumes full responsibility (moral and financial) for the statements, inferences and possible libels in this essay."[39] Lesser-known writers aimed for the same glib tone, with mixed results. In liners for *Miles Smiles* (1967), Anthony Tuttle, in an anti-intellectual move, attempts to rescue Davis from "those critics who write liner notes that go on and inexorably on about the integrity of the Artist in This, Our Complex Twentieth Century World." But in response Tuttle offers a cringey Madison Avenue riff on the album cover: "Why the smile? Because MILES SMILES happens to be the name of the album, and lo, like a smile it is – open, inviting, and, above all pleasing. Miles Smiles? Sure he does, and don't be surprised if you do, too."[40]

Espying similar excesses elsewhere, Giddins characterized "liner blurbs" for Modern Jazz Quartet LPs produced in 1968 (for the Beatles' Apple Records) as "embarrassingly *au courant*," a blatant effort to boost the relevance of a traditional outfit in a freewheeling time.[41] More and more, personal preferences percolated, and marketing angles got played. But as Benny Green wrote in liners for Coleman Hawkins' *Sirius* (1975), "no such thing as objective criticism exists anywhere."[42]

Facing systemic music industry sexism, few women wrote liner notes. Barbara Long actually begins notes for Dexter Gordon's *A Swingin' Affair* (1962) with an apology: "I hesitate to enter grounds already covered by writers more experienced than I." She also defers to Feather and Gitler, who wrote liners for Gordon LPs, and to other established critics who got to listen to Gordon in a 52nd Street scene that no longer exists. Fortunately, Long captures the vibes at the *Swingin'* show, especially when "one young tenor man, enjoying some current vogue, laughed delightedly to no one in particular, and said 'the old lion's telling us cats who's still running the jungle.'"[43] Eleanor Kennedy summons a club vibe, too, in notes for *Brother Jack McDuff Live!* (1963): "a couple of drinks and everybody digging the chick in red."[44] Nora Kelly seeks a more mellifluous range while annotating Herbie Hancock's *Empyrean Isles* (1964) and *Maiden Voyage* (1965). Her language is freely poetic, if slightly overwrought, foreshadowing New Age spirituality. Her description of folkloric mysteries involving giant serpents and mermaids is preceded by Hancock's own meditation on Atlantis and the Sargasso Sea.[45] Unfortunately, such partnerships proved rare. Englishwoman Valerie Wilmer reviewed jazz for periodicals, exhibited her photographs, and published influential books like *Jazz People* (1970) and *As Serious as Your Life* (1977), but women writing liner notes remained scarce.

Ironically, the genre accommodated men who weren't professional critics, including producer Bob Thiele, whose annotations for *Coltrane* (1962) curiously claimed "there is no need for album notes on the merits of 'Trane's music."[46] Producer Creed Taylor simply affixed his famous signature as an imprimatur. In a cameo performance, Thelonious Monk's "personal manager" supplied notes for *Misterioso* (1965): "He looked and acted like a millionaire. I liked that."[47] The most notorious liner note writer was probably Charles Mingus's psychotherapist, who on *The Black Saint and the Sinner Lady* (1963) called his client a "Black Saint who suffers for his sins and those of mankind … cognizant of a power-dominated and segregated society's impact on the underdog, the underprivileged and the minority."[48] Placed alongside *Beneath the Underdog* (1971), an autobiography Ted Gioia calls "a patchwork of braggadocio, real or fantasized sexual exploits, pop psychology, fanciful dialogue, and odd anecdotes," Mingus's outrageous liners made him the "closest jazz has come to having its own Ezra Pound."[49]

Other high-profile musicians composed liner notes as well. Pianist Bill Evans, assuming Zen mode on Davis's *Kind of Blue* (1959), references Japanese painters and calls this album's tracks "settings."[50] On *Change of the Century* (1959), Coleman likewise allies himself with painters who face queries about experimental art. The saxophonist anticipates Baraka's arguments when he says of his own music, "the only thing that matters is whether you *feel* it or not. You can't intellectualize music." As to why he plays a plastic alto, Coleman replies, "I felt it take on my emotion."[51] Here, Coleman heralds an aesthetic revolution. "To feel," his contemporary Cecil Taylor proclaimed, "is the most terrifying thing in this society."[52] As Baraka maintains throughout "Jazz and the White Critic," "attitude" and "feel" are things that cannot be taught. But they could be changed.[53]

Coleman had ample motivation to write liners. "Few musicians have been dealt with so poorly by outside commentators," Gioia says. "I can't think of another instance in jazz in which the written texts do so little justice to the body of work."[54] Coleman's peers were similarly moved. John Coltrane's praise poem, "Dear Listener," framed by a large Victor Kalin sketch, dominated the gatefold of *A Love Supreme* (1965).[55] The visual effect was sublime, indicative of the music inside. Spirituality was now the main message in jazz. Ahead of everyone, summoning interstellar mysteries on an array of LPs, Sun Ra propelled prayers to the spheres beyond. "The impossible is the watchword of the greater space age," Sun Ra notes on *Interstellar Low Ways* (1966).[56] His poetry and music communicated courage. "There is no limit to the imaginative realm-idea of the myth," Sun Ra writes in liner notes for *Space Is the Place* (1973). "Here is a challengingly frontier."[57] Yes, the man uses an adverb as an adjective, which is impossible, but also, in Sun Ra's universe, mighty real.

In the mid-1960s, the Chicago-based Association for the Advancement of Creative Musicians (AACM) took instruction from avant-garde elders and fashioned its own New Thing. Joseph Jarman, AACM musician and member of the Art Ensemble of Chicago, used a multitude of instruments and spoken-word recitations to expand the already capacious realm of African American expression. Jarman also used liner notes to affirm a network of Black musicians doing the same. Particularly moving is his description, in notes for *Urban Bushmen* (1980), of how the Art Ensemble of Chicago arrives in town with color-coded travel cases, a tight-knit brotherhood, before setting up their semicircle of instruments: "a beautiful shining object waiting to tone the infinite sound of THE ART ENSEMBLE OF CHICAGO. Finally, a huge bass drum is placed in the center of the semi-circle, the machine is ready."[58] Gary Giddins has called the Art Ensemble's music "guerilla jazz."[59] Jarman, with an insider's perspective, encompasses matters more sensitively in his liners, evoking the magic of the collective. "All that mattered for us is how musicians channeled their minds and expressed themselves spiritually," Jarman stated, serenely, elsewhere. "We were rejecting the hostility and anger you saw in the news all the time."[60]

*****

The best liner notes writers don't view their art as self-contained. Like other great jazz writers, they are more concerned with what music says to them than with what their writing says about music. "Last night I played *Meditations* / & it told me what to do / … Live!" Amiri Baraka confesses in "AM/TRAK," his poem for Coltrane.[61] Here, Brent Hayes Edwards posits, "we are with Baraka himself, beaten and jailed in the Newark uprisings in the summer of 1967, whistling Coltrane's music to keep himself sane, precisely at the moment of Coltrane's death."[62] For Baraka, as for so many listeners experiencing turbulent times, music and existence are one. You can write about this union, but only from the inside.

Notes

1 Various artists, *New Orleans Jazz* (Decca 144, 1940); Various artists, *Decca Presents an Album of Chicago Jazz* (Decca 121, 1940).
2 Charles Edward Smith, Liner notes, *New Orleans Jazz*, Decca Records, 1940, in Tom Piazza, ed., *Setting the Tempo: Fifty Years of Great Jazz Liner Notes* (New York: Anchor, 1996), 29.
3 George Avakian, Liner notes, *Chicago Jazz*, Decca Records, 1940, in Piazza, *Setting the Tempo*, 9.

Jazz Criticism and Liner Notes

4 Ibid., 12.
5 Tom Piazza, "Introduction," in Piazza, *Setting the Tempo*, 4.
6 Avakian, Liner notes, *Chicago Jazz*, 9, 20, 21.
7 Marc Meyers, *Why Jazz Happened* (Berkeley: University of California Press, 2013), 71.
8 Leonard Feather, Liner notes, Art Blakey Quintet, *A Night at Birdland* (Blue Note BLP 5037, 1954).
9 Leonard Feather, Liner notes, Paul Chambers, *Whims of Chambers* (Blue Note BLP 1534, 1957).
10 Leonard Feather, Liner notes, Cannonball Adderley, *Somethin' Else* (Blue Note BLP 1595, 1958).
11 Leonard Feather, Liner notes, Bud Powell, *The Scene Changes* (Blue Note BLP 4009, 1959).
12 Leonard Feather, Liner notes, Lee Morgan, *The Sidewinder* (Blue Note BLP 4157, 1964).
13 Gary Giddins, *Visions of Jazz: The First Century* (New York: Oxford University Press, 1998), 414. For more on this piece by Schuller, see Dale Chapman's chapter on the institutionalization of jazz in this volume (Chapter 11).
14 Gunther Schuller, Liner notes, Ornette Coleman, *Ornette!*, Atlantic Records, 1961, in Piazza, *Setting the Tempo*, 361, 362.
15 Gunther Schuller, Liner notes, Buster Smith, *The Legendary Buster Smith*, Atlantic Records, 1960, in Piazza, *Setting the Tempo*, 77.
16 Quoted in Stanley Crouch, Liner notes, Thelonious Monk, *At the Five Spot* (Milestone M-47043, 1977).
17 Ira Gitler, "Trane on the Track," *Down Beat*, October 16, 1958, 16–17.
18 Ira Gitler, Liner notes, Sonny Rollins, *Saxophone Colossus* (Prestige LP 7079, 1957).
19 Ira Gitler, Liner notes, Modern Jazz Quartet, *Django* (Prestige LP 7057, 1956).
20 Ira Gitler, Liner notes, Dexter Gordon, *Gettin' Around* (Blue Note BLP 4204, 1966).
21 Ira Gitler, Liner notes, Al Cohn and Zoot Sims, *Body and Soul*, Muse, 1976, in Piazza, *Setting the Tempo*, 124.
22 Ira Gitler, Liner notes, Wes Montgomery, *Down Here on the Ground* (A&M Records SP-3006, 1968).
23 Nat Hentoff, Liner notes, Max Roach, *We Insist! Max Roach's Freedom Now Suite* (Candid Records CJM 8002, 1961).
24 Piazza, *Setting the Tempo*, 127.
25 Nat Hentoff, Liner notes, Charles Mingus, *The Clown* (Atlantic Records 1260, 1957).
26 Nat Hentoff, Liner notes, Ornette Coleman, *Tomorrow Is the Question* (Contemporary Records M 3569, 1959).
27 Nat Hentoff, Liner notes, Donald Byrd, *A New Perspective* (Blue Note 84124, 1964).
28 Whitney Balliett, Liner notes, Gerry Mulligan Quartet featuring Chet Baker, *Gerry Mulligan Quartet* (Pacific Jazz PJ-1207, 1955).

29 Ralph J. Gleason, Liner notes, Nat King Cole and His Trio, *After Midnight* (Capitol W-782, 1956).
30 Piazza, *Setting the Tempo*, 160.
31 Robert Palmer, Liner notes, McCoy Tyner, *Sahara* (Milestone MSP 9039, 1972).
32 Robert Palmer, Liner notes, Julius Hemphill, *Dogon AD*, 1977, in Piazza, *Setting the Tempo*, 244.
33 Amiri Baraka, Liner notes, John Coltrane, *Live at Birdland* (Impulse A-50, 1964).
34 Crouch, Liner notes, *Thelonious Monk*.
35 Stanley Crouch, Liner notes, Booker Ervin, *The Freedom and Space Sessions*, 1979, in Piazza, *Setting the Tempo*, 249, 251–52.
36 Stanley Crouch, Liner notes, Wynton Marsalis, *Wynton Marsalis* (CBS FC 37574, 1982).
37 Ted Gioia, *The History of Jazz*, 2nd ed. (New York: Oxford University Press, 2011), 352.
38 Willis Conover, Liner notes, Ahmad Jamal Trio, *Volume IV* (Argo LP 636, 1958).
39 Ralph Gleason, Liner notes, Miles Davis, *In Person: Saturday Night at the Blackhawk, San Francisco, Volume II* (Columbia CS 8470, 1961).
40 Anthony Tuttle, Liner notes, Miles Davis, *Miles Smiles* (Columbia CS 9407, 1967).
41 Giddins, *Visions of Jazz*, 397.
42 Benny Green, Liner notes, Coleman Hawkins, *Sirius*, 1975, in Piazza, *Setting the Tempo*, 195.
43 Barbara Long, Liner notes, Dexter Gordon, *A Swingin' Affair* (Blue Note BLP 4133, 1962).
44 Eleanor Kennedy, Liner notes, Brother Jack MacDuff, *Live!* (Prestige LP 7274, 1963).
45 Nora Kelly, Liner notes, Herbie Hancock, *Empyrean Isles* (Blue Note BLP 4175, 1964); Nora Kelly, Liner notes, Herbie Hancock, *Maiden Voyage* (Blue Note BLP 4195, 1965).
46 Bob Thiele, Liner notes, John Coltrane, *Coltrane* (Impulse A-21, 1962).
47 Harry Colomby, Liner notes, Thelonious Monk, *Misterioso* (Columbia CL 2416, 1965).
48 Edmund Pollock, Liner notes, Charles Mingus, *The Black Saint and The Sinner Lady* (Impulse A-35, 1963).
49 Gioia, *History of Jazz*, 302.
50 Bill Evans, Liner notes, Miles Davis, *Kind of Blue* (Columbia CS 8163, 1959).
51 Ornette Coleman, Liner notes, Ornette Coleman, *Change of the Century* (Atlantic 1327, 1960).
52 Quoted in Ted Gioia, *How to Listen to Jazz* (New York: Basic Books, 2016), 134–35.
53 Amiri Baraka, "Jazz and the White Critic," 1963, in William J. Harris, ed., *The LeRoi Jones/Amiri Baraka Reader* (New York: Thunder's Mouth, 1991), 179–86.

54 Gioia, *How to Listen to Jazz*, 197.
55 John Coltrane, Liner notes: "Dear Listener," John Coltrane, *A Love Supreme* (Impulse A-77, 1965).
56 Sun Ra, Liner notes, Sun Ra, *Interstellar Low Ways* (El Saturn Records LP-203, 1967).
57 Sun Ra, Liner notes, Sun Ra, *Space Is the Place* (Blue Thumb BTS 41, 1973).
58 Joseph Jarman, Liner notes, Art Ensemble of Chicago, *Urban Bushmen* (ECM Records 1211/12, 1980).
59 Quoted in Gioia, *History of Jazz*, 361.
60 Quoted in Meyers, *Why Jazz Happened*, 200.
61 Amiri Baraka, "AM/TRAK," 1979, in Harris, *The LeRoi Jones/Amiri Baraka Reader*, 272.
62 Brent Hayes Edwards, *Epistrophies: Jazz and the Literary Imagination* (Cambridge, MA: Harvard University Press, 2017), 25.

CHAPTER 16

Jazz Autobiography

Daniel Stein

Picture Dizzy Gillespie, Charlie Parker, and Charles Mingus at a New York City jazz club in the 1950s. Dizzy wonders: "who invited all those white folks?" He then complains that there is "nothin' over there but critics." Mingus responds:

> Man, that's a lot of talent, don't you dig it? I see Leonard Feather, he's a piano player. There's Bill Coss and Gene Lees – they sing, I heard. Barry Ulanov must play drums or something, dig, with that *Metronome* beat. Martin Williams can play everything, I can tell by the way he writes. Put Marshall Stearns on bass and let Whitney Balliett score and John Wilson conduct. Let all them other young up-and-coming critics dance. How would you like to review that schitt for the *Amsterdam News*?[1]

This fantasy of a reversed power distribution between Black musicians and the white critics who professionally assess them appears in Charles Mingus's *Beneath the Underdog* (1971), an account of the bassist's life "that has taken on the status of a classic of jazz literature."[2] The passage is striking in its mockery of the critics, but it also troubles Mingus's foray into unfamiliar autobiographical territory. If critics make second-rate musicians, what about Mingus's abilities as an author? After all, *Beneath the Underdog* underwent a long process of writing, revising, and editing before it finally saw publication.[3]

The text further registers racial tensions that have shaped jazz from the beginning, as Mingus continues with a description of a performance of "Lover Man" that questions the kinds of criticism readers would have expected from the writers *Beneath the Underdog* mocks:

> Damn, Diz! You ever heard any schitt like that in your life?! Art [Tatum] backing up Bird [Charlie Parker] with left-hand solos, playing a counter-line with his right and somehow keeping the rhythm striding at the same time. Bird's laying out now.... Uh oh. Art looked up. There goes Bird. Art ain't comped him yet. Don't seem to be draggin' Bird none. Listen at them motherfuckers. Dig the critics over there still talking to each other. Don't hear a thing.[4]

Mingus conjures up a Black male world here, an onstage cosmos of competitive energy that excludes the white critics who are drowning out the music with talk.

Beneath the Underdog indicates that jazz musicians publish autobiographies to promote their own perspectives on the music, often framed as counternarratives or interventions against conventional forms of historiography and coverage.[5] Mingus employs nonstandard musical terminology (striding, laying out, comping) and slang (ain't, draggin', motherfuckers, dig) to evoke jazz's interactive thrust, suggesting that (white) critics are unable to capture the music's meanings. Other musicians' autobiographies likewise foreground the jazzman's alternative lexicon through glossaries explaining jazz lingo for interested readers. Cab Calloway's *Of Minnie the Moocher & Me* (1976) includes an updated version of his "Hepsters Dictionary," created in 1938 as a guide to the jazz musician's (in)famous jive talk. Louis Armstrong's *Swing That Music* (1936) features a glossary of swing terms, and Mezz Mezzrow's *Really the Blues* (1946) incorporates a glossary and underscores the Jewish clarinetist's claim to "Blackness" by translating a jive conversation into standard English.[6] Yet Mezzrow's self-consciousness about jive as a predominantly Black expression that white jazz musicians may learn and display as part of a cross-racial performance clashes with the vernacular language of some Black autobiographers. In *Miles* (1989), Miles Davis describes his initial encounter with Parker and Gillespie in a decidedly Black oral style that differs from Mezzrow's adopted jive lexicon: "Man, that shit was so terrible it was scary.... It was a motherfucker. Man, that shit was all up in my body."[7]

Jazz musicians thus use autobiography to narrate authoritative versions of their life stories in their own language. But jazz autobiography comes with its own complications, concerning, for instance, the creation of an authentic literary voice. Consider the following exchange between Hampton Hawes and cowriter Don Asher. When Hawes complains about the transcripts Asher made from taped interviews, "we don't want people to think we're setting them up with deliberate minority talk," Asher responds: "I took that phrase straight off the tape." Hawes counters: "I didn't mean for you to transcribe stuff directly. In this case, it's not dignified enough."[8] Here, notions of cultural status, of sophistication, refinement, and respectability complicate more strictly ethnographic approaches to writing the jazz life.

A second complication is the inability of autobiography to reproduce musical sound. "Jazz music, unrepresentable in established semantic or syntactical forms," Kevin McNeilly notes about *Beneath the Underdog*, "is overwritten in the text by conversations, verbal exchanges among musicians on the stand, whose voices tend to meld into a multitextured, indeterminate polylogue."[9] Rather than trying to grasp the music in writing, autobiographers like Mingus treat the jazz performance as an elusive phenomenon beyond literature's expressive capabilities. Instead, they portray their lives and express their opinions on the music and the culture from which it emerged.

A third complication concerns the enlisting of amanuenses to authenticate the musicians' role in jazz and transform orally rendered reminiscences into print.[10] These amanuenses include jazz critics like Irving Kolodin for Benny Goodman's *The Kingdom of Swing* (1939) or Stanley Dance for Duke Ellington's *Music Is My Mistress* (1973), who are sometimes hired explicitly to rectify the musicians' self-perceived deficiencies as writers. Paul Whiteman remarks in *Jazz* (1926), cowritten by radio host Mary Margaret McBride: "I certainly haven't tried to be literary for I am no writer, but only the conductor of a jazz orchestra."[11] Louis Armstrong notes in *Swing That Music*, partially ghostwritten by Horace Gerlach, how "hard-going writing was for a man who has lived all of his life mostly with a trumpet, not a pencil, in his hand."[12] *Beneath the Underdog* begins with a dedication: "I would like to express my deep thanks to Nel King, who worked long and hard editing this book, and who is probably the only white person who could have done it."[13] Other autobiographies connect the collaborative process with musical interaction. In *Good Morning Blues* (1985), Count Basie describes coauthor Albert Murray as "Count Basie's literary Count Basie" who "comps for me pretty much as I have always done for my soloists." Equating autobiographical creation with "four-handed piano playing," Basie validates the narrative as a music-like collaboration.[14]

Jazz autobiographies also constitute "a *reaction against* previous writing on jazz,"[15] facilitated through a collaborative writing process in which musicians, along with their amanuenses, confront an existing discourse about themselves and their music.[16] They constitute, as Ajay Heble notes, strategic attempts "at negotiating the politics of public acts of self-representation."[17] Dizzy Gillespie's chapter "Beboppers ... the Cult" in *To Be or Not to Bop* (1979), for instance, refutes "jive-ass stories about 'beboppers.'"[18] Citing a *Time* magazine article from March 25, 1946, Gillespie spends over twenty pages to "examine the charges and see how many of those stereotypes actually applied to me."[19] Davis rejects public demands for onstage propriety when he recalls about his self-understanding on and off the bandstand: "I didn't look at myself as an entertainer.... I wasn't going to do it just so that some non-playing, racist, white motherfucker could write some nice things about me."[20]

Acutely aware of such demands, many jazz autobiographers address the inadequacies of existing representations of jazz. Danny Barker's *A Life in Jazz* (1986) rejects popular depictions of jazz in the 1940s and beyond: "Many books came on the scene together with many falsehoods, lies and cooked-up stories. I read so much of this crap and then I was told I should write some truth."[21] Barker's sentiment is matched by George Foster's assertion that "[t]he critics and guys who write about jazz think they know more about what went on in New Orleans than the guys that were there.... This book is gonna straighten a lot of things out."[22] Such promises of a better jazz history, dictated or written by practitioners, underscore jazz autobiography's premise "that a good deal written about the music does not necessarily correspond with the sensibility or even lived experience of the musicians."[23] This does, however, not prevent some musicians from mentioning favorable coverage. Anita O'Day's *High Times Hard Times* (1981) is abuzz with quotes from jazz magazines and newspapers, as is Art and Laurie Pepper's *Straight Life* (1979). It makes sense, then, to think of these musicians and singers as "coconspirators in the crafting of their public images."[24]

If "the turn to jazz autobiography is regarded as a genuine opportunity to seize narrative authority,"[25] we must ask how musicians have used this authority to construct narratives about themselves and their music. "This is a story of a boy that decided on his own to make his life in music and entertainment," Clyde Bernhardt writes in *I Remember* (1986). "I tell about events and conversations that is important to me, not only because I experienced them, but because somehow it all seems to fit in a kind of bigger picture. Perhaps a picture of America. Or the Negro in America."[26] Bernhardt uses his authority as a musician to express ambiguity about the meaning of his life story. His refusal to subsume this story – and that of "the Negro in America" – into a narrative of racial progress questions notions of national greatness that appear, for instance, in Whiteman's claim that jazz "expresses the spirit of America."[27]

Rather than endorse triumphalist narratives of the national spirit, many Black jazz autobiographers detail traumatic experiences with racism. Jelly Roll Morton recalls a lynching in Biloxi, Mississippi; Roy Porter remembers "lynch talk" in Colorado Springs in the mid-1930s; Rex Stewart mentions "news of a recent lynching down South" around the same time.[28] Buck Clayton notes that "black people were still being lynched" in late-1920s Arkansas, while Garvin Bushell associates his hometown Springfield, Ohio, with a lynching in 1904.[29] Davis states that the photographs of Emmett Till, killed in Mississippi in 1955, made him "sick to my stomach" and that he "won't forget them pictures of that young boy as long as I live."[30] Milt Hinton depicts a lynching he witnessed as a boy in Vicksburg, Mississippi, as a formative event, while Billie Holiday personalizes her renditions of the anti-lynching song "Strange Fruit" in *Lady Sings the Blues*.[31] This, too, is the spirit of America, and an integral part of jazz, these writers allege.

Conceptual and Historical Overview

Jazz autobiography developed from "a small, little-known genre," as Gary Giddins observes in his foreword to Hampton Hawes's *Raise Up Off Me* (1974), to a still-growing body of work that now encompasses between around 80 and 100 texts.[32] Yet what does it mean to conceive of "this other sort of jazz literature" as a genre, a set of narratives with recurring structures and a shared self-understanding as an evolving autobiographical discourse?[33]

The first jazz autobiography, Paul Whiteman's *Jazz*, acknowledges the music's Black origins – "I did not invent jazz.... All I did was to orchestrate jazz"[34] – and recognizes its roots in slavery: "Jazz came to America three hundred years ago in chains. The psalm-singing Dutch traders, sailing ... across the ocean in 1619, described their cargo as 'fourteen black African slaves for sale in the Majesty's colonies.'"[35] Whiteman's "*apologia* for jazz"[36] is certainly suspect, as the white bandleader tends to read the music's Black roots as primitive and its white strains as modern, foreseeing a whitened "future of jazz."[37] Nonetheless, the fact that jazz autobiography begins with an acknowledgment of the first African slaves on North American soil is surprising, as it connects jazz with a history of racial exploitation in stark contrast to the animated, minstrel-saturated and blackface-like jazz origin sequence in Whiteman's film *King of Jazz* (1930). If jazz is historically rooted in the experience of enslavement (a romantic and certainly problematic idea), as Whiteman's autobiography suggests, it is still shaped by racial discrimination and segregation, as many Black musicians emphasize. "Musicians are as Jim-Crowed as any black motherfucker on the street,"[38] Mingus tells his psychoanalyst in *Beneath the Underdog*; "if you're black, there is no justice,"[39] Davis maintains.

In addition to introducing race as a factor in the music, Whiteman's *Jazz* prefigures additional genre elements. It is a collaboratively created text that includes private photographs and publicity shots, and it combines personal stories with musical and cultural commentary, accounting for "jazz and [Whiteman's] connection with it."[40] Many later jazz autobiographies also involve amanuenses, exceptions being Artie Shaw's *The Trouble with Cinderella* (1952) and W. O. Smith's *Sideman* (1991). Many amanuenses use prefaces and forewords to frame the meaning of the musician's life. Collaboration takes different forms, from taped interviews transcribed and arranged for publication to manuscripts trimmed or notes extended into full-blown narratives. Albert Murray taped his interviews with Jo Jones but delegated turning them into a book to Paul Devlin, who did a "tremendous amount of cutting, pasting, and shuffling" to produce *Rifftide*.[41] Duke Ellington "wrote slowly and haphazardly while on tour, scribbling fragments," as Brent Hayes Edwards writes about *Music Is My Mistress*.[42] Mingus produced an unwieldy 875-page draft of *Beneath the Underdog* outrageously titled *Memoirs of a Half Yellow Schitt-Colored Nigger*.[43] Holiday's *Lady Sings the Blues* (1956), allegedly written "with William Dufty," contains so many falsifications that one wonders about the distribution of authorial responsibilities in the creation of this heavily mythologized narrative.[44]

While all jazz autobiographers engage in self-mythologizing,[45] they nonetheless place on a spectrum from more documentary-minded to more fantastic narratives. According to Edwards, "collecting and documentation are clearly a central part of the work and self-conception of so many musicians."[46] This sentiment resonates with Jelly Roll Morton's hope that "since this story is for The Archives where you're supposed to give the facts, the truth may as well come out,"[47] and it is further supported by "Armstrong's passion for documenting his lived experiences across a range of media."[48] Gillespie's *To Be or Not to Bop*, Shaw's *The Trouble with Cinderella*, and Basie's *Good Morning Blues* also veer toward the spectrum's documentary end. Gillespie and cowriter Al Fraser state in the preface of their 550-page tome that their aim was to create "the best – the most complete, authentic, and authoritative autobiography of a jazz musician every published."[49] *The Trouble with Cinderella* bluntly distinguishes between "Artie Shaw," swing celebrity and "side-show freak" whom fame made "utterly miserable," and Arthur Jacob Arshawsky, the man behind the popular image.[50] Basie calls his cowriter "my main man in the research department,"[51] and references personal files as sources for his story. Many autobiographies also include interviews with family members, musicians, club owners, record producers, and critics to underscore facticity. Gillespie's *To Be or Not to Bop* and Art and Laurie Pepper's *Straight Life* choose a "multiwitness format,"[52] interspersing the autobiographer's recollections with sometimes contradictory interviews. "It's a damn lie … worst lie in the world,"[53] Dickey Wells responds to Gillespie's accusation that he had sabotaged his soloing when playing with Fletcher Henderson.[54]

Mingus's *Beneath the Underdog* and Holiday's *Lady Sings the Blues*, as well as Mezzrow's *Really the Blues* and Sidney Bechet's *Treat It Gentle* (1960), display the genre's more fantastic side. Mingus revels in chauvinistic celebrations of sexual prowess and his ambitions as a pimp, all told from a third-person perspective. His jazz world and that of many other jazz autobiographies is a male fraternity, with women playing largely subservient roles (prostitute, lover, spouse). Compare Foster's recollection of male bandstand banter – "'Gee, I know she's got good bread.' It meant she's got good pussy"[55] – with O'Day's confession that she "never considered myself a pretty girl" and that she "learned to cover up my feelings of pain beneath a hip, swinging-chick personality."[56] Holiday and O'Day expose chauvinism's flipside, recalling sexual abuse, rape, and drug addiction as well as, in O'Day's case, abortion. Reva Marin further notes a "growing list of memoirs penned by spouses of prominent jazz musicians" such as Sue Graham Mingus, Chan Parker, and Maxine Gordon as an indication of a more recent and more balanced discourse on gender in jazz.[57]

Tapping further into the fantastic, Bechet begins with a chapter on the grandfather figure Omar, recalling a Louisiana folk tale and anchoring jazz in mythical New Orleans. Mezzrow's self-presentation as jazz's "link between the races" and a convert to the "Negro race" registers the ironies of the color line even though its veracity, including depictions of Mezzrow's relationship with Louis Armstrong, is doubtful.[58] His self-portrait as an authentic jazz player may resonate with white jazz autobiographers, but many Black musicians beg to differ. Contrast the climax of Mezzrow's narrative, when "Jimmy Noone and Johnny Dodds and Sidney Bechet ... were inside my skin, making my fingers work right so I could speak my piece,"[59] with Bechet's description of Mezzrow as "a man [who] is trying so hard to be something he isn't."[60]

Whiteman's *Jazz*, Armstrong's *Swing That Music*, and Goodman's *The Kingdom of Swing* are the earliest enunciations of the genre. Whiteman makes the case for jazz as "the real American music";[61] Armstrong and Goodman trace jazz's success as a popular music. Armstrong's narrative oscillates between the trumpeter's anecdotes and didactic passages by ghostwriter Gerlach.[62] Goodman's account celebrates his career from Jewish working-class beginnings to being crowned "king of swing." The 1940s saw a more sustained effort to publish jazz memoirs, with Mezzrow's *Really the Blues*, Condon's *We Called It Music* (1947), and Wingy Manone's *Trumpet on the Wing* (1948) showcasing white musicians associated with the traditional style. In the 1950s, the genre diversified, with New Orleans players like Armstrong (*Satchmo: My Life in New Orleans*, 1954) and Baby Dodds (*The Baby Dodds Story*, 1959) publishing life stories alongside bandleaders like Shaw and singers like Holiday.[63] After a brief dip in the 1960s, when less than a handful of narratives – among them Bechet's *Treat It Gentle*, Max Kaminsky's *Jazz Band: My Life in Jazz* (1963), and Willie "The Lion" Smith's *Music on My Mind* (1964) – appeared, the genre recovered in the 1970s with a dozen narratives. Already mentioned were works by Calloway, Foster, Mingus, Ellington, Gillespie, Hawes, and Pepper, whose jazz life depictions were expanded by autobiographies like Dicky Wells's *The Night People* (1971).

In the 1980s and 90s, when jazz became more popularly recognized as a national treasure, the number of jazz autobiographies increased (two dozen in the 1980s, about twenty in the 1990s). Enticed by the establishment of jazz studies, university presses began to include them in their rosters. Heightened interest led to heightened diversity, as works published in these decades present a wide range of periods, styles, instruments, and geographical backgrounds.[64] From bandleaders like Charlie Barnet (*Those Swinging Years*, 1984), Count Basie (*Good Morning Blues*, 1985), and Woody Herman (*The Woodchopper's Ball*, 1990) to New Orleans musicians like Danny Barker (*A Life in Jazz*, 1986), pianists like Teddy Wilson (*Teddy Wilson Talks Jazz*, 1996), boppers like Miles Davis (*Miles*, 1989), and sidemen like Drew Page (*Drew's Blues*, 1980) and W. O. Smith (*Sideman*, 1991), jazz autobiography became more and more versatile. This included books like Wynton Marsalis and Frank Stewart's *Sweet Swing Blues on the Road* (1994), a collection of road stories and reflections of jazz and American culture accompanied by black-and-white photographs, as well as Marsalis and Carl Vigeland's *Jazz in the Bittersweet Blues of Life* (2001), another chronicle of the touring life. With fifteen autobiographies in the 2000s and nineteen in the 2010s, among them Oscar Peterson's *A Jazz Odyssey* (2002), Yusef Lateef's *The Gentle Giant* (2006), Horace Silver's *Let's Get to the Nitty Gritty* (2006), Clark Terry's *Clark* (2011), and Herbie Hancock's *Possibilities* (2014), the genre continues to thrive.

Toward a Genre Poetics of Jazz Autobiography

The question remains whether we can identify recurring themes, styles, and structures that warrant labeling jazz autobiography a genre. I have already mentioned "formulaic qualities"[65] from collaboration to a tendency to combine personal experience with larger narratives of jazz and nation. I have also noted the prominence of the color line, as Black musicians often address instances of racial discrimination while white musicians tend to depict their jazz education as a story of interracial inspiration. "[T]he Negro is born with rhythm. We've got to learn it," Eddie Condon claims in essentialized terms;[66] "[I] eventually came to feel more like a colored man than an 'ofay'.... I used to wish I could actually *be* Negro," Artie Shaw confesses.[67]

Beyond these elements, jazz autobiographies share a repertoire of scenes and events. This includes initial musical encounters, learning to play an instrument, first gigs and early successes, performing nationally and internationally, recording sessions, and tokens of public recognition. Typical are conversion experiences that launch the autobiographer's career. Watching Joe Oliver with Louis Armstrong, Condon recalls: "It was hypnosis at first hearing ... the music poured into us like daylight running down a dark hole."[68] Woody Herman writes: "Hearing Armstrong made you a believer in what was swing."[69] Yet the degree to which these narratives show the autobiographer's private life varies. Some – Barnet, Herman, Hawes, O'Day, Pepper, Peterson – are rather forthright about failing relationships and successive marriages and about the pitfalls of a life lived largely on the road, including drug addiction, alcohol abuse, extramarital affairs, and loneliness. Others engage in self-censure, "always [wearing] a mask in public."[70] "I just don't intend to bring up anything that might add up to a lot of gossip and speculation and that don't really have anything to do with playing music," Basie writes. "Now as for what was happening with me and the ladies during those early days in Kansas City, I figure that ain't nobody's business."[71] Ellington's multiple selves – "*me*, the thinker-writer, the okayer, the nixer, the player, the listener, the critic, the corrector" – explicitly cast the autobiography as a strategic public performance.[72]

Almost all jazz autobiographies feature photographs in order to root their narratives in a discourse of visual authenticity. Hinton's *Bass Line* is particularly interesting as it places Hinton's recollections alongside his own photography. Hinton acts as a musician-photographer-autobiographer,[73] whose images of jazz greats on the tour bus, smoking or drinking in the studio, performing onstage or relaxing backstage complicate stereotypes of the jazz life. His intimate photographs, including impressions of a frail Holiday in the recording studio shortly before her death and a snapshot of Gillespie and Mingus cracking up at Newport in 1971, recognize the limits of jazz writing as they capture a seldom seen slice of American history but also evoke a world apart from the lives of most readers.

Once we recognize autobiography as an expressive practice that can take many different shapes, additional genre variants emerge. Morton performed his life story and interspersed it with his piano playing and singing for Alan Lomax, who recorded it at the Library of Congress and used the recordings as the basis for *Mister Jelly Roll*.[74] Armstrong not only contributed to *Swing That Music*, wrote *Satchmo*, authored autobiographical essays, penned thousands of letters, and gave countless interviews, he also created an extensive archive of private recordings of himself in everyday situations as well as many photo-collages.[75] Art Hodes published *Hot Man* in 1992 but also worked for the *Jazz Record*. Rex Stewart authored articles on jazz before he drafted the manuscript Claire P. Gordon assembled into *Boy Meets Horn*. Ellington's *Music Is My Mistress* and Peterson's *A Jazz Odyssey* feature poetry by the authors. Moreover, references to songs, albums, radio and television appearances as well as live shows abound, and discographies match written narrative to the music.[76] *Swing That Music* even includes musical notation for the eponymous song, which Armstrong recorded for promotion and which the "music section" of the book features with additional scores of Armstrong's solo and solos of other musicians. The Peppers' *Straight Life* includes musical notation for the song that provides the autobiography's title, joining other autobiographies named after popular tunes: *Really the Blues, Good Morning Blues, The Woodchopper's Ball, Boy Meets Horn*, and so forth.

Finally, the fact that jazz autobiographies often reference other jazz autobiographies sanctions an understanding of these texts as a genre and evokes the music's interactive dynamics.[77] Larry Gara, who turned Baby Dodds's recollections into prose, cites *Mister Jelly Roll* as his model;[78] Barker writes that Morton "proudly boasted" about his French ancestors in "Lomax's *Mr. Jelly Lord* [sic]."[79] Discussing a show in Detroit, Basie notes that Holiday had commented on the city's hostile environment in *Lady Sings the Blues*,[80] while Jones recalls seeing Armstrong work on his typewriter after shows.[81] Buck Clayton mentions Mezzrow's *Really the Blues*,[82] as does Barnet, who also references Ellington's *Music Is My Mistress*, while Lionel Hampton's *Hamp: An Autobiography* (1989) contrasts his recollection of a band contest with Basie's version in *Good Morning Blues*.[83] Yet to designate jazz autobiography a genre should not mean to impose strict boundaries and rules on this body of works. Rather, we can recognize a shared understanding of the jazz life as an experience that inspires a specific set of story elements and a common world. It is true that jazz musicians are famously wary of categories: "I always hated categories," Davis states in *Miles*: "I always thought that music had no boundaries, no limits to where it could grow and go, no restrictions on its creativity."[84] Ellington said at a press conference in Latin America: "I don't believe in categories of any kind."[85] Yet when it comes to the category, or genre, of jazz autobiography, we can certainly discern a common poetics of the jazz life as told from the musician's perspective.

Notes

1 Charles Mingus, *Beneath the Underdog*, 1971, Nel King, ed. (New York: Vintage, 1991), 294.
2 Christopher Harlos, "Jazz Autobiography: Theory, Practice, Politics," in Krin Gabbard, ed., *Representing Jazz* (Durham, NC: Duke University Press, 1995), 138.
3 For comparisons of manuscript and book, see Eric Porter, *What Is This Thing Called Jazz? African American Musicians as Artists, Critics, and Activists* (Berkeley: University of California Press, 2002), chapter 3; Krin Gabbard, *Better Git It in Your Soul: An Interpretive Biography of Charles Mingus* (Berkeley: University of California Press, 2016), Part II.
4 Mingus, *Beneath the Underdog*, 295.
5 Ajay Heble, *Landing on the Wrong Note: Jazz, Dissonance, and Critical Practice* (New York: Routledge, 2000), 94; Porter, *What Is This Thing*, 139.
6 For more on jazz and language, see Amor Kohli's chapter in this volume (Chapter 9). For a discussion of Calloway's and Mezzrow's glossaries in relationship to American "cool," see Chapter 10 by Joel Dinerstein.
7 Miles Davis, with Quincy Troupe, *Miles: The Autobiography*, 1989 (New York: Simon and Schuster, 1990), 7.
8 Gary Giddins, "Introduction," in Hampton Hawes and Don Asher, *Raise Up Off Me: A Portrait of Hampton Hawes*, 1974 (New York: Thunder's Mouth, 2001), vi.
9 Kevin McNeilly, "Charles Mingus Splits, or, All the Things You Could Be by Now If Sigmund Freud's Wife Was Your Mother," *Canadian Review of American Studies*, 27.2 (1997), 66.
10 Reva Marin discusses the amanuenses' paratextual "authenticating function" in *Outside and Inside: Race and Identity in White Jazz Autobiography* (Jackson, MS: University of Mississippi Press, 2020), 19.
11 Paul Whiteman, with Mary Martin McBride, *Jazz*, 1926 (New York: Arno, 1974), 11.
12 Louis Armstrong, *Swing That Music*, 1936 (New York: Da Capo, 1993), 78.
13 Mingus, *Beneath the Underdog*. Jo Jones boasts: "I'll give you so much material, goddamit, you'll have to lock yourself up and be all fucked up" in Papa Jo Jones, as told to Albert Murray, *Rifftide: The Life and Opinions of Papa Jo Jones*, Paul Devlin, ed. (Minneapolis: University of Minnesota Press, 2011), 27.
14 Count Basie, as told to Albert Murray, *Good Morning Blues: The Autobiography of Count Basie*, 1985 (New York: Da Capo, 1995), xiii.
15 Harlos, "Jazz Autobiography," 137, original emphasis.

16 Daniel Stein, "The Performance of Jazz Autobiography," in Mark Osteen, ed., *Blue Notes: Toward a New Jazz Discourse*, Special Issue of *Genre* 37.2 (2004), 177. On this discourse, see John Gennari, *Blowin' Hot and Cool: Jazz and Its Critics* (Chicago: University of Chicago Press, 2006).
17 Heble, *Landing on the Wrong Note*, 103.
18 Dizzy Gillespie and Al Fraser, *To Be or Not to Bop* (New York: Da Capo, 1979), 278.
19 Ibid., 279.
20 Davis, *Miles*, 83.
21 Danny Barker, *A Life in Jazz*, Alyn Shipton, ed., 1986 (Oxford: Oxford University Press, 1988), vi.
22 George Foster, as told to Tom Stoddard, *The Autobiography of Pops Foster*, 1971 (San Francisco: Backbeat, 2005), 1.
23 Harlos, "Jazz Autobiography," 137.
24 John Gennari, "But Is It Jazz?" *Reviews in American History*, 23.1 (1995), 91.
25 Harlos, "Jazz Autobiography," 134.
26 Clyde E.B. Bernhardt, as told to Sheldon Harris, *I Remember: Eighty Years of Black Entertainment, Big Bands, and the Blues*, 1986 (Philadelphia: University of Pennsylvania Press, 1989), xv.
27 Whiteman, *Jazz*, 11.
28 Alan Lomax, *Mister Jelly Roll: The Fortunes of Jelly Roll Morton, New Orleans Creole and "Inventor of Jazz,"* 1950 (Berkeley: University of California Press, 2001), 143; Roy Porter and David Keller, *There and Back: The Roy Porter Story* (Baton Rouge: Louisiana State University Press, 1991), 25; Rex Stewart, *Boy Meets Horn*, Claire P. Gordon, ed. (Ann Arbor: University of Michigan Press, 1991), 176.
29 Buck Clayton, assisted by Nancy M. Elliott, *Buck Clayton's Jazz World*, 1986 (New York: Oxford University Press, 1989), 24; Gavin Bushell, as told to Mark Tucker, *Jazz from the Beginning*, 1988 (New York: Da Capo, 1998), 4.
30 Davis, *Miles*, 194.
31 Milt Hinton & David G. Berger, *Bass Line: The Stories and Photographs of Milt Hinton* (Philadelphia: Temple University Press, 1988), 7–8; Billie Holiday, with William Dufty, *Lady Sings the Blues*, 1956 (New York: Broadway Books, 2006), 94–95.
32 Giddins, "Introduction," vi. Marin, *Outside and Inside*, xv, identifies circa "eighty US jazz musicians [who] published their autobiographies and memoirs"; Holly E. Farrington finds over forty autobiographies by Black musicians until 1996. See Holly E. Farrington, "Narrating the Jazz Life: Three Approaches to Jazz Autobiography," *Popular Music and Society* 29.3 (2006), 375. I have located about 100 texts classifiable as jazz autobiography. The extent of the genre varies depending on one's definition of jazz and autobiography.
33 Brent Hayes Edwards, *Epistrophies: Jazz and the Literary Imagination* (Cambridge, MA: Harvard University Press, 2017), 12. On musical autobiographies more generally, see Daniel Stein & Martin Butler, Musical Autobiographies, special issue of *Popular Music and Society*, 38.2 (2015).

34 Whiteman, *Jazz*, 20.
35 Ibid., 3.
36 Marin, *Outside and Inside*, xvii.
37 Whiteman, *Jazz*, 275.
38 Mingus, *Beneath the Underdog*, 4.
39 Davis, *Miles*, 239.
40 Whiteman, *Jazz*, 11.
41 Jones, *Rifftide*, xvii.
42 Edwards, *Epistrophies*, 112.
43 Porter, *What Is This Thing*, 139; Gabbard, *Better Git It in Your Soul*, 139–46.
44 John Szwed, *Billie Holiday: The Musician and the Myth* (London: Heinemann, 2015), 13–33.
45 Stein, "Performance of Jazz," 174, 176.
46 Edwards, *Epistrophies*, 14.
47 Lomax, *Mister Jelly Roll*, 175.
48 Ben Alexander, "'For Posterity': The Personal Audio Recordings of Louis Armstrong," *The American Archivist*, 71.1 (2008), 51.
49 Gillespie and Fraser, *To Be or Not to Bop*, xvii.
50 Artie Shaw, *The Trouble with Cinderella: An Outline of Identity*, 1952 (Santa Barbara: Fithian, 1992), 341, 346. On Jewish jazz autobiography, see Marin, *Outside and Inside*, chapter 4.
51 Basie, *Good Morning Blues*, xiii.
52 Harlos, "Jazz Autobiography," 145.
53 Gillespie and Fraser, *To Be or Not to Bop*, 67.
54 Others intersperse autobiographical narration with biographical, historical, musicological segments: Lomax's *Mister Jelly Roll*, Condon's *We Called It Music*, Hodes's *Hot Man*.
55 Foster, *Autobiography of Pops Foster*, 64.
56 Anita O'Day, with George Eells, *High Times Hard Times*, 1981 (New York: Limelight, 2003), 65, 56.
57 Marin, *Outside and Inside*, 161.
58 Mezz Mezzrow, with Bernard Wolfe, *Really the Blues*, 1946 (New York: Citadel, 2001), 240. See Daniel Stein, "'Sei a mensch': Mezz Mezzrow's Jewish Hipster Autobiography *Really the Blues* and the Ironies of the Color Line," *Anglia*, 137.1 (2019), 2–32.
59 Mezzrow, *Really the Blues*, 324.
60 Sidney Bechet, *Treat It Gentle*, 1960 (New York: Da Capo, 1978), 169.
61 Whiteman, *Jazz*, 294.
62 William H. Kenney, III. "Negotiating the Color Line: Louis Armstrong's Autobiographies," in Reginald. T. Buckner and Steven Weiland, eds., *Jazz in Mind: Essays on the History and Meanings of Jazz* (Detroit: Wayne State University Press, 1991), 41.
63 Mary Lou Williams published an autobiographical essay in *Melody Maker* (1954), one of the few jazz narratives by a woman.
64 Harlos, "Jazz Autobiography," 133.

65 Kathy Ogren, "'Jazz Isn't Just Me': Jazz Autobiographies as Performance Personas," in Buckner and Weiland, *Jazz in Mind*, 112–13.
66 Eddie Condon, with Thomas Sugrue, *We Called It Music: A Generation of Jazz*, 1947 (New York: Da Capo, 1992), 162.
67 Shaw, *The Trouble with Cinderella*, 228.
68 Condon, *We Called It Music*, 107.
69 Woody Herman & Stuart Troup, *The Woodchopper's Ball: The Autobiography of Woody Herman*, 1990 (New York: Limelight, 1994), 10.
70 Gabbard, *Better Git It in Your Soul*, 131.
71 Basie, *Good Morning Blues*, xiii, 17.
72 Duke Ellington, *Music Is My Mistress*, 1973 (New York: Da Capo, 1976), 451.
73 Harlos, "Jazz Autobiography," 133.
74 Morton's performance underscores the significance of oral history for jazz historiography. One of the first books on jazz, Frederic Ramsey, Jr. and Charles Edward Smith's *Jazzmen: The Story of Hot Jazz Told in the Lives of the Men Who Created It* (1939), employs oral history to tell the history of the music.
75 Jorge Daniel Veneciano calls Armstrong an "intermedia artist" and his photo-collages "autobiography by other means." See "Louis Armstrong, Bricolage, and the Aesthetics of Swing," in Robert G. O'Meally, Brent Hayes Edwards, and Farah Jasmine Griffin, eds., *Uptown Conversation: The New Jazz Studies* (New York: Columbia University Press, 2004), 257, 258. On Armstrong's tape recordings, see Alexander, "For Posterity," 50–86.
76 I conceptualize the media-crossing convolution of the jazz musician's representation as an "intermedial autobiographics" in *Music Is My Life: Louis Armstrong, Autobiography, and American Jazz* (Ann Arbor: University of Michigan Press, 2012).
77 Cf. Ogren: "autobiographical accounts can be seen as literary 'cutting contests,' in which the musician/narrators display their storytelling skills" ("Jazz Isn't Just Me," 121).
78 William "Baby" Dodds, as told to Larry Gara, *The Baby Dodds Story*, 1959 (Alma, MI: Rebeats, 2002), xiv.
79 Barker, *A Life in Jazz*, 122.
80 Basie, *Good Morning Blues*, 205–6.
81 Jones, *Rifftide*, 96.
82 Clayton, *Buck Clayton's Jazz World*, 145.
83 Charlie Barnet and Stanley Dance, *Those Swinging Years: The Autobiography of Charlie Barnet*, 1984 (New York: Da Capo, 1992), 14, 171; Lionel Hampton, with James Haskins, *Hamp: An Autobiography* (New York: Warner, 1989), 81.
84 Davis, *Miles*, 205.
85 Ellington, *Music Is My Mistress*, 378.

CHAPTER 17

Jazz and the American Songbook

Katherine Williams

This chapter seeks to outline the debt jazz in American culture owes to the American Songbook. The American Songbook (sometimes the "great American Songbook") is the name collectively given to the popular songs from the 1920s to 1950s that entered the American popular consciousness through repeated recordings and performance then and thereafter. These songs came primarily from Broadway musicals, Hollywood films, and Tin Pan Alley, the row of music publishers on New York's 28th Street. I will show this through discussion of a series of examples of American Songbook songs, analyzing the musical content and giving a cross-section overview of the reach they had within the jazz world. Finally, I hope to show the interconnectedness of the American Songbook and jazz by illustrating how the former began to draw on the latter. In examples like Harold Arlen's "Stormy Weather," Irving Berlin's "Puttin' on the Ritz," or any number of Cole Porter compositions, we see the workmanlike creators of Tin Pan Alley incorporating not just musical elements associated with jazz, but also a more general sensibility, intended to recreate the music's blues-informed world-weariness or performative impertinence.

Many commentators refer to the quintessentially *American* nature of these songs, implying that something in their construction, in their musical components or their lyrics both contributed to and depicted the nation. Alec Wilder wrote, in his groundbreaking 1972 book *American Popular Song*, that: "the American popular song took, and consolidated, certain native characteristics – verbal, melodic, harmonic, and rhythmic – that distinguished it from the popular song of other countries."[1] Terry Teachout, writing thirty years later, concurred: "It was from the outset distinctively American in tone, colored not only by ragtime and early jazz but also by the pungent accent of what H. L. Mencken called 'the American language.'"[2]

Wilder's book outlines the life and music of the songwriters and lyricists he considers most important to the American Songbook. From the outset, his commentary and analysis support his conviction that the study of songs must consider the lyrics and music together: "One may talk about *words*, or one may talk about *music*, but one cannot talk about *song* and mean anything less than the combination of the two."[3] Again, Teachout's commentary supports this. His four-part article takes the form of a list of what he considers to be the top fifty entries to the American Songbook, and he recommends not just specific artists performing the songs, but specific performances. As this chapter concerns the significance of the American Songbook to American culture through jazz specifically, I will consider vocal performances to hold equal importance to instrumental performances of the same tune. I do so deliberately for two reasons: first, to avoid rehearsing the longstanding simplistic separation between vocal and instrumental jazz; and secondly, to respect the contributions of lyricists as distinct from performers.

Versions of many of these songs have entered the jazz canon, either through their interpretation as a jazz standard, or the use of their chord changes as a contrafact under a new melody. In either case, the harmonies and structures of the American songbook have provided a vehicle for interpretation and improvisation in the jazz community for nearly a century. The main body of American Songbook songs are love songs, "and while a good many are light in tone, even more are perfectly serious and sometimes deeply felt."[4] Moreover, as jazz musicians continued to interpret songs from the American Songbook, we can begin to see a symbiosis or self-referentiality, as composers began to adopt musical devices associated with jazz, and lyricists began to refer to the act of playing and singing.

Nearly all of the entries to the American Songbook adopt a thirty-two bar form for the chorus, and it is this that is the basis for jazz standards. Teachout explains:

> Not only are standards compositions, but nearly all of them conform to a rigid structural pattern, in which an introductory verse is followed by a 32-bar chorus that falls into four eight-bar phrases. The chorus works like this: the first of the phrases is repeated, then there follows a contrasting phrase, then there is another repetition – not always exact– of the first phrase. (This structure is known as AABA form, with the B strain called the "bridge" or "release.")[5]

This form can be observed clearly in that most famous of examples, (Ted Gioia calls it "the grandaddy of jazz tunes"[6]) the chorus of George and Ira Gershwin's "I Got Rhythm," first heard in the 1930 musical *Girl Crazy*, but originally written as a slower song for the 1928 musical *Treasure Girl*. This song is both about love ("I got my man") and about the songwriting process ("I got rhythm").

A: I got rhythm, I got music
A: I got my man, who could ask for anything more?
B: I got daisies, in green pastures
A: I got my man, who could ask for anything more?

Wilder explained the features of the thirty-two bar song form that made it attractive to jazz musicians:

> The melody should be spare, containing a minimal number of notes, and the harmony should be similarly uncluttered, almost skeletal … However, the principle jazz interest in any song lies in its "changes": its harmony. And this harmony mustn't change too quickly. For if it does, the player will be unable to fool around within the confines of the chord.[7]

Gershwin's original song was thirty-four bars, featuring a two-bar tag at the end of a standard thirty-two bar chorus. These two bars were soon dropped by jazz players absorbing it into their canon, giving musicians a thirty-two bar framework from which to hang their improvisations. Gioia comments that "the song's chords became so famous that they eclipsed the composition itself," and he explains that although the essence of "I Got Rhythm" has remained central to American musical culture, it has often been heard in an interpretation of one of the later "rhythm songs," with musicians' own substitutions and interpretations layered on top.[8]

A brief history of versions of "I Got Rhythm" illustrates the extent to which songs from the American Songbook have been adopted and appropriated across American culture, and further afield. "I Got Rhythm" is an immensely popular tune, and thousands of recordings exist. What follows is a cross section, rather than an exhaustive list, to illustrate the diversity of style and geographical reach of this song.[9]

In 1931, George Gershwin himself recorded an energetic solo piano version.[10] In the same year Louis Armstrong and His Orchestra recorded a hot jazz take, featuring Armstrong's characteristic raspy vocals and Dixieland trumpet.[11] Jimmy Dorsey and His Orchestra released a fast swing version in 1937.[12] The Duke Ellington Orchestra's "Cottontail," recorded in 1940, used the "I Got Rhythm" changes (often shortened to "Rhythm changes" in jazz parlance) to showcase the instrumental soloists and cross-section phrasing that was a feature of Ellington's writing and orchestra.[13] Charlie Parker's "Anthropology" (1945) used the rhythm changes as a bebop contrafact at breakneck speed.[14]

Numerous singers have recorded the tune, including Ethel Merman, who made the song famous in the original *Girl Crazy* performance. She later released a version set to a disco beat on the 1979 *Ethel Merman Disco Album*.[15] Ella Fitzgerald recorded a swinging and scat version with jazz orchestra and strings in 1959.[16] The Puppini Sisters recorded a close harmony slow version with big band on their 2011 album *Hollywood*.[17] The material of the American Songbook reached further than the USA, as demonstrated by Japanese pianist Hiromi's hard swinging, raucous version of "I Got Rhythm" on 2008's *Beyond Standard*.[18]

Tin Pan Alley

In around 1885, a row of music publishers had offices in the same district of Manhattan: on 28th Street, between 5th and 6th Avenue. The area became known as "Tin Pan Alley," due perhaps to the noise made by cheap pianos in the publishers' offices, or perhaps to the noise made by banging on tin pans. "Like 'Hollywood,' 'Tin Pan Alley' became a metonym for a place, an industry and a mode of production."[19] The main unit for music sold out of Tin Pan Alley was sheet music – the melody, lyrics, and piano arrangement for a song published for home performance. Wilder reflects on how the historical editorial and publication process had the potential to distort a composer's intent:

> Every publisher of popular music depends upon professional editors to supply the piano accompaniment (harmonization) for any song written by someone who cannot write his own piano part, or to "simplify" the harmonizations supplied by skilled composers who overreach the abilities of the consumer who buys the sheet music and takes it home to play. Many talented melodists have depended upon the editors to complete their work and get a song ready for publication. Contrariwise, gifted composers whose innovations grew out of their sophisticated sense of harmony have often fought with editors who were determined to eliminate the subtleties of their work in the cause of "simplification."[20]

Several phenomena helped pave the way for a shift in the way music was consumed by the general public in the mid-twentieth century. The invention of the long-playing record (LP) in 1948 and its subsequent adoption into domestic spaces signaled a move away from sheet music as the dominant form of exchanging music. Another key development was the establishment of the Brill Building as a home for songwriting in the early 1960s. The Brill Building was an eleven-story Art Deco-building at 1619 Broadway, where many individuals involved in different strata of songwriting, performance, and production could be housed in the same building. Simon Barber writes:

> The structure of the Brill Building is an example of "vertical integration"; that is to say that publishers, songwriters, arrangers, producers and performers were located at such proximity, that the entire process of writing a song, arranging it, transcribing it, recording a demo, pitching the song to a label or artist, and contracting a "plugger" to take the song to radio, could

all be done in-house. Indeed, there are stories of songwriters who would start at the top of the Brill Building and work down until a song found a home, sometimes with more than one company.[21]

Many songs that originated in the Brill Building became chart successes. Crucially, this mode of production signaled a turn towards reception of popular music through its recorded form. Consumers began seeking out specific recordings of Brill Building songs that featured particular musicians. Notable examples include Carole King (music) and Gerry Goffin's (lyrics) song "Will You Love Me Tomorrow," sung by The Shirelles, which topped the charts on its release in December 1960.[22] Another is King and Goffin's "(You Make Me Feel Like) A Natural Woman," which was released as a single by soul singer Aretha Franklin in 1967,[23] and then by King, providing her own vocals on *Tapestry* in 1971.[24]

Broadway

Broadway shows from the 1920s–50s were another source of many songs that entered the American Songbook. Of course, musicals were in themselves an important part of American culture, but when these songs were taken out of context and performed by jazz musicians as jazz standards, they gained a life of their own. Among the key contributors in this context, Jerome Kern is perhaps best known for his 1927 musical *Show Boat* (including the songs "Can't Help Lovin' Dat Man" and "Ol' Man River"). Kern followed *Show Boat* with *Sweet Adeline* (1929), *The Cat and the Fiddle* (1931), *Music in the Air* (1932), *Roberta* (1933), and *Three Sisters* (1934). From the mid-1930s, he mainly shifted his focus to composing for film musicals. An exception to this change of direction was 1939's *Very Warm for May*. The show was a critical and commercial failure. Indeed, the second night's showing had an audience of only twenty.[25] However, the ongoing success and ubiquity of "All the Things You Are" as a jazz standard ensures that the show remains a presence in American culture.

The introductory verse to "All the Things You Are," like many verses of familiar songs in the American Songbook, became inconsequential for jazz practice – improvising musicians excised this section and were quick to adopt the thirty-two bar chorus as a jazz standard. Many things ensured that this was favoured by jazz musicians for repeated treatment. The key signature, to begin, of A♭ major, hovering around the relative F minor. This puts B♭ instruments (trumpet, cornet, soprano, and tenor saxophone) in B♭ major, and E♭ instruments (alto and baritone saxophone) in F major. Both these keys lie naturally under the fingers, especially for saxophonists.

Jazz and the American Songbook

The harmony is based on the cycle of fifths, which continue for entire phrases. The ii7-V-I figure, which is such a crucial figure for jazz improvisation, is a main component of the song. Harmonically speaking, it is predominantly a straightforward song. It is a gift for improvisers, adhering to (or perhaps providing the first instance of) Wilder's description of AABA songs appropriated by jazz musicians, which I quoted above.

In his own analysis of "All the Things You Are," Wilder points to two idiosyncracies:

> The *b* natural in the sixth measure is a marvellous twist, but not easy. Of course, the *e* natural is just a half step below the preceding *f*; yet the two measures pause in an unfamiliar key, even if the listener is unobservant of harmony, must sound strange....
>
> The melodic note at the end of the release is a *g* sharp with an E-major chord supporting its first measure. The harmony of the second measure is an E-augmented chord. Then the main strain returns to its original key, F minor [I disagree, and interpret this as A flat], and its opening note is *a* flat. So here we have what is technically known as an enharmonic change. For, despite the difference in its "spelling," the preceding *g* sharp is also an *a* flat. And yet for all that, I've never known a layman enthusiast of the song to boggle at this point and fail to continue singing or whistling it.[26]

Notable recordings of the tune include the 1939 swing recording by clarinetist Artie Shaw with his orchestra and Helen Forrest on vocals.[27] Bebop trumpeter Dizzy Gillespie recorded it with his sextet in 1945, providing what became a famous descending three-note bass figure introduction.[28] The ensemble on this recording included saxophonist Charlie Parker and bassist Slam Stewart. Here the melody and changes are used as a vehicle for trading eight-bar phrases and choruses of improvisation between the members of the ensemble. Bill Evans opens a solo piano recording of "All the Things You Are" with the three-note introduction as a nod to the recorded legacy that has preceded him before departing into an improvisation in his own cool-inspired style.[29] Evans also recorded the tune with his trio in the same year on *At Shelly's Manne-Hole*.[30] Also in 1963, Ella Fitzgerald recorded a swing vocal with Nelson Riddle and his orchestra.[31] Pianist Oscar Peterson and his trio recorded a Latin version with bossa nova bass on *Another Day* in 1971, with the changes inspiring rapid scalic passages by Peterson.[32] The descending bass figure was also used by pianist Bill Charlap on alto saxophonist Phil Woods's version on *American Songbook 1* in 2002.[33] Tony Bennett sang a spartan vocal version on *The Silver Lining: The Songs of Jerome Kern* in 2015.[34]

Many of the most well-known and enduring songs in the American Songbook are the work of a songwriting pair, such as the Gershwin brothers (composer George and lyricist Ira). Other notable songwriting collaborations were composer Richard Rodgers and lyricist Lorenz Hart, who together wrote both stage musicals for Broadway and film musicals for Hollywood. Among their most notable collaborations is "My Funny Valentine," from the 1937 musical *Babes in Arms*, which was made into a film two years later. The song has been recorded and interpreted by many inspirational jazz musicians, including the famous recording by trumpeter and vocalist Chet Baker on 1954's *Chet Baker Sings*.[35] After Hart succumbed to his drug and alcohol demons, Rodgers forged a successful collaboration with lyricist Oscar Hammerstein II. Hammerstein had previously partnered with Kern on stage musicals such as *Show Boat* (1927), *Sweet Adeline* (1929) and the aforementioned *Very Warm for May*. Rodgers and Hammerstein created *Oklahoma!* (1943), *Carousel* (1945), *The King and I* (1951), and *The Sound of Music* (1959). While these songwriting collaborations contributed much material to the American Songbook, Irving Berlin was an exception, writing both the words and music himself to shows such as the *Ziegfield Follies* (1919–20), *Face the Music* (1932), *Annie Get Your Gun* (1946), and films such as *Puttin' on the Ritz* (1930), *Alexander's Ragtime Band* (1938), and *White Christmas* (1954).

Saxophonist John Coltrane absorbed "My Favorite Things" from *The Sound of Music* into his repertoire, using the melody and vamps on E minor and major as a vehicle for his complex substitutions and modal improvisation. He released it as both as a single and as the title track on his 1961 album of the same name.[36] The other tracks featured on *My Favorite Things* all began life as songs from the American Songbook: Cole Porter's "Ev'ry Time We Say Goodbye," and the Gershwins' "Summertime" and "But Not for Me." Each of these songs merit consideration as stalwarts of jazz standards from the American Songbook, and have been recorded and performed in many different styles of jazz from their creation to the present day. A brief, rather than exhaustive, overview, indicates how they have all contributed to American culture. There are versions of "Ev'ry Time We Say Goodbye" recorded by singer Ella Fitzgerald (*Ella Fitzgerald Sings the Cole Porter Songbook*, 1956),[37] Ray Charles (*Ray Charles & Betty Carter*, 1961),[38] Annie Lennox (*Red Hot & Blue*, 1990),[39] Diana Krall (*Quiet Nights*, 2009),[40] and Lady Gaga (*Cheek to Cheek*, 2014).[41] "Summertime" is an aria from the 1935 Gershwin opera *Porgy & Bess*. It was recorded in 1936 by Billie Holiday,[42] bebop saxophonist Charlie Parker in 1949,[43] and Louis

Armstrong and Ella Fitzgerald in 1959.[44] The year 1959 also saw a modal- and Third Stream-inflected collaboration for expanded ensemble between Miles Davis and Gil Evans.[45] "Summertime" has been consistently performed and recorded by jazz musicians until the present day. "But Not for Me" was originally written by George and Ira Gershwin for the 1930 musical *Girl Crazy*. Chet Baker recorded a vocal and trumpet version on 1954's *Chet Baker Sings*. Three years later Miles Davis recorded a hard bop version on *Bag's Groove*.[46] Ahmad Jamal recorded a version on *At the Pershing: But Not for Me* (1958).[47]

Film Musicals

The heyday of the Broadway musical coincided with the advent of sound films after the late 1920s. The film musical, or Hollywood musical, was a natural evolution of these two artforms. Producers of musical films took advantage of the expansive settings and locations that the medium allowed. Early hits included *42nd Street* (1933), *Top Hat* (1935), and *The Wizard of Oz* (1939). Many songs from the Hollywood musical were also absorbed into the American Songbook and entered the jazz canon as standards. Such songs included "Puttin' on the Ritz," an unpublished Irving Berlin song from 1927, which was later used in the 1930 film of the same name.

One of the most famous film musicals of the era was Metro-Goldwyn-Mayer's 1939 *The Wizard of Oz*, starring Judy Garland, with songs by Harold Arlen and Edgar (Yip) Harburg. The standout song from *The Wizard of Oz* is "Over the Rainbow," which won the Academy Award for Best Original Song in the same year. The song occurs just a few minutes into the film, as Dorothy laments her life with her aunt and uncle and sings of her desire to be "where troubles melt like lemon drops." She runs away from home after an unpleasant incident with her dog Toto, and gets hit on the head in a tornado before the fantasy journey that follows.

The song uses a thirty-two bar AABA form, with the A section's melody featuring a characteristic and memorable octave leap. The B section consists of a string of oscillations between two notes, which Arlen later claimed to have been based on a children's piano exercise. Since its debut in the film, the song has been embraced as a standard by jazz musicians. Walter Frisch's short volume for Oxford Keynote, a scholarly series that reimagines the Western musical canon, is devoted entirely to the song.[48] In chapter 5, "Ivory Rainbows," Frisch makes an analytical comparison of jazz piano interpretations of the song:

from the stride-inflected virtuosity of Art Tatum [1939], to the bebop intensity of Bud Powell [1951], to the cool, fluid elegance of Dick Marx [1955], and the harmonic and motivic intricacy of André Previn [1960], to the meditative counterpoint of Keith Jarrett [1991, 1995].[49]

In addition, "Over the Rainbow" has become a significant part of American culture in other, paratextual ways. The song is almost inextricably linked with the star of the film musical, Judy Garland. Over time, Garland, and more specifically, "Over the Rainbow," became emblematic of the LGBTQ community in America. The lyrics, referring to an alternate reality in which the troubles of one's existence are forgotten, as well as Garland's own troubles with her physical and mental health, and her substance abuse, resonated with many from the LGBTQ scene. The cultural and identity significance that "Over the Rainbow" came to carry are but one example of a song text from the American Songbook as a script for performance and interpretation. With the American Songbook's material as interpretable lead sheets, generations of performers and listeners can inscribe their own meanings, which inform the cultural understanding. One such example is the openly gay singer-songwriter Rufus Wainwright, who in 2006 recreated Garland's iconic 1961 Carnegie Hall concert. Garland's performance, and Wainwright's reproduction, consisted of songs which featured in her 1964 film *I Could Go On Singing*, as well as songs from earlier in her career, including "Over the Rainbow." In my 2016 book *Rufus Wainwright*, I discuss these performances, and consider the implications for Wainwright's career, and for LGBTQ awareness and acceptance on a wider scale.[50]

Over the last few decades, the phrase "Friends of Dorothy" has been used to refer to gay men. Frisch suggests that this may have originated in reference to the Cowardly Lion, who "is distinctly feminized with a range of stereotypes.... He occasionally shows a limp wrist, and the top of his mane gets tied with a bow during his makeover in the Emerald City. The apparent contradiction between the lion's fearsome exterior and fearful interior resonated with some closeted gay men who felt they had to appear 'straight.'"[51] "Over the Rainbow" is an example of the American Songbook infiltrating American culture in extended and nuanced ways.

Self-referential American Songbook

By the time of Kern and Hammerstein's "All the Things You Are" in the late 1930s, the interplay between the American Songbook and the jazz world was strong. The lyrics were those of a straightforward love song ("You are the promised kiss of springtime" and other lines to this effect), but the melodic and harmonic language borrowed strongly from jazz. Added chords, major sevenths, and diminished sevenths abound.

Harold Arlen and Ted Koehler's "Stormy Weather" drew on jazz in more pronounced ways. The song was written in 1933 for performance at the Cotton Club, the famous black and tan venue in Harlem. Ethel Waters, who first sang it, and recorded it in the same year, was later inducted into the Grammy Hall of Fame for the performance.[52] As well as jazz-inflected harmonies and melodies, the lyrics spoke of a melancholy yearning, and a world-weariness that is often associated with the blues:

> Life is bad
> Gloom and misery everywhere
> Stormy weather, stormy weather
> And I just can't get my poor self together
> Oh, I'm weary all the time

The lyrics to "Stormy Weather" describe the sadness and longing that is typical of blues songs. In addition, the blues are personified with the line "When he walked away/The blues walked in and met me." In addition, the song is self-referential of the blues tradition, harking back to Bessie Smith's 1924 recording of 'Rocking Chair Blues' with the line "Old rocking chair's gonna get me."[53] A film musical of the same name was created in 1943 – the plot followed the loosely fictionalized life and times of dancer Bill "Bojangles" Robinson, and the title song was performed partway through by a love interest played by Lena Horne.

Examples of the circularity of American Songbook songs that referenced the craftsmanship of songwriting and the hardships of the jazz world are common. For example, the lyrics added by Mitchell Parish in 1929 to Hoagy Carmichael's 1927 song "Stardust" proceed thus:

> Sometimes I wonder
> Why I spend the lonely nights
> Dreaming of a song
> The melody
> Haunts my reverie

This short tour of the origins and songs of the American Songbook, and examples of their incorporation into the jazz canon, explains the importance of these intertwined worlds to American culture. I have chosen not to present a comprehensive list of jazz standards taken from Tin Pan Alley, alongside an exhaustive list of recorded interpretations. An excellent example of such a list can be found in Ted Gioia's *The Jazz Standards* (2012). Instead, I have selected representative examples and sought to show the pervasiveness and infiltration of this canon through discussion of stylistically varied iterations, alongside its social and historical context.

Notes

1. Alec Wilder, *American Popular Song: The Great Innovators, 1900–1950*, 1972 (New York: Oxford University Press, 1990), xxiv.
2. Terry Teachout, "The Great American Songbook: A Critical Guide," *Commentary*, February 1, 2002, www.commentarymagazine.com/articles/terry-teachout/the-great-american-songbook-a-critical-guide/.
3. Wilder, *American Popular Song*, xxv, original emphasis.
4. Teachout, "The Great American Songbook," 57.
5. Ibid.
6. Ted Gioia, *The Jazz Standards: A Guide to the Repertoire* (New York: Oxford University Press, 2012), 183.
7. Wilder, *American Popular Song*, 78.
8. Gioia, *Jazz Standards*, 168.
9. Ibid., 167.
10. George Gershwin, piano, "I Got Rhythm," Rec. February 18, 1931, *Gershwin by Gershwin* (Mark56 Records LP 641, 1973).
11. Louis Armstrong and His Orchestra, "I Got Rhythm," Rec. November 6, 1931 (Columbia 2590-D, 1932).
12. Jimmy Dorsey and His Orchestra, "I Got Rhythm," Rec. March 3, 1937 (Decca 1508, 1937).
13. Duke Ellington and His Famous Orchestra, "Cottontail," Rec. May 4, 1940 (Victor 26610, 1940).
14. Charlie Parker, alto saxophone, "Thriving on a Riff" [aka "Anthropology"], Rec. November 6, 1945, *Bird/The Savoy Recordings [Master Takes]* (Savoy Records LP SJL-2201, 1976).
15. Ethel Merman, *The Ethel Merman Disco Album* (A&M Records SP-4775, 1979).
16. Ella Fitzgerald, *Sings the George and Ira Gershwin Song Book* (Verve Records MG V4024-8, 1959).
17. The Puppini Sisters, *Hollywood* (Verve Forecast CD B0016309-02, 2011).
18. Hiromi's Sonicbloom, *Beyond Standard* (Telarc CD 83686, 2008).
19. David Suisman, *Selling Sounds: The Commercial Revolution in American Music* (Cambridge: MA: Harvard University Press, 2009), 21.
20. Wilder, *American Popular Song*, xxvi–xxvii.
21. Simon Barber, "The Brill Building and the Creative Labour of the Professional Songwriter," in Katherine Williams and Justin A. Williams, eds., *The Cambridge Companion to the Singer-Songwriter* (Cambridge: Cambridge University Press, 2016), 68.
22. The Shirelles, "Will You Love Me Tomorrow" (Scepter Records 1211, 1960).
23. Aretha Franklin, "(You Make Me Feel Like) A Natural Woman" (Atlantic A2441, 1967).

24 Carole King, "(You Make Me Feel Like) A Natural Woman," *Tapestry* (Ode Records SP-77009, 1971).
25 Wilder, *American Popular Song*, 77.
26 Ibid., 78–79.
27 Artie Shaw and his Orchestra, "All the Things You Are," Rec. October 26, 1939 (Bluebird B 10492, 1939).
28 Dizzy Gillespie Sextet, "All the Things You Are," Rec. February 28, 1945 (Musicraft 488, 1947).
29 Bill Evans, "All the Things You Are," Rec. January 10, 1963, *Bill Evans: The Complete Riverside Recordings* (Riverside R-018, 1984).
30 Bill Evans Trio, "All the Things You Are," Rec. May 14–15 1963, *At Shelly's Manne-Hole* (Riverside RM 487, 1965).
31 Ella Fitzgerald, *Sings the Jerome Kern Song Book* (Verve V6-4060, 1963).
32 The Oscar Peterson Trio, *Another Day* (MPS 2120869-9, 1971).
33 The Phil Woods Quintet, *The American Songbook Vol. 1* (Kind of Blue Records KOB 10005, 2002).
34 Tony Bennett and Bill Charlap, *Silver Lining: The Songs of Jerome Kern* (Sony Records CD 88875145742. 2015).
35 Chet Baker, *Chet Baker Sings* (Pacific Jazz PJLP-11, 1954).
36 John Coltrane, "My Favorite Things" (Parts I & II) (Atlantic 45-5012, 1961); John Coltrane, *My Favorite Things* (Atlantic LP 1361, 1961).
37 Ella Fitzgerald, *Sings the Cole Porter Song Book* (Verve Records MG V-4001-2, 1956).
38 Ray Charles and Betty Carter, *Ray Charles and Betty Carter* (ABC-Paramount ABC 385, 1961).
39 Various artists, *Red Hot + Blue* (Chrysalis F2 21799, 1990).
40 Diana Krall, *Quiet Nights* (Verve Records B001243301, 2009).
41 Tony Bennett and Lady Gaga, *Cheek to Cheek* (Columbia B000021861-02, 2014).
42 Billie Holiday and Her Orchestra, "Summertime" (Okeh 3288, 1936).
43 Charlie Parker, *Charlie Parker with Strings* (Mercury MG 35010, 1950).
44 Louis Armstrong and Ella Fitzgerald, *Porgy & Bess* (Verve Records MG VS-6040-2, 1959).
45 Miles Davis, *Porgy and Bess* (Columbia CS 8085, 1959).
46 Miles Davis, *Bags' Groove* (Prestige 7109, 1957).
47 Ahmad Jamal Trio, *At the Pershing* (Argo LP-628, 1958).
48 Walter Frisch, *Arlen & Harburg's Over the Rainbow* (New York: Oxford University Press, 2017).
49 Ibid., 97.
50 Katherine Williams, *Rufus Wainwright* (Sheffield: Equinox Publishing, 2016), 86–87.
51 Frisch, *Arlen & Harburg's Over the Rainbow*, 8.
52 Ethel Waters, "Stormy Weather (Keeps Rainin' All the Time)" (Brunswick 6564, 1933).
53 Bessie Smith, "Rocking Chair Blues" (Columbia 14020-D, 1924).

PART V

Images and Screens

CHAPTER 18

"The Sound I Saw"
Jazz and Visual Culture

Amy Abugo Ongiri

By the end of the nineteenth century, cakewalk and ragtime music had taken the world so much by storm that Europe's major classical composers were composing ragtime and cakewalk inspired music. Both Igor Stravinsky and Claude Debussy sought to break from European classical traditions by investing in the African American vernacular forms that were introducing the Old World to New World rhythmic patterns and melodies. Debussy maintained an investment in the "primitive" nature of the new African American music by encapsulating it in the metaphors and clichés of childhood. Three of his ragtime compositions are contained within the 1908 piano suite *The Children's Corner*, written for his then three-year-old daughter. His other ragtime composition *The Little Nigar*, written in 1908, also explores elements of childhood and children's toys.[1] According to Barbara B. Heyman, Stravinsky's engagement with ragtime was much more formative for the work that would come after it. Here, Heyman quotes Stravinsky's autobiography on the impact of ragtime as a modality for a new expression as marked by Stravinsky's groundbreaking score for the 1918 *Histoire du soldat*. Stravinsky would write: "Jazz meant, in any case, a wholly new sound in my mind, and *Histoire* marks my final break with the Russian orchestral school."[2]

In the same way that the structure of classical music was being challenged by African American music, the dominant innovators in European visual culture would be rocked and reshaped by encounters with African American music that would come at first in the form of ragtime and the cakewalk craze in dancehalls, cafés, and vaudeville theaters, and later extend itself into the complex articulations of jazz in all its forms. As modern art was in formation, artists sought inspiration in the streets and music halls, and within café culture among lowly entertainers, including sex workers, circus performers, and vaudeville entertainers. Minstrelsy had become firmly established as a popular entertainment form in Europe and the United States in 1896, when Henri de Toulouse-Lautrec drew a candid portrait of comedic performer Rafael Padilla, the Cuban-born performer who became famous as France's first Black superstar, appearing as the minstrel clown "Chocolat." Padilla, who had been born into slavery in Cuba, would become one of France's highest paid entertainers as the Auguste clown, exploiting a talent for buffoonish self-deprecation as the butt of all the jokes. In Toulouse-Lautrec's sketch, Padilla appears out of the minstrel costume that he made famous, dancing informally yet elegantly at an after-hours bar frequented by nightclub performers. Toulouse-Lautrec would make many subsequent sketches of Padilla and other entertainers who comprised Parisian nightlife.[3]

The interest in performance, nightlife, the circus, and café culture was shared by artists such as Pablo Picasso, Francis Picabia, Charles Demuth, and George Grosz, all of whom explored themes and aesthetics influenced by the confluence of African American performance culture and African art available in the Western cultural capitals of Paris, New York, and Berlin. Picasso and Stravinsky would even collaborate on a ragtime-influenced production for the Ballets Russes in 1917.[4] Jody Blake argues in *Le Tumulte Noir: Modernist Art in Jazz-Age Paris, 1900–1930*, that fine art's investment in primitivism was both fed and challenged by the emergence of performers of African descent in Paris. Blake begins her study by quoting Paris art dealer Paul Guillaume's 1919 claim that "a new renaissance" that "belonged to negro art" was taking place. Guillaume continued, "there was a form of feeling, an architecture of thought, a subtle expression of the most profound forces of life, which have been extracted from negro civilization."[5] African American popular music became widely available through sheet music and recording culture just as primitivism was becoming the popular mode of understanding and representing non-Western cultures within the fine arts. Artists of the new modernism used African American music to stretch not only the traditional subject matter of visual arts but the form and function as well.

The performances of Afro-European entertainers such as Rafael "Chocolat" Padilla quickly gave way to an influx of African American performers as first ragtime and the cakewalk and then jazz and the Charleston dance craze swept through Europe. "Les Joyeux Nègres" was an ensemble company created by a white American couple who brought the cakewalk to the Nouveau Cirque in Paris in 1902 to sold-out crowds. When they first performed their act at the Nouveau Cirque they did so between comic performances by "Chocolat," whose presence literally and figuratively had paved the way for African American performers in Europe. "Les Joyeux

Nègres" prominently featured Chicago-based African American child actors Fredy and Rudy Walker, whose performance caused such a sensation throughout Europe that they performed continuously in Vienna, Berlin, Stockholm, and Copenhagen without returning to the United States for three decades. Austrian sculptor Carl Kauba, best known for his sculptures of the American West, cast the young performers in bronze, and they were featured in a short film at the birth of cinema by pioneering filmmaker Louis Lumière in 1903. The Walkers and "Les Joyeux Nègres" capitalized on interest in African American culture which had been building since the Paris Exposition in 1900.[6] While it is widely repeated that John Phillip Sousa introduced the cakewalk to European audiences at this same exposition, this has been disputed by Rainer E. Lotz, who documents the fact that African American musicians were performing throughout Europe since the 1830s, when the first African American musician took his band to England. Lotz notes that few early Black musicians were recorded and many have faded from history, but they left enough documentation to conclude that their presence had an undeniable significance. Lotz carefully documents the presence and performance histories of African American musicians throughout Europe, many of whom never returned to the United States even after they stopped performing.[7]

The cakewalk craze gave way to an even bigger phenomenon, labeled "Le Tumulte Noir" by Paul Colin, the French artist commissioned to create posters for Josephine Baker's famous performance with *La Revue Nègre*.[8] While other African American artists performed in small dance halls or cabarets, Baker would become the toast of Parisian nightlife culture. Paris was truly the song while Baker was its dancer throughout the 1920s and 1930s. She even opened her own theater in 1926 and continued to star at the Folies Bergère, becoming a European sensation. Baker would have a legendary career in France, returning to the States only for brief appearances and work with the Civil Rights Movement in the 1950s and 1960s. However, Baker also tended to exaggerate her singularity as a Black performer in France and throughout Europe. While she was one of the most successful and visible, there were legions of African American performers in far flung locales across Europe whose work paved the way for Baker's amazing ascent as a performer.[9]

New visual and cultural forms were being defined by proto-jazz performers such as "Chocolat" and "Les Joyeux Negres," whose performances were captured on screen by August and Louis Lumière. Louis Lumière would also record African American dancers performing a cakewalk in a Parisian nightclub in 1902. A year later, influential filmmaker George Méliès would set the cakewalk in hell in his imaginative short film "Infernal Cakewalk," another sign that African American performance had become a bellwether for modernity's more radical impulses. For modernist visual culture, jazz pushed the limits of possibility thematically and formally. Eventually, European and Euro-American artists such as Picasso, Piet Mondrian, Jackson Pollock, and Stuart Davis would reshape visual arts under the heavy influence of both African aesthetics and African American jazz culture. In 1915, Albert Gleizes created the Cubist painting "Jazz" in a manner that represented the body of the jazz musician at the same time that it broke down the limitations of perspective and form within existing traditions of figurative drawing. Art critic Guillaume Apollinaire would compare the innovation of the European avant-garde to the movements of modern dance innovator Loie Fuller, whose frenetic "Danse Serpentine" was also captured by the Lumière brothers in an 1896 hand-colorized short film. In 1913's *The Cubist Painters*, Apollinaire celebrated Picabia's work for its innovative dynamism, writing that Picabia had successfully "abandon[ed] static painting in order to adopt new means of expression."[10] Apollinaire continues: "You cannot carry your father's corpse around everywhere you go. You leave it behind, with all the other dead. And you remember him, you miss him, you speak of him admiringly. And if you become a father, you cannot expect one of your children to carry your corpse around with him all of his life."[11] African cultures, whether they were the performance cultures of the cakewalk or the geometry of African masks, provided the aesthetic imperatives that would be a driving force in modernism's search for a new language of form.

Cubism's brave innovations were dependent on the impulses of primitivism as an art movement that drew directly on African aesthetics. Cubism's drive to discover its newness was deeply imbedded within its deliberate mining of the aesthetic impulses of non-European cultures. When the Cubists played with the geometry of perspective, they consciously mimicked the art of the non-Western world. Apollinaire, who gave the movement its name, noted that the Cubists' refiguring of space, which they termed "the fourth dimension," was invigorated by their interplay with non-European art. He wrote: "It should be added that the imaginative use of the term fourth dimension was just a way of expressing the aspirations and concerns of many young artists who were looking at sculptures from Egypt, Africa and the Pacific Islands, thinking about scientific works and seeking a sublime form of art."[12] Cubism was one of the first Western art movements to be "modern" in its reimagining of visual representation beyond the realism of earlier periods. Gleizes's "Jazz" was one of the first paintings to specifically name African American music in its titling, but Picasso, Picabia, Henri Matisse, Fernand Léger, and Demuth all referenced African American music in some form in the early period.

By the time that author F. Scott Fitzgerald dubbed the 1920s "the jazz age" in the United States, African American music had already been influencing the trajectory of visual culture there for several decades.[13] African American influence in music and performance culture was popular in the United States as early as the 1830s when blackface minstrelsy emerged as the dominant form of American entertainment. One factor that helped jazz spread globally was the widespread dissemination of sheet music, which made popular tunes created in the specific regional contexts of New Orleans, Kansas City, New York, and St. Louis available throughout the world. Stravinsky claimed to have encountered ragtime not through recordings or live performances but solely through sheet music. Ragtime innovator Scott Joplin published the sheet music for "Maple Leaf Rag" in 1899 and it quickly became one of the most widely known examples of the new movement in American music. Joplin's and other composers' ongoing publication of their ragtime compositions popularized the African American music beyond its regional and racial roots. In his autobiography, Stravinsky noted that he was attracted to ragtime because of "its truly popular appeal, its freshness, and the novel rhythm which so distinctly revealed its Negro origins." Stravinsky desired to elevate the music beyond its origins in dance music, "giving the creation the importance of a concert piece," but in the end it was jazz that would help to remake Euro-American art traditions.[14]

Black music had played a key role in the expansion of recording technology into the twentieth century in the United States. In *Stomping the Blues*, Albert Murray notes that after the invention of the phonograph, blues music was so popular that it seemed to be the technology's reason for being.[15] Murray writes:

> Once they started making phonograph records of it you could hear it almost any time of the day on almost any day of the week and almost anywhere that was far enough away from church. Because not only did there seem to be at least one phonograph in almost every neighborhood from the very outset, but it was also as if that was music that the phonograph records were all about in the first place.[16]

Mamie Smith was the first Black artist to cut a record for commercial distribution when she recorded for Okeh Records in 1920. Several months later, she would record "Crazy Blues," and the record would sell 75,000 copies in the first month of its release. It would go on to sell a million copies in just over six months.

As white artists increasingly gained access to African American music in the first half of the twentieth century, their aesthetic choices reflected the influence of a jazz tradition that was moving away from its roots as a dance music and towards a more esoteric intellectual practice. Piet Mondrian had first tied modernity and urbanity to jazz articulations with his 1942 painting *Broadway Boogie Woogie*, a work whose title referenced the boogie-woogie craze of the 1930s and 1940s in New York City. Glenn Lowry writes: "Mondrian's appreciation of boogie-woogie may have sprung partly from the fact that he saw its goals as analogous to his own: 'destruction of melody which is the destruction of natural appearance; and construction through the continuous opposition of pure means – dynamic rhythm.'"[17] While abstract expressionism developed a formal vocabulary of dynamic visual innovation, Charlie Parker, Dexter Gordon, Dizzy Gillespie, Theolonius Monk, Max Roach, and Bud Powell were developing bebop, a jazz practice that invested in experiments with form rather than audience reaction or engagement. Though bebop developed in tandem with abstract expressionism, its impact would not be immediate on most of those artists. Instead, they continued to be influenced primarily by jazz's earlier innovations such as boogie-woogie or Dixieland.

Jazz continued to move out of dancehalls and into concert halls as experimentalists such as Albert Ayler, John Coltrane, and Ornette Coleman's free jazz movement coincided with innovations happening in other artistic forms throughout the 1950s and 1960s. The interest in abstraction away from melody, which defined the work of this era's jazz innovators, coincided with the rise of abstract expressionism in the fine arts, and the cross-pollination between the two contexts was concurrent and organic. In fact, Coleman's 1960 album *Free Jazz*, which named the jazz innovation he led, featured a Jackson Pollock painting on its gatefold cover. Pollock reportedly listened to jazz continuously while he painted, and Coleman, who was also a painter, admired Pollock. Pollock told his wife the artist Lee Krasner that jazz was "the only other creative thing happening in the country."[18] However, Pollock, like Mondrian, was a fan of boogie-woogie and listened almost exclusively to it. Ironically, given the seemingly natural overlap between these concurrent innovations in music and visual art, Pollock reportedly refused to listen to any of the contemporaneous jazz movements such as bebop or free jazz and was enamored with what painter and jazz musician Larry Rivers labeled "dopey songs" from the ragtime and boogie-woogie eras.[19] Helen A. Harrison also notes, significantly, that though Pollock's action paintings are often tied to jazz innovation, when Pollock chose music to represent his art for Hans Namuth's 1951 documentary about his work, he did not choose jazz.

While ragtime and the blues were the first African American musics to gain a widespread following outside the African American community, African American artists had been drawing inspiration from a wide variety of community musical forms. Henry Ossawa Tanner was one of the first African American painters to gain international acclaim when he was accepted into the 1896 Paris Salon. Tanner's 1893 painting "Banjo Player" captures the transference of knowledge between an elderly musician and child on the banjo, an instrument created by enslaved African Americans that would become central to American folk music. Black vernacular music like the blues had thus been influencing African American artists before the widespread popularity of ragtime and other jazz forms. In fact, the image of music teacher and student would reoccur as a major motif in African American painting in almost every era of jazz.

A. Yemisi Jimoh has noted that Black music "operated in a homological relation to modernism" because African Americans have had to operate with uneven agency in the public realm.[20] While European and Euro-American modernists were reinventing the fine arts under the influence of African American musical forms, African American artists were reconfiguring the arts in relationship to transatlantic modernism but also in relationship to distinctly African American traditions, including, most significantly, jazz and proto-jazz traditions such as the blues, ragtime, and gospel. Sargent Johnson, who along with Tanner was one of the first African American artists to gain international acclaim, had initially been sent to school to study music. Similarly, Romare Bearden took time off from painting to work as a songwriter for two years and also cofounded the Bluebird Music Company with composer David Ellis. Thus, music was thematically integral to African American visual art but also formally important to the aesthetic innovations across a wide variety of African American cultural forms. Jimoh concludes: "black people have no public voice of their own. Their voices are represented through the most abstract form – music."[21]

Artists such as Aaron Douglas in his 1927 illustration *Judgement Day* for James Weldon Johnson's poetry collection *God's Trombones*, or Romare Bearden, who created an entire series of images based on jazz, made use of the sonic form in the development of a visual aesthetic. Johnson's literary adaptation of Black vernacular preaching styles in *God's Trombones* was deeply rooted in the sonic. He labels the preacher's voice as god's trombone and constantly reiterates the importance of sound over all other modes of meaning-making including the use of written language. All elements of the sermon, including physical gestures, are subsumed into the concern for sound. Meaning-making itself through word choice is of less importance than the use of words for their sonic value. Johnson writes:

> Gross exaggeration of the use of big words by these preachers, in fact by Negroes in general, has been commonly made; the laugh being at the exhibition of ignorance involved. What is the basis of this fondness for big words? Is the predilection due, as is supposed, to ignorance desiring to parade itself as knowledge? Not at all. The old-time Negro preacher loved the sonorous, mouth-filling, ear-filling phrase because it gratified a highly developed sense of sound and rhythm in himself and his hearers.[22]

Douglas was perhaps chosen to illustrate the book because of his own great devotion to sound. Much of his work references music or the sonic, from his 1934 mural *Song of the Towers* and his 1926 print *Play De Blues* to his 1935 oil painting *Listen Lord*. In *Black Art: A Cultural History*, Richard J. Powell quotes Douglas as saying he desired to "to objectify in paint and brush ... the visual emanations that came into view with the sounds produced by the old black songmakers."[23] Douglas later enlarged the book illustrations into full-scale paintings in 1939, including *Judgment Day*, which pictures the angel Gabriel with a trumpet calling all people to face judgment, but he also explored jazz culture thematically and formally throughout his modernist illustrations and paintings.[24] *Judgment Day* is awash with a visual sense of sound and was even once owned by the avant-garde Jamaican American pop star Grace Jones.[25]

Aaron Douglas is part of a generation of artists whose modernism emerged out of a shared experience of Harlem and the "New Negro" ideology. These included sculptor Augusta Savage; painter and collagist Bearden; painter Lois Mailou Jones; painter Gwendolyn Knight; painter Jacob Lawrence; sculptor, painter, and muralist Charles Alston; and sculptor Meta Warrick Fuller. In what Jimoh has called "living in paradox," African Americans were broadly influential in shaping a modernism from which they were often systemically excluded. These artists centered musical expression and liberation politics in some of their most influential works. Savage's sensitive and intensely intimate sculptural portraits of Black children and youth culminate in her large-scale piece "Lift Every Voice and Sing" (or "The Harp"), created for the 1939 New York World's Fair. The piece drew its inspiration from the song of the same name composed by James Weldon Johnson with his brother J. Rosamond Johnson, and widely known as the Negro National Anthem. The sculpture depicts a choir of twelve Black youth in the shape of a harp, held in place by the hand of God. Though the statue was, by some accounts, the most photographed work on exhibit, it was destroyed after the fair because no plan had been made to store it. The beauty and sensitivity of the portrayal as well as the positioning of the youth in relationship to the divine challenged prevailing ideological and formal modes of portraying African American youth. Savage would go on to teach Knight, Bearden, and Lawrence at the Harlem art studio where she worked.[26]

Even artists who were situated away from the Black cultural capital of Harlem, living on the west coast and in Washington, DC, were deeply influenced by, and influenced themselves, the renaissance in the arts happening there. In the same way that European artists used African art objects to reinvigorate their art, African American artists also found meaning in African aesthetics. While European artists used African art to reinvigorate by introducing new forms and styles, African American artists explored aspects of African culture that were present throughout the African diaspora albeit in forms that were often dormant or suppressed. Lois Mailou Jones was an internationalist whose work was deeply influenced by the Harlem Renaissance. Though born in North Carolina, Jones established herself in Paris, made frequent trips to Harlem, and later traveled extensively in Haiti after marrying Haitian artist Louis Vergniaud Pierre-Noel. Her groundbreaking explorations of African forms and imagery through an interest in African masks began in 1915 when she was a teenaged apprentice in a costume design shop.[27] Jones would continue to innovate using imagery from Africa. Her 1932 painting *Ascent of Ethiopia* focuses on the relationship between Africa and African American arts, considering how the latter developed in the diaspora from an African legacy. The African past is represented by Egyptian-influenced images, while modernism appears through an urban scene that highlights the importance of jazz culture to African American life, by prominently featuring musical notes, a jazz band, and a singer.

Rebecca VanDiver notes that *Ascent of Ethiopia* was influenced by Meta Warrick Fuller's 1921 sculpture *Ethiopia*, a work in which the female figure "takes control of her own body, an act of self-awakening and liberation."[28] VanDiver notes that Jones herself attributed inspiration for this painting, as well as an awakening of a general interest in Africa, to viewing Douglas's 1934 mural series *Aspects of Negro Life*. As in much of Douglas's work, this epic series features music prominently, beginning with images of African drummers and dancers and ending with a scene of jazz life that features a trumpeter, audience, and dancer. VanDiver also notes that Jones's work was actually completed two years before Douglas's mural but suggests that Jones's misremembering of events might simply have indicated a wide embrace of African culture among that generation of artists. VanDiver also notes that the painting not only pays tribute to Fuller's *Ethiopia* but also adopts Douglas's modes of abstraction, including silhouette style. Just as jazz itself was investing in experimentation away from traditional melody, visual artists experimented with form and meaning to create what VanDiver labels "a new tradition." Charles Alston's 1949 painting *Dancers* carries this twofold tradition of experimentation with form and investment in abstraction to its logical conclusion, by capturing the experience of the dancers in a dynamic colorscape rather than through a straightforward return to realism or form.

These artists and the tradition they were forming were profoundly shaped by the important place that musical expression had within the African American community. Lawrence's painting *The Music Lesson* from his 1943 Harlem series echoes Tanner's *The Banjo Player* in its emphasis on intergenerational knowledge production and racial self-determination. Similarly, Bearden's 1983 painting *The Piano Lesson (Homage to Mary Lou)* use the intimate setting of a family's living room to emphasize the importance of music, especially the continuity of knowledge and creative exchange at the heart of African American artistic practice. While the figures in Tanner's *The Banjo Player* and Lawrence's *The Music Lesson* are anonymous, Bearden's later work pays homage to jazz pianist Mary Lou Williams. Similarly, Bearden's 1974 collage *Carolina Shout* references the title of a specific composition by innovative stride pianist and composer James P. Johnson. Bearden's 1974 collage *Empress of the Blues* celebrates the work of Bessie Smith. By the 1970s, jazz musicians and jazz references were no longer anonymous but were tied to specific innovators and performers.

By the 1980s, when Bearden created *The Piano Lesson*, jazz had become institutionalized as a primary American art form.[29] Earlier, performers like Louis Armstrong had even served as ambassadors for American culture overseas through sponsorship by the US State Department throughout the 1950s and 60s.[30] African American artists such as photographer Roy DeCarava had done much to present the figure of the jazz musician as iconic, as well as to lionize individual jazz innovators through intimate portraiture. DeCarava was already one of the best-known African American photographers, famous for capturing the spirit of Harlem through his portraits, when he began to chronicle jazz culture in New York City and beyond. DeCarava's 1955 collaboration with the poet Langston Hughes, *The Sweet Flypaper of Life*, chronicled life in

Harlem, where DeCarava had been born, with an intimacy and attention to artistic form that was rarely granted to African American subjects. When DeCarava turned his attention to jazz he applied the same artistic impulses. Sherry Turner DeCarava notes:

> Conventionally, there are two primary aspects of portraiture. The first is a likeness achieved with the intent to render the subject by pose. This can be a formulaic pursuit and it did not engage DeCarava's interest. The second seeks less tangible qualities and results in lesser verisimilitude, a shift away from the importance of physical veracity. It is this second process, an interest in an authentic, engaged persona, that ... was explored in his photographs of people.[31]

DeCarava's portraits of John Coltrane, Billie Holiday, Duke Ellington, Mary Lou Williams, Ornette Coleman, Lester Young, Sarah Vaughn, Count Basie, and Lena Horne convey an unparalleled intimacy with the subjects.[32] At the same time, DeCarava grants them the regal nobility that they had achieved in their status as American artistic innovators. Sherry Turner DeCarava describes the use of light and dark in these photographs as working to "convey an openness that invites."[33]

DeCarava's 1960 collection *The Sound I Saw: Improvisation on a Jazz Theme* offers a dynamic mix of jazz portraiture and images of everyday life in the city that masterfully touches on jazz's ability to express the American experience. For the text to *The Sound I Saw*, DeCarava wrote a long tone poem whose sound is created by the textured resonances of the jazz performances captured in the images that he offers. The performance portraits of artists such as Charlie Parker, Miles Davis, Dizzy Gillespie, Duke Ellington, and Billie Holiday are so intimate and immediate that they evoke the sound that the musicians made. The collection both reflects and reflects on the experience of jazz as once "particular, subjective and individual," while also offering a universal transcendence that promises the chance "to know an ubiquitous light in ambiguous space."[34] DeCarava's attempt to capture in visual art the experience of jazz was relentless and the images that he created record nearly every significant jazz innovator performing through the 1950s and 60s. The collection faced repeated rejections from publishers and remained unexhibited and unpublished until decades later. Radiclani Clytus suggests that DeCarava's "painterly aesthetic" and refusal of a documentary style was at odds with expectations for images of African Americans when it was first introduced.[35] However, by the time *The Sound I Saw* was available to the public, first as an exhibit at The Studio Museum of Harlem, and later as a published volume, jazz had become an accepted and even celebrated part of the everyday aesthetic fabric of American life. With its mixture of quotidian urban life and the masters of jazz, *The Sound I Saw* anticipates this; however, that is not its primary or even its secondary point. Instead, *The Sound I Saw* anticipates and participates in jazz's ability to change form, function, and style in all of the arts, including in those where the resonances were primarily visual rather than sonic.

When Coleman Hawkins released "Picasso" in 1948, it was, according to Sharon Jordan, "the first recording of an unaccompanied saxophone improvisation."[36] Hawkins's nod to modernist art in this groundbreaking work acknowledged and celebrated the rich interplay between modernism's various modalities. While not always acknowledged as such, African diasporic aesthetics often drove modernism's innovations. With its creative fluidity, investment in aesthetics, and ability to mine African diasporic cultures for its most innovative impulses, jazz has been, and always will be, perfectly poised to respond to visual culture's search for new vocabularies of form.

Notes

1 Ann McKinley, "Debussy and American Minstrelsy," *The Black Perspective in Music*, 14.3 (1986), 249–58.
2 Barbara Heyman, "Stravinsky and Ragtime," *The Musical Quarterly*, 68.4 (Oct. 1982), 543–62.
3 The story of Rafael Padilla, Europe's first Black superstar, is chronicled in Gerard Noiriel's *Chocolat: La veritable histoire d'un homme sans nom* (Montrouge: Bayard Press, 2014). Henry T. Sampson provides a history of Black performers in Europe in *The Ghost Walks: A Chronological History of Blacks in Show Business 1865–1910* (Metuchen, NJ: The Scarecrow Press, 1988), which traces the development of African American performance culture after the Civil War as African American performers began to fan out across the globe. See also Rainer E. Lotz, "From Minstrelsy to Jazz: Cross-Cultural Links Between Germans and Afro-Americans," Presentation at the International Association of Jazz Record Collectors (IAJRC) 1999 Convention, Hamburg, Germany, July 29, 1999, https://edoc.hu-berlin.de/bitstream/handle/18452/21043/pst08_lotz.pdf. For more on jazz internationally, see Jürgen E. Grandt's chapter in this volume (Chapter 12).
4 Sharon Jordan gives an account of the collaboration between Picasso and Stravinsky for the Ballets Russes production *Parade* in *Jazz and Art: Two Steps Ahead of the Century* (Hamburg: Earbooks, 2017), 56–57.
5 Jody Blake, *Le Tumulte Noir: Modernist Art in Jazz-Age Paris 1900–1930* (University Park, PA: Pennsylvania State University Press, 1999), 1–2.
6 Rainer E. Lotz, "Rudy & Fredy Walker – 'Les enfants nègres' – in Europe," *Doctor Jazz Magazine*, 44.192 (March 2006), 9–23.

7. Rainer E. Lotz, "The 'Louisiana Troupes' in Europe," *The Black Perspective in Music*, 11.2 (1983), 133–42.
8. Paul Colin, *Josephine Baker and La Revue Nègre: Paul Colin's Lithographs of Le Tumulte Noir in Paris, 1927*. (New York: Harry Abrams, 1998).
9. See Sampson, *The Ghost Walks*, for more.
10. Guillaume Apollinaire, *The Cubist Painters: Aesthetic Meditations*, 1913 (Berkeley, CA: University of California Press, 2004), 72.
11. Ibid., 7.
12. Ibid., 17.
13. F. Scott Fitzgerald, *Tales of the Jazz Age*, 1922 (New York: Vintage, 2010).
14. Igor Stravinsky, *An Autobiography*, 1956 (New York: Pantianos Classics, 2006), 60.
15. Albert Murray, *Stomping the Blues* (New York: Da Capo, 1976), 131.
16. Ibid., 131.
17. Glenn Lowry, ed., *MoMA Highlights: 375 Works from the Museum of Modern Art, New York* (New York: The Museum of Modern Art, 2019), 142.
18. Ellen G. Landau, *Jackson Pollock* (New York: Harry N. Abrams, 1989), 183.
19. Helen A. Harrison is the Director of the Pollock-Krasner House and Study Center, the residence where Jackson Pollock and Lee Krassner lived and worked, and thus had direct access to their record collection. Harrison explores Pollock's interest in jazz in her unpublished paper "Jackson Pollock and Jazz: Imitation or Inspiration," available at www.academia.edu/10164140/Jackson_Pollock_and_Jazz_Inspiration_or_Imitation, as well as in a later talk for Stonybrook University Libraries entitled "Art in Focus with Helen Harrison: Jackson Pollock and Jazz," available at www.youtube.com/watch?v=o0smplV7D5A&t=1847s. Harrison emphasizes that other artists such as Stuart Davis and Robert Motherwell had a deep engagement with more contemporaneous forms of jazz than Pollock did.
20. A. Yemsi Jimoh, *Spiritual, Blues and Jazz People in African American Fiction: Living in a Paradox* (Knoxville: University of Tennessee Press, 2002), 8.
21. Ibid., 9.
22. James Weldon Johnson, *God's Trombones: Seven Negro Sermons in Verse*, 1927 (New York: Penguin, 2008), 7.
23. Richard J. Powell, *Black Art: A Cultural History* (New York: Thames and Hudson, 2003), 44.
24. Susan Earle, ed., *Aaron Douglas: African American Modernist* (New Haven: Yale University Press, 2007).
25. Nancy Anderson, "Aaron Douglas/*The Judgment Day*/1939," *American Paintings, 1900–1945*, NGA Online Editions, https://purl.org/nga/collection/artobject/166490.
26. For more on the jazz and the Harlem Renaissance, see Fiona Ngô's chapter in this volume (Chapter 5).
27. Cheryl Finely gives an account of Jones's use of masks in "The Mask as Muse: The Influence of African Art on the Life and Career of Lois Mailou Jones," in Carla M. Hanzel, ed., *Lois Mailou Jones: A Life in Vibrant Color* (Charlotte, NC: Mint Museum of Art, 2009), 50–73.

28 Rebecca VanDiver, *Designing a New Tradition: Lois Mailou Jones and the Aesthetics of Blackness* (University Park: The Pennsylvania State University Press, 2020), 67.
29 On the institutionalization of jazz, see Dale Chapman's chapter in this volume (Chapter 11).
30 Penny M. Van Eschen explores the way that African American jazz musicians were used for diplomacy in *Satchmo Blows Up the World: Jazz Ambassadors Play the Cold War* (Cambridge, MA: Harvard University Press, 2004), 79–91.
31 Sherry Turner DeCarava, "Pages from a Notebook," in Peter Galassi, ed., *Roy DeCarava: A Retrospective* (New York: The Museum of Modern Art, 1996), 51.
32 For more on jazz photography, see Benjamin Cawthra's chapter in this volume (Chapter 22).
33 Turner DeCarava, "Pages from a Notebook," 52.
34 Roy DeCarava, *The Sound I Saw: Improvisation on a Jazz Theme* (New York: David Zwirner Books, 2019), 1, 14.
35 Radiclani Clytus, "Committed to the Image," in DeCarava, *The Sound I Saw*, 197.
36 Jordan, *Jazz in Art*, 172.

CHAPTER 19

Love, Theft, and Transcendence
Jazz and Narrative Cinema

Krin Gabbard

Because jazz is fundamentally an African American cultural practice, and because the American movie industry has almost always been completely white, racial tension inevitably hovers over movies about jazz. Although this tension often plays out in derogatory myths of Blackness, some films deploy the ostensibly "less" racist notion that African Americans have the power to show white people what it means to really feel something. So, when the advent of integrated sound allowed talking and singing to arrive at the cinema with 1927's *The Jazz Singer*, Jack Robin (Al Jolson) can best express his intense love for his mother when his face is covered with burnt cork.[1]

Although *The Jazz Singer* was his breakthrough film, Jolson truly struck gold in his second film, *The Singing Fool* (1928). Again playing a jazz singer, Jolson brings the film to its emotional crescendo – again in blackface – when he sings "Sonny Boy" to express his overwhelming grief at the death of his young son.[2] Audiences loved it. *The Singing Fool* would remain the largest-grossing film ever until it was knocked out of first place eleven years later by *Gone with the Wind* in 1939.

The First Jazz Films

White America's appropriation of jazz and African American culture was often a case of "love and theft," to borrow the title of Eric Lott's influential study of blackface minstrelsy.[3] When Jolson puts on blackface, for example, he does not suddenly embody familiar film stereotypes, like the shiftless Stepin Fetchit or the highly animated Cab Calloway. Instead, as Linda Williams suggests, Jolson was stealing Black music's cultural capital at the same time that he was forging a connection between Blacks and Jews and their shared history of suffering.[4] Significantly, *The Jazz Singer* does not directly engage with racial prejudice, nor even with antisemitism. Jack Robin's struggle is with his unyielding father, not with a culture that demeaned Jews and Blacks.

The idea of walling off a jazz narrative from its social context became the norm for many biopics and melodramas, especially in films that ignored white people. In *St. Louis Blues* (1929), a Dudley Murphy-directed short film in which whites are entirely absent, Bessie Smith sings the blues because her man abuses her.[5] That same year, 1929, Murphy also directed Duke Ellington in *Black and Tan*. Playing a sophisticated band leader and composer, the Duke of this short film does not confront racism so much as the demands of a heartless show business. And he cannot prevent his lover (Fredi Washington) from dying of heart disease.[6] Nevertheless, the association of Blackness with the highly emotional music of Ellington and Bessie Smith is essential to both.

Ellington also appears in *Symphony in Black* (1935), again playing a composer, this time who has been commissioned to write "a symphony of Negro moods."[7] Both *Black and Tan* and *Symphony in Black* are remarkable for suggesting that Ellington is thoughtful and artistic, unlike cinematic representations of virtually every other Black entertainer of the period. *Symphony in Black* cuts back and forth to (1) Ellington writing music at the piano in his studio, (2) the public performance of his music with his orchestra, and (3) dramatizations of the scenes his music depicts. Again, racial oppression is only implicit in vignettes where Blacks are doing hard labor, worshiping in church, or having a night on the town. The young Billie Holiday appears in one segment, only to be abused by her lover, much like Bessie Smith in *St. Louis Blues*. (The cinema had yet to find any other narrative for female jazz singers.) But Ellington himself was disappointed when the filmmakers abandoned his original plan to end the film with a child's funeral. Instead, the funeral scene was edited so that it is not even clear who is being mourned, and *Symphony in Black* ultimately ends with dancers, cocktails, and night life.[8]

The relationship between jazz and race is most willfully distorted in *King of Jazz* (1930), a vehicle for the white bandleader Paul Whiteman and his Orchestra.[9] The film acknowledges the African contribution to jazz early on in a strange cartoon sequence in which an animated Whiteman hunts big game in Africa with an ancient musket. Menaced by a lion, Whiteman tames the beast with music from his violin. As the lion dances, so do two stereotypical Africans in loincloths. Otherwise, Black characters appear only twice, first when several romantic young white couples are joined by Whiteman himself with a young Black child on his lap. Later, just before George Gershwin joins the Whiteman band to play his "Rhapsody in Blue," a muscular man wearing only a loincloth and black body paint dances on a gigantic drumhead. Blacks are at least acknowledged, even if they are miniaturized, infantilized, and sexualized. But when the film concludes with a production number about the great "melting pot" that gave us jazz, virtually every European country contributes to the mix. There is no acknowledgement whatsoever of Africans or Black Americans in this finale.

When Jazz Was Popular Music

In the 1930s and early 1940s, jazz orchestras, inevitably white, provided sites for familiar Hollywood melodrama, romance, and comedy. In *Champagne Waltz* (1937), *Swing High, Swing Low* (1937), *Alexander's Ragtime Band* (1938), and *Second Chorus* (1940), Blacks often appear as waiters, maids, or elevator operators.[10] More often than not, Black musicians are conspicuously absent. In *Orchestra Wives* (1942), however, Harold and Fayard Nicholas steal the show in a dance number bracketed with performances by Glenn Miller's big band.[11] Their singing and dancing to "I've Got a Gal in Kalamazoo," however, was clearly designed to be easily excised for Southerners and other groups who might be unnerved by the sight of Black people. There is a similar moment in *Carolina Blues* (1944), a film built around Kay Kyser and his swing band.[12] Kyser himself was from the South and expressed pride at leading an orchestra of (white) "gentlemen." A more thorough whitening of American jazz is difficult to imagine. Nevertheless, the ordinariness of *Carolina Blues* is interrupted briefly when Harold Nicholas takes a star turn in the "Mr. Bebee" number.

In the 1940s, with the rise of bebop and the battle it inspired between "Moldy Figs and Modernists,"[13] jazz began to have a history and the beginnings of a scholarly tradition. At the cinema, filmmakers' scrupulous skirting of racial issues began to wane. Hollywood had to confront the reality that African Americans had played essential roles in the birth of American popular music. One solution was to suggest that Blacks played the music naturally and without intellection. In these racist depictions, white people understood Black music better than its creators and were thus able to make jazz into something both thoughtful and popular, maybe even respectable. A benign example of this mythology appears in two related scenes in *Syncopation* (1942).[14] About halfway through, a middle-aged Black woman (Jessica Grayson) defends jazz by calling it "trouble music," insisting that it helps folks endure suffering. At the end, after Johnny (Jackie Cooper), the leader of a white swing band, has successfully found an audience of white dancers, his white girlfriend Kit (Bonita Granville) tells him, "They're not dancing just to forget their troubles. They're getting something they can carry away. They're dancing to music that comes from the heart.

Music that is American born." To its credit, *Syncopation* does not actually denigrate "trouble music" or Black jazz. But it definitely gives white Americans another reason to like the music they already like. At the same time, the film reassures whites that their music is more American than the music of African Americans.[15]

The superiority of white appropriations of jazz is more aggressively promoted in films such as *Birth of the Blues* (1941) when a band of Black New Orleanians plays for a group of cakewalking dancers on the bayou.[16] When the sound of a second, unseen clarinet rings out, the band's regular clarinetist stares bug-eyed at his instrument, thinking it might be playing itself. Eventually a white boy is discovered hiding just behind the band. He has "picked up" the music listening to its Black creators, but he plays it so well that the Black clarinetist asks the child for lessons. In *The Jolson Story* (1946), a young Al Jolson builds his popularity around his ingenious appropriation of the "simple" music he hears in New Orleans.[17] He tells the leader of his minstrel troupe, "Some fellows just make it up as they go along. They pick it out of the air." In *The Benny Goodman Story* (1956), another young clarinetist – in this case a teenaged Benny Goodman – becomes an accomplished jazz improviser after listening to Kid Ory's band play jazz for just a few minutes.[18] And in *Young Man with a Horn* (1950), the Black trumpeter (Juano Hernandez) who took young Rick Martin (Kirk Douglas) under his wing, eventually acknowledges that his white pupil has surpassed him and that he only taught Rick how to "hold that trumpet."[19] This tradition has persisted well into the twenty-first century in films like *8 Mile* (2002) and *Magic Mike XXL* (2015), where white heroes defeat Blacks at their own game when they improvise, respectively, rap lyrics and erotically athletic dances.

Writing Jazz History and Creating Pigeonholes

Cockeyed versions of jazz history in which whites eclipse Blacks are explicit in several films. *Birth of the Blues* ends with a montage of faces that seems to present an evolutionary history of the music. Duke Ellington and Louis Armstrong appear early in a series that culminates with George Gershwin at the piano and Paul Whiteman conducting his orchestra. In *New Orleans* (1947), a white gambler introduces Miralee (Dorothy Patrick), a naïve young white woman, to jazz by telling her that it came from "work songs, the gold coast of West Africa, Little Christian churches, river boats."[20] Miralee is taken with the music, especially when she hears her maid – played by a very game Billie Holiday – sing "Do You Know

What It Means to Miss New Orleans." Miralee later tells her staunchly conservative mother that jazz is okay because classical music was also once new and that it too "sprang up in a variety of places." The film ends with a painful performance by Miralee singing "Do You Know What It Means to Miss New Orleans" with the accompaniment of a huge symphony orchestra. (Any discussion of *New Orleans* should mention Billie Holiday singing "The Blues Are Brewin'" along with a jazz orchestra led by Louis Armstrong. It may be Holiday's finest performance on film, and at least for me, it redeems the entire film.)

The most outlandish example of Hollywood's racist jazz mythology may be the moment in *A Song Is Born* (1948) when a professor of music (Danny Kaye) invites a group of jazz musicians to help him record the music's history.[21] The professor reads into the recording a story about a music carried across the ocean, but he makes no mention of Africa. He then says, "It spread to countries that shared the Spanish language ... where the rhythm or beat assumed a new form of expression. The ever-widening cycle finally reached the shores of southern United States where the beat was momentarily lost, but the melody was woven into pure Negro spiritual." It gets worse. Although Louis Armstrong appears briefly in the history lesson, it culminates with Virginia Mayo singing a pop song with lyrics that include the phrase "The blues began with a sigh." Mayo's singing is only adequately dubbed by 1940s vocalist Jeri Sullavan.

As the sound of jazz became more esoteric, the movies increasingly depicted it as a site of deviance. In *Phantom Lady* (1944), Ella Raines plays a woman who goes undercover to help exonerate her former boss after he has been accused of murder.[22] She dresses as a floozy in order to get close to a drummer (Elisha Cook Jr.), hoping she can extract crucial information from him. With the woman's highly sexualized encouragement, the drummer plays an insanely intense solo, his teeth gleaming and his eyes bulging. In *D.O.A.* (1949), Edmond O'Brien is poisoned at a nightclub where Black musicians literally leap up and down on a stage while playing wild bebop.[23]

A dream-ballet sequence in *The 5,000 Fingers of Dr. T.* (1953) offers the inevitable association of jazz with marijuana when male dancers gyrate to the sound of an instrument that appears to be part saxophone and part hookah.[24] More egregious examples of the association are spectacularized in *The Gene Krupa Story* (1959) when Gene (Sal Mineo) takes drugs and is subsequently arrested and imprisoned.[25] A more thoughtful account of jazz and drug addiction is Shirley Clarke's *The Connection* (1961), which not only involves a self-referential plot about a director making a film of jazz artists at work, including their interactions with the man who sells them heroin, but also features onscreen performances by jazz artists Jackie McLean and Freddie Redd.[26]

Among postwar movies, where jazz musicians were often ridiculed or pathologized, *Sweet Smell of Success* (1957) is an anomaly.[27] Martin Milner plays a jazz guitarist who is the only character in the film with integrity and the only person that an egomaniacal gossip columnist (Burt Lancaster) cannot manipulate. Another anomaly may be *Pete Kelly's Blues* (1955) in which Jack Webb plays an unambiguously masculine trumpet player who even goes up against gangsters.[28] The film is a stark contrast to films such as *Young Man with a Horn* (1950), *The Five Pennies* (1959), and, later, *Mo' Better Blues* (1990) all of which show jazz trumpeters humiliated and unmanned when they falter with their instruments.[29] Webb's trumpeter, however, consistently handles his horn with as much authority as he handles tough guys.

Black Jazz Artists Move to the Center

In the 1950s, jazz artists made regular cameos in American films. Nat King Cole and Armstrong both acquired substantial filmographies. Cole even had a starring role as W. C. Handy, "the father of the blues," in *St. Louis Blues* (1958).[30] Among many other roles, the jazz pianist and vocalist played a hard-as-nails mercenary soldier in *China Gate* (1957).[31] Armstrong was featured prominently in *New Orleans* (1947), *Glory Alley* (1952), *The Glenn Miller Story* (1954), and *High Society* (1956).[32] Although his character in *Paris Blues* (1961) carries the name "Wild Man Moore," Armstrong largely plays himself as a senior jazz statesman with access to one of the most highly regarded professors in a Parisian music conservatory.[33]

Among many other examples of jazz artists appearing in feature films, we should include Benny Carter in *The Snows of Kilimanjaro* (1952), Max Roach in *Carmen Jones* (1954), Ella Fitzgerald in *Let No Man Write My Epitaph* (1960), and Gerry Mulligan in *The Subterraneans* (1960).[34] Despite these onscreen appearances, the tradition of jazz artists scoring Hollywood films does not begin until Ellington and Billy Strayhorn produced scores for *Anatomy of a Murder* (1959) and *Paris Blues* (1961).[35] John Lewis wrote the music for *Odds against Tomorrow* (1959), Quincy Jones was the composer for *The Pawnbroker* (1964), and Benny Carter provided the score for *A Man Called Adam* (1966).[36]

Jazz films took a dramatic turn in the 1960s, at least in part because the industry conceded to the burgeoning energy of the Civil Rights Movement.

For the first time, film audiences saw Black jazz artists being persecuted, as in John Cassavetes's experimental film *Shadows* (1958) and then in earnest, low-budget films such as *A Man Called Adam* and *Sweet Love, Bitter* (1967).[37] By the 1970s, the phenomenon had gone mainstream, most notably with *Lady Sings the Blues* (1972), in which Diana Ross's Billie Holiday is helpless and child-like.[38]

Holiday's cinematic infantilization is typical of a series of films about jazz artists who were, to say the least, deeply troubled. In *Bird* (1988), Charlie Parker (Forest Whitaker) is reckless and completely unreliable.[39] Much the same can be said of Dexter Gordon's character in *'Round Midnight* (1986), based on both Lester Young and Bud Powell.[40] In so many films about self-destructive jazz artists, a white character emerges as a caretaker, and often, an interpreter. In *Bird*, for example, Chan Richardson (Diane Venora) confronts a hospital psychiatrist to explain her common-law husband's violent behavior. In case we do not know why Charlie Parker might fly off the handle, Chan is there to tell us that he is without drugs and alcohol and can only "feel something" when he lashes out.

Richie "Eagle" Stokes (Dick Gregory), the character based on Charlie Parker in *Sweet Love, Bitter*, is watched over by a young white man with a troubled past played by Don Murray, and the trumpeter based on Miles Davis and played by Sammy Davis Jr. in *A Man Called Adam* has the support of an aspiring young white trumpeter (Frank Sinatra, Jr.). The French jazz connoisseur played by François Cluzet in *'Round Midnight* may be the only person who understands Gordon's character and is surely the only character who does not wish to exploit him. Even much later, in the heavily fictionalized biopic *Miles Ahead* (2015), the film introduces a white magazine writer (Ewan McGregor) to help the audience understand Miles Davis (Don Cheadle).[41] In many of these, the white characters also serve as witnesses, inevitably outliving the doomed jazz heroes and supplying gravitas as they mourn these artists' tragic passing.

Esoterica, Exotica, and Nostalgia

Perhaps audiences really did need someone to explain jazz to them. The music had been moving farther and farther from the presumed mainstream, at least since the scene in *Jailhouse Rock* (1957) when Elvis Presley storms out of a house where university types are discussing "the altered chords" in the recording of a jazz artist.[42] When asked by a faculty matron what he thinks of new developments in jazz composition, Presley's character jumps up and says, "Lady, I don't know what the hell you talkin' about."

Indeed, the idea that jazz was esoteric and exotic took hold most prominently in *Space Is the Place* (1974), which starred Sun Ra and his Intergalactic Myth Science Arkestra.[43] In a film that navigated between biopic, blaxploitation, science fiction, soft-core pornography, spaghetti western, and avant-garde art film, Sun Ra was the savior of young Blacks in Oakland, inviting them to accompany him to another world in his spaceship. In spite of the jumble of genres the film's creators recruited, Sun Ra was allowed to write all of his own speeches. As John Szwed has thoroughly documented, Ra read widely on race, Egyptology, anthropology, and the occult.[44] Much of his erudition comes through when he speaks in *Space Is the Place*.

A less flamboyant moment in cinema history also reinforces the notion that jazz is someplace out there where most of us do not live. Martin Scorsese's *New York, New York* (1977) dramatizes the moment when the big band era had played itself out and the singers who had simply been members of the band became stars in their own right.[45] After the band led by Jimmy Doyle (Robert De Niro) has broken up, Francine Evans (Liza Minnelli), Doyle's wife and former singer, goes off on her own to a successful career as a singer and actress. The film ends in 1957, shortly after Doyle has opened a jazz club. On the one occasion when audiences see a performance at the club, a band led by trumpeter Cecil Powell (Clarence Clemons) plays an atonal, barely rhythmic music. This is *not* the music of freedom and liberation. Appropriately, the camera cuts away from the band after only a few seconds. The Broadway glitz of Liza Minnelli's performances, however, is lovingly presented throughout.

One film from the end of the twentieth century dispensed with many of the old myths and found compelling ways to present the work of jazz musicians. Robert Altman's *Kansas City* (1996) grew out of the director's childhood reminiscences of Kansas City in the 1930s when the city was wide open and jazz flourished in bars and clubs.[46] Although the film's jazz musicians work in a club run by the gangster Seldom Seen (Harry Belafonte), they neither participate in criminality nor are they exploited. In one memorable scene, Seldom and his men murder one of their own in an alley, repeatedly stabbing him for betraying the boss. Altman's camera moves back and forth between this scene and the representation of the legendary tenor saxophone battle between Lester Young (played by Joshua Redman) and Coleman Hawkins (played by Craig Handy) that took place in Kansas City in 1933. While Seldom's men are knifing a man to death, the two saxophonists engage in a cutting contest of their own. After they have exhausted each other in an improvisatory battle, Young and Hawkins shake hands. Altman has cut between two cutting sessions, both with African Americans. While one group commits murder, the other engages in the richest form of collaboration.[47]

By the beginnings of the twenty-first century, jazz was often reduced to nostalgia. Perhaps the best example is Steven Spielberg's *The Terminal* (2004).[48] Tom Hanks plays Viktor, a man from an Eastern European country that ceases to exist while he is flying into JFK airport. The authorities will not let him leave the airport because he no longer has a valid passport. We eventually learn that he has come to America to acquire the signature of Benny Golson, the only musician from Art Kane's famous "Harlem 1958" photograph whose autograph he does not have.[49] Viktor's father saw the photo shortly after it came out and spent several decades writing to the musicians to get their signatures. While he died before completing his project, his loyal son has made the trip across the Atlantic to secure that last autograph. Multiple layers of nostalgia are crowded into *The Terminal*. For one, the black-and-white photograph with its fifty-seven musicians posed before a Harlem brownstone was suffused with nostalgia from the beginning, especially with the weathered faces of older musicians such Willie "The Lion" Smith, Zutty Singleton, Miff Mole, Luckey Roberts, and Red Allen.

Etymologically, nostalgia means aching for a homecoming. Hanks's character in *The Terminal* is then doubly nostalgic, first because he wants to return to the project that his father had begun, and second because he himself cannot return home because of the strange political situation he occupies. Of course, this is a Spielberg film, so Hanks does indeed escape from the airport and tracks down Golson, whom we see performing at – implausibly – a Ramada Inn. Nevertheless, we should add Golson to the prestigious list of jazz musicians with cameos in Hollywood films.

Some of the mythological trappings of jazz in the movies remain in the twenty-first century. In *Motherless Brooklyn* (2019), a Black jazz trumpeter (Michael K. Williams) somehow fancies that the body movements of a man with Tourette's syndrome (played by Edward Norton, who also directed the film and adapted its screenplay from Jonathan Lethem's novel) is evidence of his rich musical appreciation.[50] Unlike the many cinematic Black musicians who praise the achievements of white musicians, the "Trumpet Man," as he is called in the credits, simply praises the white hero for seeming to understand. At the end of the film, when Norton's character is about to be killed by a gangster, Trumpet Man intervenes and smashes the assassin over the head with his horn. Saving the life of a devotee was more important to him than the condition of his trumpet, which is badly damaged in the action. More troubling is 2018's *Green Book*, in which a working-class Italian American (Viggo Mortensen) teaches the African American jazz pianist Don Shirley (Mahershalah Ali) to appreciate Black popular music.[51] The film uses music to recreate the common racist fantasy of a white man forging a powerful individual connection with a Black man that enables an escape from white supremacy's long history.

Jazz Is Reinserted into Black Culture

A number of recent films have more assertively held white characters accountable for their complicity in American racism. *Bolden* (2019), a complex biopic for Buddy Bolden, the unrecorded cornetist who may have invented jazz, emphasizes the vicious and unprovoked violence that whites inflict upon Blacks.[52] The film is well researched, but it regularly veers off course to suggest that the judge (Ian McShane) who sent Bolden to a mental institution in 1907 was also a brutal racist who branded his Black mistress with a hot poker before killing her. He also stages a "battle royal" in which Black men with burlap bags over their heads brutalize each other until only one is left standing. At one point, Bolden stands in front of the judge while holding the legendary cylinder that may contain the cornetist's only recording. The judge seems on the verge of destroying it, even telling Bolden that no one will ever hear his music: "You have no past, no history, no culture. You come from nothin', raise your head, get people together like you some kind of ... You think we gonna let that happen?" This is one of several moments when Bolden's life is compared to the Christ story.

In the century's second decade, more work by African American filmmakers has featured jazz musicians and redressed earlier film mythologies from a Black perspective. These films often conflate jazz with Black popular music. A good example is *Sylvie's Love* (2020), written and directed by Eugene Ashe.[53] In the film, Sylvie (Tessa Thompson), an ambitious young Black woman, strives to create a life for herself in the 1950s. Because Sylvie has a long affair with the talented Black saxophonist Robert (Nnamdi Asomugha), we hear some carefully crafted music recorded for the film by Mark Turner, Uri Caine, and Sullivan Fortner, among others. But on several occasions, crucial action takes place while pop music from the 1950s and early 1960s plays in the background. The film basically revolves around Sylvie and her overcoming of an industry's built-in racism as she becomes a television producer. Although Sylvie is enchanted by Robert's music, he abandons his musical career at the end of the film.

In many of these recent films, the focus moves away from jazz, if only to remind us of the various antagonistic forces challenging the music's Black creators For example, in *Ma Rainey's Black Bottom* (2020), the most memorable scenes foreground not the music but white supremacist violence.[54] In Lee Daniels's *The United States vs. Billie Holiday* (2021) the achievements of the greatest of all jazz singers, and her frequent collaborator Lester Young, are secondary to a plot about the persecution of Holiday by racist FBI agents.[55] Like *Sylvie's Love*, these films take a larger view of the Black experience, of which jazz is a relatively small part. One other film from this historical moment deserves mention. In telling the story of Fred Hampton, the Black Panther leader assassinated by the Chicago Police in 1969, *Judas and the Black Messiah* (2021) makes startling use of Rahsaan Roland Kirk's "The Inflated Tear" and the canonical recording of "Fleurette Africaine" that featured Duke Ellington with Charles Mingus and Max Roach.[56]

Transcendence

The release of the Pixar animated film *Soul* (2020) marks an important development in the history of jazz cinema.[57] The main character is Joe, a jazz pianist whose big break comes when he auditions for star alto saxophonist Dorothea Williams. When he takes a solo during the audition, Joe leaves behind his normal life and is literally suspended in the air. The images that surround him blink like rows of dancing red candles. This is one of the few moments in cinema where a jazz artist is *shown* to be transcending his environment through jazz. In literature, there are several good examples of the music's transformative powers. These include James Baldwin's unnamed narrator suddenly understanding his brother's music at the end of "Sonny's Blues" (1957), the moment when Henry Smart first hears Armstrong in Roddy Doyle's *Oh, Play That Thing* (2004), and Art Pepper's account of his saxophone battle with Sonny Stitt in his extraordinary autobiography (1979).[58]

Several films feature comparable moments of transcendence, either for people performing jazz or for those hearing it. In the eponymous moment in Woody Allen's *Stardust Memories* (1980), Allen's character and his girlfriend (Charlotte Rampling) share a perfect moment on a Sunday morning in New York as they stare lovingly at each other and listen to Armstrong's 1931 recording of "Stardust."[59] If *Stardust Memories* uses music to signify transcendence, Damien Chazelle does it with cinematic techniques in two of his films. In *Whiplash* (2014), we know that the young hero has finally and thoroughly mastered the art of jazz drumming when the image goes into slow motion and the sound completely vanishes.[60] In *La La Land* (2016), Chazelle uses "whip pans" to zip from Seb (Ryan Gosling) playing an ebullient piano solo to Mia (Emma Stone) creating elaborate and slightly goofy dance moves.[61] In both films, the characters have moved out of their ordinary environment into a state that is uniquely related to jazz.

But in *Soul*, these moments are demystified for us, and we actually learn what this state is called. When Joe appears to have died, he finds himself in a Pixar wonderland where people float in the air bearing enchanted looks, much like Joe did in the middle of his piano solo. The place is called "The Zone." A guide tells Joe that you reach it when you "are really into something, and it feels like you're in another place." It is "the place between the physical and the spiritual."

My guess is that others will enter The Zone in jazz films that are yet to be made. As of this writing, we seem to be entering a golden age of jazz and cinema with the happy appearance of *Soul* and many other intriguing films with jazz content. A new generation of filmmakers has dispensed with many of the old jazz myths, and we can now look forward to learning how the music speaks to them.

Notes

1. Alan Crosland, dir., *The Jazz Singer* (Warner Bros., 1927). See my work on *The Jazz Singer* and many other films with a connection to jazz in Krin Gabbard, *Jammin' at the Margins: Jazz and the American Cinema* (Chicago: University of Chicago Press, 1996). For an alphabetical list of films with jazz, see David Meeker, *Jazz in the Movies 1917–1977* (London: British Film Institute, 1977). For an account arranged historically, see Kevin Whitehead, *Play the Way You Feel: The Essential Guide to Jazz Stories on Film* (New York: Oxford University Press, 2020).
2. Lloyd Bacon, dir., *The Singing Fool* (Warner Bros., 1928).
3. Eric Lott, *Love and Theft: Blackface Minstrelsy and the American Working Class* (New York: Oxford University Press, 1995).
4. Linda Williams, *Playing the Race Card: Melodramas of Black and White from Uncle Tom to O.J. Simpson* (Princeton: Princeton University Press, 2001), 141–48.
5. Dudley Murphy, dir., *St. Louis Blues* (RKO, 1929).
6. Dudley Murphy, dir., *Black and Tan* (RKO, 1929). For an extended discussion of this short film, see Fiona Ngô's chapter on the Harlem Renaissance in this volume (Chapter 5).
7. Fred Waller, dir., *Symphony in Black: A Rhapsody of Negro Life* (Paramount, 1935).

Jazz and Narrative Cinema

8. See, "Ellington on Gershwin's *Porgy and Bess* – and a Response from the Office of Irving Mills (1935/1936)," in Mark Tucker, ed., *The Duke Ellington Reader* (New York: Oxford University Press, 1993), 116–17.
9. John Murray Anderson, dir., *King of Jazz* (Universal, 1930).
10. A. Edward Sutherland, dir., *Champagne Waltz* (Paramount, 1937); Mitchell Leisen, dir., *Swing High, Swing Low* (Paramount, 1937); Henry King, dir., *Alexander's Ragtime Band* (Twentieth Century Fox, 1938); H. C. Potter, dir, *Second Chorus* (Paramount, 1940).
11. Archie Mayo, dir., *Orchestra Wives* (Twentieth Century Fox, 1942).
12. Leigh Jason, dir., *Carolina Blues* (Columbia, 1944).
13. Bernard Gendron, *From Montmartre to the Mudd Club: Popular Music and the Avant-Garde* (Chicago: University of Chicago Press, 2002), 121–41.
14. William Dieterle, dir., *Syncopation* (RKO, 1942).
15. Krin Gabbard, "Syncopated Women: Gender and Jazz History in 1942 Hollywood," Wolfram Knauer, ed., *Jazz @ 100: An Alternative to a Story of Jazz Heroes* (Darmstadt, Germany: Wolke Verlag Hofheim, 2018), 155–65.
16. Victor Schertzinger, dir., *Birth of the Blues* (Paramount, 1941).
17. Alfred E. Green, dir., *The Jolson Story* (Columbia, 1946).
18. Valentine Davies, dir., *The Benny Goodman Story* (Universal, 1956).
19. Michael Curtiz, dir., *Young Man with a Horn* (Warner Bros., 1950).
20. Arthur Lubin, dir., *New Orleans* (Majestic, 1947).
21. Howard Hawks, dir., *A Song Is Born* (Samuel Goldwyn, 1948).
22. Robert Siodmak, dir., *Phantom Lady* (Universal, 1944).
23. Rudolph Maté, dir., *D.O.A.* (Harry Popkin, 1949).
24. Roy Rowland, dir., *The 5000 Fingers of Dr. T.* (Stanley Cramer, 1953).
25. Don Weis, dir., *The Gene Krupa Story* (Columbia, 1959).
26. Shirley Clarke, dir., *The Connection* (Allen-Hodgdon, 1961).
27. Alexander Mackendrick, dir., *Sweet Smell of Success* (Norma Productions, 1957).
28. Jack Webb, dir., *Pete Kelly's Blues* (Mark VII, 1955).
29. Melville Shavelson, dir., *The Five Pennies* (Dena Productions, 1959); Spike Lee, dir., *Mo' Better Blues* (Universal, 1990).
30. Allen Reisner, dir., *St. Louis Blues* (Paramount, 1958).
31. Samuel Fuller, dir., *China Gate* (Globe Enterprises, 1957).
32. Raoul Walsh, dir., *Glory Alley* (MGM, 1952); Anthony Mann, dir., *The Glenn Miller Story* (Universal, 1954); Charles Walters, dir., *High Society* (MGM, 1956).
33. Martin Ritt, dir., *Paris Blues* (United Artists, 1961).
34. Henry King, dir., *Snows of Kilimanjaro* (Twentieth Century Fox, 1952); Otto Preminger, dir., *Carmen Jones* (Twentieth Century Fox, 1954); Philip Leacock, dir., *Let No Man Write My Epitaph* (Columbia, 1960); Ranald MacDougall, dir., *The Subterraneans* (MGM, 1960).
35. Otto Preminger, dir., *Anatomy of a Murder* (Columbia, 1959).
36. Robert Wise, dir., *Odds Against Tomorrow* (United Artists, 1959); Sidney Lumet, dir., *The Pawnbroker* (MGM, 1965); Leo Penn, dir., *A Man Called Adam* (Embassy Pictures, 1966).

37 John Cassavetes, dir., *Shadows* (Lion International, 1958); Herbert Danska, dir., *Sweet Love, Bitter* (Film 2 Associates, 1967).
38 Sidney J. Furie, dir., *Lady Sings the Blues* (Paramount, 1972).
39 Clint Eastwood, dir., *Bird* (Warner Bros., 1988).
40 Bertrand Tavernier, dir., *'Round Midnight* (Warner Bros., 1986).
41 Don Cheadle, dir., *Miles Ahead* (Sony Pictures Classics, 2015).
42 Richard Thorpe, dir., *Jailhouse Rock* (MGM, 1957).
43 John Coney, dir., *Space Is the Place* (North American Star System, 1974).
44 John Szwed, *Space Is the Place: The Lives and Times of Sun Ra* (New York: Pantheon, 1997).
45 Martin Scorsese, dir., *New York, New York* (United Artists, 1977).
46 Robert Altman, dir., *Kansas City* (Fine Line Features, 1996).
47 For more, see chapter 8 ("Robert Altman's History Lesson") in my book *Black Magic: White Hollywood and African American Culture* (New Brunswick, NJ: Rutgers University Press, 2004), 235–50.
48 Steven Spielberg, dir., *The Terminal* (Dreamworks, 2004).
49 For more on this famous photograph, see Benjamin Cawthra's chapter on jazz photography in this volume (Chapter 22).
50 Edward Norton, dir., *Motherless Brooklyn* (Warner Bros., 2019).
51 Peter Farrelly, dir., *Green Book* (Dreamworks, 2018).
52 Dan Pritzker, dir., *Bolden* (Abramorama, 2019).
53 Eugene Ashe, dir., *Sylvie's Love* (Iam21 Entertainment, 2020).
54 George C. Wolfe, dir., *Ma Rainey's Black Bottom* (Escape Artists, 2020).
55 Lee Daniels, dir., *The United States vs. Billie Holiday* (Lee Daniels Entertainment, 2021).
56 Shaka King, dir., *Judas and the Black Messiah* (Warner Bros., 2021).
57 Pete Docter and Kemp Powers. dir., *Soul* (Disney, 2020).
58 James Baldwin, "Sonny's Blues," *Partisan Review* 24.3 (1957), 357–58; Roddy Doyle, *Oh, Play That Thing* (New York: Viking, 2004), 135; Art Pepper, *Straight Life: The Story of Art Pepper*, updated ed. (New York: Da Capo, 1994), 475, 476. For more on the Baldwin story, including a reading of this same scene, see Herman Beavers's chapter on jazz fiction in this volume (Chapter 13).
59 Woody Allen, dir., *Stardust Memories* (United Artists, 1980).
60 Damien Chazelle, dir., *Whiplash* (Sony Pictures Classics, 2014).
61 Damien Chazelle, dir., *La La Land* (Lionsgate, 2016).

CHAPTER 20

Reinstating Televisual Histories of Jazz
Nicolas Pillai

Introduction

Jazz studies has neglected television. While the New Jazz Studies of the 1990s absorbed the methodologies of cultural studies, embracing film as a complex medium, it failed to account for the twentieth-century's most enduring broadcast form. This omission was likely as much about access as prejudice. While historic jazz films were finding new audiences through VHS and DVD releases, jazz television presented unique rights issues for distributors. Musician contracts and song clearances had not anticipated this new form of dissemination.

It is important, however, to counter the prevailing narrative of scarcity. Even a superficial sweep of archival holdings demonstrates that jazz is omnipresent across the history of US television: in interstitials and advertising,[1] as well as programming, providing scores and title music for every conceivable genre, generating employment and communities of practice very different to those of the nightclub or the record company. In the discussion that follows, I am interested less in how television *has treated* jazz and more in how jazz is *a part of* television. And while acknowledging the need to present a chronological history of "US jazz television," I am also concerned with testing the boundaries of that category.

European jazz scholars have led the way in studying television: among them, David Meeker, Kristin McGee, Emile Wennekes, and Bernd Hoffman.[2] In recent years, as television clips and even full episodes have reemerged on social media platforms, a new scholarship of jazz television has blossomed.[3] However, the impermanent nature of these digital platforms – and the way that they strip away production context – should give scholars cause for concern.[4] We still lack quantitative data on what has been produced, where, by whom, and how much of it has been preserved. We still lack a jazz history of television.

Mediating Jazz

The temptation to understand television as a transparent medium, something that merely "shows," is a gross simplification. All television mediates its subject. Indeed, as Stuart Hood and Thalia Tabary-Peterssen remind us, every practical decision made on set regarding shot composition and camera movement reveals the ideological positioning of television-makers towards their subjects.[5] Such positions are frequently contradictory and contested, informed by questions of institutional and industrial structure, commerce, technology, and the wider sociopolitical landscape. In the US context, Herman Gray has posited that "television representations of blackness operate squarely within the boundaries of middle-class patriarchal discourses about 'whiteness' as well as the historic racialization of the social order."[6]

We should remember that some viewed the presence of Black performance on US television as cause for unproblematic celebration. J. Fred Macdonald records *Ebony* magazine's remarkably rosy announcement in 1950 that "television is free of racial barriers."[7] Certainly, TV's inheritance from radio and the consequent centrality of music performance did create opportunities for jazz programming:

> television accommodated expanding audiences by musical variety programs' promotion of established interwar jazz genres such as swing, boogie-woogie, and blues along with newer popular idioms (pop, crooning, and rhythm and blues), as well as the occasional showcasing of innovative jazz styles such as cool jazz and bebop.[8]

At a structural level, however, the assertion that racism was absent is patently ridiculous. Indeed, McGee suggests that early network TV largely replicated Hollywood cinema's racialized systems of production and its address to a middle-class mass audience.[9] A major barrier for Black artists was "the trend of 1950s television advertisers to identify their products with television stars and personalities who seemingly embodied the all-American ideal man and woman – middle-class, white and Anglo."[10] Thus, while television could break new ground with the Black-hosted *Bob Howard Show* (1948; broadcast on the New York CBS affiliate), the pandering to corporate sponsors led to scandalous decisions such as the cancelling of the *Nat King Cole Show* (NBC, 1956–57).[11]

Predictably, jazz found greater security when it was championed by a white host, who could adjudicate and affirm its cultural importance. James Harrod records that between January and June in 1956 *Tonight Starring Steve Allen* presented fifty-nine jazz or jazz-adjacent acts, including a striking number of African Americans.[12] Allen, a radio and television polymath, was also a prolific composer and occasional film star – his authority as a jazz aficionado further validated in the public realm by his taking the lead role in the Universal feature *The Benny Goodman Story* (1956).[13] Allen used his many platforms to advocate for jazz on television, and his own expertise to educate audiences on (what he took to be) the history and appeal of the music.

Between 1956 and 1958, Channel 7 KABC in Los Angeles produced 92 episodes of *Stars of Jazz*. Budgetary restrictions encouraged visual innovation, with director Norman Abbott using low-key lighting and "an abstract pattern light-projection system that produced varied shapes of light upon a surface."[14] Lessons learned on this program would be carried over by producer Jimmie Baker and director Steve Binder when they began work on *Jazz Scene USA* (1962), financed by Steve Allen's company Meadowlane Productions. Using the *Playhouse 90* crew, Baker and Binder recorded three shows a day at CBS Television City Studios in Hollywood. Twenty-six half-hour programs were recorded, presented first by KMLA DJ Vern Stevenson and then singer Oscar Brown Jr. The show was promptly bought by Lucille Ball and Desi Arnaz's company Desilu and syndicated around the world.

Celebrity presenters' transmedia star personalities cohered the integration of jazz within variety performance contexts. David Meeker lists *Eddie Condon's Floor Show* (WNBT, 1948–49), *Art Ford's Jazz Party* (WNTA-TV, 1958), *Frankly Jazz* (KTLA, a 1962 adaptation of the popular Frank Evans radio show of the same name on KRHM), while DJ Garry Moore would present shows sponsored by Timex and DuPont. *Dial M for Music* (1967) began with musician Billy Taylor on presenter duties, later handed over to Father Norman J. O'Connor, a local radio personality known as "the jazz priest." As noted above, most of these early hosts were white, but there were exceptions: Bob Howard, Oscar Brown Jr, Nat Cole, Billy Taylor. While this list might offer the illusion of racial progress at mid-century, we should heed Gayle Wald's warning regarding that "sense of noblesse oblige on the part of liberals who offered sympathetic TV portrayals of African Americans but resisted a shift in power relations behind the camera."[15] This problematic patronage persists in the creative industries today.

The kinds of programs I have mentioned so far are, I think, what jazz studies generally takes to be "US jazz television"; that is, music or variety programming that showcases musicians in performance. Heile et al., in their introduction to *Watching Jazz*, propose a typology of jazz onscreen.[16] Concerning television, its categories are limited to "Documentary,"

"TV Variety Show," "TV Studio Performance," "Video Clip," and "Live Footage." To demonstrate the inadequacy of these categories, one might ask where to place the most visible proponent of jazz on US television in the last 30 years – Lisa Simpson of *The Simpsons* (Fox, 1989–ongoing). In what follows, I offer some new categories. While these are not exhaustive I hope that they demonstrate how much broader and richer our consideration of "jazz television" might be.

Jazz Reenactment

You Are There (CBS, 1953–57) had a cute gimmick. Presented by anchor Walter Cronkite, it reenacted historical events using the techniques of contemporary television news reportage, with CBS journalist Harry Reasoner "on the ground" in whichever time period was that week's focus. The fall 1954 season began with "The Emergence of Jazz (November 12, 1917)" and, in something of a coup, cast Louis Armstrong as King Oliver. It was an estimable production, written by Abraham Polonsky – pseudonymously as Jeremy Daniel, to dodge the blacklist – and directed by Sidney Lumet. The script ambitiously moved between vignettes in New York City, New Orleans, Paris, and California and depicted such personages as talent agent Max Hart (played by Horace McMahon), poet Robert Goffin (Ross Martin), and Jelly Roll Morton (Billy Taylor). Elsewhere on the cast list: Cozy Cole, Bobby Hackett, Barney Bigard, Arvell Shaw, and Barrett Deems portraying members of the Original Dixieland Jazz Band and King Oliver's band.[17]

Similarly, an episode of the entertainment anthology series *DuPont Show of the Week* (NBC, November 26, 1961) presented "Chicago and All That Jazz" in its eleventh episode. A combination of new performances by performers such as Lil Armstrong, Kid Ory, Milt Hinton, and Jack Teagarden sat alongside demonstrations of dance moves and a potted history from Garry Moore, illustrated with film clips of Mamie Smith, Bessie Smith, and Louis Armstrong.

Undoubtedly, placing jazz within a continuum of world history had the effect of ennobling it in the eyes of program-makers. It also canonized the music into a teleological narrative of significant events and people. By specifying "November 12, 1917" in the episode's title, *You Are There* falls in with a version of jazz history that privileges concrete dates and discrete genres over fluidity and hybridity. Of course, this kind of storytelling is endemic in jazz writing, even that which claims to be revisionist. It seeks legitimacy for jazz through strenuous claims to significance, finding parallel in a continuity of arts programming that takes in *Bernstein Philharmonic: Jazz in*

Serious Music (CBS, January 25, 1959) and Ken Burns's PBS documentary *Jazz* (2001). As Alan Stanbridge argues in his account of the Burns series, such programs tend toward classicizing, canonizing, and conservatism.[18] This is not always the case: *Jazz Casual* (KQED, 1960–68), conceived and presented by the journalist Ralph J. Gleason, balanced his professorial to-camera introductions with musicians discussing their creative practice in relation to contemporary social issues.[19]

However, by reenacting, programs like *You Are There* and *DuPont Show of the Week* introduced the possibility of contradictory and subversive readings. Using dramatic structures to represent historical events opened these events up to the affordances of fiction. Yes, to cast Louis Armstrong as King Oliver is to acknowledge a musical lineage. But the dominance of Armstrong's public persona is also so overbearing as to subsume that historicity. It might be more productive, then, to see these programs as speculative fictions, proposing alternate and destabilizing realms of Black experience. A striking example is that of Robert Altman's *Jazz '34: Remembrances of Kansas City Swing* (KQED, 1996), which followed *You Are There* by casting contemporary musicians as historic figures and was produced in parallel with his movie *Kansas City* (Ciby 2000, 1996). Altman dodged criticisms of historical inauthenticity by insisting that his own memories of growing up in Kansas shaped the film's narrative structure, and that his diegesis was designed to evoke "the memory of a fourteen-year-old kid."[20] By privileging fictionality, *Kansas City* implicitly criticizes neoclassical tendencies in jazz writing.

Let us take this idea of speculative reenactment and apply it to what is usually categorized as the most celebrated of the "musicians in performance" type of program, "The Sound of Jazz" (December 8, 1957), one episode in a CBS-TV series entitled *The Seven Lively Arts*. The series was named after Gilbert Seldes's 1924 book which had demurred the loftiness of contemporary art criticism, arguing for a wider encompassing of popular forms commonly thought to be low or beneath scrutiny. Jazz, for Seldes, was an exemplary American emanation: "It is the normal development of our resources, the expected, and wonderful, arrival of America at a point of creative intensity."[21] The 1957 television series, which coincided with the publication of a second edition of Seldes's book, might be seen then to reflect a mid-century strand of American intellectual commentary which positioned jazz as a key indigenous art form, worthy of considered attention and documentation.

Eleven programs illustrated Seldes's principles through a varied anthology of drama, documentary, and music. "The Sound of Jazz" was produced by Robert Herridge, the creator of the experimental arts program *Camera Three* (CBS, 1953–79), advisors for the show were jazz critics Nat Hentoff and Whitney Balliett, and all looked back on the production with pride.[22] As Michael Borshuk notes, this was still a mediated presentation but the spareness of the set and attention to gestural interaction produced a striking effect.

> Freed from rigid expectations about setting and costume, ... these musicians gave the show's audience a look at how they envisioned and exhibited themselves in the representative settings where the jazz aesthetic developed.[23]

Elsewhere, I have argued that claims for the program's authenticity fail to consider its "artful contrivance of the casual," particularly regarding romantic projections onto Billie Holiday's performance.[24] It is important, too, to recognize the show's reliance upon established iconography and narrative: Tim Wall and Paul Long note that depth of field and lighting recall mid-century jazz photography and compare the historical scope to Paul Whiteman's 1924 Aoelian Hall and Norman Granz's *Jazz at the Philharmonic* concerts.[25] We might also note assonance with the collision of traditions and styles in congregations such as Gjon Mili's *Life* magazine photo-stories or Art Kane's famous Harlem photo spread for *Esquire* in 1959.

"The Sound of Jazz" does not re-enact a specific event, nor does it require its musicians to take on dramatic roles. But, in attempting to re-enact the milieu of rehearsal and of the jam, it reaches for something mythical. The program enacts a version of utopia, as in the work of Mili and Kane, by staging gatherings that are precious precisely for their fleeting instance and their impossibility off-camera. We might call them white utopias for Black musicians.

Jazz Episodic

The writer Rod Serling, one of CBS's emergent stars in the 1950s, would consolidate his reputation with the eerie anthology series *The Twilight Zone* (CBS, 1959–64). In the first season of that show, the Serling-penned "A Passage for Trumpet" (May 20, 1960) gives us alcoholic jazzman Joey Crown (Jack Klugman) on the brink of death, in a crisis of masculinity more metaphysical than that which tormented his Hollywood equivalents. Steered through purgatory by an angelic trumpeter (John Anderson – who signs off, "Call me Gabe. Short for Gabriel."), the episode is a variant on Serling's preoccupation with limbo spaces and the ways the blankness of television sets might be used expressively, even horrifically.

Crown's redemption is played out spatially – retreading his abject life until he surrenders it. Redeemed, he takes to playing on his apartment rooftop. Acquaintance with a winsome neighbor immediately follows and, we may presume, freedom from the demons which pursued him.

There were dramas that made jazz central to their appeal, week after week. The most famous of these is *Peter Gunn* (NBC, 1958–60; ABC, 1960–61), Blake Edwards's rather stodgy attempt to put a private investigator in a jazz club setting. Far more interesting was *Johnny Staccato* (NBC, 1959–60), which had the advantage of saturnine John Cassavetes as its leading man. *Staccato* felt different to its contemporaries – rougher around the edges, confidently drawing from film noir's gutter poetics. The show's pilot opens with a wordless chiaroscuro sequence of jazz performance in the nightclub. Staccato's voiceover describes himself as half private investigator (PI), half jazz pianist "talent an octave lower than ambition." A gorgeous scrappy New York is captured on location by small mobile cameras filming in natural light. Indeed, Elmer Bernstein's theme for *Staccato* echoed his score for the movie *Sweet Smell of Success* (1957).

Krin Gabbard has observed that Black music regularly features in US cinema as a tool with which white protagonists can explore emotion and sexuality.[26] Episodic television dramas such as "A Passage for Trumpet" use jazz similarly. The subcultural world of jazz performance can also offer tantalizing glimpses of carnality and vice, as in TV episodes such as *Perry Mason*: "The Case of the Missing Melody" (CBS, September 30, 1961). Evidently, jazz is largely decorative when it appears in such shows, serving as a fresh milieu for television formats which require a new setting every week. This is an implicitly colonizing TV trope, especially when we see white recurring leads drop into Black worlds for a week, leading to racist and bathetic narrative situations – for example, *Land of the Giants*: "Giants and All That Jazz" (ABC, November 2, 1969), *Harry O*: "Sound of Trumpets" (ABC, January 30, 1975). But we must not assume that episodic TV drama can only use jazz in this way.

The dramatic mode can generate interesting new ways of understanding music and its affect, particularly through the use of props. So, in *Homicide: Life on the Streets*, "Son of a Gun," (NBC, February 10, 1993) a Miles Davis t-shirt and audiotape expose emotional inarticulacy and the pain of homosocial affection between cops. In *Everybody Loves Raymond*: "Jazz Records" (CBS, December 15, 2003), the loss of a treasured record collection threatens to tear open old wounds between father and son. In *Star Trek Deep Space Nine*: "His Way," "Image in the Sand," "It's Only a Paper Moon" (Paramount, April 20, 1998; September 28, 1998; December 28, 1998), a holographic nightclub becomes a space of care for traumatized or alienated crewmembers on the space station. For some programs, the deployment of jazz offers an opportunity to complicate an audience's understanding of essentially static central characters, as Elliott H. Powell demonstrates in his discussion of jazz in *The Golden Girls* (NBC, 1985–92).[27] Viewing *The Cosby Show*, Gray notes a tension between the empowering showcase of Black musicians and the restrictions imposed by the upper-middle-class setting. This ambivalence, is for Gray, "part of the show's appeal, its complexity in an age of racial and cultural politics where the sign of blackness labors in the service of many different interests at once."[28]

Beyond narrative, jazz was part of the aural landscape of television week in, week out. It was prominently there in title sequences – think of the woozy clarinet that introduced every episode of *Cheers* (NBC, 1982–93), the buoyant saxophones of *Cagney and Lacey* (CBS, 1982–88), the brassy roar of *Roseanne* (ABC, 1988–97). And jazz also provided diegetic and non-diegetic scoring to countless dramas, introduced documentaries, and segued talk shows, stunt gags in cartoons and sketch shows. CD collections like *Crime Jazz* demonstrate that television provided solid employment for composers such as Pete Rugolo and Shelly Manne and recording sessions for sidemen.[29]

Laughing at Jazz

In *Seinfeld*: "The Rye" (NBC, January 4, 1996), a pre-credits sequence shows us Elaine (Julia Louis-Dreyfus) mooning over her new jazz saxophonist boyfriend. He's dreamy, white, with long curly hair: Michael Brecker via Kenny G. We hear her internal monologue, vainly imagining herself muse to his artistry. Elaine's enthusiasm will be punctured once she discovers his shortcoming: while he may play a good head, he's not willing to *give* head (alluded to coyly as "that thing"). And when the saxophonist does relent, snatching a tryst with Elaine before he's to win a contract by playing for some big time music executives, disaster strikes. Where previously his solos were fluent, liquid, now he can barely muster a few strangulated honks. Mortified, Elaine leaves the club mid-set.

Beyond the very funny assault upon musical phallocentrism, "The Rye" is a good example of the way sitcoms tend to approach jazz. "Jazz is stupid. I mean, just play the right notes!" complains Angela (Angela Kinsey) in *The Office*: "The Target" (NBC, November 29, 2012). Similarly, Leslie Knope (Amy Poehler) in *Parks and Recreation*: "Pawnee Commons" (NBC, November 29, 2012) shows visible disgust when local radio program

Jazz + Jazz = Jazz plays "a recording of Benny Goodman played over a separate recording of Miles Davis." Each of these depicts jazz as opaque, confounding because of its adherence to a set of mysterious rules divorced from "common sense" or, as Gray would have it, middle-class patriarchal whiteness.

For a historic instance of this suspicion towards jazz, we might look to *The Phil Silvers Show* episode "Bilko's Bopster" (CBS, December 31, 1959), in which the platoon at Camp Freemont is disrupted by the arrival of white jazz drummer Skinny Sanders (Ronny Graham). Sanders is introduced in a montage of *Down Beat* and *Billboard* covers – and in person is comically loose-limbed, floating around with a beatific smile upon his face, the Platonic ideal of a grass-smoking freak. Sanders misses morning roll call because he's sleeping in to celebrate Dizzy Gillespie's birthday. At night, when Bilko needs rest after a 22-hour poker marathon, Sanders's frenzied drumming disturbs him. Bilko rushes out into the dorm, protesting, "What is this? *The Blackboard Jungle*?" It's a line that parades the episode's anxiety over delinquency within the platoon, constructing Sanders as a parody of Norman Mailer's White Negro. And it's instructive that nowhere in this episode do we see Pvt. Sugie Sugarman (Terry Carter), the only Black series regular. Perhaps Sugarman's presence would have confused this episode's disquisition on hipster posturing, on jazz as a resource to be exploited to the limits of absurdity. The episode concludes with Sanders being sent off on a State Department goodwill mission, the acceptable boundaries of whiteness restored.

We might compare the way Bilko depicts 1950s anxieties around race to the 1980s working through of issues arising from feminism. The celebrated *Moonlighting* episode "The Dream Sequence Always Rings Twice" (ABC, October 15, 1985) pastiches noir and screwball traditions, using contradictory flashbacks to an unsolved nightclub murder from the 1940s as a way of exploring the 1980s romance of model-turned-girlboss Maddie Hayes (Cybill Shepherd) and unreconstructed private dick David Addison (Bruce Willis). In Maddie's flashback, which imagines a blameless singer and a dissolute trumpeter (played by Shepherd and Willis respectively), the action is lit to resemble a black-and-white MGM musical and pivots around a big band rendition of "Blue Moon"; in David's, the singer is a femme fatale and the trumpeter a doomed schlub caught in her web – here, the lighting evokes Warner Bros' grittier visual style and Shepherd's torch singer rendition of "I Told Ya I Love Ya (Now Get Out)" references Rita Hayworth's seductive performance in *Gilda* (1946).

Early seasons of *Sex and the City* (HBO, 1998–2004) frequently used the nondiegetic soundtrack to make connections between jazz, the glamour of fairy-tale New York City and the *flâneuse* lifestyle of Carrie Bradshaw (Sarah Jessica Parker). While later seasons broadened the musical palette, still every episode was introduced by Douglas J. Cuomo's bouncy Latin theme song. Only series regular Samantha Jones (Kim Cattrall) professed a love for the music onscreen, but in the season 4 episodes "Defining Moments" and "What's Sex Got to Do with It?" (June 10, 2001; June 17, 2001), Carrie begins a relationship with jazz bassist and club owner Ray King (Craig Bierko). An entrepreneur as well as an artist, Ray presents as a less staid version of Carrie's on-off tycoon lover Big (Chris Noth). Ray's dexterity is a sexual asset – Carrie claims to have had her most intense orgasm with him – but his frantic scatting and attention deficit disorder turn her off. As an analyst of post-feminism masculinity, Carrie rejects jazz in the way that she rejects Ray: neither make sense to her. In the final moments of the episode, Carrie strolls past a Black saxophonist busking. The image feels iconic and familiar, recalling Sonny Rollins on the Williamsburg Bridge, a concluding condemnation of Ray as inauthentic. Yet it reduces the Black musician to imagery – by retreating into myth, it is another of those moments when *Sex and the City* seems to acknowledge the limits of representation open to its format.[30]

Laughing at jazz is, I would argue, a mode of television that deserves to be studied carefully and sensitively. It is one of the key methods through which white television producers have addressed simultaneous anxieties about race and their desire to be proximate to Black culture. If we feel defensive about the derisory treatment of jazz, and interpret that always as a racialized assault, we risk failing to see the nuances of tone and satire available to comedy. We also risk overlooking those moments when Black artists can invert white culture onscreen – for example, when Branford Marsalis acts jazz Cyrano to Will Smith, hilariously miming playing the sax in *The Fresh Prince of Bel-Air*: "Sleepless in Bel-Air" (January 3, 1994). Afterwards Will mugs to the camera, "There's definitely some perks to working for NBC," a meta-textual commentary on Marsalis's tenure on *The Tonight Show with Jay Leno*.

Jazz Interventions

I want to end by thinking about jazz interventions into TV flow, and the reasons why they are rare. By this, I mean moments where jazz performs disruptively or provokes explicit ideological reflection or is given agency in the processes that make television.

In a book chapter entitled "Politics, the Media and Collectivism," the British photographer and writer Valerie Wilmer recounts the efforts in the 1970s of the Jazz and People's Movement to reclaim television as a space for Black musicians. By interrupting recordings for the talk shows led by Merv Griffin, Dick Cavett and Johnny Carson, the group agitated for a greater jazz presence on television and recognition of the music's cultural importance. In the short term, some gains were made, with Cavett hosting a half-hour discussion for the group on his show and performances on NBC's *Positively Black* and *The Ed Sullivan Show*.[31] Famously, while Sullivan had requested a performance of Stevie Wonder's "My Cherie Amour," the band (Rahsaan Roland Kirk, Archie Shepp, Charles Mingus, and Roy Haynes) let loose with Mingus's fiery "Haitian Fight Song." Interventions such as these were glimpses of what was possible when the corporate power structures of television were challenged. Pain and anger could "render more broadly accessible the intimate spaces of black counterpublic performance," as in Roland Kirk's "chair act," analyzed by Wald in her study of public television program *Soul!*[32]

These are the kinds of televisual engagements around which jazz scholars feel comfortable. We like the swapping of "My Cherie Amour" for "Haitian Fight Song" because it makes us feel that jazz is edgier and more ideologically pure than television. Such moments are exceedingly rare, however, and in focusing upon them we may ignore the vastness of jazz in other modes of TV; we fail to see how jazz integrates within the "operating system" of television, its collaborative processes, and institutional demands. I have argued elsewhere that we should look beyond television as content, that, in the example of the BBC's 1960s show *Jazz 625*, "the available range of focal depth and image scale permitted an expressive visual field, bordering on the abstract."[33] Scholarship requires a closer attention to the "elusive micro-practices" of television if it wishes to contend with how the medium has presented jazz.[34] But I hope that in this short survey I have suggested ways in which the study of popular television is also the study of jazz's existence in that world. We would profit by shifting focus away from "exceptional" instances and instead considering jazz as an everyday part of broadcast culture.[35]

Where (to take just one example) is the scholarship of jazz in children's television?[36] These performances have been profound in the everyday experience of US family life: Vince Guaraldi's score for the Bill Menendez-produced *Peanuts* cartoons; Blossom Dearie's delicate rendering of "Figure Eight," one of Bob Dorough's songs for *Schoolhouse Rock*; the soundscape of *Mister Rogers' Neighborhood* informed by the jazz sensibility of musical director Johnny Costa; *Sesame Street*'s use of Joe Raposo's scores, some of which featured "Toots" Thielmans, or the Street's many jazz visitors over the years, including Cab Calloway, Gillespie, and Herbie Hancock. If we are to expand our definition of "US jazz television," perhaps we must also expand our definition of radical engagement to account for why these television songs stay with people throughout their lives.[37]

For the many who did not care to watch a program about jazz, jazz was nevertheless a part of their viewing pleasure. Through television sets, jazz sounded in houses throughout the country, an intimate part of the everyday. As television has hybridized across new platforms, it has developed an even more intimate connection with the viewer. In the era of streaming, television is watched on laptops and phones and its jazz pipes in through earbuds. Jazz television has been recycled in memes and as a token of personal status on social media. We must account for its persistence.

Notes

1 On this, see Mark Laver, *Jazz Sells: Music, Marketing and Meaning* (New York: Routledge, 2015).
2 David Meeker, *Jazz in the Movies 1917–1977* (London: British Film Institute, 1977); Kristin McGee, *Some Liked It Hot: Jazz Women in Film and Television, 1928–1959* (Middletown, CT: Wesleyan University Press, 2009); Emile Wennekes, "The Scattered Dream of 'Same Time, Same Station': *The Nat King Cole Show*," Jazz and Cinema conference, Cardiff University, November 1, 2013; Bernd Hoffman, *Rhythmen der Zeit – Jazz in Film und Fernsehen* (Westerkappeln: DerWulff, 2019).
3 For edited collections that capture this moment, see Björn Heile, Peter Elsdon, and Jenny Doctor, eds., *Watching Jazz: Encounters with Jazz Performance on Screen* (New York: Oxford University Press, 2016) and Nicolas Pillai, ed., "Special Issue: Jazz in Television," *Jazz Research Journal* 12.1 (2018).
4 See Michael Borshuk, "'The Sound of Jazz as Essential Image:' Television, Performance, and the Modern Jazz Canon," *Jazz Research Journal* 12.1 (2018), 33.
5 Stuart Hood and Thalia Tabary-Peterssen, *On Television* (London: Pluto Press, 1997), 10–11.
6 Herman Gray, *Watching Race. Television and the Struggle for Blackness* (Minneapolis: University of Minnesota Press, 2004), 9.
7 J. Fred MacDonald, "Black Perimeters – Paul Robeson, Nat King Cole and the Role of Blacks in American TV," *Journal of Popular Film and Television*, 7:3 (1979), 246.
8 McGee, *Some Liked It Hot*, 203.
9 Ibid., 207.

10 Lola Clare Bratten, "Nothin' Could Be Finah: The Dinah Shore Chevy Show," in Janet Thumim, ed., *Small Screens, Big Ideas: Television in the 1950s* (London: I. B. Tauris, 2002), 88.
11 Herman Gray, "The Politics of Representation in Network Television," in Darnell Hunt, ed., *Channeling Blackness: Studies on Television and Race in America* (New York: Oxford University Press, 2005), 159–60.
12 James A. Harrod, *Stars of Jazz: A Complete History of the Innovative Television Series, 1956–1958* (Jefferson, NC: McFarland, 2020), 4–5.
13 For more on this film, see Krin Gabbard's chapter on narrative film in this volume (Chapter 19).
14 Harrod, *Stars of Jazz*, 16.
15 Gayle Wald, *It's Been Beautiful: Soul! and Black Power Television* (Durham, NC: Duke University Press, 2015), 60.
16 Heile et al., *Watching Jazz*, 9.
17 Phil Rosenzweig, *Reginald Rose and the Journey of 12 Angry Men* (New York: Fordham University Press, 2021), 81–84.
18 Alan Stanbridge, "Burns, Baby, Burns: Jazz History as a Contested Cultural Site," *The Source*, 1.1 (2004), 84.
19 For a reenactment of this kind of show in the UK context, see Nicolas Pillai and Vanessa Jackson, "How Television Works: Discourses, Determinants and Dynamics Arising from the Re-enactment of Jazz 625," *Journal of Popular Television*, 9.1 (2021), 139–57.
20 David Thompson, ed., *Altman on Altman* (London: Faber and Faber, 2006), 9.
21 Gilbert Seldes, *The Seven Lively Arts* (New York: Harper, 1924), 84.
22 On the show's production, see Nat Hentoff, *The Jazz Life* (London: Panther Books, 1964), 149–50, and "Huckleberry Dracula, Jazz, and Public TV," *The Village Voice*, July 31, 1978, 30; and Whitney Balliett, *Collected Works: A Journal of Jazz 1954–2000* (London: Granta Books, 2001), 638–39.
23 Borshuk, "The Sound of Jazz," 16.
24 Nicolas Pillai, *Jazz as Visual Language: Film, Television and the Dissonant Image* (London: I. B. Tauris, 2016), 20.
25 Tim Wall and Paul Long, "Sight and Sound in Concert? The Inter-Relationship between Music and Television," in Andy Bennett and Steve Waksman, eds., *The Sage Handbook of Popular Music* (Los Angeles: Sage Reference, 2015), 456–77.
26 Krin Gabbard, *Black Magic: White Hollywood and African American Culture* (New Brunswick: Rutgers University Press, 2004).
27 Elliott H. Powell, "Staying Golden: The Politics of Gender, Sexuality, and Jazz in *The Golden Girls*," *Jazz Research Journal*, 12.1 (2018), 86–109.
28 Gray, "Politics of Representation," 165.
29 Jason Lee Lazell, producer, *Crime Jazz* (Moochin' About Records MOOCHIN07, 2014).
30 See Susan Zieger, "Sex and the Citizen in Sex and the City's New York," in Kim Akass and Janet McCabe, eds., *Reading Sex and the City* (London: I. B. Tauris, 2004), 96–111; Deborah Jermyn, *Sex and the City* (Detroit: Wayne

State University Press, 2009), 82–89; Jennifer Armstrong, *Sex and the City and Us* (New York: Simon and Schuster, 2018), 179–82.
31 Valerie Wilmer, *As Serious as Your Life: The Story of the New Jazz* (London: Quartet Books, 1977), 215–18; John Kruth, *Bright Moments: The Life and Legacy of Rahsaan Roland Kirk* (New York: Welcome Rain Publishers, 2000), 247–49; Wald, *It's Been Beautiful*, 117–18.
32 Wald, *It's Been Beautiful*, 114–27.
33 Pillai, *Jazz as Visual Language*, 128.
34 Pillai and Jackson, "How Television Works," 154.
35 See Nicholas Gebhardt and Roger Fagge's special issue on "Jazz and Everyday Aesthetics," *Jazz Research Journal* 13: 1–2 (2019).
36 I am only aware of Liam Maloney, "Ain't Misbehavin': Jazz Music in Children's Television," *Jazz Research Journal* 12: 1 (2018), 63–85.
37 This phenomenon is charmingly illustrated by the cast rendition of Neil Hefti's *The Odd Couple* theme in *Friends*: "The One with the Dozen Lasagnas" (NBC, January 12, 1995).

CHAPTER 21

Documentary Jazz/Jazz Documentary
Will Finch

Documentary film is a slippery category. The things we call documentaries are defined as much by press releases, reviews, and Netflix tags, as they are by form, content, or production. For documentary scholar Bill Nichols, documentary "mobilizes no finite inventory of techniques, addresses no set number of issues, and adopts no completely known taxonomy of forms, styles or modes."[1] Ideas about documentaries change with technologies, viewing experiences, and the imperatives of screen-media industries. However, they appear united in being inexorably and, at times, frustratingly *about* reality. Filmmakers intervene within and shape realities represented in documentaries, but often do so with the suggestion, or plea, that their creations carry claims to "truthfulness" and reality itself.

My chapter comprises two sections that focus respectively on documentaries *about* jazz and documentaries that *use* jazz. The first section considers documentary as the "creative treatment of [jazz] actuality," to expand John Grierson's enduringly problematic definition of documentary.[2] I ask what does it mean to document jazz on film? How and why have documentaries shaped jazz? My second section asks what happens to documentary when jazz forms part of its treatment? Considering jazz as part of filmmakers' representational toolkit, I ask what ideas does jazz make about documentary subjects? What role does jazz play in documentary aesthetics?

Scholars often focus on either side of the divide between music as subject[3] and music as an element of documentary.[4] The divide results from documentary texts categorized as *about* music or not, and resultant questions posed, and methods employed by different scholarly fields. I explore these questions throughout, rooting them in the fields from which they emerge and as they pertain to examples I introduce. I also draw attention to the instability of the categories I outline. Documentaries *about* jazz may focus attentions on other subjects used to frame jazz. Equally, leveraging jazz's signifying potential offers meaning about nonjazz subjects that shape perceptions of jazz itself. The iterative recontextualizations of jazz within documentary film pose important questions about what jazz is, was, and will be. I consider this embedment through examples from the center and periphery. I do not give a comprehensive account of jazz documentaries nor of jazz in documentary (the latter being largely undocumented).[5] Documentary stretches beyond screen-media, most notably into radio and podcasts, neither of which I address here. I have also focused where possible on examples that situate documentary as a mode of production deeply woven into the textures of jazz and US-American culture.

Jazz Documentary

"Jazz," like documentary, is ontologically slippery; as Krin Gabbard notes, "[i]f today we call something jazz, it has much more to do with the utterances of critics, journalists, record companies and club owners than with the music itself."[6] Accordingly, the films I explore in the first section are *about* jazz in part because they were advertised or received as such. Testing the category (for instance in Ahmir "Questlove" Thompson's 2021 film *Summer of Soul*) offers fertile ground to understand jazz's diversity in documentary film. I do not attempt this here, and instead explore examples of three main sub-genres of music documentary: concert films, metanarrative documentaries, and biographical documentaries. My discussion focuses on documentaries as repositories of jazz cultures and as vessels for representing and creating jazz histories and experience.

The potential to better understand jazz through documentary was first explored in earnest in the 1990s, when scholars gave sustained attention to jazz on/in audiovisual media. The "New Jazz Studies" developed understandings of jazz as a contextualized cultural form, rather than an "autonomous" music, whose aesthetic "progress" could be understood through a series of innovators and styles taking jazz from entertainment to Art.[7] It distanced itself from received taxonomies and histories[8] and from the "seductive menace"[9] of jazz phonograph, "the primary vehicle for the canonization of jazz."[10] Scholars engaged with contexts obscured in records but revealed in photography, literature, and film (e.g., dance, ethnicity, and gender).[11] Focus beyond the "purely musical" saw attentions turn to documentaries as sites of jazz history and reception, though work is still to be done to unpack the reflexive relationship of jazz and documentary.

Documentaries are primary sources of jazz. They display jazz's past through performances recorded for the film, footage exhumed from archives, and oral histories captured in interviews. Mura Dehn's film *The Spirit Moves: A History of Black Social Dance on Film, 1900–1986* (1987), for example, serves for Christi Jay Wells as a document of "applejack" dance, developed in combination with bebop and whose movements of "temporal manipulation" "allowed dancers not only to keep up with bebop musicians, but also to move in and out of time with them at will in a manner analogous to the tension between 'inside' and 'outside' playing in a jazz solo."[12] Simultaneously, Dehn's film reveals as much about jazz as it does about how filmmakers frame it. Jayna Brown employs *The Spirit Moves* in this way when addressing Dehn's attempt "to legitimate the dances as art forms, worthy of historical preservation" by using the conventions of anthropological film.[13] Karen Backstein acknowledges it, like Wells, as a historical document but also addresses how Dehn's narration impacts the representation of dance. Backstein suggests the film "set[s] the dance firmly in relation to Caucasian culture," giving as example Dehn's words when describing the Charleston's arrival as the "'shock of a complete revolution against caucasian grace and bodily unity.'"[14]

Concern over documentary's subjective mediation of jazz truths runs throughout the genre's reception. As an ostensibly objective genre, manifestations of the filmmaker's agency are understood to detract from the veracity of that same "truth." Some documentary practices like "direct cinema" and "cinema verité" sought to promote the genre's "unmediated" reputation by eschewing filmmakers' "distorting" acts.[15] Some of the most celebrated examples of this mode are concert films, shaped by the principles of observational documentary and enabled by portable cameras and high-fidelity synchronous recording equipment. Many well-known examples are "rockumentaries," which can focus on rock, blues, jazz, and hip-hop.[16] *Don't Look Back* (1967) and *Woodstock* (1970), for example, demonstrate the felicitous partnership between rock music's apparent emphasis on "authenticity" and documentary modes seeking "authentic" representation.[17] While the codevelopment of rock and observational documentary aesthetics is well documented, jazz and documentary's codevelopment has received less attention. This is perhaps due to anxieties over emphasizing jazz association with "liveness."

Jazz's identity throughout the twentieth century often revolved around understandings that jazz *was* live performance.[18] As Ted Gioia puts it, "[j]azz music lives and dies in the moment of performance."[19] This understanding grew out of complex ideas about the "immediacy" of improvisation,[20] ethnocentric and racist perceptions of Black people's "inherent" physicality,[21] and jazz's dance heritage.[22] Similar associations are identifiable in jazz's etymologies linked to enthusiasm and sex.[23] Ontological debates too present performance as the "work object" of jazz,[24] or as "the primary focus of critical attention in jazz."[25] Emphasizing that documentary offers access to the experience of live performance overlooks the mediation in documentary. It risks concealing jazz's industrial and aesthetic development with recording technologies, which paradoxically, as Philip Auslander argues, created the very notion of "liveness" as the superior antecedent to mediated experience.[26]

The idea that documentary film offered access to this experience is perhaps most identifiable in concert films, the oft-cited archetype of which is *Jazz on a Summer's Day* (1959), though there are important predecessors.[27] Roger Tilton's *Jazz Dance* (1954), for example, was advertised as a spontaneous ticket to "one of New York's noisier temples of jazz."[28] Before then, new technologies and formats like *Soundies*, combined sound and film in novel ways to sell access to music performance.[29] As Laura Niebling discusses in relation to *Vitaphone Varieties*, these short films can be understood as early examples of music documentary for their regulation and promotion of artists, their marketization of recorded performance, and their shaping of the aesthetics of on-screen jazz encounters.[30] Against this backdrop, *Jazz on a Summer's Day* emerged as a model of music documentary as a way to "witness" live performances.

In *Jazz on a Summer's Day*, Bert Stern and Aram Avakian combine footage of the 1958 America's Cup yacht races and the Newport Jazz Festival. For Thomas Cohen, cutaways from musicians to twinkling waters and sunlit audiences was an intentional, but ineffective, attempt to extricate jazz from its associations with urbanity and sinister pursuits.[31] Michael Chanan, conversely, argues attention on audience members and their surroundings results in "more than a transcription of concert performances, but an almost ethnographic portrait of the audience in its natural habitat."[32]

Evoking Christopher Small's influential idea "musicking" (something *all* persons at musical "events" do), Chanan explores the film as a document of jazz's musicking relationships.[33] Chanan asserts the film "records a moment when jazz, in all its varieties, had been accepted within the cultural mainstream of the American upper classes," glossing over distinctions made between Black and white musicians, audiences, and the music they are shown enjoying.[34] The musicking of *Jazz on a Summer's Day* is not only the relationships between musicians and audiences, but also between filmmakers, promoters, and documentary audiences, who encode and decode meaning through the film. The film's musicking is not a display of jazz in all its varieties nor of their acceptance by the white upper class. Rather, the filmmakers' sunny treatment and curatorial decisions draw into focus "the racial politics involved in debates over the merits of cool jazz vs. hard bop," genres configured by industry and critics as white and Black musics.[35] In the film Thelonious Monk joins Henry Grimes and Roy Haynes on stage to perform "Blue Monk." The filmmakers devote half the sequence to yachts, leaving less than a minute to Monk and relegating his solo to underscore a weather announcement. Stern's displacement of Monk's image and music leaves "Blue Monk" as "'music under' accompanying white people's amusements."[36] Such interpretations contrast from more popular understandings of the film as a window onto "the bliss of being alive and adult in the Eisenhower era, smoking and listening, drinking, and dancing, when jazz was not only popular but a liberating force in the American identity."[37] I return to connections between documentary, jazz, and the American democratic imaginary below.

Jazz on a Summer's Day reveals as much about the Newport Jazz Festival as it does about the filmmaker's perspectives on jazz. It omits many of the festival's well-known acts (e.g., Miles Davis, Duke Ellington, and Maynard Ferguson) while leaving time for several sequences of the "hot" group Eli's Chosen Six, a white band with collegiate connections to Columbia's George Avakian, the film's music producer. Resulting from time and contractual constraints, or Avakian's promotional ambitions, the film's spotlight on "hot" jazz's revivalists speaks to the film's vision of what jazz is, at the expense of contemporary jazz practice.[38] Documentary's claims to reality must be interrogated within the contexts of their production to understand what films say about jazz and why. While *Jazz on a Summer's Day* might conceal vivid images of jazz's racialized industrial contexts, it makes no clear claims to jazz history, instead presenting itself as a musical event merely relayed. Such illusory distance from historical critique, however, should not be ignored, especially in films that obscure their mediating forces. Films more deliberate in espousing their vision of jazz, especially through narration, are more open to the audiovisual means by which they seek to persuade audiences, and so work harder to establish their films as "truthful." This is no clearer than in historical music documentaries.

Described here as meta-narrative documentaries, these films concern not discrete jazz events or musicians, but jazz's history. The most well-known example is *Jazz* (2001, Ken Burns).[39] The nineteen-hour PBS miniseries was anticipated for its power to "fix in the minds of millions of Americans a particular set of notions when the word jazz is uttered."[40] Criticism boomed around how Burns and his collaborators wield this power and what the film really says about jazz history[41] and to whom.[42] Criticism about what the film includes and omits, most notably developments after the 1960s, are frequent and bound to meta-narratives repeated throughout *Jazz*.[43] Burns and writer Geoffrey Ward delineate existing jazz canons and refine the characteristics and contexts of key stylistic periods to illustrate the telos of jazz as US democracy. Jazz, so *Jazz* suggests, embarrassed the aesthetics of "complexity" to emerge as the embodiment of democracy and freedom and so coconstructed the sociopolitical identity of the United States.[44] That the series' chronology effectively ends with the 1960s, compacting following decades into one episode, is as much to do with difficulties apprehending the uncodified history of post-1960s jazz, as it is to do with Burns's and Ward's conceptions of jazz, which could not acknowledge incorporation of (other) popular musics in jazz fusion nor the relinquishment of jazz's core harmonic and structural properties in free jazz. As Sherrie Tucker suggests, ending in the 1960s also concludes the history of jazz as democracy with "the victories of the Civil Rights Movement and the end of Jim Crow," and so eludes the reality of post-1960 racial inequality.[45]

Jazz's democracy thesis, as Theodore Gracyk has described it, is an enduring idea in the history of jazz that Burns's film helped integrate into jazz education and popular imaginations.[46] Following Tucker, I agree that *Jazz*'s most valuable contribution to discussions of jazz and documentary is "the very fact it provides such a clear, unapologetic illustration of dominant jazz discourse and its politics."[47] *Jazz*'s model looms large in the creation and appraisal of other meta-narrative jazz documentaries and around which audiences must, inevitably, evaluate how dominant jazz narratives propagate through documentary (see, for example, 2012's *History of Jazz: Oxygen for the Ears*).[48] How, for example, does Edward Bland's dramatized documentary *The Cry of Jazz* (1959) on jazz and African American history push against or with narratives repeated in *Jazz*?[49] At its denouement, Sun Ra and Arkestra perform the figurative death of jazz at the end of the 1950s, in a sequence where the musicians repeat a fast, descending bebop lick. With successive repetitions the lick fragments and distorts into an intricate jumble, while the visual track interposes shots of the band with images of abandoned ghettos – a montage of jazz's self-strangulation and the realities of Jim Crow USA. The scene follows a scripted discussion in an interracial jazz club where Alex, the film's narrator, proclaims "the body of jazz is dead" because, "jazz for all its power, beauty, and world dominance, is too limiting. It's genteel slavery." For William Sites, the sequence "re-presents jazz – hitherto portrayed as an extraordinarily rich and powerful medium central to African American cultural survival – as a fatally constricted musical style, a sonic cul-de-sac whose rigid formal constraints signal the social imprisonment of Black America."[50]

Burns and Ward's refusal to frame free jazz as a legitimate continuation of the jazz tradition resonates here with Bland's depiction of jazz's death, but in name only. At the hands of Sun Ra, whose career challenged the "death of jazz," the sequence's music seems, paradoxically, to anticipate free jazz's breaking of constraints and realizes Alex's proposition in the film that although "the jazz body is dead," "the spirit of jazz is alive."[51]

For Tom Surgal, *Jazz*'s dismissal of free jazz was a call to "supply a cinematic corrective to right that wrong" in the documentary *Fire Music* (2021).[52] Using many of the same representational strategies as *Jazz* (notably excluding voice-of-god narration) the film tells stories of free jazz in the 1950s and 60s, a project similarly undertaken in *Imagine the Sound* (1981) and *Inside Out in the Open* (2001).[53] *Fire Music* features recollections of surviving musicians, including Bobby Bradford, Sonny Simmons, and Carla Bley; and explanations from critic Gary Giddins, who is distanced from other talking heads by being presented in black-and-white, signaling his position as a nonmusician outsider or as provider of loose meta-narratives, archival film performances, and photographs. Through these elements, *Fire Music* introduces a series of sometimes fragmented narratives establishing Ornette Coleman, Eric Dolphy, Cecil Taylor, John Coltrane, and Sun Ra as the movement's "greats" without exploring too deeply their differences. While the film includes, often in passing, a wealth of other musicians, some critics have challenged its omissions as "fall[ing] short of being fair to history."[54] Perhaps the film's most compelling aspect is its visual editing, which incorporates abstract film between and over the interviews and performances, resulting in poetic responses to the subject matter itself, and borrowing perhaps from earlier attempts to perform jazz visually onscreen.[55] Seen more positively, focus on individual anecdotes, and the omission of any strict meta-narrative, allows the film to ask more questions than it answers about the histories of free jazz. For my purposes, however, *Fire Music* demonstrates the legacy of *Jazz* as a model of jazz history and the provocation to deconstruct it.

Compared to the meta-narrative jazz documentary, which boasts a handful of well-known examples, biographical jazz films are numerous. *Chasing Trane* (2017), *Miles Davis: Birth of the Cool* (2019), *What Happened, Miss Simone?* (2015), *Billie* (2020), and *Oscar Peterson: Black + White* (2022) are recent examples that demonstrate a continued appetite for the genre. Like earlier examples, including *Ornette: Made in America* (1985), *Thelonious Monk: Straight, No Chaser* (1988), *Let's Get Lost* (1988) these films explore a different kind of jazz reality. Following John Corner's summary, biographical films tend to concern how subjects shaped and were shaped by their contexts, the interiority of an artist's personal and public personae, and a justification of greatness or infamy.[56] These concentrations are found throughout documentary, though single-subject biographical films allow opportunities to "point … inwards to the condition of the individual rather than outwards to the social structures and processes beyond them."[57]

The Long Night of Lady Day (1984) is a BBC documentary portrait of Billie Holiday. It traces Holiday's biography and career and continues, in many ways, dominant narratives of Holiday as "Our Lady of Sorrows,"[58] weaving her work through tragic stories that "have hijacked components of Holiday's artistry."[59] The story is told primarily through interviews, including with Artie Shaw and John Hammond and other figures who controlled her music and life.[60] Though the documentary seeks at times to devalue the authority of these voices, they are also given opportunity to solidify and justify their power. Holiday's friends and colleagues Carmen McRae, Thelma Carpenter, and Sylvia Syms offer different accounts that demonstrate her artistic agency and offer a foil to authoritative male voices that dominate elsewhere.

The film's remaining material archives moving and still images of Holiday, "one of the most photographed black women of her time."[61] However, diversity in Holiday's photographic representation, Matthew Duffs explains, is flattened by images that "support the Holiday legend" and jazz's wider iconography.[62] *The Long Night of Lady Day* capitalizes on the signifying potential of jazz photography, using it to authenticate and visualize the narrative. Photographs are often "animated" using rostrum cameras to create the so-called "ken-burns" effect.[63] Suspended above photographs, the camera pans smoothly across, zooms in on, or rotates images to create footage that can mask the paucity of film and "maintain a sense of ongoing motion."[64] Rostrum cameras usually move across photographs to illustrate the narrative, draw attention to the image's aesthetic and material qualities, or to foreground its connotative signification.

In *The Long Night of Lady Day*, a sequence focuses attention on William Gottlieb's photograph of Holiday singing at Downbeat Jazz Club in 1947, "her eyes are closed and her head is tipped back, while her throat bulges full with the power of her voice."[65] Following a segment on Holiday's narcotic use and the gloves she wore to conceal needle marks, the film shifts focus from the tragic to Holiday's artistic agency. The sequence begins with Milt Gabler, who signed Holiday to Decca in 1944, recounting the time he first heard her sing her hit "Lover Man." Gabler explains that Holiday insisted, despite objections, on a string accompaniment.

"She was the first Black girl singer to record with fiddles," Gabler says, as the string introduction of "Lover Man" fades into the audio track. The image cuts to Gottlieb's photograph, Holiday's face is off-center and small on the screen. Gottlieb's original image outlines a curtain behind Holiday but in this version the image's background is black, illuminating Holiday's face. The biggest difference from the original image, however, is the addition of a microphone in front of Holiday. While other images shot by Gottlieb at the club featured this microphone, the original image used does not.[66] Combined with Holiday's recording, the post-production addition of the microphone renders the image more "audible," more "live," and more affective.

However, as the sequence continues, additional interpretations present themselves. After the cut to Gottlieb's image, the film features fifty-five uninterrupted seconds of "Lover Man" while the visual-track zooms slowly in on Holiday until the microphone moves out of frame during the final line: "Lover man, oh, where can you be?" With the microphone's erasure, the object of mediation disappears, and Holiday's voice emanates from the image itself. What was once mediated through the microphone, becomes "closer" to the audience. As Laura Mulvey has explored, the tendency for films to "pause" on women in audiovisual media demonstrates their objectification under the filmic gaze.[67] Such moments reinforce this objectification and further the dominant characterization of Holiday as an entrancing product of sorrow. However, the sequence draws attention to Holiday's demands regarding her string accompaniment and the accomplishments of her artistic self-determination. My reading of this moment demonstrates not only the tension between the representation and reality of jazz in documentary, but also its collapse. Whether in didactic voice-overs, noiseless "flies-on-the-wall," or subtle manipulations of jazz's own historical image, documentary stitches representation and reality together, leaving audiences to unpick or soothe the fissures of documented jazz reality.

Documentary Jazz

For some, underscore in documentary undermines its claim to reality. As Corner explored, "*journalist rationalism* and *observational minimalism* have acted to keep many producers (and quite possibly sizeable sections of the audience) concerned about the risk of a musical ingredient somehow subverting programme integrity."[68] However, as Holly Rogers has argued, such concerns overlook the fact that, although "documentary may be underpinned by a realist aesthetic … it often remains persuasive, subjective, emotional and narrative. As soon as an aesthetic decision is made, the line between the real and the fictional begins to flex."[69] In fact, Rogers continues, "music in film is one of the most powerful illusory persuaders that what we are watching is, in fact, yet rather paradoxically, as real as possible."[70] Music in documentary destabilizes and supports the film's treatment of reality and claims to it. This enigmatic relationship may appear inconsequential; however, when we locate music not as a tool in the filmmaker's toolkit, but as the subject at the heart of documentary's reality it becomes vital. This is, in part, why I suggest the split between documentary music and music documentary has come easily to scholars. In addressing the relationship of jazz and documentary, ignoring texts that are not about jazz limits our understanding. Despite consideration given to jazz's function in fiction films not *about* jazz, when attentions turn to documentary, consideration is drawn first to documentary's power to mold ideas about jazz directly, while jazz *in* documentary is left in softer focus.[71]

In this section, I explore examples of documentaries that frame their subjects by using jazz, or as Jonathan Godsall has suggested as a more accurate term for such intertextual practices, by appropriating jazz.[72] Jazz is found in diverse documentary or nonfiction films, for example in the 2014 Virgin Atlantic in-flight safety video. Looking for jazz in nonjazz contexts is crucial to understanding the music's significance especially for "nonjazz" audiences who do not seek it but find it in the everyday. The "everyday" is a disputed yet abundant category of experience that reaches far into our socio-political structures.[73] Combining the realms of leisure and commerce, inattention, and familiarity, the everyday is vital to the cultural realities with which documentaries grapple. While I do not claim that watching documentaries is necessarily always an "everyday" experience, jazz's integration in them speaks to everyday forms of interpretation and experience naturally conversant with jazz's sliding signifiers. The documentaries I have selected below are significant in jazz's and documentary's relationship in part because their documentary subjects are bound to jazz through existing networks of meaning. However, myriad examples demonstrate jazz's prevalence in seemingly unrelated, everyday, nonfiction settings.

An offshoot of Condé Nast's food magazine *Bon Appétit* is a YouTube channel hosting a range of recipe videos, cooking challenges, reviews, and food documentaries. Between 2017 and 2020, the channel featured writer and chef Claire Saffitz recreating mass-produced foods, including Pizza Rolls and Kit Kats. The show, *Gourmet Makes*, studied those products and invented ways to recreate them with professional techniques. The show's principal music comprises a range of library music, most prominent of which are tracks foregrounding solo drum fills and short grooves, performed on a distinctly "jazzy" kit. Swing 8th notes, the use of brushes and "hot-rods," dynamic accents, and an improvisational feel all contribute to music redolent of Joe Morello, at the "cooler" end, or Art Blakey, for more be/hard-bop-inspired tracks. The show's theme, as an example of its wider sonic aesthetic, is "Bottle Banging," made by artist "Condor" on the music library JinglePunks under the genre "jazz."

Formally, this music structures the flow of images, adding rhythm and continuity, key functions of music in virtually all screen media. It signals the program's start, supports changes in focus, and smooths gaps. The tracks' fast tempos and syncopation add energy to the show, which alternates between music-free dialogue and energetic cooking scenes. Important to the show is the wider connotations jazz brings. It is not only tempo that adds energy, but the wider signification of jazz, and bebop in particular, as energetic. The show's highbrow take on lowbrow foods oscillates between refined culinary methods and populist excitement spurred by (sometimes ironic) reverence to the original product. This juxtaposition of cultural fields finds ready association with jazz's dual character as both entertainment and art, rebellious and rarefied. Meanwhile, the tracks' improvisatory feel resonates with the kitchen as a place of invention. Add to this the test kitchen's Manhattan address, and *Bon Appetit's* middle-class market, and the show's use of jazz seems effortless in supporting the show's brand and infotainment style.

Often, documentary filmmakers use and reinforce jazz's existing associations with their subject, especially chronological or geographic proximity. For example, in *Toots* (2006) on the life of Manhattan saloonkeeper Bernard "Toots" Shor, jazz grounds the narrative in New York's post-prohibition bars. *What Happened to Kerouac?* (1986) features Charlie Parker's and Dizzy Gillespie's music to situate the narrative in place and time and to demonstrate bebop as the transgressive and avant-garde sound of the Beat Generation. Francis Thompson's city-documentary of New York City, *N.Y., N.Y.* (1957) tightly integrates a Gershwinian jazz score to accompany its modernist, abstract portrait of the social and industrial motion of *the* American metropolis.[74] Jazz's use in typical and unexpected documentary contexts has resulted in myriad reflexive relationships between jazz and documentary subjects. However, I would like to return to the legacy of Burns's democracy thesis and conceptions of (certain) jazz styles as the sound of American democracy. In doing so I draw brief attention to the history of documentary as a democratic agent and suggest democracy as a central theme of the documentary/jazz relationship.

Documentary film has long been a democratic and propagandist tool. Ambitions to promote and reflect public discourse and participation in documentary is a key theme in documentary scholarship and filmmaking, especially in the documentary practice of the West.[75] Music, so American classical composer Gail Kubik explained in 1945, helps "sell" democracy and support filmmakers' and funders' democratic ambitions. Kubik's choice word and broader conception of documentary music and democracy were aimed at promoting "feelings of a free and unrestricted personality" in the opposition to European fascism.[76] While the examples I explore below concern a different idea of democracy, they evidence the longstanding use of music in documentary's democratic project.

Raoul Peck's *I Am Not Your Negro* (2016) examines James Baldwin's unfinished memoir *Remember This House*, written from c. 1979 to Baldwin's death in 1987.[77] The film-essay uses archival film and photographs to illustrate Baldwin's recollections of civil rights leaders Medgar Evers, Malcom X, and Martin Luther King Jr. The film uses pre-existing music, including Nat King Cole and Lena Horne, to situate the narrative in time and place. There is also newly written music, composed by Alexei Aigui, that includes music for jazz ensemble. The band performs improvised, quiet tracks redolent of a tempo-less "Flamenco Sketches" inspired no doubt by Peck's request for Aigui to produce a jazz score and to "listen to Miles Davis."[78] The music is often subtle in its allusion to Davis's, though no less vital to the film's attention to Baldwin's critiques of US-American democracy in *Remember This House*.

An hour and seven minutes into Peck's film, footage of the 1965 Watts Uprising is juxtaposed with the emphatic voice-over from *The Land We Love* (1966), a US Savings Bond promotional documentary.[79] In the visual-track, buildings burn and police assault at gun-point Black protesters, while the now dislocated narrator extols American life: "For all of us, there's all of America in all of its scenic beauty … all of its limitless opportunity." Next in the audio-visual flow, Martin Luther King Jr. delivers, in 1967, an anti-Vietnam-war speech before a jump cut reveals a photograph of writer and activist James Baldwin smiling and listening to King, showing their personal connection. Marking this cut is a short cue, which underscores the following sequence.

Muted trumpet, double bass, drum kit, and piano freely exchange short phrases and then fade behind the voice of Samuel L. Jackson, who reads an extract of Baldwin's work. Alongside photographs of smiling, white-picket families, Jackson says:

no other country in the world have been so fat and so sleek, and so safe and so happy, and so irresponsible, and so dead. No other country can afford to dream of a Plymouth and a wife and a house with a fence, and the children growing up safely to go to college and to become executives and then to marry and have the Plymouth and the house and so forth. A great many people do not live this way, and cannot imagine it, and do not know that when we talk about "democracy," this is what we mean.

The two-minute sequence is one of the film's more arresting and is illustrative of the film's treatment of Baldwin's critique.

What then, does Aigui's score, and evocation of Davis mean for the film's treatment of Baldwin's work? In his interview, Aigui reports that "Raoul wanted something violent, so I asked Andrey [Gontcharov, the trumpeter] to create a tense sound."[80] Little of the film's jazz score evokes the ferocity that "violence" might signal. Baldwin's words, framed by visions of the cruel hypocrisy and terror of the US-American democratic illusion Baldwin describes, speak to violence, but the score supports the film's and Baldwin's critique of American democracy. It accompanies the assertion that any vision of US-American democracy cannot coexist with power inequalities or violent injustice.[81] *I Am Not Your Negro*'s use of jazz might well be seen, therefore, as a continuation of the democracy thesis found in Burns's *Jazz* and in the writing of others, including Ralph Ellison and Stanley Crouch.[82] In this light, Aigui's evocation of Davis's music from the late 50s and early 1960s reinforces the dominant significations of 1960s jazz as perhaps the pinnacle of jazz's democratic potential. However, while Baldwin was remembering mid-century civil rights leaders, he was writing at least a decade later and thus referring to the unfinished work of the democratic project. Jazz at the time of *Remember this House* was ever more varied and irreverent to tradition. Davis was to soon return to the studio with *The Man with the Horn* (1981) and later, *You're Under Arrest* (1985). Had Aigui sought to emulate Davis's contemporaneous music, the film's framing of Baldwin's democratic critique might well have served to expand and deconstruct the received jazz-democracy thesis in productive ways that supported its wider critique of white, heterosexual democratic hegemony. However, in the light of *Jazz*, Peck and Aigui see little scope perhaps for post-1960s jazz to continue in the democratic mode. Tellingly, the film's ending, where Peck links Baldwin to contemporary Black Lives Matter activism, is underscored by Kendrick Lamar's "The Blacker the Berry" (2015), in tacit approval of the death of jazz as a vital political force.

By way of a conclusion, and seemingly in contrast to this view, I turn to Nadia Hallgren's documentary *Becoming* (2020), which offers a different kind of continuation of the democracy thesis.[83] The film tells a more carefully sanctioned story of Michelle Obama's life than the autobiography after which it is named. Both represent in their production and content the platform of resistance and democratic potential Obama fostered within the gendered and racialized politics of the twenty-first century.[84] In continuation, the film is primarily concerned with the unfinished work of democracy. As Obama says, "when Barack was first elected, various commentators had naively declared that our country was entering a post-racial era, in which skin color would no longer matter. Many were overlooking the racism and tribalism that was tearing our nation apart."

Under these words, an instrumental jazz chorale synthesizes with images of anti-Black violence provoked by Obama's presidency to establish sobriety and reflective weight. Written by the saxophonist and bandleader Kamasi Washington, the track is one of the more conspicuous examples of the film's underscore, where Washington's eclectic and melodic score succinctly demonstrates music's power to co-construct meaning. To many critics, Washington's success proves the enduring political agency of jazz practice.[85] Washington's selection as composer for *Becoming* endorses the opinions of critics that his music was intimately bound to Obama-era optimism,[86] the activism of Black Lives Matter,[87] and indeed, the very continuation of the jazz as democracy thesis.[88] Known more for the maximalism of his breakout record, *The Epic* (2015), Washington's score appears, however, muted and sanctioned. Compared to the live, socially distanced performance of the soundtrack recorded for the LA Philharmonic's concert series Sound/Stage, in *Becoming*, Washington's music is left low in the mix. This is partly due to the documentary's clean-cut approach and promotional message which reflects back onto Washington's music, softening its edges. The subtlety of approach, and its success within the film's democratic ambition, points not only to jazz's long-established signification in the cultural vernacular, easily identifiable even in quiet cues, but also to its enduring role in shaping documentary subjects and documentary aesthetics.

Notes

1 Bill Nichols, *Representing Reality: Issues and Concepts in Documentary* (Bloomington, IN: Indiana University Press, 1991), 12.
2 John Grierson, "The Documentary Producer," *Cinema Quarterly* 2.1 (1933), 8. For an overview of the impact of Grierson's definition, see Susan Kerrigan and Phillip McIntyre, "The 'Creative Treatment of Actuality': Rationalizing

and Reconceptualizing the Notion of Creativity for Documentary Practice," *Journal of Media Practice* 11.2 (August 2010), 111–30.
3 Benjamin Halligan, Robert Edgar, and Kirsty Fairclough-Isaacs, eds., *The Music Documentary: Acid Rock to Electropop* (New York: Routledge, 2013).
4 For an introduction to music and documentary, see Holly Rogers, "Introduction: Music, Sound and the Nonfiction Aesthetic," in Holly Rogers, ed., *Music and Sound in Documentary Film* (New York: Routledge, 2015), 1–19.
5 For a more comprehensive catalogue of jazz on film that includes credits to a large number of documentary films and other performances of jazz documented on film, see David Meeker, *Jazz on the Screen* (Washington, DC: Library of Congress, 2017). For a discussion of jazz performance in narrative film, see Krin Gabbard's chapter in this volume (Chapter 19).
6 Krin Gabbard, "The Word Jazz," in Mervyn Cooke and David Horn, eds., *The Cambridge Companion to Jazz* (Cambridge: Cambridge University Press, 2002), 1.
7 Scott DeVeaux, "Constructing the Jazz Tradition: Jazz Historiography," *Black American Literature Forum*, 25.3 (1991), 526.
8 Sherrie Tucker, "Deconstructing the Jazz Tradition: The Subjectless Subject of New Jazz Studies," in David Ake, Charles Hiroshi Garrett, and Daniel Goldman, eds., *Jazz/Not Jazz: The Music and Its Boundaries* (Berkeley: University of California Press, 2012), 264–84.
9 Jed Rasula, "The Media of Memory: The Seductive Menace of Records in Jazz History," in Krin Gabbard, ed., *Jazz Among the Discourses* (Durham, NC: Duke University Press, 1995), 134–62. As Peter Elsdon makes clear, the jazz records ought not be abandoned "in the face of cautions about what it represents. But we should seek to understand the recording as culturally mediated." Peter Elsdon, "The Potential of the Jazz Record," in Wolfram Knauer, ed., *Darmstädter Beiträge Zur Jazzforschung* (Wolke Verlagsgesellschaft, 2014), 117. See also Katherine Williams, "Duke Ellington's Newport Up!: Liveness, Artefacts and the Seductive Menace of Jazz Revisited," in Roger Fagge and Nicolas Pillai, eds., *New Jazz Conceptions: History, Theory, Practice* (New York: Routledge, 2017), 111–29.
10 Tony Whyton, *Jazz Icons: Heroes, Myths and the Jazz Tradition* (Cambridge: Cambridge University Press, 2013), 84.
11 For examples, see K. Heather Pinson, *The Jazz Image: Seeing Music through Herman Leonard's Photography* (Jackson, MS: University Press of Mississippi, 2014); Krin Gabbard, *Jammin' at the Margins: Jazz and the American Cinema* (Chicago: University of Chicago Press, 1996); Kristin A. McGee, *Some Liked It Hot: Jazz Women in Film and Television, 1928–1959* (Middletown, CT: Wesleyan University Press, 2009); Nicolas Pillai, *Jazz as Visual Language* (London: I. B. Tauris, 2016).
12 Mura Dehn, dir., *The Spirit Moves: A History of Black Social Dance on Film* (Dancetime Publications, 1987); Christi Jay Wells, *Between Beats: The Jazz Tradition and Black Vernacular Dance* (New York: Oxford University Press, 2021), 130–31.

13 Jayna Brown, "From the Point of View of the Pavement: A Geopolitics of Black Dance," in Nichole T. Rustin and Sherrie Tucker, eds., *Big Ears: Listening for Gender in Jazz Studies* (Durham, NC: Duke University Press, 2008), 174.

14 Karen Backstein, "Keeping the Spirit Alive: The Jazz Dance Testament of Mura Dehn," in Krin Gabbard, ed., *Representing Jazz* (Durham, NC: Duke University Press, 1995), 242.

15 For an introduction to both styles of documentary and their differences, see Keith Beattie, "The Truth of the Matter: Cinéma Vérité and Direct Cinema," *Documentary Screens: Non-Fiction Film and Television* (London: Macmillan Education UK, 2004), 83–104.

16 Gunnar Iversen and Scott Mackenzie, eds., *Mapping the Rockumentary: Images of Sound and Fury* (Edinburgh: Edinburgh University Press, 2022), 3.

17 Robert Strachan and Marion Leonard, "Reel to Real: Cinema Verité Rock Authenticity and the Rock Documentary," in Graeme Harper, Ruth Doughty, and Jochen Eisentraut, eds., *Sound and Music in Film and Visual Media: An Overview* (New York: Continuum, 2009), 284–99.

18 David Horn, "The Identity of Jazz," in Mervyn Cooke and David Horn, eds., *The Cambridge Companion to Jazz* (Cambridge: Cambridge University Press, 2003), 16.

19 Ted Gioia, *The Imperfect Art: Reflections on Jazz and Modern Culture* (New York: Oxford University Press, 1990), 86.

20 Frederick Garber, "Fabulating Jazz," in Gabbard, *Representing Jazz*, 70–103.

21 Ronald Michael Radano, "Black Music's Body Politics," in Philip V. Bohlman and Goffredo Plastino, eds., *Jazz Worlds/World Jazz* (Chicago: University of Chicago Press, 2016), 429–44.

22 Backstein, "Keeping the Spirit Alive: The Jazz Dance Testament of Mum Dehn."

23 Gabbard, "The Word Jazz," 1–6.

24 Stephen Davies, *Musical Works and Performances: A Philosophical Exploration* (Oxford: Clarendon, 2001), 16–19.

25 Andrew Kania, "All Play and No Work: An Ontology of Jazz," *The Journal of Aesthetics and Art Criticism*, 69.4 (2011), 400.

26 Philip Auslander, *Liveness: Performance in a Mediatized Culture*, 2nd ed. (New York: Routledge, 2008).

27 Bert Stern and Aram Avakian, dir., *Jazz on a Summer's Day* (Galaxy Productions, 1959).

28 Roger Tilton, dir., *Jazz Dance* (1954); "'Jazz Dance' on Film," *New York Times*, September 5, 1954, sec. Magazine.

29 Emile Wennekes, "'All Aboard!': Soundies and Vitaphone Shorts," in Björn Heile, Peter Elsdon, and Jennifer R. Doctor, eds., *Watching Jazz: Encounters with Jazz Performance on Screen* (New York: Oxford University Press, 2016), 57–72; Laura Niebling, "'I Don't Make Culture, I Sell It!': The Early History of Music Documentation 1920s-1970s," in Gunnar Iversen and Scott Mackenzie, eds., *Mapping the Rockumentary: Images of Sound and Fury* (Edinburgh: Edinburgh University Press, 2022), 24–35; Amy Herzog, "Discordant Visions: The Peculiar

Musical Images of the Soundies Jukebox Film," *American Music*, 22.1 (2004), 27–39.
30 Niebling, "I Don't Make Culture," 24.
31 Thomas Cohen, *Playing to the Camera: Musicians and Musical Performance in Documentary Cinema* (New York: Columbia University Press, 2012), 24.
32 Michael Chanan, "Music, Documentary, Music Documentary," in Brian Winston, ed., *The Documentary Film Book* (London: Bloomsbury, 2019), 339.
33 Christopher Small, *Musicking: The Meanings of Performing and Listening* (Hanover: University Press of New England, 1998), 7–9.
34 Chanan, "Music, Documentary," 339.
35 Cohen, Playing to the Camera, 32.
36 Ibid., 31–32.
37 Ben Ratliff, "Jazz as a Window on Life in the 50's," *New York Times*, July 30, 2000, sec. Arts & Leisure, AR31.
38 For a complete list of the festival's planned line up, the program can be viewed here: www.rirocks.net/Band%20Articles/Newport%20Jazz%20Festival%201958.htm.
39 Ken Burns, dir., *Jazz* (Florentine Films, 2001). For more on the Burns documentary, see Nicolas Pillai's chapter on jazz and television in this volume (Chapter 20).
40 Ben Ratliff, "Fixing, for Now, the Image of Jazz: MUSIC," *New York Times*, January 7, 2001, sec. Arts & Leisure.
41 Alan Stanbridge, "Burns, Baby, Burns: Jazz History as a Contested Cultural Site," *The Source*, 1.1 (2004), 82–100.
42 Hector Amaya, "Racialized Documentary Reception of Ken Burns' Jazz," *Television & New Media* 9.2 (March 2008), 111–30; Steven F. Pond, "Jamming the Reception: Ken Burns, 'Jazz', and the Problem of 'America's Music,'" *Notes* 60.1 (2003), 11–45.
43 Tim Wall and Paul Long, "Jazz Britannia: Mediating the Story of British Jazz on Television," *Jazz Research Journal* 3.2 (2009), 151–52.
44 Theodore Gracyk, "Jazz after Jazz: Ken Burns and the Construction of Jazz History," *Philosophy and Literature*, 26.1 (2002), 173–87.
45 Geoffrey Jacques, "A Roundtable on Ken Burns's *Jazz*," *Journal of Popular Music Studies*, 13.2 (2001), 220.
46 For pedagogical uses of *Jazz* see Tony Whyton, "Birth of the School: Discursive Methodologies in Jazz Education," *Music Education Research*, 8.1 (2006): 78–79.
47 Jacques, "A Roundtable," 213.
48 Stefan Immler, dir., *History of Jazz: Oxygen for the Ears* (Giganova Productions, 2012).
49 Edward Bland, dir., *The Cry of Jazz* (KHTB Productions, 1959).
50 William Sites, "Beyond the 'Futureless Future': Edward O. Bland, Afro-Modernism and *The Cry of Jazz*," *American Studies*, 60.1 (2021), 33.
51 Paul Youngquist, *A Pure Solar World: Sun Ra and the Birth of Afrofuturism*, illustrated ed. (Austin: University of Texas Press, 2016), 127.

52 Tom Surgal, dir., *Fire Music* (Submarine Entertainment, 2021); Steve Dollar, "'…The Parts That Were Left out of the Ken Burns Documentary': Tom Surgal on the 'Historical Corrective' That Is His Free Jazz Documentary, Fire Music," *Filmmaker Magazine* (blog), September 10, 2021, https://filmmakermagazine.com/112250-the-parts-that-were-left-out-of-the-ken-burns-documentary-tom-surgal-on-the-historical-corrective-that-is-is-free-jazz-documentary-fire-music/.
53 Ron Mann, dir., *Imagine the Sound* (1981); Alan Roth, dir., *Inside Out in the Open* (2001).
54 Steve Provizer, "Film Review: 'Fire Music: A History of the Free Jazz Revolution' – Informative but Incomplete," *The Arts Fuse*, https://artsfuse.org/235064/film-review-fire-music-a-history-of-the-free-jazz-revolution-informative-but-incomplete/.
55 See Pillai, *Film, Television and the Dissonant Image*.
56 John Corner, "Biography within the Documentary Frame: A Note," *Framework: The Journal of Cinema and Media*, 43.1 (2002), 98.
57 Ibid., 96.
58 John Jeremy, dir., *The Long Night of Lady Day* (1515 Productions, 1984); John Szwed, *Billie Holiday: The Musician and the Myth* (London: Heinemann, 2015), 3.
59 Michael V. Perez and Jessica McKee, eds., *Billie Holiday: Essays on the Artistry and Legacy* (Jefferson, NC: McFarland, 2019), 2.
60 Farah Jasmine Griffin, *If You Can't Be Free, Be a Mystery: In Search of Billie Holiday* (New York: The Free Press, 2001), 99.
61 Szwed, *Billie Holiday*, 71.
62 Matthew Duffus, "Seeing Is Believing? Reading Billie Holiday through Photography," in Perez and McKee, *Billie Holiday*, 102. See also Benjamin Cawthra, *Blue Notes in Black and White: Photography and Jazz* (Chicago: University of Chicago Press, 2011), and Pinson, *The Jazz Image*.
63 Ingrid Hölzl, "Moving Stills: Images That Are No Longer Immobile," *Photographies*, 3.1 (2010), 105.
64 Sam Billinge, *The Practical Guide to Documentary Editing: Techniques for TV and Film* (New York: Routledge, 2017), 127.
65 Duffus, "Seeing Is Believing?," 102.
66 William P. Gottlieb, "Portrait of Billie Holiday, Downbeat, New York, N.Y., ca. Feb. 1947," Library of Congress, Monographic. Photograph., www.loc.gov/item/gottlieb.04211.
67 Laura Mulvey, "Visual Pleasure and Narrative Cinema," *Screen*, 16.3 (1975), 6–18.
68 John Corner, "Sounds Real: Music and Documentary," *Popular Music*, 21.3 (2002), 358.
69 Rogers, "Introduction," 3.
70 Ibid.
71 Morris Holbrook, *Music, Movies, Meanings, and Markets: Cinemajazzamatazz* (New York: Routledge, 2011); See also Gabbard, *Jammin' at the Margins*.

72 Jonathan Godsall, *Reeled In: Pre-Existing Music in Narrative Film* (New York: Routledge, 2018), 6–7.
73 Roger Fagge, "The Politics, Aesthetics and Dissonance of Music in Everyday Life," *Jazz Research Journal*, 13.1–2 (2019): 7–18.
74 Philip Brophy, "Bring the Noise," *Film Comment*, 45.1 (February 2009), 16.
75 Jonathan Kahana, *Intelligence Work: The Politics of American Documentary* (New York: Columbia University Press, 2008), 1–4.
76 Gail Kubik, "Music in Documentary Films," *Music Journal; New York*, 3.5 (1945), 13.
77 Raoul Peck, dir., *I Am Not Your Negro* (Velvet Films, 2016).
78 Marine Wong Kwok Chuen, "Alexei Aigui on Scoring the Breakthrough Documentary I Am Not Your Negro," *Score It Magazine*, 24 February 2017, http://magazine.scoreit.org/interview-alexei-aigui-not-negro/.
79 William L. Hendricks, prod., *The Land We Love* (Warner Bros., 1966).
80 Chuen, "Alexei Aigui."
81 Katharine Lawrence Balfour and Lawrie Balfour, *The Evidence of Things Not Said: James Baldwin and the Promise of American Democracy* (Ithaca: Cornell University Press, 2001), 18.
82 David Alder, "Jazzocracy: Jazz, Democracy, and the Creation of a New American Mythology. On Jazz, Hip-Hop and Democracy," *Democratiya*, 14 (Autumn 2008), 157–65.
83 Nadia Hallgren, dir., *Becoming* (Big Mouth Productions, 2020).
84 Brittney Cooper, "A'n't I a Lady?: Race Women, Michelle Obama, and the Ever-Expanding Democratic Imagination," *MELUS*, 35.4 (2010), 41.
85 William Beuttler, *Make It New: Reshaping Jazz in the 21st Century* (Amherst, MA: Lever Press, 2019), 7.
86 Andy Beta, "Kamasi Washington: Becoming (Music From the Netflix Original Documentary)," *Pitchfork*, May 19, 2020, https://pitchfork.com/reviews/albums/kamasi-washington-becoming-music-from-the-netflix-original-documentary/.
87 George Varga, "Kamasi Washington 'the Jazz Voice of Black Lives Matter'", *Chicago Tribune*, October 4, 2016, www.chicagotribune.com/sd-et-pop-kamasi-20160929-story.html.
88 Brandon Soderberg, "Art of Cool 2016: Finding Modern Democracy in Modern Jazz," *INDY Week*, May 4, 2016, https://indyweek.com/api/content/bae9a173-97f9-5154-acf0-5c877920a3ce/.

CHAPTER 22

Two Dark Rooms
Jazz and Photography

Benjamin Cawthra

The jazz musicians assembled on a Harlem stoop for Art Kane's camera in 1958 represented generations and styles of the music gathered in one place, but also a watershed cultural moment. Made to accompany an *Esquire* spread on jazz's past, present, and future, the image also fused various strands of photography's history into one decisive moment. It is a group portrait, portraiture being a primary function of photography since its inception. It is also a documentary record made for publication in a commercial magazine, a type of photography that had flowered in the golden age of photojournalism just past. To the extent Kane was able to art direct the photograph (as he humorously recalls in Jean Bach's 1995 film *A Great Day in Harlem*), it also reaches for aesthetic value and crosses the group portrait with 1950s candid work, assisted here by the unplanned row of children seated on the curb next to the biggest kid of all, Count Basie. Jazz was enjoying a brief period of mainstream popularity in the 1950s, fueled by the sales of long-playing records, the birth of jazz festivals in the United States and Europe, changing white liberal racial attitudes, and the affluence of postwar America. That jazz would never again achieve this level of mainstream acceptance and cultural influence was not photography's fault. The camera had been there from the beginning, promoting jazz's stars, selling its club dates and concerts – and now records, probing the music's deep beauty for visual analogues and associations. The symbiotic relationship between the two forms has, if anything, been strengthened by the passage of decades since Kane's photograph.[1]

Jazz photographs are evidentiary documents, nostalgic memorials, and contributors to a romantic mythology and mystique. Sight and sound are combined and made more potent by mutual association. But classic jazz photographs do not exist in the realm of myth alone. Jazz photographs intersected with trends in portraiture, documentary, and advertising during the peak decades of the music's popularity. They described the social contours of the music – the places where it was heard and the communities formed around it. And images helped sell the music, whether promoting performances or recordings. In terms of cultural impact, jazz photographs made African American innovation more obvious even as the drive for equality in American life gained momentum.

In a sense, photography and jazz grew up together. While photography dates to the invention of the daguerreotype in 1839, its problematic relationship to traditional art forms persisted in the nineteenth century. Some photographers distanced their work from aesthetics, preferring to see themselves as technicians whose job it was to make realistic records of people (through portraiture) and places (via landscape photography). Cumbersome equipment and slow shutter speeds limited more dynamic conceptions, and the question of whether the photographer or the camera truly made the image remained an open one. With every technical advance, photography became more of an industry, with the creation and distribution of images tied to urbanization. But these advances also opened up aesthetic vistas. Some photographers, especially members of the pictorialist movement of the late nineteenth and early twentieth centuries, attempted to emulate with light and chemicals what impressionist painters had achieved in oils. When Alfred Stieglitz made his arguments for photography as an art form, it remained a private and somewhat expensive hobby for aesthetes, even as Stieglitz's own work – and that of contemporaries such as Anne Brigman and Paul Strand – revealed photography's artistic potential.[2]

Eighty years into photography's disputatious life, recorded jazz was born, and the music became a far more controversial expression due to its iconoclastic form – with roots in Black diasporic expression in an era of white consolidation in American society and politics – and cultural impact, especially on the young. Soon capturing the music visually reflected the range of photographic uses – as a form of commercial advertisement, as a document of social life, as an art form beholden only to aesthetics, and as a way for listeners to connect with their musical heroes. All of these may be seen in photography of the emerging world of jazz by the 1930s. Just as photography began to find a place in elite art institutions, technical advances made it an accessible popular hobby. At the same time, jazz bid for artistic credibility with concerts at Carnegie Hall, for example, but also became a popular music as big band swing. It is no accident that the most accomplished photographers of jazz were photojournalists and commercial photographers who had grown up amid the Great Depression and World War II – and they very quickly began blurring the lines between documentary and fine art expression. But preceding and alongside them, portraitists, photojournalists, and club photographers assisted in visually describing the jazz world.

Whatever their background or approach, photographers shared a deep love of jazz. The musicians were cultural heroes, and some of the best-known images we have of many of them were done for free or close to it, with minimal circulation at the time of their creation. Photographers had expressed not only their belief in jazz as music, but jazz as an art form able to transcend social custom and reorder racist thinking. Jazz photography could do nothing less than valorize Blackness in a countercultural sense. Indeed, throughout these decades, the camera captured the racial aspects of the music and raised uncomfortable questions for American culture. Jazz's fundamental Blackness was often at odds with acceptable visual representation in the United States, where a lynching photograph could become a postcard but Black music sequences could be cut from circulating Hollywood feature films in the 1930s.[3] This tension may also be seen in early coverage of the music in important new pictorial journalism outlets such as *Life* magazine. Perhaps more surprising, the music's Blackness was further downplayed in the leading trade magazines – *Down Beat* and *Metronome*. The album cover in the 1950s made jazz's association with Blackness obvious and unavoidable at just the moment the Freedom Movement for civil rights and racial equality began to change the American social and political landscape.

So photography made jazz, and jazz musicians, visible. But another point of contention throughout photography's history has been the extent to which a photograph relies on the subject as much as the photographer. And in this, jazz musicians were quick to see the value of their own images as promotional tools, thinking beyond their agency-commissioned publicity portraits. Whether allowing access to rehearsals or recording sessions to photographers, posing for album covers, or even occasionally taking control of their album design and photography, important musicians managed their photographic images over time. Dizzy Gillespie conspired with William Gottlieb to create a look for bebop. Sonny Rollins art directed the cowboy theater of his *Way Out West* album cover. Miles Davis seemed supremely aware of his image, and not only because he dressed well. His camera awareness – onstage and off – contributed to the mystique of "cool" that benefited his career. John Coltrane allowed Roy DeCarava close access during club performances. Some musicians, such as Gillespie and the accomplished Milt Hinton, were amateur photographers themselves. Hinton's work, made over five decades as a bassist, has the intimacy of family photographs and the aesthetic imprimatur of a creative mind at work, as multiple collections of his photographs attest.[4]

Jazz photography documents more than how important musicians looked. In the hands of visual artists, the camera reveals the emotion in the music, in the audiences as well as on stage. It shows the contexts for performance over a range of time and place, providing a feel for small clubs, recording studios, and festival venues, and where musicians stayed and how they traveled. It can make visible urban life across the country, as in the case of Duncan Schiedt's Indianapolis club photographs and his efforts to collect forgotten images by other Indianans, or painter/photographer Ralston Crawford's jazz photos from New Orleans.[5] It reveals how the music was marketed. It shows musicians in nonperformance contexts – Louis Armstrong in his pajamas and smoking jacket in a private backstage jam captured by Charles Peterson; the quiet moments with family members such as John and Alice Coltrane at a recording break in a Chuck Stewart image; Milt Hinton's snapshot of a young Dizzy Gillespie asleep on Cab Calloway's tour bus. Jazz photographs reveal an art world, one often circumscribed by race and ever in conversation with commercial interests.

Beginnings

Even before jazz had been recorded, studio portraiture captured what the musicians looked like. European exiles, most of them Jewish, came to the United States fleeing persecution in the early twentieth century, and many became studio portrait photographers who identified with the African American experience of discrimination. Publicity portraits became an important element in the jazz world over time. By mid-century Lee of Hollywood and G. Maillard Kesslere's glamour-inflected lighting techniques helped dissociate jazz from its questionable social origins and aligned jazz musicians with other celebrities in the entertainment world. In doing so, they could not help but make jazz and its practitioners part of a cultural mainstream, visually speaking.

The great era of documentary photography, the 1930s, found Berenice Abbott visiting the Savoy Ballroom and Farm Security Administration photographers like Russell Lee making photos at concerts and dances. As jazz and photography both gained in respectability and artistic credibility in the 1930s, mainstream publications began to notice. The new giant in magazine publishing, Henry Luce's photography-based *Life*, began in 1936 and intermittently reported on what the kids were up to. *Life*'s most prominent jazz photographic essays included work by former musician Charles Peterson, who covered the revival of hot jazz in the late 1930s during the height of the Swing Era, and Gjon Mili, whose wartime essays on jazz dance and jam sessions were both eye-catching technical exercises and inspirational to later photographers of the music. His short 1944 film *Jammin' the Blues* expanded the possibilities for filming jazz performance.[6]

Three Postwar Figures

The work of three photographers – William Gottlieb, Herman Leonard, and William Claxton – formed the center of a jazz photographic tradition long after they had completed their jazz work. In the 1980s and after, books and exhibitions solidified their reputations as important names in the field. They were music fans, and their timing – the late 1940s and 1950s, when enduring ideas about jazz were formed – solidified their legacy as skilled creators of memorable images.

Gottlieb worked as a journalist for *Down Beat* in the early postwar era in New York at the very moment bebop began to make its presence felt on 52nd Street. He photographed a range of musicians – his images of Billie Holiday became iconic – but he emerged as something of a renegade advocate for bebop in *Down Beat*'s pages. His images of musicians associated with the movement, including Dizzy Gillespie, Thelonious Monk and, to a lesser extent, Charlie Parker, are rare visual documents. Gottlieb's *The Golden Age of Jazz*, published in 1979 three decades after he stopped photographing jazz musicians, sparked interest in images that had only been seen cropped in poor reproductions in *Down Beat*'s tabloid pages in the late 1940s. His photographs are housed at the Library of Congress as significant historical documents.[7]

Unlike the mostly self-taught Gottlieb, Leonard was trained as a fine arts photographer, working for a time as an assistant to the Canadian master portraitist Yousuf Karsh, and became known as a fashion photographer from the 1950s on. He began photographing musicians at 52nd Street clubs around the time Gottlieb quit in 1948. Leonard gained access by allowing the clubs to use his photographs free of charge. His images of relaxed rehearsals and concentrated performances at venues such as the Royal Roost developed into a visual style and an iconography for the music. Backlighting, wafting cigarette smoke, and a sculptural sense of form made Leonard's work stand out. His photograph of Dexter Gordon in rehearsal fuses all of these elements into perhaps the one image best signifying jazz. But like Gottlieb, Leonard's jazz images were rarely seen until the 1980s, when publication of his work revealed a fugitive noir world, a jazz culture romanticized through Leonard's eye. At the time, a gallery of images in *Metronome*'s 1950 yearbook, for which he received no fee, provided the greatest exposure for Leonard's jazz work. His prints are now part of the Smithsonian Institution's collections.[8]

Operating in fast-growing southern California in the 1950s, Claxton went from amateur fan photographer to commercial chronicler of the local music scene as art director for *Theme* magazine and the Pacific Jazz record label. Shooting unobtrusively in available light during recording sessions, Claxton captured the relaxed sensibility of music made during the day in the studios of Los Angeles, where the film industry dominated. On sunny location shoots for album covers, Claxton played on the California dream years before a similar rock iconography emerged, relocating jazz from smoky East Coast basement clubs to California's beaches, deserts, and mountains and promoting a cerebral, compositionally oriented jazz made by important white musicians such as Chet Baker, who became Claxton's iconic jazz subject. Claxton's 1960 road trip with German writer Joachim Berendt resulted in *JazzLife*, a massive project containing some of the most striking jazz images ever published.[9]

The work of these three has become a visual shorthand for jazz itself, but their work does not convey the full range of jazz photography, whose practitioners come from all corners of American life and indeed well beyond its shores.

Album Covers

When the long-playing record (LP) was born in 1948, it opened up a new field for the visual expression of the music. Advances in printing meant that more elaborate art, including photography, could help sell the records and enhance the star power of the artists. Columbia, a label with international reach able to afford four-color cover photography, had developed the LP. The label had a full-time studio photographer on hand by the 1950s in Don Hunstein, who shot recording sessions and occasional album covers for every kind of artist Columbia recorded. The company also commissioned original artwork and used the images of a wide range of independent photographers such as Jay Maisel and Roy DeCarava. But jazz-based companies were much smaller operations, and often their owners made their own photographs out of economic necessity. Foremost among these was Blue Note cofounder Francis Wolff, a German émigré whose valorizing studio rehearsal shots show the deep influence of Expressionist cinema. Designers – most often Reid Miles – incorporated Wolff's photographs into inexpensive but striking two-color designs that continue to influence jazz marketing and the public perception of the music.[10] Esmond Edwards parleyed his freelance photography for Prestige into a producer's role at the company, the first of several industry jobs for this pioneering African American. Another Black photographer, Chuck Stewart, formerly an assistant to Herman Leonard, made his own name with striking photographs most closely associated with the Impulse! label in the 1960s.[11] Other key contributors to early album covers include Magnum photographer Dennis Stock (whose 1959 book *Jazz Street* is one of the first important collections of original jazz photographs); Don Schlitten, Robert Parent, and Lee Friedlander, whose early work for Atlantic came near the start of a distinguished fine art photographic career.[12]

Just as advertising and design concepts shifted dramatically in the 1960s influenced by Pop art and countercultural aesthetics, so did album art. Columbia chased the zeitgeist with Thelonious Monk's 1968 *Underground* cover designed by John Berg, in which the mild-mannered pianist is cast as a well-armed revolutionary. With the waning of acoustic jazz on major US labels in the 1970s and with American independents struggling or dying, European labels saw opportunity. ECM, the Munich-based company that became home to American musicians as well as Europeans from across the continent, signaled a shift away from the personality of the performers and toward a vision of jazz as state of mind, a private experience visually expressed in abstract designs by Tadayuki Naito and subdued portfolio landscape photography by Lajos Keresztes among others.[13] Creed Taylor's CTI label in the States had pioneered the use of portfolio photography with the colorful advertising work of Pete Turner.[14]

Despite the smaller compact disc format introduced in the 1980s, some photographers still made recording session photography into a specialty, most prominently Jimmy Katz. Furthermore, many unused or forgotten images gained life as part of compact disc reissues, including as part of lavish boxed set packages. The question of who should own the rights to images shot for record companies such as Columbia became an open question as labels started to monetize their archival images in the new century. Sony BMG extended royalty privileges to photographers like Hunstein who had contributed to the Columbia archive over the decades.[15]

Street Photography

Robert Frank, Garry Winogrand, and other "street" photographers in the postwar era had many admirers, and their candids influenced photographers associated with jazz. Herb Snitzer, who worked on *Metronome*'s staff in the late 1950s and early 60s, brought a street sensibility to his jazz photographs from the era. His 1960 photo essay covering Louis Armstrong on tour in *Metronome* is an excellent example.[16] Jerry Dantzic's dynamic candid style practiced in New York's streets bled over into the way he shot jazz. A collection of Billie Holiday images made over a single week in 1957 during a New Jersey club engagement are striking for their sense of intimacy and surprise, revealing the person behind the myth.[17] Carole Reiff, who only made jazz photographs for a few years in the 1950s, showed a remarkable ability to take artistic advantage of access to a world of musicians away from the stage. Her informal portraits of an off-duty community constitute a kind of jazz family album created with a high contrast style.[18]

The African American Eye

The jazz image has not by any means been exclusive to New York, though the city remains the center of both photography and jazz. The Black-owned newspapers that flourished around the country during the years of *de facto* and *de jure* segregation employed staff photographers who created archives detailing an entire social world of African American life, including the realm of entertainment. Key figures in this work include Charles "Teenie" Harris of the *Pittsburgh Courier*, a flagship Black newspaper with a national following. Harris made images of not only a thriving local scene, but also internationally known touring performers.[19] Charles Williams, who shot primarily in the 1930s and 1940s, and Bob Douglas, most active in the 1950s and after, worked for local Los Angeles papers, including the *California Eagle* and *Los Angeles Sentinel*, and created distinguished archives from their years of photojournalism.

Some important Black photographers were not professionals at all. Al Smith, a postal worker by day, made photographs of the Central District in Seattle, including the Jackson Street music scene. Smith took photographs of club patrons and then returned the next week to sell prints to the subjects. This informal photography documented an entire time and place and reveals not only what musicians looked like on the bandstand, but also patrons and club settings long gone. This kind of work occurred in Kansas City, San Francisco – wherever the music could be heard in nightclubs.

As for the professionals – or those who aspired to be – breaking into the photographic world was difficult. Gordon Parks began as an intern in the final days of the Farm Security Administration photography section and eventually became *Life*'s first African American staff photographer.

Parks's work was wide ranging, but he did photograph jazz musicians – including, most sensitively, Duke Ellington. But Parks was an exception, as was Ted Williams, who began photographing street life in 1940s Chicago. His 1958 Newport Jazz Festival photographs garnered a 21-page spread in *Down Beat* that led to publication in a wide range of national magazines during his long career, covering the Civil Rights Movement among other assignments. Hugh Bell's remarkable jazz photographs – some of which, such as those of Billie Holiday, did not flatter their subjects – were a small but significant portion of his fashion- and travel-based career. Bell's "Hot Jazz" is one of the remarkable jazz photos; along with work by Ed Feingersh, Roy DeCarava, and Bob Willoughby, Edward Steichen selected it for *The Family of Man* exhibition at the Museum of Modern Art in 1955, the best attended photography exhibition of all time.[20]

But many Black photographers had great difficulty obtaining work no matter how impressive their portfolios. Roy DeCarava's project photographing Harlem with jazz as a key component found resistance from galleries and publishers. His available light shots featuring deep gray tones lend a mysterious feel to images like "Dancers – New York" from 1956 – a style DeCarava denied was a "Black aesthetic." What is "Black" about his work is the treatment of his subjects – the expressiveness he finds in the lives of Harlemites as they work, play, and, in the case of jazz, perform or listen. The music functions as a kind of cultural connective tissue.[21] DeCarava and others formed Kamoinge Workshop in 1964 to pool resources, trade ideas, and advocate for Black photographers. Important work flowed from this group over the succeeding decades, including from several photographers who engaged closely with jazz: the street photographer Beuford Smith; original portraitists Anthony Barboza and Ming Smith, who documented the New York loft jazz scene of the 1970s and 80s; and versatile Frank Stewart, who eventually became the staff photographer for Jazz at Lincoln Center.[22] The work of Gerald Cyrus from the 1980s onward brings many strands of Black jazz photography together. His street work recalls that of Beuford Smith and DeCarava, while his images of patrons in Harlem jazz clubs dancing, flirting, and listening to unseen musicians capture the social scene, a soulful update of club photography.[23]

Way Out West

Besides William Claxton, Douglas, and Charles Williams, there were other important photographers operating on the West Coast. Bob Willoughby's striking candid work captured the excitement of live performance – see his famous image of Big Jay McNeely playing on his back on a Los Angeles stage while white patrons egg him on – and distinctive portraits, including striking profile shots of Gerry Mulligan and Miles Davis.[24] The Monterey Jazz Festival, beginning in 1958, became an important venue for photographers on the West Coast and eventually provided gallery space each year for themed photography exhibitions. Ray Avery was a Glendale record store owner and long-time lensman on the Los Angeles scene who contributed to records made there and who also shot at Monterey. Jerry Stoll spent eight years as staff photographer at Monterey in the 1960s, creating some of the festival's most iconic images as international stars gathered each September. Best-known for his rock photographs, San Francisco's Jim Marshall actually began his music photography in the jazz world, shooting at Monterey and at Bay Area venues through the 1960s.[25] In the 1970s and 80s, Kathy Sloane created a distinctive archive of performance photography, concentrating much of her work at the North Beach club Keystone Korner. Sloane combined her intimate club images with oral history interviews with club personnel, musicians, and patrons to create a textured, multidimensional portrait of a jazz community.[26]

Curating the Jazz Image

While book projects spearheaded by producer Orrin Keepnews and collector Frank Driggs had collected early jazz photographs by the early 1980s, curatorial work in the field began to mature in a series of significant gallery exhibitions and publications.[27] C. Daniel Dawson, himself an accomplished photographer, curated the first exhibition of DeCarava's jazz photographs for the Studio Museum of Harlem in 1982. *The Sound I Saw*, named for a book project that had yet to find a publisher, revealed in depth DeCarava's social vision of the music. Dawson continued to champion Black photographers and put together a symposium, *Jazz and the Art of Photography*, for Columbia University's Center for Jazz Studies in 2000, an effort to draw greater scholarly attention to the field. The next year, DeCarava's masterpiece finally found a publisher thanks in part to Dawson's efforts.[28]

Lee Tanner, a photographer whose day job was as an accomplished metallurgist, created an impressive archive of jazz photographs from his nights and weekends in 1950s and 60s Boston. By 1990 he had conceived of The Jazz Image, a rubric under which he licensed his own work and curated a series of multi-photographer themed exhibitions at Kimball's East Bay Area jazz club, and other venues throughout the 1990s. Tanner developed a loose international network of jazz photographers for these exhibitions, which included shows in Washington, DC, and New York galleries. For five years he curated "Indelible Images" for *Jazz Times* magazine, highlighting a half-dozen photographers each year, including less well-known practitioners such as Lou Jones and Tad Hershorn. Tanner's ultimate statement, *The Jazz Image: Masters of Jazz Photography*, brought together twenty-seven of the genre's greatest photographers between two covers.[29]

For two decades, Sam Stephenson of Duke University's Center for Documentary Studies followed the trail of renowned *Life* photographer W. Eugene Smith, master of photojournalism's war-era golden age. Stephenson catalogued and analyzed a massive visual and aural archive closely documenting in obsessive detail the troubled Smith's years living in a New York Flower District loft. The *Jazz Loft* project documents a location frequented by artists and jazz musicians ranging from the fascinating but forgotten to Thelonious Monk himself, resulting in a series of publications and exhibitions that brought a remarkable and idiosyncratic archive of a jazz community back to life.[30]

When Reggie Pettus, a barbershop owner in San Francisco, rescued a cache of photographs that had adorned Red Powell's shoeshine parlor for decades from a Fillmore Street landlord, he saved a critical visual record of the city's history. Photographer and UC Santa Cruz professor Lewis Watts assisted Pettus in exhibiting the prints in his shop and in neighborhood galleries, and soon the *Harlem of the West* project was born. Collaborating with writer and photographer Elizabeth Pepin Silva, Watts's photo restorations and curatorial choices, along with Silva's research and oral histories, reconstructed the history of the Fillmore district and its thriving music scene in its 1940s and 50s heyday. The project has resulted in touring exhibitions and the book went into its fourth edition in 2020.[31]

The International Lens

Jazz is said to be the most original cultural contribution made by the United States to the rest of the world. Passionate fans of the music met its arrival with images that documented and celebrated the liberating spirit of jazz. In fact, some took up photography so they could get closer to the music and found a life's calling behind the lens and in the darkroom. Katsuji Abé's work reflects the deep interest in jazz in Japan. Through the postwar decades, he created images for album covers and photographed visiting musicians. Abé made a significant contribution to the genre by publishing his anthology of jazz photography, *Jazz Giants*, in Japan in 1986 and the United States two years later.[32]

Among significant British photographers have been David Redfern and Val Wilmer, also an accomplished music writer. Wilmer's 1976 milestone *The Face of Black Music* offers images of African American musicians that function as interpretive sources of the Black experience, often accompanied by words from the subjects themselves.[33] In France, Jean-Pierre Leloir's photographs of French jazz clubs and culture of the 1950s and 60s, including informal musician portraits, are unequaled for their sense of ease and atmosphere.[34] His countryman Guy Le Querrec's work from the 1960s on showed a sensitivity to the music's nature – his image of Charles Mingus onstage poring over yards of lead sheets is an example of the creativity Le Querrec showed in performance settings. Swiss photojournalist Dany Gignoux also made distinctive concert photographs a part of her archive from the 1970s to the 90s.

Jan Persson captured the wave of interest in jazz in postwar Denmark, home of several expatriate American musicians and a frequent European tour stop by the 1960s, when he began photographing musicians with a distinguished eye.[35] In Milan, Italy's jazz capital, Roberto Polillo's performance work stood out in the 1960s as he shot for *Musica Jazz*.[36] Giuseppe Pino brought a fashion photographer's daring eye to photographing musicians from the 1960s on. Roberto Masotti's informal images of musicians frequently enhanced ECM's visually spare releases from the 1970s onward.

These and many others created an international subgenre in which two art forms bonded, in which people shared a cultural affinity across borders during the Cold War's time of tension and vulnerability. Jazz remains original to American culture, but musicians, listeners, and, yes, photographers from other lands remain a primary base of its ongoing support.

Notes

1 See recent research in the field: Alan Ainsworth, *Sight Readings: Photographers and American Jazz, 1900–1960* (Bristol, UK: Intellect, 2022); Benjamin Cawthra, *Blue Notes in Black and White: Photography and Jazz* (Chicago: University of Chicago Press, 2011); K. Heather Pinson, *The Jazz Image: Seeing Music through Herman Leonard's Photography* (Jackson: University Press of Mississippi, 2014).
2 Alfred Stieglitz, "Pictorial Photography," 1899, in Alan Trachtenberg, ed., *Classic Essays on Photography* (Stony Creek, CT: Leete's Island, 1980), 116–23.
3 For more on jazz and narrative cinema, see Krin Gabbard's chapter in this volume (Chapter 19).

4 Milt Hinton and David G. Berger, *Bass Lines: The Stories and Photographs of Milt Hinton* (Philadelphia: Temple University Press, 1988); Milt Hinton, David G. Berger, and Holly Maxson, *OverTime: The Jazz Photographs of Milt Hinton* (San Francisco: Pomegranate, 1991).
5 Duncan Schiedt, *Jazz in Black and White: The Photographs of Duncan Schiedt* (Bloomington: Indiana University Press, 2004).
6 W. Royal Stokes, *Swing Era New York: The Jazz Photographs of Charles Peterson* (Philadelphia: Temple University Press, 1994).
7 William P. Gottlieb, *The Golden Age of Jazz* (New York: Simon and Schuster, 1979); "William P. Gottlieb Collection," Library of Congress, www.loc.gov/collections/jazz-photography-of-william-p-gottlieb/.
8 Herman Leonard, *The Eye of Jazz* (London: Viking, 1989); *Jazz, Giants, and Journeys: The Photography of Herman Leonard* (New York: Scala, 2007).
9 William Claxton, *Jazz Seen* (Cologne: Taschen, 2000); William Claxton and Joachim E. Berendt, *Jazzlife: A Journey Across America for Jazz in 1960* (Cologne: Taschen, 2005). See also Richard Bock, William Claxton, and Nesuhi Ertegun, eds. *Jazz West Coast: A Portfolio of Photographs by William Claxton* (Hollywood, CA: Linear, 1955); and William Claxton and Hitoshi Namakata, *Jazz West Coast: Artwork of Pacific Jazz Records* (Tokyo: Bijutsu Shupan-Sha, 1992).
10 Michael Cuscuna, Charlie Lourie, and Oscar Schnider, *The Blue Note Years: The Jazz Photography of Francis Wolff*, Foreword by Herbie Hancock (New York: Rizzoli, 1995). See also Graham Marsh and Glyn Callingham, eds., *Blue Note Album Cover Art: The Ultimate Collection* (San Francisco: Chronicle, 2002).
11 Charles Stewart and Paul Carter Harrison, *Chuck Stewart's Jazz Files* (Boston: New York Graphic Society, 1985).
12 Dennis Stock, *Jazz Street: A Photographic Exploration into the World of Jazz*, Text by Nat Hentoff (Garden City, NY: Doubleday, 1960); Lee Friedlander, *American Musicians* (New York: Distributed Art, 1998).
13 Edition of Contemporary Music (ECM), *Sleeves of Desire: A Cover Story* (Baden: Lars Muller, 1996).
14 Pete Turner, *Color of Jazz: Album Cover Photographs by Pete Turner* (New York: Rizzoli, 2006).
15 Robert Levine, "Sony Taps into Photo Archive as a Resource during Hard Times," *New York Times*, May 29, 2008, www.nytimes.com/2008/05/29/arts/music/29phot.html.; Jon Pareles, *Keeping Time: The Photographs of Don Hunstein* (Chicago: Insight, 2013).
16 Herb Snitzer, *Glorious Days and Nights: A Jazz Memoir* (Jackson, MS: University Press of Mississippi, 2011).
17 Jerry Dantzic and Grayson Dantzic, *Billie Holiday at Sugar Hill* (New York: Thames and Hudson, 2017).
18 Carole Reiff, *Nights at Birdland: Jazz Photographs: 1954–1960* (New York: Simon and Schuster, 1985).
19 Stanley Crouch and Deborah Willis, *One Shot Harris: The Photographs of Charles "Teenie" Harris* (New York: Abrams, 2003).

20 Nuit Banai and Michael Valentine, *Hugh Bell: Between the Raindrops* (New York: Valentine New York, 2006); Edward Steichen, *The Family of Man* (New York: Museum of Modern Art, 1955).
21 Roy DeCarava, *Roy DeCarava: A Retrospective* (New York: Museum of Modern Art, 1996); Roy DeCarava, *The Sound I Saw: Improvisations on a Jazz Theme* (New York: David Zwirner Books, 2019).
22 Wynton Marsalis and Frank Stewart, *Sweet Swing Blues: On the Road* (New York: Thunder's Mouth, 1998).
23 Anthony Barboza and Herb Robinson, eds., *Timeless: Photographs by Kamoinge* (Atglen, PA: Schiffer, 2015).
24 Bob Willoughby, *Jazz in LA* (Kiel: Nieswand Verlag, 1990).
25 Jim Marshall, *Jazz* (San Francisco: Chronicle, 2005).
26 Kathy Sloane, *Keystone Korner: Portrait of a Jazz Club* (Bloomington, IN: Indiana University Press, 2011).
27 Orrin Keepnews and Bill Grauer, Jr., *A Pictorial History of Jazz: People and Places from New Orleans to Modern Jazz* (New York: Crown, 1955); Frank Driggs and Harris Lewine, *Black Beauty, White Heat: A Pictorial History of Classic Jazz, 1920–1950* (New York: Morrow, 1982).
28 Roy DeCarava, *The Sound I Saw: The Jazz Photographs of Roy DeCarava* (New York: Studio Museum of Harlem, 1983).
29 Lee Tanner, *The Jazz Image: Masters of Jazz Photography* (New York: Abrams, 2006).
30 Sam Stephenson, *The Jazz Loft Project: Photographs and Tapes of W. Eugene Smith from 821 Sixth Avenue, 1957–1965* (New York: Knopf, 2009).
31 Elizabeth Pepin Silva and Lewis Watts, *Harlem of the West: The San Francisco Jazz Era* (Berkeley, CA: Heyday, 2020).
32 K. Abé, *Jazz Giants* (New York: Billboard, 1988).
33 Val Wilmer, *The Face of Black Music* (New York: Da Capo, 1976).
34 Gerardo Canella and Jordi Soley, *Jazz Images by Jean-Pierre Leloir* (Barcelona: Elemental, 2010).
35 Mia Fuglsang Holm, *Musical Portraits: Photographs and Reflections by Jan Persson* (Arhaus: Ajour, 2011).
36 Roberto Polillo, *Swing, Bop & Free: Il jazz degli anni '60* (Milano: Marco Polillo, 2006).

Bibliography

Abbott, Lynn and Doug Seroff. *The Original Blues*. Jackson, MS: University Press of Mississippi, 2017.
Abé, K. *Jazz Giants*. New York: Billboard, 1988.
Adorno, Theodor. *Night Music: Essays on Music 1928–1962*. Trans. Wieland Hoban. Calcutta: Seagull, 2017.
Ainsworth, Alan. *Sight Readings: Photographers and American Jazz, 1900–1960*. Bristol, UK: Intellect, 2022.
Akkerman, Gregg. *The Last Balladeer: The Johnny Hartman Story*. Toronto: Scarecrow Press, 2012.
Albertson, Chris. *Bessie Smith*. Revised and expanded edition. New Haven: Yale University Press, 2003.
Alder, David. "Jazzocracy: Jazz, Democracy, and the Creation of a New American Mythology. On Jazz, Hip-Hop and Democracy." *Democratiya* 14 (2008): 157–65.
Alexander, Ben. "'For Posterity': The Personal Audio Recordings of Louis Armstrong." *The American Archivist* 71.1 (2008): 50–86.
Alexander, Elizabeth. "Billy Strayhorn Writes Lush Life." *Ploughshares* 28 (Spring 2002): 10–12.
Alkyer, Frank. "Inside the Detroit Jazz Festival's Bubble." *Down Beat*. September 8, 2020. https://downbeat.com/news/detail/inside-the-detroit-jazz-festivals-bubble.
Als, Hilton. "Foreword." David Margolick. *Strange Fruit: Billie Holiday, Café Society, and an Early Cry for Civil Rights*. Philadelphia: Running Press, 2000. 9–13.
Amaya, Hector. "Racialized Documentary Reception of Ken Burns' *Jazz*." *Television & New Media* 9.2 (2008): 111–30.
Anderson, Nancy. "Aaron Douglas/*The Judgment Day*/1939." *American Paintings, 1900–1945*. NGA Online Editions, https://purl.org/nga/collection/artobject/166490.
Ansermet, Ernst-Alexandre. "Bechet and Jazz Visit Europe, 1919." *Frontiers of Jazz*, 3rd ed. Ed. Ralph de Toledano. Gretna, LA: Pelican, 1994. 111–18.
Apollinaire, Guilliaume. *The Cubist Painters: Aesthetic Meditations*. Berkeley: University of California Press, 2004.

Aristotle. *The Nicomachean Ethics*. Ed. Hugh Tredennick and Jonathan Barnes. New York: Penguin, 1976.
Armstrong, Jennifer. *Sex and the City and Us*. New York: Simon and Schuster, 2018.
Armstrong, Louis. *Swing That Music*. New York: Da Capo, 1993.
Ashe, Bertram D. "On the Jazz Musician's Love/Hate Relationship with the Audience." *Signifyin(g), Sanctifyin', and Slam Dunking: A Reader in African American Expressive Cultures*. Ed. Gena Dagel Caponi. Amherst: University of Massachusetts Press, 1999. 277–89.
Asher, Don. "The Barrier." *The Jazz Fiction Anthology*. Ed. Sascha Feinstein and David Rife. Bloomington, IN: Indiana University Press, 2009. 1–16.
Attali, Jacques. *Noise: The Political Economy of Music*. Trans. Brian Massumi. Minneapolis: University of Minnesota, 1985.
Atkins, E. Taylor. *Blue Nippon: Authenticating Jazz in Japan*. Durham: Duke University Press, 2001.
Auslander, Philip. "Musical Personae." *TDR* 50.1 (2006): 100–19.
Auslander, Philip. *Liveness: Performance in a Mediatized Culture*. 2nd ed. New York: Routledge, 2008.
Avakian, George. Liner notes. *Chicago Jazz. Setting the Tempo: Fifty Years of Great Liner Notes*. Ed. Tom Piazza. New York: Anchor, 1996. 9–24.
Backstein, Karen. "Keeping the Spirit Alive: The Jazz Dance Testament of Mura Dehn," *Representing Jazz*. Ed. Krin Gabbard. Durham: Duke University Press, 1995. 229–46.
Badger, Reid. *A Life in Ragtime: A Biography of James Reese Europe*. New York: Oxford University Press, 2007.
Bakhtin, Mikhail Mikhailovich. *The Dialogic Imagination*. Trans. Caryl Emerson and Michael Holquist. Austin: University of Texas Press, 1981.
Bakhtin, Mikhail Mikhailovich. *Problems of Dostoevsky's Politics*. Ed. and Trans. Caryl Emerson. Minneapolis: University of Minnesota Press, 1984.
Bakhtin, Mikhail Mikhailovich. *Speech Genres & Other Late Essays*. Trans. Vern W. McGee. Ed. Caryl Emerson and Michael Holquist. Austin: University of Texas Press, 1986.
Baldwin, James. "Sonny's Blues." *Partisan Review* 24.3 (1957): 327–58.
Balfour, Katharine Lawrence and Lawrie Balfour. *The Evidence of Things Not Said: James Baldwin and the Promise of American Democracy*. Ithaca: Cornell University Press, 2001.
Balliett, Whitney. Liner notes. Gerry Mulligan Quartet featuring Chet Baker. *Gerry Mulligan Quartet*. Pacific Jazz PJ-1207, 1955.
Balliett, Whitney. *Collected Works: A Journal of Jazz 1954–2000*. London: Granta Books, 2001.
Banai, Nuit and Michael Valentine. *Hugh Bell: Between the Raindrops*. New York: Valentine New York, 2006.
Baraka, Amiri [LeRoi Jones]. *Blues People: The Negro Experience in White America and the Music That Developed From It*. New York: Morrow, 1963.

Baraka, Amiri. "Jazz and the White Critic." *The LeRoi Jones/Amiri Baraka Reader*. Ed. William J. Harris. New York: Thunder's Mouth, 1991. 179–86

Baraka, Amiri. "Hunting Is Not Those Heads on the Wall." *Poetics of the New American Poetry*. Ed. Donald Allen and Warren Tallman. New York: Grove, 1973. 378–81.

Baraka, Amiri. Liner notes. John Coltrane. *Live at Birdland*. Impulse A-50, 1964.

Baraka, Amiri. "Black Art." *Transbluesency: The Selected Poems of Amiri Baraka/LeRoi Jones (1961–1995)*. Ed. Paul Vangelisti. New York: Marsilio Publishers, 1995. 142–43.

Baraka, Amiri. *Home: Social Essays*. New York: Ecco Press, 1998.

Baraka, Amiri. "The Screamers." *The LeRoi Jones/Amiri Baraka Reader*. Ed. William J. Harris. New York: Thunder's Mouth, 1991. 171–77.

Baraka, Amiri. *Black Music*. New York: Morrow, 1968.

Baraka, Amiri. "AM/TRAK." *The LeRoi Jones/Amiri Baraka Reader*. Ed. William J. Harris. New York: Thunder's Mouth, 1991. 267–72.

Baraka, Amiri. "Henry Dumas: Afro-Surreal Expressionist." *Black American Literature Forum* 22.2 (1982): 164–66.

Baraka, Amiri. *Wise, Why's, Y's*. Chicago: Third World Press, 1995.

Barber, Simon. "The Brill Building and the Creative Labour of the Professional Songwriter." *The Cambridge Companion to the Singer-Songwriter*. Ed. Katherine Williams and Justin A. Williams. Cambridge: Cambridge University Press, 2016. 67–77.

Barboza, Anthony and Herb Robinson, eds. *Timeless: Photographs by Kamoinge*. Atglen, PA: Schiffer, 2015.

Barker, Danny. *A Life in Jazz*. Ed. Alyn Shipton. Oxford: Oxford University Press, 1988.

Barlow, William. *Voice Over: The Making of Black Radio*. Philadelphia: Temple University Press, 1999.

Barnet, Charlie & Stanley Dance. *Those Swinging Years: The Autobiography of Charlie Barnet*. 1984. New York: Da Capo, 1992.

Barnett, LaShonda, ed. *I Got Thunder: Black Women Songwriters on Their Craft*. Cambridge, MA: Da Capo Press, 2007.

Barrett, Lindon. *Blackness and Value*. Cambridge: Cambridge University Press, 1998.

Barthes, Roland. "The Death of the Author." In *Image-Music-Text*. 142–48, 1977.

Barthes, Roland. *Image-Music-Text*. Trans. Stephen Heath. London: Fontana, 1977.

Basie, Count, as told to Albert Murray. *Good Morning Blues: The Autobiography of Count Basie*. New York: Da Capo, 1995.

Bauer, William. "Louis Armstrong's 'Skid Dat De Dat': Timbral Organization in an Early Scat Solo." *Jazz Perspectives* 1.2 (2007): 133–65.

Bauman, Richard. *A World of Others' Words*. New York: Wiley, 2004.

Beattie, Keith. *Documentary Screens: Non-Fiction Film and Television*. London: Macmillan Education UK, 2004.

Beavoir, Simone de. *The Mandarins*. Paris: Gallimard, 1954.

Beavoir, Simone de. *America Day By Day*. Trans. Carol Cosman. Berkeley: University of California Press, 1999.
Beavoir, Simone de. *A Translatlantic Love Affair: Letters to Nelson Algren*. New York: New Press, 1998.
Bechet, Sidney. *Treat It Gentle*. 1960. New York: Da Capo, 1978.
Belgrad, Daniel. *The Culture of Spontaneity: Improvisation and the Arts in Postwar America*. Chicago: University of Chicago Press, 1998.
Bentley, Gladys. "I Am a Woman Again." *Ebony*. August 1952. 92–98.
Berendt, Joachim Ernst and Günther Huesmann. *The Jazz Book: From Ragtime to the 21st Century*. 7th ed. Chicago: Lawrence Hill, 2009.
Berger, Edward, David Cayer, Henry Martin, and Dan Morgenstern, eds. *Annual Review of Jazz Studies 12: 2002*. Lanham, MD: Scarecrow Press.
Berklee College of Music. "Berklee Institute of Jazz and Gender Justice," www.berklee.edu/jazz-gender-justice.
Berliner, Paul. *Thinking in Jazz: The Infinite Art of Improvisation*. Chicago: University of Chicago Press, 1994.
Berliner, Sasha. "An Open Letter to Ethan Iverson (and the rest of Jazz Patriarchy)." SashaBerlinerMusic.com. September 21, 2017, www.sashaberlinermusic.com/sociopoliticalcommentary-1/2017/9/21/an-open-letter-to-ethan-iverson-and-the-rest-of-jazz-patriarchy.
Bernhardt, Clyde E.B., as told to Sheldon Harris. *I Remember: Eighty Years of Black Entertainment, Big Bands, and the Blues*. 1986. Philadelphia: University of Pennsylvania Press, 1989.
Beta, Andy. "Kamasi Washington: Becoming (Music From the Netflix Original Documentary)." *Pitchfork*. May 19, 2020. https://pitchfork.com/reviews/albums/kamasi-washington-becoming-music-from-the-netflix-original-documentary/.
Beuttler, Bill. *Make It New: Reshaping Jazz in the 21st Century*. Amherst, MA: Lever Press, 2019.
Billinge, Sam. *The Practical Guide to Documentary Editing: Techniques for TV and Film*. New York: Routledge, 2017.
Blake, Jody. *Le Tumulte Noir: Modernist Art in Jazz-Age Paris 1900–1930*. University Park: Pennsylvania State University Press, 1999.
Bloom, Harold. *The Anxiety of Influence: A Theory of Poetry*. 2nd ed. New York: Oxford University Press, 1997.
Bock, Richard, William Claxton, and Nesuhi Ertegun, eds. *Jazz West Coast: A Portfolio of Photographs by William Claxton*. Hollywood, CA: Linear, 1955.
Bomberger, E. Douglas. *Making Music American: 1917 and the Transformation of Culture*. New York: Oxford University Press, 2018.
Borshuk, Michael. "'The Sound of Jazz as Essential Image:' Television, Performance, and the Modern Jazz Canon." *Jazz Research Journal* 12.1 (2018): 12–35.
Bourdieu, Pierre. *Outline of a Theory of Practice*. Trans. Richard Nice. Cambridge: Cambridge University Press, 1977.

Bourdieu, Pierre. *Distinction: A Social Critique of the Judgment of Taste*. Trans. Richard Nice. New York: Routledge, 1986.

Boyd, Herb. "Setbacks are not defeats for James Carter, Regina Carter." *Down Beat*. July 21, 2020. https://downbeat.com/news/detail/setbacks-defeats-carters.

Brackett, David. *Interpreting Popular Music*. Berkeley: University of California Press, 2000.

Bradford, Perry. *Born with the Blues: Perry Bradford's Own Story*. New York: Oak Publications, 1965.

Braggs, Rashida K. *Jazz Diasporas: Race, Music, and Migration in Post-World War II Paris*. Oakland, CA: University of California Press, 2016.

Bratten, Lola Clare. "Nothin' Could Be Finah: The Dinah Shore Chevy Show." *Small Screens, Big Ideas: Television in the 1950s*. Ed. Janet Thumim. London: I. B. Tauris, 2002. 88–104.

Briggs, Charles L. and Richard Bauman. "Genre, Intertextuality, and Social Power." *Journal of Linguistic Anthropology* 2.2 (1992): 131–72.

Brockhaus, Immanuel. "Organizing Emotions in Time: Klangästhetik und Studiotechnologie im ECM Sound der frühen Jahre, 1970–1980." *European Journal of Musicology* 16.1 (2017): 94–114.

Broecking, Christian. *Dieses unbändige Gefühl der Freiheit: Irène Schweizer – Jazz, Avantgarde, Politik*. Berlin: Broecking Verlag, 2016.

Brooks, Daphne A. *Bodies in Dissent: Spectacular Performances of Race and Freedom, 1850–1910*. Durham: Duke University Press, 2006.

Brooks, Daphne A. "1920, August 10: Mamie Smith becomes the first black woman to make a phonograph record." *A New Literary History of America*. Eds. Greil Marcus and Werner Sollers. Cambridge, MA: Harvard University Press, 2009. 545–50.

Brooks, Daphne A. "Nina Simone's Triple Play." *Callaloo* 34.1 (2011): 176–97.

Brooks, Daphne A. *Liner Notes for the Revolution: The Intellectual Life of Black Feminist Sound*. Cambridge, MA: Harvard University Press, 2021.

Brooks, Gwendolyn. "We Real Cool." *Jazz Poems*. Ed. Kevin Young. New York: Knopf, 2006. 45.

Brooks, Tim. *Lost Sounds: Blacks and the Birth of the Recording Industry, 1890–1919*. Urbana and Chicago: University of Illinois Press, 2004.

Brophy, Philip. "Bring the Noise." *Film Comment* 45.1 (February 2009): 16.

Brothers, Thomas. *Louis Armstrong: Master of Modernism*. New York: Norton, 2014.

Brown, Jayna. "From the Point of View of the Pavement: A Geopolitics of Black Dance." *Big Ears: Listening for Gender in Jazz Studies*. Eds. Nichole T. Rustin and Sherrie Tucker. Durham: Duke University Press, 2008. 157–79.

Brown, Sterling. "Cabaret." *The Collected Poems of Sterling Brown*. Ed. Michael S. Harper. Evanston, IL: TriQuarterly Books, 1980. 111–13.

Brown, Sterling. "Ma Rainey." *The Collected Poems of Sterling A. Brown*. Ed. Michael S. Harper. Evanston, IL: TriQuarterly Books, 1980. 62–63.

Byant, Clora and Buddy Collette et al. eds. *Central Avenue Sounds: Jazz in Los Angeles*. Berkeley: University of California Press, 1998.

Büchmann-Møller, Frank. *You Just Fight For Your Life: The Story of Lester Young.* Westport, CT: Greenwood, 1990.
Budds, Michael J. ed. *Jazz and the Germans: The Influence of 'Hot' American Idioms on 20th Century German Music.* Hillsdale, NY: Pendagron, 2002.
Burley, Dan. *Original Handbook of Harlem Jive.* New York: Dan Burley, 1944.
Burley, Dan. *Dan Burley's Jive.* Ed. Thomas Aiello. DeKalb, IL: Northern Illinois University Press, 2009.
Burroughs, William S. [William Lee]. *Junkie: Confessions of an Unredeemed Drug Addict [Junky].* New York: Ace, 1953.
Bushell, Gavin, as told to Mark Tucker. *Jazz from the Beginning.* 1988. New York: Da Capo, 1998.
Calloway, Cab. *Cab Calloway's Cat-ologue: A Hepster's Dictionary.* New York: Cab Calloway, Inc., 1938.
Calloway, Cab and Bryant Rollins. *Of Minnie the Moocher and Me.* New York: Thomas Y. Crowell Company, 1976.
Calt, Stephen. *Barrelhouse Words: A Blues Dialect Dictionary.* Urbana: University of Illinois Press, 2009.
Campbell, James. *Paris Interzone.* London: Secker and Warburg, 1994.
Camus, Albert. *The Rebel: An Essay on Man in Revolt.* 1951. New York: Vintage, 1991.
Canella, Gerardo and Jordi Soley. *Jazz Images by Jean-Pierre Leloir.* Barcelona: Elemental, 2010.
Carby, Hazel. *Race Men.* Cambridge, MA: Harvard University Press, 1998.
Cawthra. Benjamin. *Blue Notes in Black and White: Photography and Jazz.* Chicago: University of Chicago Press, 2011.
Chanan, Michael. "Music, Documentary, Music Documentary." *The Documentary Film Book.* Ed. Brian Winston, London: Bloomsbury, 2019. 337–44.
Charters, Ann, ed. *Jack Kerouac: Selected Letters, 1940–1956.* New York: Penguin 1996.
Charters, Samuel B. and Leonard Kunstadt. *Jazz: A History of the New York Scene.* Garden City, NY: Doubleday, 1962.
Chernoff, John Miller. *African Rhythm and African Sensibility: Aesthetics and Social Action in African Musical Idioms.* Chicago: University of Chicago Press, 1979.
Chilton, John. *Sidney Bechet: Wizard of Jazz.* 1987. New York: Da Capo, 1996.
Chinen, Nate. "SF Jazz Center Opens in California." *New York Times,* January 24, 2013, http://artsbeat.blogs.nytimes.com/2013/01/24/sfjazz-center-opens-as-temple-of-jazz-in-california/.
Chuen, Marine Wong Kwok. "Alexei Aigui on Scoring the Breakthrough Documentary I Am Not Your Negro." *Score It Magazine.* February 24, 2017. http://magazine.scoreit.org/interview-alexei-aigui-not-negro/.
Claxton, William. *Jazz Seen.* Köln: Taschen, 2000.
Claxton, William and Hitoshi Namakata. *Jazz West Coast: Artwork of Pacific Jazz Records.* Tokyo: Bijutsu Shupan-Sha, 1992.
Claxton, William and Joachim E. Berendt. *Jazzlife: A Journey Across America for Jazz in 1960.* Köln: Taschen, 2005.

Clayton, Buck, assisted by Nancy M. Elliott. *Buck Clayton's Jazz World.* 1986. New York: Oxford University Press, 1989.

Clowney, David and Robert Rawlins. "Pushing the Limits: Risk and Accomplishment in Musical Performance." *Contemporary Aesthetics* 12.1 (2014): https://digitalcommons.risd.edu/liberalarts_contempaesthetics/vol12/iss1/15/.

Clytus, Radiclani. "Committed to the Image." *The Sound I Saw: Improvisation on a Jazz Theme.* Ed. Roy DeCarava. New York: David Zwirner Books, 2019.

Cohan, Brad. "Mostly Other People Do the Killing interview: 'If we wanted to make people mad, that's easy.'" *Time Out.* November 14, 2014, www.timeout.com/newyork/music/mostly-other-people-do-the-killing-interview-if-we-wanted-to-make-people-mad-thats-easy.

Cohen, Thomas. *Playing to the Camera: Musicians and Musical Performance in Documentary Cinema.* New York: Columbia University Press, 2012.

Coleman, Julie. *The Life of Slang.* New York: Oxford University Press, 2012.

Coleman, Ornette. Liner notes. *The Shape of Jazz to Come.* Atlantic SD-1317, 1959.

Coleman, Ornette. Liner notes. Ornette Coleman. *Change of the Century.* Atlantic 1327, 1960.

Coleman, Ornette. "Harmolodic = Highest Instinct: Something to Think About." *Free Spirits: Annals of the Insurgent Imagination.* Ed. Paul Buhle, et al. San Francisco: City Lights, 1982. 117–20.

Coleman, Ornette. "Prime Time for Harmolodics." *Down Beat.* July 1983. 54–55.

Colin, Paul. *Josephine Baker and La Revue Nègre: Paul Colin's Lithographs of Le Tumulte Noir in Paris, 1927.* New York: Harry Abrams, 1998.

Collier, James Lincoln. *Jazz: The American Theme Song.* New York: Oxford University Press, 1995.

Collins, John. *West African Pop Roots.* Philadelphia: Temple University Press, 1992.

Coltrane, John. Liner notes: "Dear Listener." *A Love Supreme.* Impulse A-77, 1965.

Colomby, Harry. Liner notes. Thelonious Monk. *Misterioso.* Columbia CL 2416, 1965.

Condon, Eddie, with Thomas Sugrue. *We Called It Music: A Generation of Jazz.* 1947. New York: Da Capo, 1992.

Conover, Willis. Liner notes. Ahmad Jamal Trio. *Volume IV.* Argo LP 636, 1958.

Conover, Willis. Liner notes. Kenny Clarke and Francy Boland. *Jazz is Universal.* 1962. Rhino WPCR-27191 CD, 2012.

Conrad, Earl. Foreword. *Dan Burley's Jive* by Dan Burley. Ed. Thomas Aiello. DeKalb, IL: Northern Illinois University Press, 2009. 5–10.

"Cool." *Oxford English Dictionary,* www.oed.com/viewdictionaryentry/Entry/40978.

Cooper, Brittney. "'A'n't I a Lady?': Race Women, Michelle Obama, and the Ever-Expanding Democratic Imagination." *MELUS* 35.4 (2010): 39–57.

Corner, John. "Biography Within the Documentary Frame: A Note." *Framework: The Journal of Cinema and Media* 43.1 (2002): 95–101.

Corner, John. "Sounds Real: Music and Documentary." *Popular Music* 21.3 (2002): 357–66.

Cortez, Jayne. *Jazz Fan Looks Back*. New York: Hanging Loose Press, 2002.
Cowley, Julian. "The Art of the Improvisers – Jazz and Fiction in Post-Bebop America." *New Comparison* 6 (1988): 194–204.
Cramer, Stephen, ed. *Turn It Up! Music in Poetry from Jazz to Hip-Hop*. West Battleboro, VT: Green Writers Press, 2020.
Creeley, Robert. "Introduction." Charles Olson. *Selected Writings*. New York: New Directions, 1966. 1–10.
Creeley, Robert. "Introduction." *Book of Blues* Ed. Jack Kerouac. New York: Penguin, 1995. ix–xiii.
Cronin, Paul, ed. *A Time to Stir: Columbia '68*. New York: Columbia University Press, 2018.
Crook, Hal. *How to Improvise*. Rottenburg, Germany: Advance Music, 1991.
Crouch, Stanley. Liner notes. Thelonious Monk. *At the Five Spot*. Milestone M-47043, 1977.
Crouch, Stanley. Liner notes. Booker Ervin. *The Freedom and Space Sessions*. 1979. *Setting the Tempo: Fifty Years of Great Jazz Liner Notes*. Ed. Tom Piazza. New York: Anchor, 1996. 248–55.
Crouch, Stanley. Liner notes. Wynton Marsalis. *Wynton Marsalis*. CBS FC 37574, 1982.
Crouch, Stanley and Deborah Willis. *One Shot Harris: The Photographs of Charles "Teenie" Harris*. New York: Abrams, 2003.
cummings, e.e. "God Pity Me Whom(God Distinctly Has)." *Jazz Poetry*. Ed. Kevin Young. New York: Knopf, 2006. 31.
Cuscuna, Michael, Charlie Lourie, and Oscar Schnider. *The Blue Note Years: The Jazz Photography of Francis Wolff*. Foreword by Herbie Hancock. New York: Rizzoli, 1995.
Dantzic, Jerry and Grayson Dantzic. *Billie Holiday at Sugar Hill*. New York: Thames and Hudson, 2017.
Davies, Stephen. *Musical Works and Performances: A Philosophical Exploration*. Oxford: Clarendon, 2001.
Davis, Angela Y. *Blues Legacies and Black Feminism*. New York: Pantheon, 1998.
Davis Miles, with Quincy Troupe. *Miles: The Autobiography*. New York: Simon and Schuster, 1990.
de Barros, Paul. "SF Jazz Center a West Coast oasis for the genre." *Seattle Times*. February 3, 2013, www.seattletimes.com/entertainment/sf-jazz-center-a-west-coast-oasis-for-the-genre/.
DeCarava, Roy. *The Sound I Saw: The Jazz Photographs of Roy DeCarava*. New York: Studio Museum of Harlem, 1983.
DeCarava, Roy. *Roy DeCarava: A Retrospective*. New York: Museum of Modern Art, 1996.
DeCarava, Roy. *The Sound I Saw: Improvisation on a Jazz Theme*. New York: David Zwirner Books, 2019.
DeCarava, Sherry Turner. "Pages from a Notebook." *Roy DeCarava: A Retrospective*. Ed. Peter Galassi. New York: The Museum of Modern Art, 1996. 41–59.
Deleuze, Gilles. *Negotiations*. Trans. Martin Joughin. New York: Columbia University Press, 1995.

Derricotte, Toi. *The Black Notebooks: An Interior Journey.* New York: Norton, 1997.
Desmangles, Justin. "Bob Kaufman's African Dream." *Open Space.* November 7, 2017. https://openspace.sfmoma.org/2017/11/bob-kaufmans-african-dream/.
DeVeaux, Scott. "Constructing the Jazz Tradition: Jazz Historiography." *Black American Literature Forum* 25.3 (1991): 525–60.
DeVeaux, Scott. *The Birth of Bebop: A Social and Musical History.* Berkeley: University of California Press, 1997.
Dinerstein, Joel. "Lester Young and the Birth of Cool." *Signifyin(g), Sanctifyin' and Slam-dunking.* Ed. Gena Dagel Caponi. Amherst: University of Massachusetts Press, 1999. 239–76.
Dinerstein, Joel. *Swinging the Machine: Modernity, Technology, and African-American Culture Between the World Wars.* Amherst: University of Massachusetts Press, 2003.
Dinerstein, Joel. *The Origins of Cool in Postwar America.* Chicago: University of Chicago Press, 2017.
Dodds, William "Baby," as told to Larry Gara. *The Baby Dodds Story.* 1959. Alma, MI: Rebeats, 2002.
Dokosi, Michael Eli. "How a photo of Billy Eckstine offended the white community." *Face2FaceAfrica.* March 24, 2020. https://face2faceafrica.com/article/how-a-photo-of-singer-billy-eckstine-offended-the-white-community.
Dollar, Steve. "'…The Parts That Were Left out of the Ken Burns Documentary': Tom Surgal on the 'Historical Corrective' That Is His Free Jazz Documentary, Fire Music." *Filmmaker Magazine.* September 10, 2021. https://filmmakermagazine.com/112250-the-parts-that-were-left-out-of-the-ken-burns-documentary-tom-surgal-on-the-historical-corrective-that-is-is-free-jazz-documentary-fire-music/.
Doyle, Roddy. *Oh, Play That Thing.* New York: Viking, 2004.
Dregni, Michael. *Django: The Life and Music of a Gypsy Legend.* New York: Oxford University Press, 2004.
Driggs, Frank and Harris Lewine. *Black Beauty, White Heat: A Pictorial History of Classic Jazz, 1920–1950.* New York: Morrow, 1982.
Du Bois, W.E.B. *The Souls of Black Folk.* 1903. Oxford: Oxford University Press, 2007.
Duffus, Matthew. "Seeing Is Believing? Reading Billie Holiday Through Photography." *Billie Holiday: Essays on the Artistry and Legacy.* Eds. Michael V. Perez and Jessica McKee. Jefferson, NC: McFarland, 2019. 97–111.
Dunbar, Paul Laurence. "The Poet." *The Collected Poetry of Paul Laurence Dunbar.* Ed. Joanne M. Braxton. Charlottesville: University of Virginia Press, 1993. 191.
Dunkel, Mario. "Marshall Winslow Stearns and the Politics of Jazz Historiography." *American Music* 30.4 (2012): 468–504.
Dunkel, Mario. "Constructing the American Hugues Panassié," *America and the Musical Unconscious.* Eds. Julius Greve and Sascha Pöhlmann. New York: Atropos, 2015. 93–104.
Earle, Susan ed. *Aaron Douglas: African American Modernist.* New Haven: Yale University Press, 2007.

Edition of Contemporary Music (ECM). *Sleeves of Desire: A Cover Story*. Baden: Lars Muller, 1996.
Edwards, Brent Hayes. "Louis Armstrong and the Syntax of Scat." *Critical Inquiry* 28.3 (2002): 618–49.
Edwards, Brent Hayes. *Epistrophies: Jazz and the Literary Imagination*. Cambridge: Harvard University Press, 2017.
Elam, Harry J., Jr. "The Device of Race: An Introduction." *African American Performance and Theater History: A Critical Reader*. Eds. Harry J. Elam, Jr. and David Krasner. Oxford: Oxford University Press, 2001. 3–16.
Ellington, Duke. "Ellington on Gershwin's *Porgy and Bess* – and a Response from the Office of Irving Mills." *The Duke Ellington Reader*. Ed. Mark Tucker. New York: Oxford University Press, 1993. 116–17.
Ellington, Duke. *Music Is My Mistress*. New York: Da Capo, 1976.
Ellison, Ralph. "The Charlie Christian Story." In *Shadow and Act*, 233–40, 1964.
Ellison, Ralph. "The World and the Jug." *The Collected Essays of Ralph Ellison*. Ed. John F. Callahan. New York: Modern Library, 2003. 155–88.
Ellison, Ralph. *Shadow and Act*. New York: Random House, 1964.
Ellison, Ralph. *Living With Music: Ralph Ellison's Jazz Writings*. New York: Modern Library, 2002.
Elsdon, Peter. "Listening in the Gaze: The Body in Keith Jarrett's Solo Piano Improvisations." *Music and Gesture*. Eds. Anthony Gritten and Elaine King. Aldershot: Ashgate, 2006. 192–207.
Elsdon, Peter. "The Potential of the Jazz Record." *Darmstädter Beiträge Zur Jazzforschung*. Ed. Wolfram Knauer. Wolke Verlagsgesellschaft, 2014. 109–118.
Enstice, Wayne and Janis Stockhouse, eds. *Jazzwomen: Conversations With Twenty-One Musicians*. Bloomington: Indiana University Press, 2004.
e/Prime Media & Randy Fertel, "Musical Threads in Early Jazz." *A Closer Walk*. https://acloserwalknola.com/historical-context/musical-threads-early-jazz/.
Evans, Bill. Liner notes. Miles Davis. *Kind of Blue*. Columbia CS 8163, 1959.
Evans, David. "High Water Everywhere: Blues and Gospel Commentary on the 1927 Mississippi River Flood." *Nobody Knows Where the Blues Come From: Lyrics and History*. Ed. Robert Springer. Jackson, MS: University Press of Mississippi, 2006. 3–75.
Ewell, Philip A. "Music Theory and the White Racial Frame." *Music Theory Online* 26.2 (2020), https://mtosmt.org/issues/mto.20.26.2/mto.20.26.2.ewell.html.
Fagge, Roger. "The Politics, Aesthetics and Dissonance of Music in Everyday Life." *Jazz Research Journal* 13.1–2 (2019): 7–18.
Farrington, Holly E. "Narrating the Jazz Life: Three Approaches to Jazz Autobiography." *Popular Music and Society* 29.3 (2006): 375–86.
Faulkner, Anne Shaw. "Does Jazz Put the Sin in Syncopation?" *Keeping Time: Readings in Jazz History*. 2nd ed. Ed. Robert Walser. New York: Oxford University Press, 2014. 26–29.
Feather, Leonard. Liner notes. Art Blakey Quintet. *A Night at Birdland*. Blue Note BLP 5037, 1954.

Feather, Leonard. Liner notes. Paul Chambers. *Whims of Chambers.* Blue Note BLP 1534, 1957.
Feather, Leonard. Liner notes. Cannonball Adderley, *Somethin' Else.* Blue Note BLP 1595, 1958.
Feather, Leonard. Liner notes. Bud Powell. *The Scene Changes.* Blue Note BLP 4009, 1959.
Feather, Leonard. Liner notes. Lee Morgan. *The Sidewinder.* Blue Note BLP 4157, 1964.
Featherstone, Mike. *Undoing Culture: Globalization, Postmodernism and Identity.* London: Sage, 1995.
Feinstein, Sascha. *Jazz Poetry: From the 1920s to the Present.* Westport, CT: Greenwood, 1997.
Feinstein, Sascha. *A Bibliographic Guide to Jazz Poetry.* Westport, CT: Greenwood Press, 1998.
Feinstein, Sascha and Yusef Komunyakaa, eds. *The Jazz Poetry Anthology.* Bloomington, IN: Indiana University Press, 1991.
Feinstein, Sascha and Yusef Komunyakaa, eds. *The Second Set.* Bloomington, IN: Indiana University Press, 1996.
Ferguson, Roderick A. *Aberrations in Black: Toward a Queer of Color Critique.* Minneapolis: University of Minnesota Press, 2003.
Finely, Cheryl. "The Mask as Muse: The Influence of African Art on the Life and Career of Lois Mailou Jones." *Lois Mailou Jones: A Life in Vibrant Color.* Ed. Carla M. Hanzel. Charlotte, NC: Mint Museum of Art, 2009. 50–73.
Finkelstein, Sidney. *Jazz: A People's Music.* New York: The Citadel Press, 1948.
Fischlin, Daniel, Ajay Heble, and George Lipsitz. *The Fierce Urgency of Now.* Durham, NC: Duke University Press, 2013.
Fitzgerald, F. Scott. *Tales of the Jazz Age.* New York: Vintage, 2010.
Foster, George, as told to Tom Stoddard. *The Autobiography of Pops Foster.* San Francisco: Backbeat, 2005.
Frank, Arthur W. *The Wounded Storyteller: Body, Illness, and Ethics.* Chicago: University of Chicago Press, 1997.
Frey, William H. "The New Great Migration: Black Americans Return to the South, 1965–2000." The Brookings Institution, May 2004, 1–3.
Friedlander, Lee. *American Musicians.* New York: Distributed Art, 1998.
Friedwald, Will. *Sinatra! The Song Is You.* New York: Da Capo, 1997.
Frisch, Walter. *Arlen & Harburg's Over the Rainbow.* New York: Oxford University Press, 2017.
Fuller, Richard Buckminster. *Utopia or Oblivion: The Prospects for Humanity.* New York: Bantam, 1969.
Fuller, Richard Buckminster. *Earth Inc.* New York: Doubleday/Anchor, 1973.
Gabbard, Krin. "The Quoter and His Culture." *Jazz in Mind: Essays on the History and Meaning of Jazz.* Eds. Reginald T. Buckner and Steven Weiland. Detroit: Wayne State University Press, 1991. 92–111.
Gabbard, Krin. *Jammin' at the Margins: Jazz and the American Cinema.* Chicago: University of Chicago Press, 1996.

Gabbard, Krin. "The Word Jazz." *The Cambridge Companion to Jazz*. Eds. Mervyn Cooke and David Horn. Cambridge: Cambridge University Press, 2002. 1–6.

Gabbard, Krin. *Black Magic: White Hollywood and African American Culture*. New Brunswick: Rutgers University Press, 2004.

Gabbard, Krin. *Better Git It in Your Soul: An Interpretive Biography of Charles Mingus*. Berkeley: University of California Press, 2016.

Gabbard, Krin. "Syncopated Women: Gender and Jazz History in 1942 Hollywood." *Jazz @ 100: An Alternative to a Story of Jazz Heroes*. Ed. Wolfram Knauer. Darmstadt, Germany: Wolke Verlag Hofheim, 2018. 155–65.

Garber, Eric. "Gladys Bentley: The Bulldagger Who Sang the Blues." *OutLook: National Lesbian and Gay Quarterly* 1 (1988): 52–61.

Garber, Eric. "A Spectacle in Color: The Lesbian and Gay Subculture of Jazz Age Harlem." *Hidden from History: Reclaiming the Gay and Lesbian Past*. Eds. Martin Bauml Duberman, Martha Vicinus, and George Chauncey, Jr. New York: New American Library, 1989. 318–31.

Garber, Frederick. "Fabulating Jazz." *Representing Jazz*. Ed. Krin Gabbard. Durham: Duke University Press, 1995. 70–103.

Garber, Michael G. "Eepha-Soffa-Dill and Eephing: Found in Ragtime, Jazz, and Country Music, from Broadway to a Texas Plantation." *American Music* 35.3 (2017): 343–74.

Garon, Paul and Beth. *Woman with Guitar: Memphis Minnie's Blues*. New York: Da Capo, 1992.

Gates, Henry Louis, Jr. *The Signifying Monkey: A Theory of African-American Literary Criticism*. New York: Oxford University Press, 1988.

Gebhardt, Nicholas and Roger Fagge, eds. Special issue: "Jazz and Everyday Aesthetics." *Jazz Research Journal* 13: 1–2 (2019).

Gendron, Bernard. *From Montmartre to the Mudd Club: Popular Music and the Avant-Garde*. Chicago: University of Chicago Press, 2002.

Gennari, John. "Jazz Criticism: Its Development and Ideologies," *Black American Literature Forum* 25.3 (1991): 449–523.

Gennari, John. "But Is It Jazz?" *Reviews in American History* 23.1 (1995): 91–97.

Gennari, John. *Blowin' Hot and Cool: Jazz and Its Critics*. Chicago: University of Chicago Press, 2006.

Gennari, John. "'Wacky Post-Fluxus Revolutionary Mixed Media Shenanigans': Rethinking Jazz and Jazz Studies Through Jason Moran's Multimedia Performance." *The Routledge Companion to Jazz Studies*. Eds. Nicholas Gebhardt, Nichole Rustin-Pascal, and Tony Whyton. New York: Routledge, 2019. 117–28.

Giddens, Anthony. *Modernity and Self-Identity: Self and Society in the Late Modern Age*. Stanford: Stanford University Press, 1991.

Giddins, Gary. *Satchmo: The Genius of Louis Armstrong*. Cambridge, MA: Da Capo Press, 1988.

Giddins, Gary. *Visions of Jazz: The First Century*. New York: Oxford University Press, 1998.

Giddins, Gary. "Introduction." *Raise Up Off Me: A Portrait of Hampton Hawes.* 1974. Eds. Hampton Hawes and Don Asher. New York: Thunder's Mouth, 2001. v–xiii.

Gilbert, Andrew. "In The Bay Area, A New Jazz Mecca." *Jazz Times* (January/February 2013): 11–12.

Gillespie, Dizzy with Al Fraser. *To Be Or Not To Bop.* New York: Da Capo, 1979.

Gilroy, Paul. *The Black Atlantic: Modernity and Double Consciousness.* London: Verso, 1993.

Ginsberg, Allen. *Howl and Other Poems.* San Francisco: City Lights Publishers, 2002.

Gioia, Ted. *The Imperfect Art: Reflections on Jazz and Modern Culture.* New York: Oxford University Press, 1990.

Gioia, Ted. *The History of Jazz.* 2nd ed. New York: Oxford University Press, 2011.

Gioia, Ted. *The Jazz Standards: A Guide to the Repertoire.* New York: Oxford University Press, 2012.

Gioia, Ted. *How To Listen To Jazz.* New York: Basic Books, 2016.

Gioia, Ted. "When They Had A Contest to Rename Jazz." *The Honest Broker.* June 7, 2022. https://tedgioia.substack.com/p/when-they-had-a-contest-to-rename.

Gitler, Ira. Liner notes. Modern Jazz Quartet. *Django.* Prestige LP 7057, 1956.

Gitler, Ira. Liner notes. Sonny Rollins. *Saxophone Colossus.* Prestige LP 7079, 1957.

Gitler, Ira. "Trane on the Track." *Down Beat.* October 16, 1958. 16–17.

Gitler, Ira. Liner notes. Dexter Gordon. *Gettin' Around.* Blue Note BLP 4204, 1966.

Gitler, Ira. Liner notes. Wes Montgomery. *Down Here on the Ground.* A&M Records SP-3006, 1968.

Gitler, Ira. Liner notes. Al Cohn and Zoot Sims. *Body and Soul. Setting the Tempo: Fifty Years of Great Jazz Liner Notes.* Ed. Tom Piazza. New York: Anchor, 1996. 120–26.

Givan, Benjamin. "Gunther Schuller and the Challenge of Sonny Rollins: Stylistic Context, Intentionality, and Jazz Analysis." *Journal of the American Musicological Society* 67.1 (2014): 167–237.

Gleason, Ralph J. Liner notes. Nat King Cole and His Trio. *After Midnight.* Capitol W-782, 1956.

Gleason, Ralph J. Liner notes. Miles Davis. *In Person: Saturday Night at the Blackhawk, San Francisco, Volume II.* Columbia CS 8470, 1961.

Godsall, Jonathan. *Reeled In: Pre-Existing Music in Narrative Film.* New York: Routledge, 2018.

Gold, Robert S. *A Jazz Lexicon.* New York: Knopf, 1964.

Goldstein, Howard. "Crooning." *Grove Music Online,* www-oxfordmusiconline-com.exlibris.colgate.edu/grovemusic/view/10.1093/gmo/9781561592630.001.0001/omo-9781561592630-e-0000006867?rskey=bJFMeF&result=1.

Gonzales, Babs. *I, Paid My Dues.* East Orange: Expubidence Publishing Corp, 1967.

Gopnik, Blake. *Warhol*. New York: Ecco, 2020.
Gordon, Maxine. *Sophisticated Giant: The Life and Legacy of Dexter Gordon*. Oakland, CA: University of California Press, 2018.
Gottlieb, William P. *The Golden Age of Jazz*. New York: Simon and Schuster, 1979.
Govind, Arathi. "'An Undeniable Presence': Racial justice work among South Asian American Musicians." Ph.D. dissertation, University of California at Berkeley, 2019.
Gracyk, Theodore. "Jazz After *Jazz*: Ken Burns and the Construction of Jazz History." *Philosophy and Literature* 26.1 (2002): 173–87.
Grandt, Jürgen E. *Gettin' Around: Jazz, Script, Transnationalism*. Athens: University of Georgia Press, 2018.
Gray, Herman. *Watching Race. Television and the Struggle for Blackness*. Minneapolis: University of Minnesota Press, 2004.
Gray, Herman. "The Politics of Representation in Network Television." *Channeling Blackness: Studies on Television and Race in America*. Ed. Darnell Hunt. New York: Oxford University Press, 2005. 155–74.
Green, Benny. Liner notes. Coleman Hawkins. *Sirius. Setting the Tempo: Fifty Years of Great Jazz Liner Notes*. Ed. Tom Piazza. New York: Anchor, 1996. 193–96.
Grierson, John. "The Documentary Producer." *Cinema Quarterly* 2.1 (1933): 7–9.
Griffin, Farah Jasmine. *If You Can't Be Free, Be a Mystery: In Search of Billie Holiday*. New York: The Free Press, 2001.
Griffin, Farah Jasmine and Salim Washington. *Clawing at the Limits of Cool: Miles Davis, John Coltrane, and the Greatest Jazz Collaboration Ever*. New York: St. Martin's Press, 2008.
Guattari, Felix. *The Three Ecologies*. Trans. Ian Pindar and Paul Sutton. London: Continuum, 2007.
Gussow, Adam. "'Shoot Myself a Cop': Mamie Smith's 'Crazy Blues' as Social Text." *Callaloo* 25.1 (2002): 8–44.
Hall, Stuart. "What Is This 'Black' in Black Popular Culture?" *Black Popular Culture*. Ed. Gina Dent. Seattle: Bay Press, 1992. 21–33.
Halligan, Benjamin, Robert Edgar, and Kirsty Fairclough-Isaacs, eds. *The Music Documentary: Acid Rock to Electropop*. New York: Routledge, 2013.
Hampton, Lionel, with James Haskins. *Hamp: An Autobiography*. New York: Warner, 1989.
Harap, Louis. "The Case for Hot Jazz." *Musical Quarterly* 27.1 (1941): 47–61.
"Harlem House Parties Inspire New Play." *Negro World*. February 9, 1929. 7.
Harlos, Christopher. "Jazz Autobiography: Theory, Practice, Politics." *Representing Jazz*. Eds. Krin Gabbard. Durham: Duke University Press, 1995. 131–66.
Harney, Stephano and Fred Moten. *The Undercommons: Fugitive Study and Black Study*. Wivenhoe, UK: Minor Compositions, 2013.
Harper, Michael S. *Dear John, Dear Coltrane*. Pittsburgh: University of Pittsburgh Press, 1970.
Harrod, James A. *Stars of Jazz: A Complete History of the Innovative Television Series, 1956–1958*. Jefferson, NC: McFarland, 2020.

Harrington, Richard. "Wynton Marsalis, Young Lion of Jazz." *Washington Post.* December 15, 1984. www.washingtonpost.com/archive/lifestyle/1984/12/15/wynton-marsalis-young-lion-of-jazz/85901b90-3f36-4bd7-b300-0a9ca6e67240/.

Harris, Sheldon. *Blues Who's Who: A Biographical Dictionary of Blues Singers.* 1979. New York: Da Capo, 1981.

Harrison, Helen A. "Jackson Pollock and Jazz: Imitation or Inspiration." Unpublished paper. www.academia.edu/10164140/Jackson_Pollock_and_Jazz_Inspiration_or_Imitation.

Hart, James D. "Jazz Jargon." *American Speech* 7.4 (1932): 241–54.

Haufman, Bo. "Ray Mitchell." Duke Ellington Society of Sweden *Bulletin.* 27.4 (2019): 11.

Heble, Ajay. *Landing on the Wrong Note: Jazz, Dissonance, and Critical Practice.* New York: Routledge, 2000.

Heble, Ajay. "Introduction." *Classroom Action: Human Rights, Critical Activism, and Community-Based Education.* Ed. Ajay Heble. Toronto: University of Toronto Press, 2017. 3–38.

Heile, Björn, Peter Elsdon, and Jenny Doctor, eds. *Watching Jazz. Encounters with Jazz Performance on Screen.* New York: Oxford University Press, 2016.

Hentoff, Nat. "Pres." *A Lester Young Reader.* Ed. Lewis Porter. Washington, DC: Smithsonian Press, 1991. 157–64.

Hentoff, Nat. Liner notes. Charles Mingus. *The Clown.* Atlantic Records 1260, 1957.

Hentoff, Nat. Liner notes. Ornette Coleman. *Tomorrow is the Question.* Contemporary Records M 3569, 1959.

Hentoff, Nat. Liner notes. Max Roach. *We Insist! Max Roach's Freedom Now Suite.* Candid Records CJM 8002, 1961.

Hentoff, Nat. Liner notes. Donald Byrd. *A New Perspective.* Blue Note 84124, 1964.

Hentoff, Nat. *The Jazz Life.* London: Panther Books, 1964.

Hentoff, Nat. "This Cat Needs No Pulitzer Prize." 1965. *The Duke Ellington Reader.* Ed. Mark Tucker. New York: Oxford University Press, 1993. 362–68.

Hentoff, Nat. "Huckleberry Dracula, Jazz, and Public TV." *The Village Voice.* July 31, 1978. 30.

Herman, Woody & Stuart Troup. *The Woodchopper's Ball: The Autobiography of Woody Herman.* New York: Limelight, 1994.

Hersch, Charles. *Democratic Artworks: Politics and the Arts from Trilling to Dylan.* Albany: State University of New York Press, 1998.

Hersch, Charles. *Subversive Sounds: Race and the Birth of Jazz in New Orleans.* Chicago: University of Chicago Press, 2007.

Hersch, Charles. "Reconstructing the Jazz Tradition." *Jazz Research Journal* 2.1 (2008): 7–28.

Hersch, Charles. "Unfinalizable: Dialog and Self-Expression in Jazz." *The Routledge Companion to Jazz Studies.* Eds. Nicholas Gebhardt, Nichole Rustin-Paschal, and Tony Whyton. New York: Routledge, 2018. 367–76.

Herzog, Amy. "Discordant Visions: The Peculiar Musical Images of the Soundies Jukebox Film." *American Music* 22.1 (2004): 27–39.

Heyman, Barbara. "Stravinsky and Ragtime." *The Musical Quarterly* 68.4 (Oct. 1982): 543–62.

Himes, Chester. *A Rage in Harlem*. 1957. London: Penguin, 2011.

Hinton, Milt & David G. Berger. *Bass Line: The Stories and Photographs of Milt Hinton*. Philadelphia: Temple University Press, 1988.

Hinton, Milt, David G. Berger, and Holly Maxson. *OverTime: The Jazz Photographs of Milt Hinton*. San Francisco: Pomegranate, 1991.

"History of Jazz at Lincoln Center." http://jazz.org/history.

"A History as Rich as Jazz Itself." *Down Beat*, https://downbeat.com/site/about/P6.

"History of the Record Industry, 1920s–1950s." *Medium*. June 8, 2014. https://medium.com/@Vinylmint/history-of-the-record-industry-1920-1950s-6d491d7cb606.

Hobsbawm, Eric. [Francis Newton]. *The Jazz Scene*. London: MacGibbon & Kee, 1959.

Hodeir, André. *Jazz: Its Evolution and Essence*. New York: Grove Press, 1956.

Hoffman, Bernd. *Rhythmen der Zeit – Jazz in Film und Fernsehen*. Westerkappeln: DerWulff, 2019.

Hogg, Bennett. "Enactive Consciousness, Intertextuality, and Musical Free Improvisation." *Music and Consciousness: Philosophical, Psychological, and Cultural Perspectives*. Eds. David Clarke and Eric Clarke. New York: Oxford University Press, 2011. 79–93.

Hogg, Richard M. *The Cambridge History of the English Language*. New York: Cambridge University Press, 1992.

Holbrook, Morris. *Music, Movies, Meanings, and Markets: Cinemajazzamatazz*. New York: Routledge, 2011.

Holiday, Billie, with William Dufty. *Lady Sings the Blues*. New York: Broadway Books, 2006.

Holm, Mia Fuglsang. *Musical Portraits: Photographs and Reflections by Jan Persson*. Arhaus: Ajour, 2011.

Holmes, John Clellon. *Go*. 1952. New York: Thunder's Mouth Press, 1997.

Holmes, John Clellon. *The Horn*. New York: Random House, 1958.

Hood, Stuart and Thalia Tabary-Peterssen, *On Television*. London: Pluto Press, 1997.

hooks, bell. "Performance Practice as a Site of Opposition." *Let's Get It On: The Politics of Black Performance*. Ed. Catherine Ugwu. Seattle: Bay Press, 1995. 210–19.

Horn, David. "The Identity of Jazz." *The Cambridge Companion to Jazz*. Eds. Mervyn Cooke and David Horn. Cambridge University Press, 2003. 9–32.

Horne, Gerald. *Jazz and Justice: Racism and the Political Economy of the Music*. New York: Monthly Review Press, 2019.

Hölzl, Ingrid. "Moving Stills: Images That Are No Longer Immobile." *Photographies* 3.1 (2010): 99–108.

Hrebeniak, Michael. *Action Writing: Jack Kerouac's Wild Form*. Carbondale: Southern Illinois University Press, 2006.

Hrebeniak, Michael. "Jazz and the Beat Generation." *The Cambridge Companion to the Beat Generation*. Ed. Steven Belletto. Cambridge: Cambridge University Press, 2017. 250–64.

Hughes, Langston. "The Negro Artist and the Racial Mountain." *Within the Circle: An Anthology of African American Literary Criticism from the Harlem Renaissance to the Present*. Ed. Angelyn Mitchell. Durham: Duke University Press, 1994. 55–59.

Hughes, Langston. *The Weary Blues*. 1926. New York: Knopf, 2017.

Hughes, Langston. "Rent Party Shout: For a Lady Dancer." *The Collected Poems of Langston Hughes*. Eds. Arnold Rampersad and David Roessel. New York: Vintage, 1994. 130.

Hughes, Langston. *I Wonder As I Wander*. 1934. New York: Hill and Wang, 1993.

Hughes, Langston. *Little Ham*. 1935. *The Collected Works of Langston Hughes: Volume 5, The Plays to 1942: Mulatto to The Sun Do Move*. Eds. Leslie Catherine Sanders and Nancy Johnston. Columbia, MO: University of Missouri Press, 2002. 196–265.

Hughes, Langston. "Let America Be America Again." *The Collected Poems of Langston Hughes*. Eds. Arnold Rampersad and David Roessel. New York: Vintage, 1994. 189–91.

Hughes, Langston. "Don't You Want To Be Free." 1937. *The Collected Works of Langston Hughes: Volume 5, The Plays to 1942: Mulatto to The Sun Do Move*. Eds. Leslie Catherine Sanders and Nancy Johnston. Columbia, MO: University of Missouri Press, 2002. 538–73.

Hughes, Langston. *Montage of a Dream Deferred*. 1951. *The Collected Poems of Langston Hughes*. Eds. Arnold Rampersad and David Roessel. New York: Vintage, 1994. 387–429.

Hughes, Langston. Liner notes. Randy Weston. *Uhuru Afrika*. Roulette WPCR-29214 CD, 2017.

Hunter, Evan. "from *Streets of Gold*." *Moment's Notice: Jazz in Poetry & Prose*. Eds. Art Lange and Nathaniel Mackey. Minneapolis: Coffee House Press, 1993. 86–100.

Hurston, Zora Neale. "The Gilded Six-Bits." *The Complete Stories*. New York: Harper Perennial, 2008. 86–98.

Hurston, Zora Neale. *Their Eyes Were Watching God*. 1937. New York: Harper, 1990.

Hurston, Zora Neale. "Story in Harlem Slang." *American Mercury* (July 1942): 84–96.

Hutcheon, Linda. *A Theory of Adaptation*. New York: Routledge. 2006.

iTunes Charts, (n.d.), www.itunescharts.net/fra/artists/music/stan-getz-joao-gilberto/albums/getzgilberto/.

Iversen, Gunnar and Scott Mackenzie, eds. *Mapping the Rockumentary: Images of Sound and Fury*. Edinburgh: Edinburgh University Press, 2022.

Iyer, Vijay. "Exploding the Narrative in Jazz Improvisation." *Uptown Conversation: The New Jazz Studies*. Eds. Robert G. O'Meally, Brent Hayes Edwards, and Farah Jasmine Griffin. New York: Columbia University Press, 2004. 393–403.

Jackson, Bruce and David Demsey. "Source Uncovered for Martin Luther King Jr. Jazz Quote." *Down Beat*. January 2011. 62–63.

Jackson, Zakiyah Iman. *Becoming Human: Matter and Meaning in an Antiblack World*. New York: New York University Press, 2020.
Jacques, Geoffrey. "A Roundtable on Ken Burns's *Jazz*." *Journal of Popular Music Studies* 13.2 (2001): 207–25.
Jarman, Joseph. Liner notes. Art Ensemble of Chicago. *Urban Bushmen*. ECM Records 1211/12, 1980.
Jarrett, Michael. "The Tenor's Vehicle: Reading *Way Out West*." *Representing Jazz*. Ed. Krin Gabbard. Durham: Duke University Press, 1995. 260–82.
"'Jazz Dance' on Film." *New York Times*. September 5, 1954. Sec. Magazine.
Jermyn, Deborah. *Sex and the City*. Detroit: Wayne State University Press, 2009.
Jimoh, A. Yemsi. *Spiritual, Blues and Jazz People in African American Fiction: Living in a Paradox*. Knoxville: University of Tennessee Press, 2002.
Johnson, Bruce. "Hear Me Talkin' to Ya: Problems of Jazz Discourse." *Popular Music* 12.1 (1993): 1–12.
Johnson, Helene. "Poem." 1922. *Jazz Poems*. Ed. Kevin Young. New York: Knopf, 2006. 28–29.
Johnson, James Weldon. *God's Trombones: Seven Negro Sermons in Verse*. 1927. New York: Penguin, 2008.
Johnson, Javon. *Killing Poetry: Blackness and the Making of Slam and Spoken Word Communities*. New Brunswick, NJ: Rutgers University Press, 2017.
Johnson, Russell L. "'Disease Is Unrhythmical': Jazz, Health, and Disability in 1920s America." *Health and History* 13.2 (2011): 13–42.
Johnson-Laird, P.N. "How Jazz Musicians Improvise." *Music Perception* 19.3 (2002): 415–42.
"Jolly." "Harlem Show and Duke at Howard." *The Pittsburgh Courier*. December 10, 1932, 11.
Jones, Meta DuEwa. *The Muse is Music: Jazz Poetry from the Harlem Renaissance to Spoken Word*. Urbana, IL: University of Illinois Press, 2011.
Jones, Papa Jo, as told to Albert Murray. *Rifftide: The Life and Opinions of Papa Jo Jones*. Ed. Paul Devlin. Minneapolis: University of Minnesota Press, 2011.
Jordan, Sharon. *Jazz and Art: Two Steps Ahead of the Century*. Hamburg: Earbooks, 2017.
Josephson, Barney, with Terry Trilling-Josephson. *Café Society: The Wrong Place for the Right People*. Urbana: University of Illinois Press, 2009.
Kahana, Jonathan. *Intelligence Work: The Politics of American Documentary*. New York: Columbia University Press, 2008.
Kania, Andrew. "All Play and No Work: An Ontology of Jazz." *The Journal of Aesthetics and Art Criticism* 69.4 (2011): 391–403.
Kaufman, Bob. *The Collected Poems of Bob Kaufman*. Eds. Neeli Cherkovski, Raymond Foye, and Tate Swindell. San Francisco: City Lights Books, 2019.
Keepnews, Orrin. *The View from Within*. New York: Oxford University Press, 1988.
Keepnews Orrin and Bill Grauer, Jr. *A Pictorial History of Jazz: People and Places from New Orleans to Modern Jazz*. New York: Crown, 1955.

Kelley, Robin D.G. *Freedom Dreams: The Black Radical Imagination*. Boston: Beacon Press, 2002.

Kelley, Robin D.G. *Africa Speaks, America Answers: Modern Jazz in Revolutionary Times*. Cambridge, MA: Harvard University Press, 2012.

Kelley, William Marvin. "If You're Woke You Dig It." *New York Times*. May 20, 1962. Section SM, 45.

Kelly, Nora. Liner notes. Herbie Hancock. *Empyrean Isles*. Blue Note BLP 4175, 1964.

Kelly, Nora. Liner notes. Herbie Hancock. *Maiden Voyage*. Blue Note BLP 4195, 1965.

Kennedy, Eleanor. Liner notes. Brother Jack MacDuff. *Live!* Prestige LP 7274, 1963.

Kenney, William H., III. "Le Hot: The Assimilation of American Jazz in France, 1917–1940." *American Studies* 25.1 (Spring 1984): 1–25.

Kenney, William H., III. "Negotiating the Color Line: Louis Armstrong's Autobiographies." Eds. Reginald. T. Buckner and Steven Weiland. *Jazz in Mind: Essays on the History and Meanings of Jazz*. Detroit: Wayne State University Press, 1991. 38–59.

Kerman, Joseph. *Contemplating Music: Challenges to Musicology*. Cambridge: Harvard University Press, 1986.

Kernodle, Tammy L. "Beyond the Chord, the Club, and the Critics: A Historical and Musicological Perspective of the Jazz Avant-Garde." *Creative Black Music at the Walker: Selections from the Archives*. Eds. Danielle A. Jackson and Simone Austin. Minneapolis: Walker Art Center, 2020, https://walkerart.org/collections/publications/jazz/creative-black-music-introduction/.

Kerouac, Jack. *Mexico City Blues (242 Choruses)*. New York: Grove, 1959.

Kerouac, Jack. *Visions of Cody*. 1972. New York: Penguin, 1993.

Kerrigan, Susan and Phillip McIntyre. "The 'Creative Treatment of Actuality': Rationalizing and Reconceptualizing the Notion of Creativity for Documentary Practice." *Journal of Media Practice* 11.2 (2010): 111–30.

King, Martin Luther, Jr. "On the Importance of Jazz: Opening Address to the 1964 Berlin Jazz Festival," WCLK, www.wclk.com/dr-martin-luther-king-jr-importance-jazz.

King, Martin Luther, Jr. *Where Do We Go From Here: Chaos or Community?* Boston: Beacon, 1967.

Klein, Howard. "Ellington Denied Pulitzer Citation." *New York Times*. May 5, 1965. www.nytimes.com/1965/05/05/archives/ellington-denied-pulitzer-citation-advisory-board-turns-down-bid-by.html.

Kluth, Andrew J. "Intertextuality and the Construction of Meaning in Jazz Worlds: A Case Study of Joe Farrell's 'Moon Germs.'" *Journal of Jazz Studies* 12.1 (2019): 51–71.

Knauer, Wolfram. *"Play yourself, man!" Die Geschichte des Jazz in Deutschland*. Stuttgart: Reclam, 2019.

Kofsky, Frank. *Black Nationalism and the Revolution in Jazz*. New York: Pathfinder Press, 1970.

Korsyn, Kevin. "Toward a New Poetics of Musical Influence." *Music Analysis* 10.1–2 (1991): 3–72.
Kouwenhoven, John A. *The Beer Can by the Highway: Essays on What's "American" About America.* Garden City, NY: Doubleday, 1961.
Kouwenhoven, John A. *Made in America: The Arts in Modern Civilization.* New York: Anchor, 1962.
Kristeva, Julia. "Word, Dialogue and Novel." *The Kristeva Reader.* Ed. Toril Moi. New York: Columbia University Press, 1986. 34–61.
Kruth, John. *Bright Moments: The Life and Legacy of Rahsaan Roland Kirk.* New York: Welcome Rain Publishers, 2000.
Kubik, Gail. "Music in Documentary Films." *Music Journal; New York* 3.5 (1945): 13–54.
Landau, Ellen G. *Jackson Pollock.* New York: Harry N. Abrams, 1989.
Lane, Jeremy F. *Jazz and Machine-Age Imperialism.* Ann Arbor: University of Michigan Press, 2013.
Lange, Art and Nathaniel Mackey, eds. *Moment's Notice: Jazz in Poetry & Prose.* Minneapolis: Coffee House Press, 1993.
Lasker, Steven. Liner notes. Duke Ellington. *The Complete 1932–1940 Brunswick, Columbia and Master Recordings of Duke Ellington and His Famous Orchestra.* Mosaic Records MD11-248, 2010.
Latour, Bruno and Steve Woolgar. *Laboratory Life: The Construction of Scientific Facts.* Princeton, NJ: Princeton University Press, 1986.
Laver, Mark. "Freedom of Choice: Jazz, Neoliberalism, and the Lincoln Center." *Popular Music and Society* 37.5 (2014): 538–56.
Laver, Mark. *Jazz Sells: Music, Marketing and Meaning.* New York: Routledge, 2015.
Lazar, Kay. "Berklee let teachers quietly leave after alleged sex abuse, and pushed students for silence." *Boston Globe.* November 8, 2017, www.bostonglobe.com/metro/2017/11/08/berklee-college-lets-teachers-quietly-leave-after-alleged-sexual-abuse-students-least-one-found-another-teaching-job/yfCkCCmdJzxkiEgrQK4cWM/story.html.
Leishman, Marista. *My Father – Reith of the BBC.* Edinburgh: Saint Andrew Press, 2006.
Leonard, Herman. *The Eye of Jazz.* London: Viking, 1989.
Leonard, Herman. *Jazz, Giants, and Journeys: The Photography of Herman Leonard.* New York: Scala, 2007.
Leonard, Neil. "The Jazzman's Verbal Usage." *Black American Literature Forum* 20.1–2 (1986): 151–60.
Leonard, Neil. *Jazz: Myth and Religion.* Oxford: Oxford University Press, 1987.
Levine, Robert. "Sony Taps Into Photo Archive as a Resource During Hard Times." *New York Times.* May 29, 2008, www.nytimes.com/2008/05/29/arts/music/29phot.html.
Lewis, Eric. *Intents and Purposes: Philosophy and the Aesthetics of Improvisation.* Ann Arbor: University of Michigan Press, 2019.
Lewis, George E., "Improvised Music After 1950: Afrological and Eurological Perspectives," *Black Music Research Journal* 16.1 (1996): 91–122.

Lewis, George E. *A Power Stronger Than Itself: The AACM and American Experimental Music.* Chicago: University of Chicago Press, 2008.
Lipsitz, George. *Dangerous Crossroads: Popular Music, Postmodernism and the Poetics of Place.* London: Verso, 1997.
Liska, A. James. "Wynton and Branford Marsalis: A Common Understanding." *DownBeat.* December 1982. https://wyntonmarsalis.org/news/entry/a-common-understanding-wynton-and-branford-marsalis-interview-downbeat-december-1982.
Litweiler, John. *The Freedom Principle: Jazz After 1958.* New York: Morrow, 1984.
Locke, Alain. "The New Negro." *The New Negro*, Ed. Alain Locke New York: Touchstone, 1997, 3–16.
Locke, Alain. *The Negro and His Music.* Washington, DC: The Associates in Negro Folk Education, 1936.
Lomax, Alan. *Mister Jelly Roll: The Fortunes of Jelly Roll Morton, New Orleans Creole and "Inventor of Jazz."* Oakland, CA: University of California Press, 1973.
Long, Barbara. Liner notes. Dexter Gordon. *A Swingin' Affair.* Blue Note BLP 4133, 1962.
Lopes, Paul. *The Rise of a Jazz Art World.* Cambridge: Cambridge University Press, 2002.
Lott, Eric. *Love and Theft: Blackface Minstrelsy and the American Working Class.* New York: Oxford University Press, 1995.
Lotz, Rainer E. "The 'Louisiana Troupes' in Europe." *The Black Perspective in Music* 11.2 (1983): 133–42.
Lotz, Rainer E. "From Minstrelsy to Jazz: Cross-Cultural Links Between Germans and Afro-Americans." Presentation at the International Association of Jazz Record Collectors (IAJRC), 1999 Convention. Hamburg, Germany. July 29, 1999, https://edoc.hu-berlin.de/bitstream/handle/18452/21043/psto8_lotz.pdf.
Lotz, Rainer E. "Rudy & Fredy Walker – 'Les enfants nègres' – in Europe." *Doctor Jazz Magazine* 44.192 (March 2006): 9–23.
Lotz, Rainer E. "Early African-American Entertainers." *The History of European Jazz: The Music, Musicians, and Audience in Context.* Ed. Francisco Martinelli. Sheffield: Equinox, 2018. 642–52.
Lowry, Glenn, ed. *MoMA Highlights: 375 Works from the Museum of Modern Art, New York.* New York: The Museum of Modern Art, 2019.
Lupton, Deborah. *Risk.* 2nd ed. London: Routledge, 2013.
MacAdams, Lewis. *Birth of The Cool: Beat, Bebop, and the American Avant-Garde.* New York: Free Press, 2001.
MacDonald, J. Fred. "Black Perimeters – Paul Robeson, Nat King Cole and the Role of Blacks in American TV." *Journal of Popular Film and Television* 7.3 (1979): 246–64.
Mackey, Nathaniel. "Other: From Noun to Verb," *Representations* 39 (1992): 51–70.
Mackey, Nathaniel. *Splay Anthem.* New York: New Directions, 2006.
Madhubuti, Haki R. "For Black People." *GroundWork: New and Selected Poems* Chicago: Third World Press, 1997. 97–103.
Mailer, Norman. *The White Negro.* San Francisco: City Lights Books, 1957.

Mailer, Norman. Box 1014, Folder 1. Norman Mailer Papers, Harry Ransom Center (HRC). University of Texas-Austin.

Major, Clarence. *Juba to Jive: A Dictionary of African American Slang*. New York: Penguin, 1994.

Malone, Jacqui. *Steppin' on the Blues: The Visible Rhythms of African American Dance*. Urbana: University of Illinois Press, 1996.

Maloney, Liam. "Ain't Misbehavin': Jazz music in children's television." *Jazz Research Journal* 12.1 (2018): 63–85.

Mann, Klaus. *The Turning Point: Thirty-Five Years in This Century*. New York: Marcus Weiner, 1984.

Maréchal, Paul, ed. *Andy Warhol: The Complete Commissioned Record Covers*. 2nd ed. Munich: Prestel, 2015.

Margolick, David. *Strange Fruit: Billie Holiday, Café Society, and an Early Cry for Civil Rights*. Philadelphia: Running Press, 2000.

Marin, Reva. *Outside and Inside: Race and Identity in White Jazz Autobiography*. Jackson, MS: University of Mississippi Press, 2020.

Marsalis, Wynton and Frank Stewart. *Sweet Swing Blues: On the Road*. New York: Thunder's Mouth, 1998.

Marsh, Graham and Glyn Callingham, eds. *Blue Note Album Cover Art: The Ultimate Collection*. San Francisco: Chronicle, 2002.

Marshall, Jim. *Jazz*. San Francisco: Chronicle, 2005.

Mason, Amelia. "Berklee's Institute of Jazz and Gender Justice Aims to Combat Sexism in Jazz." *WBUR.org*. April 9, 2019, www.wbur.org/artery/2019/04/09/berklees-institute-of-jazz-and-gender-justice-sexism-jazz.

Matheny, Keith. "Techies can appear slow to embrace philanthropy." *USA Today*. June 18, 2012. Money, 5b.

Maultsby, Portia K. "Africanisms in African-American Music." *Africanisms in American Culture*. Ed. Joseph E. Holloway. Bloomington: Indiana University Press, 1990. 185–210.

McClure, Michael. "Wolf Net." *Io No.* 20 (1974): 143–300.

McCluskey, John. "Lush Life." *The Jazz Fiction Anthology*. Eds. Sascha Feinstein and David Rife. Bloomington, IN: Indiana University Press, 2009. 340–56.

McCracken, Allison. *Real Men Don't Sing: Crooning in American Culture*. Durham: Duke University Press, 2015.

McGee, Kristin. *Some Liked it Hot: Jazz Women in Film and Television, 1928–1959*. Middletown, CT: Wesleyan University Press, 2009.

McGuigan, Jim. *Cool Capitalism*. London: Pluto Press, 2009.

McKay, Claude. "The Harlem Dancer." *Harlem Shadows: The Poems of Claude McKay*. New York: Harcourt Brace, 1922. 42.

McKinley, Ann. "Debussy and American Minstrelsy." *The Black Perspective in Music* 14.3 (1986): 249–58.

McMullen, Tracy. "Jazz Education after 2017: The Berklee Institute of Jazz and Gender Justice and the Pedagogical Lineage." *Jazz & Culture* 4.2 (2021): 27–55.

McNeilly, Kevin. "Charles Mingus Splits, or, All the Things You Could Be by Now If Sigmund Freud's Wife Was Your Mother." *Canadian Review of American Studies* 27.2 (1997): 45–70.

McRae, Rick. "'What is Hip?' and Other Inquiries in Jazz Slang Lexicography." *Notes* 57.3 (2001): 574–84.

McWhorter, John. "Duke Ellington Deserves the 1965 Pulitzer Prize." *New York Times*. July 20, 2022. www.nytimes.com/2022/07/20/opinion/duke-ellington.html.

Meeker, David. *Jazz in the Movies 1917–1977*. London: British Film Institute, 1977.

Meeker, David. *Jazz on the Screen*. Washington, DC: Library of Congress, 2017.

Mellers, Wilfred. *Music in a New Found Land: Themes and Developments in the History of American Music*. London: Faber, 1987.

Mencken, Henry Louis. *The American Language: An Inquiry into the Development of English in the United States, Supplement Two*. New York: Knopf, 1962.

Merriam, Alan. *The Anthropology of Music*. Evanston, IL: Northwestern University Press, 1964.

Meyers, Marc. *Why Jazz Happened*. Berkeley: University of California Press, 2013.

Meyers, Marc. Liner notes: "Disquiet Nights of Reluctant Stars." Stan Getz and João Gilberto. *Getz/Gilberto*. 1964. Verve 80020749-02 CD, 2014.

Mezzrow, Mezz, with Bernard Wolfe. *Really the Blues*. 1946. New York: Citadel, 2001.

Michael Brecker International Saxophone Competition. https://breckercompetition.org/.

Mingus, Charles. *Beneath the Underdog*. 1971. Ed. Nel King. New York: Vintage, 1991.

Minnebach, Guy. "The bossa nova cover no one knew was a Warhol: Paul Desmond's Take Ten." *Andy Earhole*. October 13, 2019. https://warholcoverart.com/2019/10/13/the-bossa-nova-cover-no-one-knew-was-a-warhol-paul-desmonds-take-ten/.

Mitchell, Gail. "Drummer Terri Lyne Carrington Talks Berklee Institute Of Jazz, Gender Equity: It 'Is Everybody's Work.'" *Billboard.com*. May 7, 2019, www.billboard.com/articles/business/8510413/terri-lyne-carrington-talks-berklee-institute-jazz-gender-justice.

Mitchell, Nicole. "Improvisation, Community, and Social Practice." Keynote Address: Lex Non Scripta, Ars Non Scripta: Law, Justice, and Improvisation Conference, McGill University, Montreal, Quebec, 2009.

Monson, Ingrid. "Doubleness and Jazz Improvisation: Irony, Parody, and Ethnomusicology." *Critical Inquiry* 20.2 (1994): 283–313.

Monson, Ingrid. *Saying Something: Jazz Improvisation and Interaction*. Chicago: University of Chicago Press, 1996.

Moten, Fred. *In the Break: The Aesthetics of the Black Radical Tradition*. Minneapolis: University of Minnesota Press, 2003.

Moten, Fred. *Black and Blur*. Durham: Duke University Press, 2017.

Mulvey, Laura. "Visual Pleasure and Narrative Cinema." *Screen* 16.3 (1975): 6–18.

Murphy, John P. "Jazz Improvisation: The Joy of Influence." *The Black Perspective in Music* 18:1–2 (1990): 7–19.

Murray, Albert. *The Hero and the Blues*. Columbia, MO: University of Missouri Press, 1973.
Murray, Albert. *Stomping the Blues*. New York: Da Capo, 1976.
"A Negro Explains 'Jazz'." *Literary Digest*. April 26, 1919. 28–29.
Ngô, Fiona I.B. *Imperial Blues: Geographies of Race and Sex in Jazz Age New York*. Durham: Duke University Press, 2014.
Nichols, Bill. *Representing Reality: Issues and Concepts in Documentary*. Bloomington, IN: Indiana University Press, 1991.
Nicholson, Stuart. *Is Jazz Dead? (Or Has It Moved to A New Address)*. New York: Routledge, 2005.
Nicholson, Stuart. *Ella Fitzgerald: The Complete Biography*. New York: Routledge, 2014.
Nicholson, Stuart. *Jazz and Culture in a Global Age*. Boston: Northeastern University Press, 2014.
Niebling, Laura. "'I Don't Make Culture, I Sell It!': The Early History of Music Documentation 1920s–1970s." *Mapping the Rockumentary: Images of Sound and Fury*. Eds. Gunnar Iversen and Scott Mackenzie. Edinburgh: Edinburgh University Press, 2022. 24–35
Noiriel, Gerard. *Chocolat: La Veritable Histoire D'Un Homme Sans Nom*. Montrouge: Bayard Press, 2014.
Ochs, Phil. Liner notes. *Pleasures of the Harbor*. A&M 133, 1967.
O'Day, Anita, with George Eells. *High Times Hard Times*. 1981. New York: Limelight, 2003.
O'Hara, Frank. *Lunch Poems*. San Francisco: City Lights Books, 1964.
Olson, Charles. "Projective Verse." *Selected Writings*. Ed. Robert Creeley. New York: New Directions, 1966. 15–26.
Olson, Charles and Robert Creeley. *The Complete Correspondence, Volume IV*. Ed. George Butterick. Santa Barbara: Black Sparrow, 1980.
O'Meally, Robert G., ed. *The Jazz Cadence of American Culture*. New York: Columbia University Press, 1998.
Osofsky, Gilbert. *Harlem: The Making of a Ghetto; Negro New York, 1890–1930*. New York: Harper & Row, 1971.
Ott, Brian L. and Cameron Walter. "Intertextuality: Interpretive Practice and Textual Strategy." *Critical Studies in Media Communication* 17.4 (2000): 429–46.
Owens, Thomas. "Charlie Parker: Techniques of Improvisation, Vol.1." Ph.D. dissertation, University of California, Los Angeles, 1974.
Palmer, Robert. Liner notes. McCoy Tyner. *Sahara*. Milestone MSP 9039, 1972.
Palmer, Robert. Liner notes. Julius Hemphill. *Dogon AD*. 1977. *Setting the Tempo: Fifty Years of Great Jazz Liner Notes*. Ed. Tom Piazza. New York: Anchor, 1996. 243–47.
Palmquist, David. *Ellington on the Web*, http://ellingtonweb.ca.
Panassié, Hugues. *Hot Jazz: The Guide to Swing Music*. New York: M. Witmark & Sons, 1936.
Panikker, Dhirendra Mikhail. "Sound Come-Unity': Post-9/11 Brown and the Politics of Intercultural Improvisation." Ph.D. dissertation, University of California at Riverside, 2019.

Pareles, Jon. *Keeping Time: The Photographs of Don Hunstein*. Chicago: Insight, 2013.
Parker, Morgan. *There Are More Beautiful Things Than Beyoncé*. Portland, OR: Tin House Books, 2017.
Parker, Travis and Lou Gold. "The Moon, The Stars, and You." Sheet music. Travis R. Parker, 1933.
Paulo, Joaquim and Julius Wiedenmann, eds. *Jazz Covers*. Vol. I & II. Köln: Taschen, 2012.
Pellegrinelli, Lara. "Separated at 'Birth': Singing and the History of Jazz." *Big Ears: Listening for Gender in Jazz Studies*. Eds. Nichole Rustin and Sherrie Tucker. Durham: Duke University Press, 2008. 31–47.
Pepper, Art and Laurie Pepper. *Straight Life: The Story of Art Pepper*. Updated ed. New York: Da Capo, 1994.
Perez, Michael V. and Jessica McKee, eds. *Billie Holiday: Essays on the Artistry and Legacy*. Jefferson, NC: McFarland, 2019.
Perry, Imani. *May Forever We Stand: A History of the Black National Anthem*. Chapel Hill: University of North Carolina Press, 2018.
Perry, Imani. *Vexy Thing: On Gender and Liberation*. Durham: Duke University Press, 2018.
Phillips, Kyra and Deenu Zara. "Human toll of COVID-19 touches every corner of the jazz world." *ABC News*. June 12, 2020. https://abcnews.go.com/Entertainment/human-toll-covid-19-touches-corner-jazz-world/story?id=71178081.
Piazza, Tom. "Introduction." *Setting the Tempo*, 1–5.
Piazza, Tom., ed. *Setting the Tempo: Fifty Years of Great Jazz Liner Notes*. New York: Anchor, 1996.
Pillai, Nicolas. *Jazz as Visual Language: Film, Television and the Dissonant Image*. London: I. B. Tauris, 2016.
Pillai, Nicolas., ed. "Special Issue: Jazz in Television." *Jazz Research Journal* 12.1 (2018): 5–162.
Pillai, Nicolas and Vanessa Jackson. "How Television Works: Discourses, Determinants and Dynamics Arising from the Re-enactment of *Jazz 625*." *Journal of Popular Television* 9.1 (2021): 139–57.
Pinson, K. Heather. *The Jazz Image: Seeing Music through Herman Leonard's Photography*. Jackson: University Press of Mississippi, 2014.
Pocock, John Greville Agard *Virtue, Commerce, and History: Essays on Political Thought and History, Chiefly in the Eighteenth Century*. Cambridge: Cambridge University Press, 1985.
Polillo, Roberto. *Swing, Bop & Free: Il jazz degli anni '60*. Milano: Marco Polillo, 2006.
Pollock, Edmund. Liner notes. Charles Mingus. *The Black Saint and The Sinner Lady*. Impulse A-35, 1963.
Pollock, Jackson. "My Painting." *Possibilities* No. 1 (Winter 1947–488): 78–83.
Pond, Steven F. "Jamming the Reception: Ken Burns, 'Jazz', and the Problem of 'America's Music.'" *Notes* 60.1 (2003): 11–45.

Popelka, Larry. "Google and Other Tech Companies Need Lessons in Local Philanthropy." *Bloomberg Businessweek*. April 22, 2014, www.businessweek.com/articles/2014-04-22/google-and-other-tech-companies-need-lessons-in-local-philanthropy.

PopMatters Staff. "Kind of, Kind of Blue: A Conversation with Mostly Other People Do the Killing," *PopMatters*. September 14, 2014, www.popmatters.com/185662-kind-of-kind-of-blue-a-conversation-with-mostly-other-people-do-the--2495616921.html,

Porter, Eric. *What Is This Thing Called Jazz?: African American Musicians as Artists, Critics, and Activists*. Berkeley: University of California Press, 2002.

Porter, Roy and David Keller. *There and Back: The Roy Porter Story*. Baton Rouge: Louisiana State University Press, 1991.

Porter, Theodore M. "Foreword: Positioning Social Science in Cold War America." *Cold War Social Science: Knowledge Production, Liberal Democracy, and Human Nature*. Eds. Mark Solovey and Hamilton Cravens. New York: Palgrave Macmillan, 2012. ix–xv.

Porter, Tom. "Music Professor McMullen Heading to Berklee on Prestigious Fellowship." Bowdoin.edu. April 6, 2020, www.bowdoin.edu/news/2020/04/music-professor-mcmullen-heading-to-berklee-on-prestigious-fellowship.html.

Poster for the International Congress on the Dialectics of Liberation, London, 1967.

Powell, Elliott H. "Staying Golden: The Politics of Gender, Sexuality, and Jazz in *The Golden Girls*." *Jazz Research Journal* 12.1 (2018): 86–109.

Powell, Richard J. *Black Art: A Cultural History*. New York: Thames and Hudson, 2003.

Powers, John Farl. "He Don't Plant Cotton." *Hot and Cool: Jazz Short Stories*. Ed. Marcela Breton. New York: Plume, 1990. 78–91.

Pronko, Michael. "Quiet About It – Jazz in Japan." *The Routledge Companion to Jazz Studies*. Eds. Nicholas Gebhardt, Nichole Rustin-Paschal, and Tony Whyton. New York: Routledge, 2019. 271–91.

Prouty, Ken. *Knowing Jazz: Community, Pedagogy, and Canon in the Information Age*. Jackson, MS: University Press of Mississippi, 2012.

Provizer, Steve. "Film Review: 'Fire Music: A History of the Free Jazz Revolution' – Informative but Incomplete." *The Arts Fuse*. https://artsfuse.org/235064/film-review-fire-music-a-history-of-the-free-jazz-revolution-informative-but-incomplete/.

"The Pulitzer Prize for Music: It's Time to Alter and Affirm." June 1, 2004. www.pulitzer.org/files/musicchanges.pdf.

Ra, Sun. Liner notes. Sun Ra. *Interstellar Low Ways*. El Saturn Records LP-203, 1967.

Ra, Sun. Liner notes. Sun Ra. *Space Is the Place*. Blue Thumb BTS 41, 1973.

Ra, Sun. *This Planet is Doomed: The Science Fiction Poetry of Sun Ra*. New York: Kicks Books. 2011.

Radano, Ronald M. "Review: Jazz, Modernism, and the Black Creative Tradition." *Reviews in American History*, 21.4 (1993): 671–76.

Radano, Ronald M. *New Musical Figurations: Anthony Braxton's Cultural Critique.* Chicago: University of Chicago Press, 1993.

Radano, Ronald M. "Black Music's Body Politics." *Jazz Worlds/World Jazz.* Eds. Philip V. Bohlman and Goffredo Plastino. Chicago: University of Chicago Press, 2016. 429–44,

Ramsey, Frederic, Jr. and Charles Edward Smith. *Jazzmen: The Story of Hot Jazz Told in the Lives of the Men Who Created It.* New York: Harcourt Brace, 1939.

Ramsey, Guthrie. *Race Music: Black Music From Bebop to Hip-Hop.* Berkeley: University of California Press, 2003.

Rasula, Jed. "The Media of Memory: The Seductive Menace of Records in Jazz History." *Jazz Among the Discourses.* Ed. Krin Gabbard. Durham: Duke University Press, 1995. 134–62.

Ratliff, Ben. "Jazz as a Window On Life in the 50's." *New York Times.* July 30, 2000. Sec. Arts & Leisure, AR31.

Ratliff, Ben. "Fixing, For Now, The Image Of Jazz: MUSIC." *New York Times.* January 7, 2001. Sec. Arts & Leisure.

Reason, Dana. "Navigable Structures and Transforming Mirrors': Improvisation and Interactivity." *The Other Side of Nowhere: Jazz, Improvisation, and Communities in Dialogue.* Eds. Daniel Fischlin and Ajay Heble. Middletown, CT: Wesleyan University Press, 2004. 71–83.

"Record Reviews." *Down Beat* 14.14 (July 2, 1947): 14–16.

Reed, Ishmael. *Yellow Back Radio Broke Down.* New York: Doubleday, 1969.

Reed, James. "The Shrimp Peel Gig," 1997. *The Jazz Fiction Anthology.* Eds. Sascha Feinstein and David Rife. Bloomington, IN: Indiana University Press, 2009. 369–84.

Reich, Howard. "The Story Behind the First Pulitzer for Jazz." *Nieman Reports.* https://niemanreports.org/articles/the-story-behind-the-first-pulitzer-for-jazz/.

Reiff, Carole. *Nights at Birdland: Jazz Photographs: 1954–1960.* New York: Simon and Schuster, 1985.

"Reviews and Ratings of New Popular Albums." *Billboard.* July 2, 1955. 28.

Rexroth, Kenneth. "Discordant and Cool." *The New York Times.* November 29, 1959, https://archive.nytimes.com/www.nytimes.com/books/97/09/07/home/kerouac-mexico.html.

Rhode, Deborah L. "#MeToo: Why Now? What Next?" *Duke Law Journal* 69.2 (2019): 377–428.

Robinson, J. Bradford. "Jazz Reception in Weimar Germany: In Search of a Shimmy Figure." *Music and Performance During the Weimar Republic.* Ed. Bryan Gilliam. Cambridge: Cambridge University Press, 1994. 107–34.

Rogers, Holly. "Introduction: Music, Sound and the Nonfiction Aesthetic." *Music and Sound in Documentary Film.* Ed. Holly Rogers. New York: Routledge, 2015. 1–19.

Rosenberg, Bruce A. "Oral Sermons and Oral Narrative." *Folklore: Performance and Communication.* Ed. Dan Ben-Amos et al. Berlin: DeGruyter, 1975. 75–102.

Rosenberg, Harold. *The Tradition of the New.* New York: Horizon, 1960.

Rosenzweig, Phil. *Reginald Rose and the Journey of 12 Angry Men.* New York: Fordham University Press, 2021.

Ross, Lillian. "You Dig It, Sir?" *Reading Jazz*. Ed. Robert Gottlieb. New York: Vintage, 1999. 686–700.

Rouzier, Coco. Liner notes. Werner Fischer's Travelogue. *The Light Is On*. PBR Jazz PBR J300 CD, 2015.

Rusch, René. "Crossing Over with Brad Mehldau's Cover of Radiohead's 'Paranoid Android': The Role of Jazz Improvisation in the Transformation of an Intertext." *Music Theory Online* 19.4 (2013), https://mtosmt.org/issues/mto.13.19.4/mto.13.19.4.rusch.html.

Russell, Ross. *The Sound*. London: Cassell, 1961.

Russell, Ross. "Lester and Alienation." Box 5, Folder 5. Ross Russell Papers, Harry Ransom Center (HRC), University of Texas-Austin

Rust, Brian. *Jazz and Ragtime Records (1897–1942)*. Highlands Ranch: Mainspring Press, 2002.

Rustin, Nichole T. and Sherrie Tucker. "Introduction." *Big Ears: Listening for Gender in Jazz Studies*. Eds. Nichole T. Rustin and Sherrie Tucker. Durham: Duke University Press, 2008. 1–28.

Sampson, Henry T. *The Ghost Walks: A Chronological History of Blacks in Show Business 1865–1910*. Metuchen, NJ: The Scarecrow Press, 1988.

Sanchez, Sonia. "a/coltrane/poem." *The Jazz Poetry Anthology*. Eds. Sascha Feinstein and Yusef Komunyakaa, Bloomington, IN: Indiana University Press, 1991. 183–85.

Sanders, Leslie Catherine. "Introduction: *Little Ham*." *The Collected Works of Langston Hughes: Volume 5, The Plays to 1942*. Eds. Leslie Catherine Sanders and Nancy Johnston. Columbia, MO: University of Missouri Press, 2002. 196.

Saul, Scott. *Freedom Is, Freedom Ain't: Jazz and the Making of the Sixties*. Cambridge, MA: Harvard University Press, 2009.

Schechner, Richard. *Between Theater and Anthropology*. Philadelphia: University of Pennsylvania Press, 1985.

Schechner, Richard. *Performance Studies: An Introduction*. 2nd ed. New York: Routledge, 2012.

Scheinin, Richard. "Jason Moran's New Trick: Skateboarding at SFJazz." *San Jose Mercury News*. May 2, 2013, www.mercurynews.com/ci_23132144/jason-morans-new-trick-skateboarding-at-sfjazz.

Schiedt, Duncan. *Jazz in Black and White: The Photographs of Duncan Schiedt*, Bloomington, IN: Indiana University Press, 2004.

Schuller, Gunther. "Sonny Rollins and the Challenge of Thematic Improvisation." *Jazz Review* 1.1 (1958): 6–11, 21.

Schuller, Gunther. Liner notes. Ornette Coleman. *The Shape of Jazz to Come*. Atlantic SD-1317, 1959.

Schuller, Gunther. Liner notes. Buster Smith. *The Legendary Buster Smith*. *Setting the Tempo: Fifty Years of Great Jazz Liner Notes*. Ed. Tom Piazza. New York: Anchor, 1996. 69–79.

Schuller, Gunther. Liner notes. Ornette Coleman. *Ornette!*. *Setting the Tempo: Fifty Years of Great Jazz Liner Notes*. Ed. Tom Piazza. New York: Anchor, 1996. 360–65.

Schuller, Gunther. *Early Jazz: Its Roots and Musical Development*. Oxford: Oxford University Press, 1968.
Scott, William B. and Peter M. Rutkoff. *New York Modern: The Arts and the City*. Baltimore: Johns Hopkins University Press, 1999.
Sehgal, Kabir. *Jazzocracy: Jazz, Democracy, and the Creation of a New American Mythology*. Mishawaka, IN: Better World Books, 2008.
Seldes, Gilbert. *The Seven Lively Arts*. New York: Harper, 1924.
Shadwick, Keith. "Brave New World." *Jazzwise*. March 2007. 34–37.
Sharpe, Christina. *In the Wake: On Blackness and Being*. Durham: Duke University Press, 2016.
Shaw, Artie. *The Trouble with Cinderella: An Outline of Identity*. 1952. Santa Barbara: Fithian, 1992.
Shepp, Archie. Foreword. *Black Talk* by Ben Sidran. New York: Da Capo, 1981. xiii–xviii.
Shipton, Alyn. *A New History of Jazz*, Rev. ed. New York: Continuum, 2007.
Shipton, Alyn. *Hi-De-Ho: The Life of Cab Calloway*. New York: Oxford University Press, 2010.
Shklovsky, Viktor. "Art as Technique." 1917. https://paradise.caltech.edu/ist4/lectures/Viktor_Sklovski_Art_as_Technique.pdf.
Silva, Elizabeth Pepin and Lewis Watts. *Harlem of the West: The San Francisco Jazz Era*. Berkeley, CA: Heyday, 2020.
Sites, William. "Beyond the 'Futureless Future': Edward O. Bland, Afro-Modernism and *The Cry of Jazz*." *American Studies* 60.1 (2021): 33–57.
Škvorecký, Josef. "Foreword." *The Bass Saxophone*. Trans. Kaca Polackova-Henley. London: Picador, 1980. 7–21.
Škvorecký, Josef. *Talkin' Moscow Blues: Essays About Literature, Politics, Movies, and Jazz*. New York: The Ecco Press, 1988.
Sloan, Nate. "Constructing Cab Calloway: Publicity, Race, and Performance in 1930s Harlem Jazz." *The Journal of Musicology* 36.3 (2019): 370–400.
Sloane, Kathy. *Keystone Korner: Portrait of a Jazz Club*. Bloomington, IN: Indiana University Press, 2011.
Small, Christopher. *Musicking: The Meanings of Performing and Listening*. Hanover: University Press of New England, 1998.
Smith, Charles Edward. "Collecting Hot." *Esquire* (February 1934): 96, 148.
Smith, Charles Edward. Liner notes. *New Orleans Jazz. Setting the Tempo: Fifty Years of Great Jazz Liner Notes*. Ed. Tom Piazza. New York: Anchor, 1996. 25–50.
Smith, Charles Edward. "Collecting Hot: 1944." *Esquire* (February 1944): 26, 98–100.
Smith, C.W. "The Plantation Club." *Hot and Cool: Jazz Short Stories*. Ed. Marcela Breton. New York: Plume, 1990. 200–21.
Snitzer, Herb. *Glorious Days and Nights: A Jazz Memoir*. Jackson, MS: University Press of Mississippi, 2011.
Snorton, C. Riley. *Black on Both Sides: A Racial History of Trans Identity*. Minneapolis: University of Minnesota Press, 2017.

Soderberg, Brandon. "Art of Cool 2016: Finding Modern Democracy in Modern Jazz." *INDY Week*. May 4, 2016. https://indyweek.com/api/content/bae9a173-97f9-5154-acf0-5c877920a3ce/.
Southern, Eileen. *The Music of Black Americans: A History*. 3rd ed. New York: Norton, 1997.
Spellman, Alfred Bennett. *Four Lives in the Bebop Business*. New York: Limelight, 1985.
Spellman, Alfred Bennett Liner notes. *John Coltrane and Johnny Hartman*. Impulse GRD 157, 1995.
Spillers, Hortense. *Black, White, and in Color: Essays on American Literature and Culture*. Chicago: University of Chicago Press, 2003.
Stanbridge, Alan. "A Question of Standards: 'My Funny Valentine' and Musical Intertextuality." *Popular Music History* 1.1 (2004): 83–108.
Stanbridge, Alan. "Burns, Baby, Burns: Jazz History as a Contested Cultural Site." *The Source* 1.1 (2004): 82–100.
Starr, S. Frederick. *Red and Hot: The Fate of Jazz in the Soviet Union*. New York: Limelight, 1994.
Stearns, Marshall. "Rebop, Bebop, and Bop." *Harper's*. April 1, 1950. 89–96.
Steichen, Edward. *The Family of Man*. New York: Museum of Modern Art, 1955.
Stein, Daniel. "The Performance of Jazz Autobiography." Mark Osteen, Ed. *Blue Notes: Toward a New Jazz Discourse*. Special Issue of *Genre* 37.2 (2004): 173–99.
Stein, Daniel. *Music Is My Life: Louis Armstrong, Autobiography, and American Jazz*. Ann Arbor: University of Michigan Press, 2012.
Stein, Daniel. "'*Sei a mensch*': Mezz Mezzrow's Jewish Hipster Autobiography *Really the Blues* and the Ironies of the Color Line." *Anglia* 137.1 (2019): 2–32.
Stein, Daniel & Martin Butler. *Musical Autobiographies*. Special issue of *Popular Music and Society* 38.2 (2015).
Stephenson, Sam. *The Jazz Loft Project: Photographs and Tapes of W. Eugene Smith from 821 Sixth Avenue, 1957–1965*. New York: Knopf, 2009.
Stewart, Charles, and Paul Carter Harrison. *Chuck Stewart's Jazz Files*. Boston: New York Graphic Society, 1985.
Stewart, Jesse. "No Boundary Line to Art: 'Bebop' as Afro-Modernist Discourse." *American Music* 29.3 (2011): 332–52.
Stewart, Rex. *Boy Meets Horn*. Ed. Claire P. Gordon. Ann Arbor: University of Michigan Press, 1991.
Stieglitz, Alfred. "Pictorial Photography." *Classic Essays on Photography*. Ed. Alan Trachtenberg. Stony Creek, CT: Leete's Island, 1980. 116–23.
Stock, Dennis. *Jazz Street: A Photographic Exploration into the World of Jazz*. Text by Nat Hentoff. Garden City, NY: Doubleday, 1960.
Stokes, W. Royal. *Swing Era New York: The Jazz Photographs of Charles Peterson*. Philadelphia: Temple University Press, 1994.
Strachan, Robert and Marion Leonard. "Reel to Real: Cinema Verité Rock Authenticity and the Rock Documentary." *Sound and Music in Film and Visual Media: An Overview*. Ed. Graeme Harper, Ruth Doughty, and Jochen Eisentraut. New York: Continuum, 2009. 284–99.

Straus, Joseph N. "The 'Anxiety of Influence' in Twentieth-Century Music." *The Journal of Musicology* 9:4 (1991): 430–47.
Stravinsky, Igor. *An Autobiography*. New York: Pantianos Classics, 2006.
Strayhorn, Billy. "Lush Life." *Jazz Poems*. Ed. Kevin Young. New York: Knopf, 2006. 68–69.
Street, Julian. "The Jazz Baby." *The Jazz Fiction Anthology*. Eds. Sascha Feinstein and David Rife. Bloomington, IN: Indiana University Press, 2009. 415–46.
Strongin, Thodore. "2 Pulitzer Jurors Resign in Protest." *New York Times*. May 13, 1965. https://timesmachine.nytimes.com/timesmachine/1965/05/13/97200854.pdf.
Suisman, David. *Selling Sounds: The Commercial Revolution in American Music*. Cambridge, MA: Harvard University Press, 2009.
Sukenick, Ronald. *Down and In: Life in the Underground*. New York: Beech Tree, 1987.
Suzuki, Yoko. "Two Strikes and the Double Negative: The Intersections of Gender and Race in the Cases of Female Jazz Saxophonists." *Black Music Research Journal* 33.2 (2013): 207–26.
Szwed, John. *Space is the Place: The Lives and Times of Sun Ra*. New York: Pantheon, 1997.
Szwed, John. *Billie Holiday: The Musician and the Myth*. London: Heinemann, 2015.
Tanner, Lee. *The Jazz Image: Masters of Jazz Photography*. New York: Abrams, 2006.
Taylor, Clyde. "The Language of Hip: From Africa to What's Happening Now." *First World* 1 (1977): 25–32.
Taylor, Clyde. "'Salt Peanuts': Sound and Sense in African/American Oral/Musical Creativity," *Callaloo* 16 (1982): 1–11.
Teachout, Terry. "The Color of Jazz." September 1995. www.commentary.org/articles/terry-teachout/the-color-of-jazz/.
Teachout, Terry. "The Great American Songbook: A Critical Guide." *Commentary*. February 1, 2002, www.commentarymagazine.com/articles/terry-teachout/the-great-american-songbook-a-critical-guide/.
Teague, Jessica E. *Sound Recording Technology and American Literature, from the Phonograph to the Remix*. Cambridge: Cambridge University Press, 2021.
Teal, Kimberly Hannon. "Living Traditions: Embodying Heritage in Contemporary Jazz Performance." Ph.D. dissertation. Eastman School of Music, University of Rochester, 2012.
Thiele, Bob. Liner notes. John Coltrane. *Coltrane*. Impulse A-21, 1962.
Thelin, John. "Higher Education and the Public Trough: A Historical Perspective." *Public Funding of Higher Education: Changing Contexts and New Rationales*. Eds. Edward P. St. John and Michael D. Parsons. Baltimore: Johns Hopkins University Press, 2004. 21–39.
Thompson, Robert Farris. *African Art in Motion: Icon and Act*. Berkeley: University of California Press, 1974.
Thompson, Robert Farris. *Aesthetic of the Cool: Afro-Atlantic Art and Music*. Pittsburgh: Periscope, 2011.

Thurman, Wallace. *Negro Life in New York's Harlem: A Lively Picture of a Popular and Interesting Section*. Girard, KS: Haldeman-Julius Publications, 1928.
Tomlinson, Gary, "Cultural Dialogics and Jazz: A White Historian Signifies." *Disciplining Music: Musicology and Its Canons*. Eds. Katherine Bergeron and Philip V. Bohlman. Chicago: University of Chicago Press, 1992. 64–94.
Tonelli, Chris. *Voices Found: Free Jazz and Singing*. New York: Routledge, 2020.
Tucker, Mark. "Musicology and the New Jazz Studies." *Journal of the American Musicological Society* 51.1 (1998): 131–148.
Tucker, Sherrie. "Deconstructing the Jazz Tradition: The Subjectless Subject of New Jazz Studies." *Jazz/Not Jazz: The Music and Its Boundaries*. Eds. David Ake, Charles Hiroshi Garrett, and Daniel Goldman. Berkeley: University of California Press, 2012. 264–84
Turner, Pete. *Color of Jazz: Album Cover Photographs by Pete Turner*. New York: Rizzoli, 2006.
Tuttle, Anthony. Liner notes. Miles Davis. *Miles Smiles*. Columbia CS 9407, 1967.
Vance, Joel. *Fats Waller: His Life and Times*. London: Robson Books, 1979.
Vandever, Kalia. "Token Girl." Medium.com. March 16, 2018, https://medium.com/@kaliamariev/token-girl-564457c86f13.
VanDiver, Rebecca. *Designing a New Tradition: Lois Mailou Jones and the Aesthetics of Blackness*. University Park: The Pennsylvania State University Press, 2020.
Varga, George. "Kamasi Washington 'the Jazz Voice of Black Lives Matter,'" *Chicago Tribune*. October 4, 2016. www.chicagotribune.com/sd-et-pop-kamasi-20160929-story.html.
Veneciano, Jorge Daniel. "Louis Armstrong, Bricolage, and the Aesthetics of Swing." *Uptown Conversation: The New Jazz Studies*. Eds. Robert G. O'Meally, Brent Hayes Edwards, and Farah Jasmine Griffin. New York: Columbia University Press, 2004. 256–77.
Vian, Boris. *Round About Close to Midnight: The Jazz Writings of Boris Vian*. Ed. Mike Zwerin. London: Quartet, 1988.
Vicente, Eduardo. "Bossa Nova and Beyond: The Jazz as Symbol of Brazilian-Ness." *The Routledge Companion to Jazz Studies*. Eds. Nicholas Gebhardt, Nichole Rustin-Paschal, and Tony Whyton. New York: Routledge, 2019. 293–302.
Vogel, Shane. *The Scene of the Harlem Cabaret: Race, Sexuality, Performance*. Chicago: University of Chicago Press, 2009.
Von Eschen, Penny M. *Satchmo Blows Up the World: Jazz Ambassadors Play the Cold War*. Cambridge, MA: Harvard University Press, 2004.
Wagnleitner, Reinhold. "Jazz – The Classical Music of Globalization, Or: When The Cold War Morphed Into the Cool War." *Is It 'Cause It's Cool?: Affective Encounters With American Culture*. Eds. Astrid M. Fellner, Susanne Hamscha, et al. Vienna: Lit Verlag, 2013. 51–73.
Wald, Gayle. *Crossing the Line: Racial Passing in Twentieth Century U.S. Literature and Culture*. Durham: Duke University Press, 2000.
Wald, Gayle. *It's Been Beautiful. Soul! And Black Power Television*. Durham: Duke University Press, 2015.

Wall, Tim and Paul Long. "Jazz Britannia: Mediating the Story of British Jazz on Television." *Jazz Research Journal* 3.2 (2009): 145–70.

Wall, Tim and Paul Long. "Sight and Sound in Concert? The Inter-Relationship Between Music and Television." *The Sage Handbook of Popular Music*. Eds. Andy Bennett and Steve Waksman. Los Angeles: Sage Reference, 2015. 456–74.

Wallenstein, Barry. "Poetry and Jazz: A Twentieth-Century Wedding." *Black American Literature Forum* 25.3 (1991): 595–620.

Wallgren, Måns. "Sweden: 1970–2000." *The History of European Jazz: The Music, Musicians, and Audience in Context*. Ed. Francisco Martinelli. Sheffield: Equinox, 2018. 217–23.

Walser, Robert. "'Out of Notes': Signification, Interpretation, and the Problem of Miles Davis." *Jazz Among the Discourses*. Ed. Krin Gabbard. Durham: Duke University Press, 1995. 165–88.

Waterman, Ellen. "'I Dreamed of Other Worlds': An Interview with Nicole Mitchell." *Critical Studies in Improvisation / Études critiques en improvisation* 4.1 (2008): 1–7, www.criticalimprov.com/index.php/csieci/article/view/510.

Weir, Michele. "The Scat Singing Dialect: An Introduction to Vocal Improvisation." *The Choral Journal* 55.11 (2015): 28–42.

Wells, Christopher J. [Christi Jay Wells]. "'A Dreadful Bit of Silliness': Feminine Frivolity and Ella Fitzgerald's Early Critical Reception." *Women and Music: A Journal of Gender and Culture* 21 (2017): 43–65.

Wells, Christopher J. [Christi Jay Wells]. "'You Can't Dance To It': Jazz Music and Its Choreographies of Listening." *Daedalus* 148.2 (2019): 36–51.

Wells, Christi Jay. *Between Beats: The Jazz Tradition and Black Vernacular Dance*. New York: Oxford University Press, 2021.

Welty, Eudora. "Powerhouse." *The Jazz Fiction Anthology*. Eds. Sascha Feinstein and David Rife. Bloomington, IN: Indiana University Press, 2009. 452–63.

Wennekes, Emile. "The scattered dream of 'same time, same station': *The Nat King Cole Show*." Jazz and Cinema conference. Cardiff University. November 1, 2013."

Wennekes, Emile. "'All Aboard!': Soundies and Vitaphone Shorts." *Watching Jazz: Encounters with Jazz Performance on Screen*. Eds. Björn Heile, Peter Elsdon, and Jennifer R. Doctor. New York: Oxford University Press, 2016. 57–72.

Whitehead, Kevin. *Play the Way You Feel: The Essential Guide to Jazz Stories on Film*. New York: Oxford University Press, 2020.

Whiteman, Paul, with Mary Martin McBride. *Jazz*. 1926. New York: Arno, 1974.

Whitman, Walt. "Slang in America." *The North American Review* 141 (1885): 431–35.

Whyton, Tony. "Birth of the School: Discursive Methodologies in Jazz Education." *Music Education Research* 8.1 (2006): 65–81.

Whyton, Tony. *Beyond A Love Supreme*. Oxford: Oxford University Press, 2013.

Whyton, Tony. *Jazz Icons: Heroes, Myths and the Jazz Tradition*. Cambridge: Cambridge University Press, 2013.

Wilder, Alec. *American Popular Song: The Great Innovators, 1900–1950*. New York: Oxford University Press, 1990.

Willener, Alfred. *The Action-Image of Society*. Trans. A. M. Sheridan-Smith. London: Tavistock, 1970.

Wilf, Eitan Y. *School for Cool: The Academic Jazz Program and the Paradox of Institutionalized Creativity*. Chicago: University of Chicago Press, 2014.
"William P. Gottlieb Collection." Library of Congress. www.loc.gov/collections/jazz-photography-of-william-p-gottlieb/.
Williams, John A. *Night Song*. New York: Farrar, Straus and Cudahy, 1961.
Williams, Katherine. *Rufus Wainwright*. Sheffield: Equinox Publishing, 2016.
Williams, Katherine. "Duke Ellington's Newport Up!: Liveness, Artefacts and the Seductive Menace of Jazz Revisited." *New Jazz Conceptions: History, Theory, Practice*. Eds. Roger Fagge and Nicolas Pillai. New York: Routledge, 2017. 111–29.
Williams, Linda. *Playing the Race Card: Melodramas of Black and White from Uncle Tom to O.J. Simpson*. Princeton: Princeton University Press, 2001.
Williams, Martin T. *The Jazz Tradition*. New York: Oxford University Press, 1983.
Willoughby, Bob. *Jazz in LA*. Kiel: Nieswand Verlag, 1990.
Wilmer, Valerie. *The Face of Black Music*. New York: Da Capo, 1976.
Wilmer, Valerie. *As Serious As Your Life: The story of the new jazz*. London: Quartet Books, 1977.
Wilson, Carl. *Celine Dion's* Let's Talk about Love: *A Journey to the End of Taste*. New York: Continuum, 2007.
Wyss, Thomas. "Das archaische Herz der Finsternis." *Tages-Anzeiger*. November 25, 2009. 30.
X, Malcolm. "The Founding Rally of the OAAU." 1964. *By Any Means Necessary*. New York: Pathfinder, 1992. 57–96.
X, Malcolm. with Alex Haley. *The Autobiography of Malcolm X*. New York: Grove Press, 1965.
Yaeger, Patricia. "Editor's Note: Bulldagger Sings the Blues." *PMLA* 124.3 (2009): 721–26.
Yaffe, David. *Fascinating Rhythm: Reading Jazz in American Writing*. Princeton: Princeton University Press, 2009.
Young, Kevin, ed. *Blues Poems*. New York: Knopf, 2003.
Young, Kevin. *Jelly Roll: A Blues*. New York: Knopf, 2005.
Young, Kevin, ed. *Jazz Poems*. New York: Knopf, 2006.
Youngquist, Paul. *A Pure Solar World: Sun Ra and the Birth of Afrofuturism*. Illustrated edition. Austin: University of Texas Press, 2016.
Zieger, Susan. "Sex and the citizen in *Sex and the City*'s New York." *Reading Sex and the City*. Eds. Kim Akass and Janet McCabe. London: I. B. Tauris, 2004. 96–111.
Zimmerman, Brian. *Jazziz* "Song of the Day": Feb. 12, 2020 www.jazziz.com/song-of-the-day-bing-crosby-with-the-duke-ellington-orchestra-st-louis-blues/
Zwerin, Michael. "A Lethal Measurement." 1966. *John Cage: An Anthology*. Ed. Richard Kostelanetz. New York: Da Capo, 1991. 161–67.
Zwerin, Mike. *Swing Under the Nazis: Jazz as a Metaphor for Freedom*. New York: Cooper Square, 2000.

Discography

Armstrong, Louis & His Orchestra. "(What Did I Do To Be So) Black and Blue?" Rec. July 19, 1929. Okeh 8714, 1929.
Armstrong, Louis & His Orchestra. "I Got Rhythm." Rec. November 6, 1931. Columbia 2590-D, 1932.
Armstrong, Louis and Ella Fitzgerald. *Porgy & Bess*. Verve Records MG VS-6040-2, 1959.
Bailey, Derek. "Stella By Starlight." *Ballads*. Tzadik TZ 7607, 2002.
Baker, Chet. *Chet Baker Sings*. Pacific Jazz PJLP-11, 1954.
Baraka, Imamu Amiri. *It's Nation Time – African Visionary Music*. Motown/Black Forum B 457L, 1972.
Basie, Count. "Stay Cool." Columbia DC 368, 1946.
Bennett, Tony & Bill Charlap. *Silver Lining: The Songs of Jerome Kern*. Sony Records CD 88875145742. 2015.
Bennett, Tony & Lady Gaga. *Cheek To Cheek*. Columbia B000021861-02, 2014.
Big Bill and the Memphis Five. "Let Me Dig It." Vocalian 04591, 1938.
Bogan, Lucille. [Bessie Jackson]. "B.D. Woman's Blues." Rec. March 7, 1935. *Complete Recorded Works in Chronological Order, Vol. 3* (Document Records BDCD-6038, 1993).
Broonzy, Big Bill. "Going Back to Arkansas." *Big Bill Broonzy: Complete Recorded Works in Chronological Order, Vol. 8*. Document DOCD 5130, 1993.
Brooks, Gwendolyn. "We Real Cool," https://poets.org/poem/we-real-cool.
Brötzmann, Peter. *Machine Gun*. FMP CD 24 CD, 1990.
Brown, Ray. *This Is Ray Brown*. Verve LP V-8290, 1958.
Carr, Leroy. "I'm Going Back to Tennessee." *Leroy Carr Vol. 2*. Document DOCD 5135, 1992.
Carr, Leroy. "Going Back Home." *Leroy Carr Vol. 6*. Document DOCD 5139, 1992.
Charles, Ray and Betty Carter. *Ray Charles and Betty Carter*. ABC-Paramount ABC 385, 1961.
Clark, Sonny. *Cool Struttin'*. Blue Note LP 1588, 1958.
Clarke, Kenny and Francy Boland. *Jazz Is Universal*. 1962. Rhino WPCR-27191 CD, 2012.
Coltrane, John. "My Favorite Things" (Parts I & II). Atlantic 45-5012, 1961.
Coltrane, John. *My Favorite Things*. Atlantic LP 1361, 1961.
Coltrane, John. "Alabama." *Live at Birdland*. Impulse A-50, 1964.
Coltrane, John. *A Love Supreme*. Impulse A-77, 1965.
Coltrane, John. "My Favorite Things." *Live in Japan*. Impulse GRD-4-102, 1991.
Cortez, Jayne. *Celebrations and Solitudes*. Strata East SES-7421, 1974.
Cox, Ida. "Chicago Bound Blues (Great Migration Blues)." *Complete Recorded Works, Vol. 1*. Document DOCD 5322, 1995.
Davis, Miles. *Birth of the Cool*. Capitol LP T-762, 1957.
Davis, Miles. *Bags' Groove*. Prestige 7109, 1957.
Davis, Miles. *Porgy and Bess*. Columbia CS 8085, 1959.

Dorsey, Jimmy & His Orchestra. "I Got Rhythm." Rec. March 3, 1937. Decca 1508, 1937.
Easton, Amos. [Bumble Bee Slim]. "Going Back to Florida." *Bumble Bee Slim Vol. 8*. Document DOCD 5268, 1994.
Eckstine, Billy. "Everything I Have Is Yours." MGM Records 10259, 1948.
Ellington, Duke and His Orchestra. "Arabian Lover." Rec. May 3, 1929. *Duke at the Cotton Club*. RCA 6127, 2000.
Ellington, Duke and His Orchestra. "Jungle Jamboree." Rec. July 29, 1929. *Early Ellington: The Complete Brunswick and Vocalion Recordings of Duke Ellington, 1926–1931*. Decca GRD-3-640, 1994.
Ellington, Duke and His Orchestra. "Maori (A Samoan Dance)." Rec. February 21, 1930. *Early Ellington: The Complete Brunswick and Vocalion Recordings of Duke Ellington, 1926–1931*. Decca GRD-3-640, 1994.
Ellington, Duke and His Orchestra. "Jungle Nights in Harlem." Rec. June 4, 1930. *Duke at the Cotton Club*. RCA 6127, 2000.
Ellington, Duke and His Orchestra. "Wang Wang Blues." Rec. October 27, 1930. *Early Ellington: The Complete Brunswick and Vocalion Recordings of Duke Ellington, 1926–1931*. Decca GRD-3-640, 1994.
Ellington, Duke and His Orchestra. "Stars." Brunswick A-9331, 1932.
Ellington, Duke and His Orchestra. "Rude Interlude." Rec. September 26, 1933. Victor 24431, 1933.
Ellington, Duke and His Orchestra. "Dear Old Southland." Rec. December 4, 1933. Victor 24501, 1934.
Ellington, Duke and His Orchestra. "Cottontail." Rec. May 4, 1940. Victor 26610, 1940.
Evans, Bill. "All The Things You Are." Rec. January 10, 1963. *Bill Evans: The Complete Riverside Recordings*. Riverside R-018, 1984.
Evans, Bill. "All The Things You Are." Rec. May 14–15 1963. *At Shelly's Manne-Hole*. Riverside RM 487, 1965.
Fitzgerald, Ella. *Sings the Cole Porter Song Book*. Verve Records MG V-4001-2, 1956.
Fitzgerald, Ella. *Sings the George and Ira Gershwin Song Book*. Verve Records MG V4024-8, 1959.
Fitzgerald, Ella. *Sings The Jerome Kern Song Book*. Verve V6-4060, 1963.
Franklin, Aretha. "(You Make Me Feel Like) A Natural Woman." Atlantic A2441, 1967.
Gershwin, George. "I Got Rhythm." Rec. February 18, 1931. *Gershwin By Gershwin*. Mark56 Records LP 641, 1973.
Gillespie, Dizzy Sextet. "All The Things You Are." Rec. February 28, 1945. Musicraft 488, 1947.
Gordon, Dexter. "Cheese Cake." Rec. June 11, 1964. *Cheese Cake*. SteepleChase SCCD 36008 CD, 1990.
Gordon, Dexter. "Blues Up and Down." *Great Encounters*. CBS-Columbia LP JC 39578, 1979.

Halvorson, Mary. "Solitude." *Meltframe*. Firehouse 12 Records FH12-04-08-021, 2015.
Hawkins, Erskine. "Keep Cool, Fool." Bluebird B-11049, 1941.
Henderson, Fletcher. "He Wasn't Born in Araby, But He's a Sheikin' Fool." Rec. April 1924. *Fletcher Henderson and the Blues Singers: Complete Recorded Works in Chronological Order, Vol. 2, 1923–1924*. Document Records DOCD-5343, 1995.
Henderson, Fletcher. *A Study in Frustration: The Fletcher Henderson Story.* Columbia CXK 85470, 1961.
Henderson, Rosa. "Down South Blues." *Rosa Henderson: Complete Recorded Works in Chronological Order, Vol. 1*. Document DOCD 5401, 1995.
Henderson, Rosa. "Back Woods Blues." *Rosa Henderson: Complete Reocrded Works in Chronological Order, Vol. 2*. Document DOC 5402, 1995.
Hines, Earl ("Fatha") and Orchestra. *Midnight in New Orleans*. MGM Records 10329, 1949.
Hiromi's Sonicbloom. *Beyond Standard*. Telarc CD 83686, 2008.
Holiday, Billie and Her Orchestra. "Summertime." Okeh 3288, 1936.
Howell, Peg Leg. "Rock and Gravel Blues." Columbia 14320-D, 1928.
Ink Spots and Ella Fitzgerald. "Cow Cow Boogie." Decca Records 18587A, 1944.
Jamal, Ahmad Trio. *At The Pershing*. Argo LP-628, 1958.
Johnson, Alec. "Miss Meal Cramp Blues." *Mississippi String Bands and Associates, 1928–1931*. Document BDCD 6013, 1991.
Johnson, Lonnie. "Hard Times Ain't Gone No Where." Decca 7388, 1937.
Kelly, Eddie. "Goin' Back to Alabama." *Carolina Blues 1937–1947*. Document DOCD 5168, 1993.
Kerouac, Jack & Steve Allen. *Poetry for the Beat Generation*. Dot Records DLP 3154, 1959.
King, Carole. "(You Make Me Feel Like) A Natural Woman." *Tapestry*. Ode Records SP-77009, 1971.
Krall, Diana. *Quiet Nights*. Verve Records B001243301, 2009.
Lande, Art. "Angel Eyes." *The Eccentricies of Earl Dant*. 1750 Arch Records S-1769, 1977.
Lazell, Jason Lee, producer. Various artists. *Crime Jazz* (Moochin' About Records MOOCHIN07, 2014).
Marl Young's String Ensemble. "The Songs You Sing/Always To-Gether." Sunbeam S-108, 1947.
Memphis Jug Band. "Going Back to Memphis." *Memphis Jug Band Vol. 3*. Document DOCD 5023, 1991.
Memphis Minnie. "Ma Rainey." *Complete Recorded Works 1935–1941 in Chronological Order, Vol. 5*. Document BDCD 6012, 1991.
Memphis Minnie and Kansas Joe. "Goin' Back to Texas." *Complete Recorded Works 1929–1934 Vol. 1*. Document DOCD 5028, 1991.
Merman, Ethel. *The Ethel Merman Disco Album*. A&M Records SP-4775, 1979.
Mingus, Charles. *Charles Mingus Presents Charles Mingus*. Candid CJM 8005, 1961.
Murray, Sonny [Sunny Murray]. *Sonny's Time Now*. Jihad Productions 663, 1965.

Navarro, Fats and His Bop Boys. "Everything's Cool." Rec. September 6, 1946. Savoy 941, 1949.
Parker, Charlie. "Shoe Shine Boy" [aka "Yardin' with Yard"/"Shoe Shine Swing"]. Rec. February 15, 1943. *The Complete "Birth of The Bebop."* Stash Records CD ST-CD-535, 1991.
Parker, Charlie. "Thriving on a Riff" [aka "Anthropology"]. Rec. November 6, 1945. *Bird/The Savoy Recordings [Master Takes]*. Savoy Records LP SJL-2201, 1976.
Parker, Charlie. "Cool Blues." Dial 1015, 1947.
Parker, Charlie. *Charlie Parker With Strings*. Mercury MG 35010, 1950.
Peterson, Oscar Trio. *Another Day*. MPS 2120869-9, 1971.
The Puppini Sisters. *Hollywood*. Verve Forecast CD B0016309-02, 2011.
Rainey, Ma. "Sissy Blues." *Ma Rainey: Complete Recorded Works in Chronological Order, Volume 3, c. December 1925–c. June 1926*. Document Records DOCCD-5583, 1997.
Rainey, Ma. "Little Low Mama Blues." *Complete Recorded Works in Chronological Order, Vol. 4*. Document DOCD 5584, 1997.
Rainey, Ma. "Prove It On Me Blues." Paramount 12668, 1928.
Roach, Max. *We Insist! Max Roach's Freedom Now Suite*. Candid CJM 8002, 1961.
Ross, Annie. "Jackie." Rec. September 14, 1953. Prestige 879, 1954.
Shaw, Artie and his Orchestra. "All The Things You Are." Rec. October 26, 1939. Bluebird B 10492, 1939.
Shepp, Archie. *Fire Music*. Impulse AS-86, 1965.
The Shirelles. "Will You Love Me Tomorrow." Scepter Records 1211, 1960.
Simone, Nina. "Mississippi Goddam." *Nina Simone in Concert*. Phillips LP 600-135, 1964.
Smith, Bessie. "Rocking Chair Blues." Columbia 14020-D, 1924.
Smith, Bessie. "Soft Pedal Blues." Rec. May 14, 1925. Columbia 14075-D, 1925.
Smith, Bessie. "Backwater Blues." Rec. February 17, 1927. Columbia 14195-D, 1927.
Smith, Bessie. "Foolish Man Blues." Rec. October 27, 1927. *Bessie Smith: The Complete Recordings*, vol. 3. Columbia Records C2K47474, 1992.
Smith, Mamie. "Crazy Blues." Okeh 4169, 1920.
Smith, Ruby Walker, interview with Chris Albertson. "Life on the Road, I." Bessie Smith. *Bessie Smith: The Final Chapter, The Complete Recordings, Vol. 5*. Columbia/Legacy, C2K 57546, 1996.
Stewart, Rex and His Orchestra. "I'll Come Back for More." Rec. March 20, 1939. Vocalion 5448, 1940.
Strothers, Jimmie. "Goin' to Richmond." *Red River Blues*. Travelin' Man TM CD 08, 1991.
Tyus, Charles and Effie. "Good Old Bygone Days." *Vocal Duets: Complete Recorded Works in Chronological Order (1924–1931)*. Document 5526, 1997.
Various artists. *Decca Presents An Album of Chicago Jazz*. Decca 121, 1940.
Various artists. *New Orleans Jazz*. Decca 144, 1940.
Various artists. *Red Hot + Blue*. Chrysalis F2 21799, 1990.
Waldron, Mal. *Free at Last*. ECM 1001 831 332-2 CD, 1991.

Washboard Sam. "Going Back to Arkansas." *Complete Recorded Works in Chronological Order, Vol. 4.* Document DOCD 5174, 1993.
Waters, Ethel. "(What Did I Do to Be So) Black and Blue?" Rec. April 1, 1930. Columbia 2184-D, 1930.
Waters, Ethel. "Stormy Weather (Keeps Rainin' All The Time)." Brunswick 6564, 1933.
Waters, Ethel. "The Hottentot Potentate." Liberty Music Shop L-188, 1935.
Weston, Randy. *Uhuru Afrika.* Roulette WPCR-29214 CD, 2017.
Williamson, Sonny Boy. "Down South." *Sonny Boy Williamson: Complete Recorded Works in Chronological Order, Vol. 1.* Document DOCD 5055, 1991.
Woods, Phil Quintet. *The American Songbook Vol. I.* Kind of Blue Records KOB 10005, 2002.
Young, Lester. *The Greatest.* Intro Records LP 603, 1951.

Film, Television, and Video Works

Allen, Woody, director. *Stardust Memories.* United Artists, 1980.
Altman, Robert, director. *Kansas City.* Fine Line Features, 1996.
Anderson, John Murray, director. *King of Jazz.* Universal, 1930.
Ashe, Eugene, director. *Sylvie's Love.* Iam21 Entertainment, 2020.
Bacon, Lloyd, director. *The Singing Fool.* Warner Bros., 1928.
Bland, Edward, director. *The Cry of Jazz.* KHTB Productions, 1959.
Burns, Ken, director. *Jazz.* Florentine Films, 2001.
Carter, Thomas, director. *Swing Kids.* Hollywood Pictures, 1993.
Cassavetes, John, director. *Shadows.* Lion International, 1958.
Chazelle, Damien, director. *Whiplash.* Sony Pictures Classics, 2014.
Chazelle, Damien. *La La Land.* Lionsgate, 2016.
Cheadle, Don, director. *Miles Ahead.* Sony Pictures Classics, 2015.
Clarke, Shirley, director. *The Connection.* Allen-Hodgdon, 1961.
Coney, John, director. *Space Is the Place.* North American Star System, 1974.
Connelly, Marc and William Keighley, directors. *The Green Pastures.* Warner Bros., 1936.
Crosland, Alan, director. *The Jazz Singer.* Warner Bros., 1927.
Curtiz, Michael, director. *Young Man with a Horn.* Warner Bros., 1950.
Daniels, Lee, director. *The United States vs. Billie Holiday.* Lee Daniels Entertainment, 2021.
Danska, Herbert, director. *Sweet Love, Bitter.* Film 2 Associates, 1967.
Davies, Valentine, director. *The Benny Goodman Story.* Universal, 1956.
Dehn, Mura, director. *The Spirit Moves: A History of Black Social Dance on Film.* Dancetime Publications, 1987.
Dieterle, William, director. *Syncopation.* RKO, 1942.
Docter, Pete and Kemp Powers, directors. *Soul.* Disney, 2020.
Eastwood, Clint, director. *Bird.* Warner Bros., 1988.
Ellwood, Allison and Alex Gibney, directors. *Magic Trip: Ken Kesey's Search For A Kool Place.* Magnolia Pictures, 2011.

Farrelly, Peter, director. *Green Book*. Dreamworks, 2018.
Fitzgerald, Ella, vocals. "How High the Moon." March 20, 1966, www.youtube.com/watch?v=1GUmxnYheKo.
Fuller, Samuel, director. *China Gate*. Globe Enterprises, 1957.
Furie, Sidney J., director. *Lady Sings the Blues*. Paramount, 1972.
Green, Alfred E., director. *The Jolson Story*. Columbia, 1946.
Gsell, Gitta, director. *Irène Schweizer*. RECK Filmproduktion/Intakt, 2006.
Hallgren, Nadia, director. *Becoming*. Big Mouth Productions, 2020.
Harrison, Helen A. "Art in Focus with Helen Harrison: Jackson Pollock and Jazz." Stony Brook University Libraries, www.youtube.com/watch?v=0osmplV7D5A&t=1847s.
Hawks, Howard, director. *A Song Is Born*. Samuel Goldwyn, 1948.
Hendricks, William L., producer. *The Land We Love*. Warner Bros., 1966.
Immler, Stefan, director. *History of Jazz: Oxygen for the Ears*. Giganova Productions, 2012.
Jason, Leigh, director. *Carolina Blues*. Columbia, 1944.
Jeremy, John, director. *The Long Night of Lady Day*. 1515 Productions, 1984.
Jeremy, John. *Swing Under the Swastika*. Yorkshire Television, 1988.
King, Henry, director. *Alexander's Ragtime Band*. Twentieth Century Fox, 1938.
King, Henry. *Snows of Kilimanjaro*. Twentieth Century Fox, 1952.
King, Shaka, director. *Judas and the Black Messiah*. Warner Bros., 2021.
Leacock, Philip, director. *Let No Man Write My Epitaph*. Columbia, 1960.
Ledisi, vocals. "Alright." Rec. May 22, 2014, www.youtube.com/watch?v=W6prPMxTHAA.
Lee, Spike, director. *Mo' Better Blues*. Universal, 1990.
Leisen, Mitchell, director. *Swing High, Swing Low*. Paramount, 1937.
Lubin, Arthur, director. *New Orleans*. Majestic, 1947.
Lumet, Sidney, director. *The Pawnbroker*. MGM, 1965.
MacDougall, Ranald, director. *The Subterraneans*. MGM, 1960.
Mackendrick, Alexander, director. *Sweet Smell of Success*. Norma Productions, 1957.
Mann, Anthony, director. *The Glenn Miller Story*. Universal, 1954.
Mann, Ron, director. *Imagine the Sound*. 1981.
Marsalis, Wynton. "Giant Steps," Rec. July 17, 1987. www.youtube.com/watch?v=2XrdiOY_Uxk.
Marsalis, Wynton. "Jazz in Marciac 2009." Rec. August 6, 2009. www.youtube.com/watch?v=ZBJ-MmTA-eU&t=392s.
Maté, Rudolph, director. *D.O.A.* Harry Popkin, 1949.
Mayo, Archie, director. *Orchestra Wives*. Twentieth Century Fox, 1942.
Micheaux, Oscar, director. *The Girl from Chicago*. Micheaux Film, 1932.
Micheaux, Oscar. *Birthright*. Micheaux Film, 1939.
Monk, Thelonious, piano "Evidence." Rec. 1963. www.youtube.com/watch?v=qweSlfP6BtI.
Moran, Jason, piano. *In My Mind: Monk at Town Hall, 1959*. Rec. March 28, 2015 for *Jazz Night in America* (NPR), www.youtube.com/watch?v=JqhH-OUXyrY&t=683s.

Moran, Jason. "Fats Waller Dance Party: Live at Paris Jazz Festival." Rec. July 5, 2015, www.youtube.com/watch?v=z6-db4p9tL8.
Moran, Jason. "Fats Waller Dance Party – Middelheim 2015." Rec. August 2015, www.youtube.com/watch?v=TZjZ7mFir28.
Murphy, Dudley, director. *St. Louis Blues*. RKO, 1929.
Murphy, Dudley. Dudley Murphy, dir., *Black and Tan*. RKO, 1929.
Norton, Edward, director. *Motherless Brooklyn*. Warner Bros., 2019.
Peck, Raoul, director. *I Am Not Your Negro*. Velvet Films, 2016.
Penn, Leo, director. *A Man Called Adam*. Embassy Pictures, 1966.
Potter, H.C. director. *Second Chorus*. Paramount, 1940.
Preminger, Otto, director. *Carmen Jones*. Twentieth Century Fox, 1954.
Preminger, Otto. *Anatomy of a Murder*. Columbia, 1959.
Pritzker, Dan, director. *Bolden*. Abramorama, 2019.
Reisner, Allen, director. *St. Louis Blues*. Paramount, 1958.
Ritt, Martin, director. *Paris Blues*. United Artists, 1961.
Roth, Alan, director. *Inside Out in the Open*. 2001.
Rowland, Roy, director. *The 5000 Fingers of Dr. T*. Stanley Cramer, 1953.
Saturday Night Live. March 10, 1979. Guests Gary Busey, Eubie Blake, and Gregory Hines. NBC Television.
Saturday Night Live. April 14, 1979. Guests Milton Berle and Ornette Coleman. NBC Television.
Schertzinger, Victor, director. *Birth of the Blues*. Paramount, 1941.
Scorsese, Martin, director. *New York, New York*. United Artists, 1977.
Shavelson, Melville, director. *The Five Pennies*. Dena Productions, 1959.
Siodmak, Robert, director. *Phantom Lady*. Universal, 1944.
Spalding, Esperanza, bass and vocals. "On the Sunny Side of the Street." January 2016, www.youtube.com/watch?v=TQtXo4tiZxs.
Spielberg, Steven, director. *The Terminal*. Dreamworks, 2004.
Steen, Harold Heide, Jr., director. *Monk in Oslo*. Norwegian Broadcasting Corporation, 1966.
Stern, Bert and Aram Avakian, directors. *Jazz on a Summer's Day*. Galaxy Productions, 1959.
Surgal, Tom, director. *Fire Music*. Submarine Entertainment, 2021.
Sutherland, A. Edward, director. *Champagne Waltz*. Paramount, 1937.
Tavernier, Bertrand, director, *'Round Midnight*. Warner Bros., 1986.
Thorpe, Richard, director. *Jailhouse Rock*. MGM, 1957.
Tilton, Roger, director. *Jazz Dance*. 1954.
Waller, Fred, director. *Symphony in Black: A Rhapsody of Negro Life*. Paramount, 1935.
Walsh, Raoul, director. *Glory Alley*. MGM, 1952.
Walters, Charles, director. *High Society*. MGM, 1956.
Webb, Jack, director. *Pete Kelly's Blues*. Mark VII, 1955.
Weis, Don, director. *The Gene Krupa Story*. Columbia, 1959.
Wise, Robert, director. *Odds Against Tomorrow*. United Artists, 1959.
Wolfe, George C., director. *Ma Rainey's Black Bottom*. Escape Artists, 2020.
Woodberry, Billy, director. *And When I Die, I Won't Stay Dead*. Rosa Filmes, 2015.

Index

8 Mile (film), 294
16th Street Baptist Church, 22, 119, 128, 240
42nd Street (film), 269
52nd Street, 209, 242, 342
78 rpm records, 1, 3, 7, 8, 234, 235, 281
369th Infantry Regiment, 188

Abbott, Berenice, 341
Abbott, Norman, 307
ABC-Paramount, 121, 123
Abé, Katsuji, 348
ability/disability, 42
abstract expressionism, 8, 31, 282
Academy Awards, 269
Adderley, Cannonball, 167, 236
Adorno, Theodor, 138
advertising, 163, 305, 338, 344
Africa, 24, 35–36, 38–40, 44, 65–68, 99, 138, 159, 162–164, 178, 189, 192, 193, 203, 224, 278, 280, 285, 292–295
Africa/Brass (LP), 110
African American Vernacular English (AAVE), 106, 145, 147, 150, 159
"African Lady" (song), 192
"Afro Blue" (song), 120, 121
Afrofuturism, 69, 224, 298
After Midnight (LP), 239
Ahmad Jamal '73 (LP), 8
Aigui, Alexei, 330, 331
Alabama, 96, 188, 240
"Alabama" (song), 128, 240
Albers, Anni, 130
Albers, Josef, 130
album covers, 7–8, 135, 234, 236, 243, 282, 340, 343–344
Aldana, Melissa, 195
Alexander, Elizabeth, 226, 228, 230
   "Billy Strayhorn Writes 'Lush Life'" (poem), 228, 229
Alexander's Ragtime Band (film), 268, 293
Ali, Mahershala, 300
Alianza Hotel, 190

"All the Things You Are" (song), 266–267, 270
Allan, Lewis. *See* Meeropol, Abel
Allen, Red, 299
Allen, Steve, 223, 306, 307
Allen, Woody, 301
Alston, Charles, 284, 286
Altman, Robert, 298, 299, 309
Alvin Hotel, 167
American Broadcasting Company (ABC), 311, 312
American Songbook 1 (LP), 267
American Songbook, the, 7, 262–272. *See also* Broadway, Tin Pan Alley
American South, 3, 5, 22, 31, 55, 86, 90, 91, 96, 97, 102, 103, 128, 146, 164, 187, 211, 221, 237, 251, 293, 295
American Speech, 151
American West, 279
Amsterdam News, 98, 155, 248
Anatomy of a Murder (film), 296
And I Thought About You (LP), 110
And When I Die, I Won't Stay Dead (film), 231
Anderson, Ivie, 113, 115
Anderson, John, 310
Anderson, Laurie, 129
Anderson, Robert Mailer, 183
Andrews, Julie, 27
"Angel Eyes" (song), 58
Angelou, Maya, 224
Annie Get Your Gun (theatrical show), 268
Another Day (LP), 267
Ansermet, Ernst-Alexandre, 189
Anslinger, Harry, 160
"Anthropology" (song), 264
antisemitism, 44, 138, 291, 341
"Anything You Can Do I Can Do Better" (song), 52
Aoelian Hall, 310
Apollinaire, Guillaume, 280
   The Cubist Painters (book), 280
Apollo Theater, 117
Apple Records, 242

393

April in Paris (LP), 7
"Arabian Lover" (song), 88
Arbery, Ahmaud, 12
Aristotle, 55, 130
Arkansas, 96, 136, 251
Arlen, Harold, 262, 269, 271
Armenia, 196
Armstrong, Lil, 308
Armstrong, Louis, 3, 11, 23–25, 37–39, 51, 54, 69, 72, 81, 82, 86, 94, 115, 153, 163, 187, 234, 249, 250, 253–257, 264, 269, 286, 294–296, 301, 308, 309, 341, 345
Arnaz, Desi, 307
Arp, Jean, 135
Art Ensemble of Chicago, 29, 135, 244
Art Ford's Jazz Party (television program), 307
Art Pepper + Eleven (LP), 166
Ascension (LP), 118
Ascent of Ethiopia (painting), 285
Ashe, Eugene, 300
Asher, Don, 209, 210, 249
"The Barrier" (story), 208, 209
Ashgabat, 187
Asia, 196
Asomugha, Nnamdi, 300
Aspects of Negro Life (painting), 285
Association for the Advancement of Creative Musicians (AACM), 29, 30, 135, 244
At Shelly's Manne-Hole (LP), 267
At the Five Spot (LP compilation), 240
At the Pershing: But Not for Me (LP), 269
Atlantic Records, 135, 237, 344
Atomic Br. Basie, The (LP), 7
Attali, Jacques, 138
Audubon Ballroom, 128
Augusta, 119
Auschwitz, 168
Austin, 156
Austin, Gene, 38
Australia, 196
Austria, 279
autobiography, 6, 123, 153, 154, 161, 167, 243, 248–258, 281, 301, 332
"Autumn Serenade" (song), 118
Avakian, Aram, 322
Avakian, George, 234, 235, 323
Avery, Ray, 347
Ayler, Albert, 223, 282

Babes in Arms (theatrical show), 268
The Baby Dodds Story (book), 255
Bach, Jean, 338
Bach, Johann Sebastian, 210
"Back Woods Blues" (song), 97
"Backwater Blues" (song), 106

Bacon, Louis, 115
Badenko, Artem, 196
Bag's Groove (LP), 269
Bailey, Benny, 193, 194
Bailey, Derek, 58
Bailey, Philip, 124
Baker, Chet, 66, 166, 268, 269, 325, 343
Baker, Jimmie, 307
Baker, Josephine, 189, 279
Bakhtin, M.M., 49, 50, 53, 56, 59, 60
Baldwin, James, 167, 204–206, 301, 330–331
Remember This House (unfinished book), 330, 331
"Sonny's Blues" (story), 167, 204–206, 211, 214, 216, 301
Ball, Hugo, 135
Ball, Lucille, 307
Ballads (LP), 118
Ballets Russes, 278
Ballew, Smith, 114
Balliett, Whitney, 238, 239, 248, 310
Baltimore Afro-American, The, 114
Bambaataa, Afrika, 225
Bangkok, 196
Banjo Player (painting), 283, 286
Baraka, Amiri, 3, 24, 26, 44, 107, 132, 135–137, 147, 151, 219, 223–227, 239–240, 243, 244
"AM/TRAK" (poem), 226, 227, 244
"Black Art" (poem), 223
"Black Dada Nihilismus" (poem), 135
Black Music (book), 240
Blues People (book), 3, 147, 240
"Hunting Is Not Those Heads on the Wall" (essay), 132
"Jazz and the White Critic" (essay), 243
"The Screamers" (story), 135
"Speech #38 (or Y We say it this way)" (poem), 44
Wise, Why's, Y's (book), 44
"You Wants To Know Why?" (poem), 44
Barboza, Anthony, 346
Barker, Danny, 251, 255, 257
Barnet, Charlie, 255–257
Barthes, Roland, 49, 138
Barton, William, 196
baseball, 104
Basie (LP), 8
Basie, Count, 7, 160, 165, 166, 250, 253, 255–257, 287, 338
Bass Line (book), 256
Bauhaus, 7, 130
"B.D. Woman's Blues" (song), 4
Bearde, Nicholas, 123
Bearden, Romare, 283–286
Beatitude, 223

Beatles, the, 242
Beats, the, 9, 31, 130, 150, 154, 156, 159–161, 167, 168, 222, 223, 230, 239, 329
Beauvoir, Simone de, 163, 164
bebop, 8–10, 13, 23, 26, 43, 44, 52, 54, 56, 70, 116, 117, 130, 131, 133, 135, 145, 147, 154, 161, 165, 166, 176–178, 192–195, 208–210, 222, 223, 235, 250, 255, 264, 267–270, 282, 293, 295, 306, 321, 323, 324, 329, 340, 342
Bechet, Sidney, 189, 193, 194, 234, 254, 255
Beck, Julian, 129
Becoming (film), 331–332
Becton, Clarence, 194
Beijing, 196, 197
Belafonte, Harry, 298
Belgian, 193
Bell, Hugh, 346
Beneath the Underdog (book), 243, 248–250, 252–254
Benin, 196
Bennett, Tony, 267
The Benny Goodman Story (film), 294, 307
Benson, Al, 156
Bentley, Eric, 130
Bentley, Gladys, 4, 84–86, 94, 99
Berendt, Joachim, 343
Berg, John, 344
Berklee College of Music, 180–182
Berle, Milton, 75–76
Berlin, 21, 187, 197, 278, 279
Berlin, Irving, 262, 268, 269
Berliner Jazztage (JazzFest Berlin), 21, 192
Berliner, Sasha, 181
Bernhardt, Clyde, 251
Bernstein Philharmonic: Jazz in Serious Music (television program), 309
Bernstein, Elmer, 311
Bey, Andy, 123
Beyoncé, 230
Beyond Standard (LP), 265
Bierko, Craig, 314
Big Band Jazz (LP compilation), 239
Bigard, Barney, 115, 308
Bilko's Bopster (television episode), 313
Billboard (magazine), 7, 313
Billie (film), 325
Biloxi, 251
Binder, Steve, 307
Bird (film), 297
Birdland, 215
Birmingham, 22, 119, 128, 240
Birth of the Blues (film), 294
Birth of the Cool (LP), 165
Birthright (film), 96
Bishop, Walter, Jr., 55

Bizet, Georges, 51, 53
Black and Tan (film), 83, 87–90, 292
"Black and Tan Fantasy" (song), 87, 89
Black and White (film), 187
Black Arts Movement, 118, 223
"Black Beauty" (song), 89
Black church, the, 55, 100, 284, 292
Black Forum, 224
Black Lives Matter, 13, 31, 331
Black Mountain College, 129, 130
Black Nationalism, 223
Black Paine College, 119
Black Panthers, the, 301
Black Power, 223, 239
The Black Saint and the Sinner Lady (LP), 243
"The Blacker the Berry" (song), 331
blackface minstrelsy, 38, 39, 67, 97, 111, 121, 124, 252, 277, 278, 281, 291
Blackwell, Ed, 133
Blake, Eubie, 74, 114
Blake, William, 130
Blakey, Art, 235, 241, 329
Bland, Edward, 324, 325
Bley, Carla, 325
Blind Blake, 106
Blood on the Fields (composition), 10
Bloom, Harold, 49, 50, 52, 59
"Bloomdido" (song), 48
Blue (LP), 52
"Blue 7" (song), 179
"Blue Monk" (song), 323
"Blue Moon" (song), 313
Blue Note Records, 196, 235, 343
Bluebird Music Company, 283
blues, 2–4, 10, 26, 41, 56, 69, 84, 85, 92, 97–104, 113, 114, 117, 118, 135, 165, 188, 193, 196, 211, 214, 216, 220, 222, 225, 226, 230, 233, 236, 237, 239, 262, 271, 281, 283, 295, 306, 321
"The Blues Are Brewin'" (song), 295
"Bo Weavil Blues" (song), 104
Bob Howard Show (television program), 306
Body and Soul (LP), 238
"Body and Soul" (song), 58
Bogan, Lucille, 4
Boggs, Dock, 97
Boland, Francy, 193
Bolden (film), 300
Bolden, Buddy, 300
Bon Appétit (magazine), 328, 329
Bontemps, Arna, 220
boogie-woogie, 113, 282, 306
Boone, Richard, 42
Boss of the Blues (LP), 239
Boss Soul (LP), 224
bossa nova, 167, 192, 267

Boston Globe, 181
Boswell, James, 241
"Bottle Banging" (song), 329
Bourdieu, Pierre, 113, 139
Bowie, Lester, 135
"Box 703, Washington, D.C." (song), 193
Boy Meets Horn (book), 257
Bradford, Bobby, 325
Bradford, Perry, 2
Branch, James 'Plunky', 127
Brand, Dollar. *See* Ibrahim, Abdullah
Brandeis University, 236
Braque, Georges, 131
Braxton, Anthony, 26
Brazil, 167, 192
Breaking Point (LP), 137
Brecht, Bertolt, 72
Brecker, Michael, 312
Breton, Andre, 136
Bridgewater, Dee Dee, 196
Brigman, Anne, 339
Brill Building, the, 265, 266
British Broadcasting Corporation (BBC), 138, 315, 326
Broadway, 4, 74, 152, 262, 266–269, 298
Broadway Boogie Woogie (painting), 8, 282
"Broderick" (song), 236
Bronx, the, 5
Brooklyn, 187, 197
Brooks, Daphne A., 2, 72
Brooks, Gwendolyn, 82, 222
  Maud Martha (book), 82
  "We Real Cool" (poem), 222
Broonzy, Big Bill, 96, 159
Brother Jack McDuff Live! (LP), 242
Brötzmann, Peter, 194, 195
Broun, Heywood, 85
Brown, H. Rap, 128
Brown, James, 59
Brown, Michael, 12
Brown, Oscar, Jr., 111, 120, 307
Brown, Ray, 161
Brown, Sterling, 102–103, 107, 221
  "Cabaret" (poem), 221
  "Ma Rainey" (poem), 103–107
Brubeck, Dave, 8
Buber, Martin, 50
Buenos Aires, 197
Burgess, Ernest, 86
Burke, Sonny, 116
Burley, Dan, 148, 155
Burns, Ken, 11, 170, 180, 309, 323–326, 329, 331
Burroughs, William S., 162
  Junky (novel), 162
Busey, Gary, 74

Bushell, Garvin, 251
"But Not for Me" (song), 268, 269
"Buttons and Bows" (song), 51
Byard, Jaki, 59, 238, 241
Byas, Don, 194
Byrd, Charlie, 167
Byrd, Donald, 238
Byrne, David, 74

Cab Calloway's Cat-alogue: A Hepster's Dictionary (book), 153
cabaret cards, 160
Cabaret Voltaire, 135
Café Africana, 195
Café Bohemia, 9
Café CD Blues, 197
Café Society, 5
Cage, John, 129, 130, 132–134
Cagney and Lacey (television program), 312
Caine, Uri, 300
cakewalk, the, 104, 277–280, 294
California, 308
California Eagle, 345
call and response, 50, 67, 107
Calloway, Cab, 5, 42, 44, 98, 153–155, 162, 249, 255, 291, 316, 341
Camera Three (television program), 310
Camus, Albert, 167
  The Rebel: A Study of Man in Revolt (book), 167
"Can't Help Lovin' Dat Man" (song), 266
Capitol Records, 47
"Caravan" (song), 210
Carmen (opera), 53
Carmen Jones (film), 296
Carmichael, Hoagy, 271
Carmichael, Stokely, 128
Carnegie Corporation, 177
Carnegie Hall, 8, 270, 339
Carolina Blues (film), 293
Carolina Shout (collage), 286
"Carolina Shout" (song), 286
Carousel (theatrical show), 268
Carpenter, Thelma, 326
Carr, Leroy, 96
Carrington, Terri Lyne, 180–182
Carroll, Joe, 42
Carson, Johnny, 315
Carter, Benny, 46, 190, 296
Carter, James, 13
Carter, Regina, 13, 173
"The Case of the Missing Melody" (television episode), 311
Cassady, Neal, 161
Cassavetes, John, 297, 311

Castile, Philando, 12
The Cat and the Fiddle (theatrical show), 266
Cattrall, Kim, 314
Cavett, Dick, 315
Celebrations and Solitudes (LP), 224, 227
Center for Documentary Studies, 348
Center for Jazz Studies, 347
Chambers, Paul, 236
Champagne Waltz (film), 293
Change of the Century (LP), 243
Charlap, Bill, 267
Charles, Ray, 268
Charleston, the, 278, 321
Chasing Trane (film), 325
Chauvin, Derek, 12
Chavez, Carlos, 7
Chazelle, Damien, 301, 302
Cheadle, Don, 297
Cheek to Cheek (LP), 268
Cheers (television program), 312
Cherry, Don, 133, 137, 223, 225, 238
Chet Baker Sings (LP), 268, 269
Chicago, 81, 86, 96, 154–156, 225, 234, 235, 244, 279, 301, 308, 346
"Chicago Bound Blues (Great Migration Blues)" (song), 96
Chicago Defender, 96, 147, 155
Chicago Jazz (record set), 234
Chile, 195
China Gate (film), 296
Chiang, Philip, 7
Chocolate Kiddies (theatrical show), 189
Chopin, Frédéric, 86, 87, 89
Cincinnati, 114
Civil Rights Act of 1964, 22
Civil Rights Movement, 22, 28, 66, 73, 119, 128, 136, 228, 279, 296, 324, 330, 331, 340, 346
Civil War, the, 288
Clam House, 84
Clark (book), 255
Clark, Sonny, 161
Clarke, Kenny, 193
Clarke, Shirley, 295
class, 4, 12, 42, 57, 82, 87, 91, 98, 100, 105, 135, 156, 164, 187, 188, 300, 306, 312, 322, 329
classical music, 4, 9, 10, 49, 51, 52, 86, 87, 89, 97, 113, 133–136, 161, 175, 178, 179, 181, 182, 189, 210, 236, 277, 295, 330
Claxton, William, 342, 343, 346
Clayton, Buck, 251, 257
Clemons, Clarence, 298
The Clown (LP), 238
Cluzet, François, 297
Cobham, Billy, 196
Cohn, Al, 238

Cold War, 94, 163, 177–179, 191, 349
Cole, Cozy, 308
Cole, Freddie, 123
Cole, Nat "King," 116, 229, 239, 296, 306, 307, 330
Coleman, Earl, 116
Coleman, Ornette, 8, 12, 23, 31, 73–76, 117, 135, 138, 225, 236, 238, 239, 243, 282, 287, 325
Colin, Paul, 279
Collier, James Lincoln, 207
Collins, Arthur, 38
Cologne, 193
Colomby, Harry, 243
Colorado Springs, 251
Colored Vaudeville Benevolent Association, 2
colorism, 82
Coltrane (LP), 110, 242
Coltrane Live at Birdland (LP), 227, 240
Coltrane, Alice, 341
Coltrane, John, 13, 27–29, 50, 55, 56, 58, 69, 110, 117–123, 138, 224–227, 237, 240, 243, 244, 268, 282, 287, 325, 340, 341
"Dear Listener" (poem), 243
Columbia Broadcasting System (CBS), 306–311, 313
Columbia Records, 235, 323, 343, 344
Columbia University, 127–129, 139, 140, 347
Communist International (Comintern), 139
Communist Party, 187
compact discs (CDs), 344
Condé Nast, 328
Condon, Eddie, 254, 256
Condor, 329
"Confirmation" (song), 13
The Connection (film), 295
Conover, Willis, 193, 241
Conrad, Earl, 147
Cook, Elisha, Jr., 295
Cook, Will Marion, 189
cool, 66, 159–168, 340
"Cool Blues" (song), 161
cool jazz, 165–167, 267, 306, 322
"Cool Struttin'" (song), 161
"Cool Walk" (song), 161
Coon, Carlton, 38
Cooper, Jackie, 293
Copacabana, 192
Copenhagen, 194, 279
Cortez, Jayne, 224–227
"How Long Has Trane Been Gone" (poem), 227
The Cosby Show (television program), 312
Coss, Bill, 248
Costa, Johnny, 316
Cotton Club, 5, 86–88, 98, 271

"The Cotton Club Stomp" (song), 89
"Cottontail" (song), 264
"Country Gardens" (composition), 52, 53, 136
country music, 97
COVID-19, 12
"Cow Cow Boogie" (song), 41
Cox, Ida, 4, 96
Crane, Hart, 220
Crawford, Ralston, 341
"Crazy Blues" (song), 2–4, 15, 98, 281
Creeley, Robert, 130–132
Cricket, The, 232, 240
Crime Jazz (CD compilation), 312
Cronkite, Walter, 308
crooning, 110–118, 123, 306
Crosby, Bing, 114–116
Crouch, Stanley, 11, 179, 240–241, 331
The Cry of Jazz (film), 324
CTI Records, 344
Cuba, 278
Cubism, 8, 280–281
cummings, e.e., 221
    "God Pity Me Whom(God Distinctly Has)" (poem), 221
Cunningham, Merce, 129, 130
Cuomo, Douglas J., 314
cutting contests, 50, 298
Cyrus, Gerald, 346
Czechoslovakia, 138, 191

D.O.A. (film), 295
Dada, 129, 135, 136
Daddy O'Daylie (Holmes Daylie), 156
Dale, George, 235
Dallas, 159, 237
Dan Burley's Original Handbook of Harlem Jive (book), 155
dance, 64, 67, 74, 87, 91, 129, 152, 159, 189, 221, 277–282, 285, 286, 293–295, 308, 320, 321, 323, 341, 342, 346
Dance, Stanley, 250
Dancers (painting), 286
"Dancers – New York" (photograph), 346
Daniels, Lee, 301
Danse Serpentine (film), 280
Dantzic, Jerry, 345
Dark Room Collective, 225
Davis, Angela, 4, 119
Davis, Frank Marshall, 107
Davis, Miles, 10, 66, 69, 73, 74, 133, 160, 165–167, 215, 222, 230, 236, 239, 241–243, 249, 250, 252, 255, 257, 269, 287, 297, 311, 313, 323, 325, 330, 331, 340, 347
Davis, Sammy, Jr., 297
Davis, Stuart, 8, 280

Dawson, C. Daniel, 347
Day, Andra, 6
De Leath, Vaughn, 112
De Niro, Robert, 298
Dean, James, 167
"Dear Old Southland" (song), 115
Dearie, Blossom, 315
Debussy, Claude, 86, 178, 277
DeCarava, Roy, 286–288, 340, 343, 346, 347
Decca Records, 41, 47, 326
Deems, Barrett, 308
"Defining Moments" (television episode), 314
Dehn, Mura, 320, 321
Delaunay, Charles, 190
Deleuze, Gilles, 139
democracy, 14, 57, 98, 164, 170, 179, 180, 191, 216, 323, 324, 329–332
Demuth, Charles, 278, 281
Denmark, 193, 349
Depression, the, 97, 147, 339
Derricotte, Toi, 71
Desilu, 307
Desmond, Paul, 7, 166
Destination Out (LP), 137
Detroit, 12, 13, 257
Detroit Jazz Festival, 14
Devlin, Paul, 253
Devo, 74
Dial M for Music (television program), 307
Dialectics of Liberation Congress, 139
dialogism, 49–51
diaspora, African, 36, 39, 40, 65, 66, 68, 72, 159, 163, 178, 188, 285, 288, 339
Dibango, Manu, 12
Diddley, Bo, 46
Diddly, Bo, 38
Diggeth Thou? (book), 155
disco, 264
Dixieland, 161, 187, 195, 264, 282
Django (LP), 237
"Do You Know What It Means to Miss New Orleans" (song), 294, 295
documentary, 11, 163, 283, 309, 319–332, 338
Dodds, Baby, 147, 255, 257
Dodds, Johnny, 254
Dogon A.D. (LP), 239
Dolphy, Eric, 137, 325
Don't Look Back (film), 321
Dorough, Bob, 315
Dorsey, Jimmy, 264
Dorsey, Tommy, 116
Dostoevsky, Fyodor, 59
Double-V Campaign, 147
Douglas, Aaron, 283–285
Douglas, Bob, 345, 346

Douglas, Kirk, 294
Down Beat, 10, 13, 42, 151, 155, 161, 162, 196, 237, 313, 340, 342, 346
Down Here on the Ground (LP), 238
"Down South" (song), 96
"Down South Blues" (song), 96
Downbeat Jazz Club, 326
Doyle, Roddy, 301
  Oh, Play That Thing (novel), 301
Dr. Hepcat (Lavada Durst), 156
drag, 4, 84. *See also* performance
drama, 98, 99, 130, 135, 239
drawing, 7, 243, 278, 280
"The Dream Sequence Always Rings Twice" (television episode), 313
Drew's Blues (book), 255
Driggs, Frank, 347
drugs, 6, 44, 150, 152–154, 160, 165, 166, 178, 194, 204, 205, 213–215, 254, 256, 268, 270, 295–297, 326
Du Bois, W.E.B., 71, 72, 86, 128
  The Souls of Black Folk (book), 71
Duchamp, Marcel, 136
Dufty, William, 253
Duke Ellington & John Coltrane (LP), 118
"The Duke Steps Out" Out (song), 89
Duke University, 348
Dumas, Henry, 136
Duncan, Robert, 130
DuPont, 307
DuPont Show of the Week (television program), 308, 309
Duvivier, George, 5
Dyani, Johnny, 195
Dylan, Bob, 239

e.s.t., 196
Eady, Cornelius, 226
Easton, Amos, 96
Eberle, Ray, 116
Ebony, 236, 306
Eckinger, Isla, 194
Eckstine, Billy, 112, 116–117
ECM Records, 194, 196, 344, 349
Ed Sullivan Show, The (television program), 315
Eddie Condon's Floor Show (television program), 307
Edwards, Blake, 311
Edwards, Cliff "Ukulele Ike," 38
Edwards, Esmond, 344
eephing, 38–39
Egypt, 280, 285, 298
Eicher, Manfred, 194, 196
Eisenhower, Dwight, 323
El Paso, 207

Eldridge, Roy, 54, 55
Eli's Chosen Six, 323
Eliat, 196
Eliot, T. S., 97, 221
Ella Fitzgerald Sings the Cole Porter Songbook (LP), 268
Ellington, Duke, 3, 5, 10, 72, 83, 86–90, 92, 94, 98, 110, 113–117, 163, 165, 166, 189, 195, 210, 229, 237, 250, 253, 255–258, 264, 287, 292, 294, 296, 301, 323, 346
Elliott, Moppa, 53
Ellis, David, 283
Ellison, Ralph, 50, 52, 160, 164, 167, 179, 213, 331
  Living With Music (book), 167
Empress of the Blues (collage), 286
Empyrean Isles (LP), 242
England, 110, 279
The Epic (LP), 332
Ervin, Booker, 240, 241
Esquire, 98, 161, 162, 310, 338
Esquire's All American Hot Jazz (record series), 161
Ethel Merman Disco Album (LP), 264
Ethiopia, 285
Ethiopia (sculpture), 285, 286
Eubie! (theatrical show), 74
Europe, 9, 10, 38, 52, 57, 67, 68, 70, 72, 90, 104, 111, 129, 132, 138, 140, 163, 178, 189, 190, 194–196, 203, 277–280, 283, 285, 293, 299, 330, 338, 341, 344, 349
Europe, James Reese, 188
"Ev'ry Time We Say Goodbye" (song), 268
Evans, Bill, 53, 243, 267
Evans, Frank, 307
Evans, Gil, 133, 165, 166, 269
Evergreens (LP), 239
Evers, Medgar, 22, 330
"Everybody Loves My Baby" (song), 38, 220
Everybody Loves Raymond (television program), 311
"Everything I Have Is Yours" (song), 116
"Everything's Cool" (song), 161
existentialism, 165, 167, 168, 238
Expressionist cinema, 343
Eyer, Robert, 10

Fabio, Sarah Webster, 224
"Fables of Faubus" (song), 136, 228
Face the Music (theatrical show), 268
Falay, Muvaffak "Maffy," 193
The Family of Man (exhibition), 346
Farm Security Administration, 341, 345
Farmer, Art, 166
Farrell, Joe, 56
fashion, 66, 75, 83, 84, 87, 88, 105, 135, 155, 340–342, 346, 349

Faubus, Orville, 136
Faulkner, Anne Shaw, 203
   "Does Jazz Put the Sin in Syncopation?" (article), 203
Feather, Leonard, 235–237, 242, 248
Feingersh, Ed, 346
Ferguson, Maynard, 323
Festival de Vitoria-Gasteiz, 69
Fetchit, Stepin, 291
fiction, 98, 99, 135, 136, 162, 163, 167, 204–216, 301
"Figure Eight" (song), 315
film, 65, 66, 90, 96, 115, 151, 262, 266, 268–270, 279, 280, 283, 291–302, 305, 311, 313, 319, 320, 321–332, 342
Fire Music (film), 325
Fire Music (LP), 128, 136
Fischer, Werner T., 196, 197
Fitzgerald, Ella, 40–42, 47, 65, 167, 229, 264, 267–269, 296
Fitzgerald, F. Scott, 223, 281
   Tender is the Night (novel), 223
The Five Pennies (film), 296
Five Spot, 9, 133, 226, 237, 240
The 5,000 Fingers of Dr. T. (film), 295
"Flamenco Sketches" (song), 330
"Flaming Youth" (song), 89
"Flat Flat Floogie (with a Floy Floy)" (song), 44
"Fleurette Africaine" (song), 301
Florida, 96, 100
Flowers, Martha, 192
Floyd, George, 12, 31
"Flying Home" (song), 41, 42
Folies Bergère, 279
"Foolish Man Blues" (song), 84
Ford Foundation, 177
Forrest, Helen, 267
Fortner, Sullivan, 300
Foster, George, 251, 254, 255
Four Saints in Three Acts (opera), 113
"Fourth Symphony" (composition), 134
Fox Broadcasting Company, 308
France, 113, 139, 161, 188, 189, 191, 193, 196, 278, 279, 349
Frank, Robert, 344
Frankfurt, 189
Franklin, Aretha, 8, 266
Frankly Jazz (television program), 307
Fraser, Al, 253
Fred Hall's Sugar Babies, 38
Free at Last (LP), 194
Free Form (painting), 134
free jazz, 9, 10, 23, 31, 73, 129, 140, 194, 223, 224, 237, 241, 282, 324, 325

Free Jazz (LP), 8, 31, 134, 137, 138, 282
The Freedom and Space Sessions (LP compilation), 240
The Fresh Prince of Bel-Air (television program), 314
Friedlander, Lee, 344
Friends (television program), 318
Frisell, Bill, 173
From Spirituals to Swing (concerts), 100
Fujita, S. Neil, 8
Fuller, Loie, 280
Fuller, Meta Warrick, 285, 286
Fuller, Richard Buckminster, 130, 134
   "The Music of the New Life" (essay), 134
funk, 59, 74

G.I. Bill, 176
Gabler, Milt, 326, 327
Gaillard, Slim, 43, 44
Gara, Larry, 257
Garland, Judy, 269, 270
Garrison, Jimmy, 110, 122
Garry, Sid, 114
Gates, Henry Louis, Jr., 28, 50
gender, 4, 42, 75, 81–88, 91–93, 97, 98, 101, 112, 114–116, 129, 180–182, 204, 221, 230, 237, 242, 254, 270, 296, 310, 313, 314, 320, 332
The Gene Krupa Story (film), 295
The Gentle Giant (book), 255
Georgia, 103
"Georgia on My Mind" (song), 208
Gerlach, Horace, 250, 254
Germany, 138, 161, 163, 189, 191, 193, 194, 196, 343
Gerry Mulligan and His Tentette (LP), 166
The Gerry Mulligan Quartet (LP), 239
Gershwin, George, 263–265, 268, 269, 292, 294, 329
Gershwin, Ira, 5, 263–265, 268, 269
Gettin' Around (LP), 237
Getz, Stan, 66, 166, 167, 192, 194
Getz/Gilberto (LP), 167, 192
"Giant Steps" (song), 69
"Giants and All That Jazz" (television episode), 311
Giddins, Gary, 39, 236, 242, 244, 252, 325
Gignoux, Dany, 349
Gilberto, Astrud, 192
Gilberto, João, 167, 192
Gilda (film), 313
Gillespie, Dizzy, 8, 25, 26, 40, 42, 44, 48, 54, 55, 116–118, 145, 148, 191, 192, 235, 248–250, 253–256, 267, 282, 287, 313, 316, 329, 341, 342
Gillespie, William, 340
Ginsberg, Allen, 130, 219, 222, 223
   Howl (poem), 222

Giovanni, Nikki, 224
Girl Crazy (theatrical show), 263, 264, 269
The Girl from Chicago (film), 96
"The Girl from Ipanema" (song), 136, 238
Gitler, Ira, 235, 237–238, 242
Gleason, Ralph, 238, 239, 241, 309
Gleizes, Albert, 280
Glendale, 347
The Glenn Miller Story (film), 296
Gloria Hotel, 192
Glory Alley (film), 296
"Go Down, Moses" (song), 99
Godard, Jean-Luc, 129
Goebbels, Joseph, 138
Goffin, Gerry, 266
Goffin, Robert, 308
"Goin' Back to Alabama" (song), 96
"Goin' Back to Texas" (song), 96
"Goin' to Richmond" (song), 96
"Going Back Home" (song), 96
"Going Back to Arkansas" (song), 96
"Going Back to Florida" (song), 96
"Going Back to Memphis" (song), 96
Gold, Robert S., 147, 152, 162, 164
    A Jazz Lexicon (book), 147, 162, 164
The Golden Age of Jazz (book), 342
The Golden Girls (television program), 312
Golson, Benny, 299
Gone with the Wind (film), 291
Gontcharov, Andrey, 331
Gonzales, Babs, 42
Good Morning Blues (book), 250, 253, 255, 257
"Good Old Bygone Days" (song), 96
"Good Rockin' Tonight" (song), 117
Goodman, Benny, 82, 165, 250, 254, 294, 313
Gordon, Claire P., 257
Gordon, Dexter, 52, 194, 237, 242, 282, 297, 342
Gordon, Maxine, 254
Gordon, Robert, 5
Gosling, Ryan, 302
gospel, 99, 113, 135, 238, 283
Gottlieb, William, 326, 327, 340, 342, 343
Gourmet Makes (online program), 328
Graham, Ronny, 313
Grainger, Percy, 136
Grammy awards, 10, 239, 271
Granville, Bonita, 293
Granz, Norman, 310
Gray, Freddie, 12
Grayson, Jessica, 293
Great Britain, 138, 190, 349
A Great Day in Harlem (film), 338
Green, Benny, 242
Green Book (film), 300
The Green Pastures (film), 113

Greene, Gene, 38
Greenwich Village, 9, 133, 159, 177, 222
Gregory, Dick, 297
Grieg, Edvard, 51
Grierson, John, 319
Griffin, Johnny, 52, 194
Griffin, Merv, 315
Grimes, Henry, 12, 323
Grosz, George, 278
Guaraldi, Vince, 315
Guattari, Felix, 140
Guillaume, Paul, 278

Hackett, Bobby, 308
Haden, Charlie, 133
Hahn, Alex, 196
The Haig, 166
Haiti, 285
"Haitian Fight Song" (song), 315
Hall Johnson Choir, 89
Hallelujah I'm a Bum (film), 121
Hallgren, Nadia, 331–332
Halvorson, Mary, 58
Hamasyan, Tigran, 196
Hamburg, 191
Hammerstein, Oscar, II, 268, 270
Hammond, John, 100, 326
Hamp: An Autobiography (book), 257
Hampton, Fred, 301
Hampton, Lionel, 42, 257
Hancock, Herbie, 242, 255, 316
Handy, Craig, 298
Handy, John, 239
Handy, W. C., 99, 114, 222, 296
Hanks, Tom, 299
Happenings, 129
Harburg, Edgar (Yip), 269
"Hard Times Ain't Gone No Where" (song), 96
Harlan, Byron, 38
Harlem, 2, 4, 5, 26, 41, 83, 84, 86, 87, 89, 90, 98,
    99, 128, 150, 152–155, 187, 190, 193, 195, 212,
    221–223, 271, 284–287, 299, 310, 338, 346
"Harlem Blues" (song), 2
Harlem Hellfighters, 188–189
Harlem of the West (photography project), 348
Harlem Renaissance, 4, 82, 84, 92, 94, 221, 230,
    284, 285
Harper, Michael S., 227
    "Dear John, Dear Coltrane" (poem), 227
Harris, Allan, 123
Harris, Charles "Teenie," 345
Harris, Eddie, 167
Harris, Wynonie, 117
Harry O (television program), 311
Hart, Lorenz, 121, 268

Hart, Max, 308
Hartman, Johnny, 110, 115–123
Hawes, Hampton, 249, 252, 255, 256
Hawkins, Coleman, 58, 238, 242, 288, 298
Hawkins, Erskine, 160
Haynes, Roy, 315, 323
Hayworth, Rita, 313
"He Wasn't Born in Araby, But He's a Sheikin' Fool" (song), 94
"Heebie Jeebies" (song), 37–39
Hefti, Neil, 318
Hemingway, Ernest, 164
Hemphill, Julius, 239
Henderson, Fletcher, 30, 38, 94, 113, 254
Henderson, Joe, 53
Henderson, Rosa, 96, 97
Hendricks, Jon, 40
Hentoff, Nat, 10, 238, 239, 310
"Hep Cat Boogie" (song), 117
Herman, Woody, 255, 256
Hernandez, Juano, 294
Herridge, Robert, 310
Hershorn, Tad, 348
"Hesitating Blues" (song), 222
Hibbler, Al, 115
Higgins, Billy, 133
High Society (film), 296
High Times Hard Times (book), 251
Hill, Andrew, 59
Himes, Chester, 136
  A Rage in Harlem (novel), 136
Hines, Earl, 59, 92, 116, 117
Hines, Gregory, 74
Hinton, Milt, 252, 256, 308, 340, 341
hip-hop, 10, 12, 49, 156, 224, 225, 294, 321
hipness, 9, 116, 145, 148, 150–152, 156, 168, 174, 182, 219, 222, 234, 239, 241, 254
Hiromi, 265
Hiroshima, 168
"His Way" (television episode), 311
Histoire du soldat (theatrical work), 277
History of Jazz: Oxygen for the Ears (film), 324
Hobsbawm, Eric, 163
Hoch Conservatory, 189
Hodeir, André, 90
Hodes, Art, 257
Holiday, Billie, 4, 7, 69, 72, 119, 160, 165, 166, 171, 226, 228, 252–257, 268, 287, 292, 294, 295, 297, 301, 310, 325–327, 342, 345, 346
Holland, 193
Holland, Charles, 113
Hollywood, 262, 265, 268, 269, 293, 296, 299, 306, 310, 340
Hollywood (LP), 265
"Hollywood Bed" (song), 117

Holmes, John Clellon, 162
  Go (novel), 162
  The Horn (novel), 167
"The Holy City" (song), 89
Home Box Office (HBO), 313
Homicide: Life on the Streets (television program), 311
"Honeysuckle Rose" (song), 59
Hoover, Herbert, 97
Horne, Lena, 271, 287, 330
Hot Club de France, 190
hot jazz, and hot music, 96, 98, 161, 264, 323
"Hot Jazz" (photograph), 346
Hot Man (book), 257
"How High the Moon" (song), 41
Howard, Bob, 306, 307
Howard Theater, 114
Howard University, 102, 128
Howell, Peg Leg, 100
Hubbard, Freddie, 137
Hughes, Langston, 3, 43, 97–102, 107, 155, 187–188, 190, 192, 193, 195, 197, 219–222, 225, 286
  Ask Your Mama: 12 Moods for Jazz (book), 222
  "Bound No'th Blues" (poem), 99, 102
  "The Cat and the Saxophone (2 a.m.)" (poem), 220–221
  The Children's Corner (composition), 277
  "Children's Rhymes" (poem), 43
  "Cross" (poem), 99
  Don't You Want to Be Free? (play), 99
  "Dream Boogie" (poem), 43
  First Book of Jazz (book), 99
  "Flatted Fifths" (poem), 44
  "Hard Luck" (poem), 100
  "Hey!" (poem), 100, 102
  "Hey! Hey!" (poem), 100
  "Jam Session" (poem), 44
  "Let America Be America Again" (poem), 98
  "Likewise" (poem), 44
  Little Ham (play), 98
  "Maker of the Blues" (poem), 99
  Montage of a Dream Deferred (book), 43, 44
  Mule Bone (play, with Zora Neale Hurston), 98, 99
  "The Negro Artist and the Racial Mountain" (essay), 3, 220
  "The Negro Speaks of Rivers" (poem), 99
  Not Without Laughter (novel), 98, 99
  "Question [2]" (poem), 44
  "Rent-Party Shout: For a Lady Dancer" (poem), 98

"Song for a Dark Girl" (poem), 99
The Sweet Flypaper of Life (book), 286
"Tag" (poem), 44
The Weary Blues (book), 220
"The Weary Blues" (poem), 97, 99
"Trumpet Player" (poem), 197
"What? So Soon!" (poem), 44
Hungary, 189
Hunstein, Don, 343, 344
Hunter College, 177, 179
Hunter, Evan, 209, 210
  Streets of Gold (novel), 209
Hurst, Robert, 69
Hurston, Zora Neale, 98, 100, 104, 162, 169
  "Story in Harlem Slang" (story), 162
  "The Gilded Six-Bits" (story), 169

I Am Not Your Negro (film), 330–331
I Could Go on Singing (film), 270
"I Couldn't Hear Nobody Pray" (song), 99
"I Didn't Know What Time It Was" (song), 52
"I Dream of Jeannie with the Light Brown Hair" (song), 51
"I Got Rhythm" (song), 52, 263–265
I Remember (book), 251
"I Told Ya I Love Ya (Now Get Out)" (song), 313
"(I Wish I Could Shimmy Like) My Sister Kate" (song), 92
Ibrahim, Abdullah, 195
"I'll Come Back for More" (song), 115
"Image in the Sand" (television episode), 311
Imagine the Sound (film), 325
"I'm Going Back to Tennessee" (song), 96
impressionism, 339
Impressions (LP), 110
improvisation, 11, 13, 32, 51, 53, 64, 66, 90, 92, 102, 130–133, 137–139, 146, 164, 167, 168, 179, 194, 236, 237, 241, 263, 267, 268, 321, 329
Impulse! Records, 121, 122, 344
"I'm So in Love with You" (song), 114
"The Inflated Tear" (song), 301
In My Mind: Monk at Town Hall, 1959 (multimedia performance), 58
"In That Great Gettin' Up Mornin'" (song), 99
"In the Land of Oo-Blah-Dee" (song), 48
Indianapolis, 341
Indigenous peoples, 46
The Infernal Cakewalk (film), 280
Ink Spots, the, 41
Inside Out in the Open (film), 325
Institute of Jazz and Gender Justice, 180–183
Institute of Jazz Studies, 177, 182
Interstellar Low Ways (LP), 243
Interstellar Space (LP), 118

Israel, 196
Italy, 193, 349
It's Nation Time (LP), 224
"It's Only a Paper Moon" (television episode), 311
itutu (Yoruba), 159, 163
"I've Got a Gal in Kalamazoo" (song), 293
Ives, Charles, 134
Iyer, Vijay, 64

Jackie and Roy, 42
Jackson, Samuel L., 330
Jailhouse Rock (film), 297
Jamaica, 284
Jamal, Ahmad, 8, 241, 269
Jammin' the Blues (film), 342
Janco, Marcel, 135
Japan, 187, 190, 243, 265, 348, 349
Jarman, Joseph, 244
Jarreau, Al, 42
Jarrett, Keith, 270
Jazz (book), 250, 252–254
Jazz (film), 11, 170, 180, 309, 323–325, 331
Jazz (painting), 280
Jazz '34: Remembrances of Kansas City Swing (telvision program), 309
Jazz 625 (television program), 315
Jazz Age, 83, 93, 112, 113, 115, 116, 146, 219, 221, 281
Jazz and People's Movement, 315
Jazz and the Art of Photography (symposium), 347
Jazz at Lincoln Center, 11, 50, 173, 179, 346
Jazz at the Philharmonic (concert series), 310
Jazz Band: My Life in Jazz (book), 255
Jazz Casual (television program), 239, 309
Jazz Club Universitaire, 190
jazz critics, 6, 68, 162, 166, 177, 179, 235–239, 241–243, 248–251, 310
Jazz Dance (film), 322
jazz fusion, 10, 57, 196, 241, 324
Jazz Giants (book), 349
The Jazz Image: Masters of Jazz Photography (book), 348
Jazz in Marciac, 69
Jazz in the Bittersweet Blues of Life (book), 255
Jazz in the City (concert series), 173
Jazz Is Universal (LP), 193
jazz kissa, 190
Jazz Loft (photography project), 348
jazz manouche, 191
A Jazz Odyssey (book), 255, 257
Jazz on a Summer's Day (film), 322–323
Jazz Record, 257

"Jazz Records" (television episode), 311
Jazz Samba (LP), 167
Jazz Scene USA (television program), 307
jazz scholarship, 1, 41, 45, 51, 64, 76, 161, 178, 179, 182, 189, 255, 305, 307, 315, 320, 324, 347
The Jazz Singer (film), 291
Jazz Street (book), 344
Jazz Times, 239, 240, 348
Jazz Workshop, 132
Jazzhus Montmartre, 194
JazzLife (book), 343
Jazzmen: The Story of Hot Jazz Told by the Men Who Created It (book), 161
Jefferson, Eddie, 40
Jeffries, Herb, 115
Jess, Tyehimba, 225
Jim Crow, 2, 5, 86–88, 96, 160, 194, 252, 324. *See also* segregation
JinglePunks (website), 329
Jivin' in Be-Bop (film), 8
Joans, Ted, 136, 167, 223
Jobim, Antônio Carlos, 167, 192
"John Brown's Body" (song), 99
John Coltrane and Johnny Hartman (LP), 118, 120, 121, 123
John Handy Recorded Live at the Monterey Jazz Festival (LP), 239
Johnny spielt auf (opera), 189
Johnny Staccato (television program), 311
Johns, Jasper, 129
Johnson, Alec, 97
Johnson, George W., 14
Johnson, Helene, 221, 222
 "Poem" (poem), 221
Johnson, J. Rosamond, 13, 284
Johnson, James P., 92, 286
Johnson, James Weldon, 13, 283, 284
 God's Trombones (book), 283
Johnson, Lonnie, 96, 97
Johnson, Robert, 222
Johnson, Samuel, 241
Johnson, Sargent, 283
Jolson, Al, 38, 121, 291, 294
The Jolson Story (film), 294
Jones, Elvin, 110, 122, 240
Jones, Grace, 284
Jones, Jo, 253, 257
Jones, LeRoi. *See* Baraka, Amiri
Jones, Lois Mailou, 284, 285
Jones, Lou, 348
Jones, Orville "Hoppy," 41
Jones, Quincy, 296
Joplin, Scott, 281
Jordan, Sheila, 45

Josephson, Barney, 5
Judas and the Black Messiah (film), 301
Judgement Day (illustration), 283
Juju, 127
"Jungle Jamboree" (song), 88
"Jungle Nights in Harlem" (song), 88
"Just Coolin'" (song), 161

Kaap, Jack, 47
KABC, 307
Kalin, Victor, 243
Kaminsky, Max, 255
Kamoinge Workshop, 346
Kane, Art, 299, 310, 338
Kansas City, 234, 256, 281, 298, 309, 345
Kansas City (film), 298, 309
Kansas Joe, 96
Karsh, Yousuf, 342
Katz, Jimmy, 344
Kauba, Carl, 279
Kaufman, Bob, 167, 223
 "Bagel Shop Jazz" (poem), 223
 "War Memoir" (poem), 223
Kaye, Danny, 295
"Keep Cool, Fool" (song), 160
Keepnews, Orrin, 165, 347
Kelley, Robin D. G., 27
 Freedom Dreams (book), 136
Kelley, William Marvin, 164
Kelly, Eddie, 96
Kelly, Nora, 242
Kennedy, Eleanor, 242
Kennedy, John F., 31
Kenny, Bill, 124
Kenny G., 312
Keppard, Freddie, 1
Keresztes, Lajos, 344
Kern, Jerome, 266–268, 270
Kerouac, Jack, 130, 161, 162, 171, 219, 223, 329
 Mexico City Blues (book), 222
 On the Road (novel), 162
Kesey, Ken, 168
Kesslere, G. Maillard, 341
Keystone Korner, 347
Kilmer, Joyce
 "Trees" (poem), 155
Kimball's East, 347
Kind of Blue (LP), 53, 243
The King and I (theatrical show), 268
King of Jazz (film), 252, 292–293
The Kingdom of Swing (book), 250, 254
"King of the Bungaloos" (song), 38
King Pleasure, 40
King, Carole, 266

King, Martin Luther, Jr., 21, 22, 30, 31, 50, 55, 119, 128, 173, 192, 330
"I Have a Dream" (speech), 119
"Letter from Birmingham Jail" (essay), 119
Where Do We Go from Here? (book), 31
King, Nel, 250
Kinsey, Angela, 312
Kirk, Rahsaan Roland, 65, 225, 301, 315
Kline, Franz, 130
Kline, Randall, 173, 174
Klugman, Jack, 310
KMLA, 307
Knight, Gwendolyn, 284, 285
Koehler, Ted, 271
Kolodin, Irving, 250
Komunyakaa, Yusef, 225
Konitz, Lee, 12, 166
Kooning, Willem de, 130
Kouwenhoven, John A., 9
Beer Can by the Highway, The (book), 9
KQED, 239, 309
Krall, Diana, 268
Krasner, Lee, 282
Krenek, Ernst, 189
KRHM, 307
Kristeva, Julia, 49
KTLA, 307
Kubik, Gail, 330
"Kucheza Blues" (song), 193
Kyser, Kay, 293

L.H.O.O.Q. (painting), 136
La La Land (film), 302
LA Philharmonic, 332
Ladies Home Journal, 203
"Lady Be Good" (song), 42
Lady Gaga, 268
Lady Sings the Blues (book), 6, 252–254, 257
Lady Sings the Blues (film), 5, 297
Lagos, 193
Lamar, Kendrick, 12, 225, 331
Lambert, Hendricks, & Ross, 40
Lancaster, Burt, 296
Land of the Giants (television program), 311
The Land We Love (film), 330
Lande, Art, 58
Las Vegas, 166
Last Poets, 225
Lateef, Yusef, 255
Latin America, 258
Latin jazz, 59, 166, 192, 267, 314
Lawrence, Jacob, 130, 284–286
Le Querrec, Guy, 349
Ledisi, 42, 48
Lee, Don. *See* Madhubuti, Haki

Lee, Russell, 341
Lee of Hollywood, 341
Lees, Gene, 248
Lefebvre, Henri, 129
Léger, Fernand, 281
The Legendary Buster Smith (LP), 237
Leloir, Jean-Pierre, 349
Lennox, Annie, 268
Leonard, Herman, 342–344
Les Joyeux Nègres, 278
"Let Me Dig It" (song), 159
Let No Man Write My Epitaph (book), 296
Lethem, Jonathan, 299
Motherless Brooklyn (novel), 299
Let's Get Lost (film), 325
"Let's Get Lost" (song), 166
Let's Get to the Nitty Gritty (book), 255
Lewis, George E., 25, 26, 29, 50, 68, 132
Lewis, John, 296
Library of Congress, 257, 342
Lichtenstein, Roy, 8
Life (magazine), 155, 310, 340, 341, 345, 348
"Lift Every Voice and Sing (or, The Harp)" (sculpture), 284
"Lift Every Voice and Sing" (song), 13, 284
Liggins, Jimmy, 117
The Light Is On (LP), 197
Lincoln Center, 10, 11. *See also* Jazz at Lincoln Center
Lincoln, Abbey, 111, 238
Lindsay, Vachel, 220, 221
"The Jazz of This Hotel" (poem), 221
liner notes, 118, 192, 193, 227, 234–244
Listen Lord (painting), 284
"Little Low Mamma Blues" (song), 106
The Little Nigar (composition), 277
Little Rock, 136
"Little Rootie Tootie" (song), 58
Live at the Village Vanguard (LP), 110
Live in Japan (LP), 27
"Livery Stable Blues" (song), 1
Living Theater, 129
Locke, Alain, 3, 241
The Negro and His Music (book), 3
"The New Negro" (essay), 3, 15
Lomax, Alan, 257
The Long Night of Lady Day (film), 326–327
London, 189
Long, Barbara, 242
Los Angeles, 166, 196, 238, 307, 343, 347
Los Angeles Sentinel, 345
Loueke, Lionel, 196
Louis-Dreyfus, Julia, 312
Louisiana, 254
A Love Supreme (LP), 118, 121, 123, 227, 243

"Lover Man" (song), 326, 327
Luce, Henry, 341
Ludwigsburg, 194
Lumet, Sidney, 308
Lumière, August, 279
Lumière, Louis, 279
"Lush Life" (song), 120, 226, 228–230
lynching, 100, 228, 251–252, 340

"Ma Rainey" (song), 103–104
Ma Rainey's Black Bottom (film), 301
MacAdams, Lewis, 159, 167
  The Birth of The Cool: Bebop, The Beats, and the American Avant-Garde (book), 159
Machine Gun (LP), 194
Mackey, Nathaniel, 26, 204, 225, 226
  Mu (poem sequence), 225
  "Other: From Noun to Verb" (essay), 204
  Song of the Andomboulou (poem sequence), 225
  Splay Anthem (book), 225
MacLow, Jackson, 129
Mad House, 85
Madhubuti, Haki, 44, 224, 226
  "For Black People" (poem), 44
Madrid, 190
The Magic Hour (LP), 241
Magic Mike XXL (film), 294
Magnum Photos, 344
Maid of Harlem (theatrical show), 2
Maiden Voyage (LP), 242
Mailer, Norman, 9, 164
  "The White Negro" (essay), 9
Maisel, Jay, 343
The Majesty of the Blues (LP), 241
Major, Clarence, 149
  Juba to Jive (book), 149
Malcolm X, 21–23, 26, 28, 30–32, 128, 136, 223
Malcolm, Malcolm, Semper Malcolm (song), 136
Malcom X, 330
Malina, Judith, 129
A Man Called Adam (film), 296, 297
The Man with the Horn (LP), 331
Mance, Junior, 195
Mancini, Henry, 9
Mann, Thomas, 5
Manne, Shelly, 312
Manone, Wingy, 254
"Maori (A Samoan Dance)" (song), 88
"Maple Leaf Rag" (composition), 281
Marsalis, Branford, 314
Marsalis, Ellis, 12
Marsalis, Wynton, 10, 50, 57, 69–70, 170, 179, 241, 255
Marshall, Jim, 347

Martin, Ross, 308
Martin, Trayvon, 12
Marvin, Johnny, 38
Marx, Dick, 270
Masotti, Roberto, 349
Massey Hall, 8
Mathis, Johnny, 123
Matisse, Henri, 8, 281
Mau Mau, the (Kenya Land and Freedom Army), 136
May, Butler, 98
Mayo, Virginia, 295
McBride, Mary Margaret, 250
McCluskey, John
  "Lush Life" (story), 210, 216
McGregor, Chris, 195
McGregor, Ewan, 297
McGuigan, Jim, 163
  Cool Capitalism (book), 163
McKay, Claude, 221
  "The Harlem Dancer" (poem), 221
McLean, Jackie, 137, 296
McMahon, Horace, 308
McNeely, Big Jay, 135, 347
McPartland, Jimmy, 235
McPhatter, Clyde, 124
McRae, Carmen, 326
Meader, Darmon, 40
Meadowlane Productions, 307
Meditations (LP), 227, 244
Meeropol, Abel, 4–5, 228
  "The House I Live In" (song), 5
Mehldau, Brad, 56
Méliès, George, 279
"Memories of You" (song), 114
Memphis, 96
Memphis Jug Band, 96
Memphis Minnie, 96, 103, 104
Mencken, H. L., 152, 262
  The American Language (book), 152
Menendez, Bill, 315
Mercer, Johnny, 208
Merman, Ethel, 264
#MeToo movement, 181
Metro-Goldwyn-Mayer (MGM), 269, 313
Metronome, 248, 340, 343, 345
Metropolitan Opera Orchestra, 237
Mezzrow, Mezz, 154, 161, 162, 249, 254, 257
Miami, 196
Michael Brecker International Saxophone Competition, 196
Micheaux, Oscar, 96
Middle East, the, 191
"Midnight in New Orleans" (song), 117

Index

migration, African American, 3, 91, 96–97, 102, 146, 150, 169
Milan, 192, 349
Miles, Reid, 344
Miles Ahead (film), 297
Miles Davis in Person, Saturday Night at the Blackhawk, San Francisco, Volume 2 (LP), 239, 241
Miles Davis: Birth of the Cool (film), 325
Miles Smiles (LP), 242
Miles: The Autobiography (book), 249, 255, 257
Miley, Bubber, 87, 89
Mili, Gjon, 310, 342
Miller, Glenn, 293
Mills, Irving, 113, 114
Milner, Martin, 296
Milton, John, 236
Mineo, Sal, 295
Miner, Robert, 183
Mingus Ah Um (LP), 8
Mingus, Charles, 8, 63, 117, 132, 133, 136, 224, 228, 237, 238, 243, 248, 250, 252–256, 301, 315, 349
Mingus, Sue Graham, 254
Minneapolis, 192
Minnelli, Liza, 8, 298
"Minnie the Moocher" (song), 153
Minton, Bobbie. *See* Bentley, Gladys
Minton's, 26
Miss Calypso (LP), 224
"Miss Meal Cramp" (song), 97
"Miss Otis Regrets" (song), 228
Mississippi, 194, 211, 251, 252
"Mississippi Goddam" (song), 22, 31, 228
Mississippi River, 221, 234
Missouri River, 234
Mister Jelly Roll (book), 257
Mister Rogers' Neighborhood (television program), 315
Misterioso (LP), 243
Mitchell, Nicole, 30
Mitchell, Ray, 114
Mitchell, Roscoe, 135
Mo' Better Blues (film), 296
Mobley, Hank, 194
Modern Jazz Quartet, 237, 242
modernism, 8, 9, 16, 41, 52, 70, 74, 75, 102, 110, 116, 117, 119, 120, 129, 135, 136, 175–178, 219, 221, 277, 278, 280, 283–285, 288, 293, 329
Moholo, Louis, 195
Mole, Miff, 299
Mondrian, Piet, 8, 280, 282
Monk, Thelonious, 11, 25, 30, 58, 67–69, 117, 237, 240, 241, 243, 282, 323, 325, 342, 344, 348
Monroe, Bill, 97

Monroe, Marilyn, 7
Monte, Tony, 121
Monterey, 347
Monterey Jazz Festival, 347
Montgomery, Wes, 55, 238
Montoliu, Tete, 194
"Moon Germs" (song), 56
Moonlighting (television program), 313
Moore, Clement
  "A Visit from St. Nicholas" (poem), 155
Moore, Garry, 307, 308
Moran, Jason, 58, 59, 173
Morello, Joe, 329
Morgan, Lee, 236
Morrison, James, 196
Morse, Lee, 38
Mortensen, Viggo, 300
Morton, Jelly Roll, 50, 188, 225, 251, 253, 257, 308
Moscow, 187
Mostly Other People Do the Killing, 52
Moten, Fred, 225
Motherless Brooklyn (film), 299
Motherwell, Robert, 289
Motown Records, 224
"Mr. Bebee" (song), 293
Muldrow, Georgia Anne, 63
Mullen, Harryette, 225, 226
Mulligan, Gerry, 165, 166, 239, 296, 347
Mulvey, Laura, 327
Munich, 194, 344
Murphy, Dudley, 87, 292
Murray, Albert, 11, 164, 168, 179, 216, 240, 241, 250, 253
  Stomping the Blues (book), 240, 281
  The Hero and the Blues (book), 216
Murray, Don, 297
Murray, Sunny, 223
Museum of Modern Art, 7, 346
Music in the Air (theatrical show), 266
Music Is My Mistress (book), 250, 253, 257
The Music Lesson (painting), 286
Music on My Mind (book), 255
Musica Jazz (magazine), 349
"My Alice Blue Gown" (song), 85
"My Cherie Amour" (song), 315
My Favorite Things (LP), 268
"My Favorite Things" (song), 27–28, 268
"My Funny Valentine" (song), 268

Naito, Tadayuki, 344
Namuth, Hans, 283
Nat King Cole Show (television program), 306
National Association for the Advancement of Colored People (NAACP), 177

National Broadcasting Company (NBC), 73, 154, 306, 308, 311, 312, 314, 315
Native Tongues, 225
Navarro, Fats, 54, 160
Negro World, 90
neoliberalism, 176
New England Conservatory, 236
New Jazz Studies, the, 64, 65, 76, 305, 320. *See also* jazz scholarship
New Jersey, 345
New Mexico, 207
New Orleans, 10, 24, 57, 69, 86, 163, 164, 189, 194, 203, 234, 241, 251, 254, 255, 281, 294, 308, 341
New Orleans (film), 294–296
New Orleans Jazz (record set), 234
The New Orleans Mascot, 203
A New Perspective (LP), 238
New Thing, the, 240, 241, 244. *See also* free jazz
New Woman, the, 87
New York, 3, 5, 7–9, 26, 76, 81, 84, 91, 128, 129, 131, 133, 139, 153–155, 160, 164, 167, 173, 192, 196, 205, 215, 222, 226, 240, 241, 248, 262, 265, 278, 281, 282, 286, 301, 306, 308, 311, 314, 322, 329, 342, 345, 346, 348. *See also* the Bronx, Harlem
New Yorker, 171, 239
New York Police Department (NYPD), 160, 215
New York Public Library, 153
New York Teacher, The (magazine), 5
New York Times, 10, 128, 164, 239
New York University, 179
New York Voices, 40
New York World's Fair, 284
New York, New York (film), 298
Newark, 177, 244
Newley, Anthony, 238
Newport Jazz Festival, 171, 256, 322, 323, 346
Nicholas Brothers, the, 293
Nicholas, Fayard, 293
Nicholas, Harold, 293
Nichols, Herbie, 5
A Night at Birdland (LP), 235
"A Night in Tunisia" (song), 235
The Night People (book), 255
"Nine Little Miles from Ten Tennessee" (song), 114
Nippon Hōsō Kyōkai (NHK), 190
Nobel Peace Prize, 22
Nobel Prize in Literature, 228
"Nobody Knows the Trouble I've Seen" (song), 99
Noone, Jimmy, 254
North Carolina, 285
Norton, Edward, 299

Noth, Chris, 314
Nouveau Cirque, 278
"Nuages" (song), 191
N.Y., N.Y. (film), 329

Oakland, 298
Obama, Barack, 160, 332
Obama, Michelle, 331–332
Obenzinger, Hilton, 140
O'Brien, Edmond, 295
Ochs, Phil, 119
O'Connor, Norman J., 307
O'Day, Anita, 251, 254, 256
The Odd Couple (television program), 318
Odds Against Tomorrow (film), 296
Odets, Clifford
    Waiting for Lefty (play), 99
Odum, Howard W., 97
The Office (television program), 312
Of Minnie the Moocher & Me (book), 249
"Oh Come, All Ye Faithful" (song), 51
O'Hara, Frank, 226
    "The Day Lady Died" (poem), 226
Ohio, 251
Ohio River, 146
Okeh Records, 1, 4, 281
Oklahoma! (theatrical show), 268
Oliver, King, 3, 88, 256, 308, 309
"Ol' Man River" (song), 211, 266
Olson, Charles, 130–132
    "Projective Verse" (essay), 130
On the Edge, 196
Onassis, Jacqueline Kennedy, 7
One Act Play Magazine, 99
The One with the Dozen Lasagnas (television episode), 318
"OOL-YA-KOO" (song), 48
Oracle, 183
Orchestra Wives (film), 293
Organization of Afro-American Unity, 21
orientalism, 2, 88
Original Dixieland Jazz Band, 1, 308
Ornette! (LP), 236, 237
Ornette: Made in America (film), 325
Ory, Kid, 294, 308
Oscar Peterson: Black + White (film), 325
Out There (LP), 137
Out to Lunch (LP), 137
"Over the Rainbow" (song), 269–270
"Over There" (song), 51
Oxford English Dictionary (*OED*), 163

Pacific Islands, 280
Pacific Jazz Records, 343
Padilla, Rafael, 278

Page, Drew, 255
painting, 4, 129–131, 134, 243, 278, 280–286, 339, 341
Palmer, Jack, 220
Palmer, Robert, 238, 239
Panassié, Hugues, 161, 190, 191
    Hot Jazz: The Guide to Swing Music (book), 161
Paramount, 311
"Paranoid Android" (song), 56
Pardo, Don, 75
Parent, Robert, 344
Paris, 190, 278, 279, 283, 285, 296, 308
Paris Blues (film), 296
Paris Exposition, 279
Paris Opera, 190
Paris Salon, 283
Parish, Mitchell, 271
Park, Robert, 86
Parker, Chan, 254, 297
Parker, Charlie, 8, 9, 11, 13, 23, 25, 48, 51–54, 74, 116, 117, 132, 133, 136, 161, 166, 167, 215, 223, 226, 248, 249, 264, 267, 268, 282, 287, 297, 329, 342
Parker, Morgan, 225, 228, 230
    "Ain't Misbehaving" (poem), 230
    "Lush Life" (poem), 228, 229
    "So What" (poem), 230
Parker, Sarah Jessica, 314
Parker, William, 32
"Parker's Mood" (song), 13
Parks and Recreation (television program), 312
Parks, Gordon, 345
"A Passage for Trumpet" (television episode), 310
Patchen, Kenneth, 222
Patrick, Dorothy, 294
Patton, Charley, 112
The Pawnbroker (film), 296
"Pawnee Commons" (television episode), 312
Peanuts (television specials), 315
Peck, Raoul, 330–331
Pendergrass, Teddy, 123
People's Voice, 155
Pepper, Art, 166, 251, 253, 255–257, 301
Pepper, Laurie, 251, 253, 257
performance, 6–7, 64–66, 68, 70, 71, 73, 75, 76, 83, 86, 88, 92, 99, 101, 106, 107, 129–131, 135, 137, 138, 173, 204, 212, 214, 219, 222–224, 250, 262, 265, 278–281, 287, 295, 306, 310, 311, 322, 327, 341, 342, 346, 347
Performance Piece No. 1 (performance work), 129
Perry Mason (television program), 311
Persson, Jan, 349
Pete Kelly's Blues (film), 296
Peter Gunn (television program), 9, 311

Peters, Brock, 192
Peterson, Charles, 341, 342
Peterson, Oscar, 255–257, 267, 325
Pettiford, Oscar, 193
Pettus, Reggie, 348
Phantom Lady (film), 295
Philadelphia, 84
The Phil Silvers Show (television program), 313
photography, 65, 66, 242, 252, 255, 256, 286–288, 299, 310, 315, 320, 326, 327, 338–349
The Piano Lesson (Homage to Mary Lou) (painting), 286
"Piano Sonata no. 2 in B-flat Minor, Op. 35 (March Funèbre)" (composition), 87
Picabia, Francis, 278, 280, 281
"Picasso" (song), 288
Picasso, Pablo, 131, 240, 278, 280, 281
Pierre-Noel, Louis Vergniaud, 285
Pino, Giuseppe, 349
Pittsburgh Courier, 114, 155, 345
Pixar, 301, 302
Pizzarelli, Bucky, 12
Planet of the Apes (film), 48
Play De Blues (illustration), 284
Playhouse 90 (television program), 307
podcasts, 320
Poehler, Amy, 312
poetry, 43–44, 97, 99, 101, 104–107, 129–132, 135, 145, 164, 167, 219–230, 239, 243, 257, 283, 287, 308
Polillo, Roberto, 349
political ideology
    anarchy, 134
    Black Nationalism, 136
    Bolshevism, 163
    Communism, 164
    conservative, 57
    fascism, 164, 330
    left, 5, 99, 100, 119, 127, 129, 155
    Marxism, 129
    McCarthyism, 178
    Nazism, 138, 163, 190, 191
    Soviet, 138, 163, 179
Pollock, Edmund, 243
Pollock, Jackson, 8, 131, 132, 134, 135, 167, 280, 282, 283
Polonsky, Abraham, 308
Pop art, 7, 8, 344
Porgy & Bess (opera), 268
Porter, Cole, 190, 228, 262, 268
Porter, Gregory, 123
Porter, Roy, 251
Positively Black (television program), 315
Possibilities (book), 255
postmodernism, 175

post-structuralism, 49, 50, 59
Pound, Ezra, 132, 243
Powell, Adam Clayton, 155
Powell, Bud, 55, 193, 209, 236, 270, 282, 297
Powell, Red, 348
Powers, J. F.
  "He Don't Plant Cotton" (story), 211
Prague, 138
Presley, Elvis, 7, 117, 297
Prestige Records, 235, 344
"A Pretty Girl Is a Melody" (song), 52
Previn, André, 270
Prime Time, 73–76
primitivism, 39, 86, 149, 252, 277, 278, 280
Prince, 124
Prince of Wales, the, 85
Professor Calloway's Swingformation Bureau (book), 153
Prohibition, 329
A Program of Mexican Music (LP), 7
"Prove It on Me Blues" (song), 4
Prysock, Arthur, 123
"Psalm" (song), 227
Public Broadcasting Service (PBS), 309, 323
Public Enemy, 225
Pukl, Jure, 196
Pukwana, Dudu, 195
Pulitzer Prize, 10
punk, 74, 75
Puppini Sisters, The, 265
Puttin' on the Ritz (film), 268, 269
"Puttin' on the Ritz" (song), 262, 269

Quebec, Ike, 167
queerness, 4, 16, 84, 85, 92, 152, 228, 230, 270
Quiet Nights (LP), 268

Ra, Sun, 29–30, 69, 135, 224, 243, 298, 324, 325
  The Outer Darkness (poem), 224
race, 12, 22, 41, 42, 57, 65, 66, 71, 82, 83, 85–91,
  111–113, 115, 120, 132, 133, 154, 160, 165, 166,
  176, 178, 182, 187, 188, 193, 195, 204, 206,
  208–210, 212, 221, 224, 235, 249–252, 254,
  256, 279, 281, 291–293, 297, 298, 306, 307,
  310–315, 320–324, 331, 332, 338, 340, 346, 349
race records, 3, 187
racial violence, 5, 12, 22, 31, 65, 81, 119, 128,
  135, 191, 205, 215, 240, 244, 251–252, 300,
  330–332
racism, 3, 5, 9–11, 26, 27, 31, 32, 36, 39, 43, 47,
  65, 68, 71–73, 75, 76, 81, 83, 92, 96–98, 113,
  119, 127, 146, 147, 149, 156, 160–164, 168,
  175, 176, 180, 182, 203, 208, 211, 212, 215,
  251, 256, 291–295, 297, 300, 301, 306, 311,
  321, 324, 332, 340, 341

radio, 111, 112, 114, 117, 151, 156, 160, 190, 250,
  257, 306, 307, 312, 320
Radiohead, 56
ragtime, 38, 113, 188, 277, 278, 281–283
Raines, Ella, 295
Rainey, Ma, 4, 92, 103–107, 222
Rainey, Pa, 103
Raise Up Off Me (book), 252
Rampling, Charlotte, 301
Ramsey, Frederic, Jr., 161
Raposo, Joe, 316
Rauschenberg, Robert, 129
Rawls, Lou, 123
Ray Charles & Betty Carter (LP), 268
Razaf, Andy, 81
R&B, 115, 135, 156, 160, 224, 238, 306
RCA Victor, 1, 7
Reagan, Ronald, 57
Really the Blues (book), 154, 161, 162, 249, 254, 257
Reasoner, Harry, 308
Reconstruction, 203
Record, Eugene, 124
Red Hot & Blue (LP), 268
Redd, Freddie, 296
Redfern, David, 349
Redman, Don, 38
Redman, Joshua, 173, 298
Reed, Ishmael, 135
  Yellow Back Radio Broke-Down (novel), 135
Reed, James
  "The Shrimp Peel Gig" (story), 210
Rega Dance Orchestra, 1, 2
Reiff, Carole, 345
Reinhardt, Django, 191
Reith, John, 138
"Reponsible" (song), 194
Revue Nègre (theatrical show), 189, 279
Revue Romande, 189
Rexroth, Kenneth, 222
Rhames, Arthur, 53–55
"Rhapsody in Blue" (composition), 292
Rice, Elmer
  The Adding Machine (play), 99
Rice, John Andrew, 130
Richards, M. C., 130
Richardson, Lee, 116
Richmond, 96
Riddle, Nelson, 267
Rifftide (book), 253
Rio de Janeiro, 192
Rivers, Larry, 282
Roach, Max, 136, 238, 282, 296, 301
Roberta (theatrical show), 266

Index

Roberts, Luckey, 299
Roberts, Marcus, 69
Roberts, Matana, 32
Robertson, Dick, 114
Robeson, Paul, 5
Robinson, Bill "Bojangles," 271
Robinson, Earl, 5
Robinson, Smokey, 124
"Rock and Gravel Blues" (song), 100
rock music, 49, 56, 111, 113, 123, 151, 156, 224, 321, 347
Rockefeller Foundation, 177
"Rocking Chair Blues" (song), 271
Rodgers, Richard, 121, 268
Rolling Stone, 239
Rollins, Sonny, 8, 13, 65, 236, 237, 314, 340
Romany people, 191
Roney, Wallace, 12
Roost Records, 110
Roseanne (television program), 312
Ross, Annie, 171
Ross, Diana, 5, 8, 297
Ross, Lillian, 171
Rossini, Gioachino, 51
Round Midnight (film), 297
Rouzier, Coco, 196, 197
Rowe, Billy, 155
Royal Philharmonic Hall, 189
Royal Roost, 342
"Rude Interlude" (song), 115
Rugolo, Pete, 312
Russell, Pee Wee, 235
Russell, Ross, 162, 167
  The Sound (novel), 162
Russia, 187, 196, 277
Rutgers University, 177
"The Rye" (television episode), 312
Ryōichi, Hattori, 190

Sahara (LP), 239
Saint-Saëns, Camille, 190
Salaam, Kalamu ya, 30
"Salt Peanuts" (song), 8
samba, 192
"Same Train" (song), 89
sampling, 49
Samson et Dalila (opera), 190
San Francisco, 127, 168, 173, 174, 222, 345, 347, 348
San Francisco Chronicle, 239
San Francisco Renaissance, 222
Sanchez, Sonia, 107, 224, 226
Sandburg, Carl, 97
Sanders, Joe, 38
Santa Fe, 41

Santamaria, Mongo, 120
Satchmo: My Life in New Orleans (book), 255, 257
Saturday Night Live, 73–76
Savage, Augusta, 284
Savoy Ballroom, 341
Saxophone Colossus (LP), 179, 236, 237
scat, 36–45, 264
The Scene Changes (LP), 236
Schiedt, Duncan, 341
Schizo-Culture (conference), 139
Schlitten, Don, 344
Schneeman, Carolee, 129
School of American Ballet, 11
Schoolhouse Rock (television program), 315
Schuller, Gunther, 84, 133, 178, 179, 236–237, 239
  Early Jazz (book), 236
  The Swing Era (book), 236
Schweizer, Irène, 195
Scorsese, Martin, 298
Scott-Heron, Gil, 225
sculpture, 4, 279, 284, 285
Sargeant, Winthrop, 10
Seattle, 345
Second Chorus (film), 293
segregation, 3, 5, 22, 88, 111, 160, 211, 252, 345
Sehgal, Kabir, 170
Seiber, Mátyás, 189
Seinfeld (television program), 312
Seldes, Gilbert, 309
  The Seven Lively Arts (book), 309
"September Song" (song), 75
Serling, Rod, 311
sermons, 55, 135, 283. *See also* Black church, the
Sertso, Ingrid, 45
Sesame Street (television program), 316
The Seven Lively Arts (television program), 309–310
Sex and the City (television program), 313, 314
sexism, 75, 86, 97, 98, 180–182, 237, 242, 254
sexuality, 4, 9, 57, 81–86, 91–93, 115, 149, 221, 243, 254, 277, 295, 311, 321, 331
SFJAZZ, 173–174, 182
Shadows (film), 297
Shakespeare, William
  Hamlet (play), 155
The Shape of Jazz to Come (LP), 133, 236, 239
Sharp, Alex, 124
Shaw, Artie, 253–256, 267, 326
Shaw, Arvell, 308
sheet music, 2, 37, 153, 265, 278, 281
"The Sheik of Araby" (song), 69
Shepherd, Cybill, 313
Shepp, Archie, 128, 136, 148, 224, 315

Shihab, Sahib, 193
Shirelles, The, 266
Shirley, Don, 300
Shklovsky, Viktor, 120
Shor, Bernard "Toots," 329
Show Boat (theatrical show), 266, 268
Sideman (book), 253, 255
The Sidewinder (LP), 236
signifying, 25, 28, 50–52, 57
Silicon Valley, 174, 183
silkscreen, 7. *See also* painting, visual art
Silva, Elizabeth Pepin, 348
Silver, Horace, 255
The Silver Lining: The Songs of Jerome Kern (LP), 267
Simmel, Georg, 212
Simmons, Sonny, 325
Simone, Nina, 22, 31, 228, 325
The Simpsons (television program), 308
Sims, Zoot, 235, 238
Sinatra, Frank, 5, 116, 166, 167
Sinatra, Frank, Jr., 297
The Singing Fool (film), 291
Singleton, Zutty, 299
Sirius (LP), 242
Sissle, Noble, 38, 114
Six Gallery, the, 222
Škvorecký, Josef, 163
slam poetry, 225
slang, 43, 44, 145–156, 159, 162–164, 168, 208, 225, 249
slavery, 10, 25, 65, 101, 104, 111, 128, 146, 252, 278, 283, 324
"Sleepless in Bel-Air" (television episode), 314
Sloane, Kathy, 347
Slovenia, 196
Smalley, Webster, 98
Smith, Al, 345
Smith, Bessie, 3, 4, 84, 86, 92, 106, 187, 220, 222, 226, 271, 286, 292, 308
Smith, Beuford, 346
Smith, Buster, 237
Smith, C. W., 209, 210
    "The Plantation Club" (story), 207
Smith, Charles Edward, 161, 234
Smith, Mamie, 1, 98, 281, 308
Smith, Ming, 346
Smith, Ruby Walker, 92
Smith, W. Eugene, 348
Smith, W. O., 253, 255
Smith, Will, 314
Smith, Willie "The Lion," 92, 255, 299
Smithsonian Collection of Classic Jazz (LP compilation), 180
Smithsonian Institution, the, 239, 343

Snitzer, Herb, 345
The Snows of Kilimanjaro (film), 296
Snyder, Gary, 168
"Soft Pedal Blues" (song), 92
"Solitude" (song), 58
Somethin' Else (LP), 236
A Song Is Born (film), 295
Song of the Towers (painting), 284
"Son of a Gun" (television episode), 311
"Sonny Boy" (song), 291
Sonny's Time Now (LP), 223
Sony BMG, 344
Soul (film), 301, 302
soul music, 196, 266
Soul! (television program), 315
soularfone, 45
Soultrane (LP), 237
"Sound of Trumpets" (television episode), 311
The Sound I Saw (exhibition), 347
The Sound I Saw: Improvisation on a Jazz Theme (book), 287, 288
"The Sound of Jazz" (television episode), 309–310
The Sound of Music (film), 27
The Sound of Music (theatrical show), 268
Sound/Stage (concert series), 332
Soundies, 322
Sousa, John Phillip, 279
South Africa, 195
South Carolina State University, 128
South Pacific, the, 86
Southern Christian Leadership Conference, 119
Space Is the Place (film), 298
Space Is the Place (LP), 224, 243
Spain, 69
Spalding, Esperanza, 160
Spellman, A. B., 118, 237
Spielberg, Steven, 299
The Spirit Moves: A History of Black Social Dance on Film, 1900–1986 (film), 320–321
spirituals, 86, 100, 128, 146, 295
Spotlite Club, 241
Springfield (Ohio), 251
Srinivasan, Srinija, 174
St. Louis, 86, 135, 235, 281
St. Louis Blues (1929 film), 292
St. Louis Blues (1958 film), 296
"St. Louis Blues" (song), 99, 114
Stanley, Ralph, 97
Star Trek Deep Space Nine (television program), 311
"Stardust" (song), 271, 301
Stardust Memories (film), 301
Starr, S. Frederick, 163
"Stars" (song), 115
Stars of Jazz (television program), 307

State Department Jazz Ambassador tours, 179, 191, 286
"Stay Cool" (song), 160
Stearns, Marshall, 177–179, 182, 248
  The Story of Jazz (book), 178, 179
SteepleChase Records, 194
Steichen, Edward, 346
Stein, Gertrude, 113
Steinbeck, John, 97
  The Grapes of Wrath (book), 97
"Stella by Starlight" (song), 58
Stephenson, Sam, 348
Stern, Bert, 322
Stevenson, Vern, 307
Stewart, Chuck, 341, 344
Stewart, Frank, 255, 346
Stewart, Rex, 251, 257
Stewart, Slam, 42, 267
Stieglitz, Alfred, 339
Stitt, Sonny, 301
Stock, Dennis, 344
Stockhausen, Karlheinz, 196
Stockhausen, Simon, 196
Stockholm, 279
Stoll, Jerry, 347
Stone, Emma, 302
Stormy Weather (film), 271
"Stormy Weather" (song), 262, 271
Straight Life (book), 251, 253, 257, 301
Strand, Paul, 339
"Strange Fruit" (song), 7, 119, 228, 252
Strauss, Johann, II, 51
Stravinsky, Igor, 51, 53, 277, 278, 281
Strayhorn, Billy, 120, 226, 228–230, 296
Street, Julian
  "The Jazz Baby" (story), 206
stride piano, 74, 92, 221, 270
Strothers, Jimmie, 96
Student Nonviolent Coordinating Committee (SNCC), 128
Students for a Democratic Society, 127
Students' Afro-American Society, 127
Studio Museum of Harlem, 287, 347
A Study in Frustration (LP compilation), 113
The Subterraneans (film), 296
Sukenick, Ronald, 136
  Down and In: Life in the Underground (autobiography), 136
Sullavan, Jeri, 295
Sullivan, Ed, 315
Summer of Soul (film), 320
"Summertime" (song), 268, 269
Surgal, Tom, 325
Surrealism, 129, 136
"Swanee River" (song), 124

Swapp, Felice, 173
Sweden, 193, 196
Sweet Adeline (theatrical show), 266, 268
"Sweet Georgia Brown" (song), 85
Sweet Love, Bitter (film), 297
Sweet Smell of Success (film), 296, 311
Sweet Swing Blues on the Road (book), 255
swing, 10, 56, 113, 116, 135, 151, 161, 166, 176, 190, 210, 239, 249, 253, 254, 264, 267, 293, 306, 339
Swing Era, 23, 115, 116, 176, 342
Swing High, Swing Low (film), 293
Swing Kids (film), 163
Swing Landscape (painting), 8
Swing That Music (book), 153, 249, 250, 254, 257
Swing Under the Swastika (film), 163
A Swingin' Affair (LP), 242
Swingin' with Zoot Sims (LP), 235
Switzerland, 189, 196, 197, 349
Sylvie's Love (film), 300, 301
Symphony in Black (film), 292
Syms, Sylvia, 326
Syncopation (film), 293, 294

Tacuma, Jamaaladeen, 75
"Take Me Out to the Ball Game" (song), 53
Take Ten (LP), 7
"Take the A Train" (song), 229
Talking Heads, 74
Tanner, Henry Ossawa, 283, 286
Tanner, Lee, 347
Tapestry (LP), 266
"The Target" (television episode), 312
Tatum, Art, 208, 209, 270
Taylor, Billy, 239, 307, 308
Taylor, Breonna, 12
Taylor, Cecil, 59, 195, 224, 243, 325
Taylor, Creed, 243, 344
Taylor, Shooby, 42
Teagarden, Jack, 308
"Tears for Johannesburg" (song), 238
Teddy Wilson Talks Jazz (book), 255
television, 9, 58, 66, 75, 76, 154, 236, 239, 257, 300, 305–316, 326–327
Tennessee, 96
"Tenor Madness" (song), 13
The Terminal (film), 299
Terry, Clark, 45, 255
Texas, 96, 133, 235
theatricality, 6–7, 64–67, 69, 70, 72, 74, 88, 135.
  See also performance
Thelonious Monk: Straight, No Chaser (film), 325
Theme (magazine), 343
Thiele, Bob, 122, 242
Thielmans, "Toots," 316

Third Stream, 236, 269
Thomas, Leon, 45
Thompson, Ahmir "Questlove," 320
Thompson, Francis, 329
Thompson, Lucky, 194
Thompson, Robert Farris, 66, 159, 162, 163
Thompson, Tessa, 300
Thomson, Virgil, 113
Thornhill, Claude, 165
Those Swinging Years (book), 255
Threadgill, Henry, 12
"Three Blind Mice" (song), 51
Three Sisters (theatrical show), 266
Thurman, Wallace, 91
  Negro Life in New York's Harlem (book), 91
"Tiger Rag" (song), 191
Till, Emmett, 252
Time (magazine), 22, 30, 155, 250
Time Out (LP), 8
"Times Square" (song), 73, 74
Timex, 307
Tin Pan Alley, 25, 69, 85, 86, 228, 262, 265–266, 271
"Tishomingo Blues" (song), 88
To Be or Not to Bop (book), 250, 253
Tokyo, 28, 190, 192
Toledo, 192
Tolson, Melvin, 221
Tomorrow Is the Question (LP), 133, 238
Tonight at Noon (LP), 237
Tonight Show with Jay Leno (television program), 314
Tonight Starring Steve Allen (television program), 306
Toomer, Jean, 221, 225
Toots (film), 329
Top Hat (film), 269
Torin, Symphony Sid, 156
Torme, Mel, 46
Toronto, 8
Toulouse-Lautrec, Henri de, 278
Travelogue, 197
Treasure Girl (theatrical show), 263
Treat It Gentle (book), 254, 255
"Trouble, Trouble, I Has 'Em All My Days" (song), 99
The Trouble with Cinderella (book), 253
Trumpet on the Wing (book), 254
Tucker, Sophie, 1
Turkey, 193
Turkmenistan, 187
Turner, Big Joe, 117
Turner, Joe, 239
Turner, Mark, 300
Turner, Pete, 344

Tuttle, Anthony, 242
Twilight Zone, The (television program), 310
Tyner, McCoy, 110, 122, 239, 240
Tyus, Charles, 96
Tyus, Effie, 96
Tzara, Tristan, 135

Ubangi Club, 98
Uhuru Afrika (LP), 192, 193, 195
Ulanov, Barry, 248
Umbra, 232
Underground (LP), 344
Union of Soviet Socialist Republics (USSR), 163, 168, 187
The United States vs. Billie Holiday (film), 6, 301
Universal, 307
University of California, Berkeley, 127
Urban Bushmen (LP), 244

Van Vechten, Carl, 85
Vandross, Luther, 123
Variety, 153, 155
vaudeville, 1, 2, 38, 98, 101, 111, 277
Vaughn, Sarah, 42, 287
Venora, Diane, 297
Very Warm for May (theatrical show), 266, 268
Vian, Boris, 165
Vicksburg (Mississippi), 252
Victor, Fay, 45
Vienna, 193, 279
Vietnam, 127, 330
Vigeland, Carl, 255
Village Vanguard, 9
Village Voice, 238, 240
Virgin Atlantic Airways, 328
vocalese, 37, 40, 43
Vogel, Eric, 191
Volume IV (LP), 241

Wagner, Richard, 51, 178
Wainwright, Rufus, 270
Waldron, Mal, 194, 226
Walker, Fredy, 279
Walker, Rudy, 279
Waller, Fats, 5, 59, 81, 92, 211, 221, 230
"Wang Wang Blues" (song), 88
Ward, Geoffrey, 324
Warhol, Andy, 7–8
Warner Bros., 113, 313
Washboard Sam, 96
Washington, DC, 128, 191, 196, 285, 348
Washington, Fredi, 87–89
Washington, Kamasi, 32, 225, 332
Waters, Ethel, 4, 38, 82, 86, 115, 187, 271
Watson, Leo, 42

Watts Uprising, 330
Watts, Jeff "Tain," 69
Watts, Lewis, 348
Way Out West (LP), 8, 340
We Called It Music (book), 254
We Insist! Freedom Now Suite (LP), 136, 238
Webb, Jack, 296
Webster, Ben, 153, 194
Weill, Kurt, 75
Weimar Republic, 189
Weinstock, Bob, 235
Weitz, Alex, 196
Wells, Dickey, 253, 255
Welty, Eudora
  "Powerhouse" (story), 212, 216
"West End Blues" (song), 51
Western Swing, 41
Weston, Randy, 192, 193
"(What Did I Do to Be So) Black and Blue?" (song), 82
What Happened to Kerouac? (film), 329
What Happened, Miss Simone? (film), 325
"What's Sex Got to Do with It?" (television episode), 314
Whetsol, Arthur, 87
Whims of Chambers (LP), 236
Whiplash (film), 301
Whitaker, Forest, 297
White Christmas (film), 268
White Light (painting), 8, 135
White, Barry, 123
Whiteman, Paul, 57, 250–254, 292–294, 310
Whitman, Walt, 145
"Who Can I Turn To" (song), 238
"Why Was I Born" (song), 51
"Will You Love Me Tomorrow" (song), 266
Willener, Alfred, 129, 130, 136, 137, 139
  The Action Image of Society: On Cultural Politicisation (book), 129
Williams, Bert, 38
Williams, Charles, 345, 346
Williams, Clarence, 3
Williams, John A.
  Night Song (novel), 215
Williams, Martin, 88, 179, 180, 238, 239, 248
  The Jazz Tradition (book), 239
Williams, Mary Lou, 286, 287
Williams, Michael K., 299
Williams, Ned, 153
Williams, Sherley Anne, 107
Williams, Spencer, 220

Williams, Ted, 346
Williams, William Carlos, 219
Williamson, Sonny Boy, 96
Willis, Bruce, 313
Willoughby, Bob, 346
Wilmer, Valerie, 242, 315, 349
  As Serious as Your Life (book), 242
  Jazz People (book), 242
  The Face of Black Music (book), 349
Wilson, John, 248
Wilson, Teddy, 255
Winogrand, Garry, 344
The Wizard of Oz (film), 269
WNBT, 307
WNTA-TV, 307
Wolff, Francis, 343, 344
Wonder, Stevie, 315
Wood, Aja Burrell, 182
The Woodchopper's Ball (book), 255, 257
Woodberry, Billy, 231
Woods, Phil, 267
Woodstock (film), 321
World War I, 4, 74, 91, 96, 97, 135, 188, 203
World War II, 28, 115–117, 130, 132, 153, 154, 159, 161–163, 165, 166, 168, 175–177, 179, 190, 222, 223, 234, 296, 338, 339, 342, 344, 348
Wright, Richard, 107
Wynton Marsalis (LP), 241

Yahoo!, 174
Yale University, 177
"Yellow Dog Blues" (song), 88
You Are There (television program), 308, 309
"You Are Too Beautiful" (song), 121–122
"(You Make Me Feel Like) A Natural Woman" (song), 266
You're Under Arrest (LP), 331
Young Man with a Horn (film), 294, 296
Young, Kevin, 225
  "Errata" (poem), 225
  Jelly Roll: A Blues, 225
Young, Lester, 7, 54, 66, 153, 159, 161, 165, 166, 171, 222, 287, 297, 298, 301
Young, Marl, 117
YouTube, 328

Zenón, Miguel, 173
Ziegfeld Follies (theatrical show), 268
Zimmerman, George, 12
Zurich, 195, 197